INTRODUCTION TO INVESTMENTS

Introduction to
INVESTMENTS

John C. Clendenin, Ph.D.

PROFESSOR OF FINANCE
UNIVERSITY OF CALIFORNIA, LOS ANGELES
RESEARCH CONSULTANT
LOS ANGELES STOCK EXCHANGE

SECOND EDITION

McGRAW-HILL BOOK COMPANY, INC.

New York   Toronto   London

1955

INTRODUCTION TO INVESTMENTS

v

PREFACE

This book is intended primarily as an introductory textbook for college-level classes in investments. However, its subject matter and its brevity may combine to make it useful for adult-education classes and for individual reading as well. I have tried to include both sound investment philosophy and practical investment detail, in order to make the book broadly useful.

In preparing this second edition, as in the original edition five years ago, I have been influenced by the experiences of many years' contact with the investments field. The completed book is therefore certain to reflect many of the ideas and prejudices which I have accumulated through these years, both in the choice of subject matter and in the conclusions reached. With respect to the latter, I have made a conscious effort in most passages to subordinate my personal convictions to the conventional viewpoint, for it seems to me that a beginning course in any field should be built around the generally accepted philosophy and nomenclature of that field. But in the choice of subject matter and in the mode of presentation I have felt less constrained. I hold firmly to five central convictions about the nature of an effective introductory course in investments and have followed them closely in preparing this book.

In the first place, I am convinced that my students make more progress in a course based on a concise textbook supplemented as time permits by periodical readings, outside readings, and problems than they do by other methods. I have therefore made the book short and laconic. Second, I note that most students are concerned with investments chiefly as a personal and family problem, rather than from the viewpoint of an investment dealer or a financial institution. I have accordingly stressed the development of personal investment plans. Third, I believe that a broad perspective is more valuable to a beginner in investments than thorough coverage of a few subjects. I have therefore included a wide variety of topics, among them life insurance, real estate, trusts, tax planning, and savings institutions, in a short book whose principal focus is on security investments. I doubt if I shall have time to discuss all of these topics in my classroom, but there will be time for the student to read the chapters in the book, and the course will therefore provide an integrated survey of the many elements which fit into a modern investment program. Fourth, I am convinced that market prices and their behavior constitute one of the major problems of investment management. Consequently, the book makes a determined attempt to point the way to the evaluation of investment assets. Fifth, I believe that a textbook on investments should provide a considerable amount of descriptive detail on market procedure, types of securities, and analytical mechanics. The student who does not have these is usually uncertain and dissatisfied, and the instructor who must provide them in class is intolerably burdened. I have therefore included them in the book.

Although the above policies pointed the way rather clearly to the material to be covered, they obviously did not solve all the problems of the book. I was compelled to omit far more in the way of financial history, discussion of public policy, and analytical elaboration of points mentioned than I wished. I also had to assume that my readers would know a little of corporate procedure and securities and a little of accounting, but I have not assumed a high degree of proficiency in either.

It is a pleasure to acknowledge the aid and advice so generously given me during the preparation of this book. Many of my friends in the securities business in Los Angeles and in the Los Angeles banks have read chapters and provided illustrative material; I am particularly indebted to President W. G. Paul of the Los Angeles Stock Exchange for help of this type. I have also received material from Eastern banks, securities firms, and from stock exchanges in all parts of the country. My colleagues on the local faculty have given me needed advice and criticism on many points, as have numbers of my students and other friends. To all these people I owe a debt of gratitude. Their contributions have been of inestimable value.

JOHN C. CLENDENIN

CONTENTS

Chapter 1: INVESTMENT OBJECTIVES

During the past century the average American has found it necessary to devote an ever-increasing amount of time to the management of his financial resources. This is a very gratifying fact, for it is a direct consequence of the nation's rising standard of living, which has made the accumulation of savings possible to most citizens. But wealth brings its problems, too. The utilization of great resources requires the development of great corporations, great governmental activities, complex securities markets, and many other mystifying institutions and procedures. Taxes, inflation, depression, labor relations, and countless other social phenomena affect the productivity and value of invested savings. All these things combine to present the investor with a formidable array of problems, which demand an amount of technical information on financial matters far beyond the requirements of earlier times.

While it would be foolish to assume that the investment needs of different families and institutions conform to any standard pattern, it seems rather clear that all investors have three tasks in common. First, they should plan the types of investments to be used and the proportions of each to be acquired, in order to assure the security, stability, income, and other advantages which their situations require. Second, they must select specific investments of the desired types, making sure that quality, stability, and other features are obtained as needed. Third, they should study the long-run values of suitable investments and time their purchases and sales with due regard for price behavior in the characteristically unstable investment markets. The proper handling of this threefold task is an assignment of no mean proportions. It requires technical knowledge, diligence, and some experience, but it is the essence of successful investment management for either an individual or an institution.

The Nature of Investment

In the broad and customary sense of the term, an investment is any asset or property right acquired or held for the purpose of conserving capital or earning an income. This comprehensive definition does not distinguish between safe and hazardous investments, tangible and intangible investments, or direct and institutional investments. It simply recognizes that savings accounts, bonds, mortgages, life insurance, corporate stocks, real estate, business equities, and other earning assets all fulfill the same basic function, that of employing their owners' funds. Furthermore, this definition does not limit the term investment to property intended to return a cash income or cash profit. Indeed, the most satisfactory investments held by many people are their homes, which yield their returns in family satisfaction and in exemption from rent payments.

The merit of this broad definition of the term investment will become clear when the problem of investment proportioning, commonly referred to as investment programing or portfolio planning, is further discussed. The discussion will show that the proper balancing of any investor's resources among various types of assets, such as life insurance, bonds, stocks, homeownership, or business ownership, is a completely unified problem—an investment problem. The nature or quality of any individual investment which seems desirable must necessarily influence the nature and quality of the others which are selected, in order that a sound balance may be achieved.

In a narrower sense, the term investment is sometimes used to suggest a commitment which is relatively free from risk of loss. Thus, high-quality bonds are said to be "of investment grade." In this sense the label investment would be restricted to situations promising stability of value and income, a modest rate of return, and relatively little chance of spectacular capital appreciation. People who seek high-income yields or large capital gains are therefore said to forsake investment for speculation.

Speculation means the deliberate assumption of risks in ventures which offer the hope of commensurate gains. The hoped-for gains may come in the form of larger incomes than a safe investment would supply. More probably the speculator hopes that his "investment" will rise greatly in market price, as its earning power increases or becomes more secure. Or he may expect its value (and possibly that of the whole stock market or real estate market) to "go up" because of existing conditions. It is commonly said that the owners of speculative commitments are more interested in profits from price appreciation than they are in the incomes from their properties. This may or may not be true, but the radical variations in price of some speculative assets (50 per cent declines or 100 per cent increases in a year's time are not unusual) suggest that in most speculations the value of the principal should be of prime concern.

There is nothing immoral or undesirable about reasonable speculation. The difference between investment and speculation is only a matter of degree of risk, and few personal investment programs need be confined exclusively to ultrasafe items. Indeed, the nation would never have new industries or progress at all if speculators did not venture into untried projects. But sensible speculators do not gamble. They choose their ventures with care, they risk only what they can afford, and if possible they diversify their speculations enough to prevent errors in selection from resulting in burdensome losses. However, every investment dealer knows that many people "speculate" heavily on the strength of idle "tips" or gossip or plunge into situations which they do not understand. This is gambling, not speculation, even though the commitment is of reasonable speculative quality.

Experienced investors generally believe that for most people extensive speculation is not profitable. Casual gambling in securities or real estate most assuredly is not. On the other hand, the successful operation of insurance companies, trust funds, and many private estates through the years indicates that conservative investments can usually be kept safe and productive. Ways can be found to justify the inclusion of a portion of promising speculations in a sound investment portfolio, and proper timing of purchases and sales can do much to improve investment results, but these are merely incidents of sound investment administration, not arguments in favor of reckless risk taking. The histories of big-time and small-time financiers alike point the moral: the way to get money is to work for it, and the way to have money is to keep it by investing soundly.

Risks of Investment

There are four distinct, though related, types of risk to which investments are subject in varying degree. Some of these risks scarcely exist at all in certain investments, and they vary greatly in intensity from one investment to another. No investment is free of all of them. In fact, the most highly regarded investment in the average investor's portfolio, his United States government bonds, is acutely subject to one of these risks.[1]

The first and most dangerous risk is the *business* or *functional risk*. Every business or piece of property is subject to the possibility that its earning power or usefulness may wane because of competition, change in demand, uncontrollable costs, managerial error, government action, or some similar circumstance. Likewise, any individual debtor may suffer a shrinkage in earning power or capacity to pay. Investments such as the bonds of the United States government or populous states, or the bonds of a far-flung and well-financed corporation such as the American Telephone and Telegraph Company, are little subject to this risk, at least in the foreseeable future. But the stock of the average business corporation, or real estate in a given neighborhood, or a farm whose money source is cotton or any other single crop—these are always vulnerable in greater or less degree. It is a major task of investment management to watch for business hazards and to take appropriate steps to avoid loss if the risk increases and to profit from the change if it decreases.

The second risk is the *market risk*. This hazard arises from the fact that market prices and collateral values of securities and real property may vary substantially, even when their earning power does not change. The causes for these price uncertainties are varied. At times many markets are simply "thin"—that is, buyers and sellers appear only intermittently, and one who wishes to do business at a given time may obtain a satisfactory or a disadvantageous price, depending on the accidental condition of the market. More commonly, investment prices vary because investors vacillate in their opinions about the future desirability of the property in question, or because they vacillate in their preferences for alternate or com-

---

[1] For a comprehensive discussion of investment risks see George W. Dowrie and Douglas R. Fuller, *Investments,* John Wiley & Sons, Inc., New York, 1950, Chap. 7.

peting forms of investment, or simply because they sometimes have
money to invest and sometimes have not. Fluctuation in the market
value of one's investments is not so damaging as impairment of their
earning power, if one does not have to sell them or borrow on them,
but it is imperative to most investors that at least a portion of their
holdings be capable of quick liquidation without loss. Emergencies
and once-in-a-lifetime business opportunities must be anticipated.
The extensive vagaries of the stock market, the uncertainty and
slowness of real estate markets, and the irregular markets for mortgages and second-grade bond issues all indicate the presence of the
market risk. The only investments which are completely exempt
from the market risk are those which are always available in cash,
such as savings accounts, Series E bonds, and life insurance reserves.
In addition, top-grade governmental and corporation bonds enjoy
fairly steady sales markets and fluctuate in price very little except
as a result of interest-rate changes.

The third risk, the *money-rate risk,* applies most definitely to the
values of fixed-income securities of long or indefinite maturity, such
as high-grade bonds, mortgages, and preferred stocks. It may also
apply in lesser degree to common stocks and real estate. The money-
rate risk refers to the fact that long-term securities paying fixed income (the standard $1,000 bond pays a fixed contractual rate of in-
terest on its face value) are worth a premium if the interest rates
on new issues decline but are worth less if interest rates on new
issues rise. For example, the Union Pacific Railroad in 1946 sold a
large issue of 2½ per cent bonds due in 1991. These bonds are
superbly secure in quality, and as long as interest rates remained
low their market price remained close to their par value. But in later
years a shortage of loan funds developed, and in 1953 borrowing
corporations were selling new high-class bonds paying as much as
3¾ per cent interest. Since no investor would pay par value for a
2½ per cent bond when he could get 3¾ per cent on comparable
new bonds, the market price on the Union Pacific bonds dropped
to 80 per cent of par. This is a drastic decline—from $1,000 to $800—
for a security which is almost free of the business risk. Of course,
it can be argued that the owner of such bonds can hold them to
maturity and complete the contract just as he originally planned it,
but this does not alter the fact that his original commitment subjected him either to a capital loss or to an income below subsequently

available rates for a long period of years. This hazard is theoretically balanced by the possibility of gain if interest rates fall instead of rise, but is nonetheless a source of concern to those interested in the market values of high-grade long-term investments. Insurance companies, banks, and trustees are among those most acutely concerned. Selection of very short-term bonds and mortgages would minimize the effect of money-rate changes on the value of the investment, since the early maturity would release the funds for reinvestment at prevailing market rates; but this is not a wholly attractive solution, since the expense of constant reinvestment would be considerable and the interest rates on short-term investments would probably average lower than long-term ones anyway.

The fourth risk, the *price-level risk,* is the factor which at times makes the best investments exceedingly hazardous. The most highly rated investments available—government bonds, savings deposits, life insurance, and others—are without exception payable in definite dollar sums. Receipt of the dollars is sure, but the buying power of those dollars is very uncertain. The people who bought government bonds in 1941 had by 1953 lost almost half of the purchasing power they invested, though the bonds were still worth the original number of dollars. The dollars themselves were worth less. Since most investors are acutely concerned with the real buying power of their investments and the incomes from them, this price-level hazard is of outstanding importance. There is no perfect solution to the problem, either, since investments which are theoretically protected against the price-level risk are frequently not so protected in fact and are, in addition, seriously subject to the business risk. It is usually argued that, since real estate and common stocks represent tangible "commodities," their prices and earning power in dollars should rise and fall proportionally with all commodities and with the cost of living. This is probably vaguely true in the long run, if the real estate and stocks are wisely selected and widely diversified over many locations and industries. It is not likely to be true of individual stocks or real estate parcels, and it is most definitely not true over short periods of time.

Material of Investments

As has been indicated, the commitments which may qualify as desirable investments are infinite in variety. Some are not even acquired voluntarily, since employers frequently require savings into a retirement fund and the United States government compels many people to invest in social security. The following 12 classifications of investments do not enumerate all the important items employed by individual investors, but they illustrate all the significant types. Most of these will be discussed at greater length in later chapters, but the features which are most significant to investors will be pointed out at this time. Note that investments which offer the greatest security from the business risk tend to be stable in dollar value (hence dependable as a source of emergency cash) but low in percentage yield and vulnerable to the price-level risk, while those which promise compensation for price-level changes tend to be characterized by business risks, market-price instability, and better income returns.

1. Savings bank deposits. Savings deposits are accepted by the savings departments of commercial banks, by mutual savings banks, by post offices (into postal savings accounts), and by certain other less important agencies. Savings accounts are always payable in dollar sums, are extremely liquid (the deposit contract usually permits the bank to demand 30 days' notice of intent to withdraw the money, but payment is practically always available instantly), and yield relatively low interest rates. Most small depositors receive 1 to 2½ per cent, but larger accounts often receive less. The interest is fully subject to income taxes, and the principal is commonly subject to property taxes to some extent.

2. Life insurance policies. The typical individual (not group) life insurance policy is a combination of decreasing insurance protection plus increasing savings account. The insured is charged an annual premium which is sufficient to pay his share of the death benefits incurred by his age group, to pay his share of the operating expenses, and to contribute a definite sum to the reserve or savings account embodied in his policy. In subsequent years his share of the cost of the death benefits to his age group will be reduced because the amount of insurance protection he pays for is measured by the difference between the face of the policy and the reserve already accumulated in it—that is, when his $1,000 policy has accumulated a $400 reserve he will be charged for only $600 of insurance protection. In addition, his policy is credited with the interest earnings on its accumulating reserve. The principal difference between a high-premium 20-year endowment or 20-pay life policy and a low-premium ordinary life policy is found in the fact that the high-premium policy accumulates a large reserve rapidly, while the low-premium policy accumulates its reserve more slowly and is therefore subject to larger insurance protection costs for a longer period. High-premium policies are suitable for people who wish to use them as savings accounts, with insurance protection which diminishes as the savings are completed, while low-premium policies are suitable for people who wish chiefly insurance protection at a minimum cash outlay.

Life insurance policies are desirable investments when properly chosen to meet the insured's needs. They are very poor investments if poor selection results in the purchase of unneeded protection or in the assumption of high premium burdens which prevent other desirable investments. Life insurance reserves are very safe investments which usually earn between $2\frac{1}{2}$ and 3 per cent for their owners. They are available only as dollar sums, hence are fully subject to the price-level hazard. They are quite liquid, since almost the full reserve can be borrowed from the company at reasonable rates, at short notice, repayable whenever the insured chooses; or the policy can be canceled and the reserve recovered. Life insurance policies have other advantages in varied fields, including the procurement of retirement annuities, the liquidating of business interests, and the handling of tax problems; but discussion of these must be deferred to a later chapter.

3. Savings and loan accounts. Most communities have savings and loan associations whose function is to accumulate investors' savings and invest them in local mortgage loans. Since the associations are supervised by state or Federal agencies, and since they are usually conservatively managed, their safety record is good. Many of them also insure the first $10,000 of each investor's account by means of membership in the Federal Savings and Loan Insurance Corporation. Interest-dividends paid on savings and loan accounts (technically the investors in most of these organizations are shareholders and owners, not creditors) generally range between 2½ and 3½ per cent. Immediate liquidity is not guaranteed, since the associations are intended to employ their funds in long-term mortgages, but in practice accounts may be withdrawn on demand or after short notice most of the time. The income is fully subject to income taxation. The property tax position varies, but is not usually burdensome.

4. United States government securities. Treasury bonds, notes, certificates, and bills, together with the Series E, H, J, and K savings bonds, represent the largest group of securities available to the American public and are probably the group least subject to the business risk. Maturities ranging from 90 days to 40 years are available, and interest yields vary from about 1 per cent to approximately 3.25 per cent. The market risk on government securities is negligible, and the money-rate risk on long-term bonds is less than it would be on any other similar security. Only the price-level risk is serious. Government obligations are exempt from state and local property taxes, and their interest payments are not subject to state or local income taxes. However, the bonds are subject to Federal and state estate, inheritance, and gift taxes, and the interest is usually subject to Federal income taxation. Like life insurance policies, government bonds are so varied in their terms that a proper choice must depend on the needs of each individual investor.

5. State and municipal bonds. This category includes the obligations of scores of thousands of public agencies, some rich, some poor. Most of them are conscientious, though a few are on occasion inclined to be evasive. Debt service (*i.e.,* payment of interest and principal) may be promised from tax revenues, from public business revenues, from special assessments on real estate, or from a combination of these. Most public obligations are good quality, and many are top grade. All are payable only in dollars. Long-term bonds are subject to the money-rate risk, and many issues are subject to the market risk. Lower quality issues are also subject to the business risk. Since state and municipal interest payments are exempt from the very heavy Federal income tax, they are attractive to corporations and individuals in the higher tax brackets. This causes the bonds to sell higher and pay lower interest yields than corporate bonds of similar quality and maturity dates; good ones yield less than taxable Federal bonds, possibly averaging 2½ per cent in 1954 on 20-year maturities. Each state usually exempts its own and its municipalities' bonds from income and property taxes within its borders, but the bonds are subject to Federal and state inheritance, estate, and gift taxes.

6. Corporate bonds. Corporate bonds are the debts of business concerns. They are usually sold to investors in $1,000 units. The bondholders as creditors usually have no voice in management and are entitled to little more than the regular payment of interest and the ultimate repayment of the principal, all in fixed dollar sums. Corporate bonds vary widely in contract terms and quality but, in general, are subject to the price-level and money-rate risks in varying degree. Some issues have very dependable markets and are of unquestioned quality; others are doubtful on both points. There are no significant tax exemptions available on corporate bonds as a class. For the past ten years the best grade bonds have yielded from $\frac{1}{4}$ to $\frac{1}{2}$ per cent more than United States Treasury bonds of similar maturity date. In 1954 the ruling rate on top-grade long-term corporate bonds was close to 3 per cent, but lower quality bonds could be bought at prices which promised yields up to 8 or 9 per cent.

7. Corporate stocks. Stockholders are owners, and corporate stocks represent the residual ownership and control of corporations. The business risks inherent in the enterprise naturally fall with full force on the stockholder, who bears them because he may also hope for the extraordinary gains which success may bring him. The market risk is obviously high in stock ownership, the money-rate risk is an uncertain factor. With respect to the price-level risk, it may be assumed that indirect property ownership through the holding of stocks is a satisfactory approach to the objective of owning buying power instead of merely money, but no single stock can be expected to fluctuate in close proportion to the price level. Only an average of many stocks in many industries can hope to do this. Certain types of stocks, such as those of rate-regulated utilities, will not experience changes in dollar earning power when the price level changes; these are useless as purchasing-power hedges. And preferred stocks, which in general have accepted maximum limits on their dividend rights in return for priority of claim to dividends out of the corporate earnings (the common holders will get more or less, depending on how much is earned), are also poor price-level hedges. Good common stocks fluctuate considerably in price, and a typical group may be expected to yield between 4 and 7 per cent, depending on market conditions at the time. Because the corporations usually pay something less than two-thirds of their earnings in dividends, common stockholders may also expect to receive some long-run advantage from the additional earnings which will be reinvested in the business. Corporate stocks and their dividends do not ordinarily receive any favorable tax treatment except a relatively minor income tax advantage provided in the Revenue Act of 1954 and the low-rate property taxation (or failure to assess) which is common to all intangibles.

8. Mortgages and loans. Though this form of investment is resorted to by thousands of individuals and institutions, the types of loans and the circumstances surrounding them are so varied as to preclude accurate generalizations. It is probable that skillful lenders find this type of investment very satisfactory, and the average uninitiated investor probably has better luck with mortgages than he has with corporate stocks. However, mortgages and loans are often too large to permit much diversification for small investors who use them. Mortgages and loans are often exempted from the property taxes, but the income from them is taxable.

9. Homeownership. This type of investment has always been popular with Americans and has received additional impetus in recent years through the activities of the Federal Housing Administration. Homeownership is probably financially profitable to a family which finds a fixed location feasible and whose members can perform the small incidental functions of maintenance and repair. Otherwise, the case is doubtful. There may, of course, be important psychic advantages stemming from security, stability, and the prestige of proprietorship, which will weigh heavily for homeownership. From a strictly financial viewpoint, homeownership permits an investment from which substantial income in the form of free rent is assured, since the family's use of the premises is certain. A price-level hedge is thus obtained without the necessity for assuming heavy business risks. Market risks in real estate are always substantial. Homeownership affords an income tax advantage, since the family's occupancy of a home is not measured as taxable income. In general, it may be guessed that a properly chosen home investment, bought for a normal 80 to 120 times its normal monthly rental value, will yield the average family a tax-free 5 per cent return after allowing fair amounts for depreciation, property taxes, maintenance, and insurance.

10. Real estate ownership. Like mortgage lending, this form of investment takes so many forms that reasonable generalizations are impossible. Good results undoubtedly depend on skilled supervision and, in many cases, require the performance of incidental maintenance by the owner to keep costs down. Many owners find real estate ownership a convenient way of realizing both profit and a slow return of capital (out of depreciation allowances) in cash, when they are "living up" their estates after retirement. With respect to risk factors, general real estate ownership is similar to homeownership and also has the disadvantage of affording only fairly large individual parcels, thus precluding wide diversification. Profits from rental real estate are fully taxable.

11. Business ownership. Ownership of one's own business or farm is one of the great sources of psychic satisfaction in life. For many people the investment is profitable in varying degree; for many others, perhaps for most, the financial commitment yields little more than an opportunity for self-employment at a modest wage. The risks are obviously specific to each case. The paramount claim of an investor-proprietor's own business of course poses a problem when he attempts to diversify and balance his investment portfolio, since this unique and preponderant commitment is necessarily prized above all other considerations.

12. Pension rights. Many investors are now accumulating substantial pension and social security expectations in the course of their employment. These rights are extremely valuable and must be carefully included in the development of any investment plan. Since most of them are payable in dollars, it must be conceded that they are subject to the price-level risk, and to the extent that their fulfillment depends on future interest earnings, they are subject to a money-rate risk. Few are affected by the market risk or the business risk.

The Investment Program

Enough has been said in preceding pages about investment risks and needs to indicate that a systematic investment plan is in order.

Whether the investor is an individual, an insurance company, or a bank, he can identify certain objectives to be reached and certain hazards to be met. Since it is unlikely that any specific investment or type of investment will meet every need, an assortment of investments is called for—an assortment which is suited to the specific case and time.

This idea may seem a bit unreasonable to a young man who does not have much money. After all, a three-man army which has an air corps, a tank corps, and an artillery corps cannot be expected to have much infantry. But at least a scientifically planned expansion program is possible, and so it is with an investor. If a sound investment program is to be set up out of earnings, a sequence of general requirements can be planned. Individual selections can then be made as funds are available.

Planning a Personal Investment Program

Although the first chapter of a book on investments is hardly the proper place for a discussion which must assume familiarity with the entire subject, it seems desirable at this point to elaborate on the nature of a lifetime financial plan. It can perhaps be compared to a military campaign—the principal objectives are allowed for, and the whole procedure is kept sufficiently flexible so that contingencies may be met and opportunities may be seized.

The financial aspirations which an investor may hold for himself are unquestionably his own affair. He may choose to emphasize complete family security and peace of mind, or he may make the upbuilding of his own business his major interest, or he may undertake to enhance his wealth by trading for profit in securities or real estate. Other likely ambitions will come readily to mind. In any case, the investor's hopes are likely to come closer to fulfillment if he is clear on what his desires are and if he has a systematic plan for reaching them.

This book will not undertake the thankless task of telling its readers what their investment objectives ought to be, though it may on occasion comment favorably or adversely on some of them. It will, however, offer a four-step plan for framing an investment program, which may help the reader to outline a comprehensive portfolio designed to attain his chosen goals. This will be supplemented in later chapters by discussions designed to aid in the choice of suitable individual investments and the timing of purchases and sales.

The four steps to be taken in organizing an individual's investment program call for the acquisition of (1) adequate life insurance, (2) a highly liquid emergency fund, (3) business and home investments, and (4) a general investments portfolio. These four steps should ordinarily be considered and financed in the order named:

1. Necessary insurance. Life insurance protection on the family breadwinner is desirable to assure his family the savings he may not live to earn. This protection is often needed in largest amount when the family is relatively young, before much saving has been possible. Other life insurance to protect the family budget against death and readjustment expenses should be considered, and provision for business life insurance, estate tax liquidity, and peculiar personal estates such as life tenancies may also be needed. Again—and this is of outstanding importance—insurance providing disability income in case the breadwinner is sick or injured for long periods should be provided. The amounts needed for all these purposes will often appear too great to be afforded in the average family budget, but account can be taken of available assistance from relatives in dire emergencies, and the passage of time and the accumulation of savings will ultimately bring resources closer to needs for most people.

2. A quick-recourse fund. Next on the high-priority list is the accumulation of a fund which will always be available for emergencies. For purely family use, readily available resources amounting to half a year's income, kept in insurance reserves, bank deposits, or government savings bonds, might suffice. Since this fund will doubtless be used and replaced a good many times in the history of the average family, it should be in a highly convenient form and location, and available without any delay, embarrassment, or heavy costs.

3. Investments to meet personal needs. Third on the priority list are the investments in a home and in a personal business, if needed. From a purely financial viewpoint these might not rank so high, but personal urgency outweighs financial theories. Also, modern installment financing makes it possible to control very substantial investments in homes, especially, without having to omit everything else.

4. General fund. This fund receives all sums not allotted to the preceding ones. In general, its function is a balancing and proportioning one, to bring the entire investment program into line with sound principles. Its fundamental tasks are to provide safety through wide diversification and to bring about a reasonable balance between investments in dollar-value items and in equities. The principles involved are discussed at length in the next section.

Features of a Personal Program

In choosing his specific investments the investor will need definite ideas regarding a number of features which his total portfolio should possess. These features should be consistent with his general objectives and, in addition, should afford him all the incidental conveniences and advantages which are possible in his circumstances. The following eight features are suggested as the ingredients from which many successful investors compound their selection policies. They are not offered in any order denoting importance, except that the first is clearly the most vital.

1. Safety of principal. Although safety of principal does not necessarily require that the market prices of one's investments never shrink below their cost, it does require that the investor avoid unsound and profitless risks. It calls for careful review of economic and industry trends before choosing types of investments or the time to invest. It demands careful selection of the individual commitments. Finally, it recognizes that errors are unavoidable and requires extensive diversification.

Adequate diversification means assortment of investment commitments in five different ways—by industry, geographically, by management personnel, by financial type (that is, between dollar receivables and equities), and by maturities. If this is accomplished, losses due to the decline of any industry, to disaster in any geographic region, to error or defalcation by any management group, to changes in the price level, and to changes in interest rates would all be minimized. This is desirable, even if it also diversifies against fortuitous gains.[2] Since adequate diversification should balance fortui-

[2] This is a point on which violent difference of opinion exists. Most textbook writers, investment counselors, investment companies, and bank trust officers take the viewpoint indicated here, but some hold that safety lies in a few holdings carefully chosen and closely watched. One very successful investor argues that nearly all investments are subject to risk; that such investments fluctuate in price to an amount which overshadows any possible dividend or interest income; that careful and intelligent specu-

tous gains against fortuitous losses, it may justify a reasonable proportion of speculative stocks in the average portfolio—or better yet, the inclusion of investment company stocks which represent a portion of speculative commitments.

Diversification can be wasteful if carried to extremes. Too many securities and real estate and mortgage holdings—possibly over 20 for the average individual—give him too many to watch, unless he makes a profession of supervising them or employs someone to do it for him. Too small commitments in securities are uneconomic because of excessive commission charges and other costs in transactions. Securities commitments should probably range between $500 minimum and half a year's family income as a maximum, except for items of superlative quality, such as government bonds.

2. Adequate liquidity and collateral value. Emphasis has already been laid on the necessity for a minimum quick-recourse fund. In addition, a sound fortfolio will look to the sure and quick availability of additional funds which may be needed for business opportunities, stock market opportunities, or estate taxes. Whether money raising is to be done by sale or by borrowing, it will be easier if the portfolio contains a planned proportion of high-grade and readily salable investments such as government or big-corporation bonds. Real estate, personal businesses, or speculative securities are not ideal for this use.

3. Stability of income. This factor is important in arranging an investment portfolio for an individual who depends closely on the income; it is less important for others. Though income stability helps greatly in stabilizing the prices of corporate stocks, it can be found to a high degree only in certain industries, and insistence upon it therefore restricts the available choices. Probably stable income payers also cost a trifle more than other investments, hence should not be overemphasized by those who do not need them.

4. Adequacy of income after taxes. There are really two problems involved here, one concerned with the amount of income paid by the investment and the other with the burden of income taxes upon

---

lators can anticipate these price changes in a majority of cases; and that successive speculations, not widely diversified but always carefully studied, will employ funds more profitably than is possible through diversified investing. See G. M. Loeb, *The Battle for Investment Survival,* Barron's Publishing Company, Inc., Boston, 1952.

that income. When the investor's income is small, he is usually eager to obtain maximum cash returns on his investments and is prone to take excessive risks and to prefer immediate dividends to greater benefits at a later date. It is unfortunate to have to choose between adequate income and adequate security; but it is possible, to some degree, to seek out good stocks which pay practically all their earnings in dividends and real estate which nets its owner both real earnings and depreciation funds in cash.

The investor who is not pressed for cash income often finds that income taxes deplete certain types of investment incomes less than others, thus affecting his choices. For example, neither the rental value of an owner-occupied home nor the interest paid by a state or municipal bond is subject to Federal income tax. Furthermore, corporate earnings which are not paid out in dividends are not taxable to the stockholders, even though when used to add to the company's resources they presumably enhance the value of the stock.

5. Purchasing-power stability. The price-level hazard has already been explained. There remains to state the conclusion that the average personal or family portfolio is well-balanced in normal times when it consists half of dollar-sum holdings, such as bank deposits, life insurance, and bonds, and half of ownership equities such as real estate and common stocks. In making this computation some investors would regard mortgage and other debt as negative dollars—that is, as subtractions from the dollar-sum investments.

From a purely theoretical viewpoint it would appear that a portfolio consisting entirely of real estate and stocks would balance price-level changes more perfectly than the 50-50 program recommended. Perhaps it might, with luck, but the instability of equity prices plus other considerations previously mentioned commend the 50-50 choice in the average case. Obviously, such factors as the quality of the investments, the adequacy of insurance protection, the stability of personal earnings, family needs, and estate tax hazards could affect this ratio. Many investors are also guided in this respect by their judgments of the country's economic condition. Clearly, if a business boom and inflationary trends are in prospect, investments in common stocks and real estate have more than average attraction; but if depression and price declines seem likely, conservative dollar-type investments would be wiser.

The indicated preference for a 50-50 ratio between dollars and equities would not apply to an institution such as a bank or insurance company, whose assets must be in dollars to offset obligations which are payable in dollars.

6. Possible appreciation. It is neither necessary nor desirable, in making investments, to forswear hope for market profits in a search for security. Both real estate and stock markets are highly irregular, and the individual who sticks closely to quality investments can still profit by choosing well, buying at the right time, and switching wisely from overpriced to underpriced items. Not many people will profit greatly by these devices, but reasonable acumen will be rewarded, and some of the inevitable losses can be offset. Ventures into speculative commitments may be similarly approached, with the expectation of more and greater losses which may be balanced by more and larger gains, if the investor has the diligence and skill which successful speculation demands.

7. Freedom from care. The existence of important risks in every class of investment makes it impossible to "buy good things and forget them." Constant skilled supervision is necessary to avoid losses and to obtain good returns. But the pitfalls which await the uninitiated are much less dangerous in commitments of investment grade than in speculations. One who wishes to minimize the attention required by his investments should therefore make quality his watchword. This emphasis will doubtless reduce the amount of income available and tend to direct the bulk of the portfolio to dollar-sum items. Alternatively, a professional investment counselor or the investment management services of a trust company can be employed, at a cost approximating one-half of one per cent per year on sums of reasonably substantial size.

8. Legality. Investments of trusts, estates, children, and incompetents must consist of types approved by law. State laws and precedents vary, but in all cases the plans must include complete compliance with requirements.

Legal Ownership and Tax Problems

Investment plans and decisions are often affected by the legal aspects of property ownership and by tax problems involving both incomes and ultimate estates. For example, a plan for developing a number of living trusts for members of the family by making gifts into the trusts at annual intervals will require the planning of a whole series of independent portfolios. In another case, the decision of a high-salaried individual to retire from active business may justify switching extensively from tax-exempt to taxable income sources. Legal title and estate tax matters are most troublesome to people of substantial wealth, but every investor must deal with them to some extent, if only to decide if the joint tenancy laws of his state hold any advantage for him. Some of the principles involved are discussed in later chapters of this book.

Institutional Investment

Like individuals, financial institutions find it desirable to choose investments which are appropriate to their needs. Banks, savings banks, life insurance companies, and savings and loan associations need investments which are almost exclusively payable in dollars. They must also have items which are very safe and free from market price fluctuation, because their obligations customarily total between 90 and 95 per cent of their total assets and a relatively small shrinkage in asset values would endanger their solvency. Banks and savings banks, and to a lesser degree the life insurance companies, must also consider the ready marketability of a portion of their investments, since their customers have the right to demand the prompt return of the money in their custody, and it is important that such demands be met without the necessity of selling securities or property at a loss.

Other institutions, such as endowed hospitals and colleges and trust companies administering the funds of others for a fee, are under less pressure to secure value stability but usually feel bound to obtain steady income and long-run security. Nearly all institutional investments are to some extent regulated by public authority, although in varying degree.

It must be concluded, therefore, that the investment policies of financial and endowed institutions are likely to vary greatly with the type of business conducted and the legal restrictions imposed, as well as with the preferences of their managements. Investors seeking to pass judgment upon them must therefore consider all these factors.

QUESTIONS AND PROBLEMS

1. Would you say that the stock of General Motors Corporation, which sold under 25 and above 90 in the years 1947–1954, should be called a speculation?

2. Would the individual who carefully studied General Motors' prospects in 1954 and estimated that the company's future annual earnings and dividends would average $6 per share and $4 per share, respectively, be investing or speculating if he bought the stock at 75?

3. Is it reasonable to say that a great oil company such as Texas Company (maker of Texaco products) is significantly subject to the business risk? What could happen to it?

4. Are United States government bonds subject to the market risk? To the money-rate risk?

5. Would a well-diversified collection of residential properties have afforded an investor a satisfactory price-level hedge during the 1942–1953 inflation? Would farm properties have done so? Industrial stocks? Oil stocks? Will these precedents be followed during the "next" inflation? What will probably happen to all of these in a depression?

6. Why is life insurance enumerated as a form of investment?

7. Is there any real difference between the investment functions performed by postal savings deposits and by insured savings and loan accounts?

8. Are the interest incomes from savings accounts and government bonds subject to income taxation? Are the tax rates high enough to make any real difference?

9. Why is there so little difference between the yields of corporate bonds and United States Treasury bonds? Why should there be a difference at all?

10. Why are public utility common stocks and nearly all preferred stocks regarded as poor price-level hedges?

11. Explain why homeownership yields a "tax-free" income. Would this be true of rental property?

12. How can an investor "live up" his investments in real estate after retirement? Could this be done with common stock investments? How?

13. If you were retiring on social security plus employers' pensions totaling $150 per month, and had $40,000 in cash of your own, what types of investments would you regard as most suitable for your savings?

14. If you were an attorney aged 30, with a wife and two children, no

relatives capable of giving financial support, no savings other than household furniture and office equipment, but with earnings now averaging $6,000 per year, how much life insurance and how much disability income insurance would you consider proper? (Assume that ordinary life insurance costs $20 per thousand per annum, of which half may be regarded as savings, and that total-and-permanent disability income coverage costs $60 per year for a disability income amounting to $100 per month.)

15. As this man begins to accumulate savings, what should he do with the first $5,000, assuming it to be saved $1,000 annually?

16. Would the purchase of a $15,000 home be advisable, if the rental value was $120 per month, if the annual taxes were $250, average depreciation $300, average maintenance costs $200, and insurance $20?

17. When the attorney is aged 50, earning $10,000, and has $50,000 saved, how much insurance protection does he need? How much when he is 60 and has $75,000 saved?

18. If the attorney at age 60 had no life insurance, no dependents except his wife, and continued in his profession, and you were asked to recommend investments for his $60,000 (the $15,000 home is assumed already purchased), what would you select? List amounts beside the following, and where corporations are involved indicate how many different ones you would invest in: savings deposits, savings and loan, government bonds, telephone bonds, electric power company bonds, telephone stocks, electric power stocks, motor company stocks, electric equipment stocks, steel stocks, food stocks, chemical stocks, bank stocks, oil stocks, building material stocks, insurance stocks, residential (rental) property.

REFERENCES

Badger, Ralph E., and Harry G. Guthmann: *Investment Principles and Practices,* Prentice-Hall, Inc., New York, 1951, Chaps. 4, 28.

Bellemore, Douglas H.: *Investments Principles and Practices,* B. C. Forbes and Sons Publishing Co., Inc., New York, 1953, Chaps. 1, 18.

Dowrie, George W., and Douglas R. Fuller: *Investments,* John Wiley & Sons, Inc., New York, 1950, Chaps. 3, 6, 7, 12.

Financial Handbook, The Ronald Press Company, New York, 1948, pp. 213–270.

Graham, Benjamin: *The Intelligent Investor,* Harper & Brothers, New York, 1954.

Grodinsky, Julius: *Investments,* The Ronald Press Company, New York, 1953, Chap. 1.

Jordan, David F., and Herbert E. Dougall: *Investments,* Prentice-Hall, Inc., New York, 1952, Chaps. 7, 8, 11.

Robbins, Sidney M.: *Managing Securities,* Houghton Mifflin Company, Boston, 1954, Chaps. 7, 8.

Sauvain, Harry C.: *Investment Management,* Prentice-Hall, Inc., New York, 1953, Chaps. 10–13.

Chapter 2: BASIC DETERMINANTS
OF INVESTMENT VALUES

One of the most troublesome problems confronting investors is that of estimating the values to be paid or accepted for investment assets. The market prices for most types of investments vary considerably through the years, and some of the very important types, including real estate and common stocks, fluctuate sharply as business conditions change. Because of the importance of the sums involved, no investor can afford to ignore these price fluctuations, and many investors are interested in profiting from them if they can. An understanding of the basic factors affecting investment values is therefore of general interest.

Later chapters of this book will deal in detail with the characteristics of specific types of investments. The task of the present chapter is to explore some of the fundamentals which affect all investment values. These fundamentals are pertinent to the determination of both long-run value trends and cyclical fluctuations in value.

In approaching this task, it is essential to realize that investment values are in the last analysis simply prices, and that prices are made by demand and supply. The real problem, therefore, is to explain how people arrive at their decisions to pay certain prices when they buy or to accept certain prices when they sell. Viewed in this light, it is clear that no answer can be complete, for a complete answer would have to explain the ideas of many people who buy and sell on impulse or as the result of faulty reasoning, in addition to the presumed majority whose decisions are informed and sensible. But if it is assumed that most investors are reasonably informed and sensible, it would appear that the major influences determining investment values can be identified with four fundamental concepts.

The first of these is a mathematical approach to the subject, which suggests that the prices people will pay for an investment asset are largely determined by their appraisals of the future dividends and other benefits which the investment may be expected to produce. This approach requires the estimation of future benefits, both in amount and time of receipt, and appraises them on a present-value basis by means of compound discount tables. The second concept involves an economic interpretation of capital supplies, profit margins, interest rates, the interrelationships among them, and the impact of the whole upon investment values. The third concept stresses the fact that supply and demand for investment assets are greatly affected by personal preferences, the customs of financial institutions, legal restrictions on institutional investment, the distribution of the nation's wealth and income, and the national money supply. Finally, it must be conceded that the uncertainties of the future explain, if they do not justify, rapid fluctuation in the markets for securities and real estate at times; and, since these fluctuations are familiar and expected, their violence is often accentuated by speculators seeking to exploit them.

These four fundamentals, then, will be presented here as the logical basis for investment valuation. They are neither complete nor perfect in this chapter, but it is believed that they will provide a reasonable introduction to the subject of investment values and their causes.

The Present-value Theory

It is often said that the reasonable present market value of any investment is the total of future benefits (whether as income or return of principal, in cash or in services would not matter) expected from it, discounted down to the present at an interest rate consistent with the risk. By this measure it could be computed that a share of stock deemed likely to pay $6 annually in dividends *forever* is worth $100 if the hazards justify a yield of 6 per cent on the bargain; or that a bond promising $30 per year interest plus a return of $1,000 principal after 20 years is now worth $864.10, if the risk is commensurate with a 4 per cent yield.[1] These statements appear to be

---

[1] Table 1 indicates that $1 per year for the next 20 years is worth $13.59, if the appropriate discount rate is 4 per cent. Since the bond pays $30 per year, the total present value of 20 years' interest payments is $407.70 (30 × $13.59). The principal sum is to be repaid after 20 years; Table 2 indicates that a $1 sum due in 20 years has a present value at 4 per cent discount of $.4564, and the $1,000 bond principal

fully logical. No investment is intrinsically worth more or less than the present value of the expected future benefits from it.

Competent economists will immediately observe that at any given time the market value of an investment asset depends on demand and supply, which in turn reflect the estimates of a number of people concerning the future paying power of the investment and the degree of risk [2] involved. In other words, the market price is the result of a consensus about the future of the investment. This is unquestionably the proper viewpoint. It must also be noted that, although this market consensus vacillates as people change their opinions about the future, it is certain to adjust itself to reflect the actual situation as the future unfolds. The individual who wishes to invest profitably must therefore base his decisions at least in part upon accurate appraisals of the income to be expected and the rate of discount which the risk requires.

It would appear that the first step in determining the dollar value of an investment must of necessity be to estimate the amount and timing of the benefits to be received from it from now until the end of time—unless, of course, it is appraised purely by guess. After all, the only advantages the owners will ever get out of an investment asset are the payments or services it brings them, after expenses and taxes are deducted. It is immaterial, in making these estimates of future benefits, whether the investment in question is a contractual obligation such as a bond or an annuity, which promises fixed sums in dollars, or whether it is an equity item such as stock or real estate, whose payments might be irregular in amount and timing. In either instance the first step in valuation is to make the best possible forecast of future benefit receipts.

In many instances the future benefits expected by investors consist of attractive selling prices rather than long years of dividend or rental income. However, it may be argued that the most likely basis for expecting an increased selling price is the conviction that either the earning power or the safety of the investment is increasing and that the improvement will shortly be recognized by others and be

---

must therefore have a present value of $456.40. The two present values, $407.70 on the interest payments and $456.40 on the principal, total $864.10.

[2] The term should probably be *distaste* rather than risk, since an investor's insistence on a high yield rate as an inducement to buy a certain investment may spring from his dislike of its long-term nature, of the supervision required, of its lack of marketability, or any of a number of other factors.

reflected in the price.[3] The underlying source of value is still the discounted value of expected future receipts.

It is clear that, as time passes and differing aspects of the future appear, revisions of investors' estimates of benefits to come will cause constant changes in their appraisals of many investments. Obviously, those which wear out or become obsolete as time passes will have progressively smaller or fewer contributions to make in the future, and their values will decline progressively. Those which encounter severe competition or adverse political developments or any of a multitude of other hazards will also seem to promise less. And of course those whose advantages are ascendant will appear to offer more than was previously anticipated. All of this is clearly evident in the fluctuation of real estate and stock market values.

When the best possible estimates of future benefits have been made, it is next necessary to discount these estimates down to the present at a proper rate of interest, to determine what they are worth. The proper rate of interest or discount is said to be a composite of two factors: the basic rate of interest on low-risk loans, which reflects chiefly the supply of and demand for funds, and the extra return which investors demand of an investment which they deem to be hazardous or inconvenient. Thus, long-term United States government bonds in 1953 yielded about 3¼ per cent, but good electric power company common stocks were regarded as sufficiently objectionable to justify a 6 per cent rate. (Both of these rates are before allowance for income taxes; the net returns would therefore be considerably less.) Investment values will obviously depend almost as much upon the degree of hazard which investors believe attaches to a commitment as on the amount they believe it will earn; for a stock estimated to pay $4 per share per year into the indefinite future is worth $100 per share if its quality justifies a 4 per cent discount rate, but only $50 if uncertainty demands an 8 per cent yield. Furthermore, it is clear that the future of any investment will look less secure at certain times than at others. Business conditions, political conditions, and variations in public confidence will inevitably produce changes in the rate of compensation people

[3] There are occasional irrational markets in which this is not true. For example, investors in 1929 borrowed money at 7 per cent and bought stocks at prices to yield 3 per cent, not in expectation of any dividend increase but rather in the hope of selling the already overpriced stock to "some other sucker" at a still higher price. Who cares about dividends when the principal appreciates 25 per cent per year?

will demand for bearing risks; and this means changes in the values they attach to their investments.

Tables 1 and 2 illustrate the ideas being presented here. These tables are small excerpts from very large tables which enable the investor to obtain at a glance the present-day theoretical value of sums which are expected to be paid in the future. Thus Table 1 indicates (in the 5 per cent column, fourth entry) that a share of stock

Table 1. Present Value of a $1 Annual Payment for Specified Numbers of Years, at Various Discount Rates

Years	2%	4%	5%	6%	8%
5	$ 4.71	$ 4.45	$ 4.33	$ 4.21	$ 3.99
10	8.98	8.11	7.72	7.36	6.71
15	12.85	11.12	10.38	9.71	8.56
20	16.35	13.59	12.46	11.47	9.82
30	22.40	17.29	15.37	13.76	11.26
40	27.36	19.79	17.16	15.05	11.92
50	31.42	21.48	18.26	15.76	12.23
60	34.76	22.62	18.93	16.16	12.38
80	39.74	23.92	19.60	16.51	12.47
100	43.10	24.50	19.85	16.62	12.49
Forever....	50.00	25.00	20.00	16.67	12.50

expected to pay $1 per year in dividends for 20 years, and to pay nothing thereafter, is worth $12.46 if the risk is such that the investor wants a 5 per cent return on his money. If the expected dividend is $2.50 per year, it is only necessary to multiply the $12.46 value for each $1 of income by 2½ ($12.46 × 2½) to arrive at the correct appraisal of $31.15. One further item of explanation is required here: since these indicated values assume that the income (dividend, net rent, or whatever it is) will be paid for the indicated number of years only (in this example, 20 years), the values are computed so that the investor gets his principal back out of the annual dividends, in addition to his 5 per cent income. Thus the $2.50 dividend expected on the share of stock selling for $31.15 is far more than 5 per cent on $31.15. It is this 5 per cent plus an installment of returning principal. It will therefore be necessary to exercise caution in comparing the "yields" cited in some professional literature with the percentage returns shown in Table 1, for the yields on stock investments are commonly computed by dividing expected income by present price, *thus assuming that the earning power of the principal will last forever and need not be amortized.*

Table 2 indicates the value of single payments to be collected in the future. This table is commonly used in evaluating future contractual payments to be made in lump sums, and may also be used

Table 2. Present Value of a Single $1 Payment to Be Collected at a Future Time, at Specified Rates of Compound Discount

Years to payment date	2%	4%	5%	6%	8%
5	$.9057	$.8219	$.7835	$.7473	$.6806
10	.8203	.6756	.6139	.5584	.4632
15	.7430	.5553	.4810	.4173	.3152
20	.6730	.4564	.3769	.3118	.2145
30	.5521	.3083	.2314	.1741	.0994
40	.4529	.2083	.1420	.0972	.0460
50	.3715	.1407	.0872	.0543	.0213
60	.3048	.0951	.0535	.0303	.0099
80	.2051	.0434	.0202	.0095	.0021
100	.1380	.0198	.0076	.0029	.0005

in two-part calculations such as that illustrated in footnote 1 on page 24.

One of the very significant aspects of investment valuation is the relative emphasis which must be attached to imminent dividends or other income, as compared with the relative unimportance of receipts expected in distant years. For example, a share of stock expected to pay a $1 dividend annually for 100 years (and to be valueless thereafter) is worth $19.85, if the risk is one which justifies a 5 per cent yield; yet the dividends for the first 20 years are worth $12.46, leaving a value of only $7.39 for those of the next 80 years. Other examples can be deduced from Table 1; it will be noted that the higher the yield rate expected, the greater the relative importance of the early receipts. Evidently an investor need not estimate the far-distant incomes from his investment with extreme accuracy; if he is right about what it can do for the next 20 years his value conclusions can be substantially accurate. The importance of early receipts also emphasizes the investment weakness of idle land or non-dividend-paying stocks. Long-deferred incomes have only a limited current value, especially if the risk justifies a high discount rate. Table 2 illustrates this situation.

Two more detailed aspects of present value calculations should be noted. First, it is clear that the more imminent income expectations are usually far more certain of collection than the later ones and might reasonably be discounted at a lower rate. For example, if one estimated that General Motors common stock would produce a $4 per share dividend annually for 40 years, and thereafter produce nothing, the 40 years' payments at 6 per cent discount would have a present value of $60.20 (Table 1). But if the first 15 years' payments at $4 were deemed so sure that 4 per cent discount was sufficient, they alone would be worth $44.48; and if the remaining 25 years' payments were regarded as sufficiently uncertain to warrant 8 per cent discount, they would be worth $13.44. Adding the $44.48 and the $13.44 produces a present-value estimate of $57.92 on this basis.

The second detailed aspect of present values is based upon the fact that many investments seem very certain to produce a limited amount of dividends but are likely to produce much more. The more certain portion of the income may reasonably be evaluated at a lower discount rate than is applied to the remaining portions. For example, the 40-year, $4 per share, estimated income from General Motors stock need not all be regarded as of equal quality; possibly $1 per year is highly dependable, justifying a 4 per cent discount rate; perhaps $1 more is deserving of a 5 per cent rate, and the final $2 may be uncertain enough to justify a discount rate of 8 per cent. On this basis Table 1 indicates that the income portions would have present values of $19.79, $17.16, and $23.84, respectively, to total to an appraisal of $60.79.

Calculations of the sort indicated here are seldom made by amateur investors, though they are common enough in connection with major real estate and bond transactions. Perhaps the reason amateurs do not make such calculations is that they dislike to "guesstimate" incomes for long periods into the unknown future and, therefore, prefer to choose in a more casual way between the values which the market provides. The simplified "rule-of-thumb" appraisal methods ordinarily used will be presented in later chapters.[4]

It is not to be expected that market prices, which reflect the current judgments of fallible men, will at all times show accurate appraisals of investment assets. By the same logic, it is not to be expected that accurate appraisals by investors will always obtain immediate market profits. But there is hardly room for doubt that good judgment in appraising future earning power and in assaying economic hazards will have its reward in the long run. Even if market prices never reflect the values which the prescient investor identifies and acquires, the investor will obtain the income benefits which his wisdom enables him to foresee; and in most instances the market prices will sooner or later recognize the true situation. Market prices are often slow and erratic in arriving at logical levels, but they are forever searching for them.

The Value of Improbable Possibilities

The theory that investment values may be appraised by capitalizing the best available estimate of future income receipts fails to work in cases in which the probable income is small but in which large gains are possible but unlikely. People are usually willing to pay good sums for such items as speculative oil land or doubtful-quality corporate stocks which probably will never pay any return but which may possibly produce large amounts. This speculative attitude also affects the price of some types of medium-grade real estate and stocks, for people are often willing to pay more than normal dividend capitalizations for assets with enticing additional long-shot possibilities.[5]

Although it is difficult to prove the point or to make any quantitative measures of the amounts, it seems reasonable to conclude that most real estate and stock values are based upon the capitalized

---

[4] These methods generally involve an attempt to predict average annual corporate profits and dividends per share of stock, and appraise the stock by multiplying the expected earnings and dividends by capitalization factors which past value history indicates to be reasonable.

[5] It has been suggested by some writers that the real basis for these speculative prices lies in the mathematical probability that the contemplated dividend will be paid. Thus, if an oil-producing bonanza is a 1-chance-in-4 probability, the stock of

values of estimated future incomes from them plus the speculative value attached to their improbable possibilities. It also seems reasonable to guess that the values of stable and profitable properties are mostly based upon capitalized anticipated incomes—this can be deduced from the fact that their values seem reasonably related to projected earnings and dividends—while the values of undependable or losing ventures are based mostly on their speculative possibilities. Finally, it is clear that values based on stable incomes are far more dependable than those based upon vague possibilities, for the prices of productive real estate and steady-dividend-paying stocks fluctuate much less than those of their speculative counterparts.

On the strength of these deductions it would seem wise for the investor in secure and stable properties to concentrate most of his attention on estimates of earnings and dividend distributions and for the owner of highly speculative items to take special cognizance of market behavior. The values of extreme speculations often border on the irrational and are, consequently, extremely subject to market whims and fancies.

Sunk Capital

Most investments in business ownership, stocks, real estate, and to some extent mortgages and bonds represent interests in *sunk capital*. That is, these investments depend upon assets which, because of their nature or location, are definitely committed to one industry or type of service. If that industry or type of service produces a return, the investment will have value; if no returns can be had, the investment is a failure and will have only a speculative value based on the possibility of some future improvement in its position. The returns which investors obtain from their properties may consist of returns of capital or payments from net income or both.

For example, a poorly located apartment house costing $50,000

---

the oil company ought to sell at about one-fourth the price it would bring if the bonanza were already a proven fact. The author believes that the salability of bright dreams varies greatly from time to time, but that on the average they sell higher than true mathematical probabilities would justify. Hope springs eternal in the speculator's breast—and the net result is a pattern of stock and real estate prices which often makes speculative opportunities higher in price than they should be.

might enable its owner to pay all operating expenses and recover $1,000 annually for 50 years. No net income would be earned in this case; yet the apartment house would have a value based chiefly upon the discounted present value of $1,000 annually for the remainder of its useful life. Most buildings and many other "wasting asset" investments make returns consisting of recovered capital plus whatever net income is earned.

But a large percentage of business investments cannot make payments to their owners except out of real earnings, because of the necessity for constant modernization and improvement. The typical business finds that depreciation funds—the portion of cash receipts from sales which represent recoveries of original capital—must be steadily reinvested and even supplemented by outlays from earnings and new sales of securities, if competitive efficiency is to be maintained. Capital committed to such industries is forever "sunk" in them, and the investments must be evaluated largely on the basis of the distributions from earnings which can be expected.

Earning Power of Capital

The earning power of any group of business assets, including the monopoly position, prestige, and good will which management will attempt to develop in the business, depends chiefly on the urgency of demand for the products and the extent of competition which must be met. A nation which is growing vigorously, and which affords many new or inadequately developed industries where available new capital may be invested, is likely not to be too sharply competitive in any field. Profit margins will therefore be high. On the other hand, a nation which is growing slowly, which lacks the impetus of new inventions or new industries and which has adequate amounts of new savings seeking investment, is likely to be well supplied with competitors in every line. Average profit margins under such conditions will be relatively low.

Of course, it is not to be expected that different businesses would have identical profit margins under any of these conditions. After all, skillfully managed concerns in all lines may be expected to do better than others. And it is to be expected that relatively secure lines of business, or those better known or easier to enter or easier to finance, may be somewhat more crowded and more competitive than the average. Logical differentials in earnings rates are certain to occur. Investors who are estimating the future dividend-paying power of a company must therefore consider both the general earning power of capital and the particular competitive position of the company and its industry.

As new savings become available for business use their owners naturally tend to invest them in the industries in which future earnings seem likely to compensate most generously for the degree of risk involved. This is an individual and competitive process in which errors in judgment constantly occur, yet it seems to allocate new capital reasonably well between industries. Each industry tends to be built up competitively until its probable average earnings rate matches all others, allowing for differences in risk and convenience. Although this building-up process does not work out with complete accuracy, it does tend to establish an average profit margin, or group of related profit margins in different industries, which provide a measure of the potential earning power of uninvested funds.

Because many of the owners of existing capital investments are constantly seeking to sell them, investors with free funds usually have a choice between the acquisition of existing properties or the construction of new ones. This is true whether the desired investments are in corporate stocks, small businesses, farms, residential real estate, or something else. As a rule, also, there are enough competing sellers and buyers in each field so that the prices paid for existing investments are reasonably related to the cost of constructing equally profitable new ones. This means that, if the probable average earning power of new funds invested in business is 7 per cent, an existing business could be bought at a price upon which its average earnings would amount to a somewhat similar figure. To be more definite about it, if a new apartment house can be constructed at a cost upon which 7 per cent can be earned, a similar existing apartment house should bring a price upon which its earnings will approximate 7 per cent.

Investors may make two practical deductions from these facts. First, they may expect that the long-term average rate of business profits will tend to reflect the adequacy or shortage of the nation's capital supply, as measured against its rate of growth and development. If the nation is able to save at a rate in excess of the sums needed to expand old industries and develop new ones, average profit rates will fall and the investor who holds long-term fixed-income bonds, preferred stocks, and mortgages, or who owns patent-protected or other monopolistic businesses, will retain a constant income, while the investor who depends on the diminishing profits of competitive enterprise will get less. If the nation's savings are small compared to the business opportunities available, the relative advantage will be reversed. The second deduction is that, since the yield rates at which investment incomes of all sorts are capitalized will be related to the average rate of business profits, fixed-income investments will rise or fall in value as general profit rates change, while the value of a typical competitive investment will be subject to two offsetting influences: a tendency for profit rates and income capitalization rates to rise and fall together. For example, a decline in its profit rate from 8 to 6 per cent would not affect the investment value of a competitive enterprise if investors' savings increased in volume so that all comparable investment opportunities were crowded down to a 6 per cent basis. A $6 annual income capitalized at 6 per cent is worth as much as an $8 income capitalized at 8 per cent.

Although these deductions based upon capital supply and profit margins are true as general long-run tendencies, their effects are obscured and importantly distorted by other influences. Paramount among these influences are the economic disturbances known as business cycles, which affect all aspects of investment values, and the variations in investor preferences for different types of investments, which cause relative values to change sharply frome time to time. These factors will be noted in succeeding sections.

Interest Rates and Stock Yields [6]

When business concerns or property owners wish to borrow money for long-term business use, they normally offer to pay interest rates which are somewhat lower than the sums they expect to earn with the assets the borrowed money will purchase. However, they must offer high enough rates to get the desired money, in competition with others in whose hands it would have similar earning power. Thus the interest rates offered for borrowed money will normally be re-

[6] Yield may be defined roughly as the percentage of net income (dividend or interest payment) to the price of the security. More detailed definitions will be developed later.

lated to but somewhat less than the average earning power which the money might have in business. The suppliers of loan funds are of two types: those whose preferences or legal position compel them to make loans instead of owning business investments direct, and those who can choose either loans or ownership. Banks and life insurance companies are chiefly in the first category; they must lend. But individuals and many other agencies have a choice; they may either lend or own. Thus the suppliers of loan funds have not only the opportunity of playing one borrower against another, to obtain a rate commensurate with the earning power of newly constructed capital; some of them are also in a position to weigh the advantages of owning versus lending and to choose the most attractive.

It would follow from all this that long-run trends in interest rates should be somehow related to the earning power of common stock investments, which are a form of property ownership. This relationship is illustrated in Chart 1, which reproduces a study on the subject made by the Cleveland Trust Company. It will be noted that the yields on both bonds and stocks tended to rise, with certain cyclical interruptions, from 1904 until about 1923. From 1923 to 1948 the tendency was generally downward, though the influences of depression and war distort the trend considerably. The rising trend of 1904–1923 coincided with a period of great growth in the country, in which investment opportunities outstripped saving, creating a scarcity of capital. This scarcity was magnified by the wearing out of existing facilities during World War I.

The period 1923–1948 began with the gradual overcoming of the capital shortages during the twenties and continued through the economic doldrums of the thirties, when new capital was not very profitable and existing capital did not appear very safe. The declining interest rates of 1934–1941 can be in large part ascribed to the fact that available funds were offered for loan on good security at a time when high-quality borrowers were unable to find profitable business uses for them. Less secure investments yielding much more did not appeal to safety-minded investors; hence, stocks remained relatively low in price and generous in yield.

The final period on the chart, that of 1942–1953, continued low bond yields and relatively high stock yields under decisively changed conditions. War boom and postwar expansions caused an enthusiastic demand for funds to finance new capital facilities. Beginning in

1947 sporadic attempts were made to limit the rate of bank credit expansion, and the consequent rise in interest rates (reflecting moderately lower bond prices) can be seen on the chart. The stock market, meanwhile, had a checkered history. Prices gradually rose and yields consequently fell during and immediately after the war, but large-scale corporate sales of new stock to finance postwar expansion

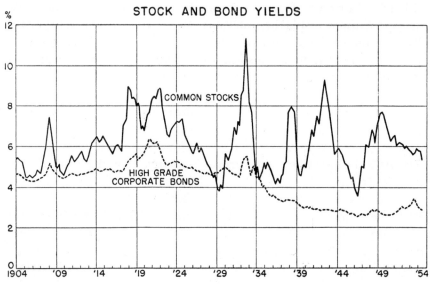

CHART 1. (*Reproduced from the Cleveland Trust Company Bulletin, June 16, 1954.*)

overwhelmed the limited buying demand for stock in 1946–1948, drove stock prices down and again raised stock yields to high levels. These high yields naturally attracted buyers, the stock market recovered in the years 1949–1953, and in 1953 both stock and bond yields were low enough to reflect the nation's ample supplies of capital and savings. Clearly, investments in this wealthy country will not often yield as generous returns as they did back in 1920–1925.

Further inspection of Chart 1 discloses two other noteworthy facts. First, during most of the period 1904–1937 the yield on the stocks did not greatly exceed that on the bonds. This fact may be credited in part to the perennial optimism of the average stockholder, and in part to the fact that the chart shows only the *dividend yield* on the stocks. The *earnings* of the corporations probably averaged 50 per cent more than the dividend payments, and it was reasonable for the stockholder to hope for some long-run advantage from the retained portion of the earnings. But it is clear that since 1937 stock yields have remained far above bond yields. This persistent situation must be ascribed in part to artificially low interest rates on the bonds, but it also reflects a relative lack of demand for stocks, which was due partly to personal investors' preferences and partly to the fact that institutional investors were diverting most of the nation's savings into other investments. This situation has inspired a notable advertising campaign by the securities dealers in the years 1949–1954, through which the dealers hope to add many new stock buyers to their lists.

Second, the yields of the stocks increased much more sharply in depressions than did those on the bonds. The reasons are threefold: stocks are more hazardous than bonds, hence have less appeal when people are frightened by hard times; bonds are widely held in institutions, whose finances and policies are more stable than those of individuals; and good bonds are not commonly subjected to erratic speculative buying and selling. It may be noted in passing, however, that bond yields as well as stock yields often fall with good times and rise with poor ones. The reason lies in part in the desire of many people to sell securities and retain cash in hard times, when cash is most difficult to obtain, as contrasted with a willingness to keep their resources fully invested in good times.

The Importance of Institutions and Customs

A large percentage of the funds available for investment in the United States is invested through institutions such as insurance companies, banks, savings and loan associations, and investment companies. It is sometimes asserted that the people who invest through these institutions do so because of the business practices followed by them and that the money which the institutions offer for loan or stock investments is therefore going into channels insisted upon by the original savers. To some extent this is undoubtedly true; yet it is probable that investors use these institutions more because of the service, convenience, and tax advantages afforded, and because of the effort they make to sell their services, than because of any specific investment policies.

The very large sums now invested through institutional channels are being guided into types of investments which law and custom deem suitable for the institutions. It is certain that these funds exert a major force in determining the market prices and relative yields of bonds, stocks, real estate, and mortgages, because they constitute a major portion of the demand for investment assets.

If and when the controlling statutes and the judgment of leaders in an institutional group justify new types of investments for the institutions, some of the money controlled by these institutions will go into those investments. For example, until a few years ago banks limited their residential mortgage loans to 60 per cent of appraised value and a final maturity not exceeding 10 years. Now, with the assistance of the Federal Housing Administration, 80 per cent loans for 20 years are common, and the banks compete vigorously for the business. The loan money is available and freely used, and mortgage interest rates and real estate values have both been affected noticeably.

The desire of life insurance companies to earn larger incomes on a portion of the funds entrusted to their care is now causing these institutions to experiment with investments in common stock and real estate. Trust companies are placing important portions of trust funds in common stocks. These two great reservoirs of capital probably aggregate close to 120 billion dollars; and if even a modest portion of this sum is shifted from bonds into equities, the change may have important effects on the prevailing levels of bond, stock, and real estate prices. And there are other institutions, including the fast-growing pension trust movement, which could have similar effects on the capital markets.

The significance of these institutional practices in the investment markets is probably not a fast-changing one, but it is unquestionably important enough to warrant observation by investors interested in framing long-range plans for themselves. Of greater immediate importance is the disposition of individuals to increase or decrease the percentages of their savings which they invest through institutions. From 1930 through 1954 institutional channels have been popular. As a result the supply of funds for bond and mortgage investment has been increased and that for stock investment has been sharply limited.

Central Banking Policy

During the past generation the Federal Reserve System has grown greatly in power and authority. From its original conception as a bankers' bank with the function of aiding commercial banks to provide a restrained but steady credit supply to the country, the Reserve System has developed into a major financial regulatory agency. It cooperates with the United States Treasury in matters affecting fiscal policy, but its discretionary powers over the credit supply, stock market finance, and bond yield rates are very great indeed. And with respect to most of its powers the Reserve System operates with no statutory mandate or limitation except the most general admonitions to "maintain sound banking conditions" and "prevent excess use of credit."

Federal Reserve authority impinges upon the investment field in a number of ways, of which four may be specifically noted here. First, the System has the technical capacity to supply the commercial banks copiously with lendable funds or to cause a great scarcity of such funds. This power is obviously equivalent to an effective control of short-term interest rates and may have a considerable effect on bond prices, on business cash positions, and on the availability of all forms of bank loans. The principal devices by which the System can affect bank lending are its open market operations, its power to change member bank reserve requirements, and its control of rediscount rates. Second, the Reserve System can exert great influence on high-class bond prices by open market dealing in government bonds. Extensive purchases of such bonds will keep them high in price and yielding relatively low rates; in consequence, private bond buyers seeking better yields will bid up corporate and municipal bonds, thus reducing their yields also. Obviously, sales by the Reserve System would cause government bond prices to drop, which would in turn drag down corporate bond prices and increase the interest yields available on all classes of bond investments.

The third sphere of Reserve authority which affects investors is its control over stock market credit. By specific statute the System is authorized to limit the percentage of value which any member bank may lend on stock exchange securities when the purpose of the loan is to finance the purchase or holding of such securities; and similar restrictions may be placed on margin transactions under which a securities dealer is the lender.[7] The stock market has always made considerable use of credit in financing rising markets, especially when large amounts of new securities are being sold. This credit control power appears to be very effective in restraining stock prices when new stock issues are being sold in quantities, even when large corporate earnings and dividends provide reason for higher prices. Corporate bond prices would probably be sensitive to it also at any time when they were not assisted by Reserve System support of the government bond market. The Reserve System seems disposed to restrict stock market credit vigorously, even when it attacks inflationary credit expansion in no other way.

The fourth major application of Reserve authority upon investors is by means of moral suasion. Presumably the Reserve System speaks mainly to the commercial banks when it comments upon business conditions, credit policies, and banking practices, but its power over both banks and investment markets is so great that Reserve attitudes are always an influence in shaping private decisions on financial policy.

The foregoing comments are not intended to suggest that the Reserve System is capable of dominating stock prices and interest rates at will, without any attendant effects on business prosperity or the general price level. It is evident that the System is powerful enough to affect the relative levels of stock yields, long-term interest rates, short-term interest rates, and other such categories, by exerting its influence on the credit supplies available in each field; but even in this respect its control is limited, because private loan funds will still be directed to the investment areas in which private lenders find the greatest attraction and will neglect others which appear less attractive. When the Reserve authorities undertake still more ambitious tasks, such as providing unlimited loan funds with which to fight a war or finance a postwar reconstruction period, there is no doubt but that they can supply the money, as indeed they have done; but the resultant effects of inflation and price-level distortion even they cannot prevent. Investors therefore cannot view the Reserve System as a maker of economic laws. It is, instead, a manipulator of

7 These powers were given the System by the Securities Exchange Act of 1934, which is discussed at some length in Chap. 12.

money rates and credit supplies, with enough power to affect investment values greatly but not enough to control them completely.

Supply and Demand

Preceding sections of this chapter have noted logical basic relationships between bond yields, stock yields, and net earnings on real
estate investments, but have also noted that these relationships do
not remain constant. For example, bond yields may decline while
stock yields rise and real estate yields remain unchanged. In the
discussion of institutional and Federal Reserve policies it was observed that these agencies may affect the prices and yields of various
classes of investments by making heavy investments in one class
and little or none in another.

But institutions are not the only unstable factors in the investment markets. Individuals, too, have their peculiarities. Their
tendencies to change their investing policies radically, emphasizing
reckless cupidity or unreasoning fear as business conditions are good
or bad, are familiar to all. Less widely recognized but tremendously
important are the tendencies of investors to give preference to temporarily favored industries or investment types and to neglect to
invest in others; this may result, for example, in sharp depreciation
in the stocks of growing industries which attempt to sell new shares
and relative strength in others. And what is true of industries or
investment types is even more true of individual companies' stock
issues.

The essence of the matter is that there is a separate supply-and-
demand market for each of many types of investments. In each case
the supply consists of both old items—shares, bonds, or properties—
offered for resale and new ones which may be issued or constructed.
The demand is represented by new savings augmented by credit
expansion, if any, and is expressed by institutions and individuals,
each motivated by a separate set of convictions, prejudices, and legal
limitations and each capable of changing his investing habits from
time to time. As a matter of fact, the nature of the demand for investment assets may be changing fundamentally as this is written,
because steeply progressive taxes and government measures to re-
distribute the national income may be changing the identities of
the groups who have savings to invest.

It is therefore not practical to assume that there are exact permanent or normal relationships between the yields available on bonds, stocks, real estate, or subclasses of these, nor between long-term and short-term money rates, nor between the yields on safe and speculative investments. Within reasonable limits these relationships may be expected to vary as supply and demand establish the various yields independently.

Market Fluctuations

This chapter has thus far dealt with the general level of investment values and the rate of return upon them, and with the human and institutional preferences which account for differences in price and rate of return between different types of investments. It is now desirable to give brief attention to the *fluctuation* in these prices and percentage returns. The space devoted to this problem will be brief at this time because detailed treatment will be necessary later.

It is obvious that fluctuations in investment prices are the results of changes in the bids of buyers and the offers of sellers. Apparently either the buyers vary as the will-o'-the-wisp in their appraisals of the future, or they are engaged in frantic speculative attempts to outguess near-term market prices, or their actions are governed by their varying money supplies. Practically the same words could be said of sellers in the investments markets. The keys to investment prices can therefore be found in the general attitude toward the distant future, in people's guesses on the price outlook for the next few months, and in the money supplies of business firms and investors.

Clearly, these situations will not be the same at all times—politics, taxes, wars, inflation, new inventions, and other factors will intervene —so that neither various types of investments nor various industries nor specific geographic areas will retain their same relative desirability. And it is very obvious that different kinds of investors—for example, bond-buying insurance companies and stock-buying families—will not have investable funds which are always proportional in amount or even comparable in year-in-and-year-out stability. These are some of the factors which lead to relative stability in the bond market and occasional wild instability in the stock market.

Summary

The investor who would really appreciate the idiosyncrasies of the investment markets has a Herculean task in his hands. He must appreciate the intricacies of compound discount, grasp the relationships between the rate of savings and the technical outlets for capital, understand the workings of the nation's institutional and credit structure, follow the preferences and prejudices of the people who have money to invest, and translate the whole into a pattern of supply and demand for each separate type of investment. The whole of this task is preliminary, if the job of investing is to be done properly, to the two main functions assigned to this book—those of surveying the functioning of the investment markets and reviewing the merits of the principal types of investments available in them.

QUESTIONS AND PROBLEMS

1. If you estimated that Swift & Co. stock would average $2.50 per year in dividends for the next 50 years, and be valueless after that, how much would you pay for the stock if the risk justifies a 5 per cent yield?

2. If you estimated that General Electric would average $2 per share in dividends for the next 50 years, and be valueless thereafter, and if you believed its quality justified a 4 per cent yield, at what figure would you appraise it?

3. Which of the above is the better buy, General Electric at $50 or Swift at $45?

4. If you were offered an apartment house for $80,000, and if you estimated that it would net you $4,000 per year after expenses and taxes (but before depreciation) for the next 40 years, would it be a better investment than General Electric stock at $60? (Assume the premises of question 2.)

5. What is the value of a residential building lot whose services are worth $200 per year after taxes and expenses, in perpetuity, allowing for a 5 per cent return on the investment? Could you afford to pay this sum for the lot and then hold it idle for 10 years (assuming a tax cost of $50 per year meanwhile) until you were ready to build on it?

6. Find an example of a common stock whose value is mostly based on its improbable possibilities. What is the principle involved here? Do improbable possibilities exist in real estate? In bonds? Illustrate.

7. Would it be reasonable to say that a commitment justified by the discounted value of its most probable future dividend payments was an investment, while one justifiable only by its improbable possibilities was a speculation?

8. Would you call a railroad sunk capital? A wholesale grocery business owning chiefly inventory? Which is the better investment?

9. If a flood of new inventions afforded many new investment opportunities in new industries, what would happen to the average profit margins in business? Why? What would happen to the value of the stock of a corporation whose earnings and dividends remained unchanged? Why?

10. If the savings of the American people increase greatly during the next few years, but relatively few new industries appear, what will happen to the level of rents? To the value of rental properties? Why?

11. Why are bond prices more stable than stock prices?

12. If a selling campaign by stockbrokers convinced many people that they should invest more in stocks and less in life insurance and savings bonds, would this change the long-term level of stock prices? Would it affect bond values? Mortgage interest rates?

13. Is it possible that the Federal Housing Act, which makes it easier for middle-class investors to buy homes, has contributed to the weakness of stock values during the last 15 years?

14. How can the Federal Reserve System affect the prices and yields of corporate bonds? Can it keep bonds up and stocks down? How?

15. What would happen to stock prices in an important industry—for example, electric power—if a great need for expansion required the sale of new stock in amounts greater than investors desired to buy at the moment? After the expansion was complete, what would happen?

16. Why does the demand for stocks and real estate fall off in periods of depression? If new stocks are not sold and new houses are not constructed in depressions, why does the supply of these items for sale appear to be so large?

REFERENCES

Badger, Ralph E., and Harry G. Guthmann: *Investment Principles and Practices,* Prentice-Hall, Inc., New York, 1951, Chaps. 2, 22.

Bellemore, Douglas H.: *Investments Principles and Practices,* B. C. Forbes and Sons Publishing Co., Inc., New York, 1953, Chaps. 2, 3, 7.

Dowrie, George W., and Douglas R. Fuller: *Investments,* John Wiley & Sons, Inc., New York, 1950, Chap. 2.

Evans, George H., and George E. Barnett: *Principles of Investment,* Houghton Mifflin Company, Boston, 1940, Chaps. 2, 10.

Financial Handbook, The Ronald Press Company, New York, 1948, pp. 1175–1210.

Grodinsky, Julius: *Investments,* The Ronald Press Company, New York, 1953, Chap. 20.

Jordan, David F., and Herbert E. Dougall: *Investments,* Prentice-Hall, Inc., New York, 1952, Chaps. 9, 10.

Williams, John B.: *Theory of Investment Value,* Harvard University Press, Cambridge, Mass., 1938.

Chapter 3: CORPORATE PRACTICES AND THE INVESTOR

The securities of business corporations represent the second largest group of intangible investment values in America today, being exceeded in value only by the great total of the Federal debt. Corporation bonds and term debt outstanding at December 31, 1953, were estimated to total 79 billion dollars,[1] and the value of outstanding corporate stocks in mid-1954 totaled well over 150 billion dollars.[2] At least 6.5 million people owned corporate securities directly,[3] and a majority of the rest of the population had an indirect interest in them through their life insurance investments, bank deposits, and other holdings.

These impressive figures explain the preoccupation of investors with corporate affairs and justify the inclusion of a considerable discussion of corporate technicalities in any textbook on investments. The function of the present chapter is to describe certain corporate procedures which are of importance to investors, in order to provide an essential background for later discussions of the value of corporate securities.

Nature of a Corporation

A corporation may be defined as an artificial entity created by right of sovereign governmental authority and having the powers,

---

[1] U.S. Dept. of Commerce, *Survey of Current Business,* October, 1954, p. 14.

[2] Stocks listed on the New York Stock Exchange had a total value of 138 billion dollars. This value is reported regularly in the *Survey of Current Business.* The 150-billion-dollar figure may be small, but allowance must be made for duplication in totals which include the entire capitals of holding companies, investment companies, etc., and also the issues owned by them.

[3] Estimated as of Mar. 31, 1952, by Lewis H. Kimmel in *Share Ownership in the United States,* Brookings Institution, Washington, 1952. The figure has doubtless grown since 1952.

privileges, and limitations stipulated by that authority.[4] Corporations usually have the right to own property, make contracts, sue and be sued, borrow money, employ people, and conduct their affairs much as a natural person would his own. In one sense the corporation is a sort of partnership of many people, who put their money into the venture and get back salable interests in it; but the investor does not own the corporation's property, nor is he responsible for its debts. The corporate entity owns the property and owes the debts. If the investor becomes a stockholder he receives "shares" of stock in the corporation, is technically regarded as one of the owners of the business, and is entitled to such dividends, voting rights in selecting the management, and other privileges as the law and the corporation's financial progress may make possible. If the investor is a bondholder, he is a creditor of the corporation, not of its stockholders, and will receive the payments to which the bond contract entitles him if the corporation is able to pay them.

Business corporations are usually created under state law, though national banks and a few other specialized enterprises are Federal creatures. General business corporations are permitted to incorporate (that is, to obtain a corporate identity) under the laws of any one state and then do business in any or all of the others, subject to the commercial laws and taxes of the states where business is done. However, the corporation laws of the incorporating state control the corporation in all matters affecting its corporate status, which would include stockholders' rights, dividends, borrowing of money, and many like items of concern to investors.

Investors as a rule display no particular interest in their corporations' states of origin or in the corporation laws of the states. This is no doubt a satisfactory policy 99 per cent of the time, but in the hundredth case it may not be sound, for there are situations in which statutory provisions make an important difference to investors. While it must be admitted that the state laws are far more like than unlike, significant differences exist on the following points: [5]

4 Compare the famous definition of Chief Justice Marshall in the Dartmouth College Case, 4 Wheat. 518 (1819): "A corporation is an artificial being, invisible, intangible, and existing only in contemplation of law. Being the mere creature of law, it possesses only those properties which the charter of its creation confers upon it either expressly or as incidental to its very existence. . . ."

5 The best comparative summaries of state laws on these and other corporate matters

1. Methods by which corporations may amend their articles of incorporation

2. Classes of stock and par values which may be used

3. Protective features for preferred stock

4. Voting rights on all stock

5. Powers which must be conferred on directors, powers which may be conferred on directors, and powers which must be exercised by stockholder vote

6. Rights of stockholders

7. Right of the corporation to purchase and retire its own common shares

8. Definitions of surplus and eligibility to pay dividends

9. Method of authorizing new issues of securities and the prior rights of stockholders to buy them

10. Method of authorizing and consummating merger, reorganization, or dissolution and the rights of dissenting stockholders when these things are done

Corporations come into being when chartered under the state code by the proper state official. This is done as a routine matter when the original incorporators file an application, together with the proposed *articles of incorporation,* certain other documents, and the necessary fee. This procedure is important to investors because the articles of incorporation (which may also be referred to as the corporation's *charter* when officially accepted for filing) constitute a contract between the state and the stockholders outlining in considerable detail what the corporation is to do and the rights of the parties concerned. Each group of incorporators may write up a set of articles to suit themselves, subject only to the broad limitations of the law, and the investor who subsequently buys the stock automatically subscribes to these articles.

Amendments to a corporation's articles may usually be made by an affirmative vote at a stockholders' meeting, effective as soon as a formal notice is filed with the proper incorporation officials. However, the state codes usually stipulate the procedure which must be followed and often forbid changes adverse to the interests of any special group of stockholders, such as preferred stockholders, unless this group concurs in the action. Sometimes the corporate articles

---

will be found in the United States Corporation Company's annual *Corporation Manual,* a large reference volume which is available in law and large general libraries.

contain clauses which protect stockholders by forbidding certain types of amendments, as well as mergers and other similar actions, unless large majorities of each class of stockholders consent.

The nature of corporate articles may be seen from the following outline, which is taken from the Nevada corporation code. Nevada was chosen because its law is typical and conveniently concise. The articles are required to state: [6]

1. The name of the corporation. . . .

2. The name . . . of the city . . . in which its principal office or place of business is to be located in this state. . . .

3. The nature of the business . . . to be transacted . . . by the corporation. [In writing this section banks, insurance companies, and utilities usually indicate their intentions, but general corporations usually enumerate every transaction they can imagine and then add "all other lawful business."]

4. The amount of the total authorized capital stock . . . and the number and par value [including no par value] of the shares. . . . If the corporation is to issue more than one class of stock . . . a description of the different classes thereof [with regard to number of shares authorized, and to voting and other rights], . . . as to amount of preference . . . , rate of dividends, premium on redemption, conversion price, or otherwise. . . .

5. Whether the members of the governing board shall be styled directors or trustees, and the number. . . .

6. Whether . . . stock . . . shall be subject to assessment. . . .

7. The names . . . of the incorporators. . . .

8. Whether or not the corporation is to have perpetual existence. . . .

9. The . . . articles . . . may also contain . . . provisions for the regulation of the business and for the conduct of the affairs of the corporation, and [on] the rights, powers or duties of the directors or stockholders, or any classes of stockholders, or holders of the bonds or other obligations of the corporation, or providing for the . . . distribution . . . of the profits of the said corporation; provided such provisions are not contrary to the laws of this state.

The importance of the corporate articles to investors can scarcely be overstated, particularly in connection with items 4 and 9 on the above list. Although prospective stockholders frequently believe that corporations are so orthodox in framing their articles that special

[6] Explanatory phrases in brackets are added by the author.

investigations are unnecessary, this cannot be accepted as a sound conclusion. Important differences occur, and frequently. Since the outstanding features of all important corporations' articles are summarized in the investment reference manuals and in the prospectuses which offer new securities for sale, it is foolish for an investor to ignore this aspect of any prospective investment. Desirable and objectionable features in corporate articles will be discussed at several later points in this book.

Issuance and Transfer of Stock

The corporation laws of most states provide that new shares of corporate stock may be issued only when they are (1) authorized in the articles of incorporation, (2) approved for issuance by the stockholders, and (3) ordered sold and issued by the directors. In some cases new issues must also be approved by the corporation commissioner or some other regulatory agency. When all requirements have been met, the process of stock issuance in nearly all cases consists of filling out a stock certificate for the stockholder and entering the proper record on the stock ledger for the corporation.

A stock certificate is usually an engraved or lithographed document about 8 by 11 inches in size on which are entered the stockholder's name, the number of shares, and the date the certificate is issued. The face of the certificate will state the name of the corporation, the state of incorporation, the class of stock, and various other details about the company and stock. It will bear the printed signature of company officers and the manual signatures of a transfer agent and (usually) a registrar. On the reverse side of the certificate there is usually a verbatim copy of the portion of the corporation's articles outlining the features of the different classes of stock (this will be omitted if only one class is authorized) and a form for the stockholder to fill out when he assigns his stock to a purchaser, donee, or other transferee.

Corporations are careful about issuance of stock certificates. Due precautions are taken against forgeries, all certificates are numbered and recorded by number, and the number of shares is either engraved on the certificate or punched out in a forgery-proof manner. The transfer agent who issues new certificates may be a company official or employee, but most large corporations engage a bank or trust company to perform this service. The transfer agent is instructed not to issue new certificates unless certificates for a corresponding number of old shares are returned to him properly endorsed, for reissue, or unless he has proper evidence that new shares are to be issued as requested. The registrar is always an officer of a bank or trust company and independent of both issuing corporation and transfer agent; his job is to countersign the transfer agent's new certificates, if a corresponding number of old shares are canceled out or if evidence of the propriety of an additional issue is presented.[7]

When a stockholder sells his stock, or when for any reason he wishes to assign it or to have all or part of it reissued in another name, he must sign the assignment form on the back of the certificate. The certificate can then be sent in to the transfer agent, who will issue new certificate(s) as instructed. However, large corporations do not find it convenient to keep signature files on their stockholders; so most of them decline to accept transfer instructions unless the stockholder's signature is guaranteed by the added endorsement of a bank, trust company, or securities broker.

Stockholders frequently wish to assign their stock certificates to banks or other lenders as collateral for loans. Since it is not desirable to endorse such a temporary assignment on a stock certificate, the banks have developed a separate assignment form for this purpose. When the note is repaid this separate form can be destroyed, and the original certificate remains unimpaired. The corporation does not even need to be notified of the loan transaction. It continues to send corporate notices and pay dividends to the stockholder without interruption.

Lost stock certificates are not salable or negotiable by the finder, since they can be transferred only by the signed order of the stockholder of record or by his agent. However, transfer agents will usually refuse to issue replacements to holders who claim to have lost their certificates, unless they are furnished with a surety bond which

---

[7] Investors sometimes learn about these things in the hard way. In Los Angeles in 1927 the Julian Petroleum Corporation failed, after company officers had issued and sold over 3,000,000 preferred shares, of which only 600,000 were authorized. There was no registrar, or this could not have happened. In this case the catastrophe was compounded by the fact that there was also no audit by independent accountants, and someone managed to steal or dissipate most of the company's assets. At the present time many important corporations do not have stock registrars or adequate audits.

will indemnify the transfer agent if the "lost" instrument turns up in the hands of a legitimate holder.[8]

The corporation's stock ledger will show at all times the name and address of each stockholder and the number of each certificate he holds, the date of its issuance, and the number of shares represented. A different stock ledger will be kept for each class of stock.

Most corporations never "close" their stock ledgers. That is, they never refuse or delay the transfer of stock when endorsed certificates are presented on regular business days. Since the stockholder list is constantly changing, it is necessary for dividends, stock purchase rights, voting privileges at stockholders' meetings, and other benefits to be assigned by the directors to stockholders "of record" at the close of business on stated days. These days are known as "stock-of-record" days. For example, if the directors of United States Steel Corporation decide at a meeting on March 1 that they wish to pay a dividend of $1 per share about April 1, they might order the treasurer to pay $1 per share on April 1 to stockholders of record at the close of business on March 20. The list of stockholders would be determined as of that date, thus giving the treasurer 10 days to prepare the checks before the designated mailing date on April 1.

Stockholders are privileged under any reasonable circumstances to have access to the stockholders' ledger or to the information it contains. This is to permit any stockholder who wishes to communicate information to the other stockholders or to solicit their votes at stockholders' meetings to know who they are.

These normal corporate procedures suggest a number of personal policies for wise investors. Clearly, it is unnecessary to invest in the stocks of corporations which do not employ disinterested registrars and competent external auditors to check on the issuance of stock;

---

[8] Recently a typical corporate transfer agency reported that it replaced lost bonds and preferred stock when furnished with a perpetual surety bond in amount equal to two times the face value of the lost certificate; the premium on the surety bond would be 2 per cent of the amount of the surety bond. On a lost common stock or convertible bond, the perpetual surety bond had to be written for an indeterminate amount, at a premium cost of 6 per cent of the value of the lost certificate. These surety bond premiums were payable only once, but the loser of the certificate had to agree to reimburse the surety company if the surety ever had to pay a claim. If the surety company doubted the moral or financial integrity of the professed loser of a certificate, it simply declined to issue him a surety bond unless provided with collateral sufficient to absorb any possible claim.

there are plenty of stocks available which have these protective devices. Second, it is important to guard securities from fire, theft, and misplacement, by keeping them in a safe deposit box, in a good safe, or in the custody of a securities broker. Third, it is neither necessary nor desirable to sign the assignment form on the back of a stock certificate until it is finally delivered for sale or transfer. Fourth, it is important to notify the corporation immediately if any security is lost or mislaid, so that sale or transfer to an innocent third party can be prevented.

Dividends: Nature and Types

While the term dividend is ordinarily used to mean a cash payment to stockholders out of the past or present earnings of the corporation, it is also used on occasion to designate distributions of stock, bonds, or property of various kinds. These latter distributions may be made out of earnings, but frequently are not. In view of the multitude of factors which may motivate noncash dividends, it seems best to discuss them separately under the headings Stock Dividends and Property Dividends and to confine the present section to the ordinary variety of cash dividends.

As noted in a preceding page, cash dividends are usually disbursed by check on a "payment date" to "stockholders of record" a few days earlier. The great majority of successful American corporations pay four dividends yearly on each class of stock, at approximate quarterly intervals. A few pay monthly, semiannually, or annually, and a similar few make disbursements at irregular intervals. Concerns with erratic earnings obviously must pay when they can. These remarks apply equally well to both preferred and common stocks.

As respects the amounts paid on each successive distribution, corporate policies vary considerably. Preferred stocks usually get regular and equal periodic dividends, unless poor earnings, payments on arrears, or participations cause differences. Common stocks usually receive payments based on one of four identifiable plans:

1. *Stabilized regular dividends:* payments based on a rate which the directors feel the corporation can afford over a period of time. The excess earnings of good years will compensate the corporation for narrow margins or shortages in bad years. Suitable for utilities, banks, insurance

companies, and other types with steady earnings. Examples: American Telephone and Telegraph, Bank of America, Pacific Gas and Electric Company.

2. *Regular dividends at rates occasionally revised as earnings vary:* payments based on the average level of current earnings. Suitable when earnings are reasonably steady but subject to some growth or cyclical change. Examples: Continental Oil Company of Delaware, R. H. Macy, Dresser Industries.

3. *Moderate regular dividends plus extras as warranted:* very widely used when a stable basic dividend is warranted but extra payments are desired as earned. Examples: Standard Oil Company of Indiana, Swift & Co., Simmons Company.

4. *Amount (and time) of each dividend based on the situation at the time:* not so popular with investors as the other methods, but used considerably by concerns operating in cyclical industries. Examples: Libby, McNeill & Libby, Great Northern Iron Ore Properties, Pittsburgh & Lake Erie Railroad, New York Central Railroad.

Dividends: Corporate Objectives

Affirmative decisions with respect to dividend payments are made in practically all instances by the directors of the corporation. Neither preferred nor common stockholders have any contractual rights which entitle them to receive dividends. They will get them, in the order of preference as established in the corporation's articles, when and if the directors order the payments.

The fact that the corporation's directors have authority over dividend policy does not mean, of course, that an established and capricious board can refuse indefinitely to make payments when the corporation is in a position to pay. If a corporation should and normally would pay dividends, minority stockholders can get a court order which will compel payments.[9] But the directors' preferences are entitled to great weight in such matters, and the courts will not interfere unless the directors' attitude amounts almost to an abuse of discretion.

It is to be expected that directors will order dividend payments only after reviewing the interests of both the corporation and its stockholders. If the corporation has accumulated some surplus out of earnings, and if there is presently a more than adequate cash

[9] *Dodge v. Ford Motor Co.,* 204 Mich. 459 (1919).

balance, and if the cash is not soon to be needed for working capital, plant expansion, debt retirement, or possible losses, dividends are in order. If the corporation has attained its full growth and is virtually debt-free, as is National Biscuit Company, almost the entire current earnings may be distributed. If money for expansion is still needed, a corporation whose stock is widely held might find a liberal dividend policy advantageous because the attractive dividend would make the stockholders willing to buy new securities from the corporation at frequent intervals. The American Telephone and Telegraph Company is the outstanding exponent of this principle. However, a corporation whose stock is held in large blocks might find new prorata share offerings not acceptable to many of its large holders; such a corporation is likely to limit dividends and retain its earnings, if it needs money for expansion or debt retirement. Large stockholders are likely to prefer low dividends for another reason: dividends are fully subject to personal income taxes. If earnings are retained by the company and invested in expansion, the stockholder's personal income tax does not reach them, even though they cause his shares to rise in value; and if he ultimately realizes these gains in cash by selling some of his stock, he will pay only a relatively modest "capital gains" tax. These considerations, as well as others less commonly encountered, are likely to shape each corporation's dividend policy. The investor who understands such policies before buying stock may avoid unwelcome surprises.

Dividends: Legal and Contractual Factors

Attention has already been directed to the fact that cash dividend payments are usually made only out of accumulated earned surplus (prior earnings) or current earnings, since law and business practice discourage the payment of dividends out of paid-in funds. However, many states permit payment of preferred dividends from paid-in funds, and common stock payments may be made in some instances, if the directors feel that such action is advisable.

A second legal factor of note involves the corporation's own contractual commitments. It has become customary for bond indentures and bank loan agreements to forbid corporate dividends, especially those paid on common stock, when the corporation's cash holdings or net current assets fail to exceed a prescribed sum. Also such agreements commonly require dividends to be paid only from earnings subsequent to the date of the loan or forbid them unless surplus exceeds a stated sum. In a few cases preferred stocks are protected by clauses in the corporation's articles forbidding dividends on common stocks except when similar cash and surplus conditions are fulfilled. Few of these restrictions have affected payments during the boom of 1946–1953, but many may become significant in future years.

A third legal factor which has important bearing on corporate dividend practice is embodied in corporate tax law.[10] These influences are varied. For example, certain types of investment companies can escape *corporate* income taxes if they pay all of their net income out in dividends to their stockholders; consequently, most eligible ones do this. As an example with opposite effect, double taxation of subsidiary and parent corporations successively on the same income under certain conditions induces the parent company to cause the subsidiary to limit its dividends, thus reducing the parent's income and its capacity to pay. Another possible tax factor is found in the much-discussed Section 102 of the Internal Revenue Code. This measure imposes a heavy tax on "improper accumulation of surplus," ostensibly to compel any earnings not actually needed in the business to be disbursed in dividends. However, it is legitimate to accumulate earnings for future debt repayment or for future expansion, so the Section is very difficult to enforce.

The fourth major legal factor affecting dividend policy is limited

---

[10] The Federal corporate income tax at 1954 rates absorbed 52 per cent of taxable corporate income if such income exceeded $50,000 and lesser percentages if the income was less. Deficits incurred in any year could be "carried back" into the two previous years to offset the taxable income of those years and gain a tax refund, or "carried forward" into the five succeeding years to cancel out future taxes. Net long-term gains on sale of equipment, real estate, or securities held as operating facilities or investments and not as inventories were taxed separately at 26 per cent and not included in taxable corporate income.

Taxable corporate income included earnings from business operations after deduction of all proper expenses, including depreciation, general taxes, state income taxes, and bond interest; plus interest earned on receivables, corporate bonds, and most Federal bonds; plus (approximately) 15 per cent of dividends received. Income from state and municipal bonds was not taxable. Holding companies and subsidiaries could file a "consolidated return" (*i.e.*, as though they constituted one corporation) if 80 per cent of the subsidiaries' common stocks were owned by the group, but the tax rate in this case was raised from 52 to 54 per cent for all corporations except railroads and public utilities.

to public utilities, banks, insurance companies, and similar institutions whose finances are regulated by public authority. The regulatory agencies often have discretionary authority to order or to suggest firmly that dividend policy be subordinated to expansion or debt retirement. The corporation has little choice but to comply.

Cash Dividend Policy: Summary

Since the dividend prospect is very important in establishing the value of a stock and in determining whether it is suitable for a given portfolio, it is important for an investor to review and understand the controlling factors in each case. Information can be had from the usual sources—prospectuses, annual reports, newspapers and periodicals, financial services—and facts not specifically stated may usually be deduced from the corporate history. The salient points to seek would appear to be:

1. Adequacy of net current assets and cash
2. Adequacy and stability of earnings
3. Requirements for expansion and debt retirement
4. Directors' policies re expansion and debt retirement
5. Directors' attitudes toward dividend payments
6. Preferences (or circumstances) of dominant stockholder groups
7. Adequacy of earned surplus
8. Contractual restrictions on dividends
9. Restrictions imposed by regulatory agencies
10. Effect of dividend policies on the corporation's own taxes

Although the practices of individual corporations varied widely, the average big American corporation in prewar years paid out about 65 per cent of its earnings in dividends. The ratio declined during the war, and in the inflationary boom which followed the war most firms devoted most of their increased earnings to plant construction and augmentation of working capital. The 1948 dividend distributions averaged less than 40 per cent of earnings. However, the end of the boom and the stabilization of earnings will tend to restore prewar dividend policies; the 1953 payout of earnings by leading companies exceeded 55 per cent.

Stock Dividends

Stock dividends may be defined as prorata payments to common stockholders of additional amounts of common stock. Such payments increase the number of shares in each stockholder's hands but do not alter his aggregate investment in the corporation, nor his prorata interest in it.

Stock dividends may be classified roughly into two groups: big ones and small ones. A big-percentage stock dividend, say from 10 per cent on up, will reduce the per share price of the stock, since the same corporate assets and earning power must now be divided among more shares. This may be desirable to the stockholders, since lower priced shares sometimes sell more readily and at a relatively higher price. Such a change may pave the way for a corporate offering of new stock, by establishing a per share price which is within the reach of more prospective purchasers. Stock dividends may also be used to bring the value of the stock into equality or proportionality with that of another company, to facilitate a merger or combination by exchange of stock.

Small stock dividends, ranging from 10 per cent down, are usually used when an expanding corporation needs most of its cash earnings in the business but feels that it should give its stockholders a reasonable dividend. Eastman Kodak Company and Dow Chemical Company are examples of firms which were doing this in 1953. Inasmuch as the stockholders already own the corporation, the logic of a prorata distribution of a few extra shares in it is a little hard to see. Presumably the payees can keep their original shares and sell the new ones in lieu of cash dividends—incidentally, the stockholders would encounter little or no income tax in this case, since a stock dividend per se distributes nothing and is not taxable—but brokerage fees on the trifling sales would make them uneconomical, and the income tax calculations to determine the adjusted cost on the new and old shares would be a nuisance. As a crowning absurdity, a small stock dividend either would require the distribution of a large number of warrants for fractional shares or would require the corporation to sell all fractions and remit the proceeds to the entitled stockholders. Neither expedient is free of trouble. The warrants would have to be "matched up" into whole shares by purchase or sale among the shareholders, possibly with the assistance of the corporation, and a cash distribution from the sale of fractional shares would present the stockholders with difficult income tax accounting problems.

Stock dividends require the corporation to transfer an amount representing the par value or the stated value of the new stock from its surplus account to its capital stock account.[11] Paid-in surplus may sometimes be used for this purpose, and even if earned surplus is used, the amount transferred is usually exempt from any dividend limitations imposed by bond or bank loan contracts.

Dividend Payable in Property

Dividends payable in property usually fall into three categories: (1) those paid in the bonds or preferred stock of the paying corporations, (2) those paid in the securities of other corporations, and (3) those paid in merchandise. Ordinarily, none of the three is common. In the past few years, however, the liquidation or voluntary reorganization of many corporations has been accomplished by the distribution of subsidiaries' stocks to the stockholders of the parent company. A distribution which sets up a former subsidiary or business department as a new independent company is termed a "spin-off."

The procedures involved in the payment of property dividends are similar to those followed in the payment of ordinary cash or stock dividends, with the addition of proper approval by stockholders if the dividend is a liquidating one. To the receiving stockholders, the income tax situation could be quite complicated. Generally speaking, securities received as a liquidating dividend or in a spin-off are not taxable income but must be identified and recorded as representing a portion of the original investment, at a proper portion of the original cost. In most other cases property dividends are ordinary taxable dividend income, to be recorded at market value. Because of the complexity of these situations, corporations paying property dividends usually obtain rulings from tax authori-

[11] In recent years leading theorists have argued that small stock dividends paid in lieu of cash dividends should be charged to earned surplus at market value. The New York Stock Exchange now insists that the market value of such small stock dividends plus the cash payments made concurrently should not exceed the company's earnings, since stockholders tend to regard both as income.

ties and advise their stockholders on the proper accounting procedures.

Stock Splits

The term stock split is applied to a case in which a corporation reduces the par value or stated value of its stock and gives its stockholders a larger number of shares having the same aggregate par value or stated value in exchange for their old shares. For example, General Motors Corporation in 1950 split its $10 par common stock 2 for 1, giving each holder two new $5 par common shares for each $10 par share previously held. Similarly, the United States Steel Corporation in 1949 split its no par stock 3 for 1, by the simple process of issuing to stockholders two additional no par shares for each share previously held, without making any change in the aggregate stated value of its capital account. Thus stock splits increase the number of shares outstanding without in any way affecting total capital or total surplus. The result is to reduce the per share value of the stock accordingly. Indeed, this is the purpose of the split, for stock whose value exceeds $70 or $80 per share is often neither as popular nor as salable as its quality deserves. Stock splits are fairly common actions, especially in bull markets or when new stock sales are contemplated. Frequently they are followed by establishment of a new dividend rate which is proportionately greater than that paid before the split. As a rule investors regard stock splits as bullish gestures reflective of expansion, good earnings, prospects for higher dividends, and hopes for higher share prices.

The additional shares received in a stock split are not regarded as taxable stockholder income. It is assumed that the total shares held after the split represent the initial investment, whose cost must now be prorated over the larger number of shares.

Assessments

Relatively few corporations now have legal power to impose assessments on their stockholders, and even in cases of insolvency the device is little used. Only in mining and small promotional concerns, where initial capital may need to be supplemented under possibly adverse operating conditions, is the assessment economically feasible.

When state law and corporate articles permit assessments, the usual provision authorizes the directors to require the additional cash contribution on a per share basis on or before a date which they designate. Proper notice must be sent to the stockholders. In event of nonpayment, the defaulting shares may be seized and sold by the directors, the assessment deducted from the sales price, and the balance (if any) remitted to the expropriated stockholder.

Rights

Corporations frequently raise money for expansion by selling additional securities to their common stockholders. Usually the additional securities are common stocks, but preferred stocks or bonds are sometimes sold in this way also.[12] Since the common stockholders are the residual owners of the corporation, no injustice is done if the new securities are offered pro rata at a price below their market value. The low price will assure the sale of the securities, thus obtaining the money for the corporation, and the stockholders may even feel that the privilege of buying the new securities at a low price is analogous to a special dividend.

When stockholders are offered the privilege to subscribe pro rata to new securities, the privilege accruing to one old share is termed a *right*. If the offer permits the purchase of one new share for each 10 held, a stockholder owning 100 old shares would receive 100 rights, which would entitle him to buy 10 new shares. The offering may be a large one, permitting the purchase of as much as one new share for each two held, or it may be a small one, such as one new for each 20 held.

Technically, rights are handled in a manner similar to dividends. Assuming that the charter properly authorizes additional stock and that a stockholders' meeting has approved it, the directors would then order rights to be sent to stockholders of record at the close of business on a stipulated date. The rights themselves would consist

12 A favorite device is to sell convertible bonds or preferred stock under rights. The bonds or preferred stock will be good grade, and if the conversion terms are attractive they will be eagerly bought. Later piecemeal conversion into common stock will complete the plan for ultimate common stock financing without the depressing effect on the stock market which the direct sale of the new stock might bring. The American Telephone and Telegraph Company is the foremost exponent of this technique, using debenture bonds convertible into stock.

of transferable lithographed certificates entitling the holder to return them within the prescribed period (usually 2 or 3 weeks) accompanied by his check, to obtain the promised stock. Rights not exercised within the prescribed period usually "expire" and become valueless. Stockholders who do not wish to exercise their rights should consequently sell them promptly, so that the purchaser may have time to use them before they expire.

It is obvious that rights to purchase new stock below its market price would have value. The nature of that value may be illustrated as follows: Assume that the stock of the Example Corporation is selling at $30 per share on July 25, after announcement that stockholders of record July 30 will receive rights to subscribe to one new share at $24.50 for each 10 shares held. It may reasonably be calculated on July 25 that any 10-share block of stock now worth $30 per share, or a total of $300, is about to be supplemented by a $24.50 cash investment, making a total value of $324.50. This new total will, however, then represent 11 shares, or $29.50 per share. If the future value of the stock is to be $29.50 and the subscription price is $24.50 when accompanied by 10 rights, it is clear that the 10 rights save the subscriber just $5, or 50 cents per right. It is equally clear that the 50 cents per right, or total of $5 needed to bring the new $24.50 share up to an equality of $29.50 with each of the other shares, will be raised by chipping 50 cents off each of the old $30 shares on the stock-of-record date.[13] The value of the right is therefore no mys-

---

[13] The securities markets have a formula for the evaluation of rights to buy additional common stock, which is worked out as follows: Let M equal the market price of the stock, S the subscription price, N the number of rights needed to obtain the privilege of buying one new share, and R the value of a right. Before the stock-of-record date,

$$R = \frac{M - S}{N + 1}$$

In the case of the Example Corporation, M is $30, S is $24.50, and N is 10. Consequently,

$$R = \frac{(\$30 - \$24.50)}{10 + 1} = \frac{\$5.50}{11} = 50 \text{ cents}$$

After the stock-of-record date the formula becomes

$$R = \frac{M - S}{N}$$

In this case the market price of the stock has already declined because the value of the right has been separated from it, but if no other market change has occurred we would compute

$$R = \frac{\$29.50 - \$24.50}{10} = \frac{\$5}{10} = 50 \text{ cents}$$

CORPORATE PRACTICES AND THE INVESTOR   63

terious bonus from Santa Claus; it is just a portion of the stockholder's original equity, which he can salvage only by exercise or sale.

It is a familiar fact that the market price of a stock subject to rights usually declines by approximately the value of the right, when the right is separated from the stock at the stock-of-record date. The same phenomenon is observed on dividend record dates. Since a purchaser after this date no longer obtains the right or the dividend, he pays less for his purchase.

Rights to purchase stocks which are actively traded on the public markets usually have an active market themselves. In most cases the prices on stock and rights will be mathematically related, since no careful purchaser would pay more for stock than a rights purchase plus a subscription would cost him, or vice versa. Obviously, the value of the rights will rise and fall in proportion to the difference between the market price of the stock and the subscription price for the new shares. Since the latter is usually a fixed sum, the rights must fluctuate as the market price of the stock fluctuates, and in much greater proportion.

When preferred stocks or bonds or the securities of subsidiaries are offered to stockholders under a rights arrangement, it is clear that the relationship between the value of the right and the value of the stock will not be necessarily close. The value of the stock will decline by something approximating the value of the right after the stock-of-record date, but related market fluctuations cannot be expected.

In most cases a right is not taxable income when received by a stockholder from a corporation but represents instead the return of a portion of his original investment.[14] This is true in nearly all cases in which the right carries the privilege of buying additional common stock, bonds or preferred stock convertible into common stock, or the common stock of an important subsidiary. Rights to buy nonconvertible bonds or preferred stock are usually regarded as taxable income to the full extent of their value.

Although the rights technique frequently offers stockholders subscription privileges requiring investment of important sums of money on very short notice, the practice is popular with most investors. In fact, corporations like American Telephone and Tele-

---

[14] Income tax accounting having to do with rights and the related stocks is intricate beyond the scope of this book.

graph Company and Pacific Gas and Electric Company, which have used this device again and again, are popular with many investors because they accept occasional additional investments in this way, free of brokerage charges and other incidental costs to the investor. And if the investor is unable or unwilling to exercise rights when they are sent to him, they are usually salable through brokers at a reasonable cost. The only real investment objection to the rights device comes from small investors whose few rights do not permit either economical subscription to whole shares or sale of rights in economical quantities and from holders of large blocks of stock who find the added investments asked of them to be burdensomely large.

Exchanges or Recapitalizations

Occasionally corporations find it advantageous to attempt to retire certain outstanding securities in exchange for others, or to rewrite their articles to make major changes in their outstanding stocks, or to merge with subsidiaries in a manner which effects a major financial readjustment. Such action may be taken in order to eliminate securities with obsolete or undesirable features, or to simplify the group of securities which constitute the capital structure, or to eliminate securities whose preferential rights prevent successful new financing, or to retire preferred stock with burdensome accumulated dividends attached, or possibly to scale down the entire capital structure to a size proportional to a shrunken earning power. In any of these situations, the usual procedure calls for the adoption of a "plan of reorganization" by the directors, the voting stockholders, and (usually) by each affected class of stockholders, voting separately. The plan will amend the corporate articles to authorize the desired new securities and order their issuance in exchange for the outstanding ones which are to be retired. Sometimes the plan will be binding upon all stockholders, once it is formally adopted. In other instances the exchange provided in the plan is optional to each stockholder; or there may be a choice of exchange offers.

Procedures of this sort are of great concern to the investor, because they may result in either advantage or disadvantage to him. The state corporation laws and to a lesser extent the articles of incorporation should have provisions designed to prevent injustice in framing such plans. However, plans which inflict considerable sacrifice on classes of securityholders are possible in many states, if the proper majorities can be persuaded to vote for them. Investors owning stocks in weak corporations, and particularly the owners of preferred stocks, are vulnerable to this hazard. Such investors have reason to be familiar with their rights under the state code and their own corporate articles.

An exchange or recapitalization does not give rise to a taxable gain or loss to the stockholder, provided the corporation undertook it for normal business reasons. The new securities received by the stockholder would simply replace those surrendered by him, and for income tax purposes their cost to him would be the cost of his original holdings.

Repurchase of Stock

Practically all corporations have the legal right to repurchase shares of their own stock from their stockholders. Such transactions must of course be made at fair prices and under conditions which give all stockholders reasonable opportunity to participate in them, and the corporation must not expend so much on them that creditors or other stockholders are jeopardized. In addition, some states further discourage repurchase of common stock by requiring that sums so expended be charged against earned surplus. Large repurchases in such cases would soon exhaust the surplus and effectively prevent further dividend payments.

Stock repurchased by the corporation ceases to draw dividends or to vote while it is held in the corporate treasury. It may be resold by the corporation, however, after which it again attains full status as outstanding stock.

Corporations buy their own stock for various reasons. During the stock market break of 1929, Transamerica Corporation bought large quantities of its own stock in an attempt to keep the market price up to what the officers regarded as the "true" value of the stock. In 1931, Pacific Finance Corporation bought quantities of its own stock at $15 per share, knowing that the corporate assets amounted to $25 per share and that every share retired at $15 netted a $10 gain to the remaining stockholders. During most of 1948 the Adams Express Company bought and sold its own stock to stabilize the market. Swift & Company buys stock for resale to its employees on the installment plan. In 1950 Paramount Pictures, Inc., sold some of its theater interests for cash and used the proceeds to buy in and retire a portion of its stock, thus eliminating capital no longer needed in the business.

Corporate stock repurchases are made in various ways. Most common is the ordinary technique of purchase through a broker, in the securities markets. Occasionally a corporation planning to buy stock may ask its stockholders for "tenders" at asking prices named by the stockholders; the corporation would then accept the cheapest tenders. Or the corporation may offer to buy, from each stockholder who cares to sell, a stated fraction of his holdings at a stated price. If the stock in question is common stock, the corporation may not compel any stockholder to sell, except by an elaborate process of stockholders' meeting, amendment of the articles, and recapitalization, which would affect every stockholder proportionately. If a preferred stock were involved, the situation would be the same, unless the preferred stock were subject to a sinking fund or to a redemption provision in the articles. These features of preferred stocks are discussed in Chapter 5.

Purchase or sale by a corporation of its own stock is chiefly significant to the investor because of its effect on the market price of his stock. However, such important matters as the company's cash position, its surplus position, and the remaining assets and earning power per share of stock may be affected by repurchases of stock.

Corporate Combinations: Three Methods

Two or more corporations frequently desire to combine their business or financial affairs into a single ownership or management unit. The object is often larger-scale operation, the unification of complementary product lines, the integration of a raw-material source with a processing operation, or some similar business advantage. The proposal to combine may originate with the managements of the companies, with important stockholder groups, or in some other way; but however the idea may originate, it is likely to be brought finally to the majority of the stockholders as a well-developed proposal to which the managements and large stockholders have already agreed. Such proposals are usually about as equitable as two bargaining managements with diverse investor interests are able to make them, but they are unlikely to seem entirely fair to everyone concerned.

The methods which may be used for combining corporations are capable of almost infinite variation. Since space here is limited, it seems best to survey the situation only from the viewpoint of an investor whose corporation is to be bought out or absorbed by another. In this case, the corporation's independent existence is likely to be terminated in one of three ways: (1) its assets can be sold to the successor company in return for either new stock or cash, which could then be distributed to the stockholders as a liquidating dividend; (2) its stockholders could be persuaded to sell their shares to the combined company, receiving in return either cash or stock in the combined company; or (3) the terminating corporation could be *merged* with one or more others into a combined company, which would then operate as one unit having all the assets, liabilities, and net worth of the constituent companies. The choice between these methods will be affected by the cash positions of the separate companies, the debts of the companies, the extent to which all stockholder groups are willing to cooperate, and especially by the income tax problems of the companies and their important stockholders.

The most common method of corporate combination, the sale of the entire assets of one company to the other, usually requires the approval of the directors of both companies and a majority vote of the stockholders of the selling corporation. If the selling corporation is to be liquidated, the plans must include the payment of all debts and the retirement of preferred stock before the final liquidating distribution is paid to the common stockholders. When the sales proceeds are received in cash the corporation will have no problem in financing the necessary payments to creditors and preferred stockholders, but it may have to pay substantial capital gains taxes if its assets bring more than their adjusted cost. After a cash sale the common stockholders would presumably also receive their liquidating dividend in cash; this could result in a taxable gain or loss to most of them also. This complicated tax problem might be avoided if the selling corporation arranged to exchange its property for new securities in the purchasing corporation. Under 1954 laws the exchange would probably not give rise to a corporate gain or loss for tax purposes, and a final liquidating distribution of such stock to the stockholders of the selling corporation would constitute a tax-exempt substitution of one security for another. But this simple avoidance of the tax hazard might create at least one other problem: it could leave the selling corporation with debts and preferred stock requiring redemption, and no cash holdings with which to make the payments. This difficulty is not insurmountable, but it often makes the whole process of corporate combination more complex than it might seem at first glance.

Instead of purchasing its assets, an acquiring corporation may obtain control of another by purchasing its stock. This may be done by purchase in the open market, but the purchasing company generally prefers not to buy any stock unless it can obtain almost the entire issue, and at a reasonable price. Consequently, the acquiring corporation usually negotiates first with the management and large stockholders of the other company and, when agreement is reached, opens an escrow in a bank or trust company through which the same terms are offered to other stockholders. The escrow terms usually stipulate that no transaction will occur and the offer will be withdrawn unless the desired amount of stock reaches the escrow by a certain date. The offer-in-escrow may name a cash price, or, more likely, it may propose payment in stock of the acquiring company. A cash offer obviously means that the seller may sustain a capital gain or loss; an exchange of stock for stock generally will not. It is clear that there would be no way for a dissatisfied stockholder to keep others from selling their stock to an acquiring company, which could then elect its own officials and run the acquired company virtually as a division of its own business; but the dissenting holder could keep his own stock and obtain his usual prorata share of such dividends as the new management might disburse, as long as his corporation remained in business.

The third method of combining independent corporations, by merger, is a statutory process which joins all the identities, assets, liabilities, and stockholder interests of the predecessor firms into a single successor firm. Mergers are worked out very exactly by contract between the merging firms, subject to all the restrictions imposed by law, and subject also to ratification by the voting stockholders. The process is roughly as follows: the directors of the firms to be merged work out a merger agreement which includes a complete set of articles of incorporation for the successor corporation [15] and a procedure for issuing stock in the new firm to the stockholders of each of the old ones. Bondholders need not be provided for; the new firm is automatically obligated on the debts of all of its predecessors, and the merger process will not impair the validity of mortgages. The merger terms must satisfy the statutory requirements in each state in which any merging concern is incorporated. Large majorities of the voting stock of each merging corporation must usually approve the merger, and if state laws or corporate articles or bond indentures so require, the consent of majorities of preferred stockholders and bondholders may be necessary also. When all consents have been obtained, the merger may be declared consummated; but at this point many states, though not all, require that any dissenting preferred or common stockholder be given a reasonable time to refuse the merger and demand that his equity be appraised and paid to him in cash. The appraisal will not be generous, since it must be based on an assumed liquidation of the company; but if the dissenter does not demand this option promptly, he will perforce participate in the merger on the terms thereof, for the original companies lose their identities and existence completely in the new one.

In general, it may be stated that few stockholders find it good business to demand cash payment as the means of avoiding participation in a merger. It is usually more profitable to sell the stock. Of course, the vast majority of stockholders do not disapprove proposed mergers. They usually agree with the managements that the mergers are desirable; and in the occasional instances in which vigorous stockholder opposition to a proposed merger develops, the deal is more than likely to be dropped. If a proposed merger plan is definitely unfair, an aggrieved stockholder can usually get the courts of the incorporating state to forbid it.

The terms of merger arrangements very commonly provide for the issuance of new securities, similar to those previously held, to the stockholders of the merging firms. That is, common stockholders usually get new common stock, and preferred stockholders usually get new preferred which is at least somewhat similar in privileges and dividend rights to their old stock. This practice naturally re-

---

[15] The successor corporation might be one of the old firms, with its articles amended suitably, or it might be a new entity.

duces resistance to the merger. However, it must be conceded that the combined firm will usually be different in size, nature of business, and capital structure from any of its predecessors; and in the process of framing new articles, many of the features of the old stocks may be dropped. Mergers are thus likely to change both the legal features and the quality of the securities held by some of the participants, even when every effort is made to do justice to all concerned. Investors who chose the old securities to obtain these specific features and qualities may therefore be disappointed in the new arrangement; but a definite financial loss is not often to be expected.

Ordinarily the securityholders involved in a merger will not realize a gain or loss for income tax purposes when they receive their new securities, as a merger is regarded as a tax-free reorganization under present Federal law.

All these methods have been used frequently in recent years. Two interesting 1954 cases of formal merger are those of Nash-Kelvinator Corporation and Hudson Motor Car Company, in which Nash-Kelvinator was continued as the surviving combined corporation, but with its name changed to American Motors Corporation; and of Chemical Bank and Trust Company and Corn Exchange Bank Trust Company, which became the Chemical Corn Exchange Bank of New York, operating under the Chemical Bank's original charter as amended. Purchase and sale of assets combined the Kaiser Motors Corporation and Willys-Overland Motors, Inc., in 1953, in a complicated transaction in which a subsidiary of Kaiser bought the Willys name and properties for cash and assumed the Willys liabilities, leaving Willys to dissolve and distribute the cash to its stockholders; and in 1954 Packard Motor Car Company changed its name to Studebaker-Packard Corporation, issued 3,542,187 new shares to Studebaker Corporation and assumed Studebaker's liabilities in return for Studebaker's assets, leaving Studebaker to dissolve and distribute Studebaker-Packard shares to its stockholders. Purchase of stock is illustrated in two 1954 acquisitions by Burlington Mills Corporation. In the first case Burlington bought 467,402 out of 556,000 outstanding shares of Goodall-Sanford Inc. through an escrow in which Burlington offered $20 per share for Goodall-Sanford stock, provided that at least 380,000 shares accepted; in the second case, Burlington offered to exchange one-third share of its

$4.50 dividend Second Preferred plus 1.2 shares of its common stock for each share of Pacific Mills common, through a similar escrow.

Holding Companies

Holding companies are concerns whose business includes investment in and control of other corporations through ownership of their securities. The corporations thus controlled are referred to as subsidiary companies. Holding companies do not always own all of the securities of their subsidiary companies; in fact, they seldom own large percentages of the subsidiaries' bonds. But the essence of holding company control lies in the ownership of most of the stock, especially the common stock, and it is usual for holding companies to own all or most of their subsidiaries' common stocks. A publicly owned portion of a subsidiary's common stock is regarded as occupying a somewhat unique financial position and is termed a minority interest.

Investors are interested in holding company problems because a large percentage of the nation's important corporations are holding companies and because the holding company form of organization poses certain financial problems which do not exist in a business operated by a single corporation. The problems center about the fact that all the corporations in a holding company system are still legally separate concerns. Their managements may be the same people and their policies may be coordinated, but their assets, incomes, and obligations are legally independent. Thus the cash holdings of a subsidiary are not available to the parent (holding) company, unless the subsidiary pays a dividend, buys something from the parent, or makes a loan to it.[16] Likewise, the parent's cash is available to the subsidiary only by means of a loan or other formal transaction.[17] Dividends paid by a subsidiary are paid equitably (pro rata) on the stock held by the parent company and on that held by minority in-

16 The Associated Gas and Electric Corporation was forced into bankruptcy in 1940 when regulatory authorities ordered its subsidiaries to cease paying dividends and to use the money for other purposes. Associated controlled the money but could not get it.

17 The most common reason for new financing given by holding companies in their sales prospectuses is "to finance loans to subsidiaries and purchase of additional stock from them. . . ." See, for example, New England Electric System Prospectus, Sept. 29, 1954, p. 3.

terests. If a subsidiary with substantial earnings is legally prevented from paying dividends (for example, by a provision in a bank loan agreement), the holding company has no means of obtaining these earnings as dividends, hence cannot credit them to its own earned surplus. Lacking a surplus, it cannot pay dividends itself, even though its indirect earnings in the subsidiary are adequate.[18] Obviously, a subsidiary without earnings or surplus could not pay dividends, even though other subsidiaries of the same holding company and the holding company itself were prosperous.[19] The debts of a subsidiary company are not the debts of the parent, and vice versa. To be sure, the parent company which permits a subsidiary to be forced into bankruptcy will probably lose its investment in the subsidiary, but the parent company is ordinarily under no obligation to throw good money after bad by paying the debts of an unsuccessful subsidiary which is not worth salvaging.[20] Similarly, a sound subsidiary has no more duty to pay the debts of a faltering holding company than it has to pay those of any other stockholder.

This emphasis on the legal independence of different corporations should not blind the reader to the fact that holding systems are usually substantially unified for financial as well as for operating purposes. For example, the American Telephone and Telegraph Company has on many occasions drawn dividends from prospering subsidiaries and loaned or invested the money in other subsidiaries, to finance expansion or to pay debts. It has sold its own securities to obtain additional money for similar purposes. It draws its dividend income each quarter from the subsidiaries best able to provide it and leaves other possible sources untouched. The creditors of subsidiaries are fully aware that the whole resources of the system will support any sound subsidiary, and for that matter the parent

[18] General Public Utilities Corporation comments in its 1946 annual report that its subsidiaries' dividends during the year were limited "by reason of regulatory commission orders or for other reasons," thus restricting its own accumulation of earned surplus.

[19] In 1947 The Pacific Telephone and Telegraph Company encountered increased expenses which for a time almost obliterated earnings. Other units of the American Telephone system, including the parent company, were not so seriously affected. But Pacific Telephone had to solve its own problem by reducing dividends temporarily.

[20] In 1933 the Deep Rock Oil Corporation, whose common stock was owned by Standard Gas and Electric Company, could not pay its bond interest and current expenses. Standard did not find it convenient to save Deep Rock, so simply allowed it to go into bankruptcy.

company also, up to the limits indicated by law and business discretion. Unity is definitely a fact.

Holding companies commonly furnish their stockholders two sets of financial statements, one on a "corporate" basis and one on a "consolidated" basis. The statements on a corporate basis show the assets, liabilities, incomes, and expenses of the corporations separately, just as they legally stand. In that case the parent company's assets include the stocks it owns in the subsidiaries, and its income includes the dividends received from the subsidiaries. On the other hand, the consolidated statements show the entire group of companies as though they were one business.[21] On a consolidated balance sheet all the companies' cash, receivables, and physical assets are shown as assets, and all the debt claims and stock owned by "outsiders," including the holding company's securityholders, are shown on the liabilities side of the statement; but intercompany debts and securities holdings are not shown, since they are meaningless if the companies are considered as one unit. On a consolidated income statement all the companies' sales, expenses, and net incomes would be combined, except that intercompany payments would not be shown.

The simplified statements on page 74 involving subsidiary corporations A and B and holding company H will illustrate the contrast between corporate and consolidated statements. In this case it is assumed that in addition to its own business H owns 90 per cent of the common stocks of A and B but none of B's preferred. A and B each pay $1,000 per year in common dividends. The dividends paid by H are not shown, since they do not affect the consolidation.

Examination of the statements on page 74 will make clear the separate corporate positions of companies A, B, and H, with respect to such vital matters as cash holdings, debts, surplus, earnings, and the like. Their activities will be much influenced by these positions. But the aggregate position of the system as a whole, and particularly the scope of its earning power, will be shown by the consolidated statements. For example, it is only on the consolidated income statement that the entire $4,080 of earnings on the holding company stockholders' equity is clearly shown; and it is only on the consolidated

[21] There are exceptions. "Consolidated" statements sometimes consolidate certain subsidiaries fully but treat the securities owned in others as investments. This is discussed in Chap. 14.

Corporate and Consolidated Balance Sheet, December 31, 1954

	Subsidiary A	Subsidiary B	Holding Co. H	Consolidated companies
Assets				
Cash....................	$ 1,000	$ 2,000	$ 500	$ 3,500
Other Current Assets........	5,000	9,000	3,000	17,000
Fixed Assets (net)...........	9,000	15,000	6,500	30,500
Stocks of Subsidiaries at Cost Price....................	......	......	23,000	
Total.................	$15,000	$26,000	$33,000	$51,000
Liabilities				
Debts, etc...................	$ 3,000	$ 5,000	$ 1,000	$ 9,000
5% Preferred Stock..........	0	6,000	4,000	10,000
Common Stock..............	10,000	10,000	25,000	25,000
Minority Interest in A and B Common.................	......	......	......	2,700
Surplus...................	2,000	5,000	3,000	4,300
Total.................	$15,000	$26,000	$33,000	$51,000

Corporate and Consolidated Income Account, Calendar Year 1954

	Subsidiary A	Subsidiary B	Holding Co. H	Consolidated companies
Sales.....................	$20,000	$45,000	$12,000	$77,000
Expenses and Taxes..........	18,000	42,500	11,500	72,000
Dividend Income...........	0	0	1,800	
Net Income................	2,000	2,500	2,300	5,000
Minority Share (A and B Common)...................	......	......	......	420
Preferred Dividends..........	0	300	200	500
Earned for Common.........	2,000	2,200	2,100	
Earned for H Common.......	......	......	......	4,080

balance sheet that their $29,300 of total equity ($25,000 stock account plus $4,300 surplus) is shown and compared with total system assets of $51,000. Most investors place particular stress on consolidated earnings as the true measure of the earning power of a holding company investment, on the theory that earnings retained for capital expansion by a subsidiary are just as advantageous to a holding company stockholder as they would be if paid into the holding company and retained by it.

Holding company securities and the securities of their subsidiaries are not unsound or otherwise dangerous to investors, as a rule. There are, as has been noted, some legal intricacies in the use of multiple corporations which may make the shifting of cash through the system a little more difficult than in the case of a single corporation. This is especially true if the subsidiaries are publicly regulated utilities in which intercompany loans and dividends are subject to the approval of the regulating commissions. Also, minority holders of subsidiaries' common stocks may sometimes find that the plans and objectives of the holding company are not entirely in their best interests. Finally, there are certain regulatory measures, especially in the public utility and banking fields, which discriminate against the holding company form of organization. However, these factors do not seem important enough to justify the rejection of otherwise satisfactory investment choices.

QUESTIONS AND PROBLEMS

1. Is a corporation in default on its contract, and thus liable to lawsuit, if it ceases to pay dividends to its stockholders? What if it ceases to pay interest on its bonds? Why is the latter case different?

2. Could California businessmen incorporate a corporation in Delaware and cause it to do all its business in Colorado? If they did so, which state laws would govern it with respect to its power to pay dividends, repurchase its stock, or merge with another corporation? With respect to the meaning of its contracts for the sale of merchandise?

3. Why are investors indifferent to the terms of the corporation laws under which their companies operate? If you had stock in a Maryland corporation and the management proposed a merger plan which seemed unfair to you, where could you ascertain your rights under the law?

4. Who frames a corporation's articles? May they ever thereafter be changed? How?

5. What does a registrar do? Why is this important to a stockholder?

6. How much would it cost to obtain a replacement certificate if a 100-share certificate for General Motors stock was lost?

7. If U.S. Steel were to pay a $1 dividend on May 1 to stockholders of record on April 20, and if you bought stock on April 19 but did not get the indorsed certificate to the transfer office until April 21, who would get the dividend?

8. Investigate and classify the dividend policies of several leading corporations, for example, Consolidated Edison, Chrysler Corporation, Allis-Chalmers, Pennsylvania Railroad, Louisville and Nashville Railroad, Wilson and Co., Container Corporation, Columbia Gas System.

9. Enumerate several reasons for omission or limitation of corporate dividends. Are all of these signs of corporate weakness?

10. Why are stock splits more common than large stock dividends? What is the difference?

11. If you held stock in a successful corporation which needed all of its earnings in the business, would you advocate (a) no dividends, (b) small stock dividends, or (c) sale of additional stock under rights, with cash dividends continued? Why? Which system would keep the price of the stock the highest?

12. Why are stock dividends, stock splits, and liquidating dividends not regarded as taxable income to the stockholder?

13. Is there any fundamental difference between an assessment and the sale of new stock under rights?

14. Should the value of a right be regarded as a taxable dividend income to the investor? Why?

15. Why does stock usually decline in price a day or two before the stock-of-record date? Would this happen if the stock market were rising strongly?

16. Why is it difficult to work out a merger which does not disappoint at least some of the stockholders? If outstanding bonds were left unchanged in their contractual features, but through the merger became the obligations of the new corporation, could they be improved or weakened in quality by the change? Explain.

17. Assume that the Imaginary Textile Company has 100,000 shares each of First Preferred, Second Preferred, Third Preferred, and common stock. All preferreds are 5 per cent cumulative, $20 par. The common is no par. Assume also that the corporate articles now limit each issue to 100,000 shares. Assume further that the earnings range between $600,000 and $200,000 annually, averaging $400,000, and that the common stock usually gets 50 cents per share annually in dividends. The market prices of the stocks are First Preferred, $20; Second Preferred, $17; Third Pre-

ferred, $15; common, $8. Expansion needs require the sale of additional stock, but it is clear that additional stock cannot be sold until existing preferred dividend requirements are reduced to approximately half the average earnings. Outline a recapitalization plan which these stockholders will vote for, remembering that no stockholder will want any reduction in his income, preferential position, market value, or prospects for gain.

18. What advantages may accrue to investors as a result of purchases of its own common stock by their corporation? What errors and frauds might occur?

19. Do you agree that investors in holding companies will find consolidated financial statements more illuminating than corporate ones? Are the latter needed at all?

20. Does the consolidated balance sheet shown in the simplified example on page 74 give an accurate picture of the cash position of company H?

21. Would you like to be a minority stockholder in a subsidiary which the controlling company wishes to expand greatly by use of reinvested earnings? Why?

REFERENCES

Dice, Charles A., and Wilford J. Eiteman: *The Stock Market,* McGraw-Hill Book Company, Inc., New York, 1952, Chap. 2.

Financial Handbook, The Ronald Press Company, New York, 1948, pp. 379–455.

Hoagland, Henry E.: *Corporation Finance,* McGraw-Hill Book Company, Inc., New York, 1947, Chaps. 3, 5, 36.

Husband, William H., and James C. Dockeray: *Modern Corporation Finance,* Richard D. Irwin, Inc., Homewood, Ill., 1952, Chaps. 4, 14, 15, 24, 28, 29.

Robbins, Sidney M.: *Managing Securities,* Houghton Mifflin Company, Boston, 1954, Chap. 6.

Shultz, Birl E.: *The Securities Market and How It Works,* Harper & Brothers, New York, 1946, Chap. 4.

Spengler, Edwin H., and Jacob Klein: *Introduction to Business,* McGraw-Hill Book Company, Inc., New York, 1948, Chaps. 2, 3.

Chapter 4: COMMON STOCKS
AND THEIR VALUE

Common stock may be defined as the residual ownership of a corporation, which is entitled to all assets and earnings after the other limited claims have been paid and which has the basic voting control. In short, common stock is the fundamental ownership equity. No private business corporation is without common stock, most of them draw the major portion of their funds from their common stockholders, and nearly all are managed basically in the interests of the common stockholders.

The investor in common stock thus occupies a position directly comparable to that of the owner of a farm or a factory. Successful operation means in either case good income from the business and increased value for the investment; losses mean the opposite. Common stock bears the main burden of the risk of the enterprise and also receives the lion's share of the advantages of success; it is the potent and dynamic element in corporate financing and the one which commands the highest concentration of investor interest.

Perquisites of the Common Stockholder

Since the common stockholders usually control the corporation, it is to be expected that corporate policies will be developed to further their interests. Such corporate actions as dividend payments, stock dividends, stock splits, recapitalizations, mergers, expansion, sale of new securities, and use of rights are normally planned by management with particular reference to their effect on the common stock. Bondholders and preferred stockholders are not disregarded, of course; but it is assumed that they will be content with the exact preferences and advantages stipulated in the bond indenture and the corporate articles, so that management discretion may be applied chiefly in the interests of the common stock.

For example, when a drought in the fall of 1947 impaired the earnings of the New England Electric System at a time when money was urgently needed for expansion, the bondholders would probably have chosen to eliminate dividends as a means of conserving cash. But since the common stock interests were in control, the available earnings were used to continue the dividends and the funds needed for expansion were borrowed. Again, the planning of recapitalization plans may be cited. When the Armour and Company management in 1954 advanced a plan for eliminating dividend arrearages on the 6 per cent preferred stock, the plan called for the issuance of new 5 per cent income bonds plus common stock purchase warrants in exchange for the principal plus the back dividends on the old preferred. It was not an unjust plan, but its basic purpose was to reduce the annual preferred dividend burden and clear away the arrearages from past years, thus paving the way for resumption of dividends to common stockholders. Other examples involving other phases of financial and business policy might be mentioned, but the point has been made: business corporations are run by the common stockholders in the interests of the common stockholders.

Investment Characteristics

Before proceeding further with the study of common stocks it will be desirable to summarize the investment features usually attributed to them. These features are in several cases generalizations which are subject to exceptions, but on the whole a common stock may be said to have the following characteristics:

1. It normally has control of the corporation and will exercise that control in its own interests.

2. It has unlimited ownership rights to the remaining gains from the business, after other securityholders have received their (usually) limited contractual payments.

3. It bears the principal hazards of the business, since other securityholders, creditors, and employees usually have prior claims, and its quality depends importantly on the amount and nature of the prior claims.

4. Common stock may be sold by its holder to any willing buyer, but in the ordinary course of business it does not come "due," hence need never be redeemed by the corporation; nor may the corporation ordinarily "call" it for redemption or force the stockholder to surrender

it against his wishes. (A formal recapitalization or merger or final liquidation may be an exception.)

5. The earnings on the common stockholders' equity may be unstable. Not only will the corporation's total earnings fluctuate as business conditions change and its own affairs progress, but all the creditors and preferred stockholders must be allowed prior rights, thus making the residual share more unstable than the total.

6. Dividends may fluctuate. Dividends must depend on earnings, cash position, surplus position, expansion needs, debt situation, and management policy. Even if management desires a stable dividend rate, it may not always be feasible, for expansion, debt retirement, and cash accumulation are often more important to the corporation.

7. Dividends are normally less than the earnings on the common stockholders' equity; hence the value of that equity should grow as a result of the investment of the undistributed earnings in the business.

8. Common stocks in general are a price-level hedge. That is, they tend to earn, pay dividends, and bring market prices at levels which are vaguely related to the general commodity price level. However, this is only a long-run general tendency, subject to numerous exceptions, as will be noted later.

9. Common stock prices fluctuate extensively. These fluctuations are so extreme that even in high-grade stocks the timing of purchases and sales is a major investment problem. Large profits or losses on such investments are therefore commonplace.

Investors in common stocks are thus afforded commitments which are interesting, useful, potentially profitable, and hazardous. The selection of such commitments requires more than average care and competence, but is not so difficult that a careful investor should not attempt it. In fact, the average careful investor needs common stocks in order to create a balanced investment program. He must therefore either learn to select them himself or accept the alternative of placing that function in the hands of a friend, an investment counselor, or some other informed person, or on the managers of an investment company whose shares he may buy.[1]

---

[1] An investment company is an organization which sells its own shares to the public and invests the proceeds in a diversified list of other securities. The investments are bought and sold as conditions warrant. See Chap. 19.

Stock Prices

Shares of stock of ordinary investment types range in price between $10 and $200 per share. A few sell higher, and a number of good issues mingle with the more speculative types valued between $1 and $10 per share. Great numbers of small and speculative corporations have shares worth less than $1 each.

It is conventional for shares selling in normal price ranges to be quoted in terms of dollars and eighths rather than dollars and cents per share. Thus Eastman Kodak was quoted in 1954 at $57\frac{1}{8}$, meaning $57.12\frac{1}{2}$ per share, and Celotex Corporation at $19\frac{1}{2}$, or $19.50 per share. Pricing intervals smaller than eighths of a dollar are not used on stocks worth much in excess of $2 per share. Shares selling below $2 are sometimes quoted in dollars and cents, with pricing intervals of 5 cents or 1 cent. In other markets they may be quoted in sixteenths or thirty-seconds of a dollar.

Shares of stock are always quoted at prices which contemplate transferring to the purchaser the ownership of the share and all future dividends or other disbursements except those already of record and in process of payment. Even accumulated back dividends on preferred stock are transferred from seller to buyer. The price of the stock must be determined with this in mind.

Fundamental Calculations

Investors in common stocks make constant use of five fundamental calculations for gauging the merit of a common stock and testing the reasonableness of its price. These calculations are in no sense final determinants of quality or value, but they are convenient preliminary indicators which, taken in conjunction with the investor's general knowledge of the industry and the company, tell whether the stock is worthy of further investigation. Although the actual arithmetic is usually done by securities analysts, so that the investor may take the figures directly from securities manuals and analytical reports, it seems best to review the processes briefly. The calculations in question determine (1) the earnings per share, (2) the net asset value (or book value) per share, (3) leverage, (4) the price-earnings ratio, and (5) the yield.

In computing earnings per share, assets per share, and other such measures, it is customary to divide the appropriate sum of earnings or assets by the number of shares *outstanding*, that is, owned by the stockholders. The corporate articles may authorize additional shares which have never been issued, and reacquired shares may be held as treasury stock by the corporation, but these do not receive dividends and would not share in the assets in the event of liquidation, hence need not be included in the per share calculations.

Earnings per Share

Since the common stock is the lowest ranking security and the residual claimant to the earnings of a corporation, it is usually possible to compute its earnings per share by taking the net corporate profit after expenses, interest, and taxes, subtracting the preferred dividend requirement for the period (whether paid or accumulated unpaid would not matter), and dividing the remainder by the number of common shares outstanding. This may be illustrated by reference to the 1953 income statement of Celotex Corporation. In that fiscal year the company had a profit of $3,024,844 after payment of all expenses, interest, and taxes. Preferred dividend requirements for the year were $256,677. The remaining $2,768,167 amounted to $3.06 earned per share on the 905,472 common shares outstanding, computed simply by dividing $2,768,167 by 905,472. Earnings per share are computed in the same manner for quarterly or semi-annual periods, when the data are available.

If the company does not earn enough to pay the full preferred dividend, the amount of the deficiency is regarded as a deficit to the common stock. For example, if the Celotex Corporation had had a profit of only $200,000 in 1953, it would have been $56,677 short of covering its preferred requirements of $256,677. Dividing this $56,677 deficiency by 905,472, the number of common shares, would indicate that the deficit per common share was 6 cents. If the situation had been worse—for example, if there had been a $200,000 *loss* after payment of all expenses—the deficit to the common stockholders would have been $200,000 plus the $256,677 preferred dividend requirement. The total of $456,677 divided among 905,472 common shares would show a deficit of 50 cents per share.

Two special cases should be noted. When a corporation issues new stock for property or cash during a business year, the new assets contribute to earnings during only part of the year. In such cases analysts often compute earnings per share on the weighted average number of shares outstanding, rather than on the total number outstanding at the year end. Second, when there are participating preferred stocks or special classes of common stock outstanding, it is sometimes necessary to devise special calculations to show the proper per share allocations of the earnings. The nature of such special calculations must obviously depend on the rights to earnings as established in the corporate articles.

If the stock under consideration is that of a holding company, earnings per share may be computed from either the corporate or the consolidated income statement. The earnings of the corporate statement will include the dividends received by the holding company from its subsidiaries, plus the profits from its own operations; this may be a measure of the holding company's capacity to pay dividends from current earnings. Earnings per share computed from a consolidated statement will show the per share profits of the business as a whole, regardless of whether the subsidiaries paid dividends to the holding company. This is the calculation most commonly used by investors, because most investors wish to measure as earnings per share the total earned increment accruing on their investment, in both holding company and subsidiaries. Any minority interests in subsidiaries' earnings must of course be allowed for.

In calculations which appraise stock values on a per share basis the investor must make mental allowance for any situation which threatens to dilute his per share earnings or assets. This dilution problem often occurs when corporations sell bonds or preferred stocks which are convertible into common or have stock purchase warrants or options outstanding which permit their holders to buy new stock at a fixed price. Usually the conversion of bonds or preferred stock into common stock will reduce the senior claims to income by a relatively modest amount. Stock purchase options may call for prices which add relatively little to the earning assets of the corporation. In either instance, therefore, the number of outstanding common shares might increase greatly while the total earnings available for the common stock increased very little. The result would be a decline in per share earnings.

Investors generally place very great emphasis upon earnings per share and the trend of earnings per share, arguing that both present and future dividends are dependent upon earnings. This is probably a well-founded position, especially if the earnings statements are studied to make sure that they are fairly presented and free from distortions due to nonrecurring incomes or expenses and if proper attention is given to other developments in the company or the industry which are not yet reflected in the earnings figures.

Net Asset Value per Share

The net asset value per share, sometimes referred to as the book value per share, attempts to measure the amount of assets which the corporation has working on behalf of each share of common stock. It is arrived at by taking the net (after allowance for depreciation and depletion) balance sheet value of the corporate assets, subtracting the face value of creditors' and preferred stockholders' claims, and dividing the remainder by the number of outstanding common shares. The Celotex Corporation at December 31, 1953, had total assets carried at $44,670,197, after allowances for depreciation. Debts and preferred stock amounted to $15,469,212. The remaining $29,-200,985 indicated a net asset value of $32.25 for each of the 905,472 common shares.

Students of accounting will observe that this method of calculating net asset value per share makes no deduction from assets for such balance sheet credit items as contingency reserves, inventory value reserves, and self-insurance reserves. The reason is that these items are usually tantamount to appropriated surplus and thus truly a part of the stockholders' net worth, unless there is definite reason to regard them as offsets to assets which are likely to be lost in the near future.

In any business in which available assets are a good measure of earning power, the asset value per share may be highly significant. However, it must be conceded that (1) corporate book values are usually based on cost, not earning power, and (2) intangible assets not on the books may be more significant than book values, in determining earning power. Asset value figures should thus not be overstressed, though the solid dependability of good assets in assuring future earnings should not be belittled.

Because some corporations with very valuable patents, trade

names, good will, and other intangible assets do not show them on their financial statements at all, it has become customary in recent years to compute net asset values based on tangible assets alone. That is, intangible assets are not included among the assets at all, for this purpose. This practice sometimes results in very small book values per share for some highly valuable stocks, but in other cases it avoids distortion by excluding the dubious intangible values which some corporate statements contain.

In computing book values for holding company stocks, consolidated balance sheets are generally used. If minority interests exist, they are allotted a proper share of subsidiary net worth.

The Leverage Factor

The leverage factor indicates the number of dollars employed in the business for every dollar invested by the common stockholders. Thus, if a $3,000,000 business employed $1,000,000 of creditors' money, $1,000,000 from preferred stockholders, and $1,000,000 from common stockholders, it would have a leverage factor of 3; there would be $3 of total assets for every $1 of common stockholder investment. Leverage factors in large industrial concerns usually range from about 1.1, in very conservative enterprises, to about 2 or 2.5.[2]

In a low-leverage enterprise the interest and preferred dividend claims are small or nonexistent, and the bulk of the earnings are available for the common stock. If the earnings are good, the dividends can be large; if the earnings are small, a small dividend may still be possible. Low leverage thus tends toward stability, security, and high quality in the common stock. In a high-leverage enterprise, however, the common stock position is dynamic but speculative. If

[2] Leverage factors computed with regard to holding company stocks are sometimes misleading, if the equity of the holding company common stock is regarded as junior to all other securities in the system. For example, assume that holding company H, which has only common stock outstanding, owns all the common stocks of subsidiaries A and B. Subsidiary A has no securities outstanding except the common stock owned by H; subsidiary B is financed 80 per cent with bonds which are in public hands and 20 per cent with the stock held by H. If the two subsidiaries are of equal size, a consolidated balance sheet would show 40 per cent in bonds preceding a 60 per cent common stock equity, or a leverage factor of 1.67. Actually, the holding company's common stock has an absolute first claim (leverage 1.0) with respect to A's property and a very junior claim on B. This is unquestionably a stronger position than a simple 60 per cent equity in the whole system.

the earnings are good, the creditors and preferred stockholders receive their limited income, leaving the large remainder to the common; but if the earnings are small, the entire amount or more may be needed to pay the prior claims. A high leverage factor means that the common stock is taking a large risk in anticipation of a large profit.

This may be illustrated in an imaginary $5,000,000 business. If common stockholders invest the whole $5,000,000, their equity earns just what the business earns, possibly 8 per cent or possibly 2 per cent. But if the funds are raised by borrowing $2,000,000 at 4 per cent, selling $2,000,000 of 6 per cent preferred stock, and selling $1,000,000 of common stock, the case is far different. In this second instance an 8 per cent return on the $5,000,000 of invested funds would amount to $400,000. The lenders would get $80,000 in interest, the preferred stockholders would get $120,000 in dividends, and the earnings on the common stock equity would be $200,000, or 20 per cent. If the business earned only 2 per cent on its funds, however, the interest requirements would be covered by only a small margin, the preferred dividend would not be fully earned, and the high-leverage common stock would show a deficit for the year.

Because balance sheet values do not always reflect accurately the true values of corporate assets, some analysts prefer to measure leverage by comparing the *market* value of the common stock (obtained by multiplying the market price per share by the number of outstanding common shares) to a total obtained by adding the market value of the common plus the par or reasonable liquidation value of the preferred plus the face value of all debts. This process would give a better measure of true leverage in a concern whose assets included valuable patents or good will not listed on the balance sheet, or whose assets were listed on the balance sheet at figures far in excess of their true value.

It would be just as logical, or perhaps more so, to base the measurement of leverage on corporate income rather than on capitalization. After all, the most perfect demonstration of low leverage would be in the concern whose interest and preferred dividend obligations absorbed only a small fraction of its business earnings in the average year. Conversely, high leverage would be illustrated by the firm whose interest and preferred obligations took a large percentage of its average earning power.

Before leaving the subject of leverage it is desirable to note that the use of leverage varies greatly from one type of business to another. In the very stable electric power business, in which the earnings needed to pay large bond interest and preferred dividend requirements are very dependable, the common stockholders usually contribute only 20 per cent to 50 per cent of the invested capital; leverage factors in this industry thus range between 5 and 2. In ordinary competitive industry, as was noted earlier, most cases fall between 2.5 and 1.1. In banking, in which stable earnings and very stable and secure assets are normal, the stockholders' investment normally amounts to only 5 to 10 per cent of the total assets of the bank, and the leverage factors therefore range between 20 and 10. It is clear, therefore, that the degree of leverage found in any business concern must be judged in the light of a full understanding of the firm and its industry, with particular regard to the stability of its earnings and the liquidity and safety of its assets.

Price-earnings Ratio

The price-earnings ratio is simply the market price of the stock expressed as a multiple of the per share earnings of the corporation. Thus, General Electric stock would be selling for *sixteen times earnings* if it sold for $40 per share at a time when the annual earnings amounted to $2.50 per share. The price-earnings ratio is a conventional and highly regarded measure of stock value, because it gives an excellent indication of corporate success measured against the price of the stock.[3]

As an indication of typical price-earnings ratios on good-quality stocks, Chart 2 has been compiled over the period 1928–1953 inclusive. The chart shows the ratio of a weighted aggregate of prices to earnings of 20 stocks, all of which are so high grade that each company earned profits and paid dividends in every year of the period. Neither earnings nor dividends fluctuated extremely during the period; so market values had no occasion to fluctuate because of such changes. In short, Chart 2 is designed to show the variation in value of dependable corporate earning power.

---

[3] Instead of the commonly used price-earnings calculations some writers invert the ratio and compute the *earnings yield*—that is, the percentage which the annual per share earnings figure bears to the price of the stock.

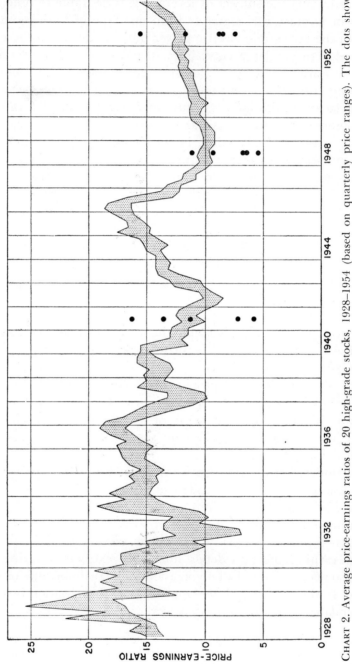

CHART 2. Average price-earnings ratios of 20 high-grade stocks, 1928–1954 (based on quarterly price ranges). The dots show average price-earnings ratios of A, Baa, Ba, B, and Caa stocks at three dates.

It will be noted that the average price has been around 13 to 14 times earnings. Ten times earnings has been a fairly low figure, and 18 times earnings has been very high. This chart provides a basic clue to the values of high-grade common stocks. Unfortunately, it is difficult to provide so clear an indication of the value of lower grade stocks. Their earnings and dividends are so erratic, and their futures at any given time are so obscure, that it is not reasonable to attribute their prices over a period of time to any measurable sustained earning power. For stocks whose earnings possibilities seem well-defined and stable, as those in Table 3 (page 92), it can be assumed that lower quality will result in a lower price-earnings ratio; but in the cases of many dynamic speculations, even high-leverage ones, the possibility of great gain attracts enough buyers to cause a moderately high ratio of price to probable earnings and dividends.

In an attempt to gauge price-earnings ratios in stocks of different qualities, average ratios were computed for five quality groups at their average prices in 1941, 1948, and 1953. The results are shown by black dots arranged in the respective year columns on Chart 2. The highest dot represents the very best investment stocks, which seem normally to bring about 16 times their stable earning power; the lowest dot represents about the poorest category which could be counted upon for reasonably regular dividends, and it seems normally to bring about seven or eight times earning power.

Yield

The yield refers to the percentage which the annual dividend bears to the current price of the stock. If General Electric stock pays dividends at the rate of $1.60 per annum and sells at $40, the yield is 4 per cent. Investors often compute yields in terms of the prices they paid when they bought their stocks, even when both prices and dividends have since changed. This may be satisfactory from a personal historical standpoint, but it is rather pointless in a current review of one's investments. The significant yield factor in determining whether to buy or sell *now* is the yield based on the present price and the present or prospective annual dividend rate.

Chart 3 traces the long-term yield history of the same 20 stocks whose price-earnings ratios appear in Chart 2. In addition, the average yield record of a group of high-grade bonds is also shown. For

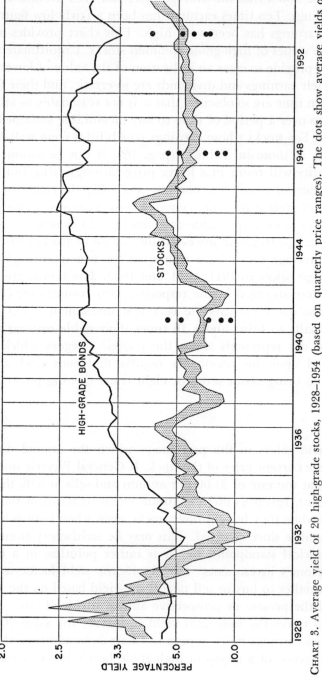

CHART 3. Average yield of 20 high-grade stocks, 1928–1954 (based on quarterly price ranges). The dots show average yields of A, Baa, Ba, B, and Caa stocks at three dates.

the sake of convenience the yield scales have been charted upside down; so the charted curves are high when stock and bond prices are high, and vice versa. If allowance is made for abnormal inflation in 1929 and abnormal deflation in 1932 and 1942, it appears that a long-run normal average yield on these stocks slightly exceeds 5 per cent. Yields under 4 per cent and over 7 have been exceedingly transitory.

Chart 3 also includes black dots in the year columns for 1941, 1948, and 1953 to illustrate the average yields obtainable on top-grade and lesser stocks. As in Chart 2, the lowest grade shown is about the poorest which can produce reasonably regular dividends in normal times. It appears that the very best common stocks generally yield between 4 and 5 per cent, but that lesser ones at times average 8 per cent or even more.

The relatively low bond yields shown on the chart since 1938 raise a question as to the permanence of both bond and high-grade stock yields at their present levels. The supply-and-demand analysis presented in Chapter 2 explains the situation, but the existing disparity between bond and stock yields is unprecedented in modern history and causes many analysts to believe that the bond yields must ultimately rise or the stock yields fall.

Only the Future Is Significant

If yields and price-earnings ratios are to give a true index to the present highness or lowness of the price of a stock, they must be based on estimated dividend and earnings rates of the foreseeable future, coupled with the present price of the stock. To today's seller or purchaser, it is almost completely immaterial whether the stock did well in the past or did poorly. It is future performance which is being sold and bought. Of course, the past and the present may give some indication of the future, and for that reason it may be significant to study them carefully and to compare present prices with past dividends and earnings.

In most practical investment literature, yields and price-earnings ratios are calculated using the present annual dividend rate and the rate of earnings as shown by some recent report. This is a satisfactory approach if it is assumed that the immediate present is the best clue to the future; but it gives absurd results when the immediate present is far out of line with any reasonable future expectations. For example, the stock of the Cudahy Packing Company sold at $12 in early 1948, shortly after reporting earnings of $4.32 per share for the 1947 fiscal year. The stock was then said to be selling for less than three

Table 3. Yields and Price-earnings Ratios on Common Stocks of Different Qualities

Stock	Quality rating *	Average price, 1954 † (1)	Average earnings, 1952–1953 (2)	Dividend rate, 1954 (3)	Price-earnings ratio ‡ (4)	Yield, per cent § (5)
American Telephone......	Excellent	163	$11.58	$9.00	14.1	5.5
Boston Edison............	Excellent	51	3.13	2.80	16.3	5.5
Chase National Bank.....	Excellent	45	3.95	2.00	11.4	4.4
du Pont.................	Excellent	116	4.82	4.00	14.1	3.4
General Electric..........	Excellent	40	1.83	1.60	21.9	4.0
Consolidated Edison......	Very good	43	2.78	2.40	15.5	5.6
General Motors..........	Very good	66	6.47	4.00	10.2	6.1
International Harvester...	Very good	30	3.61	2.00	8.3	6.7
Swift...................	Very good	45	5.19	3.00	8.7	6.7
Union Pacific............	Very good	120	14.75	6.00	8.1	5.0
California Packing........	Good	26	3.20	1.50	8.1	5.8
Motor Wheel............	Good	23	3.30	2.00	7.0	8.7
National Supply..........	Good	28	6.28	2.00	4.5	7.1
New England Electric.....	Good	14½	1.23	.90	11.8	6.2
Southern Pacific..........	Good	41	6.66	3.00	6.2	7.3

* Quality ratings adapted from those of a leading advisory service.
† Mean of highs and lows for first half of year.
‡ Ratio Column (1) to Column (2).
§ Ratio Column (3) to Column (1).

times earnings. Actually, Cudahy's rosiest hopes for the future did not contemplate an average earning power much in excess of $2 per share per year; 1947 was a fluke of high order, and a price-earnings ratio based on it was meaningless, as subsequent earnings history has proved.

To repeat: yields and price-earnings ratios must be based on reasonable estimates of average future dividends and earnings, if they are to be meaningful in indicating which stocks are the most attractively priced. Past and current earnings and dividends are chiefly significant as indexes of what can be expected in the all-important future.

Quality and Price

Table 3 illustrates the tendency for high-quality stocks to sell at a higher price-earnings ratio and at a lower yield than stocks of lesser quality. The 15 stocks in the table were chosen for illustrative purposes because their earnings and dividend rates seem reasonably stable, but it must be presumed that they will fluctuate, as will the prices of the stocks. Consequently, the price-earnings and yield figures shown here are subject to considerable variation. The quality classifications used are based on those assigned by one of the leading investment advisory services.

The degree of price stability to be expected in stocks of varying quality is illustrated in Tables 4 and 5. The stocks included are substantially the same in both tables. All are large issues, most are

Table 4. 1946 Price Ranges of 239 Leading Stocks, Grouped by Quality

Range as per cent of average price	Quality of stocks					
	Best	Excel-lent	Very good	Good	Fair to good	Fair
Below 20.0	..	..	..	1		
20–29.9	3 *	11 *	5	..	2	
30–39.9	2	2	14	12	2	1
40–49.9	..	2	12 *	14	11	2
50–59.9	..	1	11	12 *	12	6
60–69.9	..	..	6	7	21 *	9
70–79.9	..	..	..	11	11	10 *
80–89.9	..	..	2	1	8	8
90–99.9	..	..	..	1	2	3
Over 100	..	..	..	..	1	
Number of stocks	5	16	50	59	70	39

* Median group.

Table 5. 1937–1944 Price Ranges of 297 Leading Stocks, Grouped by Quality

Range as per cent of average price	Quality of stocks					
	Best	Excel-lent	Very good	Good	Fair to good	Fair
Below 40.0	..	..	..	..	..	1
40– 49.9						
50– 59.9	..	1	2			
60– 69.9	1	..	6	2		
70– 79.9	4 *	8 *	10	1		
80– 89.9	..	3 *	7	3	..	1
90– 99.9	..	2	11	1	2	1
100–109.9	..	2	8 *	6	1	
110–119.9	..	1	13	..	2	
120–129.9	..	1	12	13	7	5
130–139.9	..	..	6	9 *	6	10
140–149.9	..	..	3	2	9	13
150–159.9	..	..	1	12	10 *	14 *
160–169.9	..	..	..	6	10	18
170–179.9	..	..	..	4	6	10
180–189.9	..	..	..	2	6	1
190–199.9						
Over 200	..	..	..	..	1	
Number of stocks	5	18	79	61	60	74

* Median group.

listed on the New York Stock Exchange, the industries represented are widely assorted, and the quality ratings are based on those assigned by a leading financial service in 1947. The year 1946 was a year in which stock prices fluctuated only a little more than in the average year of the decade 1940–1949, and only twice as much as in the very stable year 1953. The period 1937–1944 produced stock price ranges no greater than those of many relatively mild boom-and-depression cycles of the past. While an optimist is entitled to hope that future economic disturbances may be less extensive than those reflected here, a careful investor is forced to note two things: (1) that the price fluctuations in stocks can be disturbingly large, so much so that investors must time their purchases and sales and plan their portfolios accordingly; and (2) that the fluctuations of typical stocks in the "fair" category, which is undoubtedly good enough to warrant consideration even in moderately conservative portfolios, are two to three times as great as those in the "best" classification.

There is no evidence to show that low-priced stocks fluctuate more extensively than high-priced ones of the same quality. All of the stocks studied in Tables 4 and 5 were regrouped to test this theory, and the results were very clear. If low-priced and high-priced stocks of the same quality are compared, their percentage fluctuations above and below their mean prices will average about the same. There are many low-priced stocks which fluctuate violently, and most high-priced stocks are relatively stable; but the reason is found in the fact that most low-quality stocks are low-priced, and vice versa.

Market Factors

Though earning power, dividend prospects, and quality are the major factors determining the value of a stock, there are market factors which may cause its price to depart extensively from a long-run norm. These market factors are numerous. They may affect all stocks, or an entire industry, or an individual stock issue. For example, a reduction in margin requirements might provide enough additional buying demand to drive the general stock market upward; or an exceptionally heavy expansion program by the electric utilities might deluge the markets with so much new utility stock that such stocks would be in great oversupply and therefore weak; or an attempt by a large stockholder to liquidate a block of unseasoned stock might find few buyers, hence depress the market for that particular stock. Market factors are so important in the study of common stocks that they must be mentioned at this point, but a discussion of them is reserved for another chapter.

Determinants of Quality in Stocks

Because investors do not all prefer stocks with identical characteristics, it is not feasible to define quality with mathematical exactness. Many investors, for example, do not require that a stock pay large or regular dividends. To others such a dividend practice is the exact measure of desirability. But all will agree that a high-quality stock must of necessity represent a profitable and an enduring equity. For present purposes, therefore, a high-quality common stock is one upon which the corporation appears able to earn and pay reasonable (though not necessarily completely regular) dividends into the indefinite future, while maintaining its financial strength, its competitive position, and the vigor of its business. This definition implies that a public utility stock with very stable earnings and dividends, such as Pacific Gas and Electric Company common, may be similar in quality to an industrial like Allis-Chalmers Manufacturing Company, whose earnings are less stable but appear equally sure into the long-run future. A low-quality stock, by obvious contrast, is one whose future contributions to its owner's welfare are uncertain because of weaknesses in the industry, the business, or the corporation's finances.

There are two general approaches which an investor may make in appraising quality. First, he may assemble all available information on the industry and the company and undertake a comprehensive and technical study covering stability, growth, profit margins, costs, capital structures, and many other such items. This is not an impossible task, even for an amateur, though it requires time, patience, and for accuracy, some experience. Security analysts regularly study and compare corporate prospects along these lines, to determine both quality and the probable actual amounts of future earnings and dividends. Some of the techniques and criteria employed will be suggested in a later chapter.

For the present, it will be sufficient to suggest that a high-quality common stock is likely to be found in a well-entrenched and profitable large concern, which has a low-leverage capital structure and which operates in an enduring and preferably growing industry. If the stock is really high quality, earnings per share will probably have been reported in at least nine out of the last ten peacetime years, and dividends in all ten; and the average earnings and dividends, making reasonable allowance for the postwar inflation of prices, will constitute very satisfactory returns upon the value of the stock as reported in the initial years of the period. Obviously, the company and its industry must be promisingly situated for a prosperous future.

If the investor has not the time or the facilities for conducting his own investigation into the qualities of stocks, he may with reasonable safety employ the conclusions of others. Financial advisory services, financial periodicals, and brokers all prepare lists of stocks which are classified or otherwise labeled as to quality and which may also contain "guesstimates" respecting future earnings and dividends. Because the prediction of the future is an uncertain process, the conclusions reached by different analysts may differ, but they should be sufficiently alike to confirm each other to a satisfactory degree. Some analysts report their quality findings by assigning very candid and comparable "grades," such as A, B, C, to the stocks studied; others use word terms, such as "investment grade," "good quality," or "speculative"; while others use less categorical but more illuminating descriptive paragraphs. In any event, it will not be difficult for the inquiring investor to obtain a consensus of informed opinion as to the quality of any well-known stock in which he is interested. This consensus may then be checked against his own conclusions or accepted as a guide to action.

Comparing Stocks for Investment

Most careful investors find it convenient to select common stocks for investment by comparing price-earnings ratios, yields, and asset values per share in the light of available information on market factors and quality. Since there are thousands of issues available for consideration, some systematic method of choice is a practical necessity. Probably the best first step is a review of the stocks already in the portfolio, in order to choose the industries in which added holdings would be most appropriate and to determine the most desirable quality. Other preferences, such as the desire for stability of dividend rate, for the stock of a large concern, for a low-priced stock, for a listed market, or for a certain geographic location might further guide the selections.

A knowledge of the economic and financial behavior of industries is invaluable at this point. Familiarity with the capital structures, earnings and dividend stability, and stock market reputations of such diverse industries as electric power, banking, steel production, oil refining, and the like will assist the investor in determining his needs. Knowledge of the relative importance of various cost factors, such as labor, fuel, and materials, and of the sales opportunities available will make his judgments more accurate. Some introduction to these industry factors will be provided in later chapters of this book, and further sources of information will be cited; for the present, it is sufficient to note that an acquaintance with industries will assist in making basic decisions.

Having decided upon the quality and detailed features of the desired stock, the investor may next look for issues which meet his specifications. The most convenient source of inspiration will probably be the "recommended" lists of financial advisory services, investment periodicals, and securities brokers, which, as was previously noted, are likely to include data on quality and other statistical information. Other suggestions can no doubt be drawn from quotation sheets, friends, and the investor's own broker. From these numerous sources it should be easy to select several stocks which appear to be suitable and attractively priced. These may then be compared to arrive at a final choice.

The final step is, obviously, one of comparing values. If the investor is so minded, this may become an elaborate task, involving extensive economic and financial research. If the investor is disposed to spend his money on another's recommendation, the job can be done very simply yet reasonably well by reviewing a good analyst's summary of each stock and making a decision based on the summaries plus a very few fundamental statistical measures. The most vital convenient statistical measures are:

1. The price-earnings ratio between the present price per share and the estimated average per share earnings of the next five to ten years
2. The yield of the stock, based on the present price and the probable average dividend of the next five years
3. The net asset value per share
4. The range (high and low) of the stock's price during each of the past several years

The first two of the foregoing measures require the investor to estimate future earnings and dividends.[4] Admittedly, this cannot be done with great accuracy, but since future earnings and dividends are the foundation of future investment values, the investor must

---

[4] Many professional analysts would probably argue that the market does not estimate earnings and dividends into the distant future but tends to capitalize current rates instead. Certainly the market often responds sharply to an unexpected change in earnings or dividend rates. But an investor must always remember that it is the future, not the present, which must justify his investment.

either predict them or abandon hope of gauging investment values at all. But it is not impossible to make intelligent predictions of earnings and dividends; the present figures are available as a starting point, the trends up or down in recent years are known, and definite further impressions of progress or decline can be drawn from studies of the industry and the company. The net asset value per share is not important for its own sake, but in many lines of business it is an important indicator of the earnings and share values which can be expected. Past prices for the stocks are included because they reflect the market's consensus on the value of the stock over a period of time and thus indicate something of its quality, reputation, and general price behavior.

For purposes of illustration, the suggested method of comparison may be applied to the stocks of three imaginary companies A, B, and C, as shown in the accompanying table. It is assumed that all three are in acceptable industries, that their characteristics and policies meet the present requirements, but that some slight superiority in quality is conceded to company A because it has no debt or preferred stock. The figures compiled for comparison are shown on a per share basis in the accompanying table.

Company	Estimated future earnings	Estimated future dividends	Present price	Price-earnings ratio	Yield, per cent	Net asset value	Price ranges, 1951–1953
A	$2.50	$2.00	34	13.6	5.9	$33.00	42–29 (1951) 37–28 (1952) 36–30 (1953)
B	4.00	2.50	48	12.0	5.2	38.00	60–40 (1951) 52–41 (1952) 53–40 (1953)
C	2.00	1.40	21	10.5	6.7	25.00	31–19 (1951) 27–18 (1952) 25–19 (1953)

These figures clearly indicate that the market recognizes company A's superiority in quality, as they bring out its greater market price stability and its higher price-earnings ratio. The yield of company

A's stock is relatively high because it is able to pay 80 per cent of its earnings in dividends, a ratio which is usually possible only to mature and strong concerns. The market prices in the table show that the public respects the value of A's stock; the annual lows (that is, the lowest prices during each year) are not far below the present price, and the highs have exceeded the present price in each year. The net asset value appears to be adequate to support continued earning power at the estimated rate. Company B's stock is selling on a price-earnings basis which recognizes a quality somewhat lower than A's. Company B's stock yields less than A's, possibly because earnings are retained in the company for expansion or debt retirement; this is not necessarily a long-run disadvantage, but the stock would probably bring higher and more stable prices if a larger dividend were paid. The net asset value is far enough below present stock prices to require further investigation; the market price record is satisfactory, though the present price is much closer to the highs of the past two years than to the lows. The third stock, that of company C, is selling at 10.5 times estimated earnings and promises a yield of 6.7 per cent. These are attractive ratios for a good-quality stock; they suggest that the stock may have drifted down in price as a result of one of the temporary aberrations referred to as "market factors." A glance at the recent price ranges indicates that the stock is much closer to its recent lows than to its highs and that it is definitely capable of selling higher, in line with its earnings and dividends. The net asset value lends support to the impression that the stock is undervalued. As between companies B and C, assuming that they appear to be of equal quality, the investor would unhesitatingly choose C; and unless the quality differences seem great, C is probably a better choice than A.

Appraising a Common Stock

It is never advisable to buy a common stock just because it is the best of an available group. There have been times, for example in 1929, when nearly all stocks were grossly overvalued. It is therefore desirable to have a method of appraisal which is independent of current market prices.

In Chapter 2 it was suggested that a stock might be appraised by estimating the future benefit payments to be expected from it and discounting them down to the present at a reasonable discount rate. Several methods of discounting the estimated future payments were suggested. These methods are logical and worthy of consideration.

However, securities analysts commonly base appraisals of common stocks on the same four factors which were considered as criteria for comparing stocks in the preceding section. The fundamental basis for the appraisal will be estimated future earnings and dividends, capitalized by the use of price-earnings ratios and yields which seem appropriate for the quality of stock being considered. The net asset values and market price histories will then be used to modify or confirm the values based on earnings and dividend estimates.

Obviously, an appraisal of a common stock can be based either on "average" stock market conditions or on "current" ones. The charts on price-earnings ratios and yields shown on a preceding page indicate that in an average market a typical good stock sells for about 14 times earnings and yields about 5 per cent but that at various times the same stock might sell at 18 times earnings and yield 4 per cent or for 10 times earnings and yield 7 per cent. Investors make appraisals on either an average or a current basis, to suit their immediate purposes. The average market basis probably has the greatest practical value, for current market appraisals are chiefly useful in deciding whether to acquire or hold one specific stock instead of another, and this can be done more readily by comparison of price-earnings ratios and yields; but the decision as to whether to buy or hold the best stock in a compared group involves an appraisal of its long-run probable value. This calls for an appraisal based on average or normal stock market conditions.

The appraisal process involves not only the estimating of long-term future earnings and dividends, but also the determination of price-earnings ratios and yields which would be typical for the stock to be appraised. This latter is no small task; "normal" price-earnings ratios and yields for the average high-class stock may be deduced from Charts 2 and 3, but similar normal figures for a specific oil stock may be higher or lower, both because the stock is an oil stock and because its quality is not identical with that of the average represented on the chart. These questions can be answered, in a rough way, by extensive research and comparison of the past records of many stocks, including the one under study.

To illustrate the appraisal process, it may be assumed that the imaginary company C of the preceding section appears worthy of selling at 13 times earnings and on a 5 per cent yield basis, in a normal market. At 13 times earnings its future earning power of $2 per share per year indicates an appraisal of $26 per share. The expected average dividend of $1.40, on a 5 per cent yield basis, appraises at $28; this is a normal occurrence, for the earnings and yield appraisals commonly differ by several dollars and must be averaged to obtain the basic appraisal. The $27 basic appraisal (average of $26 and $28) is justified by the $25 net asset value figure. The stock price ranges shown in the table do not concur in the $27 appraisal, but it is a well-known fact that stock prices frequently drift away from logical values for extended periods of time. This situation is one which may well cause the investor to review his analysis to make sure that he has not overlooked some basic weakness in the stock, but it need not cause him to reject a carefully developed conclusion.

If the stock of company C has a value of $27 per share by normal market standards, it should be a satisfactory investment at $21.

It is not fantastic to use an illustration in which a good stock normally worth $27 sells for $21. Stock market prices fluctuate so extensively through the years that the prices of fine-quality stocks are sometimes halved or doubled, and individual stock prices constantly deviate above and below the group average. It has been said that an alert investor need never pay more than 75 per cent of their normal value for his high-grade stock investments and may count on selling them at 125 per cent of normal value, if his purchases and sales are not hurried. This is probably an overoptimistic statement, and it clearly makes no allowance for errors, wars, and other unpredictable events; but it serves to emphasize the importance of appraisal methods which give at least some impression of what the normal value of a stock is.

Common Stocks as Price-level Hedges

During the 1941–1952 inflation investors were much concerned to know whether common stocks actually live up to their theoretical capacity to serve as a price-level hedge. The issue was hotly debated in 1947 and 1948 by many investment experts, but it is perhaps reasonable to conclude that the evidence of the 1941–1948 period was

*Table 6. Common Stocks as Price-level Hedges—Increases in per
Share Prices, Earnings, and Dividends, Compared with
Increases in Commodity Price Levels*

(1936–1941 average = 100%)

	1952–1953 prices per share, %	1952–1953 cash dividends per share, %	1952–1953 earnings per share, %
Consumer price index..............	188.2		
Wholesale price index..............	209.4		
Moody's 125 industrials...........	214.0	269.0	310.0
Moody's 24 utilities..............	128.9	128.8	151.5
Moody's 25 railroads.............	179.0	264.0	528.0
S & P's 19 banks.................	121.6		
S & P's 18 insurance companies....	208.8		
Byron Jackson...................	177.18	137.61	233.33
Stewart-Warner..................	184.36	327.77	400.00
Studebaker......................	382.29	......	457.57
Oliver..........................	186.58	3000.00	497.43
Pillsbury Mills..................	138.57	131.57	280.92
Hormel.........................	180.09	166.66	166.78
California Packing...............	196.66	326.08	293.80
Best Foods......................	327.07	328.94	390.90
Pennsylvania Railroad............	79.48	150.60	121.64
Chesapeake & Ohio Railroad......	87.19	95.23	133.25
Louisville & Nashville Railroad....	198.01	167.84	340.16
Union Pacific Railroad...........	230.00	200.00	193.06
American Telephone & Telegraph..	101.37	100.00	113.81
Commonwealth Edison...........	118.02	128.57	102.21
Consolidated Edison..............	127.97	110.25	128.11
Pacific Gas and Electric..........	124.55	105.75	100.00
Allis-Chalmers..................	119.04	223.46	268.63
General Electric.................	183.78	222.92	329.34
General Motors..................	254.22	231.21	314.07
International Harvester...........	146.11	232.55	254.22
Borden.........................	255.87	191.78	275.62
General Foods...................	138.64	121.15	167.84
General Mills....................	229.33	304.65	240.78
Swift...........................	170.51	169.23	426.36
Chase National Bank.............	127.88	142.85	196.51
Continental Insurance...........	212.58	193.91	162.87
Home Insurance.................	128.59	136.36	166.36
Security-First National Bank......	213.38	134.98	290.08
Socony Vacuum Oil..............	269.11	365.51	388.97
Standard Oil (Of Indiana).........	244.50	151.51	293.68
Texas Company..................	256.83	313.72	364.48
Union Oil.......................	217.61	183.83	425.18

not complete at the 1948 year end, since corporate stock prices, earnings, and dividends had not been finally stabilized on a new postwar price level. Whether anything approaching stability has been
achieved even by 1954 is an unsettled question, but at least enough
time has elapsed that it is logical to test the matter statistically.

It seems reasonable, in considering this issue, to conclude that a
common stock might give evidence of service as a price-level hedge
if (1) its price rose or fell permanently with a change in the price
level, or (2) its earnings per share changed with the price level, or
(3) its dividends changed with the price level. A really good price-
level hedge would have to do all three.

Table 6 presents a fragment of evidence on this subject. It compares the postwar levels reached by stock prices, earnings, and dividends with postwar cost of living and wholesale price indexes. In
order to have a stable basis for comparison, postwar prices and earnings and dividends are given at average levels for 1952–1953 and
are stated as percentages of their 1936–1941 averages. On the whole,
it appears that the industrial and insurance stock prices have caught
up to the price level, and that the earnings and dividends of the
industrials and railroads have done so. (The railroad showing is due
in part to the very low base period in the late thirties.) But the utility
and bank stocks and the prices of the rail stocks have not matched
the doubled price level; evidently these are not acceptable inflation
hedges. Among the individual stocks in the table there are several—
Hormel, Pillsbury, and General Foods, for example—which would
naturally have been expected to be good inflation hedges, and which
have not gained satisfactorily. Others, such as Best Foods, have done
extraordinarily well. Some of these differences are doubtless due to
abnormalities in the figures of the particular years, but in large part
they are due to fundamental but unpredictable differences in the
growth and profits of the industries and companies. And an examination of the year-by-year record of these companies discloses that the
timing of the stock price and dividend increases did not coincide
with the price-level changes, but instead lagged far behind.

The sensible conclusion, which coincides with theory and previous
experience, is that the common stocks of most nonregulated competitive industries are potentially good price-level hedges, but that
a widely diversified collection of stocks would be needed in order
to assure reasonably typical results, even in the long run.

Growth Stocks

It has been noted in a preceding chapter that corporations normally distribute between 50 and 75 per cent of their earnings as dividends and retain the balance to add to their operating resources. This practice should and normally does result in a slow growth in corporate earning power. But there are always certain industries in which technological progress or rapid growth of sales opportunities affords, for a span of years, a chance for aggressive concerns to do exceptionally well. A rapidly growing demand often eliminates the need for sharp price competition and makes generous profits possible, which can be used to build up large and efficient resources to add to future earnings. During such a growth period it is also possible to develop brand names, specialized products, and customer contacts. Better yet, a period of technological progress makes it possible for research-minded concerns to make tremendous profits out of a constant stream of new products and processes. In the past two decades the chemical and electronics industries, among others, have been conspicuous as growth industries.

But spectacular growth is not confined to industries exploiting new technologies. Aggressive and pioneering managements have produced great growth by developing new methods and greater efficiency in chain-store management, automobile manufacturing, food packaging, and other industries, for their companies. The essential characteristic of a growth situation, then, is a generous and rising earning power which is building up the resources and trade position which will contribute to large earnings and dividends in the future. Such a situation is almost certain to be accompanied by improving quality (*i.e.*, assurance of future strength) in the company as well. It is very obvious that the stock market would respond vigorously to evidence of increasing earnings coupled with increasing stock quality. Stocks in those situations often rise in price rapidly until they sell for 15 to 25 times current earnings and yield only 2.5 to 4 per cent on their current dividends. As the expected growth builds up the earnings and dividends the increased stock price should ultimately be justified by normal price-earnings and yield ratios at the higher level.

Growth often continues for a long time, but in a competitive economy it can hardly be expected to be a perpetual phenomenon in any company or industry. Consequently, the investor who pays a high price-earnings ratio for a growth stock must be convinced that the growth will continue long enough to justify the price he is paying, and to compensate for the low initial rate of dividend. The investor who buys into a growth situation before the impending growth is fully reflected in the price will of course obtain this ultimate increase in the dividend, and in addition a very handsome increase in the price of his stock, but the investor who pays a price which fully allows for the expected growth will find little profit in it, even though the growth subsequently develops as he expected.

Because of the melodrama popularly attached to growth situations, which of course stems from recognition of the enormous gains made by those who bought in time into such stocks as du Pont and International Business Machines, investors and brokers are much attracted to them. This eagerness to participate in growth results in rather high prices for many growth stocks, with consequent risks of disappointment for people who buy them. As in many another dynamic situation, therefore, it must be conceded that the opportunities and the pitfalls in this area are both substantial.

Does Common Stock Ownership Pay?

The answer to this question is not an unequivocal one. The people who manage their stock investments with diligence and skill should ordinarily find them profitable. Others who invest without either knowledge or luck probably do very badly. Although he has no adequate data to support his belief, the author is under the impression that the average small stockholder does rather poorly except in occasional periods of price-level inflation. The reasons are to be found mainly in the choice of mediocre-quality stocks and in poor timing of purchases and sales. Amateurs are notorious for buying stocks when market prices are high, and for selecting doubtful promotions or historically successful concerns whose futures are unpromising. And it must be admitted that the market choices at nearly all times include large numbers of stocks which will not prove to be good investments.

But there is no doubt that many corporate ventures do very well. The 20 good stocks included in the price-earnings and yield charts have earned and paid consistently. So have many others. Some have gained spectacularly in earnings and market value. Most of the time in recent years it has been possible to buy good common stocks which pay 50 to 100 per cent more than good bonds and whose earnings are far in excess of the dividends paid. These are surely potentially profitable. Even if it be admitted that the reinvested earnings of recent years have not added pro rata to corporate stock values as reflected in market prices, they have nevertheless had a pronounced effect on both stock prices and earning power.

Careful statistical studies made by a number of persons indicate that holders of diversified stock investments in relatively large American corporations (such as those listed on the New York Stock Exchange) have fared very well if their stocks were held on a long-range basis.[5] Even lists chosen at random under varying conditions of prosperity and depression were usually more profitable than bond holdings, if retained for a reasonable span of years and sold under any conditions except those of deepest depression. These results reflect, in the main, the (1) better dividend yields available on the stocks, (2) growth due to reinvested earnings, and (3) gains attributable to price-level increases.

The conclusion to be drawn from this and other evidence is that common stocks should be profitable to those who diversify wisely, identify quality and value correctly, and succeed in avoiding calamitous errors. However, errors are possible; predicting the future is not an exact science, and even the economic expert may be wrong. And the chances for error as well as the damage an error may cause increase in geometric proportion as the investor forsakes quality for the speculative grades of stocks.

One other factor which lends some attractiveness to good common stocks is embodied in the Revenue Act of 1954. This measure recognizes that all corporate net income is rather severely taxed in the hands of the corporation, and that further full-scale income taxation of the stockholder's dividend receipts is discriminatory. Consequently, the law permits each taxpayer to exclude the first $50 of his dividends from his total of taxable income, thus obtaining it tax-free; and an amount equal to 4 per cent of the remainder of his dividends may be subtracted from his tax. For a typical stockholder

[5] See Chelcie C. Bosland, *The Common Stock Theory of Investment*, The Ronald Press Company, New York, 1937, or Edgar L. Smith, Common Stocks as Long Term Investments, The Macmillan Company, New York, 1928.

whose top tax bracket is 26 per cent, this will reduce the levy on $1,000 of dividends from $260 to $209, and increase the amount retained from 74 per cent to 79 per cent. This is a minor advantage, and the principle may not long survive in the political wrangle over it, but in 1954 it is an element in investors' evaluation of stocks.

Personal Policy in Stock Investment

For the great majority of reasonably well-informed and financially middle-class investors, the best possible stock investment policy could be summed up in three simple rules: First, buy only good-quality stocks; second, buy stocks only when they can be had at attractive prices; third, diversify well. More detailed ideas on procedure will be presented in another chapter, but these are the essentials. The choice of good-quality stocks is made because they yield almost as much as speculative stocks and offer much greater security. It is to be assumed that middle-class investors are too preoccupied with other things to devote constant attention to speculation and that they should not risk serious losses. Some minor speculation through the medium of investment company shares might be an exception to the rule. The reasons for stipulating attractive prices and adequate diversification are obvious.

For the investor whose stake in the stock market must be small, say under $5,000, adequate diversification is a difficult problem. The solution may be found in investment company shares, provided the investment companies in turn confine themselves for the most part to conservative stocks. The investor of limited means has no occasion to risk his funds in other than quality commitments which are most carefully selected for assured future and attractive price.

The investor who has not the ability or the interest to study stocks must turn to others for guidance, if he owns stocks at all. There are professional investment advisers and bank trust officers in every city who will undertake the management of a stock fund of $25,000 or more for a moderate fee. Alternatively, the investor may obtain professional guidance in the assembling of a portfolio and thereafter simply retain it; or he may rely on periodic coaching by his broker or banker. In this case, too, the investment company may be of value. Of all these alternatives, the investment adviser or the bank trust seem to offer the best solutions, even if they cost money. Somehow, the idea of a dependent and gullible investor accepting free advice about stocks suggests the image of a blind man following a road map. If he is lucky, he may get there.

Finally, some comment may be made about the stock investment policies of competent and well-financed investors. These are the investors who should, from the point of view of social welfare, invest in part in promotional and speculative enterprises. They have the ability to understand them, the influence to control them, and the resources to diversify widely against the risk. Many speculative enterprises are dominated by such investors. But these investors will also find it desirable to make most of their smaller stock investments, which are not to be supervised personally and intensively, in good-grade stocks. Less care is needed with these, and they are less vulnerable to price fluctuations, errors, and trouble.

The reader will note that these suggestions to stock investors lean heavily toward the better grade stocks and that nothing is said about trading for profit, aggressive and defensive policy, and similar ideas. The reason for emphasis upon quality stocks is that the discussion has to do with investment, which consists of keeping funds secure and employing them profitably. Twenty years' experience has convinced the author that amateurs can be taught to do reasonably well with good stocks but that even professionals fail to invest with consistent success in speculative ones. This appears to be sufficient reason to advise people to choose conservative stocks; and the advice will not deprive the nation of needed investment in new and speculative industries, for people will not follow it.

As respects stock market fluctuations and trading for profit, these will be considered in another chapter. Investors will find that some added knowledge of market behavior will make for more successful investing. Most market traders will ultimately also discover that investing is a far more profitable process than trading.

QUESTIONS AND PROBLEMS

1. Are some common stocks better quality investments than some bonds? Why?

2. Are the perquisites of ownership of any value to a middle-class small-investor family?

3. Why would a middle-class small-investor family want to own com-

mon stock? When the hazards and the necessary effort of supervision are considered, is it worth while?

4. At December 31, 1953, the Allis-Chalmers Manufacturing Company had net tangible assets amounting to $401,503,323. Its debts totaled $175,148,638, its preferred stock at par value was $12,072,800, and the balance represented the equity of the 3,267,209 no par common shares. What was the book value per share? What was the leverage factor? Is this high or low leverage?

5. Allis-Chalmers's 1953 profit after allowance for income taxes was $21,943,569, out of which preferred dividends of $450,881 were paid. What was earned per share on the common stock?

6. At a price of $55 per share, what was the price-earnings ratio? The dividend rate was $4 per share. What was the yield on the $55 price?

7. Allis-Chalmers is a quality stock, despite its heavy postwar indebtedness, and probably is entitled to sell in an average market for 12 times earnings and to yield about $5\frac{1}{2}$ per cent. It will probably earn an average of about $6 and pay about $4 for the next few years. Its 1953 price range was 60–41. Appraise it for investment purposes on a normal market basis.

8. Would the fact that Allis-Chalmers has 120,728 shares of $100 par $3\frac{1}{4}$ per cent preferred stock, each of which is convertible at the holder's option into two shares of common, affect your appraisal in any way? How?

9. Are earnings per share computed on a consolidated or a corporate basis? Why?

10. Should a business which is acutely subject to the business cycle (for example, jewelry manufacturing) have a high-leverage or a low-leverage capital structure? Why?

11. Could one speculate successfully in very high-class stocks by buying them when they sold for 10 times earnings and paid 7 per cent and selling them when they sold for 16 times earnings to yield 4 per cent? Would there be much risk in this?

12. Would it not be more profitable to speculate in medium-grade and speculative stocks, because they fluctuate more and the profits could be greater? Why do not all investment professors get rich by doing this?

13. What is meant by market factors? What kind of market factors could cause Allis-Chalmers to sell at a price out of line with other similar stocks?

14. If you wanted to compare the stocks of Allis-Chalmers, International Harvester, Caterpillar Tractor, and Westinghouse Electric as respects quality, but did not have time for extensive study, where could you get information?

15. Are all stocks good price-level hedges? What kinds are not? Would

a high-leverage stock have any advantages in a time of inflation? Of deflation? How about an investment company stock?

16. The Caterpillar Tractor Company in early 1954 had total assets $261,000,000, debts $99,000,000, preferred stock $23,500,000, and 3,974,-000 common shares. It was paying an annual dividend rate of $2 plus 4 per cent in stock, earned $4.84 per common share in 1953, and appeared capable of averaging $4.50 to $5 per share in earnings for the next few years. Its business seemed generally comparable with that of Allis-Chalmers. Appraise it as of January, 1954, when Allis-Chalmers brought $50, and in a subsequent "normal" market.

17. Look up the subsequent market records of both stocks and see if your January, 1954, conclusions were sound.

REFERENCES

Badger, Ralph E., and Harry G. Guthmann: *Investment Principles and Practices,* Prentice-Hall, Inc., New York, 1951, Chaps. 5, 6.

Bellemore, Douglas H.: *Investments Principles and Practices,* B. C. Forbes and Sons Publishing Co., Inc., New York, 1953, Chap. 5.

Bosland, Chelcie C.: *The Common Stock Theory of Investment,* The Ronald Press Company, New York, 1937.

Dice, Charles A., and Wilford J. Eiteman: *The Stock Market,* McGraw-Hill Book Company, Inc., New York, 1952, Chap. 29.

Dowrie, George W., and Douglas R. Fuller: *Investments,* John Wiley & Sons, Inc., New York, 1950, Chaps. 29–31.

Graham, Benjamin, and David L. Dodd: *Security Analysis,* McGraw-Hill Book Company, Inc., New York, 1951, Part IV.

Grodinsky, Julius: *Investments,* The Ronald Press Company, New York, 1953, Chaps. 21, 22.

Hoagland, Henry E.: *Corporation Finance,* McGraw-Hill Book Company, Inc., New York, 1947, Chap. 6.

Robbins, Sidney M.: *Managing Securities,* Houghton Mifflin Company, Boston, 1954, Chaps. 21, 25.

Chapter 5: PREFERRED STOCKS
AND THEIR VALUE

Corporate managements have learned that some stock-buying investors prefer the type of fundamental ownership equity represented by common shares, while others prefer to accept limited rights to dividends and other corporate benefits in exchange for the greater security afforded by a prior claim. Preferred stocks have been devised for the benefit of the investor who wants priority. Preferred stocks are ownership shares which typically are entitled to a limited annual dividend out of available earnings before the common stock gets anything and in case of liquidation to a limited sum out of the assets before the common stock gets anything. Some corporations create more than one class of preferred stock; such classes may rank in sequence (first, second, third, etc.) in priority of claim, or they may be equal in this respect.

Since preferred shares are definitely a part of the ownership, their claims are inferior to those of bondholders and other creditors. Furthermore, the corporation does not *owe* them anything; they may be entitled to receive dividends before other stocks get them, but the dividends will be available only if the directors declare them, and this should be done only if the corporation can afford the payment.

The investment merits of any class of stock in a corporation issuing more than one class will depend importantly on the special features and privileges granted to that class by the articles of incorporation. Preferred shares are not all alike; aside from the question of priorities, they may be voting, callable, convertible, cumulative, and participating, or they may have some of these features, or none of them; and there are many other features which they may or may not have. Every state permits its general business corporations to issue such classes or types of shares as the corporate managements deem advisable, if the shares follow certain basic legal requirements and are properly authorized in the corporate articles. The legal requirements are usually very general in nature, being concerned chiefly with fairness and fraud prevention; in consequence, the powers and privileges of the various classes of shares are established by detailed provisions in the articles. The articles will also indicate the maximum number of shares of each class of stock which the corporation is authorized to issue.

Investors in preferred stocks ought to be familiar with their rights under the corporation code and the articles of their corporation. However, the state codes are lengthy, technical, and inaccessible documents; so most investors assume that the law will be fair and just and confine their inquiries to the corporate articles. The important provisions in the articles are summarized in official prospectuses and in the major financial reporting services, such as Moody's or Standard & Poor's. These sources are usually adequate.

Authorized Stock

One of the very important determinants of the quality of preferred shares is the number of shares outstanding or authorized by the articles. Prior rights to earnings or assets can assure a high degree of safety, if the number of shares enjoying the priority is small and if the articles limit the number which may be issued. In checking the number of authorized and outstanding shares it is desirable to note all of the classes of stock which the articles permit, since several classes with equal or varying preferences could be authorized.

Dividend Provisions

Preferred stocks nearly always have some sort of preference as to dividends. The usual provision calls for quarterly dividends which must be paid up to date before a dividend may be paid on any lower ranking preferred or common stock. Most modern issues are also cumulative; that is, preferred dividends which are not paid cumulate and must be paid up in full before dividends may be resumed on the lower ranking stocks. Issues on which dividends are noncumulative never get their payments if the corporation is forced to omit them at the regular payment time. A few preferreds have special variations, such as the provision that unpaid dividends cumulate up to a limited amount only or to the extent earned but no more; these provisions are designed to forestall the possibility of excessive accumulations which might embarrass the company.

When corporations issue preferred stocks which rank sequentially —that is, a first preferred, a second preferred, etc.—the first preferred is usually entitled to all accumulated and current dividends before any payments may be made on the second preferred. The second preferred will then have similar preferences over the next ranking issue. Sometimes a junior or lower ranking preferred will be noncumulative, when the senior (high-ranking) preferred is fully cumulative.

Clearly, a cumulative preferred is a more satisfactory investment vehicle than a noncumulative one. There are times when even strong corporations must omit preferred dividends temporarily, and it is better for the investor that these be merely deferred rather than lost. Furthermore, there is greater incentive for the management to try to pay dividends regularly if unpaid ones cumulate; for cumulated dividends presumably must be paid sometime, whereas unpaid noncumulative dividends embarrass no one but the unpaid stockholder.

When preferred dividends have accumulated unpaid, they are regarded as being attached to the stock. If the stockholder sells his stock, the purchaser obtains title to the dividend accruals. If the corporation itself acquires the stock, the dividend rights are retired.

Preferred stocks are ordinarily entitled to their preference dividends and no more. They seldom receive rights or other special disbursements. Exceptions are found in the case of participating preferreds, which will be discussed later.

Asset Preferences

Most preferred stocks are preferred as to assets. That is, if the firm is liquidated, they receive their par value or a stated sum plus all cumulated unpaid dividends, plus a premium or bonus in some instances, before lower ranking stock gets anything. Very commonly the articles specify that in case of involuntary liquidation (under compulsion of law or because of insolvency) the asset preference is limited to par or stated value plus cumulated dividends but that if the liquidation is voluntary a premium must be paid also. This premium may vary from nothing to 25 per cent, but it is generally between 5 and 10. These three items—par or stated value, possible premium, and cumulated dividends if any—are all that most preferreds are entitled to receive.

Voting Power

In a majority of corporations preferred stock does not vote on ordinary management matters or to elect directors. This feature was probably written into the articles in most cases by men who regarded preferred shareholders virtually as creditors, with limited risk and limited rights. There is at the present time a pronounced trend toward full voting rights for preferred shares. However, it must be admitted that common shares usually far outnumber preferred shares, so the usual one vote per share provision will not give the preferred holders much power; and it must be further conceded that most of them will not be much interested in voting anyhow.

Preferred stockholders are much more likely to take an interest in management when they do not receive dividends than when they do. Consequently, the considerable number of corporations which give unpaid preferred holders (1) the right to elect certain directors, or (2) the right to elect a majority of the directors, or (3) some other significant voting power are placing their preferred stockholders in a position where they can at least become vocal in self-defense. This is a sound provision. The preferred stock will seldom undertake to displace a management which is conscientiously battling adversity, but neglect and fraud can be summarily chastened. The usual provision giving preferred stockholders these powers makes them effective only after omission of several consecutive quarterly payments or when total payments are 2 or 3 years in arrears.

Even more important than a vote on management matters is the preferred stock's right, voting as a single class of stock, to veto certain types of proposals. The veto power should extend to all such matters as (1) amendment of the articles to change the preferred stock's own privileges, (2) amendment of the articles to authorize more preferred or higher ranking preferred, (3) issuance of bonds or preferred stock, (4) mergers or substantial change of business. Action adverse to its interests on these matters could greatly weaken a preferred stock without at all injuring the common. State laws in a number of states specifically give each class of preferred stock a veto on some of these matters, but not all states do so. Stronger protection is afforded in the articles of many corporations.

Investors are probably justified in indifference to their preferred stocks' voting rights in 95 cases out of 100, for most managements are scrupulously fair toward their senior securityholders, but in scattered instances very unjust measures are attempted. The preferred stock which does not have sound voting or veto rights has inadequate defenses in such cases. Since there are many preferred shares on the market, the wise investor will merely choose among those whose voting and veto powers are adequate. There is no point in being unnecessarily vulnerable.

Call Features

Most modern preferred stock is callable or redeemable. That is, the corporation reserves the right to pay it off at prices specified in

Table 7. Price Ranges on Callable and Non-callable Preferred Stocks

Issue	Annual dividend	Call price	Price range	
			1934	1953
Archer-Daniels-Midland...	$7.00	115	117–110	Retired
Atlas Powder............	6.00	110	107–83	Retired
Beatrice Creamery........	7.00	110	100–55	Retired
Glidden Company........	7.00	105	107½–83	Retired
General Motors..........	5.00	120	109–89¾	123½–112½
Montgomery Ward.......	7.00	N.C.	133–88	176–157
Midland Steel Products....	8.00	N.C.	85¼–44	139–125¼
U.S. Steel..............	7.00	N.C.	99½–67¼	144¼–135

the articles and retire it. Many old preferreds are non-callable, however, either because the articles say so or because the articles do not mention redemption at all.

Some preferreds may be called in part—that is, in blocks consisting of 10 or 20 per cent or some other fraction of the original issue —but some must be called in their entirety or not at all. Usually the stockholder must be given 2 or 3 months' notice prior to the call date. The call price, which is specified in the articles, consists of par or a stated value, plus a possible premium, plus all cumulated unpaid dividends. The premium is usually the same as that payable in voluntary liquidation, any amount from nothing to 25 per cent, but generally between 5 and 10 per cent. Sometimes the call premium declines or rises with the passage of time.

A call feature in a preferred stock is of no advantage to the investor, but it enables a prosperous corporation to retire high-rate preferreds. The call price thus limits the advantage an investor can gain by purchase of preferreds in corporations whose financial standing is improving, for it is clear that the market price is unlikely to go very far above the call price. Investors are understandably reluctant to pay much more than the call price for any callable preferred, even if it is of high quality. Table 7 illustrates the effect of call prices on some high-grade preferreds which were outstanding in 1934.

Convertible or Warrant-bearing Preferreds

About one-fourth of all preferred shares are convertible into the common stock of the company at the option of the individual stockholders. This privilege permits the preferred holder to participate more fully in the company's success if it succeeds but to retain his preferred position otherwise. Very seldom does the company have the option to compel conversion.

Corporations sell convertible preferreds in order to attract money at lower dividend rates than would otherwise be possible. Also, this may be a means of obtaining new common stock capital in the long run, for the preferred stock will tend to be converted into common whenever conversion offers an opportunity to obtain higher dividends on stock having at least as much market value or a higher market value with no reduction in dividend income. Convertible preferreds have been very popular with investors since 1934, for the combination of senior rights to income plus opportunity to convert to common stock in case of price-level inflation seems to meet a definite need. In fact, this popularity is so great that preferreds with options to convert into common stock at prices far above current market values usually sell at higher prices and yield much less than comparable ordinary preferreds.

Convertible preferred shares are usually exchangeable for common shares in amounts indicated in the corporate articles. In most cases the ratio of exchange—the number of common shares received for each preferred share—decreases through the years, and in some instances the conversion right lapses altogether after a time. If the stock is both convertible and callable, the stockholder may usually exercise his conversion option after he receives notice of a call but before the payment date.

Conversion rights should be protected against *dilution*. The corporation's articles should specify that, if the value of the common stock is altered by splits, stock dividends, mergers, or rights, the conversion terms will be proportionately adjusted. Sometimes the problem of rights is solved by offering them to convertible preferred stockholders and to common stockholders simultaneously.

Instead of making a preferred issue convertible, some corporations have attached common stock purchase warrants to their preferred certificates. These can be detached and submitted with a check for the indicated amount to buy new common stock. When such warrants are valuable, contracts for the purchase and sale of preferred must stipulate whether the stock is to be transferred *with warrants* or *ex-warrants.*

Participating Preferreds

A few preferred issues are made participating, which means that in case other stockholders get large dividends or special benefits the preferred participates in them also. For example, the Southern California Edison Company's Original Preferred has a preferential right to a 5 per cent cumulative dividend; but in case any other stock issued by the company gets a larger dividend or a special disbursement (including rights) the Original Preferred gets an equal rate. This preferred is non-callable. A slightly different provision is found in the case of the Poor & Co. $1.50 Cumulative Participating Class A stock. This issue has a preference to its $1.50 cumulative dividend, but after the common has received an equal amount, any further payment goes to both classes alike except that the preferred need never be paid more than $2 in any year. This preferred is callable at $26.25. A third variation is found in the Macfadden Publications $1.50 Participating Preferred, which has a preference to its basic $1.50 dividend and in addition receives in full all per share payments made on the common. This one is callable at $30 per share.

Participation occasionally extends to the matter of asset distribution if the corporation is liquidated, but this is much less common and normally much less important than dividend participation.

Par Values

Most preferreds have par values, even when the issuing company's common stock is no par. In such cases the asset preferences, call prices, and dividend rights are usually calculated as percentages of the par value. But there is no necessary relationship between these basic rights and par values. For example, Pillsbury Mills has a no par preferred which is entitled to cumulative dividends of $4 per annum, is callable at $101.50, and would receive $100 in involuntary liquidation. Again, Providence Washington Insurance Company has a $10 par preferred which receives a $2 cumulative dividend, is callable at $54, and would get $50 in involuntary liquidation. It seems reasonable to conclude that par values are not fundamentally significant investment attributes.

Sinking Funds

A considerable number of preferred issues obligate the corporation to purchase and retire some of the shares annually. The amount to be retired may be fixed at a definite sum, or it may depend on the sales volume or earnings. It may be a large amount or a relatively small one. Usually there is provision for selecting shares by lot, to be redeemed at a stated call price, if the corporation cannot buy stock on the open market at or below the call price. Sinking funds are important to the investor because they progressively reduce the number of preferred shares outstanding and thus improve the security behind those remaining. Sinking fund purchases also help both to stabilize and to keep up the price of the stock on the market, because the purchase of shares which are offered for sale will remove them from the market.

The corporation is not under any inflexible legal obligation to pay into a preferred stock sinking fund. The usual provision in the articles requires the stipulated sinking fund to be provided after payment of the preferred dividend but before payment of dividends on any lower ranking class of stock. Unpaid sinking fund installments may or may not cumulate.

Restrictions on Common Dividends

In recent years it has become common practice to write into the corporate articles certain limitations on dividends to common stock and on disbursements to repurchase common stock, to be effective during the time that the preferred stock is outstanding. These limitations usually forbid such outlays except when (1) the corporate working capital exceeds a stated amount and (2) the accumulated earned surplus exceeds a stated amount. Such restrictions add substantially to the quality of the preferred stock, for they prevent the weakening of the business by payment of ill-advised dividends on the common.

Accumulated Preferred Dividends

When a corporation is compelled to omit preferred dividends for several years, the amount of unpaid accumulations is often large enough to pose a serious problem. Efforts to pay current dividends and several years' arrears in a short period would drain working capital severely; and a conservatively slow payment program would tax the patience of junior preferred and common stockholders. Corporate managements are therefore likely to try to settle large dividend arrearages by offering the stockholders new securities, if an acceptable plan can be found. Small arrearages are usually paid up in cash.

If a substantial dividend arrearage is to be settled by issuance of new securities, it is usually not best to do it by simple declaration of a dividend payable in the new securities, for two reasons. In the first place, such a dividend need not be accepted in lieu of cash by any stockholder who does not wish to do so, and inevitably some would refuse; thus not all the arrearages could be cleared. Second, the value of the new securities distributed as a dividend would be taxable income to the stockholders.

The method of settling large preferred arrearages commonly involves some such procedure as the following: (1) After earning power is sufficiently recovered to make the project feasible, a formal "plan of recapitalization" is adopted by directors and stockholders. (2) The corporate articles are amended to create a new class of preferred stock superior in priority to the existing preferred. (3) Dividend payments are announced on the new prior preferred but not on the old preferred. (4) Old preferred holders are offered the option to exchange their shares for an equal amount of new prior preferred plus some extra new preferred or common to compensate for the accrued dividends attached to the old stock. They will do this because (a) they want dividend-paying stock, (b) the extra stock received in lieu of back dividends is not taxable as income, and (c) the new preferred will be prior in claim to the old. (5) After a year or two, when the exchanges have been largely completed, the arrears can be paid up on the remaining old preferred, and regular dividends may then begin on it and the common.

There are infinite variations to this general plan for eliminating dividend arrears. Sometimes several classes of stock are involved, and sometimes the privileges or dividend rates of the new preferreds differ from the old. Sometimes the recapitalization is not consummated by voluntary exchange of stock but, instead, becomes mandatory upon all stockholders when approved by the requisite majorities. In general, it may be stated that the recapitalization plans of the past few years have been approved by heavy majorities of preferred stockholders. The plans have seldom been generous to preferred holders, but usually they have not been excessively harsh.[1]

Fundamental Calculations

There are four basic calculations ordinarily used in indicating the investment merit of a preferred stock and gauging the reasonableness of its price. These calculations determine (1) the earnings per share, (2) the adequacy of dividend coverage on the over-all basis, (3) the asset coverage per share, and (4) the yield.

[1] For typical examples, see those consummated by Radio Corporation of America in 1936, by Curtis Publishing Company in 1940, by Barker Brothers Corporation in 1936, and by Armour and Company in 1934.

Earnings per Share

The earnings per share as ordinarily computed on preferred stocks show the number of earned dollars per share out of which the preferred dividend may be paid. The figure does not purport to show how much could legally be paid to the preferred shares. For example, if a corporation having 100,000 preferred shares outstanding has $1,000,000 in profits left after paying all expenses, interest, and taxes, the earnings per preferred share would be $10. If the annual preferred dividend rate is $5 per share, that is the dividend rate which would be paid; the $10 earnings figure merely indicates that ten dollars was available where five would suffice.

When corporations have more than one issue of preferred stock outstanding, it is customary to divide the available profits by the total number of such shares, if the two issues are of equal priority. For example, General Motors at year-end 1953 had 1,000,000 shares of $3.75 dividend preferred and 1,835,644 shares of $5 dividend preferred. The corporation had $598,119,478 in profits in 1953; divided among the 2,835,644 preferred shares, this indicated earnings of $210.93 per preferred share.[2]

But corporations frequently have issues of preferred stock which rank successively rather than equally. In such case it is customary to regard all of the profits as available to the first preferred; dividing total profits by the number of outstanding first preferred shares produces the desired figure of earnings per share. The profits available to the second preferred are those remaining after the first preferred dividend requirements are subtracted from total profits; this remaining sum is then divided by the number of second preferred shares. The process may be illustrated by the figures of the National Lead Company. This company in 1953 reported profits in the amount of $30,848,928. There were outstanding 234,293 shares of Class A $100 par 7 per cent preferred stock and 90,185 shares of Class B 6 per cent preferred, and the charter terms clearly established a dividend priority in favor of the Class A preferred. Earnings per share on the Class

[2] Despite the difference in dividend rate these General Motors shares are regarded as being equal in claim, since both are no par and their call prices are not far apart. However, when two equal-ranking preferreds of substantially different par values or income rights are involved, special arithmetic techniques are required.

A stock were therefore computed by dividing the available $30,-848,928 by 234,293, and a figure of $131.67 was obtained. Earnings available for the Class B shares were next determined by subtracting the $1,640,051 actually needed for the first preferred dividend from the total earnings of $30,848,928; the $29,208,877 thus available amounted to $323.88 per share on the 90,185 Class B preferred shares.

The technical weakness in the earnings per share calculation is apparent in the National Lead illustration. Because the number of Class B preferred shares is small, the earnings appear to cover the Class B dividend by a wider margin than they do the prior require-ment. Such is not the case, since it is clear that the Class A stock has absolute priority. The truth of the matter is that an earnings per share figure is a reliable index of earnings adequacy on preferreds only when the corporation has no interest-bearing debt and when the calculation is applied to first preferreds only. Despite these limi-tations, earnings per share figures on preferreds are generally re-ported in leading analytical services.

Dividend Coverage on the Over-all Basis

Analysts desiring a better measure of preferred stock quality than the earnings per share figure have developed a figure generally re-ferred to as "times dividend earned, over-all basis." The computa-tion involves dividing the business earnings *actually available for the securityholders* by the *total amount of interest and preferred dividend requirements*. That is, if a corporation had $1,500,000 of earnings left after paying all operating expenses and taxes, and if its bond interest required $500,000 and its preferred dividend $250,000, the total of $750,000 required to meet all prior requirements and the preferred dividend would be earned 2.0 *times*. Obviously, this computation could be easily adapted to measure the coverage for a second preferred stock also. If a second preferred requiring another $250,000 of annual payments existed in the above case, it is apparent that $1,000,000 annually would be needed to meet interest and both preferred requirements. That sum divided into the $1,500,000 actu-ally available indicates a coverage of 1.5 times for the second pre-ferred as compared with 2.0 times for the first preferred.

The logic of this method is supported by the fact that the earning power of a going business is properly measured by what it can earn for its investors after payment of operating expenses and taxes.[3] After all, interest payments on bonds are normally part of the earnings from business operation, regardless of accounting definitions. If these earnings are applied first to the payment of interest, then to a first preferred dividend, and then to a second preferred dividend, the adequacy of the earning power to meet each requirement is properly measured by checking to see how many times over all the cumulative required sum is earned.

In comparing the quality of preferred stocks in similar concerns in similar industries, the "times dividends earned" figure is a good one. In comparing preferreds in different industries, however, it is necessary to bear in mind that the amount of available earnings fluctuates far more in some industries than others. In the electric power industry a preferred whose requirements are earned two times over all in the average year is of investment grade; but in the steel or railroad industries such a preferred would be rated little better than fair, for the earnings would doubtless fall below the preferred dividend requirement in bad years.

Assets per Share

A figure showing net assets per preferred share, or book value per preferred share, is of value in some instances. It is computed by taking the net assets after depreciation and other allowances, subtracting all debts, and dividing the remainder by the number of preferred shares outstanding. The result indicates the book value of the net assets available to support each preferred share. The computation may be adapted to a situation involving more than one class of preferred stock by procedures similar to those used in computing earnings per share. The book value idea is useful in indicating whether earnings depend on solid assets or chiefly on the intangibles of good will and going-concern value, and it is highly significant in investment companies and other concerns dealing in securities and receivables; but it is open to all of the criticisms noted in connection with the book value of common stocks.

[3] Some lapse of logic may be detected in that this method treats the entire income tax as an expense prior in claim to the bond interest, instead of as an addition to the sum required for dividends on each successive class of stock. However, orthodoxy and convenience combine to recommend the technique here indicated.

Yield

The yield of a preferred stock, measured by expressing the annual dividend rate as a percentage of the price of the stock, is fundamental in gauging its attractiveness for investment. In fact, the yield and the quality of the stock are the main determinants of its attractiveness. In the case of common stocks it is customary to give great attention to undistributed earnings, which are reinvested to improve fu-

Table 8. Earnings Coverage and Yield on Industrial Preferreds

Stock	Times dividend earned, over-all basis, 1953	Yield on market price, 2/28/54, %
American Can $1.75...........	6.5	3.8
International Harvester $7.00..	6.5	4.2
National Lead $7.00.........	18.8	4.0
Midland Steel $8.00..........	4.0	6.0
U.S. Rubber $8.00...........	4.1	5.6
U.S. Steel $7.00.............	8.1	4.7
Armour $6.00...............	1.7	6.8
Butler Bros. $4.50...........	2.9	5.3
United Stores $6.00..........	2.6	7.6

ture earnings, and to the possibility of market profits; but since these factors are not usually of prime importance to preferred holders, the yield and quality (certainty of payment) factors receive greater emphasis.

Table 8 provides an indication of the relationship between quality, as evidenced by over-all dividend coverage, and yield. The statistics in the table are not perfect, since they are based on 1953 earnings without any reference to future prospects, but their implication is clear.

Investment Position of Preferred Stocks

Prior to the stock market boom of 1927–1929 preferred stocks were regarded as the small investors' province. They were widely held in comparatively small blocks. However, the situation now seems to be changing, at least with respect to the better grades of preferreds. The better grades are now sought by insurance companies, endowed institutions, trustees, and other conservative large holders who want security and a reasonable income. Lower grade preferreds are still sold to members of the general public who are willing to bear speculative risks for a somewhat higher return.

Table 9. Extent of Price Fluctuation in Preferred Stocks of Different Qualities

Stock, annual dividend, and call price	Quality	Price range, 1937–1953	Price range, 1953
American Can $1.75 (N.C.)	Excellent	52⅝–37½	45⅛–40⅛
International Harvester $7.00 (N.C.)	Excellent	202–138	166¼–148½
National Lead $7.00 (N.C.)	Excellent	207–145	173½–155¼
Midland Steel $8.00 (N.C.)	Good	173–76	139–125¼
U.S. Rubber $8.00 (N.C.)	Good	187–43½	144¾–127¾
U.S. Steel $7.00 (N.C.)	Good	160–91¾	144¼–135
Armour $6.00 (115)	Fair	139–28¼	93–77
Butler Bros. $4.50 (103)	Fair	110–60	86–79
United Stores $6.00 (115)	Fair	128–34⅝	90–72½

The slow change which is taking place in the ownership of high-grade preferreds may make their market steadier and more similar to the bond market than has been the case in times past. However, high-class preferreds have always been reasonably resistant to market fluctuations, as is indicated by the price ranges shown in Table 9. Lower grade preferreds are inclined to fluctuate violently in price, almost as much as common stocks of similar quality. The very low prices recorded for the Armour and Company preferred in the 1937–1953 period were the result of temporary dividend omissions, coupled at times with general weakness in the stock market. This was a characteristic performance, which will no doubt be repeated with this or other stocks in future market slumps. The very high price reached by the Armour stock in 1945 reflects not only a period of prosperity to the company, but also the imminent payment in cash of substantial dividend accruals.

The prices and dividend rates in the table indicate that the best preferred stocks yield about one-third more than the best corporate bonds, while poorer ones may yield as much as speculative common stocks. Preferreds which suspend or appear likely to suspend dividend payments usually drop drastically in price; dividend stability seems much more important in preferred stocks than in common issues. This principle is illustrated by the decline of the Armour preferred to 50 in early 1949, when working capital problems and an earnings deficit forced suspension of dividends.

A considerable number of investment analysts believe that preferred stocks are not suitable investments for most people who hold them. Their arguments usually include the following statements: (1) Preferred stockholders bear ownership risks with only a limited return available if the business succeeds. (2) Preferred holders can lose their capital, but the chance of market appreciation is severely limited, unless the stock is bought speculatively on a very low market. (3) Preferred holders have no legally enforcible right to dividends. (4) Accrued dividends are seldom settled in a fully satisfactory way. (5) Price instability is far greater in a preferred stock than in a bond yielding only moderately less. The obvious implication of these statements is that there is no reasonable compromise between the creditor position of a bondholder and the residual ownership position of the common stockholder. This is hardly a conclusion which can be accepted unqualifiedly; there are many cases on record in which the priorities of preferred stockholders have saved them from substantial losses which have fallen upon the common stockholders. However, there do seem to be many preferred shares in second-grade corporations which sell in good times at prices out of proportion to the limited benefits they can confer, in view of the risks to which they are subject.

The author is convinced that many people who require a steady income of somewhat larger amount than can be had in high-grade bonds might do well to consider preferreds. The preferreds will fluctuate a little in price, so they should not be regarded as completely liquid assets, and they should be purchased only at times when reasonably satisfactory prices can be had, but their good yields and dividend stability will justify the effort. Very fine-grade preferreds—the stocks of large, strong concerns with ample working capital and long unbroken dividend records, which never encounter serious earnings deficits, whose average earnings cover the preferred dividend at least 5 times over on the over-all basis in the case of a typical industrial and 2.5 times or better in a utility—can usually be bought to yield rates about midway between those of the best corporate bonds and the best common stocks.

Slightly lesser grades of preferreds, such as those labeled "good" in Table 9, will yield about as much and fluctuate about as much as the best grades of common stocks, but as compared with commons they are easier to evaluate as to fairness of price and offer greater dividend stability. They also offer substantial assurance against the ultimate losses of principal which so many investors sustain in common stocks. Industrial preferred stocks of this quality would typically cover their dividend needs 3.5 times on an over-all basis in an average year, and utilities would cover theirs 1.75 times. Naturally, this applies only to large, strong, established companies with good records.

Lesser grades of preferred stocks tend to behave much like common stocks in the market, fluctuating with the speculative tides and with the quarter-by-quarter business progress of the issuing companies. In such cases the nature of the industry and the competitive position of the company are of great importance to the investor. Naturally, the legal position of the preferred, as respects call price, convertibility, and other special details, will be important in all cases.

Guaranteed Stocks

The railroad, telegraph, and certain other industries afford investors a considerable number of "guaranteed" stocks. These are stocks whose dividend payments are either guaranteed by a parent or affiliated company or are contractually paid as a lease rental by the guarantor corporation. The latter type is the most common. In these cases the guarantor has leased the entire property and business of the lessor concern and has agreed to pay as a lease rental all operating expenses, maintenance costs, taxes, interest, and a stipulated dividend on the lessor's stock. The legal arrangements vary greatly as to technical details and duration, but most such leases run for very long periods.

Guaranteed stocks may originally have been either common or

preferred, but if their dividends under a contract are guaranteed and fixed in amount, the preferences will be immaterial for the life of the contract. If the guarantor is financially strong and the contract has many years to run, any guaranteed stock is of good quality. If the guarantor is not strong or if the contract is nearing completion, the future of the guaranteed stock may depend on the earning power of the property and on the capital structure of the property-owning corporation.

Most guaranteed stocks are products of the railroad and telegraph merger era, from 1875 to 1914. By modern standards they are relatively small issues. Most of them are traded over the counter, and apparently trading is not active. A few of the larger issues, such as Cleveland & Pittsburgh Railroad Company (guaranteed by Pennsylvania Railroad), are listed on the New York Stock Exchange. Needless to say, some guaranteed stocks are of prime quality and some are very speculative.

QUESTIONS AND PROBLEMS

1. Would it be legal to issue a preferred stock which is preferred as to income but not as to assets? (Note: Investigate the Midland Steel Products Company's $2 preferred.)

2. How would you determine the protective features of the law of Delaware, as they apply to preferred stock? What manner of provision might be there?

3. If you owned a preferred stock, and the management proposed a very unjust recapitalization plan, and a majority of the other preferred stockholders voted to approve it, could you do anything about it? In this case would there be any advantage in investing in a large issue, whose holders would be sure to include some competent and well-financed large holders, trustees, and institutions?

4. Where would you look to find out about such things as call prices, cumulation of unpaid dividends, voting power, and the like?

5. Look up the essential charter provisions of Merck & Co. $4 Second Preferred, American Car and Foundry Company $7 preferred, U.S. Steel preferred, Empire District Electric Company preferred, and Union Pacific preferred. Do you think that investors should ever buy preferred stocks without studying these provisions?

6. Why would anyone ever pay more than the call price for a preferred stock?

7. Would you care for a convertible preferred if you thought the in-

flation was over and that stock prices in general should not rise much in the next few years? Why?

8. Do stock purchase warrants attached to preferred shares need protection against dilution? How could it be done?

9. Are par values fundamentally important to preferred shareholders? Why not?

10. If you held 100 shares of a 1,000,000-share preferred issue which you knew to be high quality, would you regard a sinking fund provision requiring the company to retire 10,000 shares annually as of any particular importance?

11. What kind of dividend restrictions might be imposed on common stock for the benefit of the preferred? Why is this done?

12. Would you regard a chance to buy a medium-grade preferred with 4 years' accumulated back dividends at 70 per cent of par as a bargain?

13. Describe the preferred stock recapitalization plan worked out by Armour and Company in 1934. Was it a fair plan?

14. The earnings per share on American Tobacco $6 preferred were reported as $78.10 for the year 1953. What dividend did the stock receive?

15. Assume that an imaginary Million Dollar Corporation earned $1,000,000 in 1953 after payment of all expenses and taxes. If it had outstanding $10,000,000 of 3 per cent bonds, a 100,000-share issue of $3 dividend First Preferred, a 50,000-share issue of $3 dividend Second Preferred, and 10,000 common shares, what were the earnings per share on the First Preferred? On the Second Preferred? Which is the best quality stock? Prove this.

16. If the First Preferred was good enough in quality to sell on a 5 per cent yield basis, what would its price be? If the Second Preferred yielded 7 per cent, what would its price be?

17. List a number of criteria, both legal and economic, which would enable you to classify a preferred stock as high quality.

18. Which is the strongest security: a guaranteed stock or the preferred stock of the guarantor?

19. Look up the Cleveland & Pittsburgh Railroad 7 per cent guaranteed stock and the same road's Special 4 per cent stock. Is there any difference in quality between them? How do they compare with the Southern Railway Mobile & Ohio certificates?

20. Do you agree with the critics of preferred stocks who say that they have neither the unconditional promise of a bond nor the speculative possibilities of a common stock but that they have the major disadvantages of both types?

REFERENCES

Dowrie, George W., and Douglas R. Fuller: *Investments,* John Wiley & Sons, Inc., New York, 1950, Chap. 28.

Graham, Benjamin, and David L. Dodd: *Security Analysis,* McGraw-Hill Book Company, Inc., New York, 1951, Chap. 27.

Grodinsky, Julius: *Investments,* The Ronald Press Company, New York, 1953, Chap. 8.

Hoagland, Henry E.: *Corporation Finance,* McGraw-Hill Book Company, Inc., New York, 1947, Chaps. 7, 8.

Robbins, Sidney M.: *Managing Securities,* Houghton Mifflin Company, Boston, 1954, Chap. 20.

Chapter 6: CORPORATE BONDS
AND THEIR VALUE

In essence, corporate bonds are the promissory notes of the debtor corporation. They are called bonds instead of notes or mortgages chiefly to indicate that they are part of a mass borrowing arrangement, termed a bond issue, through which the corporation borrows the sum it needs. Corporate bond issues normally range in amount from $100,000 to $100,000,000; smaller or larger ones are not unknown.

All bonds of the same issue are part of a single elaborate bond contract and will therefore be similar or identical in their terms. Thus, all of the Socony-Vacuum Oil Company 2½s of 1976, which were sold in amount of $100,000,000, have the same interest rate, maturity date, protective covenants, and other features. Individual bonds are usually of $1,000 denomination, though an issue may include some units as large as $100,000 and some as small as $100. Interest is usually payable semiannually, though quarterly or annual payments are sometimes found.

Most bonds are issued in *bearer* form, that is, payable to bearer. The bond therefore does not show the owner's name and may be transferred to a new owner by the simple act of delivery. At each interest date the owner clips the appropriate printed and dated coupon from his bond and collects it through his bank, which handles the coupon in a manner somewhat similar to that used in collecting checks. In recent years an increasing number of bonds have been sold in *registered* form, which means that they are issued to specific named bondholders and must be returned to a transfer office for reissue when acquired by a new owner. Holders of registered bonds receive interest by check. Bonds *registered as to principal only* represent a compromise between the bearer and the fully registered forms; in this case the bond bears the owner's name and the principal will be payable only to the registered owner, but interest coupons payable to bearer are attached to the bond.

As might be expected in a field where borrowers and lenders are free to contract on any basis they desire, bonds vary greatly in their terms. With respect to maturity, the choice ranges from perpetual bonds, which never come due, to the early maturities of equipment obligations, which have a term of only a few months. With respect to pledged security, some bonds are secured by liens on real property, some by pledge of collateral or chattels, and some are unsecured. With respect to investment quality, some bonds are superbly certain and others are highly dubious. With respect to special contractual features, such as the right of the bondholder to have his bond converted into stock or the right of the debtor to pay off the bond before maturity, bond contracts are so diverse that an entire section of this chapter must be devoted to an enumeration of commonly used devices.

Bondholders are creditors, with rights and privileges which are definitely fixed in the bond contract. They ordinarily have no voice in the management of the debtor enterprise, and they usually receive only stipulated interest earnings and the return of their principal at maturity. Since they are in no sense owners or partners, their rights are contractual and enforcible at law. If the proper payments are not made or if other agreements are not fulfilled by the debtor, the bondholders' representatives may take action in court. Remedies may include a court order forcing the debtor to perform, appointment of a receiver to administer the business for the benefit of creditors, bankruptcy proceedings, or a foreclosure and sale of property belonging to the debtor.

The Corporate Bond Contract

There are three parties to a corporation bond contract, the borrowing corporation, the bondholders, and the trustee. The trustee is a bank or trust company, which is chosen and paid by the corporation but serves mainly to protect the bondholders.[1] The trustee's functions usually include (1) countersigning the bonds to assure authenticity, (2) collecting interest and principal payments from the debtor and distributing them to those entitled, (3) acting as mort-

---

[1] Most bond indentures also provide for a cotrustee who is a natural person, in whose name certain types of legal action may be taken, but the corporate trustee usually performs all the trust duties.

gagee or collateral holder if the bonds are secured, (4) verifying the performance of the debtor corporation's promises on behalf of the bondholders, and (5) taking legal action on behalf of the bondholders if necessary. Obviously, the bondholders cannot usually be parties to the framing of the bond contract, but they adopt its provisions when they choose to acquire bonds.

The contract itself, known as the *bond indenture,* is a complete lengthy legal document which constitutes the agreement between the parties. The bonds themselves are certificates of participation in this contract. In the indenture the corporation promises to pay principal and interest, promises to pay the trustee, promises to pay its taxes and other debts, and promises to maintain its property and conduct its business prudently. It will usually also agree not to enter a merger, sell its property, or change its business greatly, except under certain conditions; and it may agree to make sinking fund payments, to limit its indebtedness, and to limit its dividend payments. The trustee will promise to fulfill his functions faithfully throughout the entire life of the bond issue. The bondholders agree to allow certain grace periods in event of default, to abide by majority rule in certain situations, and to look only to the corporation's assets, not to the personal assets of directors or stockholders, for their payments.

The bond indenture will contain many other provisions, including: (1) the total amount of bonds authorized to be issued under the indenture or a statement that the authorized amount is *unlimited;* (2) statement that additional bonds may be issued in the future (*open indenture*) or that the first sale of bonds is the only one permitted (*closed indenture*); (3) statement of the purposes for which additional bonds may be issued, such as for construction or acquisition of property; (4) stipulation that all bonds must be of the same issue or that a *series* of issues, possibly having different interest rates, maturity dates, and call prices, may be sold under the basic indenture [2] (in the latter case each series issue would have a supplemental indenture detailing its special features); (5) details of the collateral or mortgage security to be provided; (6) mechanics of interest pay-

[2] Pacific Gas and Electric Company recorded its First Refunding Mortgage indenture and sold the Series A issue under it in 1920. Series A through I have now been retired. Series J through V, all issued in 1941 or later, were outstanding in June, 1953. They all have different maturity dates and call prices, and most of them pay $3\frac{1}{8}$ per cent or less interest instead of the $3\frac{1}{2}$ to 7 per cent paid by earlier series.

ments, registration of bonds, and principal repayments; (7) terms of special features such as sinking funds, call provisions, and conversion options.

During the depression of the thirties there was complaint to the effect that bond indentures did not sufficiently protect the bondholders' interests and that bond trustees were too slow in acting when defaults occurred. Under the provisions of the Trust Indenture Act of 1939, which is one of the series of Federal reform measures known as the Securities Acts, new bond issues must avoid these faults. The trustee must be financially independent of the debtor, and vigilance and positive action must be made obligatory on the trustee by the terms of the indenture.

Secured and Unsecured Bonds

Creditors often find it advantageous to have a legally enforcible lien on the property of a corporate debtor, so that in case of default they may have prior rights secured by that property. Such liens have no function unless default occurs, hence add little to the attractiveness of bonds sold by very strong borrowers such as the American Telephone and Telegraph Company. However, the economic turbulence of the thirties has proved that moderately good borrowers can quickly become weak ones, in which case a prior claim is superior to an unsecured one.

In modern practice a corporate enterprise is seldom liquidated when business disaster forces it to default on its debt. Instead, the corporate properties are placed temporarily in the possession of a trustee in bankruptcy while the corporation is "reorganized." Reorganization consists of (1) determining what amount of bonds and stocks the future earning power of the firm will support, and (2) distributing these new securities to the old securityholders in order of priority. Creditors who have liens on a sufficient amount of valuable and profitable corporate property will get full value in new securities. Creditors who have liens on property of insufficient value, or who have second liens, may get lower grade securities in whole or part. Unsecured creditors, preferred stockholders, and common stockholders will get progressively less favorable treatment, each group in turn, and some groups may get little or nothing.

A second advantage in a well-secured position is experienced if the corporation pays interest during the bankruptcy proceedings. Sometimes a corporation is placed in bankruptcy because it cannot meet a large maturing debt or because it cannot pay all of its interest and rent obligations during a time of poor earnings. In that case, even while the bankruptcy trustee is in charge, there may be earnings sufficient to pay some interest. If interest is to be paid, however, it will be paid only to claimants who are so well secured that the ultimate bankruptcy adjustment would have to pay them anyhow. Such situations are not uncommon.

In the event that it seems best to liquidate a defaulting corporation instead of reorganizing it, lien-protected bondholders will have first claim to the sale proceeds of the property covered by their liens and a prorata share with other creditors in a general claim against all corporate assets for any uncovered balance. In this case the bondholder will often be better off if his lien covers assets which are not single-purpose assets but, instead, are generally useful to other firms and other industries, hence salable at a good price.

Mortgage Security

The most common method of providing security for a bond issue is to mortgage some or all of the corporation's property for the purpose. This is accomplished by a trust deed, which gives the bond trustee a lien on the property. Bondholders formerly preferred mortgage-secured bonds issued under a closed indenture, but experience has shown that this leads to an undesirable proliferation of indentures and liens and occasionally to difficulties in financing expansion, if all available property is already encumbered. Also, the problem of determining the quality and relative priorities of bond issues secured by different portions of the same corporation's properties was frequently a baffling one.

The modern trend is toward large open indentures secured by mortgages covering all or most of the debtor corporation's property. If bonds of different qualities are desired, any number of open indentures ranking in sequence may be created, for example, one secured by a first mortgage, one secured by a second mortgage, and one unsecured. Each indenture may then provide for successive series of bonds to be issued under it, when the corporation needs the money. All series issued under the same indenture would have equal priority.

Mortgage-secured open indentures usually also carry an *after-acquired property clause,* which obligates the corporation to bring under the mortgage all property acquired subsequent to the date thereof. This clause is intended to assure the bondholders that their lien will cover new and added property as it is acquired, not just the depreciating original assets. While clever attorneys have devised ways to defeat the clause—for example, property can be bought subject to an existing mortgage, or subsidiaries can be set up to acquire and mortgage the new property, or a purchase money mortgage can be created,[3] or after a merger the successor corporation can deny that the clause applies to it—most corporations comply with it faithfully. Also, modern indentures often specifically obligate the debtor corporation not to use these evasive devices.

In order to prevent reckless issuance of bonds under an open indenture, the authorization of new bonds is often forbidden except (1) to obtain money to retire equally secured or better secured bonds, (2) to finance not over 75 per cent of the cost of new property, and (3) to obtain a very limited amount of working capital. This latter provision is for use in emergencies. Additionally, the new bonds are often forbidden in any case unless the corporate earnings during the past three or five years have been adequate to cover the total proposed interest charges by a safe margin.

Mortgage bonds are said to have either *senior* or *junior* liens, depending on the priority of their claims. The senior liens are those which have the most advantageous positions. They include *first mortgage* bonds, such as the Chicago and North Western Railway First 3s of 1989; *purchase money mortgage* bonds, which take senior rights against property acquired with the bond proceeds, even though another indenture contains an after-acquired property clause; and *prior lien* bonds, such as the Missouri-Kansas-Texas Railroad Prior Lien 4s of 1962, which were given a preferential position as a part

---

[3] A purchase money mortgage is one which is given to the seller as part of the payment for newly purchased property or one which is given to a lender who provides the money to pay the seller. In either instance the purchasing corporation acquires the property subject to the purchase money mortgage, hence cannot give its old bonds a first mortgage on it.

of a reorganization plan. It is also customary to class as senior bonds certain apparently junior issues, which are really well secured because of the adequacy of the mortgaged property, because the preceding lien is small in amount, because prior liens previously outstanding have been retired, or because the issue in question has a junior lien on part of the property and a first lien on other parts. For example, the $49,000,000 Pennsylvania Railroad Consolidated Mortgage 4½s of 1960 are now junior to only $1,810,000 of prior bonds, other senior claims having been retired. Since their mortgage covers property of ample value, these bonds are regarded as senior claims.

Junior bonds are those whose claim is subordinate to a first lien on the property. They may be either secured or unsecured. The lien status of junior bonds is often clearly defined in the bond title, as is that of the Chicago, Indianapolis & Louisville Railway Second 4½s of 2003. But corporations often dignify the position of junior issues by other labels such as *general,* or *consolidated,* or *first refunding,* or *first leasehold.* All refunding mortgages are likely to be originally junior mortgages; their function is to secure new bonds which will provide money as needed for expansion and for retirement of existing senior bonds. They may eventually become senior bonds, but the wise investor will appraise them on the basis of their immediate position rather than on their expectations.

One form of junior bond which should be understood by all bond buyers is the *leasehold mortgage* bond. Such bonds are commonly used to finance the construction of office buildings, hotels, apartment buildings, and other structures *erected on leased land.* The debtor corporation first leases the land at long term from a fee owner, agreeing to pay all taxes plus a lease rental; then it mortgages its lease plus the building it plans to erect, as security for *first leasehold mortgage* bonds. If the rental income from the building proves sufficient to pay the expenses, taxes, land rental, and principal and interest on the bonds, all will be well; but if the building earns less than expected the bondholders may lose, for operating expenses and taxes must be paid and *if the landowner is not paid he can repossess his land and the attached building together.* Thus a leasehold mortgage is clearly a junior lien. If trouble develops, the bondholders may have to forgo their interest, take over the ownership, or even pay the ground rent, to save their investment.

Collateral Security

Bonds which are secured by deposit of other bonds and stocks are termed *collateral trust notes* or *collateral trust bonds*. The pledged securities are generally assigned and delivered to the trustee of the collateral trust bonds, but the rights to receive the income and to exercise the voting powers of the pledged securities are usually retained by the debtor corporation. The pledged collateral may consist of (1) stocks and bonds of subsidiary and affiliated corporations, (2) stocks and bonds held as investments, or (3) portions of closed or limited senior issues of the borrowing corporation. In every instance, the relative quality of a collateral trust bond will be judged by the adequacy and quality of the deposited collateral.

Collateral trust bonds as a class did not perform very satisfactorily for investors between 1925 and 1935, chiefly because the device was ideal for use in much of the reckless and ill-advised finance of that period. Loosely drawn indentures permitted the withdrawal or substitution of good collateral, collateral was sometimes vastly overvalued, and indenture terms were not carefully observed. But previous misuse of a sound device is not necessarily a good reason for mistrusting it now; many completely satisfactory collateral trust issues are outstanding, such as the Potomac Edison Company 3s of 1974 and the Northern Pacific Railway 4½s of 1975, and the collateral trust method seems as reliable a method of providing security as any other.

Chattel Security

The only common use of chattels for bond security is found in the widespread practice of financing locomotives, railway cars, busses, large trucks, and similar equipment by selling serial notes or certificates secured by them. Equipment obligations, as such securities are called, have an enviable record for soundness and are usually bought by banks and insurance companies on a low yield basis.

The usual equipment purchase transaction requires the purchasing concern to make a down payment of 15 to 25 per cent of the cost. The balance is financed by the sale of equipment obligations which are secured by the equipment itself. The equipment obligations will be arranged to mature a few at a time over the next 5 to 15 years, so that interest and principal can be paid conveniently as the

---

$1,705,000

Chicago, Milwaukee, St. Paul and Pacific Railroad Company

2¼% Equipment Trust Certificates. Series KK
(Philadelphia Plan)

To mature each April 1 and October 1, 1953 to 1962, in amounts as listed below.
Semi-annual dividends April 1 and October 1.

*To be unconditionally guaranteed as to payment of par value and divi-
dends by Chicago, Milwaukee, St. Paul and Pacific Railroad Company.*

These Certificates are to be issued under an Agreement to be dated as of October 1, 1949, which will provide for the issuance of $4,500,000 par value of Certificates to be secured by nine 4500 H.P. and one 1500 H. P. Diesel freight locomotives, three 1000 H. P. Diesel road switching locomotives, one 2000 H. P. Diesel transfer locomotive and ten 1000 H. P. Diesel switching locomotives, all estimated to cost approximately $6,000,000.

AMOUNTS, MATURITIES AND YIELDS
(accrued dividends to be added)

$25,000	Apr. 1, 1953	1.60%		$150,000	Apr. 1, 1958	2.15%
15,000	Oct. 1, 1953	1.65		145,000	Oct. 1, 1958	2.20
50,000	Apr. 1, 1954	1.70		110,000	Apr. 1, 1959	2.25
20,000	Oct. 1, 1954	1.75		150,000	Oct. 1, 1959	2.30
150,000	Apr. 1, 1955	1.85		150,000	Apr. 1, 1960	2.35
140,000	Oct. 1, 1955	1.90		150,000	Oct. 1, 1960	2.35
50,000	Apr. 1, 1956	1.95		35,000	Apr. 1, 1961	2.40
40,000	Oct. 1, 1956	2.00		150,000	Oct. 1, 1961	2.40
50,000	Apr. 1, 1957	2.05		35,000	Apr. 1, 1962	2.45
40,000	Oct. 1, 1957	2.10		50,000	Oct. 1, 1962	2.45

Delivery on or about October 24, 1949

Harris, Hall & Company
(Incorporated)

Blair & Co., Inc.	Equitable Securities Corporation
Phelps, Fenn & Co.	Schoellkopf, Hutton & Pomeroy, Inc.
Robert W. Baird & Co.	Hayden, Miller & Co. Weeden & Co.
Incorporated	Incorporated
Adams & Peck	William Blair & Company
Kebbon, McCormick & Co.	Martin, Burns & Corbett, Inc.

CHART 4. Newspaper advertisement of October 17, 1949, offering equipment obligations for sale to the public.

equipment is used. Maintenance of the equipment is the obligation of the purchaser.

There are two well-known legal arrangements for handling equipment obligations. Under the most common *Philadelphia,* or *equipment lease,* plan the legal title to the equipment is placed in the trustee. The equipment obligations are not bonds, but certificates of beneficial interest, each entitled to semiannual dividends and to principal repayment at a stated date. The trustee leases the equipment to the purchaser for a rental sufficient to meet the scheduled dividends and maturities, and upon retirement of the last certificates the equipment is given unconditionally to the purchaser. Under the *New York,* or *conditional sale,* plan the trustee receives the equipment from the manufacturer and sells it to the purchasing corporation in return for a series of equipment trust notes. These notes are interest-bearing and of serial maturities; when sold to investors they provide the money to pay the manufacturer. When the notes are paid off by the purchasing corporation, the conditional sale becomes final and complete.

The good record of equipment obligations is probably due to (1) the fact that the equipment is essential and must be retained at any cost by the purchaser; (2) the mobility of the equipment, which makes repossession easy; (3) the gradual improvement in the security, since the debt is liquidated faster than the property depreciates; and (4) the ready salability of repossessed equipment. Receivers and bankruptcy trustees usually pay interest and principal installments on equipment obligations even when mortgage bonds are in default.

Debentures

Debentures are bonds which are not secured by any kind of lien or pledge. Such bonds would ordinarily be the lowest ranking obligations of a company which also had secured bonds outstanding. For example, in early 1954 the $2,000,000 of California Electric Power Company Debenture 3s of 1960 were junior to over $35,000,000 of other bonds. But not all debentures are inferior in rank. The United States government, most of our states and municipalities, and many of our strongest corporations issue no bonds except debentures. Some great corporations—such as Socony-Vacuum Oil Co., Standard Oil Company of New Jersey, and Texas Company, to name but three —prefer to finance with debentures to avoid the nuisance of property mortgages, but they assure debenture holders of seniority either by (1) agreeing not to mortgage their property while the debentures are outstanding, or (2) promising to secure the debentures equally under any mortgage which may be created. This latter promise, which is known as the *equally secured* or *ratably secured* clause, sometimes results in an issue of debentures acquiring mortgage security and ultimate seniority over other bonds.

Features of Bond Contracts

Reference has already been made to the multitude of features which appear in bond contracts. Several of these are discussed in ensuing paragraphs. In addition, it seems desirable to review certain fairly common situations in which bonds are issued jointly by several debtors, guaranteed by corporations other than the debtor, assumed by successor corporations, or extended or adjusted by joint agreement between debtor and bondholders.

Maturity Provisions

Most bond issues have definite maturity dates on which all outstanding bonds are due and payable. These maturity dates are unconditional and may ordinarily be deferred only by individual agreement between the bondholder and debtor or by a bankruptcy adjustment. However, a few bond indentures may obligate bondholders to accept majority rule in "amending" the indenture to extend the maturity date, if extension is requested by the corporation.

For the past twenty years the normal life term provided in new corporate bond issues has ranged from 10 to 50 years. The longer maturities have been sold by well-established railroad and utility companies and have usually been high quality, either mortgage bonds or covenant-protected debentures. The Southern Pacific Railroad First Mortgage Series F 2¾s of 1996 and the Southwestern Bell Telephone Debenture 2¾s of 1985 are good examples. However, the majority of recent rail and utility bond offerings have ranged from 25 to 35 years' term. Industrial bonds usually have shorter terms; 10 to 25 years would be typical. Of these, the shorter maturities may represent debt which the companies hope to repay out of earnings or convertible bonds which are expected to be exchanged for stock at an early date; or they may be low-quality bonds which would not sell advantageously at long term. Recent government bond offerings have ranged from 90 days to 40 years.

Outstanding issues include old bonds nearing maturity and old bonds of very long maturity. The latter include many issues sold prior to 1925 or created in corporate reorganizations, which do not mature until long after the year 2000. Examples are the New York Central 5s of 2013 and the Northern Pacific Railway 3s of 2047.

On a minority of bond issues, and notably on equipment obligations, building bonds, and municipal bonds, the maturities are made *serial*. That is, the bonds mature in installments over the life of the issue. Each bond has its own definite maturity date and bears interest up to that date, but by paying each batch of bonds as they mature the debtor is able to pay off the entire issue in installments planned to suit his own convenience. Serial bonds are regarded as ideal for borrowing municipalities which wish to amortize debts out of tax revenues and for corporate debtors who expect to pay out of the earnings of the financed property. Serial maturities also afford the bond buyer a chance to select a repayment date which is exactly to his taste. However, they have two patent disadvantages: (1) the small number of identical bonds (same maturity) outstanding limits the market and tends to reduce the salability of the bonds, and (2) the inflexibility of prearranged maturities sometimes embarrasses the debtors when business conditions are bad. Despite these disadvantages the serial maturity idea seems to be gaining in popularity since the war, especially among industrial concerns seeking funds for expansion. Serials may be secured or unsecured, high quality or speculative.

Sinking Funds

About one bond issue out of every eight provides for a sinking fund. This is an arrangement under which the debtor pays annual or semiannual contributions into a fund designed to retire some or all of the bonds before maturity. Obviously, this arrangement is not used on serial issues.

Sinking fund provisions usually require the debtor to make annual or semiannual payments to the trustee. Each payment may be a definite sum, or it may be a percentage of the debtor's gross sales, a percentage of his net earnings, or some other sum based upon his ability to pay. The payment may be required in cash, or it may be optionally in bonds which the debtor has purchased in the open market. The trustee is usually required to purchase bonds if he receives cash payments, in order to reduce the outstanding debt; and if the bonds are not available at a fair price, the trustee is authorized to select certain bonds by lot. These will then be retired by payment of face amount plus a small premium, probably not exceeding 5 per cent.

Sinking funds are found on both high-grade and speculative bond issues. They may be designed to retire all or a large portion of the issue by the maturity date, or they may retire only a small percentage of it. In various situations, the sinking funds are intended to (1) retire the bonds as rapidly as the debtor's finances will permit, (2) increase the security behind the bonds by a steady retirement program, and (3) keep the market buoyant by sending the debtor or the trustee out to purchase bonds for the sinking fund. Small sinking fund requirements are sometimes attached to long-term utility and railroad bonds by regulatory commissions, in order to compel the company to reduce its indebtedness out of earnings.

There is little disadvantage for the investor in purchasing a sinking fund issue, unless the bonds are callable for sinking fund purposes at unfairly low prices, or unless the sinking fund is so ill-designed as to threaten the debtor's solvency. The latter difficulty is not often met, but the former is common. See, for example, the Consumers Power Company 2⅞s of 1975, which were marketed in 1945 at 102⅜ and were quoted in 1946 as high as 108¾ but are callable for sinking fund at 102.

Call Provisions

Bond issues which may be paid off before maturity at the option of the debtor are said to be *callable* or *redeemable*. Most corporate bond issues are callable, as are most of the newer state and municipal issues. United States government long-term bonds are usually callable during the last two to five years of their terms, but not earlier.

Callable issues may be callable in part or only as an entire issue. Corporate bonds are usually entitled to a *call premium* of 3 to 10 per cent if called soon after issuance, but the premium often diminishes year by year and disappears entirely in the last years. This is desirable, since it permits necessary refunding to be done in advance of final maturity, which might occur during a depression when selling new bonds was impossible.

PROSPECTUS

Northern States Power Company

(a Wisconsin corporation)

$10,000,000

First Mortgage Bonds, 3% Series due March 1, 1979

Dated March 1, 1949   Due March 1, 1979

The Bonds in the first instance will be in temporary form later exchangeable for definitive Bonds. Temporary Bonds will be delivered at the office of Halsey, Stuart & Co. Inc., 35 Wall Street, New York, N. Y. Interest will be payable on March 1 and September 1 of each year at the office of the Trustee in Milwaukee, Wisconsin, or at the agency of the Company in Chicago or New York. The definitive Bonds will be in coupon form in the denomination of $1,000, registerable as to principal only, and in fully registered form in the denominations of $1,000, $5,000, $10,000 and authorized multiples of $10,000 Coupon and registered Bonds are to be interchangeable.

The Bonds will be redeemable, other than for the Sinking Fund, at the option of the Company as a whole at any time or in part from time to time prior to maturity, upon at least 30 days' notice, at the principal amount thereof plus the regular redemption premiums set forth on page 3 hereof. The Bonds will also be redeemable upon like notice for the Sinking Fund on June 1 in each year beginning with the year 1950 at the Sinking Fund redemption prices set forth on page 3 hereof, plus accrued interest in each case.

THESE SECURITIES HAVE NOT BEEN APPROVED OR DISAPPROVED BY THE SECURITIES AND EXCHANGE COMMISSION NOR HAS THE COMMISSION PASSED UPON THE ACCURACY OR ADEQUACY OF THIS PROSPECTUS. ANY REPRESENTATION TO THE CONTRARY IS A CRIMINAL OFFENSE.

	Price to Public (1)	Underwriting Discounts and Commissions (2)	Proceeds to Company (1)(3)
Per Unit	102.75%	0.55%	102.20%
Total	$10,275,000	$55,000	$10,220,000

(1) Plus accrued interest from March 1, 1949, to the date of delivery
(2) In the Purchase Contract referred to herein the Company has agreed to indemnify the several Underwriters against certain liabilities in connection with the Registration Statement and Prospectus.
(3) Before deduction of expenses payable by the Company estimated at $80,000.

The Bonds are offered when, as and if issued and subject to acceptance by the Underwriters, to approval of counsel, to prior sale and to withdrawal, cancellation or modification of the offer without notice.

The list of Underwriters set forth under the caption "Underwriting", subcaption "Underwriters" includes:

HALSEY, STUART & CO. Inc.

DICK & MERLE-SMITH   OTIS & CO.   WM. E. POLLOCK & CO., INC.

AUCHINCLOSS, PARKER & REDPATH   LAIRD, BISSELL & MEEDS

The date of this Prospectus is March 2, 1949.

CHART 5. Cover page of prospectus dated March 2, 1949, offering bonds for sale to the public.

There is little advantage to an investor in having a call provision in his bond. If interest rates fall, the company may retire the bond at a premium, but he will have to reinvest at lower interest rates. If interest rates rise, the bond will not be called, but he will not gain anything. And always the call price remains as a virtual ceiling to the market value of a bond, a figure which a purchaser exceeds only at his peril. For example, the well-secured non-callable Great Northern Railway Series D 4½s of 1976 were selling in 1946 at 125: but the almost identical Series E 4½s of 1977 were selling at 108, because they were callable at 105. The Series E bonds were called later that year at 105, at a time when new bonds of equal quality were paying about 3 per cent.

Conversion

Convertible bonds are those which may be exchanged for stock at the option of the holder. About one issue in twenty contains a conversion option. Nearly all conversion options provide for conversion into common stock, though occasionally the exchange is into preferred stock. Convertible bonds are sold to investors who believe that the corporation's position may improve, and who therefore hope to profit from future conversion, or to people who prefer bond security but who wish the option of taking stock if inflation reduces the buying power of bond dollars. Corporations sell convertible bonds because they find that they sell more readily or at a lower interest rate than equally well secured ordinary bonds, or because they hope to get the bonds converted into stock the next time the stock market is high.

Bonds may be convertible during the entire life of the issue, as is the case in the Standard Factors Corporation 4¾% Debentures of 1960, or conversion may be available for only a limited time, as in the case of the Inland Steel Company 3¼% Debentures of 1972, which cease to be convertible after March 15, 1967. Usually the conversion option permits the conversion of a $1,000 bond into a definite number of shares of stock, as in the above cases; but variations are found, such as the privilege of exchanging $1,000 American Telephone and Telegraph 3¾s of 1965 plus $360 in cash for 10 shares of stock in the company. It is common practice to provide in the indenture that the number of shares obtainable for a $1,000 bond shall decline as time passes. For example, a $1,000 bond may be exchangeable for 40 shares during the first five years, 30 shares during the second five years, and 20 shares thereafter. In most cases the conversion terms are such that conversion is unattractive at the time the bonds are sold but would be profitable if the stock rose sharply in price; but there is no uniformity on this point. Consequently, some convertibles are always on the point of being converted, and some are never near it. Conversion usually takes place at a rapid rate when the total market price of the shares into which a bond is convertible is greater than the value of the bond *as a bond;* but if the stock is not paying a dividend, conversion will be delayed.

It should be noted that convertible bonds have the priorities and contractual rights common to all bonds, hence should remain valuable in a depressed market in which stocks decline sharply. On the other hand, the bonds should have as great a value in a strong market as the shares into which they are convertible.

Conversion options are usually elaborately protected against dilution. That is, the indentures provide that if the company splits its stock, pays a stock dividend, issues stock under rights, or merges, an appropriate adjustment will be made in the conversion terms. Investors who buy convertible bonds should make sure that the dilution provisions are adequate.

Mention should be made of two devices somewhat related to the conversion privilege, which are infrequently used with bond issues. The first is to attach a *warrant* to the bond. This warrant entitles the bondholder to purchase for cash a certain number of shares of stock in the company at his option, at times and prices stated in the warrant. The warrant may be detachable, in which case the bondholder could sell it and retain his bond; or it may be exercisable only by the bondholder himself. The second device is to make the bond *participating,* somewhat after the manner of a participating preferred stock, so that the bond would get larger interest payments in case the company had large earnings or paid large dividends.

Income Bonds

Income bonds are bonds on which the payment of interest is mandatory only to the extent of current earnings. If earnings are sufficient to pay only a portion of the interest, that portion must be paid, but if the corporation is able to pay the unearned balance out of its cash resources, it is of course free to do so. Income bonds are not often offered for sale as new financing, but are often issued in reorganizations or recapitalizations to replace other securities. This is especially true in cases involving railroads and building corporations.

Sometimes a portion of the interest is mandatory and a portion is contingent upon earnings, as in the Baltimore and Ohio Railroad 2s–5s (2 per cent mandatory, 5 per cent if earned) of 1995. Usually any unpaid portion of the contingent interest accumulates and is payable if and when earned in the future, though there are many and various exceptions. Frequently interest on income bonds is paid only once a year. The income bond has the merit of being a realistic instrument, which will not force a concern with intermittent or limited earnings into bankruptcy, yet will definitely compel payment when earnings are available. It is probable that many of the income bonds arising out of reorganizations between 1935 and 1945 will prove to be good investments. They are now parts of acceptable capital structures, have sound indentures, and many have mortgage security.[4]

Debt-limiting and Dividend-limiting Covenants

Among the features often found in corporate bond indentures are covenants in which the corporation binds itself not to incur additional long-term debt or to pay dividends except under certain conditions. Debt-limiting covenants usually do not prohibit bank loans or other short-term debt, but they often limit new bond issues to 75 per cent of amounts required to buy or build new fixed assets and require that total debt be limited to a sum whose interest charges would have been amply covered by recent earnings. Sometimes covenants attached to the indentures of senior bonds do not limit additions to junior issues. Any covenant is likely to apply to the subsidiaries of a covenanting corporation as well as to the corporation itself.

[4] The Atchison, Topeka & Santa Fe Railway Adjustment 4s of 1995 were issued in 1906; they have worked out well. Similar hopes may be entertained for new issues such as Chicago, Milwaukee, St. Paul & Pacific 4½s of 2019; the Gulf, Mobile & Ohio 5s of 2015; the Wabash 4s of 1981; and the Erie 4½s of 2015.

Dividend limitations usually take the form of prohibiting cash payments except from earned surplus accumulated since the date of the bonds and at any time when the remaining net working capital would be less than a stipulated sum. Variations on these limitations are numerous. Sometimes the limitations apply only to dividends on common stock and sometimes to all dividends.

Debt-limiting and dividend-limiting covenants are seldom damaging to corporate efficiency, though they might be if they were too severe. They do afford the bond investor protection against a speculatively minded corporate management and must be regarded as valuable to bondholders. However, stockholders who prize continuity of dividends may not appreciate this bondholders' advantage.

Modification of Indenture

Considerable numbers of bond indentures now carry provisions permitting modification of the bond indenture when proposed by the company and consented to by two-thirds or three-fourths of the outstanding bonds. Usually these majority-rule modifications may not alter the principal sum, interest rate, or due dates of either principal or interest. They are most commonly used to release from the mortgage property which the corporation wishes to sell, to increase the amount of bonds issuable under the indenture, to release the corporation from its promise not to incur other debts or pledge its property, to modify dividend restrictions or sinking fund provisions, and for other similar purposes.

However, any provision of any bond contract may be altered by private agreement between debtor and creditor. Corporations frequently propose changes in bond contracts when there are no indenture provisions permitting the changes. These changes often *extend* the maturity date, for mutual advantage, as was done in the case of the Atlantic Ice Manufacturing Company First 6s of 1960; or they may make interest payments contingent upon earnings for a time in order to avoid defaults. Such private agreements affect only the bonds which consent to them. The bonds are usually overprinted to evidence the changes and are subsequently known as *extended* bonds, *stamped* bonds, *assented* bonds, etc.

Assumed Bonds

When a debtor corporation sells its assets to another, the successor firm may by proper declaration *assume* the bonds and make them its own. If the debtor is merged into the successor corporation, the assumption is automatic. In either case the bonds will continue to bear the name of the original debtor, but they are fully binding upon the successor for payment. If the bonds are secured by lien, the sale of the property or a merger will not affect the lien; it remains in full effect. Thus the Pere Marquette Railway First 3⅜s of 1980 are now the obligation of the Chesapeake and Ohio Railway, a successor by merger; but they retain their original title and their original lien.

Guaranteed Bonds

A considerable number of corporate bonds, especially in the railroad field, have been guaranteed by firms other than the debtors. Some of the guaranties assure payment of both principal and interest, some assure interest only. The guaranty may be extended to enable the guarantor's subsidiary to borrow at lower interest rates, as has been done for the bonds of the Cincinnati Union Terminal by the railroads which own the terminal company's stock; or it may be extended as part consideration for a lease of the debtor's property, as in the case of the New York & Harlem Railroad 3½s of 2000, guaranteed by the New York Central. An effect somewhat similar to a guaranty is achieved when a lessee company agrees to pay a long-term rental which is more than sufficient to service the lessor's bonds; this is illustrated by the Northern Central Railway 5s of 1974, serviced from lease rentals paid by the Pennsylvania Railroad.

A guaranty or a lease contract will add strength to a bond if the guarantor or lessee is financially powerful. However, the legal effects of guaranties and lease contracts are not usually so potent as those of outright assumptions, and an assumption undertakes only an unsecured obligation. Consequently, many guaranteed or lease-assured bonds are strong because of their own lien security rather than because of guaranty or lease.

Bond Terminology

Corporate bond issues are commonly given titles which undertake to describe the terms of the contract. Thus, promissory instruments running 5 years or longer are bonds or debentures; shorter maturities are *notes*. An equipment obligation (Philadelphia plan) may be a *trust certificate*. To identify the type of lien, the words *mortgage, leasehold mortgage, collateral trust,* and *secured* are used; for further clarification, adjectives such as *first, second, refunding, consolidated, general, divisional, prior,* and *adjustment* may be used singly or in combination. To describe the pledged property, such words as *bridge, terminal,* or *equipment* may be included. Additionally, such descriptive terms as *income, sinking fund, purchase money, extended, series, serial, participating,* and *convertible* are used.

Since a bond title conventionally includes the corporate name, interest rate, and maturity date, a not unusual bond is described as *Chicago and North Western Railroad Second Mortgage Convertible Income 4½s of 1999.* Another is *Shawinigan Water and Power Co. First Collateral Trust Sinking Fund Series N 3s of 1971.*

Computation of Bond Yields

As has been previously noted, the yield on any investment is one of the determinants of its attractiveness. This is especially true of bonds. Yet the concept and the calculation of bond yields are both difficult.

A bond usually promises payment of a definite principal sum on its due date, plus interest at a stated rate on that maturity value during the interim. Thus, a $1,000 4 per cent bond due in 1975 would pay $40 interest per annum until 1975 and $1,000 principal at that time. There is a further possible complication, in that the bond may be called for redemption at a premium (that is, at a price in excess of face value) before 1975. These circumstances lead bond investors to compute, on occasion, at least four types of yields: the *nominal* yield, the *current* yield, the *yield to maturity,* and the *yield to call date.*

The nominal yield is simply the percentage which the annual in-

terest payment bears to the face of the bond, in brief, the rate named
in the bond, otherwise known as the *coupon rate*.

The current yield is the percentage the annual interest payment
bears to the price of the bond. Thus, the current yield on a $1,000
4 per cent bond priced at $900 would be measured as $40 divided
by $900, or 4.44 per cent. The current yield is commonly used in

*Table 10. Bond Prices at Which a Bond Due after 20 Years Will
Produce Indicated Yields*

Yield to maturity, per cent	Nominal interest rate paid					
	2%	2½%	3%	3½%	4%	4½%
2.90	86.41	93.96	101.51	109.06	116.60	124.15
3.00	85.04	92.52	100.00	107.48	114.96	122.44
3.10	83.69	91.10	98.52	105.93	113.34	120.75
3.20	82.38	89.72	97.06	104.41	111.75	119.09
3.30	81.08	88.36	95.63	102.91	110.19	117.47
3.40	79.81	87.02	94.23	101.44	108.66	115.87
3.50	78.55	85.70	92.85	100.00	107.15	114.30
3.60	77.32	84.41	91.50	98.58	105.67	112.75
3.70	76.13	83.15	90.17	97.19	104.21	111.24
3.80	74.95	81.91	88.86	95.82	102.78	109.74
3.90	73.79	80.69	87.58	94.48	101.38	108.28
4.00	72.64	79.48	86.32	93.16	100.00	106.84

Source: Excerpted from Rollins Tables.

appraising speculative bonds whose repayment at maturity is doubtful. It is not much used on good bonds.

The *yield to maturity* is the most common measure of yield on
good bonds. For purposes of approximation it may be visualized as
follows: assume that on July 1, 1955, a $1,000 4 per cent bond due
July 1, 1975, is priced at $900. The purchaser who holds that bond
to maturity will obtain an annual cash income of $40, plus an aver-
age annual appreciation of $5 on his principal, as the bond rises from
its present value of $900 to its maturity value of $1,000. The combined annual gain is therefore $45. The average investment in the
bond during the 20 years consists of the mid-point between the $900
cost and the $1,000 maturity value, or $950. (This assumes that the

$5 annual appreciation adds itself to the principal in daily install-
ments during the whole 20 years.) The yield to maturity is the percentage which the *combined annual gain* bears to the *average investment*—in this case $45 divided by $950, or 4.74 per cent.

If the bond is bought above par the formula is the same: yield =
combined annual gain divided by average investment. Assume a

*Table 11. Bond Prices at Which a 3 Per Cent Bond Will Produce
Indicated Yields*

Yield to maturity, per cent	Years to maturity					
	19	19½	20	20½	21	21½
2.50	107.53	107.68	107.83	107.98	108.13	108.28
2.60	105.97	106.09	106.21	106.33	106.44	106.56
2.70	104.44	104.52	104.61	104.70	104.78	104.87
2.80	102.93	102.99	103.05	103.10	103.16	103.21
2.90	101.45	101.48	101.51	101.54	101.56	101.59
3.00	100.00	100.00	100.00	100.00	100.00	100.00
3.10	98.57	98.54	98.52	98.49	98.46	98.44
3.20	97.17	97.12	97.06	97.01	96.96	96.91
3.30	95.79	95.71	95.63	95.56	95.48	95.41
3.40	94.44	94.33	94.23	94.13	94.03	93.93
3.50	93.10	92.98	92.85	92.73	92.61	92.49
3.60	91.79	91.64	91.50	91.35	91.21	91.07
3.70	90.51	90.34	90.17	90.00	89.84	89.68
3.80	89.24	89.05	88.86	88.68	88.50	88.32
3.90	88.00	87.79	87.58	87.38	87.18	86.98
4.00	86.78	86.55	86.32	86.10	85.88	85.67

Source: Excerpted from Sprague Tables.

$1,000 bond due in 15 years, paying a 3 per cent coupon rate, and
priced at $1,060. The combined annual gain would be $30 cash
interest *minus* $4 annual depreciation (one-fifteenth of the $60 premium), or $26. The average investment would be $1,030, the mean
of $1,060 and the $1,000 maturity value. The yield to maturity by
this (approximate) method is therefore $26 divided by $1,030, or
2.52 per cent.

In commercial practice the yield to maturity is computed by a slightly different method, as the discount rate which, compounded semiannually, will reduce all future interest and principal payments to a present value equal to the quoted price. Since this is rather difficult to compute by arithmetic, yields to maturity are usually taken from *bond tables,* which are published in great detail and in a number of forms. Excerpts from bond tables are shown on pages 152 and 153. All the tables show the bond price as a *percentage of face value,* show the number of years remaining before the bond matures, indicate the nominal or coupon interest rate of the bond, and show a yield rate based on semiannual compounding. Though the tables are usually detailed enough to permit an approximate yield or bond value to be read directly from the columns, it is sometimes necessary to interpolate—that is, estimate a figure part way between two shown in the table—if fractional years or fractional bond prices are involved.

Since the compound-interest calculations embodied in the bond tables are the conventional and preferable ones, bond yields should be computed from the tables if possible. However, the arithmetic approximation is reasonably accurate if the bond price is between 90 and 110 and the maturity date is within 10 years. Less accurate but still significant results can be had for prices between 80 and 120 or maturities up to 20 years, provided one of these values remains within the narrower range noted in the previous sentence.

A *yield to call date* is the percentage rate which will discount future interest and principal payments back to the present quoted price, assuming the bond to be called for redemption at a definite future date. If the call price at the assumed date is the par value of the bond, the yield calculation is easy; a bond table will provide the answer if "years to call date" is substituted for years to maturity. However, if the call price is above par, the yield must be either approximated by the arithmetic method or estimated by proportioning in bond tables. A formula for this process is included in many bond tables.

Transactions in Bonds

Corporation bonds and most public bonds are quoted in *percentages of par value.* That is, a $1,000 bond selling for face value would be quoted at 100; if it were to sell for $900 it would be quoted at 90.

The rule would also hold for $500 or $100 bonds; at a price of 90 a $500 bond would sell for $450 and a $100 bond for $90.

When it is desired to quote bonds in percentages *and fractions,* it is conventional to use *eighths.* Thus Northern Pacific Railroad 4½s of 1975 were quoted at 102⅞, meaning $1,028.75 for a $1,000 bond, and Pennsylvania Railroad 4¼s of 1981 were quoted at 99½, meaning $995 for a $1,000 bond. Quotations in United States government bonds are an exception in the matter of fractions; they are traded in percentages and *thirty-seconds.* Certain short-term Federal bonds and municipal issues are also commonly quoted by yields; that is, a bond might sell on a 2.25 per cent basis. The actual price would be computed as the one which would allow a 2.25 per cent yield to maturity.

It is also conventional in the securities markets to assume that the quoted price for a bond covers only the principal of the bond. A purchaser would pay extra for any interest which had accrued since the last interest date. Thus a 4 per cent $1,000 bond bought 3 months after the last semiannual interest payment at a price of 90 would cost the purchaser $910—$900 for the principal and $10 for 3 months' accrued interest. If at the end of another 3 months the corporation failed to pay the 6 months' interest, that would be the purchaser's misfortune. He could not get his $10 back from the seller.

An exception to the "price plus accrued interest" rule is made in the case of bonds which are already defaulting their interest payments and on income bonds which may not be able to pay at the next interest date. Such bonds are traded *flat,* that is, with the understanding that no accrued interest will be added to the stated price. It is customary to mark a flat quotation with a small letter "f" or some other identifying mark.

Whether a coupon bond is traded flat or "and interest," it is expected that the seller will deliver it with all unpaid coupons attached; past due and unpaid coupons and all future ones become the property of the buyer. No question can arise if the bond is registered; transfer of ownership will automatically transfer all subsequent payments of every sort.

In order to compute the accrued interest on corporation bonds which are traded, certain standard rules are followed. They are as follows: (1) A bond coupon or interest check pays the interest through the day of its due date. (2) The period from an interest date through the corresponding numbered day of the next month is one full month, and is counted as 30 days, regardless of actual elapsed days. Each successive month is similarly counted. (3) The seller receives and the buyer pays interest for days elapsed in addition to full months since the last interest date, up to but not counting the day when the buyer's broker pays for the bond. (4) In prorating a year's interest, a year is assumed to be 360 days. For example, if a $1,000 4 per cent bond which pays interest on February 1 and August 1 is traded on May 15 but payment is to be made on May 17, accrued interest for 105 days would be computed; 3 months or 90 days would accrue through May 1, and May 2 to 16 inclusive would add 15 more. The accrued interest would be $105/360$ of $40, or $11.67.

Investment Position of Bonds

Except for the relatively few issues which are convertible or which bear stock purchase warrants, bonds entitle their holders to stipulated income and principal payments in dollars, and nothing else. Such an investment is obviously a speculation on the general price level. If the price level rises, the bond dollars will buy less; if it falls, they will buy more. Bondholders who buy long-term bonds also speculate on the future of interest rates; if interest rates rise, a fixed-interest bond will decline in value; if interest rates fall, such a bond will tend to rise, unless limited by a call price.

Despite these uncertainties, bonds have long been regarded as the most conservative type of securities investment. They are creditor instruments, enjoying a creditor's seniority of position. Good bonds have records of consistent payment and freedom from trouble which cannot be equaled in stocks, real estate, or mortgages. They provide investment outlet for 50 per cent of life insurance funds, 45 per cent of commercial bank funds, 50 per cent of mutual savings bank funds, and a probable 50 to 60 per cent of endowment and trust funds.

Of course, not all bonds are good bonds. One authority estimates that in the middle thirties interest payments were suspended on 6 per cent of the outstanding utility bonds, 16 per cent of the railroad bonds, 38 per cent of the foreign bonds, and 2 per cent of the municipals.[5] Most of these were the obligations of overbonded railroads, speculatively financed building corporations, pyramided hold-

[5] Charles Clark, *Barron's,* July 29, 1940.

ing companies, and foreign public projects. Careful investigation would have disclosed their speculative nature; in fact, it did for those who took the trouble to study the subject. However, even the reckless or blundering bondholder usually salvages something, for reorganizations or adjustments are much less severe on creditors than on the lower ranking stockholders.

Ownership of Corporate Bonds

Corporation bonds range in quality all the way from near perfection to long-shot speculations. The best issues often yield only ¼ per cent more than United States government bonds of similar maturity. The poorest may yield 15 per cent or default their payments entirely.

Obviously, bonds of such diverse qualities would not appeal uniformly to all investors. The better grades, those yielding 3½ per cent and less in the 1954 markets, are held in huge sums by insurance companies, endowment funds, corporate trustees, savings banks, commercial banks, and conservative private investors. The bulk of these holdings are in fairly large blocks and would appear to be in strong hands—that is, they are not in the possession of people likely to be forced to liquidate them. Commercial bank holdings consist largely of short-maturity obligations.

High-quality bonds, especially the corporate issues, are bought in very large quantities by trust funds and mutual savings banks whose bond investments are restricted by law to issues which meet very high legally prescribed standards. Commercial banks, insurance companies, and many nonregulated investors also choose from bonds which meet the "legal list" requirements of leading states, thus further augmenting the demand for these bonds. Many analysts believe that the heavy demand for "legal list" bonds causes them to sell higher and to yield less than they should, even admitting their high quality. Chart 6 illustrates the tendency for superior corporate bonds (the first two grades, in particular) to sell well above lesser ones. It is often said that the best corporate bonds yield so little more than government bonds (and even less than Series E bonds at times) and tax-exempt municipal bonds that it does not pay the average individual to select them.

The speculative grades of bonds are much more widely scattered in ownership and are generally held by individual investors and investment companies who are more interested in price than income. These bonds are therefore certain to respond quickly to variations in stock market prices and speculative psychology.

Since the war the very substantial growth of pension trusts and private trusts established in bank trust departments, coupled with an unprecedented expansion in corporate bond holdings by life insurance companies, has produced an almost incredible demand for good-grade corporate issues. This demand has been met by an almost equally incredible volume of new bond sales by corporations engaged in postwar expansion. Despite the large supply of new bonds, however, the demand has been so insistent that the "spread" between the yields on good corporate bonds and on government bonds has remained smaller than before the war.

The heavy demand for good long-term corporates by life insurance companies and pension and endowment funds reflects the fact that such investors have (1) legal or contractual limitations on type and quality of their investments, (2) a desire for maximum income with minimum administrative costs, (3) relatively slight emphasis on liquidity, and (4) little or no income tax liability. They are able to choose between long-term government bonds and high-grade corporates, with risk and yield as the factors controlling their choices. Consequently, the highest grade corporates follow a yield pattern very similar to that which Federal Reserve policy establishes for government bonds. Slightly lower grade corporates are influenced by this pattern, but each successive lower grade is more sharply affected by business risks and speculative attitudes.

Bond Yields

Because of the peculiar effects of length of term on the prices of bonds their values are perhaps best shown in terms of yields. Table 12 presents a comparison of corporate bond yields with other leading forms of conservative investment. As shown by the table, the best long-term corporate bonds in 1954 yielded about one-eighth more than long-term United States government bonds. Yields on the "good" category, which are the weakest bonds considered suitable for banks and other conservative institutions, are substantially below those available on the very best preferred and common stocks. Bonds lower in quality than those in Table 12 often yield little more than high-class common stocks and bank stocks but seem to be much less reliable as investments. They are bonds of companies which are currently solvent but do not appear strong enough to face a depression with confidence.

Table 12. Percentage Yields on Selected Investments

(Bond yields include amortization to maturity)

Investments	End of year				
	1927	1932	1936	1941	1953
U.S. Treasury notes *	3.44 †	2.45 †	0.98 †	0.62 †	1.63
Long-term U.S. bonds *	3.21 †	3.43 †	2.43 †	{ 1.97 †, 2.21 }	2.70
Long-term municipal bonds *	3.90 †	4.37 †	2.76 †	2.25 †	2.58 †
Best (Aaa) corporate bonds ‡	4.46	4.59	3.10	2.80	3.13
Very Good (A) corporate bonds ‡	4.92	6.61	3.78	3.27	3.40
Good (Baa) corporate bonds ‡	5.32	8.42	4.53	4.38	3.74
High-grade bank stocks	2.89	6.55	3.68	5.80	4.61
High-grade common stocks	3.92	8.11	4.62	6.90	4.77
High-grade pfd. stocks *	5.40	5.89	4.26	4.15	4.20

* From *Standard Trade and Securities Service.*
† Exempt from Federal income tax.
‡ From *Moody's Investors Service.*

The easy money conditions prevailing since 1935 have caused a sharp contrast between the yields on long-term and short-term bonds. Both government and corporate short-term bonds afforded yields almost as high as long-term bonds in late 1928, and the corporates did so in 1932. In subsequent years, however, investors' search for profitable short-term investments in a money market which Federal Reserve policy kept well supplied with funds drove short-term yields down to extremely low levels. Long-term yields also declined, but not nearly so far, for investors preferred short-term holdings at fractional rates of interest to long-term bonds on which the return would remain low for many years. This is a normal attitude; short-term interest rate bargains can be made at very low or very high rates under extreme market conditions, for neither borrower nor lender is burdened with an onerous arrangement for very long. But long-term bond transactions establish yields which endure through many years, hence are not ordinarily made at yield rates reflecting temporary extremes of credit shortage or abundance.

The influence of risk on bond yields is illustrated in Chart 6. The chart shows the yields of various classes of corporate bonds through the depression of 1938, the unsettled period 1939–1942, the war episode, and the postwar boom. The most impressive lesson to be

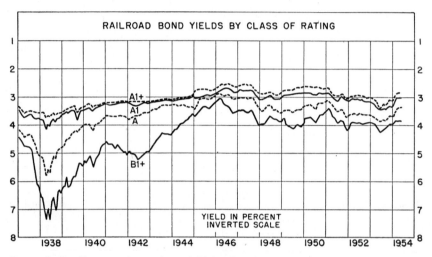

CHART 6. Quality as a factor in stabilizing bond prices. Yields on railroad bond indexes, 1937–1954. (*Standard & Poor's Bond Guide.*)

gained from Chart 6 is that all bonds tend to look good when business is good. When all corporations make money and maintain sound working capital positions second-grade bonds look secure, rise in price, and their yields approach those of quality bonds. But when business is not so good the weaknesses become apparent and the low-grade bonds decline in price, while the good issues retain their high estate. The moral to be pointed is this: second-grade bonds may be good speculative vehicles when bought at a major discount by an expert, but when business is good and bond yields are low it is unwise to compromise on quality when the objectives are safety and price stability. The wise investor will get the very best; the yield will be almost as good, and the risk will be small. The price of any bond is subject to basic changes in interest rates, but this hazard is small compared to the business risk on a mediocre bond.

Bond Prices

If the yields on bonds are the measure by which the market evaluates them, then bond prices must be regarded simply as the mathematical product of yield, nominal interest rate, and years remaining before maturity. It will be apparent at once that a bond maturing within a few years will fluctuate less in price as its yield changes than will a long maturity. There is thus greater security for one's

Table 13. Bond Prices Necessary to Permit a 3 Per Cent Bond to Produce Indicated Yields

Yield, per cent	Years to maturity				
	2	5	10	20	30
2.0	101.95	104.74	109.02	116.42	122.48
2.5	100.97	102.34	104.40	107.83	110.51
3.0	100.00	100.00	100.00	100.00	100.00
3.5	99.04	97.72	95.81	92.85	90.76
4.0	98.10	95.51	91.82	86.32	82.62
5.0	96.24	91.25	84.41	74.90	69.09
6.0	94.42	87.20	77.68	65.33	58.49
7.0	92.65	83.37	71.58	57.29	50.11

principal in a short maturity, assuming quality to be good. Table 13 illustrates this principle. It will be observed that a 3 per cent bond maturing in 2 years or even 5 years need not fluctuate extremely in price if market conditions cause it to yield 2 per cent or even 5. But a 3 per cent bond with 30 years to run depreciates drastically if it must yield 5 per cent. In view of the present low yields at which corporates are being sold, it is especially important that long-term bonds be good ones. To add the hazard of higher yield because of poor quality to the obvious hazard of a rise in basic interest rates would seem to belie any interest in security of principal.

Table 13 will serve to illustrate another interesting feature of bond markets. It has already been noted that bonds of long maturity are likely to fluctuate more in price than equally good bonds of short maturity. This feature is distasteful to many bond investors, and, in consequence, long-term bond issues must normally pay a somewhat higher interest rate than shorter ones of equal quality. But as a high-quality long-term bond becomes a shorter term bond with the passage of time, it becomes acceptable to more holders and has a tendency to sell on a lower yield basis. Table 13 indicates that a 30-year 3 per cent bond with only 10 years left before maturity would bring a price of 104.40 if it sold on a 2½ per cent yield basis, and 5 years before maturity it would bring 104.74 on a 2 per cent basis. Naturally, the possibility of a call before maturity would affect these figures. But it is clear that the investor who is willing to ignore possible price fluctuations in long-term bonds will often have a chance to sell them at a good profit in the years preceding their final maturity. This practice, which is sometimes possible in shorter term government securities as well, is known as *playing the pattern of rates.*

Interest Coverage

One of the important criteria by which analysts judge any bond is the adequacy of its interest coverage—*i.e.,* how many times the necessary interest payment has been earned. This is measured by dividing the annual interest requirements into the business earnings after all expenses but before income taxes. If its bonds are to be classed as good, the typical utility or railroad must earn its fixed interest charges four times; a typical industrial must earn them six times or more in the average year. It is very important that interest charges be small enough so that poor years' earnings will usually cover them, or at least so that unearned interest charges will not deplete working capital disastrously.

If the corporation has two or more issues of bonds which are successive in priority, it is significant to compute the coverage for the first lien bonds by dividing their interest alone into the available earnings. A high ratio of coverage would of course indicate a well-secured first lien. The coverage for the second lien is then computed on the over-all basis, by dividing its interest plus that of the senior issue into the earnings. Coverage for a third lien could be similarly figured. However, this process of computing interest coverage on successive liens has one weakness; it may show a senior bond as being amply covered by earnings, hence quite secure, when the junior bonds are not even fully covered. It must be remembered that if any mandatory bond interest is defaulted a bankruptcy proceeding could ensue. Bankruptcy might cause temporary suspension of interest payments and declines in the prices of well-secured senior bonds.

When a corporation such as a railroad operates both owned and leased properties, its fixed charges will consist of interest and lease

Table 14. Earnings Coverage in 1953 for Bond Interest and Other Fixed Charges, Selected Corporations

Corporation	Earnings available,* thousands	Interest and charges, thousands	Times earned
Chesapeake & Ohio.......	$ 83,466	$13,398	6.23
New York Central.......	88,477	49,142	1.80
Southern Pacific.........	173,376	51,564	3.36
Boston Edison...........	18,652	2,965	6.29
Consolidated Edison......	110,943	17,167	6.46
California Electric Power..	5,825	1,006	5.80
R. H. Macy.............	16,039 †	5,965 †	2.69
Socony-Vacuum Oil......	250,308	5,258	47.60
Swift..................	71,598	2,958	24.65

* Before income taxes.
† Includes $4,280,000 in rentals paid.

rentals. In some cases the lease rentals exceed the bond interest in amount. Interest coverage on railroads is computed as "coverage for fixed charges," with fixed charges including both interest and lease rentals Usually it is not easy to determine whether the lease rentals should be regarded as prior to, equal to, or junior to the bond interest.

An increasing number of bond issues carry sinking funds whose requirements are mandatory on the corporation. In the case of many railroad issues arising out of bankruptcy reorganizations, these sinking funds must be provided out of earnings before the remaining earnings can be applied to junior bond interest. In these cases analysts often compute the earnings coverage on *bond charges* rather than bond interest, including in the bond charges the mandatory sinking fund as well as the interest. The times-charges-earned figure on a junior bond thus gives a realistic measure of the adequacy of pre-tax earnings to cover senior bond interest, senior bond sinking fund, and junior bond interest.

When interest coverage on holding company bonds is being considered, it should be remembered that subsidiary bonds, subsidiary preferred stock, and possibly subsidiary income taxes will be senior to holding company bonds, if the holding company derives its income from subsidiary common stock dividends.

Criteria of Quality

Quality in a bond might well be defined as certainty of payment. A high-quality bond is one in which there seems little chance of difficulty but which is amply protected by lien and indenture terms if difficulty should arise. Quality of a bond is further enhanced if it seems likely to be stable in price, readily salable, and useful as collateral.

The principal tests by which experienced bond men appraise corporate bonds are as follows:

1. Adequacy of earnings to cover interest and charges, in average years and poor years
2. Lien protection, including priority, adequacy of amount of property under lien, durability of value of property, provisions regarding additional bonds, and provisions for release or substitution of lien
3. Indenture provisions, especially on limitations on new debt, dividends, repurchase of stock, merger, sale of business, and amendment of indenture
4. Nature of the industry, including its permanence, growth, earnings stability, competitive situation, labor problems, and relations with government
5. Strength of the company, competitively and financially
6. Marketability of the bonds, including size of the issue, market in which traded, sinking fund if any, eligibility for banks, legality for savings banks and trustees

The individual who is thoroughly familiar with the bond features discussed in this chapter, and who is willing to make point-by-point comparison of these features as they occur in different bond issues, will have no trouble in classifying bonds into quality groups. The yields available on bonds of similar maturity and quality may then be compared and checked against the bond yield indexes published by the financial services. However, the individual investor will probably find it easier to accept the guidance of the quality ratings and the bond analytical summaries prepared by leading financial services such as Moody's or Standard & Poor's. These are well done and will also provide price and yield comparisons for convenient study. Good dealers' and brokers' surveys may serve the same purpose.

Bond Policy for the Individual Investor

In these times of low yield rates on good-grade corporate bonds, it would appear that the individual investor would select them only because he wanted safety, price stability, and relative freedom from need to supervise them. To get these things, he would need to confine his holdings to very high-grade issues, those which Moody classifies as Aaa, Aa, and A and which Standard & Poor's label A1+, A1, and A. These would yield at long term somewhere around 3 per cent, as compared with 3 per cent available in Series E governments, 2.6 per cent in other governments, and perhaps 2.25 per cent in good tax-free municipals. In many situations the good corporates will serve just as well as the government bonds, and the slight advantage in income may make them a logical choice.

It should always be remembered, in considering bond policy, that the price stability obtainable in long-term bonds is only a *relative* stability in comparison to low-grade bonds and stock. As Table 13 shows, a high-grade 3 per cent bond can drop 9 per cent in market price if a scarcity of loan funds causes interest rates on new bonds of this sort to rise to 3.5 per cent. And money-rate changes of this magnitude are not uncommon, as Chart 6 indicates. In fact, such high-grade bonds as the Pacific Gas and Electric Company 3s of 1983 dropped from 98 to 91 during the tight money period in mid-1953, and rose again to sell at 101 under the easy money conditions of 1954. Long-term bonds are obviously not appropriate investments for emergency funds or other money likely to be needed in a hurry.

Fixed-interest bonds in the B categories (Baa, Ba, and B) range from the reasonably good to the definitely speculative. In practically all cases, however, they should be watched as carefully as the typical common stock, for their value is not so free from impairment as is the case in the A groups. In good times the yields on these bonds will range between 3 and 5 per cent, depending upon quality and maturity date, but in bad times their price declines may be drastic, as indicated in Chart 6, and the bonds are not free from the chance of permanent loss. Since high-grade preferred stocks can be had at prices which yield as much or more than these medium-grade bonds, and since the preferreds do not burden the company with inflexible fixed charges in bad years, it would seem that they should often be considered instead of medium bonds. Definitely, medium-grade bonds do not afford the safety, price stability, and freedom from care which are sought in the superior bonds.

Finally, the case of speculation in bonds may be considered. Bonds rated B, Caa, Ca, C, and D may be expected to fluctuate widely in price, and the investor who buys them "right" may make money on them. This is particularly true of issues in default of interest, or in danger of defaulting, and of income bonds. The latter, particularly, may fluctuate sharply when interest omission is not imminent, and it should be noted that temporary omission on an income bond is not damaging to a corporation, since it does not force bankruptcy proceedings. Bonds of these types, held strictly as speculations, are often more appropriate to individual portfolios than the Baa and Ba grades of fixed-interest bonds.

QUESTIONS AND PROBLEMS

1. What are the basic differences between the rights of bondholders and preferred stockholders?

2. Which would yield the most, safe bonds or equally safe preferred stock? Why?

3. What is in a bond indenture? How would you discover the terms of a bond in which you were interested?

4. Why are bond buyers interested in lien security? May a debenture issue have any of the advantages of lien security? How?

5. Are open indentures as satisfactory to the bondholder as closed ones? Why? What special added feature is important to make sure that the lien always covers ample property, if the indenture is open?

6. Suppose that a $100,000,000 corporation has three bond issues, one a $20,000,000 first mortgage on half of its property, another a $5,000,000 first mortgage on the second half of its property, and the third a

$10,000,000 second mortgage on the second half of its property. Rank these bonds in order of quality.

7. Under what conditions might a leasehold mortgage bond be high grade?

8. Why is the Philadelphia plan for financing equipment regarded as stronger legally than a simple chattel mortgage on equipment to which the debtor has received title?

9. Would you want the 60-year bonds of a merchandising firm owning chiefly inventory and doing business in leased premises? Why would a railroad or telephone bond be different? Or would it?

10. Would serial bonds be a good choice for an individual investor? Who would want them?

11. What are the advantages of a sinking fund to the investor? Are there any possible disadvantages?

12. Would you ever buy a bond above its call price? How far above?

13. Would a policy of investing in high-grade convertible bonds be a means of combining investment safety with inflation insurance?

14. What advantage could mortgage security have for an income bond maturing in 2015?

15. Does unpaid income bond interest accumulate?

16. Explain the meaning of the italicized terms: Shawinigan Water and Power Co. *First Collateral Trust Sinking Fund Series N 3s of 1971.*

17. Assume that a 3 per cent bond due in exactly 20 years is selling at 94. Determine the nominal yield, the current yield, and the yield to maturity. Obtain the yield to maturity by the arithmetic method, from the Rollins table, and from the Sprague table. Then price the bond at 105 and make the computations.

18. Assume that the 3 per cent bond above pays interest on March 1 and September 1. You bought the bond on June 12, and the transaction was paid for on June 14. Neglecting commissions, taxes, and mailing costs, how much was your total payment?

19. Why does deterioration in the quality of a long-term bond cause a drastic change in its price?

20. Why do fixed charges as reported on railroad statements include lease rentals?

21. What kind of bond investments do you regard as appropriate for a middle-class family? For a wealthy family?

22. Would you expect a 2½ per cent bond due in 20 years selling at 92 to be better quality or worse than a 40-year 3 per cent bond selling at 102? Why?

REFERENCES

Bellemore, Douglas H.: *Investments Principles and Practices,* B. C. Forbes and Sons Publishing Co., Inc., New York, 1953, Chap. 6.

Dowrie, George W., and Douglas R. Fuller: *Investments,* John Wiley & Sons, Inc., New York, 1950, Chaps. 4, 21.

Financial Handbook, The Ronald Press Company, New York, 1948, pp. 468–525.

Graham, Benjamin, and David L. Dodd: *Security Analysis,* McGraw-Hill Book Company, Inc., New York, 1951, Chap. 22.

Jordan, David F., and Herbert E. Dougall: *Investments,* Prentice-Hall, Inc., New York, 1952, Chap. 5.

Pickett, Ralph R., and Marshall D. Ketchum: *Investment Principles and Policy,* Harper & Brothers, New York, 1954, Chap. 6.

Robbins, Sidney M.: *Managing Securities,* Houghton Mifflin Company, Boston, 1954, Chaps. 12, 13.

Chapter 7: EMBARRASSED OR
INSOLVENT CORPORATIONS

When a corporation encounters financial difficulties, its securities may offer both a problem and an opportunity. The bad news will usually cause both stocks and bonds to decline sharply in market price, thus forcing the owners to choose between painfully severe losses and the further hazards involved in waiting for a possible future recovery. Speculatively minded purchasers, on the other hand, may buy the securities at prices far below their long-run values, if they can correctly anticipate the outcome of the situation. The securities markets usually continue to trade in the stocks and bonds of an embarrassed or bankrupt concern; so decisions to buy or sell can be implemented without difficulty.

Embarrassment and Insolvency

Financial embarrassment exists when the corporation is so short of liquid assets that it finds constant difficulty in meeting its obligations, or when its earnings are so deficient that debt service (*i.e.,* the regular contractual payment of interest and sinking fund and principal maturities if any) tends to impair its cash position, or when large-scale debt maturities are impending and must be refunded in markets where bonds are difficult to sell. Financial embarrassment thus presents a situation in which the corporation is not bankrupt, is still meeting its obligations, and in which the stockholders are still in control, but in which some emergency adjustment of the corporation's affairs is needed. Such an adjustment may be made in various ways, either by voluntary agreement between the corporation and individual creditors, or in some cases by agreements between the corporation and its bondholders acting as a group.

Insolvency exists when the corporation is definitely unable to pay currently maturing debts or when its property at a fair valuation is worth less than the amount of its debts. Insolvency might possibly be cured by a voluntary adjustment between a corporation and its creditors, but when matters have reached this critical stage it is usually necessary to resort to court supervision through receivership or bankruptcy proceedings. Court supervision prevents the corporate assets from being seized piecemeal by unpaid creditors while negotiations are proceeding, sees that a fair adjustment is planned, and compels greedy claimants to accept a fair plan.

Financial Problems

Corporate financial troubles have many causes, including such diverse ones as management incompetence, embezzlement, depression losses, loss of markets, errors in financial planning, and simple inability to sell securities in adverse markets. The necessary corrections are also diverse in nature. If the concern is so ineffective that little hope for successful operation exists, a plan to liquidate the assets or to sell operating units to other concerns will be best. If more working capital is required, ways must be found to sell new securities or to subordinate existing claims so that new borrowing will be possible. If impending bond maturities constitute the difficulty, the bonds must be extended or exchanged for others maturing at a later date. If inadequate earning power is the source of trouble, it may be necessary to convert bonds into income bonds or stock and to reduce or eliminate the old stockholders' equity in accordance with the probable real net worth remaining in the company.

In relatively few instances will it be advantageous to liquidate a large-scale corporate enterprise. Sale of the assets in most cases would net so little that almost any alternative is preferable. The obvious solution is to correct the concern's present financial troubles and try again.

The details of corrective plans developed in different cases vary considerably, but the general procedures and the methods of evaluating the rights of the securityholders in an embarrassed corporation are now quite definite. Investors who are familiar with these matters and who are capable of appraising the potentialities of an embarrassed corporation's business are therefore able to obtain a fair idea of the outcome of the average situation.

Protective Committees

When securityholders learn that a corporation is encountering serious difficulties, they sometimes form protective committees to consult with the management and to participate in court proceedings if any occur. Protective committees are self-appointed and usually develop around interested investment bankers and a few large holders of the securities. Normally a committee represents only one class of securityholders—i.e., first mortgage bondholders, debenture holders, preferred stockholders, etc.—so there may be a different committee for each class and, quite possibly, two or three competing committees for some classes.

A protective committee may choose to represent only the closed group who organized it, or it may offer its services to all holders of its class of securities. In the latter instance it may ask the holders for an indication of their approval of its ideas, or it may ask them for a proxy or power of attorney, or it may even ask them for possession of their securities plus a power of attorney to vote them or submit them for exchange in an adjustment or reorganization proceeding. A protective committee which has the authority to speak for and commit a large group of securityholders is obviously a potent force in planning any corporate adjustment, for it can provide many assenting votes to a plan it approves or an almost insurmountable block of dissenting votes if it disapproves.

Investors who are asked to support a protective committee should scrutinize its personnel and ideas, to make sure that their interests are compatible with those of the committee and that they approve its program. It is desirable that the committee members be aggressive in the interests of the securityholders, for a group which is not determined in its own behalf may be asked to make undue sacrifices, but it is also important that they display a reasonable spirit of compromise, for uncompromising attitudes may delay a reconstruction program and cause further losses.

When a protective committee enters into extensive negotiations, securityholders are often asked to deposit their securities with the committee and to authorize expenditures for legal and other costs by the committee. If the negotiations are successful, the corporation or its successor will probably pay the committee's expenses, but this is not always the case. While the negotiations are in progress, the depositing security owners will possess the committee's deposit receipts instead of their bonds or shares. These deposit receipts are transferable but are usually not so easy to sell as the original securities would be. In general, it may be concluded that an investor will risk distinct disadvantages if he deposits his securities too hastily; but, on the other hand, he may help to delay the solution of his problems if he withholds his cooperation too long.

The contumacious attitude of many protective committees during the financial troubles of the early thirties, and the excessive expenses which many of them incurred, led Congress in 1935 and 1938 to limit the activities of protective committees in Federal bankruptcy cases. These legal limitations have greatly reduced the scope of committee activities but have not eliminated them.

Voluntary Adjustments

Embarrassed corporations often believe that they can avoid defaults and expensive court proceedings if their bondholders will accept temporary reductions in interest rates, or conversion of their bonds into income bonds, or deferments of maturities on early-maturing bonds, or some other change of bond terms which will help to solve the immediate problem. Proposals along these lines are commonly advanced by managements after consultation with representative bondholders or protective committees. From the standpoint of the bondholders it is worth while to make reasonable concessions to avoid the expense, delay, and probable cessation of interest payments which a corporate bankruptcy would entail, but it is important to make sure that the proposed adjustments are fair, that they can actually be consummated, and that they will save the situation if consummated.

Most bond indentures provide that certain changes may be made in the indenture if the holders of a large majority (possibly 75 per cent) of the outstanding bonds agree, but the permitted changes seldom include matters affecting interest payments or maturity dates. Adjustments on these matters must therefore be made between the corporation and each bondholder individually. There are two ways of doing this: the corporation may offer to exchange new securities having the desired features for those currently outstanding, or it may ask the bondholders to send their bonds back to the trustee to be stamped as agreeing to the desired modifications of the original indenture.

Under either of the above procedures only the consenting bondholders will be bound, and if their sacrifice is successful they will assure full and prompt payment to the noncooperating minority, who will continue to have a legal right to collect on the original basis. Because these facts are well known it is often difficult to persuade bondholders to join in a voluntary adjustment; each holder would prefer to profit as a member of a noncooperating minority. Corporations meet this problem by making the proposed adjustments as attractive as possible—for example, if an extension of a bond maturity is sought, a cash bonus of 1 to 5 per cent may be paid to bondholders who consent to the change. The proposal will be vigorously urged upon all bondholders in advertisements and by mail and by use of salesmen.

It is usually not best to rush to comply with a corporation's request for voluntary adjustment. Even though the bondholders are merely asked to deposit their bonds in escrow, with no exchange or stamping permitted unless enough bonds are obtained to assure success, the depositing bondholder has surrendered his freedom of action. And after the exchange or stamping is completed, the new or stamped bond is a new security, unlike the old, and salable or pledgeable only as a new issue. There is usually plenty of time, after mature consideration and consultation with others, to accept a sound exchange or modification plan. Such proposals are usually analyzed at length in investment periodicals and advisory services; these should be consulted before any plan is accepted or rejected.

Adjustment by Majority Rule

Corporations whose financial troubles are limited to embarrassment may sometimes obtain adjustments which are binding on all of the affected classes of creditors, providing the requisite majorities can be persuaded to approve them.

As noted in the preceding section, corporate bond indentures commonly provide that indenture terms relating to sinking funds, working capital, limitation of debt, nonpledging of property—in fact, almost anything other than interest payments and maturity dates—may be altered by request of the corporation and approval of two-thirds or three-fourths or some similar fraction of the bonds. This type of indenture modification is binding on all of the bonds, since the indenture itself provides the method for doing it. In the proper circumstances relief from sinking funds or freedom to borrow needed working capital might make the difference between surviving a crisis and becoming insolvent.

A second though infrequently used device for obtaining financial adjustments by majority rule is found in Section 5 of the Delaware Corporation Laws. This Section permits a Delaware corporation to include in its articles a clause providing that any financial adjustment agreed to by certain majorities of its stockholders and creditors, and approved by the Delaware Court of Chancery, shall be binding upon all. As a part of the corporation's very existence, this clause thereafter is a part of every contract the corporation may make and is automatically accepted by every stockholder and every creditor.

The third procedure under which creditors' claims may be adjusted by majority rule is applicable only to railroads. Under the so-called Mahaffie Act, which the President signed in April, 1948, a railroad may propose a readjustment of the terms of any or all of its outstanding securities, or an exchange of existing securities for new ones of a different nature, in order to forestall financial difficulties. The proposal must first be addressed to the Interstate Commerce Commission, which will investigate to see if the plan is equitable and in the best interests of all concerned. If the ICC decides affirmatively, the proposal is submitted for the approval of each class of securityholders affected by it. If 75 per cent of the holders approve, the ICC may then order the adjustment placed in effect. Dissenting securityholders may carry an appeal to the courts, alleging that the plan is inequitable or improper, but there can be no bargaining advantage gained by refusing to cooperate in a fair plan.

The Mahaffie Act procedure may also be tried by railroads which are already in receivership or bankruptcy, if the supervising judge approves the attempt.

The Mahaffie Act is a streamlined successor to Chapter XV of the Bankruptcy Act, which was placed on the statute books experimentally in 1939–1940 and again in 1942–1945. The most important readjustment handled under Chapter XV was that of the Baltimore and Ohio Railroad Company, which was completed in 1945, approximately two years after the plan was first undertaken.

Equity Receivership

When a corporation is insolvent or unable to pay its obligations, it becomes important to prevent creditors from dismembering it to their own and others' ultimate disadvantage by attaching portions of its property or commencing foreclosure suits. The corporation or a friendly creditor may accomplish this by requesting a Federal or state court to appoint a receiver to take over the corporation's properties. The function of a receiver is to conserve the properties and to operate the business, if that is the best method of conserving it, while the stockholders, the creditors, and the judge work out a sound method of settling the corporation's affairs.

If it appears that the corporation's property should be liquidated, the judge will order this done and the proceeds paid to creditors and stockholders in order of priority. If it appears that the claimants will be better compensated as bondholders and stockholders in a continuing business, the judge will agree with the claimants and their protective committees that a reorganization plan is in order. The reorganization plan will usually call for the formation of a new corporation with a capital structure which the protective committees deem suitable; the plan will allot the new securities to the old bondholders and stockholders and, possibly, may provide other new securities to be sold for cash. The plan must be equitable in that it allots the well-secured claimants more or better grade securities than lower ranking claimants get, and all creditors must be allotted the full value of their claims if stockholders are to receive anything. If the earning power of the reorganized corporation does not appear promising, the old stockholders may get little or no participation in it unless they contribute new money. When a reorganization plan has been outlined, agreed to by a large majority of the entitled claimants, and decreed "equitable" by the judge, the next step is a "sale" of all of the old corporation's property at auction "for the benefit of creditors." The sale allegedly must be for spot cash; so usually the only bidder is the group consummating the reorganization plan, who represent most of the creditors and who therefore do not need to raise cash to pay themselves. Dissenting creditors who will not participate in the reorganization plan must be given their fair share of the sale price in cash, and the reorganization managers must somehow raise this money; but the amount is usually small, since a nonparticipant in the reorganization plan is entitled only to a share in the sale proceeds, and the reorganization managers need not bid much more than the liquidation or junk value at the sale.

Equity receiverships and reorganizations were common in both Federal and state courts up to 1933. Since that time most large corporate insolvencies have been handled in Federal bankruptcy courts, for the bankruptcy courts have been given the power to compel recalcitrant minorities to share in equitable reorganization plans; this supposedly speeds up the reorganizations, for minorities cannot demand special advantages as the price of cooperation, cash to pay dissenters does not have to be raised, and the fiction of a sale is unnecessary. Equity procedures are still used in small corporate insolvencies handled in state courts, when no serious dissents arise.

It is important to note at this point that equity reorganizations and bankruptcy reorganizations are available only in cases of actual insolvency, in which the corporation definitely either cannot pay its immediate obligations or in which its assets are worth less than the amount of its debts. A corporation which is merely short of funds or which foresees insolvency at some future date may try to work out an adjustment as outlined in preceding sections, but it cannot resort to equity or bankruptcy reorganization until insolvency is actually upon it.

Railroad Bankruptcy Reorganizations

An insolvent railroad may be reorganized under Section 77 (Chapter VIII) of the Federal bankruptcy law. Section 77 was enacted in early 1933 in the hope that it might expedite the reorganization of a large number of railroads which were in trouble at that time. It was amended in 1935 into its present form.

Either the insolvent railroad or a creditor may initiate reorganization proceedings under Section 77. If the judge hearing the case is satisfied that the facts justify procedure under the Section, he will appoint a bankruptcy trustee to operate the properties until re-organization is completed. Plans for reorganization may then be submitted to the ICC by the debtor railroad, by the trustee, by groups of stockholders or bondholders, and by protective commit-tees; and the commission must ultimately recommend one of these plans or one of its own to the judge, who will then hold hearings to review its practicability and fairness. A plan simply consists of a proposed capital structure which is suitable to the future earning power of the corporation, plus an equitable apportionment of the new securities to each class of old creditors and stockholders, plus any necessary provision for raising cash and meeting reorganization costs. If the judge believes the plan to be proper he will order it submitted to each class of creditors and stockholders who are en-titled to participate (that is, whose claims are high enough in pri-ority to share in the assets), and if two-thirds in amount of each class of claimants approves, the judge will order the plan carried out by delivery of the new securities to all claimants. Even if the desired two-thirds majorities cannot be had, the judge may in his discretion order a plan carried out.

Most reorganizations under Section 77 have required 5 to 12 years to complete. This has been due in part to the debtors' complicated financial structures; because of the interlacing of first, second, and third liens on different portions of property, collateral, and equip-ment, it has been very difficult to determine which securities are entitled to priorities. A second reason for delay is found in earnings experience during the years 1934–1948. Neither depression, war, nor boom gives a dependable indication of future normal earning power, either to plan a capital structure or to measure the value of a lien on a given portion of a railroad. Shortages of cash have not delayed Section 77 reorganizations. The trustees have simply suspended in-terest and sinking fund payments on all but the best secured claims and have used the earnings to improve the properties and the rail-roads' cash positions.

In order to guard Section 77 reorganizations against the delays and multiplied expenses which excessive protective committee ac-tivity would entail, the law forbids such committees to solicit proxies or deposits of securities except with the consent of the ICC. This is generally withheld until the official plan is ready for acceptance or rejection. Small groups of 25 or fewer securityholders may form their own protective committees at any time if they do not engage in general solicitation of proxies or deposits.

Industrial and Utility Reorganizations

Bankruptcy reorganizations for general corporations may be conducted under Chapter XI or Chapter X of the Federal bankruptcy act. General corporations may be defined as corporations which are not doing a railroad, banking, insurance, or savings-and-loan business. Chapter XI is intended for the simpler cases in which adjustments on only unsecured debts are required. In Chapter XI cases the debtor initiates the proceedings by admitting insolvency and proffering a reorganization plan to the court. The judge must investigate the situation, consult with the creditors, and may appoint a receiver or a bankruptcy trustee if that appears necessary. If a majority in number and amount of each affected class of creditors accepts the debtor's plan, and if the judge finds it equitable and feasible and otherwise proper, it may be made binding on all concerned.

Where secured creditors are affected by the insolvency, resort must be had to a Chapter X reorganization. Under this Chapter the proceedings may be initiated by either the debtor corporation or its creditors. The judge will appoint a trustee to manage the property and prepare a plan of reorganization. Creditors and stockholders may confer with the trustee as he prepares his plan and may prepare others of their own. After hearings on the plans, the judge must ask the advice of the Securities and Exchange Commission, if the corporation is a large one, and may do so in any event. Finally, the judge must approve a plan as being equitable and feasible and order it submitted to the claimants. If two-thirds in amount of each class of creditors and a majority of each (participating) class of stockholders approve, the judge confirms the plan and orders it carried out.

Chapter X limits the activities of protective committees in a manner somewhat similar to Section 77. Committees are forbidden, unless by consent of the judge, to solicit any approval or disapproval of any plan or to collect any proxies along such lines, until the judge orders the official plan submitted for the acceptance of the securityholders. Furthermore, the judge may in some cases invalidate proxies or deposit agreements empowering the committees. Under these circumstances protective committees do not exist at all in many cases and develop only as small groups representing a few large claimants in others. Only when opposition to a submitted plan is undertaken by determined groups will there be any extensive protective committee work under Chapter X.

The average Chapter X reorganization is completed in 2 to 3 years, though complicated cases have taken 5 or 6.

Adjustment and Reorganization Plans

Because of the noncompulsory nature of most nonbankruptcy adjustment plans their terms cannot be made severe. Consequently, most of them feature such mild expedients as 2- to 10-year extensions of maturing bonds, conversion of interest payments to an income bond basis for a limited period, or modification of indentures to eliminate sinking fund payments or to permit other borrowing. Usually these voluntary adjustment plans are not operative unless a minimum of 80 to 90 per cent of affected bondholders will consent. Typical cases include the Laclede Gas Light Company's 1934 plan for a 5-year extension of its 5s of 1934 in which cooperating bondholders received a cash bonus of $21.60 per $1,000 bond; the Associated Gas and Electric Company's 1933 plan for exchanging new income debentures for old fixed-interest bonds; the Baltimore and Ohio Railroad Company's 1938 plan for placing part of its fixed charges on an income basis for 8 years and deferring certain maturities; and the New York, Chicago and St. Louis Railroad Company's 1932 plan for extending its 6s of 1932, which involved payment of 25 per cent in cash and the balance in 6s of 1935.

Bankruptcy reorganizations are commonly made of sterner stuff. A corporation which becomes bankrupt should emerge from the reorganization with a sturdy capital structure which reflects the real value of its properties and earning power, even if this means that old stockholders are dropped out entirely and old bondholders have to become stockholders. A drastic reorganization of this sort is often resisted by the claimants but must be sought by the court and commissions under the terms of the bankruptcy laws.

Any bankruptcy reorganization should be planned with the following criteria in mind:

1. The capital structure of the new concern must be such that (a) fixed-interest requirements can be met easily, (b) income-bond interest and preferred dividends can be paid most of the time, and (c) there is at least a possible equity in earnings for the common stock. A speculative possibility of increased earnings may be reflected in the amount of common stock authorized.

2. Priorities in the old capital structure must be strictly observed—creditors must be fully compensated in new securities (at potential, not current, market values) before any stockholder is allotted anything, and preferred stockholders are fully compensated ahead of the common. Secured creditors are given preference over other creditors according to the earning power or importance of the property pledged to them.[1]

3. Unpaid interest usually is added to the bondholder's claim. If the company has earnings to spare during the bankruptcy period, and if senior creditors are certain to be paid in the long run anyhow, the trustee may pay such interest regularly.

4. Well-secured senior bonds which receive interest during bankruptcy

[1] To illustrate this principle: assume that a corporation financed by $4,000,000 of mortgage bonds, $3,000,000 of unsecured debt, and $6,000,000 of stock has failed because of inability to meet its obligations when due. Bankruptcy appraisal shows that the business can earn $100,000 annually of dependable income, another $100,000 most of the time, and an average of $200,000 more intermittently; this is held to justify a new capital structure consisting of $2,000,000 in bonds, $2,000,000 in preferred stock, and $3,000,000 in common stock. Appraisals indicate that the mortgage bonds covered a portion of the property which earned all of the dependable income, half of the "most of the time" income, and half of the intermittent income. In the reorganization, the new bonds would be allotted first; the old bondholders would get all or nearly all of them, since the old mortgage covers all of the property from which the bond-quality income is derived. In allotting the preferred stock, half of it must be set aside at once for the old bondholders, since their lien covers half of the income sources upon which the new preferred depends. The other $1,000,000 of new preferred goes pro rata to the next-ranking claims, which consist of the remaining $1,000,000 of old bond claim plus the $3,000,000 of unsecured creditors; the division is therefore $250,000 and $750,000. The $3,000,000 of new common is next divided; the old bondholders have a lien priority to half of it, but $750,000 of it pays them up in full; that leaves $2,250,000 of common to meet the remaining unsecured creditors' claims of exactly that amount. The old stockholders therefore get nothing.

A recapitulation of the above example indicates that the $4,000,000 of old bonds got $2,000,000 in new bonds, $1,250,000 in new preferred, and $750,000 in new common. Each bond received $500 in new bonds, $312.50 in new preferred, and $187.50 in new common.

In this example, extreme emphasis has been laid upon the future earning power of specific properties, on the assumption that no great sums could be realized by selling these properties to other concerns. It must be noted, however, that the unsecured creditors in this reorganization could have claimed better treatment if the unmortgaged properties in the example had been salable at a good price to outside interests.

may be permitted to continue undisturbed as the obligations of the reorganized company. This happened to most equipment obligations and to some first mortgage bonds when the debtor railroads failed during the thirties.

A good example of a bankruptcy reorganization is that of Paramount Publix Corporation (now Paramount Pictures, Inc.) in 1935, which continued $57,000,000 of subsidiary and senior debts undisturbed, allowed $59,000,000 of holding company creditors 50 per cent in new debentures and 50 per cent in new preferred stock, and allowed each old share of stock one-fourth share of new stock plus warrants permitting the purchase of additional preferred and common stock at attractive prices. Another typical example is that of the Associated Telephone Utilities Company, a holding company which failed in 1933. Two years later the bondholders of the old company received all the common stock of the successor General Telephone Corporation, investigation having proved the subsidiaries' debt to be so heavy that senior securities in the holding company were undesirable. A third example is that of the Denver & Rio Grande Western Railroad Company, whose bankruptcy period extended from 1935 to 1947. In this case the equipment obligations were continued without default; one well-secured old bond issue was fully compensated in cash and new bonds; less adequately secured old bonds got new fixed-interest bonds, income bonds, preferred stock, and common stock in varying proportions; and an issue of debentures got a small amount of new common stock. The old stockholders got nothing.[2]

Bankruptcy Reorganizations and the Investor

In most modern bankruptcy reorganizations the small investor is strictly a bystander. Large investors may enter protective groups and consult with trustees or the court, but the small holder is usually well advised to avoid such groups, watch what goes on, and retain his position or sell out as the situation warrants. As a rule, he should also stay out of groups which form to contest official reorganization

---

[2] Complete descriptions of these plans will be found in the appropriate *Moody's Investors Service* manuals for the year of consummation. For an unbelievably fantastic story of a bankruptcy case, investigate the history of the Missouri Pacific Railroad, which failed in 1933 and was in 1954 still embroiled in litigation and confusion over reorganization plans, though its business had been solidly prosperous for many years.

plans or to press for modifications. There are a number of reasons for this. In the first place, protective committee efforts are expensive, and depositing securityholders may have to pay for them. Second, controversies involving protective committees are likely to drag on for years; the large holders who control a committee may prefer to contest a minor point rather than compromise. Third, protective committee deposit receipts are usually less salable than free securities and usually bring a lower price, if the holder subsequently decides to sell. Fourth, a feasible and equitable reorganization plan is likely to be developed and confirmed without the services of a protective committee, and in less time. Finally, most protective committee efforts to resist or modify reorganizations are fruitless, anyhow.

The best sources of general information on the progress of reorganizations will be the financial reporting services, the financial newspapers and periodicals, and the daily newspapers. When plans are submitted to securityholders for final approval or rejection, a complete presentation of the situation will accompany the forms.

QUESTIONS AND PROBLEMS

1. Do stock exchanges and over-the-counter markets conduct trading in the securities of bankrupt corporations?

2. What happens to the prices of its securities when a concern fails? Why would these securities be likely to fluctuate in price during the bankruptcy period?

3. How long does a bankruptcy reorganization take? Do you approve of the Mahaffie Act? Is there a counterpart to the Mahaffie Act which may be employed by general corporations?

4. If you held a bond which was due to mature in 6 months, and if the corporation wrote you saying that it could pay the interest but not the principal at this time and requested you to agree to a 5-year extension of maturity, would you comply? Under what conditions?

5. If a protective committee wrote to you about the situation in question 4, requesting that you give them your bond so that they might negotiate effectively with the management, would you do it? Why?

6. Why was the equity receivership procedure inadequate to deal with corporate insolvencies during the depression of the early thirties?

7. What is the procedure followed in a Chapter X reorganization?

8. What are the guiding principles upon which bankruptcy reorganizations are based?

9. Assume that an established meat packing corporation has just sustained very severe losses as a result of inventory price declines, is unable to meet the principal of a bond issue which is currently due, and is therefore in bankruptcy under Chapter X. It needs $10,000,000 of additional working capital, which can be obtained at 4 per cent by selling new bonds secured by a first mortgage on its two meat packing plants. At present the corporation's assets consist of two packing plants and $10,000,000 of other assets; their total earning power is estimated for the future at $1,500,000 per year after all taxes and is credited in equal portions (thirds) to the two plants and the other assets. With the new working capital added, earning power will average about $1,900,000; of this $700,000 will be very dependable, $600,000 will be available four years out of five, and $600,000 will be irregular. The old capital structure consisted of a $15,000,000 first mortgage on the two packing plants, $10,000,000 of unsecured debt, and 1,000,000 shares of stock. Recommend a reorganization plan.

REFERENCES

Financial Handbook, The Ronald Press Company, New York, 1948, pp. 893–951.

Hoagland, Henry E.: *Corporation Finance,* McGraw-Hill Book Company, Inc., New York, 1947, Chaps. 40–43.

Husband, William H., and James C. Dockeray: *Modern Corporation Finance,* Richard D. Irwin, Inc., Homewood, Ill., 1952, Chaps. 31–34.

Investment Bankers Association of America: *Fundamentals of Investment Banking,* Prentice-Hall, Inc., New York, 1949, Chaps. 14, 15.

Plum, Lester V., and Joseph H. Humphrey: *Investment Analysis and Management,* Richard D. Irwin, Inc., Homewood, Ill., 1951, Chap. 6.

Securities and Exchange Commission: *Report on the Study and Investigation of the Work, Activities, Personnel, and Functions of Protective and Reorganization Committees,* Washington, 1936–1940.

Chapter 8: SECURITIES MARKET ORGANIZATION

The securities markets of the United States function through some 4,000 securities houses or firms, a number of trade associations, 16 national securities exchanges and several other informal ones, and a number of banks which deal in public bonds. These agencies handle or participate in investor transactions which probably exceed 25 billion dollars annually, exclusive of dealings in short-term government securities.

From the investor's viewpoint the functions of the securities business can best be analyzed by classifying them as (1) investment banking, which has to do with procuring money for corporations and government bodies by marketing new securities; (2) dealing in securities, which means buying and selling existing securities as merchandise with the firm's own money; and (3) brokerage, which means handling transactions as the customer's agent, strictly on a commission basis. Many securities firms engage in all three of these functions, and practically all of the others engage in two. In fact, it is often difficult to determine where one function leaves off and another begins.

As might be expected, there are both statutes and industry organizations which attempt to enforce sound practices in the securities field. Most of the states require all securities firms and personnel to be licensed and have enacted antifraud and regulatory statutes. Since 1933 the Federal government has also operated in this area, enacting no less than eight major statutes in the period 1933–1940. These measures regulate many aspects of corporate practice and control practically all phases of the securities business, in so far as honesty, full publicity, and fair dealing are concerned. Although a thorough study of securities regulation will be deferred to Chapter 12, it will be necessary to include certain of its aspects in the present description of the securities business itself.

Investment Banking

Investment banking has been defined as the business of obtaining money for corporations or government bodies by marketing their new securities. The definition should perhaps say "assisting in marketing . . . ," for few houses do the entire job of marketing even a small new issue, except when the issue is sold in a private transaction to a few large buyers, such as insurance companies. The investment banking function is usually accomplished in one of three ways, which may be called (1) underwriting corporate offerings, (2) purchasing-distributing, and (3) agency marketing.

Underwriting Corporate Offerings

When corporations undertake to sell stock or bonds to their existing securityholders on a "rights" or similar basis, they are sometimes urgently in need of the money which a successful sale would provide. To guard against failure, a group of investment bankers is often asked to *underwrite* the offering—that is, to agree in advance to buy at a stipulated price all of the securities which the original offerees or their assigns do not take. The investment bankers would then organize a sales campaign to dispose of any stock which they might buy pursuant to the underwriting agreement.

A successful rights offering usually attracts subscriptions to 95 per cent or more of the proffered securities.[1] However, reasonable certainty of success with an offering will require most or all of the following circumstances: (1) an offering price at least 5 per cent below market value on stocks, or 3 per cent below on bonds; (2) a reasonably stable securities market during the offering period; (3) an offering which does not exceed in value 15 per cent of the offerees' existing investment in the company; (4) a well-distributed group of stockholders, so that subscription will not exceed the buying capacity of too many of the stockholders, as it would if the stock were held in large blocks; and (5) a seasoned group of stockholders who have faith in the company. It is often possible for an offering to be successful with one or more of these requirements unfulfilled, but each departure adds to the hazard. The entire problem is accentuated by

[1] The technique of a rights offering is described in Chap. 3.

the fact that any new offering of a security inevitably adds to the supply offered for sale on the market during the offering period and ensuing weeks, thus tending to depress the price.

The fee which underwriters obtain for assuring success of a rights offering is ordinarily stated as a "stand-by" fee per share on all the stock to be offered. In about half the cases there is an additional fee per share on all stock actually purchased by them. The total of the two fees will range from 1½ to 6 per cent of the value of the new issue for a well-known corporation, depending on the quality of the stock and the chances for success with the offering. For example, Long Island Lighting Company paid underwriters a single stand-by fee of 29 cents per share on a 685,648-share offering in October, 1953. Old stockholders were offered one new share at $16 for each 7 held, at a time when the market stood at $17. Subscribers other than the underwriters took about 668,000 shares; the underwriters bought the remainder at the very attractive $16 subscription price. The Bridgeport Brass Company underwriting of November, 1953, was on the double-fee basis. In this case the corporation offered stockholders 240,672 shares on a 1-for-4 basis at $21.50 per share, at a time when the stock sold at about $22.75. The underwriters received a stand-by fee of 50 cents per share on 240,672 shares, plus an additional fee of 60 cents per share actually taken by them. In this case 37,974 shares were left to the underwriters.

The securities firms which underwrite a rights offering do not stand idle during the offering period. They often undertake to persuade large stockholders to exercise their rights, and to induce non-stockholders to buy rights and exercise them. They may buy rights and exercise them themselves, and then attempt to sell the stock to their customers. And they will most certainly buy stock if necessary to prevent the price from declining seriously during the offering period. All these things help to assure the success of the offering.

Although both investors and corporate managers may be impressed with the heavy cost of underwriting services, the advantages should also be apparent. If the corporation needs the money, the partial failure of a securities offering may leave the concern in a position in which its existing investment is imperiled. Whether the new offering is made on a rights basis or through investment banking firms, it is important for an investor to consider the possible consequences, if the transaction is not underwritten. As an alternative to the relatively costly underwriting process, some corporations endeavor to enlist the cooperation of the entire securities business in a rights offering by paying a small per share fee to any securities firm which forwards a subscription. However, many rights offerings are conducted without any arrangements of any kind with securities firms.

Purchasing-distributing

A major portion of the investment banker's business is concerned with purchasing entire new issues of securities from the issuing corporations and reselling them to investors. This process is also known as underwriting, and the purchasing group of investment bankers are called underwriters. This is the common method of marketing bonds and preferred stocks and is also used extensively when better grades and large issues of common stocks are to be sold.

Securities issues offered for marketing in this manner may range in size from $100,000 to $100,000,000 or more. Most of the important ones will exceed $1,000,000, and $50,000,000 is not uncommonly large. These sums are so large that few investment bankers find it either convenient or prudent to buy entire new corporate issues for their own accounts. Instead, they form *purchasing syndicates* consisting of several firms willing to share the responsibility. A separate syndicate is formed for each issue, though securities firms commonly ally themselves in cooperating groups which handle one issue after another.[2] Small issues may be underwritten by two or three firms; large ones may require fifty to a hundred. In each case the syndicate members will indicate the portion of the entire issue for which they take responsibility; that is, one member may take 10 per cent, another 5 per cent, etc. A *purchase group agreement* among the participating firms outlines the syndicate's plan of procedure and delegates authority to one firm to act as agent for the group in making the purchase and organizing the selling effort.

When the purchasing syndicate has been formed, the corporation and the syndicate enter into a formal *agreement to purchase and sell*. Under this agreement the details of the security to be sold are

[2] Because the leading firms tend always to form their syndicates among their own groups, it is difficult for a new or "outside" firm to compete effectively in the business. In the years 1948–1952 a number of firms were prosecuted under the antitrust laws because of this situation, but were adjudged not guilty.

outlined, and the corporation agrees to print the securities, pay the cost of audits and other surveys required for the registration statement, "register" the issue with the Securities and Exchange Commission, obtain clearances with state securities commissions, and provide descriptive prospectuses for distribution to interested investors. Sometimes the corporation's officers and leading stockholders will agree not to sell their stock for a period of months and to assist in electing a representative of the underwriters to the board of directors. The commitment of the underwriters is usually somewhat less positive; they agree to make the purchase if no legal barriers to the issuance and sale of the securities develop and if no substantial adverse changes in the condition of the corporation or the securities market appear before the date for the public offering. Sometimes the exact price of the security is left for last-minute determination on the basis of market conditions.

If an issue is expected to sell readily to a few large insurance companies or other major investors, the purchasing syndicate members may feel that no extensive sales campaign is necessary. Possibly the syndicate manager can sell the entire commitment by telephone in a few hours. If he can do so by offering the securities to a relatively few potential buyers, so that it is a private and not a public offering, a significant saving in time and money can be had because registration under the Securities Act of 1933 will not be required. If a public offering is necessary, it may still be possible for the syndicate members to find buyers for the entire issue through their own sales forces. But if the issue is very large, or if it consists of common stock or medium-grade securities which must be sold widely to individuals, it will be necessary to have many firms and many salesmen participate in the sales campaign. This calls for a *selling group*—an organized group of securities firms with substantial sales forces and clientele to which the securities can be sold. The purchasing syndicate's manager usually organizes and directs the selling group. He plans the sales program, furnishes the literature and advertising, sets the date of the offering and the price, and offers the proposed members of the selling group a quota of securities which they may obtain at a "concession" below the public offering price. The selling group members need not obligate themselves to sell or otherwise dispose of their quotas, but their opportunities to participate in future offerings may depend on the success of their efforts. They may and do split their concessions with other firms which assist them in selling their quotas. The selling group usually includes most of the firms in the purchasing syndicate, plus as many more as are deemed necessary to assemble an adequate sales force.

One of the essential elements in a successful public offering is *price stabilization*. It is therefore customary for the issuing corporation or the underwriting manager to stabilize prices by buying or selling in the open market any securities of the corporation whose prices might conceivably affect the success of the new offering. These transactions would be fraudulent if they deliberately manipulated the prices of the securities in question, but if they merely stabilize them the process is legitimate. With respect to the new securities the selling group manager will sustain the market price during the sales campaign by purchasing any of them which are offered on the market below the established price. The selling group members will be under obligation not to cut the price on any new securities offered by them during the selling period, which may extend for 30 to 60 days. When the selling effort is complete, both the purchasing syndicate and the selling group will be dissolved, unsold securities will be turned over according to agreement to the members of the purchasing syndicate, and all securities prices will be free to seek their own level.

Investors sometimes feel that new issues are priced high when offered by a selling group and that purchases can be made to better advantage later when the "pressure is off." There are good reasons why this might be true on occasion, for it is to be expected that corporations will try to make their new offerings when the market is high, to get the best possible prices; and everyone knows that after the original sale many securities tend to drift about on the market until they "find homes" where they are respected and cherished. However, it is hardly to be expected that selling group members would make a consistent policy of selling overpriced securities to their regular customers, if careful analysis could discover the excessive pricing; nor is it reasonable that underwriters would hazard their capital in buying issues which they believed to be overpriced. Table 15 casts some light on the subject. At the date of the table the market in bonds and preferred stocks stood at about the average

Table 15. Comparison of Subsequent Market Prices of Securities Issues with Original Offering Prices

Bonds

Issue	Offering price	Bid	Asked
California Oregon Power 3¼s, 1984....	102.9159	101½	102
Central Power & Light 3⅛s, 1984......	100.486	100	100⅜
Commonwealth Edison 3s, 1984........	100.3948	100	100⅜
Consolidated Natural Gas 3⅛s, 1979...	101.833	102	102¼
Detroit Edison 2⅞s, 1984.............	99¼	97⅝	98
Georgia Power 3⅛s, 1984.............	101.467	100¼	100¾
Houston Lighting & Power 3s, 1989....	102.89	100	100½
Iowa Public Service 3s, 1984..........	98⅜	98⅛	98½
Laclede Gas 3⅜s, 1974...............	101.827	100¼	101
Michigan Consolidated Gas 3⅜s, 1979..	100.759	103½	104
Northern Natural Gas 3¼s, 1973......	101.45	102½	102¾
Pennsylvania Electric 3⅛s, 1984.......	101.665	100½	101½
Montana Power 3¼s, 1979............	101.721	101¾	102
Montana Power 3⅛s, 1984............	102.66	101⅜	101¾
N.J. Bell Telephone 3s, 1989...........	101	100¼	100½
Public Service Electric & Gas 3¼s, 1984	102.915	103⅝	103⅞
Public Service of Oklahoma 3s, 1984....	99.021	99¾	100¼
N.Y. State Electric & Gas 3¼s, 1984...	102.42	103	103½
San Diego Gas & Electric 2⅞s, 1984...	98.90	97⅝	98
Southern Counties Gas 3¼s, 1984......	101.931	101¼	102
Southern Natural Gas 3⅛s, 1974.......	100	100¼	101
Utah Power & Light 3¼s, 1984........	101.931	102	102¾
Virginia Electric 3⅛s, 1984............	102.4612	101¾	102¼
West Penn Power 3s, 1984.............	100.50	99⅞	100¼
Wisconsin Electric 3⅛s, 1984..........	102.461	102	102¾

Preferred Stocks

Issue	Offering price	Bid	Asked
Dallas Power & Light 4%.............	102.56	98½	99½
El Paso Natural Gas 5.65%...........	100	107½	108½
Long Island Lighting 4.35%...........	101	99½	100½
Mississippi Power & Light 4.36%......	101	99½	100½
Louisiana Power & Light 4.16%.......	102.21	99	100
Ohio Power 4.08%...................	102	99	100
Tennessee Gas Transmission 5.85%.....	100	104	105½
Tennessee Gas Transmission 5.12%.....	100⅜	97½	98½

Source: *Wall Street Journal*, June 14, 1954.

level of the preceding six months, and the table shows that at that time there were few significant differences between the market prices of recent issues and their original offering prices.

The gross profit margin between the price of new securities to the investor and the price received by the corporation is known as the

Table 16. Size of Underwriters' Commissions on Large Purchase-Distribution Ventures in 1953 and 1954

Issue	Commission as Per Cent of Public Offering Price
$10,231,000 Columbus and Southern Ohio Electric Company 3⅝% Bonds, 1983.	.67%
$40,580,000 Northern Natural Gas Company 3¼% Debentures, 1973........	.69
$40,000,000 Commonwealth Edison Company 3⅝% Bonds, 1983............	.85
$301,500,000 General Motors Corporation 3¼% Debentures, 1979...........	.99
$100,000,000 Aluminum Company of America 3% Debentures, 1979.........	1.00
$12,500,000 Food Fair Stores, Incorporated, 4% Debentures, 1973...........	1.25
$10,000,000 Fruehauf Trailer Company 4½% Subordinated Debentures, 1973.	2.50
$6,120,000 The Montana Power Company $4.20 Pfd......................	1.57
$5,000,000 Iowa Power and Light Company 4.35% Pfd....................	1.65
$4,000,000 The Empire District Electric Company 4¾% Pfd...............	1.90
$35,700,000 Allis-Chalmers Manufacturing Company 4.08% Pfd............	1.96
$25,750,000 Pacific Gas and Electric Company 4.50% Pfd.................	2.21
$2,120,000 California Water Service Company 5.2% Pfd..................	4.15
$5,500,000 General Contract Corporation 6% Pfd.......................	9.09
$34,282,821 Fireman's Fund Insurance Company Common..................	3.51
$14,700,000 General Telephone Corporation Common.....................	3.78
$1,800,000 California Water and Telephone Company Common..............	5.00
$6,332,440 Gulf States Utilities Company Common.......................	5.25
$1,901,250 Hoffman Radio Corporation Common.........................	7.69
$1,775,000 The Fluor Corporation, Ltd., Common.......................	8.45

underwriting commission or *spread*. The amount of this margin varies. On an issue of $90,000,000 Refunding Mortgage 3s due 1981 marketed in 1948 by New York Telephone Company, the spread was $4.55 per $1,000 bond, or .45 per cent. On the other hand, 20 per cent is not an unprecedented figure, if the offering consists of common stock in an untried venture. Table 16 indicates the amount of the underwriting commissions on several important offerings in 1953 and 1954. None of the items listed in Table 16 represents financing by a new or untried concern, but it is clear from the size of the commissions on one of the preferred and two of the common offerings that the underwriters were concerned about the risks and sales problems involved. The size of the spread obviously will depend on the risk the underwriter takes, considering the quality of the issue; on the condition of the markets; on the extent of the selling effort which will be required; on the size of the issue; and on the intensity of the competition for business between underwriters. The first, second, and third of these factors are the most important, and in that order.

Agency Marketing

Instead of purchasing and reselling a new securities issue, an investment banker may merely market it as the agent of the issuing corporation. In this instance the investment banker bears no financial risk and the corporation gets its money only if the banker succeeds in selling the securities. The commission or fee to the banker will therefore range between one-third and one-half the fee for underwriting and marketing similar securities.

Agency marketing is usually undertaken under one of three conditions. Either the corporation feels that it can safely economize on the cost of underwriting by having a banking firm make a public offering on an agency basis; or the securities are so speculative that no underwriter cares to buy them, though he will sell them for a commission; or the corporation asks the investment banker to find a few major buyers who will take the entire issue after details have been arranged by negotiation.

Agency marketing for reasons of economy is illustrated by the public offering in 1948 of $25,000,000 Swift and Company 25-year debentures. Swift and Company paid Salomon Brothers and Hutzler, an investment banking firm, a commission of .40 per cent to organize and conduct the selling effort. This commission compares with .99 per cent paid by Westinghouse Electric Corporation and 1.38 per cent paid by R. H. Macy & Co., Inc., for a complete purchase-distribution service on bonds of similar quality at about the same time.

On small promotional ventures of every sort—brickyards, canneries, stores, small industrial plants generally—the cost of underwriting services on stocks would be prohibitive. Consequently, many such local issues are marketed by investment bankers on a sales commission ranging from 7 to 15 per cent. Very commonly the corporations are ones in which the investment banker has a continuing interest as promoter, heavy stockholder, or holder of stock purchase options.

Investment bankers are frequently asked to find a limited group of institutional investors, usually life insurance companies, who will buy an entire issue of new bonds. This is not difficult to do if the issue is of good quality, for the growth of insurance companies, trust funds, and endowments makes single investments of $1,000,000 to $5,000,000 readily salable. A small group of such investors can absorb a large issue. Within the space of a few days in June, 1954, the *Wall Street Journal* reported the following: Hornblower & Weeks and Union Securities Corporation placed $7,000,000 of 3⅜% and 3⅞% Promissory Notes for the Celotex Corporation; Salomon Bros. & Hutzler placed $15,000,000 of 3½% Debentures due 1979 and $10,000,000 of 5¼% preferred stock for Libby, McNeill, & Libby; and Blyth & Co. placed 100,000 shares of $25 par preferred stock for West Coast Telephone Company. These and similar issues were not and will not be offered to the general public. The issuers therefore need not undertake the task of registering with the SEC, preparing a suitable prospectus, and qualifying with state blue-sky-law commissions. Other expenses incident to a sales campaign are also avoided, and the investment banker who finds the buyers and handles the negotiations bears no financial risk and need receive only about .25 per cent of the sum involved. This economical form of agency marketing is known as *private placement*. It is popular with corporations, certain securities houses, and large insurance companies and is used in marketing large numbers of bond issues, but it is regarded rather bitterly by smaller institutions and private investors, who are denied access to such issues.

Competitive Bidding

Prior to 1935 it was customary for corporations to negotiate with investment bankers over the nature, terms, and prices of new securities issues. Most large corporations maintained continuing banker-client relationships with investment houses which handled all their business as a matter of course. On the other hand, state laws commonly required municipalities, school districts, road districts, and other public issuers to plan bond issues having statutory features and to sell these bonds to the highest bidder.

Subsequent to 1935 the Federal Power Commission, SEC, ICC, and a number of state regulatory commissions began to require public service corporations under their jurisdictions to sell their new securities issues to the highest bidder. This rule does not usually apply to securities sold to existing stockholders on a rights basis, nor to the underwriting of such an issue, but it does apply on issues sold to bankers or placed privately by them.

It is still possible, through discussions undertaken while a stock or bond issue is being planned, for the investment banker who hopes to bid on a public utility or railroad issue to have some voice in the terms of the security to be offered. This no doubt is done. It is also possible for an investment banker to interest a group of insurance companies in a forthcoming utility bond offering and by entering a bid to obtain the entire issue for private placement with them. However, it must be conceded that competitive bidding makes private placements much more difficult and awkward than they were.

Nonregulated corporations continue to negotiate the sale of their securities to investment bankers in the traditional manner. The majority of private placements are the issues of such concerns.

Controversy over the merits of competitive bidding has been raging for a decade. There is some evidence to indicate that direct competition of this sort is keeping underwriting margins in the utility field below those obtained in the less competitive industrial field.[3] However, there are some drawbacks, one of which was noted in a preceding paragraph. From the investor's standpoint the difference appears to be insignificant.

Regulation of Securities Offerings

New securities offerings are regulated mainly by the states under their *blue-sky laws* and by the Federal government under the Securities Act of 1933. These laws are considered more extensively in Chapter 12, but their impact on investment banking will be noted briefly here.

---

[3] See *The Problem of Maintaining Arm's-length Bargaining and Competitive Conditions in the Sale and Distribution of Securities of Registered Public Utility Holding Companies and Their Subsidiaries,* by the Public Utilities Division of the SEC, 1940.

The state blue-sky laws are antifraud statutes in the main, designed to forbid the sale of doubtful or improperly presented securities and to exclude dishonest firms or personnel from conducting a securities business. The usual enforcement methods require (1) that the issuing corporation obtain a permit or file explanatory data before any new securities are offered for sale in the state, and (2) that each securities firm and each securities salesman obtain a license before entering the business. The commissioner in charge of enforcement is given substantial discretion in the issuance of permits and licenses.

The Federal Securities Act of 1933, sometimes called the truth-in-securities act, was designed to obtain full and complete disclosure of pertinent information about new corporate securities when they are offered publicly. Government, state, municipal, bank, railroad, and certain other securities are exempted. The act requires *registration* of any nonexempt new issue of stock or bonds with the SEC. Registration consists of filing a large mass of data about the corporation and the proposed security and the preparation of a *prospectus* which summarizes the registration data for public use. If within 20 days (or in less time with the positive consent of the commission) the commission does not object to registration statement or prospectus, the securities may then be offered for sale. Every investor who is offered any of the securities by the corporation, an underwriter, or any dealer must also be handed a copy of the prospectus.

During the period preceding the date when a security may legally be offered for sale, no orders may be taken for it and no promises for its delivery may be made. However, information as to the nature of the forthcoming security may be circulated, and a tentative "red-herring" prospectus may be given to investors for their consideration. It is also legitimate to record investors' "indications of interest" in the forthcoming security, to obtain an active prospect list for the actual offering.

Needless to say, corporations and underwriters are very careful about the facts and figures included in the prospectus. Very little editorial opinion and no excited praise about either company or security will be included. In fact, a prospectus comes close to being a voluminous compilation of dry facts. Nevertheless, the facts are there for one who has the diligence and the capacity to interpret them.

Neither the state blue-sky laws nor the Securities Act of 1933 can prevent an incompetent individual or a lazy one from buying hazardous securities. They are not intended to; speculative business ventures are needed and must be financed. These laws do prevent fraud and misrepresentation, however, and they see that substantial information is available on the issues which are subject to their jurisdiction. Competence to judge that information and the diligence to study it are up to the individual investor.

Investment Bankers and the Public

Investment banking firms are of many types, ranging from the austere big-money institutions which specialize in large-scale purchases to the small firms which function exclusively in retail distribution. The typical firm would be one which operates chiefly at retail and also does some business as broker and over-the-counter dealer.

Most firms are keenly interested in maintaining customer good will and in building a reputation for sagacity in selecting only good issues for their representatives to sell. This does not mean that they will avoid speculative securities, but they will try to avoid unpromising ones and ones which are unsoundly priced. However, there are situations which induce well-intentioned investment bankers to suppress their doubts at times. Corporations depending upon the banker for financial assistance and advice may need funds at unpropitious times. Other investment houses with which the banker works may need his assistance in purchasing or selling groups, and he may wish to retain their good will. Or his own organization may be in need of a job to do. This conflict of interests is in no way unique to the business of investment banking. It is a situation which every manufacturer and retailer meets constantly and which must be resolved in accordance with the policies of the firm.

In most instances the ordinary investing public will deal with investment bankers through the banking firms' salesmen. The larger firms will also have statisticians or technical investment advisers who are available for consultation without charge to the investor, and statistical and financial service libraries are available in all offices. The personnel in most houses are competent and sincere. They will furnish available information candidly and will add personal opinion and advice when solicited. However, investors should realize that investment house salesmen are not omniscient, nor are they professional securities analysts. They must of necessity depend on the opinions of the firm's analysts and those of the purchasing group.

Salesmen naturally have a desire to make sales, for their compensation depends upon it. Some of them may therefore urge their wares upon the prospect with greater enthusiasm and in greater suggested amounts than the situation warrants. Others are very temperate on these points. Many salesmen keep records of their clients' portfolios and suggest additions and changes needed to maintain proper balance; this is helpful to the investor if the salesman is competent. However, it is a well-known fact that a salesman may utilize his knowledge of a client's holdings to suggest shifts from present holdings into whatever the salesman is offering at the moment. The firm for which the salesman works might or might not be aware of such an abuse of trust. On such matters the investor should make his own studies and act accordingly.

The conclusion to be drawn is that in dealing with investment bankers the investor may rely substantially on their facilities and on their advice, but the responsibility for sound decision rests fundamentally upon himself.

Marketing of Investment Fund Shares

Investment banking of a unique type is found in the marketing of the stocks of open-end *investment funds*. These funds are institutions which invest their assets in diversified lists of stocks and bonds, thus providing their own shareholders with a diversified and competently managed securities investment in a single package. Most of them continuously sell new stock and also continuously redeem existing stock in cash if the stockholder so requests.

Since new stock is sold continuously by the open-end funds, it would not be feasible for syndicates to buy and resell it. Instead, a single investment banking house—possibly one which does nothing else—functions as a perpetual selling wholesaler operating on an agency basis. The wholesaler will allow a concession from the public offering price to any other broker or dealer who may sell some of the stock. The stock is priced daily at the net asset value per share of the fund's assets, plus a fee of 4 to 8 per cent which covers selling costs. Stock is redeemed upon request at approximately net asset value, computed at the date of redemption.

Secondary Distributions and Special Offerings

When a large block of a security already in public hands must be resold by the holder, the task is similar to that of marketing a new issue. A simple offering of the stock or bonds on the market would depress the price and defeat its purpose. The situation requires an organized sales effort which will create an additional demand and place the securities, just as a selling group would do with a new issue. Two techniques are used: (1) the secondary distribution, in which a firm or selling group follows very closely the procedure which would be used with a new issue; and (2) the special offering, in which the members of a stock exchange are invited to solicit their customers' orders in the security at a stated price, out of which the member would be paid a "concession" somewhat larger than the regular commission.

The stock or bonds to be placed through one of these offerings may come from a single large stockholder, an investment company, an estate, a trust, an insurance company, or a holding company. They may be purchased by the investment banker making the offering, or they may be offered on an agency basis. If the securities come from the holdings of an influential stockholder or a holding company, they may have to be registered with the SEC just as though they constituted a new issue.

If the investment bankers controlling the offering are not members of a prominent stock exchange upon which the security is listed, the secondary-distribution technique is certain to be used. A selling group will be formed if needed, a definite offering price and offering date will be set, and ethical securities houses generally will be given an opportunity to submit orders for their customers and earn a "concession" for themselves. Even if stock exchange firms and a listed stock are involved, a secondary distribution is likely to be made if very large amounts are involved.

Special offerings are organized selling efforts in a listed security conducted from the stock exchange floor. Approval of the exchange must be obtained, but this will be granted if it appears that the quantity to be sold is too large to be placed by regular trading methods. The special offering must be announced by a member of the exchange during regular trading hours at a definite selling price, less a concession to any exchange member who produces a buying order. The stated selling price is net to the purchasing customer; the concession paid by the sellers to the member firms submitting orders is their compensation.

Obviously, secondary distributions and special offerings would not succeed if the offering prices were any higher than the familiar everyday quotations in the security. It seems probable that most of them are made at prices fractionally lower than the regular market would have recorded on the same day if no secondary or special were in prospect. However, it must be remembered that firms planning specials or secondaries are permitted to stabilize the market, and they may also choose their offering dates to get the best possible prices. No one can say that in the long run an investor either gains or loses as a result of buying on these offerings instead of on the everyday markets. Probably there is not much difference.

Dealers and the Unlisted Market

The unlisted or over-the-counter market is the very extensive resale market maintained by dealers who buy and sell securities as merchandise. In this market the participating firms buy stocks and bonds which are offered for sale by the general public and resell them to others who wish to buy. Any security may be bought or sold by any securities firm which cares to do so. Actually the bulk of such business is done in securities which are not actively traded on the stock exchanges, by a relatively limited group of dealers who have elected to carry inventories and "make" both buying and selling markets in the securities in which they specialize, and by brokers.

Mechanics of the Market

The fundamental cog in the over-the-counter market is the *dealer* who elects to make a market in a given security or group of securities. The firm acting as dealer is prepared to buy for its own account at its "bid" price any reasonable quantities of the security offered to it by the public or other securities houses, and it will sell in the same manner at its "asked" price. The difference between the bid and asked prices is the firm's "spread," or gross profit margin.

Since a dealer expects to get most of his business through other securities dealers or brokers, he makes available to them prices known as the "wholesale" or "inside market" prices—in other words, bid and asked prices which are not available to the general public. When a broker buys unlisted securities for a customer, he may buy from the dealer as the customer's agent, in which case he will charge the customer the dealer's asked price plus a commission, or he may buy from the dealer and resell to his customer at a small profit to himself. If the customer is selling, he may receive the dealer's bid price minus a brokerage commission to his own broker, or his broker may buy from him at less than the dealer's bid price and then immediately resell to the dealer.

If a customer appears in the dealer's own offices the dealer cannot charge him a commission for arranging a transaction with himself. Neither does he wish to give him the inside market price as a net price, for the brokers who provide the bulk of the dealer's business would regard that as unfair competition. As a matter of fact, dealing with the public at retail would not be profitable on gross profit margins as narrow as those which prevail in the inside market. The obvious solution is to give the customer who appears in the dealer's office a net bid approximately equal to the inside market bid minus a commission, or an asked price equal to the inside asked price plus a commission.

It is obvious that no dealer could make a market or even trade in all of the thousands of unlisted securities which the market handles. Dealers therefore specialize, either by type of security such as municipal bonds, bank stocks, or utility preferreds, or in the local securities of a particular community, or in a given list of securities. Their advertisements and quotations quickly familiarize other dealers and brokers with their intentions and attract business in their chosen specialties. Such dealers may from time to time also trade in securities other than their specialties, and investment bankers and brokers who ordinarily do not function as dealers at all may buy and sell as opportunity offers.

In addition to the more important issues on which dealers' markets are continuously available, the over-the-counter market handles thousands of transactions in smaller issues. In many cases dealers familiar with the concern or with the industry will buy lesser known securities at a negotiated price and then list their holdings for resale on quotation sheets which are widely circulated among dealers and brokers. In other instances dealers will decline to commit their funds to slow-moving securities but will take options on them or act as agents in an attempt to market them. Brokers or dealers interested in obtaining lesser known securities often find them by telephoning other dealers or by publishing offers on the quotation sheets.

The over-the-counter market is well-equipped mechanically to do its job. The larger dealers maintain trading rooms in which their traders are connected by private telephone lines with other dealers and brokers in the same city. Teletype facilities on which bids or offers can be dispatched to a number of dealers simultaneously, either locally or on an intercity hookup, are widely used. Leading dealers circulate daily or weekly "want-and-offer" sheets detailing their active bids and asks. One nationwide reporting service, the National Quotation Bureau, makes a business of collecting dealers' wants and offers on a nationwide basis and reporting them, along with the dealers' names, on properly classified daily and weekly quotation sheets. Newspapers and magazines carry quotations on the more active over-the-counter securities.

Securities Traded

The over-the-counter market operates chiefly in United States government bonds, state and municipal bonds, bank stocks, insurance company stocks, and issues too small, too inactively traded, or too closely held to have successful stock exchange markets. These latter include serial bonds, building corporation bonds, utility preferred stocks, and issues of small corporations generally. There is also an active over-the-counter market in many bond and preferred stock issues which are listed on the stock exchanges. Large blocks of good bonds or preferreds which could hardly be sold on the listed markets without breaking the price are often sold on the over-the-counter market.

The bonds of the United States government are listed on the New York Stock Exchange, but the bulk of the business in them is done over the counter. This is probably because the commercial banks of the country and a few other large dealers make very good markets in Federal bonds and their huge inventories plus their close contact with Federal Reserve policy enable them to dominate the market. Other dealers in governments perforce deal with and follow these leaders. State and municipal bonds are seldom listed on the stock exchanges because (1) many of them are serial, hence there are not enough identical bonds to make a satisfactory listed market in serial issues; (2) such bonds do not change hands often, so a listed market would be too dull to be efficient; and (3) commercial banks trade in this market also. Dealers and banks together can make an excellent market in these bonds, providing bids and offers when asked on almost any bond of satisfactory quality.

Bank stocks and insurance company stocks are nearly all traded unlisted because most such institutions traditionally refuse to have their stocks listed on the exchanges. The reasons given are that (1) listing would automatically associate the banks and insurance companies with the speculative aura of the stock exchanges; (2) listing would subject them and their stocks to more detailed regulation under the Federal securities acts; (3) listing would make their stock fluctuate more in value, in keeping with the performance of the listed market; (4) listing would cause more buying, selling, and transferring of stock and would call for fees to stock exchanges, all of which is unnecessary expense; and (5) listing would cause dealers who now stabilize stock prices from day to day by buying for inventory or selling from inventory to lose interest, thus permitting the uneven flow of public buying and selling orders to cause an unstable market. There may be some germ of truth in the last two of these arguments, but the entire presentation seems to do a better job of rationalizing than justifying the nonlisting tradition, at least where the large institutions are concerned.

Price Behavior on the Unlisted Market

Experience shows that prices on active over-the-counter securities do not fluctuate much from hour to hour, since dealers absorb irregularities in the timing of public orders by adding to or reducing inventories. However, any substantial day-to-day or week-to-week fluctuations in the listed stock market have their repercussions in public bids and offers in the unlisted market and thus compel dealers to adjust their prices. From an inspection of long-term price ranges recorded by listed and unlisted securities, it would appear that actively traded securities of comparable qualities fluctuate about as much in one market as they would in another. Table 17 shows recent price ranges of four groups of high-quality stocks, two on listed and two on unlisted markets.

Table 17. Comparison of Price Fluctuations of Listed and Unlisted Stocks

Stock	Market	Price range		
		1937–1946	*1953*	*January–February, 1954*
General Motors	NYSE	80⅜–25½	69¾–53⅝	65–58¾
General Electric	NYSE	64⅞–21½	92¼–66¼	100½–87
General Foods	NYSE	56⅛–22⅞	61¾–50⅞	60¼–56⅝
American Telephone	NYSE	200¼–101¼	161¼–152⅛	163⅛–156
Boston Edison	BSE	55–19¼	53½–46	52½–49¼
Commonwealth Edison	NYSE	36⅛–17⅜	37½–32⅛	39⅝–36⅞
Chase National Bank	Unlisted	64⅝–19½	50–42¾	45¾–43⅝
Manufacturers Trust	Unlisted	70¼–26¼	66¾–58½	65⅝–62
National City Bank	Unlisted	60¾–19	55½–46¾	52⅜–50⅜
Aetna (Fire) Insurance	Unlisted	69–35	64½–50¾	59½–56
Great American Insurance	Unlisted	35⅞–16½	32–26½	33¼–32¼
Home Insurance	Unlisted	41–19½	42⅝–37⅛	41¼–38¾

Note: The decade 1937–1946 was a period which included both high and low markets. The year 1953 was one in which price variations were substantial but not extreme. The first two months of 1954 were fairly typical.

It would be impossible to prove or disprove the oft-repeated statement that prices on the unlisted market average a little lower than those on the listed market. When securities are traded in both markets, arbitrage transactions naturally keep the prices at the same level. On actively traded securities of similar type and quality little difference is apparent, though listed securities usually have somewhat greater collateral value. On inactive securities no sure generalization is possible, for on either listed or unlisted markets a determined effort to buy or sell in large quantities may distort prices considerably. However, because of the existence of many very inactive securities in the unlisted market, because these securities are little known and therefore not regularly sought by buyers, and because such securities lack marketability and collateral value, it is a fair guess that in these categories the unlisted market may offer better quality securities for less money than can be had on the listed markets.

Price Making in the Unlisted Market

The bid and asked prices in the unlisted market are established from hour to hour by the dealers who make the market. However, these prices must be set at levels which will result in the dealers' purchases roughly equaling their sales, unless the dealers wish to increase or decrease their inventories for speculative reasons. Usually dealers do not change their inventories much for speculative reasons; so it can be said that their prices are set approximately at levels where public demand equals public offering. If a dealer's inventory rises or falls by reasonable amounts from hour to hour but balances out over a few days' time, he will regard his price as being right; and even if he has an excess of sales over purchases or vice versa, he will consider his prices right if other dealers have contra balances and will buy or sell with him. However, if dealers generally find that they are buying more than they are selling of a particular security, they will reduce both their bid and asked prices; and if they are selling more than they are buying, both figures will be raised.

Dealers in the unlisted market must not only establish the level of prices in each issue traded, they must also determine the spread between the bid and asked price. To the dealer the spread represents the gross profit margin out of which he must pay his expenses and earn his living. To the customer, it is a differential which makes his probable selling price somewhat lower than the best available buying price. In general, it appears that four factors govern the size of the spread a dealer establishes.

1. *Activity of the security.* If the dealer's inventory can be turned over rapidly, thus earning the regular gross profit at frequent intervals, the profit on each transaction can be low.

2. *Quality of the security.* If the security is of high quality, or if for any other reason a decline in its value is unlikely, a dealer can afford to

handle it at a low gross profit, for he is not likely to sustain a severe inventory loss.

3. *Dividend or interest payments.* If the security pays dividends or interest regularly, its inclusion in inventory does not hold the dealer's capital idle and he can afford a lower margin than otherwise.

4. *Competition.* The over-the-counter market is sharply competitive, and a dealer's expenses consist largely of overhead costs. He cannot afford to let other dealers take his business by making closer markets—that is, by paying slightly more and asking slightly less—and he will establish his spreads accordingly.

It is customary, when a dealer is asked for a market price on a security, for him to quote his bid and asked prices and indicate the quantities he will trade without knowing whether the inquiring broker wishes to buy or sell. The inside market quoted by the dealer then becomes the basis for negotiations. It is usually the dealer's final price on transactions ranging between a few hundred and a few thousand dollars; no better or worse prices are made on large or small transactions unless the amounts involved are extreme. However, a dealer is a principal, and if he can be persuaded to pay a little more or sell for a little less in a given instance, that is his privilege. He does not have to treat everyone alike.

On securities in which the dealer does not maintain a regular market, or in which a good market does not exist, any dealer or broker may offer to buy from or sell to a customer at a price satisfactory to himself. If the broker or dealer knows that his asking price is higher or his bid price is lower than a fair competitive price, he is duty-bound to say so to a nonprofessional customer; he is in a position of trust in such a case. However, a great many over-the-counter securities do not have steady and close markets; this forces both dealer and investor to negotiate as best they can.

The dealer's bids and asks shown in Table 18 are copied from a sheet distributed by a leading dealer on June 24, 1954. Only a few of the quotations offered by the dealer are shown here, but they illustrate well the size of the spreads in issues having good and fairly good markets. None of these issues is regarded as lacking a regular and dependable market. The quotations published by dealers in this manner are not intended as bids or offers which others can accept at their pleasure. These are *nominal* quotations, to show what the dealer is doing or expects to do. To get a *firm* bid or asked quotation, which is legally binding on the dealer, it is necessary to ask him expressly for a firm quotation on the desired quantity of the security.

Table 18. Sample Quotations from a Dealer's Inside Market Compared with Newspaper Over-the-counter Quotations, June 24, 1954

Issue	Dealer		Newspapers	
	Bid	Ask	Bid	Ask
Commonwealth Edison 3s of 1984........	99⅞	100¼		
Detroit Edison 2⅞s of 1984.............	97⅜	97¾		
Northern Natural Gas 3¼s of 1973......	102¼	102¾		
Southern Counties Gas 3¼s of 1984......	100¾	101¼		
Allied Chemical & Dye 3½s of 1978.....	104½	105		
Pacific Finance 4s of 1959..............	104	104½		
Sinclair Oil 3¼s of 1983...............	106½	107¼		
General Telephone 4.75% Pfd..........	84¾	85½		
Kaiser Steel $1.46 Pfd..................	20⅞	21¼	20⅞	22¼
San Diego Gas & Electric 4.50% Pfd.....	21	21½	21	22⅝
Texas Eastern Transmission 4.75% Pfd...	106	106¾	106	107
American Express Common.............	21⅝	21⅞	21⅝	22⅝
Bullock's Common....................	27	27½	27	29
Cleveland-Cliffs Iron Common..........	19¾	20⅛	19⅞	21⅛
Mohawk Petroleum Common...........	21	22	21	23
Bank of America.....................	35¾	36⅛	35¾	37¼
Chase National Bank..................	45⅞	46¼	45⅞	47⅝
Security-First National Bank...........	51¾	52¾	51¼	53¼
American Insurance Company..........	30	30⅜	29¾	31
Home Insurance Company.............	44½	44⅞	44½	46½
Phoenix Insurance Company...........	114	115½	114	118

Investors familiar with newspaper quotations on unlisted securities know that the spreads between the bid and asked prices as published are much greater than those quoted by dealers. Table 18 illustrates this situation. The reason is that the newspaper quotations purport to be customers' net prices—*i.e.*, what the customer would actually receive or pay, including commissions—whereas the dealers quote only their own wholesale buying and selling prices. The newspaper prices are on the whole not very realistic, being based on tradition rather than fact. Usually the published bid prices are just a little below the dealers' bids, but the published asked prices are often well above the dealers' asked prices plus a broker's commission.

Investing in Unlisted Securities

For the investor who buys securities for income or long-term gain the facilities of the unlisted market are as satisfactory as those of the listed market, if he finds securities appropriate to his needs. The dealer's spread on the inside market is not usually great enough to do any harm, brokerage commissions are about the same as on the listed markets, price ranges are about the same, and values appear to be established at about the same level. Purchases and sales are made on a dealers' stabilized market and can be negotiated to a definite figure, and there are no odd-lot differentials for small investors to pay. For short-term traders the unlisted market is slightly less advantageous; the lack of hour-by-hour irregularity limits the chances for adventitious bargains, and the dealer's spread cuts down the chances for quick profits on small changes in market prices.

Investors buying or selling anything other than the most active over-the-counter securities can often save a little money when dealing through a broker by asking that broker to "shop around" among competing unlisted dealers. The dealers are often a fraction of a point apart in their bid or asked prices, and the broker who is willing to make the effort can find the best price.

Brokers and dealers who transmit their customers' buying and selling orders to other dealers who make a market in the security are now tending to handle the transactions as agents of their customers. In such cases the customer pays or receives the inside market and is charged a standard brokerage commission by his own broker or dealer. However, some brokers or dealers sell to or buy from their customers as principals and then make a profit instead of a commission by immediately selling to or buying from a regular dealer at a different price. This is perfectly legitimate, provided the risk-free profit taken by the broker does not exceed 5 per cent. The profit may be voluntarily limited to or be less than a standard commission (*i.e.*, from 2 to .5 per cent on stocks) if the broker chooses. Despite the good intentions of brokers, it would seem to be wiser on the customer's part to ask his broker or dealer to function as an agent rather than as a principal in such cases. This is the customer's privilege.

QUESTIONS AND PROBLEMS

1. Define (a) investment banking, (b) dealing, (c) brokerage, (d) underwriting, (e) private placement.

2. Under what conditions do you believe a rights offering should be underwritten? When is this not necessary?

3. Would a selling group be formed to distribute 250,000 shares of a utility company's common stock which an underwriting group was purchasing from a holding company? Why?

4. Do you think that price stabilization should be forbidden by law? Why or why not?

5. Would it be desirable or feasible to forbid private placement by law?

6. How much would the Consolidated Edison Company of New York have to allow as commissions if it sold a $25,000,000 bond issue to underwriters? What would the cost be on a preferred stock issue? What determines these rates? Do these represent the entire cost of obtaining needed funds?

7. Would you be willing to invest in a new bond or stock issue just being marketed by an underwriting group? Why or why not? Where could you get adequate information about the quality of a new issue?

8. As an investor, would you feel assured of better value in buying an issue which the underwriters had obtained by competitive bidding, or would you prefer one on which the price was negotiated?

9. Do you think that the blue-sky laws and the Federal Securities Act of 1933 are properly designed to protect the investor? Should they require that every security be labeled A, B, C, etc., or in some other manner to identify its quality? Should the price of new offerings be subject to veto by a regulatory authority?

10. Would you trust a securities salesman who recommended sale of a stock which you held and purchase of another now being offered by his firm? Would a good salesman ever make such a proposal?

11. Would the same securities be sold on both listed and over-the-counter markets? What kinds of securities are chiefly traded over the counter? Why?

12. Does the dealer's "spread" constitute a price disadvantage to the investor who considers unlisted stocks? Why?

13. How does a broker who wishes to sell a bank stock for a client find a buyer?

14. Why can the over-the-counter market absorb an offer to sell 100

Union Pacific bonds when there might be danger that such an offering would depress the stock exchange price?

15. If you were a stockholder in the Continental Insurance Company, would you want the company to withdraw its stock from the New York Stock Exchange and depend upon the unlisted market exclusively?

16. Is it likely that the actively traded insurance stocks (see Tables 17 and 18) would sell any higher, on the average, if they were on the stock exchanges? Would the less actively traded ones (for example, the Phoenix Insurance Company) have as good markets as they now have?

17. Why is the "spread" on the Mohawk Petroleum common so much greater than that on the Cleveland-Cliffs Iron common (see Table 18)?

18. Look up the over-the-counter quotations in your daily newspaper. Are these accurate representations of the market? Are they firm bids and offers?

19. If a client asked a broker about Chase Manhattan Bank stock, which the broker knew was quoted by dealers at $43\frac{3}{4}$ bid, 44 asked, and if the broker owned no stock, would it be legitimate for the broker to say "I'll sell it to you at 45"? Is this ever done?

REFERENCES

Badger, Ralph E., and Harry G. Guthmann: *Investment Principles and Practices,* Prentice-Hall, Inc., New York, 1951, Chap. 23.

Bellemore, Douglas H.: *Investments Principles and Practices,* B. C. Forbes and Sons Publishing Co., Inc., New York, 1953, Chap. 8.

Dowrie, George W., and Douglas R. Fuller: *Investments,* John Wiley & Sons, Inc., New York, 1950, Chap. 4.

Financial Handbook, The Ronald Press Company, New York, 1948, pp. 3–62, 114–118.

Investment Bankers Association of America: *Fundamentals of Investment Banking,* Prentice-Hall, Inc., New York, 1949, Chaps. 16–18, 20.

Jordan, David F., and Herbert E. Dougall: *Investments,* Prentice-Hall, Inc., New York, 1952, Chap. 14.

Leffler, George L.: *The Stock Market,* The Ronald Press Company, New York, 1951, Chap. 29.

Loeser, John C.: *The Over-the-counter Securities Market,* National Quotation Bureau Incorporated, New York, 1940.

Robbins, Sidney M.: *Managing Securities,* Houghton Mifflin Company, Boston, 1954, Chap. 2.

Shultz, Birl E.: *The Securities Market and How It Works,* Harper & Brothers, New York, 1946, Chap. 5.

Chapter 9: BROKERAGE AND
THE STOCK EXCHANGES

Practically every firm engaged in the securities business does some brokerage. Some firms do nothing else. A broker's business consists of searching out buyers when his customer wishes to sell and sellers when his customer wishes to buy and arranging transactions in accordance with his customer's instructions. Usually those transactions are arranged with other brokers representing their customers. The brokers do not function as principals in these transactions; they are agents only. A broker charges a commission on each purchase and each sale which he executes, but he ordinarily gets nothing unless he can complete a transaction.

In order to fulfill his function and earn commissions, a broker must develop his business along three lines: First, he must provide an office with adequate financial information sources, current quotation facilities, and salesmen-advisers, to enable investors to make the decisions upon which he acts. Second, he must know where to find the best unlisted markets for his customers and how to obtain new securities currently being offered by underwriters and distributors. Third, he must arrange memberships in or contacts with the principal stock exchanges of the country, for a very large percentage of all securities buying and selling is done on the stock exchanges. He must also offer his customers incidental services in the financing of their transactions and in the storage of their securities. Brokers need not be investment bankers, over-the-counter dealers, or even stock exchange members, but they find great advantage in being stock exchange members, and their close contact with investment bankers and dealers encourages them to participate in these functions also.

Nature of a Stock Exchange

A stock exchange is an association of brokers formed to provide improved facilities for the execution of customers' orders. The main function of an exchange is to operate a trading room to which all of the brokers may bring their orders in a given list of securities. With a large number of customers' buying and selling orders thus brought together, it is expected that many transactions can be completed. The customers will get good service and the brokers will earn commissions.

Stock exchanges conduct trading in both bonds and stocks. However, only the New York Stock Exchange and the American Stock Exchange (formerly known as the New York Curb Exchange) have any significant amount of business in bonds, and all exchanges do most of their business in stocks. In order not to clutter their facilities with futile attempts to do business in inactive stocks, the exchanges limit their operations to a stated list of securities in which their members hope to have a reasonable number of orders.

Each brokerage house which belongs to an exchange has the privilege of placing a trader and assisting clerks on the trading floor and operating a private telephone line from the floor to the brokerage office. All the business on the trading floor is done by the brokers, as the exchange is a facilitating agency only. The expenses of the exchange are defrayed by monthly dues paid by the member brokers, plus minor sums collected as fees for services done for the brokers and the corporations whose stocks are listed on the exchange.

A stock exchange is a private association with a closed membership. In order to obtain a membership a brokerage firm usually must buy one from a member who is willing to sell. A membership on a successful stock exchange is an expensive asset. In 1954 a New York Stock Exchange membership cost about $60,000, an American Stock Exchange membership about $10,000, and the regional exchange memberships varying but mostly lesser amounts. When a membership has been arranged for, the prospective member must next apply for admission. If the governing board of the exchange finds the applicant's financial stability and business reputation acceptable, he will be admitted to full privileges. Successful brokers often have memberships on many stock exchanges and branch offices scattered throughout the country.

Stock exchanges generally have visitors' galleries from which visitors are permitted to watch activities on the trading floor. However, no business may be transacted from such galleries, nor does any exchange accept trading orders from anyone. Orders must be placed with brokers at their brokerage offices for transmission to the exchange floor.

Every stock exchange has extensive rules governing the business practices of its members and the methods of trading on its floor. Many of these rules are intended for the protection of the public, while others are chiefly valuable to protect and develop the exchange and its members. The floor trading rules are highly technical, but in general they provide for a well-organized routine in which all orders are handled equitably. Brokers are permitted to trade on the floor for their own accounts as well as for customers, but their "professional" trading is limited to keep it from dominating the market. Brokerage practices and stock exchange operations are subject to the supervision of the Federal Securities and Exchange Commission, under the terms of the Securities Exchange Act of 1934.

The American Stock Exchanges

The New York Stock Exchange and the American Stock Exchange are national in their scope. They conduct trading in securities which are nationwide in ownership, their broker members have offices from coast to coast, and their members also execute orders forwarded to them by banks and nonmember brokers everywhere. Most of the New York Stock Exchange members are also members or associate members of the American Stock Exchange. The securities traded on these two exchanges are all different; no stock or bond is traded on both. The New York Stock Exchange usually has the securities of the larger, older, and stronger corporations, and the American has the others. However, there are conspicuous exceptions; the big board (New York Stock Exchange) has some very poor issues, while the American has such solid successes as Carnation Company, Duke Power Company, Pepperell Manufacturing Company, and Singer Manufacturing Company, to name but four.

The other stock exchanges are properly called *regional* exchanges, for their principal service is to provide trading markets for local brokers and investors. The most important of these exchanges are located in Boston, Chicago, Los Angeles, Philadelphia, and San Francisco. The regional stock exchanges not only provide markets for local stocks but also trade in the stocks of nationally owned corporations which originated in their regions or are closely affiliated with them, even when such stocks are traded in New York. In addition, they often trade in the stocks of national corporations which have enough local stockholders to enable the local exchange to maintain a market. The members of the regional exchanges are mostly local brokers with local offices and customers, but every regional exchange has members who also hold memberships in the New York and other exchanges.

The rapid growth of the Canadian economy since 1945 has attracted the interest of investors in the United States as well as Canada. This growth has induced important outlays in Canadian branches by corporations originating in the United States, but it has also brought about extensive purchases of Canadian securities both by Canadians and by citizens residing south of the border. With the growth of Canadian securities has come a corresponding growth in Canadian over-the-counter and stock exchange markets. The Toronto Stock Exchange, the Montreal Stock Exchange, and the Canadian Stock Exchange (also in Montreal) are now important regional exchanges.

Listed Stocks and Bonds

A stock exchange must have an understanding with the corporate issuer of each stock or bond in which it trades, regarding such matters as the transfer of securities, the timely announcing of dividends and rights, and the publication of data about the corporation's affairs. These and other matters are often covered in a *listing* contract between the corporation and the exchange. The leading exchanges try to impose good corporate practices—for example, the use of registrars for stock certificates and the publication of audited financial statements—as conditions precedent to listing. The New York Stock Exchange even goes so far as to refuse to list nonvoting common stocks and preferred stocks without adequate contingent voting power, as a gesture of disapproval.

The American Stock Exchange and the regional stock exchanges have formal listing contracts with many corporations, but a considerable number of their "listings" are traded without benefit of a contract. In these instances the corporation usually consents to the trading procedure, cooperates in furnishing information and handling transfers, but does not sign any formal agreement. The securities traded without listing contracts are said to be "traded unlisted," but the trading is handled in exactly the usual manner, and most people do not know or need to know the difference.

Stock exchange trading methods are not usually satisfactory even on a regional market in issues having less than 300 to 500 stock-

Table 19. Securities Traded and Number of Members, Leading American Stock Exchanges

Exchange	Value of securities transactions, year ended Dec. 31, 1952, millions of dollars		Number of issues traded, 6/30/53	Number of members, 6/30/54
	Stocks	Bonds		
American..................	1,274	20	889	808 *
Boston....................	192	†	428	111
Los Angeles...............	181	†	353	58
Midwest...................	462	†	516	400
New York.................	14,720	769	2,491	1,366
Philadelphia-Baltimore......	165	†	569	201 *
San Francisco.............	200	1	413	64
All registered exchanges.....	17,328	791	4,042	
All exempted exchanges.....	7	†	115	

* Includes associate or special members having limited privileges.
† Less than $50,000.
Source: Data from the 1953 *Annual Report* of the SEC and from the exchanges.

holders, for a good listed market requires enough interested people to maintain a constant flow of bids and offers to the trading floor. If there are enough holders, however, the stock exchange market is usually preferred by both investors and corporations. The publicity given to stock exchange markets widens interest in the stock, the prestige of the market enhances its collateral value, and the supervision of exchanges and regulatory agencies compels good corporate and trading practices.

The Securities Exchange Act of 1934 undertakes to enforce sound conditions relating to annual audits, publication of financial reports and other data, proxy systems, "insider" trading in securities, and similar topics as conditions precedent to listing or trading on the exchanges.[1] The SEC makes rules to implement the statute and must approve the addition or dropping of any security by any of the exchanges. Though there have been conflicts, the exchanges have generally welcomed government enforcement of sound corporate practices. The smaller exchanges had been unable to compel corporations to adhere uniformly to good rules prior to passage of the act, for the only sanction available to an exchange was suspension of trading in the security, and this often hurt the exchange members more than it did the corporation.

Since 1929 many of the regional exchanges have found it difficult to obtain enough total business to maintain their facilities. Several reasons help to explain this. First, the amount of speculative trading has declined, and the decline has been especially marked in the securities of local corporations. Second, many of the larger local corporations found that the trading boom of 1927–1929 caused their stocks to scatter widely over the country. They therefore obtained listing or unlisted trading markets in New York, and local trading in their stocks diminished. Third, the over-the-counter markets have been greatly improved, so that they now offer many moderate-sized issues closer and steadier markets than the exchanges can provide.

The SEC wishes to maintain the effectiveness of the regional exchanges and has endeavored to do so by encouraging them to expand unlisted trading in nationally owned stocks which have large numbers of stockholders in their regional areas. As a result, leading stocks are traded on many exchanges; in early 1954 General Motors was on 10, General Electric on 8, Radio Corporation of America on 8, and American Telephone on 10. The purpose of sustaining the regional exchanges as useful local markets is a sound one, for their services are needed to widen public interest in the securities of growing local concerns and to develop the marketability of such concerns' stocks. The regional exchanges also serve as economical local markets for nationally known securities, especially in small quantities (odd lots). Although it might be argued that the efficiency and stability of the market in a nationally known security would be improved by collecting all the bids and offers on it in one market place, it must be remembered that many of the bids and offers appearing

[1] The Securities Exchange Act and other measures for the protection of investors are reviewed in Chap. 12.

216   INTRODUCTION TO INVESTMENTS

on the local exchanges exist because local brokers have encouraged their customers' interest in the stocks. Local trading therefore cannot be said to consist exclusively of business diverted from a central market place. Arbitrage transactions, through which profit-seeking brokers buy on one exchange and sell on another, keep the prices on different exchange markets virtually uniform and have the effect of synthesizing the bids and offers on all markets into a single resultant price.

Several of the regional exchanges have considered mergers as a means of improving their trading markets. Some members believe that mergers may improve the quality of the markets by (1) combining the bids and offers on stocks traded on both the merging exchanges, and (2) widening brokerage and investor interest in strictly local stocks by introducing them into other cities. Improvement and broadening of the markets for the listed stocks would of course improve their collateral value. Combined facilities might also reduce expenses and produce more commission earnings. The Philadelphia and Baltimore stock exchanges were merged in March, 1949, and the Chicago, Cleveland, St. Louis, and Minneapolis-St. Paul exchanges were combined into the present Midwest Stock Exchange on September 15, 1949.

Floor Trading

The "post trading" system now used by most stock exchanges is a continuous auction arrangement under which any security may be traded at any time while the exchange is open. Basically, the plan provides for the assignment of the securities to a number of different posts or areas on the trading floor. When any trader has an order to buy or sell a security, he goes to the assigned area, calls out his bid or offer, and hopes for an acceptance from another broker who has a corresponding order to sell or buy. When a number of brokers are interested in the same security, each will be desirous of buying at a low price or selling at a high price for his customer. Competitive raising of bids and lowering of asking prices should then produce transactions at prices representing truly free markets. All bidding, offering, and accepting is done verbally. When a transaction is completed, the traders enter each others' names on the "buy" and "sell" tickets, turn these over to their clerks for bookkeeping purposes, and send reports to their offices by telephone. Stock exchange pages who watch the post report the number of shares and the price to the ticker operator, so the transaction can be reported immediately in brokerage offices everywhere via the ticker tape.

The stock exchanges adhere to the general practice of quoting stocks in dollars and eighths per share and bonds in percentages and eighths of par value. No splitting of eighths is permissible, with two exceptions. United States government bonds are quoted in percentages and thirty-seconds, since that is the accustomed practice elsewhere, and very low-priced stocks are allowed smaller trading intervals than eighths of a dollar. On low-priced stocks the New York Stock Exchange trades in dollars and small fractions such as sixteenths and thirty-seconds; some of the regional exchanges turn to dollars and cents quotations, using 5-cent and 1-cent intervals.

To avoid confusion in floor transactions, the exchanges require that regular trading be done only in standard quantities, termed *board lots* or *round lots*. The board lot in stocks is usually 100 shares, though 50-share, 25-share, and 10-share board lots are established when investigation shows that those units would accommodate buyers and sellers to best advantage. The standard bond unit is one $1,000 bond. Floor transactions may be made in multiples of board lots, and it is a bidder's or seller's privilege to offer a trade in several board lots as a unit, "all or none"; but small numbers of shares, *odd lots,* are handled by a separate process through an odd-lot dealer.

Since it would be impossible for a member firm to keep a trader at each of the posts at all times, two facilitating services are made available to traders who need assistance on the floor. One is that of the so-called *two-dollar broker*. A two-dollar broker is a stock exchange member who does not have a brokerage office but, instead, makes a business of executing buy or sell orders handed to him by others. For this he receives a share of the commission. The other service is that of the *specialist*. A specialist is a member who stays continuously at one trading post, handles other brokers' orders in one or more stocks on the same basis as a two-dollar broker, and occasionally buys or sells for his own account also. Because a specialist is always at his post the traders usually hand him all their orders to buy or sell at prices remote from the ruling market price, as well as a substantial amount of ordinary business. He usually has a considerable number of orders in his possession and is likely to figure in a large percentage of the transactions at his post. When transactions take place, the specialist gives priority to the highest bids and the lowest offers. Orders at the same price rank in sequence of arrival. A specialist can often judge the strength of the market in his stock by the number of buying and selling orders accumulated in his "book." This is top-secret information. The specialist can and will disclose the highest bid and the lowest offer in his possession and may indicate the number of shares bid for or offered at those prices, but that is all he can say. Detailed rules prevent him from profiting from this inside information by trading excessively for his own account, but he is expected to buy or sell for his own account in order to prevent needless erratic fluctuations in market prices.

Delivery and Settlement

Transactions in stocks and bonds require a clear understanding of the time for transfer and payment. Stock exchange rules are rather elaborate on these points, but it suffices here to say that transactions are made on three bases: (1) *cash,* requiring settlement on the day of the contract; (2) *regular way,* requiring settlement on the third full business day thereafter; and (3) *seller's option,* requiring settlement within 60 days but as specified in the contract. Over-the-counter transactions involve similar understandings. The primary obligations to meet delivery and payment dates rest upon the brokers or dealers involved, but their customers must of necessity fulfill their commitments on time.

The most critical problems concerned with delivery of securities involve transfers of stock or bonds before the record dates for distribution of dividends, interest, rights or other privileges. When it appears that delivery of a stock can be had in time for a transfer before a forthcoming dividend, the stock is said to sell *with dividend* at a price which both buyer and seller regard as inclusive of stock and dividend. On a date believed too late to permit a purchaser to get the dividend, the stock sells *ex-dividend,* usually at a lower price which reflects the fact that the dividend is not being transferred. Stock exchanges are accustomed to set the dates on which stocks will be quoted ex-dividend, ex-rights, or ex-distribution.

Rights, Warrants, When-issued Contracts

Both stock exchanges and over-the-counter markets have occasion to trade in these instruments. Rights, as has been noted in previous chapters, are short-term privileges for the purchase of securities. Warrants are more difficult to define, for the term is used in the securities business in two ways: in a technical sense, a warrant is a piece of paper which evidences the ownership of rights, fractional shares of stock, or some other claim or privilege which does not quite attain the stature of a security. However, the term warrant is also used to mean a long-term right, usually one whose purchase privilege is valid for several years; it is this meaning which is implied when the securities markets report transactions in Tri-Continental Corporation warrants, for example. When-issued contracts are agreements for the future delivery, at the price named in the contract, of pending rights or securities which have been authorized but are not yet issued. Securities traded on a when-issued basis include those to be issued in connection with mergers, recapitalizations, reorganizations, and liquidations, and newly marketed ones which have not been physically delivered.

Because of their short lifetime, rights are often sold or bought on a when-issued basis before the certificates (warrants) evidencing them are mailed out by the company. A seller on this basis simply contracts to deliver his expected rights when he receives them. His broker may require him to make a cash or securities "margin" deposit to guarantee that he will actually provide the rights, since the broker obligates himself to deliver them to the purchaser's broker. Similarly, the purchaser of the rights makes a margin deposit with his broker. When the rights become available all when-issued contracts are settled by payment and delivery, and subsequent transactions in rights are made regular way or on a cash basis.

Long-term warrants offer no technical problem, for they can be sold and delivered as easily as any stock or bond.

Trading in when-issued securities is quite common over the counter, but technicalities interposed by the Securities Exchange Act and the SEC make it difficult to qualify them for stock exchange trading. When-issued contracts of all types are invalidated if the right or security is not issued substantially as expected. This factor, coupled with the margins required and the uncertainty of the time element in reorganizations, frequently results in when-issued contract prices which are inconsistent with the prices of other securities. For example, the old Denver & Rio Grande 4s of 1936 sold at 62½ ($625) on November 13, 1946, while the when-issued prices of securities shortly to be issued in exchange for them totaled $670.

Brokerage Orders

Brokers receive a number of different types of buying and selling orders from their customers, for execution either on the exchanges or the over-the-counter market. Brokerage orders vary as to the price at which the order may be filled, as to the time for which the order is valid, and as to contingencies which affect the order. In addition, the customer may further specify how his order is to be handled— for example, he may instruct the broker to function as an agent only, not as a principal, if the transaction is over the counter; or he may designate the exchange to which the order is to be sent, if the security is traded on several. The customer's desires are followed explicitly.

Market orders are instructions to a broker to buy or sell, as the case may be, at the best reasonable price obtainable. The broker will regard a market order as evidence that the customer wishes a transaction completed within a few hours at most and is leaving the price to the broker's discretion in order to be sure that the deal can be made. The broker should not abuse his discretion by paying too much or selling for too little, if the market is abnormal, but the emphasis is on completing the deal, not on bargaining for price. Market orders are commonly used by investors when trading in active stocks or when a desire to buy or sell is urgent; but they can be damaging in "thin" markets, in which a temporary absence of either bids or offers could result in a market order being executed at an extreme price.

Limit orders are instructions to a broker to buy or sell at a stated price "or better." If a customer instructs his broker to buy General Motors at 84 or better, the broker will buy at a lower price if one is immediately available, but he will bid up to 84 if necessary, since the customer specifically authorized that figure. If the order is to sell General Electric at 39, the broker will try for more, but if he does not get it he will offer on down to 39 in search of a buyer. If the limit makes an immediate trade impossible (*i.e.,* a limited bid is too low or a limited offer is too high), the broker will leave the order with the specialist (or dealer if the market is over the counter) with instructions to execute it if the opportunity occurs. A limit order protects the customer against paying more or selling for less than he intended, but it may cause disappointment if it results in a desired purchase or sale being "missed" by a trifling margin.

Open or *G T C* orders are orders which are "good till canceled" by the customer. Limit orders to buy at a low price or sell at a high one may be left indefinitely on this basis; the author saw a specialist on the Los Angeles Stock Exchange fill an open buy order in 1930 which had been handed to him in 1927. Most stock exchanges require that brokers send customers a monthly memorandum of outstanding open orders, and most of them automatically reduce the limit on an open bid by the amount of the dividend, each time the stock sells ex-dividend. Instead of an open order, the customer may give his broker a "day" order, only valid for one day, or a "fill or kill" order which is to be tried immediately and either filled or canceled. Needless to say, these time specifications are most important when they are in conjunction with orders which are limited as to price.

Stop-loss orders are orders which are not effective until another transaction takes place at an indicated price. The stop-loss order then becomes a market order. For example, a stockholder who held Standard Oil of Indiana when the market price was 45 might hope to get 50 for it, but might also want to sell out quickly if the market started down. He could place a stop-loss selling order at 41. This would instruct his broker to sell the stock at market if ever a regular trade took place at 41 or less. If the desired sale at 50 could be made, the customer would cancel his stop-loss order. Stop-loss orders are also used on the buy side of the market. A customer might wish to buy Union Oil because he anticipated a major rise in its price. If the current price was 48, he might still hope to buy at 46 or 47 within a few days; but to guard against being left out on the rise, he might enter a stop-loss buy order at 51. If a regular transaction took place at 51 or higher his stop-loss buying order would become a market order and would soon be filled at 51 or at the lowest price his broker could obtain.

Stop-loss orders are useful to both speculators and investors. Stop-loss selling orders can be used (1) to sell out holdings automatically in case a market drop deemed large enough to indicate the beginning of a major decline takes place; (2) to sell short if the ominous market drop occurs; or (3) if placed close to the market, to assure ultimate sale of stock which is now offered on open sell order just above the market. Stop-loss buying orders can be used (1) to limit possible losses on a short position; (2) to buy if a market rise seems to indicate a major upswing; or (3) if placed close to the market, to assure purchase of a stock which is being sought on an open bid just below the market. It will be noted that item 3 in each case requires entering two selling orders or buying orders when only one transaction is desired. However, the chance of two executions is fairly remote, for each order can be made subject to an automatic cancellation if the other is filled.

Stop-loss orders can sometimes be assured of execution at their effective price by a process known as "stopping stock." If, for example, a stock exchange specialist has several bids for Standard Oil of Indiana at 41 when the market is 45, he may be willing to earmark one of his bids to cover a stop-loss selling order at 41. He can then assure the broker placing the stop-loss order that, unless the bidders withdraw their bids and in the absence of market orders (which take precedence), the stop-loss sale at 41 is guaranteed as soon as the first regular sale takes place at that price. By a similar process an above-market selling offer may be earmarked to cover a stop-loss buying order.

Odd Lots

Thousands of stockholders own listed stock in quantities smaller than the standard board lots, and about 25 per cent of the buying and selling done on stock exchanges is in these so-called *odd lots*. Because the odd lots appear in definitely odd quantities—8 shares, 10 shares, or 15, 20, 25, 35, whatever the customer wants or has—it would be almost impossible to match buying and selling orders in them. Also, the confusion arising from verbal trading in odd lots would lead to errors. The problem has been solved by permitting designated members of the stock exchanges to operate as dealers in odd lots. These odd-lot dealers agree to buy odd lots which other members have for sale and to sell odd lots which other members need to buy. If the dealer buys more than he sells or sells more than he buys, he can clear his position by engaging in board-lot transactions.

Stock exchange member brokers who receive odd-lot orders in listed stocks usually hand them immediately to an odd-lot dealer in the stocks. Each time a board-lot transaction takes place, the odd-lot dealer in that stock is obligated to buy all odd-lot offerings in his book, which are offered below the board-lot price, at a transaction price exactly one-eighth below the board-lot price.[2] Simultaneously, he must fill all odd-lot buying orders willing to pay more than the board-lot price, at one-eighth above the board-lot price. For example, when a board lot in Columbia Gas System stock sells at 14, all odd-lot bids at market or at 14⅛ or higher are filled at 14⅛, and all odd-lot offers at market or 13⅞ or lower are bought at 13⅞. The odd-lot dealer's privilege of buying below the market and selling above it affords him a margin for expenses and profit. This *differential* between the board-lot price and the odd-lot dealer's price is raised to one-fourth on stocks which sell at 40 or above, and to 50 cents or $1 in a few instances where stocks are inactive or very high in price.

Investors who trade in odd lots should understand that neither a buying nor a selling order at "14 or better" would be filled when a board lot sold at 14. The odd-lot dealer will buy at 14 only when a board lot sells at 14⅛, and he will sell at 14 only after a board-lot sale at 13⅞. The price limit set by an odd-lot customer in his order is the price limit at which his transaction may take place, not that at which the basic board-lot transaction takes place.

The foregoing description indicates that odd-lot purchasers pay more for their shares than board-lot purchasers do and sell them for less. However, the differential is not large enough to be significant except on very cheap stocks, and few people need to resort to odd-lot transactions in them.

A relatively new variant of the odd-lot service provided for small investors is the so-called Monthly Investment Plan (or some other such label) which is intended to permit the frequent investment of small stated sums in shares and fractions of shares of a single stock.

[2] Under certain unusual technical conditions a limit order to buy or sell might be filled at its limit price instead of at a price one-eighth point removed from the board-lot price.

The transactions are handled by stock exchange member brokers in the usual course of their business. The plans vary a little on the different exchanges, but typically each monthly or quarterly investment of $40 or more is charged a 6 per cent brokerage fee, after which the balance is applied to buy shares and fractions of shares from the odd-lot dealer at the next odd-lot transaction price. Dividends are credited to the buyer's account, and when the arrangement is finally terminated any existing fraction of a share is cleared by purchase or sale of a fraction, and the buyer obtains his accumulated purchases in whole shares.

Over-the-counter stocks, some of the inactive stocks on regional exchanges, and bonds are not on an odd-lot basis. Over-the-counter dealers usually trade in shares or bonds at the same price regardless of quantity taken or at an individual negotiated price in each case. Odd lots of inactive stocks on regional exchanges and the $500 and $100 bonds which appear on the New York exchanges are simply offered and bid for in the quantities which appear. Brokers who buy and sell for their own accounts frequently trade in these issues. There is no assurance that odd lots in such securities will have a market price closely related to the board-lot prices.

Short Sales

One who sells short sells something he does not own in the hope of buying later at a lower price and delivering the later purchase against his short sale. Obviously, it would be profitable to sell a stock short at 50 and obtain the stock to deliver to the buyer by a later purchase at 40.

The fact that securities sales customarily require delivery within a few days introduces a slight mechanical complication for one who sells short. In order to deliver on the short sale, the seller must have his broker *borrow* stock for the purpose. The broker will either provide the stock from his own portfolio or get it on loan from another broker. In either instance, the borrowing customer must (1) provide cash equal in value to the stock, to be delivered to the lender as "collateral" for the loan of the stock; [3] (2) make good to the lender the value of any lost dividends or rights or other disbursements; and

---

[3] The cash proceeds of the short sale may be used for this purpose, but in this case the short seller must deposit adequate margin in cash or other securities, to assure his broker against loss and to meet SEC margin requirements.

(3) pay any daily rental or "premium" which may be agreed on if the borrowed stock is scarce. Most stocks usually loan "flat"—that is, the use of the money collateral is regarded as a fair rental for the stock—but a premium of $1 or $2 per day per 100 shares is not uncommon on some issues. On infrequent occasions when stock is plentiful but money is scarce, the lender of the stock may pay a small interest rate on the money collateral in addition to lending the stock without premium.

In order to prevent undue pressure on weak markets, the SEC has issued an order forbidding short sales in board lots in listed securities except at a price at least as high as the preceding sale and higher than the last (preceding the proposed short sale) regular-way sale which brought a price different from the proposed short-sale price. Some of the exchanges also require short sales in odd lots to be based on board-lot transactions which conform to these rules. Every selling order which is sent to the floor of a stock exchange must be identified as "long" or "short," so that proper trading procedure may be followed. Subject to the rules, orders to sell short may be market orders or limit orders, they may be open orders or time limit orders.

Before the rule forbidding short sales on declining markets it was conceded that speculative short selling sometimes drove securities prices down to unreasonably low levels with disastrous speed. However, it was also argued that speculative short selling in normal markets would prevent bullish enthusiasm from driving prices up too high and that in any case "short covering" (the purchase of stock by short sellers to close out their positions) would support prices at reasonable levels. At the moment, questions regarding the merits and demerits of unrestrained short selling would seem to be moot, but it is still significant to note that issues in which a large short interest is outstanding have potential market strength, for the short sellers must cover eventually. The total of member and customer short positions outstanding in offices of New York Stock Exchange firms is published monthly, for each listed stock.

Margin Trading

For many years it has been customary for brokers and dealers to handle either purchases or short sales for their customers on *margin*. In a margin transaction the customer does not provide enough money to finance his deal completely; he provides enough to absorb any probable loss, and the broker lends him the balance. On a margin purchase of 100 shares of stock at 80, the customer might provide 60 per cent margin, or $4,800, and the broker would finance the remaining $3,200, holding the stock as collateral. The chief purpose of the arrangement would be to enable the customer to acquire and hold $8,000 worth of stock on an investment of only $4,800. This introduces a leverage factor which cumulates the customer's profits if the stock rises and his losses if it falls.

It is obvious that a severe shrinkage in the value of the stocks held in a margin account would compel the broker to ask his customer for more margin and that if the customer failed to produce the margin the stocks would have to be sold. To guard against such forced sales the stock exchanges have made rules requiring their members to obtain reasonably substantial margin deposits from their customers. The Securities Exchange Act of 1934 gives the Board of Governors of the Federal Reserve System the power to set minimum margin requirements on listed securities.[4] Since 1934 the initial margin required by the Board has varied from 40 to 100 per cent. In 1954 it was 50 per cent on either a purchase or a short sale. The initial margin must be present after each additional transaction, but the Board rules do not require that it be maintained by additional deposit if the stock declines in price. Brokerage houses will generally insist that additional margin be deposited if the customer's equity falls below 40 per cent of the value of the securities carried.

Brokers charge their customers interest on the debit balances in their accounts. The rate is usually 2 to 3 per cent above the low call loan rate which the brokers themselves pay. A customer who buys on margin is required to authorize the use of his securities as collateral for the broker's borrowings from banks. Dividends and interest on such securities are credited to the customer's account.

In order to prevent evasion of margin requirements through the use of bank loans, the Board of Governors limits the bank loan value of a security to the same amount a broker could advance on it, if the purpose of the loan is to purchase or carry listed securities. Bank loans in lieu of margin accounts are not very satisfactory, unless the

___

[4] Except for public bonds, unlisted securities may not be included in margin accounts.

loan is to be liquidated from income or other funds. Bank loans, unlike brokers' advances, usually have definite maturity dates; sale of the securities and acquisition of others is less convenient; and banks usually demand evidence of capacity to repay by some means other than sale of the collateral.

Margin transactions were a very important part of the securities business in the robust markets of 1928–1929. They were of substantial importance also in 1935–1937. However, they have not been important since the war, for until 1949 the margin requirements were held at 75 per cent or higher and the leverage available on 75 per cent margin is not great enough to elicit much interest. If the Board of Governors should conclude that corporate financing needs the added market buying power which 50 per cent margins make possible, it seems very likely that speculators will in time again avail themselves of the privilege. Brokers generally welcome good margin accounts, though they do not encourage them if the customer's equity is under $1,000 or if excessively speculative stocks are carried.

Commissions and Taxes

The stock exchanges customarily adopt schedules of minimum commission rates to which their members are obliged to conform on stock exchange transactions. In practice, the prescribed minimum is usually the actual amount charged. Each exchange has its own minimum commission schedule, but the variations between them are not usually great. Brokers may charge any reasonable commission rate for their services on over-the-counter transactions, but they usually follow a schedule similar to that adopted by one of the exchanges. When banks or nonmember investment houses originate brokerage orders which must be executed on an exchange, they sometimes charge the customer service fees of their own, in addition to the regular commissions which are paid to the broker. However, many nonmember brokers and dealers do not do this. Instead, they send their stock exchange business through a friendly member firm which will reciprocate by extending favors in its over-the-counter and new-issue business.

In 1954 the New York Stock Exchange schedule of minimum commissions was summarized as follows:

STOCKS, RIGHTS, AND WARRANTS SELLING AT $1.00 PER SHARE AND ABOVE

A. Round Lots

For a unit of trading, a combination of units of trading, or a combination of a unit or units of trading plus an odd lot, amounting to 100 shares or less:

Money Value	Commission
Under $100.00	As mutually agreed
$100.00 to $1,999.00	1% plus $5.00
$2,000.00 to $4,999.00	$\frac{1}{2}$% plus $15.00
$5,000.00 and above	$\frac{1}{10}$% plus $35.00

To compute the commission on multiples of 100 shares, multiply the 100-share rate by the number of hundreds involved.

B. Odd Lots (Less than the Unit of Trading)

Same rates as on round lots, less $2.00 on each transaction.

C. Special Cases

The round lot and odd-lot rates above are further modified as follows:

1. On transactions under $100 in amount, commission shall be any amount agreed upon between broker and customer.

2. On transactions over $100, commission shall not be less than $6, but except for this shall not exceed $1 per share. Commission on a single round lot or odd lot shall not exceed $50.

3. When a single security is purchased and sold within 30 days under certain conditions, the commission on the second transaction is 50% of the regular rate plus $2.50 on a round lot or $1.50 on an odd lot.

STOCKS, RIGHTS, AND WARRANTS SELLING BELOW $1.00

[A schedule somewhat different from the above is prescribed in these cases.]

BONDS

Commission per $1,000 Bond (Excepting Governmental, Short-term or Called Bonds)

	1 or 2 bonds	3 bonds	4 bonds	5 or more bonds
Selling at less than $10 (1%)	$1.50	$1.20	$0.90	$0.75
Selling at $10 (1%) and above but under $100 (10%)	2.50	2.00	1.50	1.25
Selling at $100 (10%) and above	5.00	4.00	3.00	2.50

In addition to the commission charges on transactions, buyers will encounter a postage and mailing charge, ranging from 20 cents to $1 on typical transactions, and a stock transfer tax on odd-lot purchases. Sellers will have to bear a postage and mailing charge and transfer taxes in all cases. The Federal transfer tax is levied on all transactions; state transfer taxes reach only transfers or sales made within the state. Only a few states have transfer taxes, but New York is among them. Tax rates in effect in 1954 were as follows:

STOCK TRANSFER TAX

Federal Tax

$0.05 per $100 of total par value, if selling under $20 per share.

$0.06 per $100 of total par value, selling above $20.

Note: For tax purposes no par stocks are considered to be $100 par.

New York State Tax

$0.01 per sh. selling under $5.

$0.02 per sh. selling at $5 but under $10.

$0.03 per sh. selling at $10 but under $20.

$0.04 per sh. selling at $20 and over.

Transfer tax, on other than by sale, $0.02 per sh.

BOND TRANSFER TAX

Federal Tax

$0.05 per $100 par value.

A Federal "registration fee" amounting to 2 cents per $1,000 of transaction value is also levied on sellers using the facilities of a national securities exchange.

These commission and tax rates are modest costs to an investor who operates a stable investment program. However, they are large enough to burden one who trades excessively, unless he has more than average skill in obtaining market profits. It will be noted that commission costs are a larger percentage of the sums involved in stock trading than in bond trading and on low-priced stocks as compared with high-priced ones.

Options

Brokers and dealers in securities sometimes sell options to buy securities from them or to sell securities to them at a fixed price, for a limited period of time.[5] Such options are usually exercisable by the holder at any time during the stipulated period, which may run for 30, 60, or 90 days or 6 months. An active market in options on leading stocks is maintained in New York by members of the Put and Call Brokers and Dealers Assn., Inc. Options are bought and sold over the counter.

An option to buy stock from the dealer at a fixed price is termed a *call*. It is chiefly of interest to individuals who expect the price of the stock to rise. An option to sell stock to the dealer is a *put*. It is of interest to one who expects the stock to decline. An option entitling the holder either to a call or a put is a *spread* or *straddle*. It is a speculative position desired by one who expects a major change in the market but is not sure whether such a major change will be up or down.

Options permit a speculator to take a very substantial market position on a small cash outlay. They may also be used as a hedge against loss on other commitments which cannot conveniently be liquidated, or against extreme loss in speculative positions taken during the option period. Of course, there is some cost to so valuable a privilege. If a call is exercised, the total cost of the stock must be reckoned as the purchase price plus the cost of the option. On a put the net realization is the sale price minus the cost of the option. In either case there will also be taxes and a standard brokerage commission to pay. The commission compensates the customer's broker, who usually attends to the mechanical process of procuring the option and later exercising it.

The prices charged for options obviously depend on the purchase or sale price guaranteed in the option and the dealers' opinions of the market. In a lively bull market calls are high and puts are cheap. In a weak market puts are high and calls are cheap. Calls ordinarily sell higher than puts because the options require delivery of any dividends which go ex-dividend during the option period to the buyer of the stock, if the option is exercised. The *Wall Street Journal* of June 22, 1954, reported that 90-day options to buy or sell 100 shares at the June 21 market prices had sold at the following prices for the options:

[5] The real maker of the option may be an individual or a corporate investor on whose behalf a broker is acting.

June 21

Stock	Market	Puts	Calls
U.S. Steel...............	$48.75	$225.00	$287.50
New York Central.......	22.62½	175.00	200.00
Southern Pacific.........	42.75	237.50	275.00
Standard Oil (N.J.).......	88.50	375.00	450.00
Chrysler................	61.37½	300.00	350.00
General Motors..........	72.12½	325.00	375.00
Goodyear...............	63.25	387.50	425.00
Radio Corporation.......	28.00	162.50	187.50
Westinghouse Electric....	70.87½	375.00	425.00
American Tobacco.......	59.50	325.00	300.00

Obviously, the purchaser of an option will lose his investment if he does not exercise the option before it expires. A put will always be exercised before it expires if the market price on the last day is more than a small fraction below the option. A call will be exercised if the market is similarly above the option.

Brokerage Facilities

Brokers and dealers offer the public many services, which may be grouped conveniently as information and advice, trading facilities, and general service.

Investors in securities have need for much information about corporations, their capital structures, earnings, dividend policies, and prospects. They need to know about economic events and what they portend, and they often need information and advice about taxes, portfolio planning, and investment management. Brokers and dealers can provide a good deal of help on these matters. In the first place, they equip their offices with very expensive financial services, financial periodicals, and files of prospectuses and annual reports. Second, they prepare advisory literature and analyses which are often extremely valuable. Third, they have "customers' men" or sales staffs who are competent to assist customers with most of their problems. Fourth, they have analysts and investment experts to whom difficult problems can be taken. Fifth, some of them operate investment advisory departments where detailed investment supervision can be had for a fee. Except for the most detailed and continuing type of personal service all these information and advisory services are provided without charge.

Trading facilities offered to customers vary considerably. Brokers who cater to stock exchange traders customarily provide a "board room" where customers may sit and watch stock exchange sales prices marked up on blackboards or electrically operated quotation boards as the sales take place. Such board rooms are also usually equipped with *tickers* (teleprinters) which report transactions and quotations from an exchange floor by typing out the stock ticker symbols (abbreviations) and prices per share on paper tape. A well-equipped board room may have a New York Stock Exchange ticker, an American Stock Exchange ticker, one from the local exchange, and probably one or two from the commodity exchanges. Some of the tapes may be projected on a translucent screen called a *translux* as they come from the ticker, so the customers may see the tape reports without leaving their seats. A Dow-Jones news ticker, which teleprints a laconic version of the day's corporate and financial news as it happens, is standard equipment. Needless to say, the customers' men will be on hand, ready to take orders or discuss the market with those present or with anyone who telephones in. The board room doubtless will have reasonably direct telephone or teleprinter connections with the exchanges it serves, so that an obliging customers' man can speedily obtain the prevailing bid or ask on the exchange floor, the specialist's report on the number of orders on hand at the prevailing bid and ask quotations, or the specialist's reaction to a request to "stop stock." Such board rooms can also obtain over-the-counter quotations or statistical information by telephonic or teleprinter request. A market order in a reasonably active stock could be originated in Los Angeles, forwarded to New York, executed on the stock exchange, and reported back to the Los Angeles board room in less than five minutes.

Brokers and dealers who serve an investment-minded clientele frequently do not have board rooms. A market ticker and a news ticker may be in evidence, but possibly not. Quotations may be obtained by telephone. The financial services and periodicals will be on hand. Customers meet the salesmen in the calm and privacy of an office or by appointment in their own homes or offices. This type of organization is likely to stress new issues or over-the-counter securities, rather than listed ones.

Any broker or dealer is usually willing to provide free storage for a customer's securities if the customer trades often enough to give the firm some revenue from the account. The securities can be kept in the broker's name, with interest and dividends being credited to the account or remitted to the customer as received; the broker can then execute telephoned selling orders without the customer's sig-

CHART 7. Two segments of New York Stock Exchange ticker tape. The top piece reports sales in General Electric at 47⅜, Anaconda Copper at 37¾, U.S. Steel at 48¾, Curtis Publishing Company (500 shares) at 7¾, and Spiegel Preferred (120 shares totaling 12 board lots) at 57¾. The second piece reports sales in Johns-Manville, Chrysler, Westinghouse Electric (one board lot plus another sale of 300 shares), and Charles Pfizer & Co. Odd-lot transactions do not appear on the ticker tape.

nature. Brokers can also lend money to customers on their securities collateral, either for securities trading or general business purposes, at low rates and without maturity date, subject to the Federal margin regulations only if the loan is for the purpose of buying or carrying securities. This service is sometimes a highly convenient one, especially if the broker's own loan practices are generous.

In choosing a brokerage connection each individual should seek out the type of establishment which best serves his need. One who makes little use of analytical publications need not search for the firm with the best library. An investment-minded individual who is not technically skilled himself might do well to find a house with a capable and accommodating analyst. In any event it will be wise to find a congenial and diligent salesman; a friend who will trouble to ask for quotes from the stock exchange floor, who will shop around for the best market over the counter, or who will telephone his customer when interesting news appears, is worth having. Other bases for discriminating choice, including reputation for fairness and financial strength, will no doubt suggest themselves.

Brokerage Accounts

Because of the substantial sums involved brokers are very careful of their accounts. Each new customer is carefully identified before his orders are accepted. His account is correctly labeled with his full name or established as a joint account between himself and his wife. If a customer and his wife have both separate and joint holdings, three accounts are generally used, for transfers of either securities or money from one account or name to another cannot be accomplished without a written order from the transferor. As a further complication, the transfer of stock bought in John Doe's brokerage account into the joint names of John Doe and Mary Doe, husband and wife, would be regarded by Federal officials as a second transaction and subjected to a transfer tax.

When an account is opened, the customer may choose between one which is available for cash transactions only and one which is designed to permit either cash or margin operations. The broker will prefer the latter, for it paves the way for all possible transactions without committing either customer or broker to undertake them. The broker will ask his customer to fill out a signature card and a personal data card, for identification purposes; a margin card, which accepts the terms of the margin account, authorizes the broker to hold the securities as collateral, and permits the securities to be used as collateral for the broker's debts; an authorization to solicit his margin business by telephone; and written instructions for the transfer or custody of securities which are to be acquired. These documents will be needed for each account. When the accounts are those of trustees, executors, attorneys-in-fact, or corporations, the legal ramifications may be extensive.

Instructions to a broker or dealer to make transactions are commonly given by telephone, after the account is established. When the account is regarded as reliable, the instructions are carried out even if the account has no credit balance. A few days' grace, usually two to five, are allowed the customer to get sold securities or a cash purchase price into the office. The cash proceeds of a sale are available to a customer in three days, provided they are not required as margin in his account.

Brokers or dealers may be given *discretionary* accounts, in which the firm is authorized to use its own discretion in buying or selling for the account. The stock exchanges generally disapprove of this practice; the New York Stock Exchange does not permit a member firm to accept a discretionary account unless a partner in the firm manages it. However, the exchange does not object if an employee is instructed by a customer to buy or sell a specific amount of a specific security at a time and price which are left to the employee's discretion.

QUESTIONS AND PROBLEMS

1. Could a brokerage business be done by a firm which owned no stock exchange memberships?

2. Would you want to do business with a broker who declined to handle over-the-counter orders?

3. Why do nonmember firms not organize stock exchanges of their own?

4. Why would the New York Stock Exchange and the American Stock Exchange not trade in the same stocks?

5. Why would an investor prefer a listed stock to an unlisted one? Are there any advantages to the corporation in having a listed market?

6. What would happen to the price of Bethlehem Steel stock if, for no good reason, most of the day's buying orders reached the stock exchange in the morning and most of the selling orders came in in the afternoon? Would stock exchange members interested in trading for their own accounts help or hinder in this case?

7. What does a specialist do?

8. Does the post system of stock trading produce fair prices? Does it produce stable prices? (Note: Obtain three or four days' consecutive financial pages, and observe the behavior of prices.)

9. Would a stock exchange ex-dividend date fall before, on, or after the corporation's stock-of-record date for the dividend?

10. What is a when-issued contract? Why would investors want to buy or sell rights on a when-issued basis?

11. Would you use a "buy at market" order in an excited, fluctuating market?

12. Would a conservative investor ever have occasion to use a stop-loss order?

13. Would you expect limit orders to be open orders or day orders?

14. As a practical investment matter, should one whose funds are limited try to select stocks in which he can afford board lots or should he invest freely in odd lots?

15. Which is the largest sum, the commission on 100 shares of $9 stock,

or the commission on 10 shares of $90 stock plus an odd-lot differential on 10 shares?

16. Can an odd lot be bid for by means of a market order? By means of a limit order? By an open order? Can it be bought on margin? Can an odd lot be sold short?

17. Explain the SEC rule limiting short selling. How does this prevent "bear raiding"?

18. Would an investor—as distinguished from a speculator—ever have occasion to sell short?

19. Explain how a margin purchase works. Would an investor ever have occasion to buy on margin? Which would you prefer, if you were investing money due to be paid to you in two months, a margin purchase using your own free securities as margin or a purchase with money borrowed from your bank?

20. Would an investor ever have occasion to buy an option? Would a large investor who was willing to sell just a little above the current market ever find it advantageous to sell calls? Could he ever find it advantageous to sell puts?

21. What brokerage facilities would seem most important to you as an investor in securities?

22. Do you think that brokerage houses should be permitted to accept discretionary accounts? Do you approve of custody accounts, in which the securities are kept in the broker's name, though earmarked as the customer's property?

REFERENCES

Badger, Ralph E., and Harry G. Guthmann: *Investment Principles and Practices,* Prentice-Hall, Inc., New York, 1951, Chap. 23.

Bellemore, Douglas H.: *Investments Principles and Practices,* B. C. Forbes and Sons Publishing Co., Inc., New York, 1953, Chaps. 10, 11.

Dice, Charles A., and Wilford J. Eiteman: *The Stock Market,* McGraw-Hill Book Company, Inc., New York, 1952.

Dowrie, George W., and Douglas R. Fuller: *Investments,* John Wiley & Sons, Inc., New York, 1950, Chap. 4.

Financial Handbook, The Ronald Press Company, New York, 1948, pp. 65–129.

Investment Bankers Association of America: *Fundamentals of Investment Banking,* Prentice-Hall, Inc., New York, 1949, Chap. 19.

Jordan, David F., and Herbert E. Dougall: *Investments,* Prentice-Hall, Inc., New York, 1952, Chaps. 15, 16.

Leffler, George L.: *The Stock Market,* The Ronald Press Company, New York, 1951.

Plum, Lester V., and Joseph H. Humphrey: *Investment Analysis and Management*, Richard D. Irwin, Inc., Homewood, Ill., 1951, Chap. 7.

Robbins, Sidney M.: *Managing Securities*, Houghton Mifflin Company, Boston, 1954, Chaps. 3–5.

Shultz, Birl E.: *The Securities Market and How It Works*, Harper & Brothers, New York, 1946.

BROKERAGE AND THE STOCK EXCHANGES 237

Blum, Loren V., and Joseph H., Humphrey [illegible] Investment Analysis and
Management, Richard D. Irwin, Inc., Homewood, Ill, 1951, Chap. 3.
Robbins, Sidney M., [illegible] Managing Securities [illegible]
Boston, 1954, Chaps. 3-5.
Shultz, Birl [illegible] [illegible] [illegible] Wall Street, Harper &
Brothers [illegible]

Chapter 10: BEHAVIOR OF THE
SPECULATIVE MARKETS

All common stocks and the lower grades of preferred stocks and
corporate bonds may be classed as speculative in greater or less
degree. As has been stressed in previous chapters, this does not mean
that they are not fit commitments for thoughtfully planned investment portfolios. The contrary is true. But it does mean that these
securities bear some of the business risk and that their market prices
will fluctuate to a significant degree.

The prices of all securities, nonspeculative and speculative alike,
are the product of the familiar forces of demand and supply. Previous chapters have noted that the demand for nonspeculative securities is heavily institutional and depends chiefly upon (1) the funds
furnished by the public for institutional investment, (2) the competing demands for mortgage and short-term business and personal
loans, and (3) the pressure for expansion or contraction of bank
credit which stems from reserve bank policy at the moment. The
supply of institutional grade corporate securities at any time depends on the amount of new corporate financing under way, plus
occasional selling of existing securities when anticipated interest rate
or tax policy changes suggest it. Price changes in these securities are
relatively modest in amount, though changes of 10 to 15 per cent in
the prices of good long-term bonds may occur as a result of changes
in money market conditions.

Speculative securities, on the other hand, fluctuate extensively
and often rapidly in market price. The demand for them is affected
not only by the savings people have to invest in them and the competitive attractiveness of other investments, but also by the margin
credit available, the business outlook, and the speculative enthusiasm
of the moment. The supply of speculative securities is at all times
potentially large, for a very large amount of existing stock is capable
of becoming "supply" if its holders lose faith in business prospects
or the immediate future of stock prices or have urgent need of

money for other purposes. To this resale supply must be added at times the very considerable amount of new stock which industry must sell when expansion programs are under way.

The stocks of every industry and every company are affected by some of the forces which act upon the stock market. Changes in margin credit rules, for example, make it easier to own more stock or more difficult to do so, hence affect the buying or selling pressures in many issues. And boom or depression in important groups of securities naturally communicates itself to others; buyers in a rising market naturally seek the undervalued issues, thus raising them also, and sellers in a weak market tend to sell those not yet depressed, thus driving them down. As a matter of experience, it can be said that the ups and downs of the stock market are experienced in varying degree by nearly all industries and individual stocks.

The investor in stocks is confronted by a number of problems and a number of choices. He needs an investment policy which will guide him in choosing and timing his commitments. Should he attempt to take advantage of the major swings in the market, by buying when the market appears to be at a cyclical low spot and selling when it appears to be high? Should he attempt to ferret out the industries and companies which have "growth" prospects and confine his investments to them? In view of the uncertainty of market prophecies, is it ever justifiable to sell a promising holding just because the market appears high or to buy an unpromising one just because it or the market is low? Which is easiest for the layman, to pick good industries and good stocks, or to pick profitable times to buy and sell? Is it not sensible investing for a layman to buy a good stock in a good industry when the price-earnings ratio and yield prospects are right and ignore market behavior?

These and other policy questions could be answered easily if the investor were omniscient in the matter of forecasting market movements. Unfortunately, not even professionals are good at that. Most of them have to work as investment bankers or stockbrokers or investment counselors to make a living, which pretty well proves the point. And the constant study which market trading requires would consume time beyond the nonprofessional trader's ability to afford it. The problem, then, has no easy answer.

Measures of Market Behavior

Because securities prices often seem to rise or fall concertedly in response to "general conditions," investors and speculators have developed great interest in index numbers or "averages" which measure these general market price movements. These indexes are valuable, and their use is essential to any study of securities market behavior. But it is equally essential to note their limitations. They are at best only totals or averages based on the prices of certain securities, and they are capable of obscuring or misrepresenting the situation if they are inappropriate for the purpose for which they are used. Securities prices reflect differences in attractiveness between individual concerns, between industries, between large and small concerns, between high-grade and low-grade issues, and in many other ways. One who compares a specific situation to an average must always take care.

The most widely used securities indexes are simple price index numbers, which show the composite rise and fall in price of a selected group of issues.[1] On bonds, preferred stocks, and to a limited extent on common stocks, a *yield* average may be the best measure of market price. To a limited extent, but very significantly, average *price-earnings* ratios are coming into use.

Stock price indexes are compiled and published by many sources and on a number of bases. Indexes representing the whole market, computed either from a limited group of representative stocks in diverse industries or by use of a very large number of stocks, are available. Indexes representing groups of industries with certain common characteristics, such as industrial or utility, are compiled; and there are detailed price indexes by industries, such as telephone, steel, meat packing, and chain stores. Some indexes are classified by quality of security, though this is more common in bond than stock computations.

[1] The technical problems presented in compiling these indexes are beyond the scope of this book but should be studied by anyone making serious use of the indexes. There is, for example, the problem of weighting. Another problem is posed by the fact that a daily or hourly total will never catch all of the stocks at peak or bottom simultaneously; therefore the average will have a smaller range than most or all of the constituent stocks. In preparing a bond price average should one compute yields to maturity, average them, and reconvert this average yield to a price for an assumed coupon and maturity? Or is it better to average the prices of somewhat similar bonds?

The most famous indexes of stock prices are those compiled by Dow, Jones & Co., Inc., publishers of the *Wall Street Journal* and other financial services. The Dow-Jones Industrial Average consists of the total market price of one share each of 30 representative stocks, divided by a denominator which was originally 30. Through the years it has been necessary to substitute stocks in the list for various reasons or to make adjustments because of stock splits and similar changes. Continuity of the index has been maintained when these changes occur by adjusting the denominator by which the total is divided; in June, 1954, this denominator was 5.92. The second well-known Dow-Jones index is the Railroad Average of 20 representative rail stocks, compiled by the same system as the Industrial Average. Dow-Jones also compute an average of 15 utility stocks and a composite average of 65 stocks, but these have not caught the public fancy as the others have done.

The most comprehensive collection of stock price indexes is that maintained by Standard & Poor's Corporation and published in their *Standard Trade and Securities Service.* This collection contains industrial, rail, utility, and composite averages, some averages based on comprehensive large groups of stocks, and a large number of stock price averages by specific industries. A somewhat less ramified but carefully compiled collection of stock-price averages is maintained by *Moody's Investors Service.* Another good recollection is maintained by *Barron's,* a subsidiary of Dow, Jones & Co., Inc. The *Barron's* indexes include some good work on yields and price-earnings ratios; these and other Dow-Jones figures are available in a loose-leaf service called *The Dow-Jones Averages.* Other organizations also contribute to the voluminous literature in this field.

Bond and preferred stock averages are usually maintained on both a price and a yield basis. Bond indexes are classified by quality, time to maturity, and by groups of issuers, such as industrial, rail, utility, municipal, and Federal government. The best collections of indexes are published by the agencies already mentioned.

Stock Price Movements

Students of stock market performance have long been aware that the market averages are subject to three types of market movements.[2]

___

[2] In addition, Chart 8 clearly shows a general upward growth trend which has prevailed over the past fifty years. This growth trend has occurred chiefly because stock

First, there is the relatively long-range tendency, usually conforming to business cycle stages in normal times, for the market to move in a general upward or downward direction for many months or years at a time. Market analysts usually refer to this as the *basic trend, primary trend,* or *long-term trend.* Chart 8 clearly shows long-term upward trends in the industrial average in 1932–1933, 1934–1937, 1938, 1942–1946, 1949–1952, and a sharp upswing in 1954. Declines appear in 1937–1938, 1940–1942, and 1946. The period 1946–1949 shows an unusually long sidewise movement or *line.*

Superimposed on the primary trend are frequent shorter cycles of 3 months' to a year's duration, during which the averages may fluctuate 5 to 15 per cent in value. These short-range cycles also show clearly on the chart; for example, the low points in October, 1946, May, 1947, and February, 1948, interlace the high spots in February, 1947, July, 1947, and June, 1948. The up, down, and sidewise movements of the averages in forming these shorter cycles are termed *secondary,* or *short-term, trends.*

A third type of market movement is observable in the day-to-day fluctuations of the averages. For example, in the week ending August 27, 1948, the Dow-Jones Industrial Average fell 1.85 points on Monday, gained .83 on Tuesday, fell .17 on Wednesday, gained .11 on Thursday, and gained .69 on Friday. On every single day the range of fluctuation within the day greatly exceeded the net change for the day. This is typical. No cyclical pattern can be found for these hour-to-hour, day-to-day, and week-to-week fluctuations, except to suggest that extremely sharp gains or declines for a few hours or days seem usually to be "corrected" by rebound movements in the opposite direction.

It must be emphatically stated that in recognizing these three types of market movements, and in identifying some apparent periodicity in them, no conclusions can be drawn respecting the extent and timing of market changes. Such factors as wars, inflation, taxes, labor problems, and economic conditions generally are far too complex to permit the mechanical forecasting of stock prices. However, some knowledge of typical market behavior and its causes may help in avoiding obvious mistakes and in making an occasional sound decision.

values have been augmented by reinvested earnings and because the dollar has been cheapened by inflation.

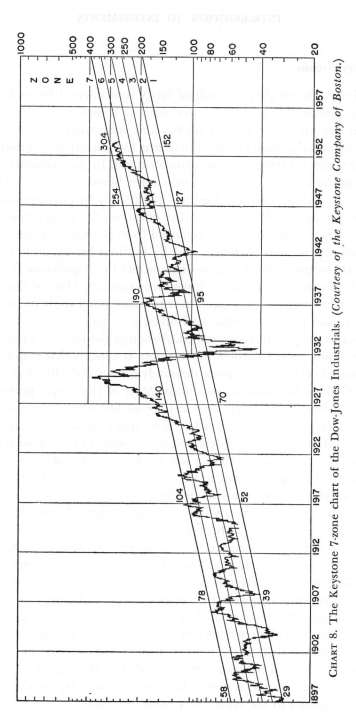

CHART 8. The Keystone 7-zone chart of the Dow-Jones Industrials. (*Courtesy of the Keystone Company of Boston.*)

Primary Trends

Primary trends are the result of fairly fundamental forces in economic affairs. They must be, for market trends and price levels which prevail for years in a logical and competitive market must have substantial foundation. There are five interrelated groups of forces which contribute to the primary trend. In the apparent order of importance they are (1) the outlook for business activity and stability, (2) the outlook for business profits, (3) speculative attitude and expectations, (4) the availability of money for stock investment, and (5) the amount of money removed from the stock market by investors who need it elsewhere and by business for expansion.

Little argument is needed to demonstrate the importance of items 1 and 2 to any student of the investment markets. Most of the space in financial periodicals is given over to painstaking study of business activity and business profits, and investment policies are constantly shaped by the conclusions reached. Although the investor's emphasis is constantly on the *outlook* for business, it appears that major securities market changes are more definitely concurrent with than ahead of variations in business conditions. Most of the major periods of business downtrend or uptrend in the past fifty years have also been periods of parallel stock market downtrend or uptrend, and the peaks and bottoms of business and stock market cycles have seldom been separated by more than a few weeks. It may therefore be concluded that primary trends in the stock market are in large part reflections of the movements of the business cycle.

Primary trends are also vitally affected by item 3, speculative attitude and expectations. There is a very large group of investors who are more interested in market profits than in future dividends. They are therefore constantly studying economic history and market patterns in the hope of recognizing coming events in time to profit from them. When they conclude that price-earnings ratios are too high or that history indicates a repetition of the 1921 postwar depression, as they did in 1946, their actions can greatly influence the market trend. The pessimistic drift of the market through 1941 unquestionably reflected the general investor conviction that business prosperity portended nothing for the stockholder while a war lay in the offing. More examples to the same effect could be cited.

Item 4, the availability of money for stock investment, is also an important factor in establishing the primary trend. The amount of money seeking investment in stocks is affected chiefly by the size and distribution of the national income; the attractiveness of competing investments such as government bonds, life insurance, real estate, and savings accounts; and the availability of credit for stock purchasers. The great bull market of 1927–1929 was aided by a national income distribution which favored the well-to-do and middle-class professional men, who are likely stock buyers; by a high level of interest in stocks, which temporarily eclipsed life insurance and other outlets; and by the ready availability of margin credit, which enabled stock buyers to buy on credit to the extent of 9 billion dollars. The contrast with the 1946–1949 situation is notable. Though the well-to-do and professional classes had satisfactory earnings in 1946–1949, high progressive taxes reduced their surpluses for investment to modest amounts, and the substantial incomes going to farmers and wage earners did not find their way to the stock market. Life insurance, home investment, and savings accounts were popular competing outlets for savings, and many people were using their funds to build up their own businesses. Credit for the stock market was almost a thing of the past. And the 1946–1949 stock market did not advance despite prosperity, profits, and dividends. The period 1949–1954, in contrast, was characterized by a strongly rising stock market. This was a period in which the money demand for stocks was very great, for several reasons: first, institutional investors, especially corporation pension funds, began to invest large sums in stocks; second, a successful sales-promotion campaign by securities firms attracted thousands of new stock buyers; third, many stock-buying families completed their planned postwar improvements to their homes and family businesses and began to divert larger sums to stock investment; and fourth, during most of this period 50 per cent margin credit was available. The importance of this available-funds aspect of the stock market is particularly noticeable in the first half of 1954; although the business situation did not promise increased profits or dividends, people had substantial incomes and somewhat less than average need for the money for consumption and capital goods uses. They therefore bought stocks, and the stock market rose vigorously.

Item 5, the withdrawals from the stock market, represents two separate influences on the stock market trend. First, there are always people who must sell their stocks, to finance their businesses and their personal affairs. The market must find replacement money to finance these retirements. Second, business corporations frequently must sell new stock to finance expansion or debt repayment. This financing removes from the market substantial amounts which otherwise would bid for existing stocks. Unless margin credit or unusually large amounts of new savings or both are available, the market has difficulty in advancing while absorbing new corporate financing. This factor contributed importantly to the 1946–1949 doldrums. However, the increased demand for stocks in the 1949–1954 period absorbed a large amount of new stock sales without serious effect on the advancing market trend.

Secondary Movements

It seems probable that most of the secondary movements in the stock market can be attributed to hasty speculators who "overdo it" in attempting to take advantage of impending price changes and who then overdo it in the opposite direction in attempting to correct their errors. After all, speculative advantage can be had by identifying the bit of news which indicates that the market should go up or down and acting upon it substantially and quickly. Perspective is limited when time is of the essence, and it is not unlikely that many reversals of opinion will take place. Also, people are very prone to become accustomed to a market level in a few weeks' time. If the natural trend of the market is up, they are inclined to seize quick profits by selling after a few weeks of rising prices. This will reverse the direction of movement, stampede panicky speculators, and "touch off" an extensive market "correction." Presently the natural rise will be resumed, with another correction to be expected in due time. Market declines show the same phenomena in reverse.

The existence of secondary movements can unquestionably be laid to the fact that the forces shaping primary trends are difficult to evaluate except in retrospect. In attempting to appraise them prospectively the market blunders and vacillates. The vacillations themselves—the secondary movements under consideration—are very likely to be set off by news events whose significance is exaggerated by current prominence. Because of their infinite variety and scope, it is extremely difficult to anticipate the behavior of secondary movements to any extent. There is a saying that a typical secondary decline in a rising market will retrace 30 to 70 per cent of the gain since the last secondary bottom and that the following advance will gain one and one-half to three times as much as the secondary decline lost. In a declining market the ratios are reversed. However, not many secondary movements are typical, a fact which helps to make the way of a prophet somewhat similar to that of the proverbial transgressor.

Day-to-day Movements

Stock prices often fluctuate sharply from hour to hour, day to day, and week to week. These gyrations are usually not at all predictable, except that "spot" news of considerable moment, such as the threat of war, the outcome of a presidential election, the settlement of a critical strike, or a dividend increase by an important corporation, is almost certain to elicit a response. The listed market's daily and hourly quotations are produced by the flow of bids and offers to the trading floor. Any news which halts or accelerates either of these flows will change market prices. If, after an hour or so of reflection, traders come to the conclusion that the news was not so important after all, its effect will soon die out. If the impression created by the news disturbs the balance of bids and offers for several days, the market effect will last just that long. Of course, any impetus of this sort may be the beginning of a substantial secondary movement. But the day-to-day movements themselves, constituting indexes of the accidental or transitory impressions of buyers and sellers for fleeting hours, do not seem to be of fundamental importance.

The Dow Theory

There are many authors with many ideas for anticipating stock market movements and profiting from them. By far the best known system is built around the Dow theory, a doctrine developed by the editors of the *Wall Street Journal* in the early years of the century and much elaborated by others since. First, the Dow theory proceeds on the assumption that if profits are to be made in the stock market they must be made by taking advantage of the primary trend, not by resisting it. Since a primary trend "usually" lasts 1 to 4 years and produces changes of 25 to 90 per cent or even greater in the market averages, there is ample time and ample room to make profits, for well-selected individual stocks should move farther than the averages.

The next fundamental assumption in the Dow theory is that, when the primary trend is up, each secondary cycle will produce a peak higher than the last preceding one, and a trough higher than the last preceding one. Conversely, when the primary trend is down, each secondary peak and trough will be lower than the preceding ones. If these facts are usually correct, they provide a basis for determining the direction of the primary trend, for every secondary rise which surpasses the previous peak will clearly signal a rising basic trend, and every secondary decline which drops lower than a preceding trough will indicate a basic downward trend.

The third fundamental assumption of the Dow theory is that any true indication of primary trend will be "confirmed" by similar action in different stock price indexes within a short time. The Dow-Jones Industrial Average and the Rail Average are usually used for this purpose. If the Industrial Average signals the beginning of a bull market, the faithful wait to see what the Rail Average will do. If it shortly produces a bull signal also, they mortgage the old homestead and buy every stock in sight. A bear market signal by either average must similarly be confirmed by the other before it is regarded as authentic.

The earlier Dow theorists seem to have regarded the secondary swings as too unpredictable to be profitable in themselves but as very useful in indicating the primary trend. Some of the less conservative later writers have attempted to use day-to-day and week-to-week market fluctuations as indications of the continuation or reversal of secondary trends, thus corrupting the Dow method to a different purpose. Although some good logic on market behavior has been mustered in support of this idea, it does not seem to be so well grounded as the original doctrine.

It is sometimes argued that the Dow theory is ineffective even if correct, for it fails to signal a change of basic trend until a distinct breakthrough of a preceding peak or trough occurs. This means that the trend will have changed weeks or months before. The criticism is true; but the obvious rejoinder is that the average primary trend is generous in scope and of long duration; so signals which are quite late can still salvage most of the cyclical gain and avoid most of the loss. A much more serious criticism is found in the fact that the Dow theorists have difficulty in identifying the key peaks or troughs which must be surpassed or broken through; the secondary movements are not clean-cut. Finally, the Dow theory is criticized because its predictions do not always work out. This also is true; but it must be admitted that in retrospect over the long primary movements of the past three decades it has not done badly.

There are two reasons why the Dow theory has elements of merit. In the first place, a great many people believe it and will act upon it. In acting upon it they can help to cause the upward or downward trend the theory predicts. For example, the market in August, 1946, was drifting slowly downward because of "recession" gossip, heavy corporate financing, and lack of margin credit. On September 1 it broke through the level of a secondary trough recorded the preceding February, and on that and ensuing days the followers of the theory created a selling panic of major scope, though no evidence of a business decline had been seen. The second reason for the appeal of the Dow theory is that it has a sensible core of logic. It is a familiar and reasonable fact that the stock market reflects the ups and downs of business conditions, which usually take some time to work themselves out. The major swings of the business cycle are related to the primary trends of the market. The secondary trends of the market merely reflect the excesses of human nature superimposed on and following the primary trend. That successive secondary peaks and troughs should follow the direction of the primary trend is obvious; if most of them did not, there would be no primary trend.

Other Market Doctrine

Stock traders discuss many generalities and rules of thumb regarding market fluctuations and, apparently, disbelieve most of them. However, there are three widely held bits of dogma regarding (1) volume of trading, (2) resistance points, and (3) lines, which must be mentioned. They are presented here as widely held ideas, not as proved rules.

It is often said that a market movement accomplished on a large or rising volume of trading reflects the consensus of opinion of the whole market and is therefore substantial, unlikely to be retraced, and likely to continue in the same direction. If the market moves up or down on small or diminishing volume, the move is likely to be ephemeral because the majority of traders is not concurring. This interpretation of trading volume is most widely used when a market which has been temporarily stationary suddenly rises or falls for two or three or more consecutive days. Another common interpretation of trading volume is found in the case of a rise or fall which has continued sharply for several days or intermittently for weeks or months. If a definite up or down movement slows to a halt or reverses itself slightly on large volume, many will hold that a market consensus shows the movement to be over and possibly ready for substantial reversal.

As a rule the market averages do not progress steadily either up or down. They rise, fall, hesitate, rise again, and generally progress haltingly and intermittently. In this process, they seem to establish *resistance points* from time to time, at which levels the week-to-week rises and declines are halted by increased selling or buying, as the case may be. When the market remains for some time in a restricted trading range, as it did in 1946–1949, there may be several known (?) resistance points on the downside and as many on the upside. Weak rallies or slumps will be turned back at the first resistance point; strong ones will progress farther. Needless to say, a market movement which breaks through a resistance point tends to gain impetus, because doubting Thomases who observe the breakthrough become convinced that an obstacle has been overcome and that further progress is to be expected. They therefore lend the weight of their buying or selling orders and help to make their expectations happen.

A *line* is a substantially sidewise movement of the market averages, that is, a lack of substantial rise or decline, which has continued for weeks or months. Since it is held that business conditions and the future outlook are constantly changing, the line simply marks a period of delay in adjusting the market to fundamental values. The longer the line continues, the more substantial will the change be when a breakout finally occurs.

Stock Prices in Different Industries

Previous paragraphs have noted that the primary, secondary, and day-to-day market fluctuations all have noticeable effects on the

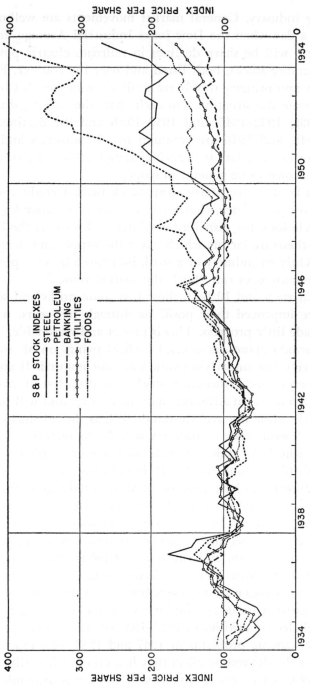

CHART 9. Stocks of leading industries follow the market cyclical pattern but also reflect differences in industry growth and outlook. (This chart shows indexes for March, June, September, and December of each year.)

stocks of every industry. General market movements are well-nigh universal. On a day when the Dow-Jones Industrial Average drops two points there will be sharp declines in railroad, electric power, bank, and insurance stocks, both listed and over the counter. Full-scale secondary and primary trends are similarly widespread. Charts 9 and 10 illustrate the situation. On each chart the major gains of 1935–1936, 1938, 1942–1946, and 1949–1954, and the declines of 1937, 1940–1942, and 1946 are common to all industries and all stocks. The shorter secondary swings—for example, those of 1947 and 1948—are also shown to be general in scope.

The reasons for this are pretty clear. Stock market credit conditions, speculative psychology, changes in the tax laws, labor legislation, foreign relations, the distribution of national income, the level of prosperity—these are factors which affect the supply and demand for all stocks. Only an industry or a stock influenced by very powerful unique circumstances can "buck the market trend."

However, Charts 9 and 10 both show that some stocks and some industries have improved their positions through the years, while others have made little progress. This is proper and reasonable. The stock market superimposes its general cyclical swings on all stocks and all industries, but underlying values are not ignored. If an industry is prosperous and growing, its stocks will drop less in market declines and gain more on advances than the average and will probably gain a little while the average stands still, as the oil stocks did in 1947–1948. A weak stock or industry will do the opposite.

An industry whose stocks do better than the general market at any time will probably be one which (1) is enjoying relatively good earnings, or (2) seems to have promise of an unusually good future, or (3) has a "vogue" among stock buyers, or (4) is comparatively free of financing problems. In 1948 excellent examples of industries whose stocks were high because of good current earnings were paper manufacturing, petroleum, and rug manufacturing. Industries facing very promising futures included chemicals and natural gas. An industry enjoying a vogue among stock buyers was the building materials manufacturing industry; similar vogues for oil companies in 1935–1936 and electric utilities in 1928–1930 colored the markets in those stocks. Financing problems in 1947 and 1948 were especially conspicuous for the depressing effect they had on electric utility and telephone stocks. An excessive quantity of stock was available for

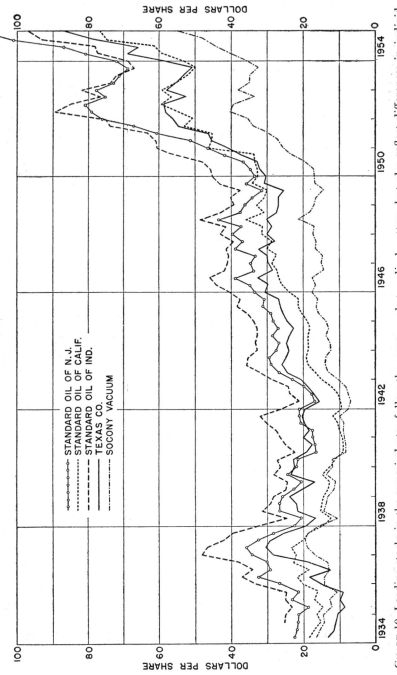

CHART 10. Leading stocks in the same industry follow the same market cyclical pattern but also reflect differences in individual progress. (This chart shows market prices on the last day of each calendar quarter.)

DOLLARS PER SHARE

STANDARD OIL OF N.J.
STANDARD OIL OF CALIF.
STANDARD OIL OF IND.
TEXAS CO.
SOCONY VACUUM

253

sale, because of new issues to finance expansion and because of the liquidation of holding companies. The market simply did not want so much utility stock, and the prices sagged.

Some industries, such as electric power, banking, and insurance, are sometimes said to be "noncyclical," that is, less subject to business cycle and general stock market trends than others. Very high-quality stocks of all types are often said to be in this category. The truth of the matter is that these stocks are mostly in industries or companies in which the earnings are both stable and predictable. With earnings and dividends stabilized, stock price fluctuations are lessened both because people understand more clearly the long-run values inherent in the stock and because they are assured of continuity of earnings and dividends in the short run. However, these stocks must not be thought immune to primary and secondary movements; they are only relatively stable.

Prices of Individual Stocks

What has been said of whole industries applies with equal force to individual stocks. Good quality and stable earning power will tend to limit the scope of price fluctuations. Regardless of quality, good current earnings, promise of future prosperity, a vogue or a following among stock buyers, and freedom from need to sell new stock will all help to sustain the price of a stock. Opposite influences will exert depressing effects. Aside from these factors and the familiar influences of dividend policy, stock dividends, splits, and the like, there are several *market* elements which contribute to the price behavior of a stock. These include

1. *Accumulation and distribution.* Important financial interests, including officers and major stockholders, investment companies, and trusts, frequently undertake to acquire or dispose of substantial amounts of a stock. Whether this is done on over-the-counter markets, on the regular exchange markets, or by special offering or secondary offering, the amount of stock for sale to the public will be affected, and unless the transactions are handled with great skill, there may be immediate effects on the market price. The market price effects may be present for months, for if accumulation mops up the "floating supply" of a stock, or if distribution adds to it greatly, it may be a long time before the disturbed supply-and-

demand relationship is adjusted. The floating supply is the portion of the stock which is likely to appear for sale on either a market rally or decline, because its holders regard it as a trading position rather than as a permanent investment. A stock with a small floating supply is likely to be buoyant; an excessive floating supply will cause market weakness.

2. *Stockholder confidence.* There are many stocks, for example, General Electric or General Foods, whose holders have confidence in them because of their long records and good reputations. These holders are disinclined to sell on market declines and are disposed to buy "bargain" offerings if the price drops. If such stocks as these are widely distributed in many hands, and if few excessive concentrations exist to give rise to frequent secondary distributions, the market price should be relatively steady. On the other hand, stocks whose earnings performances or market price histories have not earned their holders' confidence and stocks of new concerns or corporations recently reorganized in bankruptcy are likely to be unstable under selling pressure and to be unable to advance as fast in a rising market as their intrinsic merit would justify. For excellent examples, the performances of the General Public Utilities and Southern Natural Gas Company issues in 1947–1948 will suffice.

3. *Market sponsorship.* Individual stocks can be kept in stronger position marketwise if large floating supplies are not allowed to accumulate and if urgently offered stock is bought up and resold to new holders by use of security salesmen. This is undertaken by dealers and underwriters in some instances and by company managements and interested stockholders in other cases. It is not illegal manipulation if the transactions are carried out with stabilization rather than deception in mind.

4. *Profit and tax factors.* Stocks whose market value changes sharply in a short time may be vulnerable to several types of buying and selling adjustments. First, a stock or group of stocks showing a definite improvement or decline in value is likely to be carried too far in the sweep of speculative enthusiasm, thus paving the way for a "correction." Second, a substantial rise will create paper profits for many holders who will be eager to "take" them and who will hastily sell when a correction appears. The short sellers who gain on the down side will be similarly quick to buy in when a correction halts the decline. Third, any stock which has experienced a sharp decline during any calendar year, especially in the last half of the year, and most especially in a year when many people have capital gains, will be a target for "tax selling." Tax selling by investors consists of selling stocks which are priced below the investor's cost, in order to realize losses which may be used to reduce income tax liability for the year. This type of selling nearly always reduces the price of some

stocks between November 15 and December 24. Often it depresses whole segments of the market and provides excellent buying opportunities for discriminating investors.

Because both industry and individual stock features affect the market for each stock, it is unlikely that all stocks will fluctuate in parallel fashion throughout a stock market cycle. Some will reach their "peaks" ahead of the averages and some later; and the same will be true of "bottoms," as well as of "climbs" and "declines." Furthermore, this timing will not necessarily be consistent, either from one cyclical phase to another or from one cycle to another.

Investor Policy

Much of what has been said about market movements emphasizes the fact that it is more profitable to take advantage of them than to resist them. Even the careful selection of companies and industries cannot afford so much gain as relatively casual selections will if bought and sold at the right times. Of course, no sensible investor will make his selections casually, but he can add to careful selection some diligent effort to time his purchases and sales for profit.

Just what an investor should do about market timing is a hard-to-answer question. One possibility is to do nothing except to limit new commitments to times when market prices are reasonable and the outlook appears promising. A second possibility, somewhat more aggressive in nature, is to increase portfolio holdings of good stocks when market conditions appear promising and retire to the security of bonds and savings accounts when the outlook is adverse. A third and still more aggressive policy suggests the purchase of "dynamic" stocks—high-leverage or second-quality issues which fluctuate very widely in price—when the outlook is promising and a shift to "defensive" securities—bonds and relatively stable stocks—when conditions are uncertain. The pursuit of an aggressive policy would require the investor to study market and economic conditions and risk his future on his findings. This would be a sound decision if the investor could be sure that, with reasonable effort, he could be right.

But therein lies the rub. Economic affairs respond to so many stimuli that forecasts of coming events are little better than guesses. Despite time and money spent endlessly on the study of the subject, even the best informed investors must depend chiefly on investment selection and diversification for preservation of their savings. Market studies are not dependable enough to serve as the major framework of investment policy.

Formula Plans

Admitting the futility of forecasts, a number of shrewd investment managers have recently attempted to develop *formulas* which will automatically adjust an investment portfolio by limiting or reducing stock holdings when the market is high and buying them vigorously when it is low. The stocks for either purchase or sale are carefully chosen, but the timing and quantities of the transactions are pointed out by a logically framed, unemotional formula. The formulas in use vary greatly, but there are only four general types—dollar averaging, the constant ratio type, the fixed dollar sum type, and the variable ratio type.[3] These will be reviewed in order.

In the brief discussion of formula plans which can be undertaken here, it will be assumed that the stock market fluctuates cyclically but does not have a long-term tendency to trend either up or down. Most of the formula plans are designed to profit from cyclical fluctuations, and attention must therefore be focused on this aspect of market behavior. However, a long-term rising trend of stock prices, due to reinvested corporate earnings, rising commodity price levels, or other causes, would have an effect on the profitableness of each of these plans.

Dollar Averaging

Dollar averaging is a very simple system intended to make sure that the stock investor who is accumulating stocks out of income will buy them at less than the average market price. First, the prospective investor chooses a definite dollar sum which he proposes to invest in common stocks at regular periodic intervals, possibly every three or six months. Excess savings go into a bank account or bonds, to

[3] The ideas presented here are drawn from a number of sources, but the best detailed summaries of actual plans are found in two small books: (1) *Investment Timing: The Formula Plan Approach*, by C. Sidney Cottle and W. Tate Whitman, McGraw-Hill Book Company, Inc., New York, 1953, and (2) *Practical Formulas for Successful Investing*, by Lucile Tomlinson, Wilfred Funk, Inc., New York, 1953.

make sure that the budgeted stock investment will be available each time as planned. Second, the periodic stock investment may always be made in the same stock, or, alternatively, in whatever stock seems most attractive at the time. Instead of choosing individual stocks the investor might "buy the whole market" by investing his quarterly installments in investment company stocks. Third, switches from one stock to another more promisingly situated can be made at any time.

Over a long period of time this system assures that the investor will buy his stocks at a very favorable average price, unless he chooses poorly or unless the market trends down continuously. Consider, for example, what happens if the market in the long run proves cyclical, trending neither up nor down, and if the investor buys average stocks. If he invests $300 quarterly, each market "cycle" might give him two investments (one on the way up, one on the way down) at an average price, say $10 per share; perhaps another two at high prices, say $15 per share; and another two at low prices, say $5 per share. At $10 he would buy 30 shares on each purchase, or 60 shares in all. At $15 he would buy 20 shares twice, or 40 shares in all. At $5 he would buy 60 shares twice, or 120 shares in all. His total cost would be six times $300, or $1,800; his purchases would total 220 shares; and his average cost would be $8.18 per share, or $1.82 below the average price. The mathematical legerdemain here stems from the fact that the constant sum buys more shares at low prices than at high ones. This holds down the average cost per share.

Dollar averaging is a more sensible plan than that followed by most people, if pursued over a long period of years, for it will prevent the bulk of the investments being made in high markets. It is not fantastically profitable—the 18 per cent saving in the example is much too large to be typical and would be the product of a several-year period, not a single year—but even a small gain is better than a loss. The plan does not guarantee against poor choices of investments, and it cannot prevent a long down trend in the market, but it does not cause these things either. Dollar averaging will of course be unprofitable if the low-cost investments in the depression years are not made, but its average investment budget is the best possible guarantee that the money will be available to make the low-cost purchases. Finally, dollar averaging can be made more profitable if the investor will simply decline to commit his quarterly investment budget when average yields are too low or price-earnings ratios too high or when business conditions are obviously deteriorating. This last suggestion may seem to negate the basic mechanical principle of dollar averaging, but mechanical principles should be abridged when they conflict with common sense.

The mathematics of dollar averaging promise greater profits if the installments are used to buy speculative stocks whose prices fluctuate greatly, rather than stable, conservative stocks. However, the advocates of the dollar averaging system have stressed it as a means of savings accumulation and have usually advocated it as a means of acquiring conservative investment company shares for more or less permanent retention. On this basis the plan deserves approbation, particularly for amateur investors and busy people of modest means.

Many investment companies will sell their shares on periodic investment plans designed to make use of dollar averaging. The stock exchange plans for monthly or quarterly investment in a single stock are similarly designed.

Constant Ratio Plan

The constant ratio plan is a system for administering a portfolio of common stocks, bonds, and savings accounts in a manner designed to obtain some advantage from stock market fluctuations without the necessity of forecasting market behavior. The basic idea is to keep a constant percentage of the dollar value of the fund in stocks at all times, by shifting funds from stocks into bonds when stock prices rise and shifting back again when stock prices fall. This will require the sale of stocks when they are disproportionately high and the purchase of additional stocks when they are low. Therein lies the profit.

The mechanics of the plan are developed along these lines: First, a definite fund consisting of stocks, bonds, and cash is set apart, to be managed under the plan. Second, the fund's ideal ratio between common stocks on the one hand, and bonds and cash on the other, is established in accordance with the investor's circumstances and desires. The bond and savings account portion should be of high quality and highly liquid, for it must finance the purchase of stocks when all securities are depressed in price. Third, a decision is made as to the amount of change in the ratio of stock value to total value which should be tolerated before correcting sales or purchases are undertaken. If the ideal stock ratio has been set at 60 per cent, for example, no corrections should be made until the ratio changes by a significant amount, possibly up to 65 or down to 55 per cent. Then a change to restore the normal 60 per cent stock ratio would be in order. Constant trading to correct discrepancies of lesser magnitude would be unprofitable. Fourth, the portfolio of stocks should be normally diversified, carefully selected, and switched from less attractive to more attractive stockholdings when opportunity offers.

One important qualification of the mechanical theory of the plan should be noted. If the stock portfolio is small, speculative, or lacking in diversification, its fluctuations may not parallel those of the general market. In that case it might be desirable to *assume* that the stocks held were performing in proportion to the Dow-Jones Industrial Average or some similar index and to increase or decrease the stocks actually held as the assumed total value declined or rose. In other words, the movements of the general market would be used to indicate when to adjust the specific portfolio.

The gains from the constant ratio plan as thus far outlined would be relatively small. However, several supplementary devices might augment them somewhat. First, a rule not to make any shift from stocks or into stocks within 3 months of the last previous shift and never to shift more than 5 per cent of the total fund at any one time should be profitable. This rule will delay sales of stocks as the market rises and delay purchases as it falls. Second, additional stocks should not be bought unless the dividend yield on Barron's 50-stock Average exceeds that on the highest grade long-term corporation bonds by at least $1\frac{1}{2}$ per cent, in order to avoid buying them when they are too high. Third, stocks should not be bought when business conditions are deteriorating rapidly—for example, do not buy when the last published Federal Reserve Board Index of Industrial Production shows a decline of more than 1 per cent from the preceding month's index.

Enthusiasts for this plan believe that it will earn 1 to 3 per cent of the fund annually in extra market appreciation, in addition to the normal earnings due to dividends, interest, and profits from advantageous selection. It has the additional merit of keeping the investor's stock-bond ratio in a normal balanced position, regardless of whether the market is high or low. The plan is intended for use with a diversified and conservative stock portfolio, but theoretically it would be sound and much more profitable with speculative stocks which would fluctuate more widely.

Fixed Dollar Sum Plan

The fixed dollar sum plan is very similar to the constant ratio plan except that it is slightly less conservative. The basic idea is that out of each $10,000 available for securities the investor should determine the *amount* he wishes to keep in stocks. If the amount so chosen is $6,000, the project would be launched with $6,000 in stocks and $4,000 in bonds and savings accounts. If stock market declines reduced the stockholdings by a significant sum, say to $5,400, the bond and savings fund would be drawn upon to buy stocks and restore the $6,000 total. If the stocks rose to a predetermined sum, say $6,600, a correction would be made by selling $600 worth and placing the proceeds in a bond or savings account.

In order to make this plan profitable it will be necessary to follow delaying rules similar to the second and third of those suggested for the constant ratio plan. If this is done, the market gains should exceed those of the constant ratio plan, for the fixed dollar sum plan might readily shift all of the fund into stocks in a depressed market, and it will cause a larger percentage of the stocks to be sold in a high market. This feature is not conservative, for it discards the security of bonds and cash when business is bad and limits stockholdings in booms when inflation threatens. However, the plan never sells out all of the stockholdings, and if the investor protects his cash position by retaining some insurance or cash outside of the plan, this will be a simple and effective formula system.

Variable Ratio Systems

There are several formula investing plans which undertake to earn substantial profits by varying the *percentage* of a stock-bond fund which is kept in stocks. The percentage in stocks is reduced greatly when the formula shows the market to be high and increased greatly when the market appears low. Various devices are used to delay sales on rising markets and purchases on falling ones.

Since the variable ratio plan cannot be self-correcting—that is, adjustments cannot be made to restore a constant percentage or a constant sum—some outside measure of high or low markets must be found. Two general ideas have been suggested. First, the excess of stock yields over bond yields, or the excess of earnings-price percentages over bond yields, or an average of the two, may provide an index of the highness or lowness of stock prices. For this purpose only very high-class and stable stocks, such as those in Barron's 50-stock Average, could be used. Second, one might measure the stock market as high or low by computing ratios of the present position of a market price index to a trend line or moving average fitted to that same price index. Chart 8 shows how this might be done. On Chart 8 the central trend line was fitted mathematically to the charted Dow-Jones index; then the other six parallel lines were drawn. By the formula plan the percentage of stocks in the fund is changed each time the Dow-Jones index moves across one of the lines on the chart.

Many of the variable ratio plans compute a "median line" or a "median level" for stock prices. The median may be based either on a group of price-earnings ratios and yields or on a trend or moving average fitted to a stock price index. The intention is that stock-holdings will be increased but seldom decreased when the markets are below the median and that they will be decreased but not increased above the median. Under this plan a declining stock market might provide the occasion for purchase of stocks, but all purchases would be deferred until stock prices dropped below the median; after that the percentage of stocks held would be increased as long as the market declined. When the market began to rise, all stocks would be retained until the median line was passed; beyond this point each further rise would require reduction of the percentage of the fund kept in stocks. Switching from one stock to another is always permissible.

It is clear that a skillfully handled variable ratio plan might be very profitable. It is also clear that much more statistical work and much more good judgment would be required to execute one successfully than would be needed on the other plans and that errors might produce severe losses. No reasonable estimate of the profitableness of a variable ratio plan can be made, but it may be guessed that a fund restricted to good-grade stocks and bonds would reflect brilliant management if it averaged 5 per cent per year in profits in addition to the usual interest and dividend income.

Appraisal of Formula Plans

The formula plans are advocated as devices which remove basic decisions on investment policy from the confusing background of current events. It is argued that policy can be reasonably predetermined on the basis of market history and carried out effectively when the immediate decisions are limited to matters of selection between issues. Actually, many of the formula plans require some degree of policy making day by day, but the nervous pressure on the manager is doubtless reduced in part by the guidance of the formula.

There are no long-established formula-plan investment funds which can be used as examples of the performance of the idea. Several actual cases exist—the Tomlinson and Cottle-Whitman books mention plans used by Yale University, Oberlin College, Vassar College, Kenyon College, and several investment counsel firms which advise endowed institutions—but the plans all seem to have originated in comparatively recent years and to have been constantly modified. Appraisals of their capabilities must therefore be based on hypothetical cases. This is done quite extensively in the books previously mentioned.

The formula plans have mathematical and historical merit. They promise a satisfying though not spectacular profit performance if the investor selects his stocks successfully and interprets the formula's timing steps properly. They promise a chance at very substantial profits under the same conditions, if speculative stocks are used luckily. But if the market does not follow historical patterns or if the formula's timing proves impossible to interpret, the formula is useless, and speculative positions taken in pursuit of it are dangerous. The obvious conclusion is that a formula plan may be useful in any given instance, but that it cannot be considered a royal road to riches.

QUESTIONS AND PROBLEMS

1. Would a good-grade common stock fluctuate in price as much as the Dow-Jones Industrial Average? Why? How much does the Average vary during a 10-year period?

2. What elements contribute to the demand for stocks? To the supply?

3. Why do most stocks participate in a primary market upswing or

decline? Why are there significant differences in the extent to which stocks participate, in any particular case?

4. How would you learn the extent to which stocks of a particular quality or industry participate in market movements?

5. What are the basic causes of primary stock market movements? Is it possible for a business boom to proceed while the stock market remains unchanged? Why?

6. Would it be reasonable for an investor to try to avoid purchases at secondary highs or sales in secondary troughs? How?

7. Could the Dow theory possibly work out in a period in which business news and prospects are chiefly concerned with political policies and wars? Would it be sound to follow Dow theory "signals" which call for the buying of stocks only when the market seems generally undervalued and the selling signals only when stocks seem overvalued?

8. Is it wise to buy stocks which seem to be definite bargains at a time when the general market appears to be weak?

9. Would you recommend that an individual who believed business conditions to be deteriorating should sell all his stocks or merely shift from dynamic to defensive types?

10. Explain tax selling. Why is early December often a bargain season for stock investors?

11. If you wanted to try dollar averaging, how would you select your stocks? Would commissions and odd-lot differentials obliterate any possible gain? Would you buy dynamic stocks in low markets and defensive ones in high markets?

12. Would you call the constant ratio plan a speculative device or just a procedure for sound investment management? How about the fixed dollar sum plan?

13. Explain how the suggested supplementary rules could make the constant ratio plan more profitable.

14. Would the necessity of keeping some of the funds devoted to a formula plan invested in savings accounts or low-yield bonds not be adverse to total results, in that these would yield relatively little?

15. Why would a variable ratio plan promise greater gains than a constant ratio plan, if successful? Would you approve of a "median line" as a part of a variable ratio plan?

16. Does it seem that stock market fluctuations are dominated more by the values involved or by speculators' attempts to sell and buy when they think market movements down or up are impending? Are there other important market influences?

REFERENCES

Badger, Ralph E., and Harry G. Guthmann: *Investment Principles and Practices*, Prentice-Hall, Inc., New York, 1951, Chap. 25.

Bellemore, Douglas H.: *Investments Principles and Practices*, B. C. Forbes and Sons Publishing Co., Inc., New York, 1953, Chaps. 15, 16.

Cottle, C. Sidney, and W. Tate Whitman: *Investment Timing: The Formula Plan Approach*, McGraw-Hill Book Company, Inc., New York, 1953.

Dice, Charles A., and Wilford J. Eiteman: *The Stock Market*, McGraw-Hill Book Company, Inc., New York, 1952, Chaps. 18, 24, 26.

Drew, Garfield A.: *New Methods for Profit in the Stock Market*, The Metcalf Press, Boston, 1950.

Graham, Benjamin, and David L. Dodd: *Security Analysis*, McGraw-Hill Book Company, Inc., New York, 1951, Chap. 3.

Grodinsky, Julius: *Investments*, The Ronald Press Company, New York, 1953, Chap. 23.

Leffler, George L.: *The Stock Market*, The Ronald Press Company, New York, 1951, Chaps. 31–34.

Plum, Lester V., and Joseph H. Humphrey: *Investment Analysis and Management*, Richard D. Irwin, Inc., Homewood, Ill., 1951, Chaps. 17, 18.

Robbins, Sidney M.: *Managing Securities*, Houghton Mifflin Company, Boston, 1954, Chaps. 11, 37, 38.

Tomlinson, Lucile: *Practical Formulas for Successful Investing*, Wilfred Funk, Inc., New York, 1953.

Tomlinson, Lucile: *Successful Investing Formulas*, Barron's Publishing Company, Inc., New York, 1947.

Chapter 11: INVESTMENT INFORMATION AND ADVICE

There is probably no other industry or type of business as abundantly supplied with trade literature and reference materials as is the securities business. Periodicals, books, and special reports by experts are available on every hand. The quantity and quality of the information available are almost incredible to newcomers in the business. It is not possible to say that any reasonable question about any proffered security can be answered, but it is possible to say that adequate information can be had on so many topics that there is no reason to invest where reasonable questions remain unanswered. It does not follow, of course, that an amateur investor or a careless one can obtain information which will guard him from loss, for even an experienced and diligent man must expect some error in a field where every transaction involves a forecast of the future. But the diligent amateur can, with the assistance of a modicum of professional help and knowledge, make very practical use of most of these materials.

For those who do not care to undertake the study which sound securities investing requires, there are several varieties of professional investment counsel which may be obtained. Much free advice can be had from brokers and dealers, both on securities selections and on personal portfolio problems. There are also commercial advisory publications, which undertake to report the results of their staffs' analytical work in condensed form to their clients. For clients who prefer personal consultations, professional investment advisers and bank trust departments offer consulting or investment management services for a fee. Since all these types of services are varied and combined in many forms, an investor has a wide choice of services available to his needs.

Because there is no clear line of demarcation between the purveyors of investment information and the investment advisers who sell their clients a service of investment analysis and advice, this chapter will present the two functions as related and overlapping, as indeed they are.

Types of Information

The information available to investors falls readily into two classifications, that dealing with general economics, market behavior, and industries, and that dealing with specific corporations and public debtors and specific securities. The investor must be interested in both types. If he holds Wilson & Co. preferred stock, he is interested in general prosperity, the trend of commodity prices, the market for preferred stocks, and the outlook for the meat packing industry; but he must also watch Wilson's profit progress, working capital position, dividend policy, and the position of its stock.

The sources of investment information used may also be divided into two groups, according to their reporting practices; one group presents facts as dispassionately as possible, leaving all interpretation to the investor, while the other presents an analysis which offers interpretations and conclusions. Uncolored facts are demanded by an analyst who is seeking specific information or testing a hypothesis of his own, but most investors like to read arguments and opinions which they can then accept or reject. After all, it is easier to review the conclusions of others than to formulate one's own. Also, the editors of an analytical report can be expected to call attention to the most important factors in the situation, thus assisting the reader to make his own decision.

Decisions by individual investors or their investment advisers will still be necessary, however. The editors of investment literature are not so infallible that their advice can be followed without hesitation. In fact, they do not agree with each other; two leading advisory services recently published their lists of the 150 best buys chosen from the same 3,200 stocks. Only 18 stocks appeared on both lists. Very few of the selections favored by one service were given low ratings by the other, but the divergences are nevertheless significant. Investors must also base their choices to a considerable extent on their own needs for stability of income, quality standards, diversification in certain industries or areas, and other matters of which the editor of an advisory publication can have no knowledge.

Sources of Information and Advice

Investors in securities obtain information and advice from a great variety of sources. However, it seems desirable to classify these sources for brief review into seven groups and to discuss each in turn. The first group consists of the publications of the three large financial publishers, Standard & Poor's Corporation, Moody's Investors Service, and the Fitch Publishing Company. These firms sell a number of informational and advisory publications, most of which are quite expensive. Many investors subscribe to them, but most people use them without cost in brokerage offices or public libraries. The second important group of sources consists of a number of investment advisory publications, which offer printed investment advice in condensed form, based on extensive analytical work, for a rather high annual subscription price. A third group of sources provides help through personal consultation and counsel, rather than advice in printed columns; the service may be free or it may cost a fee; it is provided by brokers, banks, attorneys, accountants, and professional investment counselors. The other important source groups will only be mentioned at this point but will be discussed in detail later; they are (4) newspapers and periodicals, (5) annual reports and prospectuses, (6) literature provided by brokers and dealers, and (7) certain specialized sources and reference works.

Standard & Poor's Corporation

Standard & Poor's Corporation, one of the leading financial publishing firms, offers nine major financial reporting services and several minor ones. Subscribers include securities firms, banks, insurance companies, libraries, and private investors, among others. Since the services are sold separately and overlap to some extent, few subscribers buy them all. The major services are quite expensive, ranging up to $240 per year for the *Standard Corporation Records*.

The best known of the S and P services is the *Standard Corporation Records*. This service consists of six large loose-leaf manuals in which descriptions of all important corporate and many public issuers of securities are maintained. Each description is revised annually, and later information is added by a monthly supplement and a daily supplement which are indexed separately. The *Corporation Records* coverage is very broad; it includes nearly all important issuers of both listed and unlisted securities. On the smaller concerns the material presented is somewhat sketchy, but very comprehensive descriptions of important concerns are offered. The descriptions will include the firm's address, state of incorporation, officers and directors, business history, property and business, important provisions of articles and bylaws, bond indenture provisions, comparative financial statements, financial ratios and per share figures, and market price history of each issue. The descriptions in the *Corporation Records* are completely factual and without editorial comment of any kind, except that most of the bonds are given a quality rating by letter and number.

The next most extensive S and P services are the *Standard Listed Stock Reports,* the *Standard Over-the-counter Stock Reports,* and the *Standard Bond Reports.* Each of these services consists of a set of several hundred advisory reports on important securities. The individual reports are revised two to four times annually, to keep them up to date. Each report is on two sides of a single page and consists of certain statistical data on sales, earnings, dividends, market history, and financial position, coupled with a description of the company, its business, its prospects, and an appraisal of the market outlook for the issue. The stock report is a candid editorial opinion throughout and includes a summary comment on the stock's attractiveness at the current market price relative to other stock prices. The bond report is less definitely advisory, but rates the bond as to quality and eligibility for institutional holding, and frequently expresses a brief opinion of the bond's market position.

A fourth major S and P service, and one which is of paramount significance to amateur investors, is the *Standard Trade and Securities Service.* This service consists of three loose-leaf volumes, one of which is given over to business and financial statistics, including a fine collection of securities price and yield indexes. The other two volumes—sometimes sold separately as the *Industry Surveys*—contain treatises on the history, status, and prospects of 46 important industries—steel, petroleum, chain stores, banking, insurance, and the like. These industry descriptions are designed to acquaint the investor, in 15 to 30 concise pages, with the important features of each industry which make for stability, profitableness, and growth. These factors are then reviewed in appraising the current outlook for the industry. The presentations include brief comments and comparisons of the leading companies in each industry and are critical and advisory throughout. The loose-leaf sections are frequently revised to keep them up to date.

Other S and P services include the *Outlook,* a weekly printed periodical which is developed as an investment advisory service. It carries articles on market behavior, the outlook for various industries, important individual issues, lists of securities on which purchase or sale is recommended, and suggested groups of stocks and bonds which are deemed suitable as complete portfolios. The *Outlook* at $65 per year is much less costly than S and P's major services and is intended for individual investors. S and P also compile monthly a *Stock Guide* and a *Bond Guide,* which are 150 to 200-page booklets in which all important corporation securities are listed. The books show earnings, dividend, yield, capital structure, working capital, and market price data and rate stocks as to attractiveness for purchase and bonds as to quality and eligibility. These books may be purchased on subscription but are often distributed free to customers by brokers and dealers. S and P have several other publications which are bought chiefly by brokers and dealers and, in addition, offer a personalized service in planning and supervising portfolios for either individuals or institutions.

Moody's Investors Service

The Moody publications consist of three parts: the manuals, the manual supplements, and the stock and bond surveys. The manuals are five large books of 1,500 to 3,000 pages each, one on industrials, one on utilities, one on transportation companies, one on governments (all public issuers), and one on financial (bank, insurance company, investment company, real estate company) issuers. They are published annually and include corporate descriptive data very similar to that provided in the *Standard Corporation Records.* In addition, each volume has a special features section which includes very valuable summaries of legislation, industry history, standard financial ratios, and other material. The manuals are completely factual and nonadvisory, except that most bonds are given a quality rating and an opinion is expressed as to their eligibility for institutional investment. Each manual is brought down to date weekly by an accompanying *manual supplement,* which is a loose-leaf volume containing factual information subsequent to the date of the manual.

Moody ventures into the opinion and advisory field in two loose-leaf volumes entitled *Moody's Stock Survey* and *Moody's Bond Survey.* Each volume addresses itself in weekly releases to general business and securities market conditions and prophecies concerning them. Additional articles discuss the problems and prospects of individual industries and express opinions concerning specific corporations and their securities. Suggestions for switches from one stock or bond to another are commonly made. New securities offerings and recapitalization proposals are discussed, the securities are appraised as to quality, and suggestions as to purchase or rejection are made. On the whole, the Moody opinions give the impression of a relatively conservative editorial outlook. As a separate service, Moody's also publishes a twice-monthly pocket reference manual on bonds, which contains the usual statistics on call price, market history, earnings coverage, quality rating, and current market price.

In a more personalized vein Moody's offers to individuals an advisory reports service, through which the subscriber receives analytical reports and advice several times a year on the stocks and bonds in which he is interested. Only the securities on which the subscriber has requested reports are included in his service. For people who want more positive guidance, Moody's will undertake the responsibility of planning portfolios and recommending specific purchases and sales.

Fitch Investment Service

The Fitch Investment Service, the third of the large investment publication services, does not offer a basic information service comparable to Moody's *Manuals* and the *Standard Corporation Records.* The principal Fitch publications are three loose-leaf services consisting of one-page summary digests of (1) listed stocks, (2) unlisted stocks, and (3) bonds. These reports are editorial and advisory in nature and very similar in most respects to the *Standard Stock Reports.* A second group of Fitch services includes the *Fitch Stock Record,* the *Fitch Bond Record,* and the *Fitch Stock Summary,* all of which are pamphlet statistical summaries issued monthly or more often. They assign one line in a tabular form to each security and indicate its price history, earnings coverage, dividend, place in the capital structure, quality rating, and other data. These publications are sold to brokers and dealers for distribution to their customers. A third Fitch publication is the *Weekly Survey,* a printed advisory service presenting articles on financial affairs and specific investments, along with advice on these subjects. The Fitch organization also operates a personal investment advisory or management service for individuals and firms who wish to employ them in this capacity.

Other Published Services

Investors are offered other publications and services almost too numerous to mention. Most of them have merit, though some are apparently based on theories of stock market performance which are almost as fantastic as the economic panaceas which were so common a few years ago. These services can be roughly classified into four groups: First, there are several whose main contribution is to chart the price history of selected stocks, usually comparing price with dividends, earnings, other stocks in the same industry, and certain market averages. From these graphic and tabular presentations the investor is expected to draw his own conclusions. Second, there are several, of which the *Investograph Service* and the *Value Line* are among the best known, which employ technical and mathematical formulas to analyze both general market positions and fundamental values for specific stocks. The results are integrated with conventional research and published periodically as loose-leaf pages, to form a concise but substantial advisory and reference service. Third, there are a number of services which report the results of economic and investment studies to their subscribers in highly condensed printed letters. These letters usually offer advice both on market policy and on individual stocks. Typical of these would be the Babson, Brookmire, and United Business services.

Finally, there are many services which offer, by means of secret formulas or the personal prescience of the staff, to determine for the investor when the next rise or fall in the market will occur and how far it will go. Sometimes the stocks which will move farthest and fastest are also identified. These mystic auguries are distributed by air mail or telegram in time to permit the subscribers to profit greatly in the market. Strangely, the possessor of the crystal ball continues to eke out a paltry sustenance in the publishing business.

A survey of these services leaves the impression that most of them are primarily concerned with attempts to gain stock market profits, since the advertisements frequently feature such offerings as "our list of ten fast-moving stocks for the next rise" or "our supervised list which consistently out-performs the general market." However, the better grade services usually present well-developed opinions on (1) the position of the general market, (2) the positions of individual industries, and (3) stocks and bonds recommended for profit or for income or for price stability, and (4) portfolio policy and selections for investors of different means and tastes. Some of the services, for example *Value Line,* provide their subscribers with extensive analytical studies of industries and the leading companies in them. Other services merely mention their investment selections by name in their advisory letters, leaving the subscriber to investigate elsewhere if he chooses, or to accept their advice on faith.

Many services offer supplementary personal accommodation to subscribers desiring it. This extra service, which usually costs an extra fee, may range all the way from answering questions by letter to complete portfolio management. Without supplementary accommodation, the services range in cost from $25 to $200 per year; including personal consultation, the fee is usually much higher.

Personalized Investment Advice

An investor in securities needs to procure or to supply at least six types of investment supervision. He must keep his securities physically safe from fire or other loss; he must give them a mechanical supervision which will take care of rights, conversion and exchange options, maturing bonds and coupons, and similar matters; he must have accounting records, for income tax and other purposes; he should have an estate plan, which will allow for adequate liquidity and divisibility; he needs a general portfolio policy, incorporating his estate plan but allowing also for other objectives, such as diversification, general liquidity, price-level protection, and possible appreciation; and the selections of individual securities must be made. These six functions must be performed either by the investor or by persons paid to perform them. Parts or all of these functions may be obtained from brokers, investment service organizations, investment counselors, banks, and accountants or attorneys.

Brokers are accustomed to give all their clients a considerable amount of free advice on tax matters, estate and portfolio planning, and selection of securities. They also furnish library facilities which will contribute to an investor's efforts to solve his problems for himself. Finally, they often provide free safekeeping for securities held in customers' accounts. For large accounts brokers often do considerably more; for example, one typical firm announces its willingness to accept custody of portfolios aggregating $50,000 or more, to assist the customer in planning the portfolio to his needs, to keep accounting records on it, to handle such details as rights and exchanges after consultation with the customer, and to review the portfolio occasionally and recommend changes in conformity with market conditions and the customer's expressed policy. All this is done without charge. Other firms make a charge of $\frac{1}{10}$ to $\frac{2}{10}$ per cent per year for such services.

The publishers of investment services offer a wide variety of personalized advice. The less costly types are usually limited to an annual or semiannual review of the client's portfolio in the light of the client's desires and needs as disclosed on a questionnaire submitted by him. The client is usually also entitled to submit occasional letters of inquiry about his policies or his holdings. More elaborate personal service may include detailed portfolio planning in accordance with the client's needs, continuous supervision of the client's holdings by the organization, day-by-day recommendations to the client, and return reports by him to the organization. The most elaborate of these services may include management supervision of a portfolio in the custody of a broker or a bank by the advisory organization, which will order purchases and sales under a power of attorney and perhaps maintain the accounting records itself. The cost of thorough supervisory service is likely to run as high as $\frac{1}{2}$ per cent of the principal per annum on amounts under $1,000,000, with a minimum of $500 to $1,000. Such services are often used by small insurance companies and endowed institutions as well as by individuals.

The term investment counsel is applied to investment advisers whose services are sold to the public on a personal basis, not in conjunction with a publication which is regarded as a vital part of the service. Investment counselors render a service very similar to the more elaborate types furnished by the publisher-advisers described in the preceding paragraph, for the same types of clientele, at about the same cost. Because most investment counselors are local professional men serving local clients, there is often a more intimate contact with clients than is possible to nationwide publishing organizations. Most investment counselors find it impractical to accept clients with portfolios under $50,000, although some undertake to service small accounts by recommending "standard" portfolios or by operating open-end investment companies into which such funds may be directed.

Banks have developed several types of services which investors may use. The simplest of these, which is sometimes termed the custodian account, obligates the bank to maintain physical care of the securities, keep accounting records, collect income, call the owner's attention to such matters as rights and bond maturities, and execute transactions at the owner's request. No advice or counsel is included; the annual fee is about one-fourth of one per cent of the market value of the portfolio, with a minimum of $50. A second and somewhat more elaborate type of bank service may be termed the limited management agency. It includes all the services of the custodian account but, in addition, obligates the bank to review the holdings periodically and to make recommendations for changes if needed. Because the bank accepts some responsibility for choice of investments, these accounts are usually not desired if the customer insists upon speculating extensively. The annual cost of this service will range between one-fourth and one-half of one per cent of the principal involved, with a minimum of $50 specified, although the exact sums will depend on the amount of service promised. A third type of service is termed the full management agency. In this case the bank offers all of the custodian services, promises continuous investment supervision upon the basis of agreed policies, and undertakes to buy and sell securities as needed for the account under a power of attorney. This is not a trust, but the cost approximates that of a trust service, ranging between three-tenths and three-fourths of one per cent per annum, typically. A fourth service furnished by a few banks is that of investment supervision without custody, similar in nature to the service of an investment counselor. This service seems to be intended mainly for conservative institutions such as insurance companies, hospitals, and schools. Finally, banks offer investment supervision in connection with their trust functions. Funds or property may be delivered to a bank as trustee under the terms of a voluntary deed or a will; the bank takes title as trustee, manages the property as directed in the deed of trust or will, bears responsibility for proper custody and supervision, and pays out income and principal when and as directed in the trust instrument. This arrangement is normally more stable and enduring than an agency contract, and the cost is about the same as that for a full management agency. Trusts are accepted in amounts much smaller than the $50,000 minimum usually desired for an agency account. Small trust funds are now pooled by many banks in "common trust funds" which afford diversification as well as professional selection and management. All bank investment policy appears to lean definitely to the conservative side.

Accountants and attorneys are often in a position to render investment services to clients, particularly in relation to tax matters, estate planning, and portfolio planning. Their contributions are too varied to permit any adequate description here.

Public Regulation of Investment Advice

Abuses of trust by investment advisers led the Congress to enact the Investment Advisers' Act of 1940,[1] which undertakes to impose sound principles of conduct upon persons who sell investment advice, and to bring their activities under the supervision of the SEC. Many states have laws with a similar purpose. These laws ordinarily do not apply to banks and brokers, who are separately regulated, nor to newspapers and magazines of general circulation, nor to attorneys, accountants, and certain others. Also, the statutes do not attempt to assure the competence of the advisers or the accuracy of their conclusions; public responsibility ends with the prevention of fraud and deception.

Appraisal of Investment Advice

A number of attempts to tabulate the results of "buy" and "sell" instructions to clients by leading advisory services have led the tabulators to the conclusion that the clients would have done as well if

[1] This act is examined in more detail in Chap. 12.

they had merely held diversified portfolios of good securities throughout the period and had made no effort to improve results by buying and selling as the experts suggested. The experience of the investment companies, whose carefully managed portfolios have just about paralleled the performance of the market averages during the past few years, lend support to this view.[2] The investment experts have all made wise decisions, but they have also made many compensating bad ones, particularly in their attempts to prognosticate on the future of economic affairs and the trend of the general market.

However, there are other factors to be considered. Investment portfolios do not appear, ready planned, as gifts from heaven; they have to be developed to suit the individual need. Furthermore, investment securities which will parallel the general market in performance must be chosen; it would be easy to do much worse than the general market, as many investors have learned to their sorrow. Again, the relative certainty and peace of mind which should accompany the use of competent professional investment management is worth having, and the long successful history of endowments and similar funds under professional management indicates that success is almost totally possible. Finally, the technical administration and record keeping which some investment supervision embraces is a worth-while service for the preoccupied or the uninitiated.

In general, it is easier to have faith in investment advice which is primarily concerned with security, and only secondarily interested in attempts to make market profits, than in advice geared to an ambition to "beat the stock market." It is easier to choose profitable, enduring investments than it is to find the securities most likely to rise in price, and less risks need be taken in pursuing the objective. But it must be admitted that stock market fluctuations are often the logical results of ascertainable causes, and even here an expert ought to be right more often than he is wrong. Experts ought to have better performance ratings than rank amateurs. Consequently, good logic will not permit the decrying of investment advice of any type which is soundly conceived and not too reckless.

All this leads inevitably to the conclusion that good investment advice or supervision may be in order for many people. The type of service each person should have and the identification of the good adviser whose services should be chosen are problems deserving care-

2 See Table 34, Chap. 19.

ful thought; but they are not problems which should burden an intelligent man unreasonably. The investor must inevitably shoulder at least this responsibility.

Newspapers and Periodicals

Most metropolitan daily newspapers include a financial section of fair quality, and some of them, like the *New York Times,* contain very good ones. Good daily financial sections include sales quotations from the New York and local stock exchanges, a limited number of quotations from the unlisted markets, earnings and dividend announcements by major corporations, a report on the market averages, highlights from the business news, editorial or syndicated commentaries on market and business affairs, and announcements of new securities offerings. Except for the very best ones, it is probably fair to say that newspaper financial sections do a better job of reporting securities market affairs than they do of acquainting their readers with the progress of industries and economic affairs. American finance also enjoys the services of two outstanding daily financial newspapers, the *Wall Street Journal* and the *New York Journal of Commerce.* These dailies do a somewhat more elaborate job of reporting stock and bond quotations than the general newspapers do, but their outstanding sphere of excellence is that of reporting news of corporations, industries, products and commodities, financial affairs, taxes, labor, public policy, and foreign relations from a financial viewpoint. Much of their reporting is interspersed with interpretation, to give their readers perspective on the significance of the news. Daily reading of a financial newspaper by a nonprofessional investor is a time-consuming task, but the contribution which such study can make to a grasp of financial and business affairs is substantial.

Six general-purpose financial periodicals are best known to investors. The *Commercial and Financial Chronicle,* also known as the *Financial Chronicle,* is a combination magazine and financial newspaper. One of its two weekly issues is chiefly used for articles on business and financial affairs. The articles include many on securities markets and industries but also place heavy emphasis on Federal Reserve policy, public finance, labor, and other public policy matters. The second of the two weekly issues is a weekly financial newspaper which provides an excellent coverage of both stock exchange and unlisted quotations, as well as condensed news of corporations, industries, and business affairs. *Barron's* is a weekly investment magazine published by Dow, Jones & Co., publishers of the *Wall Street Journal*. It contains extensive editorial commentaries on investment and financial affairs; articles on corporations, industries, and products from an investment point of view; excellent tabular reports on stock exchange quotations; other stock and bond price data; and limited over-the-counter reports and business news notes. The *Financial World* is a weekly investment magazine which carries editorial comment and articles on industries and individual investment. It offers specific advice to investors on policy and individual investment, features brief sketches of corporations and quality ratings on their securities, but does not carry quotations. Subscribers also receive an annual descriptive reference manual on leading stocks and a monthly pocket statistical manual which rates listed stocks according to quality. The *Magazine of Wall Street* is published on alternate weeks. Like the *Financial World,* it carries no quotations but does an excellent job as a purveyor of financial information and investment advice to its readers. The investment advice is definite and specific. *Forbes* is a business and financial magazine, with only a portion of its pages given to finance and investments. It is published twice monthly. Its comments on the investments field are both informative and advisory. *United States Investor,* a weekly publication, devotes its issues mostly to general articles and brief advisory comments on investments and insurance. Subscribers to the *Investor* may also subscribe to a supplemental weekly *Investment Counsel Edition,* which carries detailed recommendations on portfolio policy and individual securities and industries.

These financial and investment periodicals are widely read and are of good quality. Their subscription prices range from $4 to $45 per year. The investor who buys and reads one or more of them regularly will obtain many sound suggestions and increasing competence as an investment manager, at a cost of a moderate amount of money and a considerable amount of time.

Specialized Sources

The specialized sources of information available to the investor and actually studied by many professionals in the investment field are almost too numerous to mention. Almost every trade journal, such as *Steel, Railway Age,* and *Oil and Gas Journal,* has information and statistical data which are of value. A long list of trade associations and research organizations, such as Edison Electric Institute, American Petroleum Institute, F. W. Dodge Corporation, and Automobile Manufacturers' Association, furnish ideas and data. Government sources such as the ICC, U.S. Department of Commerce, and SEC have much that is pertinent and helpful.

A considerable number of specialized information sources are regarded as the outstanding reference works in their particular fields. For example, the *Dun and Bradstreet Municipal Reports* are a primary source of data on the indebtedness, tax position, and general credit standing of most of the larger borrowing municipalities. These reports are not published in book form but are purchased individually by municipal bond dealers. The Alfred M. Best Company is the publisher of manuals on fire insurance stocks, casualty insurance stocks, life insurance companies, and insurance statistics. In addition, the firm has an insurance stock reporting service and two monthly journals on property insurance and life insurance finance. No other source provides as extensive material on insurance finance. Arthur Wiesenberger & Co., New York securities dealers, have developed their annual volume *Investment Companies* until it has become an institution in its field. The volume carries information on legislation, taxes, and administrative policies in the field, has comprehensive statistical comparisons of leading companies, and describes each one separately. Between issues the Wiesenberger firm is a prolific source of news and figures about investment companies. *Walker's Manual of Pacific Coast Securities* is an annual reference manual after the manner of Moody's, but on a much smaller scale. In view of the more detailed coverage of large business concerns in other reference sources, the significance of Walker's is greatest as a convenient reference source covering approximately one thousand publicly financed Pacific Coast corporations, including many which are not adequately described elsewhere. The firm also publishes an excellent weekly newsletter which is devoted chiefly to analytical reports and studies of Pacific Coast securities.

Annual Reports and Prospectuses

Corporate annual reports plus the proxy reports, digests of annual meetings, and special interim reports which are often sent to stockholders are often extremely illuminating. Modern reports to stockholders are becoming quite comprehensive. Financial statements in the better reports are thorough and well explained, operating policies are outlined, hopes and problems are explained. Though much of this material gets into the securities manuals, a great deal does not. A careful investor would do well to study annual reports obtained from the company or borrowed from brokers before buying stock, and he most certainly should study them when he receives them as a stockholder.

Prospectuses are issued by corporations as descriptive literature in connection with the sale of new securities. Most of them are now issued under SEC regulations, in compliance with the Securities Act of 1933. The better ones are gold mines of information, containing corporate history, description and appraisal of property, descriptions of current problems and affairs, descriptions of securities, and other matters. Prospectuses are issued only when securities are sold, so are not kept up to date, but subsequent data can be had from other sources. Prospectuses may also be difficult to obtain except on loan from dealers' files, after the initial offering period has passed.

Brokers' and Dealers' Literature

Some of the best and some of the worst investment literature is provided by brokers and dealers. Securities firms generally are eager to enhance their own prestige by offering their customers good analytical work and sound advice. They may on occasion be biased, through a desire to sell their own wares, but poor literature and advice seems more commonly to stem from haste or incompetence than from selfish bias. It is difficult to tell good literature from bad unless the subject matter is intimately known to the reader, but the reputation of the firm and the quality of its personnel should afford a clue.

Investment house literature can be divided for present purposes into three types, which may be called (1) specific analyses, (2) statistical comparisons, and (3) pamphlets on industry or market conditions. Any of these may be elaborately printed or very inexpensively mimeographed, as the firm's plans may dictate. Specific analyses are discussions of the position and prospects of individual securities. These analyses may contain definite statements of opinion that the security is attractive for investment, or the presentation may avoid giving advice. In most cases firms will not bother calling their customers' attention to a security unless an express or implied recommendation of some sort is intended. Statistical comparisons of the stocks of similar or competing concerns are among the interesting contributions which securities firms make to investment literature. Such studies may tabulate types of property held, capital structures, sales, expenses, earnings, dividends, price history, and other items. Outstanding examples of this type of work are found in comparisons of bank, insurance, investment company, public utility, and oil company securities. Investment house letters and pamphlets about industry conditions or securities market conditions range from brief notes suggesting a course of action to extensive treatises presenting the state of the nation and the comparative condition of all industries. Most investment house literature is distributed free to clients and other inquirers.

Reading the Financial Page

Reading the hieroglyphics of a newspaper's financial page is frequently a problem to the neophyte in the investments field. The structure of financial pages is by no means uniform, but there is so much of conventional meaning to the forms used that they are rarely explained in detail. Comprehension by the reader is taken for granted. The following small section from a tabulation of New York Stock Exchange transactions on September 2, 1948, is more complete than most, but it will serve to illustrate the devices used:

1948		*Stock and*						*Net*	*Closing*	
High	*Low*	*Dividend Rate*	*Sales*	*Open*	*High*	*Low*	*Close*	*Change*	*Bid*	*Ask*
10	6⅜	Jacobs, F. L.	1	7¼	7¼	7¼	7¼	−⅛	7¼	7½
48	39½	Jewel Tea 3.00xd	4	46½	46¾	46½	46¾	+1⅜	46	47½
99	92	Do. Pfd. 3.75	.40	95	95	95	95		93½	95
42¼	34¼	Johns-Manville 1.60	12	36½	36½	36⅛	36½	+¼	36⅛	36½
113⅞	100½	Do. Pfd. 3.50	2	104	104½	104	104½	+½	104	105

The 1948 high and low columns list the highest and lowest prices paid for board lots of stock thus far in the year. The stock and dividend rate column names the stock and the apparent annual dividend rate. The Do. Pfd. shown under the Jewel Tea and Johns-Manville items is an abbreviation for "ditto (the company name) preferred." If no dividend is being paid, as was the case with the F. L. Jacobs Company, the dividend space is left blank. The xd following the Jewel Tea dividend rate indicates that the stock was selling ex-dividend the current payment on this date for the first time If any stock in the list was paying irregularly, a sum accompanied by a footnote reference would have disclosed the fact. The sales column in this case lists the number of 100-share transactions which took place, except that only 40 shares of Jewel Tea preferred were traded. The Open, High, Low, and Close columns indicate the price of the first, highest, lowest, and last sales of the day, respectively. The Net Change column shows the difference in price between the last sale on this date and the last on the preceding day, except that in the case of a stock selling ex-dividend the net change is adjusted for the amount of the dividend; a blank space means no change. The Closing Bid and Ask figures represent the ruling proposals on the floor at the close of trading.

Corporate bond transactions are reported in almost identical fashion. Sales are reported in units of $1,000 bonds, and the bonds are identified by corporate name, coupon rate, and maturity date, as, for example, Delaware and Hudson 4s of 1963. Prices are quoted as usual in percentages and eighths. Government long-term bond transactions are similarly reported, with three exceptions: First, the various issues are usually footnoted to show whether their interest is taxable and whether the bonds are eligible for commercial bank ownership. Second, the bonds are usually shown with two dates, for example, Treasury 2¾s, 1960–65. The bonds are callable at par on and after the first date and are due on the second. Third, government bonds are quoted in percentages and thirty-seconds. For convenience, the number of thirty-seconds is written after a decimal point in the price figure. Thus a government bond quotation of 101 and seven thirty-seconds would be written 101.7; one quoted at 101 and one-half would be 101.16.

The over-the-counter quotations in short-term government issues and certain municipals are often expressed in yields rather than prices. Thus on September 1, 1948, the United States Treasury bills maturing December 2, 1948, were quoted at 1.08 per cent bid, 1.04 per cent asked. The asking price was obviously higher than the bid, because it yielded less.

Over-the-counter quotations in stocks or bonds seldom show sales reports, since these are private transactions. The quotations usually consist of bid price, asked price, bid price the previous day, and net change in the bid. Sometimes the year's range in bid prices is also shown. Published over-the-counter bids are usually at or close to a true inside market; the published asked prices are usually too high to be realistic.

Dividends declared by corporations are usually reported in tables which show the name of the stock, the amount per share to be paid, the stock-of-record date, and the payment date.

QUESTIONS AND PROBLEMS

1. In considering Monsanto Chemical Company stock for investment, would you prefer a factual description or an editorial presentation? What would be the worst hazards in the former? In the latter?

2. What materials and services would you want to consult before investing your money in Monsanto? Are all of these concerned with the company and its affairs?

3. Where would you find investment-minded comments on the state of the nation and on the position of the stock market? Are these proper topics for investment analysts to ponder?

4. Would it be feasible to choose promising securities by selecting only those recommended by several published services? How would you go about this?

5. If a busy professional man asked your opinion, would you advise employing an investment counselor to manage a $100,000 fund? Why or why not?

6. If a middle-aged widow unskilled in business informed you that she was considering having her bank manage her $100,000 fund, would you recommend a limited management agency, a full management agency, or a trust? Why?

7. Why are annual reports and prospectuses highly prized by investors who supervise their own investments?

8. Obtain a newspaper financial page and examine every table of figures in it. If United States Treasury bills were quoted 1.16 per cent bid, 1.12 per cent asked, would this mean that someone was offering to pay more than someone else was asking for the bills? Explain.

9. If a table headed Dividends Announced contained the data "Adams Express Company $.50 June 22–July 2," what would it mean?

REFERENCES

Bellemore, Douglas H.: *Investments Principles and Practices,* B. C. Forbes and Sons Publishing Co., Inc., New York, 1953, Chap. 13.

Financial Handbook, The Ronald Press Company, New York, 1948, pp. 201–212.

Grodinsky, Julius: *Investments,* The Ronald Press Company, New York, 1953, Chap. 24.

Jordan, David F., and Herbert E. Dougall: *Investments,* Prentice-Hall, Inc., New York, 1952, Chaps. 12, 13.

Leffler, George L.: *The Stock Market,* The Ronald Press Company, New York, 1951, Chaps. 3, 30.

Pickett, Ralph R., and Marshall D. Ketchum: *Investment Principles and Policy,* Harper & Brothers, New York, 1954, Chap. 9.

Plum, Lester V., and Joseph H. Humphrey: *Investment Analysis and Management,* Richard D. Irwin, Inc., Homewood, Ill., 1951, Chap. 8.

Robbins, Sidney M.: *Managing Securities,* Houghton Mifflin Company, Boston, 1954, Chap. 10.

Chapter 12: PROTECTING THE INVESTOR FROM LOSS

Although state authorities and the responsible elements in the securities business had attempted for many years to enforce reasonable ethical standards, the practices current in the late twenties left much to be desired. Misrepresentation and sharp practices were rife, and some of the procedures followed by the great organized markets were neither fair to their customers nor sound in their effects on the economy as a whole. As long as the markets were buoyant, there was little chance for reform; but when the stock market debacle of 1929–1933 inflicted great losses on investors, the demand for remedial action became too strong to be ignored. New laws were passed by states and by the Federal government, new regulatory commissions were established, and industry agencies for self-policing were established or strengthened.

In general, it appears that the ethical tone of the securities business has been lifted to a confidence-inspiring level. Fraud and deception have been almost eliminated, misleading or exaggeratedly optimistic sales presentations have been curtailed, and the old attitude of *caveat emptor* has been replaced by the viewpoint that securities firms occupy a position of trust in transactions with their clients. The better elements in the business are unquestionably dominant, and they now have powerful legal support in their attempts to suppress questionable practices.

Most of the measures developed to protect the securities investor have been intended to enforce honest and fair practices and have not been concerned with either the quality or the pricing of securities offered for sale. This is in accordance with American tradition; government does not deny its citizens the right to buy or sell as they choose, though it may insist on an honest description of the merchandise. However, even this rule is discarded at times; some of the states refuse to permit corporations pursuing certain objectionable financial practices to sell stock within their borders, and the Federal government presumes to manipulate both stock and bond values through its control of credit facilities and to protect individuals against themselves by limiting their use of credit for speculative purposes.

The modern investor is thus assured of a securities market whose mechanical functioning is reasonably fair and just and whose firms and personnel are in the main committed to high ethical standards. He has prompt and easy redress if he is unfairly treated. Some attempt may be made to keep reckless financial promotions from being offered to him, and he may be restrained from excessive speculative use of credit himself, but other than that his choices of investments remain his own.

Measures taken for the protection of the public may best be reviewed by classifying them by sources—the securities business, the states, and the Federal government. The Federal activities in particular are extensive.

Industry Measures

The securities business has always had to cope with fraud and sharp practices within its ranks. The large amounts of money involved make the business an enticing one to practitioners with elastic consciences, and the surprising gullibility of the public makes protective measures difficult. Securities firms generally contribute freely to better business bureaus and similar agencies, which in turn keep a close watch on dubious promotions and questionable practices in the business. Complaints from the public are analyzed by the better business bureaus and sponsored with the proper prosecuting authorities if such measures are warranted. Frequently the intervention of the bureau can obtain adjustment of a dispute without legal steps. Needless to say, the prosecution of sharp practices by state or Federal authority obtains the full sympathy and support of most elements in the securities business. Because of their fear of libel suits the ethical securities firms will not usually advise or assist the injured clients of unscrupulous firms except to direct them to better business bureaus or prosecuting authorities, but they will cooperate quietly in any steps that these agencies take.

Stock exchanges are usually vigilant in policing the activities of their member firms, for difficulties involving member firms are likely to reflect upon an exchange and all its members. Every exchange has rules covering both floor trading and the members' relations with their customers, and member firms' accounts are audited to see that the firms both obey the rules and maintain standards of financial strength. Employees of member firms are required by some exchanges to pass proficiency tests and sign an agreement to follow certain standards of conduct, if they deal with the public. Complaints involving member firms are investigated by the stock exchanges, and infractions are punished by fine or suspension. The majority of the complaints concern either misunderstandings or technical violations of rules by employees, but all are investigated and settled impartially and promptly.

Trade associations, notably the National Association of Securities Dealers, constitute a third type of industry activity for the protection of the public. Such associations develop ethical codes and standards of procedure which must be adhered to by all members. The NASD has been especially effective in establishing written codes for the guidance of firms and their employees. Customers' disputes with member firms will be investigated upon request by either local or national offices of the organization.

The investing public thus has three powerful private agencies, the better business bureaus, the stock exchanges, and the NASD, to turn to in case of a dispute with a securities firm. In most instances it will not be necessary to seek their help in order to obtain fair treatment from a reputable firm, but they should be used, and promptly, when needed. They make no charge for their services.

State Blue-sky Laws

Though general statutes and common law in every state are available to punish securities frauds, every state except Nevada has seen fit to enact special legislation dealing with the securities business. The state of Kansas pioneered in such legislation in 1911. Early discussion of this field made much use of a vernacular phrase which characterized fraudulent securities as "pieces of the blue sky." The term has stuck. State laws dealing with fraud prevention and punishment in this field are universally known as blue-sky laws.

The blue-sky laws are composed, in varying proportions, of five types of provisions: (1) those establishing commissions or special functionaries in the office of the secretary of state, attorney general, or corporation commissioner to administer this work; (2) those requiring licensing of securities firms and salesmen; (3) those requiring the filing of data on new securities which are offered for sale; (4) those requiring new securities to meet certain standards before offering is permitted; and (5) those defining securities frauds and specifying penalties. Nearly all of the states build their statutes around items 1, 2, and 3, with item 4 imposed upon securities of new corporations or of corporations having no securities listed on a national exchange. In a few states, notably New York, no official permit must be obtained before an issue is offered to the public, but an explicit and vigorously enforced antifraud statute provides a deterrent to objectionable practices.

Under many of the blue-sky laws the enforcing authorities have a great deal of discretionary power. The statutes commonly authorize denial of licenses to firms or salesmen with objectionable records and authorize or require exclusion of securities when the expense of selling exceeds a certain amount, when promoters or insiders receive large amounts for intangible assets or services, when control is peculiarly distributed, and in various other cases. Application of these provisions often becomes a matter of judgment for the enforcing authorities. One or more states banned the offerings of Kaiser-Frazer stock in 1946 and Tucker Corporation in 1947, to cite two very conspicuous examples.

It is probable that the blue-sky laws are stronger and more enforcible now than ever before. They are less conspicuous and less needed, however, because of the extent of Federal regulation under the securities acts. The state authorities are very conveniently located and empowered to handle consumer grievances. In this they are probably less hampered by local politics than ever before, and if the problem has interstate aspects they now have the aid of the SEC rather than the fetters of limited authority. Many of the blue-sky laws exempt numerous types of securities, such as bank issues, public bonds, and railroad securities, but there is enough power in most of the laws to make the enforcing authorities very useful to the investing public.

The Federal Securities Acts

The Federal securities acts consist of a series of eight measures passed in the period 1933–1940 inclusive. These statutes are not exclusively concerned with the regulation of the securities business, but they are all related to the subject of investments in one way or another. During the period 1933–1937 it appeared to many that the Federal legislation was conceived in bitterness and administered with a fervor that was more political than economic. However, attitudes on both sides have been tempered by experience and responsibility. The securities industry has discovered that the Federal authorities will use their power to discourage unsound practices and encourage good ones; and the authorities have demonstrated their willingness to cooperate in businesslike fashion with the industry. There are still problems, to be sure, but few responsible leaders in the securities business would now be willing to see the securities acts repealed or materially weakened.

Securities Act of 1933

This measure, which is sometimes referred to as the truth-in-securities act, was the first of the Federal securities acts. It is concerned chiefly with the requirement that new securities offered to the public be fully and clearly described in the offering literature and sales presentation. The act does not attempt to control the quality of any issue, or the method of distribution, or any phase of corporate business practice. In this it differs from some of the state blue-sky laws under which securities may be disqualified from sale because of some of these factors. The principal features of the act may be summarized as follows:

1. The act applies to all new securities offered to the public by the issuer or by an underwriter or dealer and also to substantial blocks of old securities offered from the corporate treasury or by major stockholders. It does not apply to securities offered privately to a limited number of institutions or people, whether the securities are new or old. Issues under $300,000 may be exempt from the provisions of the act with the consent of the SEC, which administers the law. The following are always exempt: (a) bonds of Federal, state, and local governments and their agencies;

(b) national and state bank stocks; (c) short-term commercial paper; (d) securities issued by nonprofit organizations; (e) building-loan and similar investments, and insurance policies; (f) securities of common carriers; (g) securities issued by a receiver or bankruptcy trustee; (h) securities issued after court approval in a corporate reorganization; (i) securities exchanged for others by the same issuer; and (j) securities sold wholly within one state by a locally incorporated and locally operating concern.

2. The act requires that nonexempt securities be "registered" with the SEC at least 20 days before they are publicly offered. Registration consists of paying a small fee and filing with the SEC a "registration statement" containing a mass of information concerning the legal, commercial, technical, and financial position of the issuer, together with a prospectus which summarizes this information for public use. The commission is required to delay or stop the public offering if any of the information is inadequate or misleading. It may shorten the 20-day waiting period before registration becomes effective, under certain conditions.

3. Until registration becomes fully effective it is illegal to offer the securities for sale or to take subscriptions for them. After registration is effective, no offering may be made or subscription invited unless the offeree is handed a copy of the prospectus. However, a preliminary "red-herring" prospectus may be given to a prospect for his consideration before the effective date, and he may be asked if he is interested in hearing about the forthcoming issue.

4. Any purchaser of a registered security who sustains loss in it may sue for damages if the registration statement or prospectus contained false or misleading statements on material facts. Liability may fall upon the issuer, its officers, directors, accountants, engineers, appraisers, other experts, or any underwriter. However, anyone except the issuer may exonerate himself by proving that his own work in connection with the matter was performed with due care and diligence. Severe penalties as well as civil liabilities are prescribed where the procedure of the act is violated or where fraud is committed in the sale of either registered or exempt securities.

The act as originally passed in 1933 was much more rigorous in imposing civil liabilities and more arbitrary in certain administrative details than the present law. Amendments in 1934 made the liability sections more moderate, and other changes in 1940 enabled the commission to accelerate the effective date of registration or to accept supplements to registration statements without delaying the effective date. In its original form the act was regarded as extremely hazardous to directors, underwriters, accountants, appraisers, and others, and some refused to have any part in the distribution of registered securities. However, this attitude no longer exists. Registration is still expensive, because of the extensive descriptions, legal opinions, appraisals, engineering reports, audits, and printing costs entailed; but analysts are glad to have the information, and the ultimate advantage to the public is probably substantial. The improvement in reported financial statements is especially noteworthy. The commission has insisted on reasonably detailed statements using standard or fully defined accounting methods with adequate explanatory notes and auditors' certificates.

As was noted in a previous chapter, the prospectus developed in connection with a new issue is not only a source of valuable information to an investor who considers purchasing the new security, it is a reference source for years to come. Its thoroughness and dispassionate presentation make it more than ordinarily useful for one who wishes to study his investments carefully. The prospectuses used during the first 15 years of the Securities Act were especially voluminous and led many investors to complain that they were excessively tedious and dry. In fact, many people believed that the lengthy prospectus defeated its own end because investors would not read it. Since 1950 there has been a noticeable trend toward shorter and simpler prospectuses, mainly at the urging of the SEC; in this instance the underwriters and corporate officers hesitated to shorten the prospectuses, for fear of the lawsuits which might develop if any material facts were omitted.

Securities Exchange Act of 1934

In this act Congress extended Federal regulation of the securities business to include all phases of trading in existing securities. The act contains the following principal features:

1. The SEC, consisting of five members appointed by the President with the consent of the Senate, was established to administer this and other related measures. Until the SEC was established the Securities Act of 1933 was administered by the Federal Trade Commission.

2. All stock exchanges of substantial size are required to "register" with the SEC as national securities exchanges. The SEC is given authority over (a) listing or delisting of securities; (b) short selling; (c) floor

trading techniques, including trading by members, specialists, and odd-lot dealers; and (d) general rules and practices of the exchanges.

3. Corporations whose securities are listed on any exchange must file registration statements somewhat similar to those of the 1933 act with the SEC and the stock exchange and must keep them up to date by periodic supplementary reports.

4. Each officer, director, and major stockholder of a corporation whose stock is listed on an exchange must file an initial report disclosing the amount of stock owned and thereafter monthly reports of any changes in his holdings of the stock. If any such person makes a profit in the stock on a transaction which is completed entirely within a 6 months' period, the profit is considered to be due per se to inside information and must be surrendered to the corporation, if it or any stockholder sues to compel such surrender. No officer, director, or major stockholder may sell the stock short.

5. Proxy requests and other consents solicited by managements from owners of listed securities are subject to SEC rules. Such requests must give stockholders an opportunity to instruct their proxy holders how to vote on issues to come before the meeting. Any salaries or fees or other payments made to directoral candidates by the corporation, as well as their stock holdings, must be stated in the proxy material. Opposition proposals and candidates must be given space in the management's proxy material, to present their case.

6. All securities brokers and dealers must register with the SEC, whether affiliated with stock exchanges or not. They must all conduct their affairs in accordance with prescribed standards, must limit their borrowings to reasonable amounts, must keep certain records, and are subject to audit by the SEC.

7. In all securities transactions the act forbids market manipulation, misrepresentation, deception, and any fraudulent practice.

8. The Board of Governors of the Federal Reserve System is authorized to fix the maximum credit which brokers or dealers may extend on margin transactions and which banks may extend by loan, for the purpose of buying or carrying listed securities. The act itself forbids the extension of credit by brokers and dealers on any securities other than listed or "exempted" securities. The latter include only public bonds.

It will be noted that the requirements dealing with registration by corporations, proxy requirements, and stock transactions by insiders apply only to concerns having listed securities. This no doubt has caused some corporations to refuse to list their securities. The SEC in 1946 and 1950 recommended extending these measures to cover certain unlisted securities, but Congress has not yet done so. In its early years the SEC engaged in numerous controversies with the stock exchanges and leading securities houses. In more recent years greater cooperation has been maintained, and substantial progress has been made in improving the techniques and the ethics of the business.

Because this act is long, detailed, and inclusive of many topics, there are few people who endorse it completely. In the main, it is working well. Brokers and dealers both inside and outside the scope of stock exchange authority are controlled, and general standards within the industry have been improved. The limitations imposed on short selling are salutary. Some people will question the desirability of the sweeping control over margin credit, and many dispute the wisdom of driving "insiders" away from trading in their own corporation's stock, but few informed persons will deny that the act now accomplishes most of the good intentions of its framers. There is some evidence that the SEC stretches its regulatory activities under this and the other securities acts well beyond both the intended scope of the law and the need for regulation, but this is to be preferred to error in the direction of laxity.

Public Utility Holding Company Act of 1935

This act is easily the most controversial of the group of eight securities acts. It was passed in a confusion of honest indignation and partisan politics and fought over in the press and in the courts for several years before its outcome could be clearly seen. Meanwhile the uncertainty cost investors billions in honest investment. The industry has emerged from this episode with stronger capital structures, better accounting systems, and a higher moral tone than it had in 1935, but has been permanently subjected to a heavy burden of detailed bureaucratic control.

The speculative development of great public utility holding company systems in the 1920s was accomplished in part by the purchase of stocks and properties at excessive prices. This caused many of the systems to evaluate their assets at excessive figures, to resist proper rate reductions, to exploit the sale of electric and gas appliances for the benefit of holding companies, to seek intercompany profits on construction and advisory services, and to utilize unsound capital structures. Some of the holding company systems were very large, and some controlled widely scattered properties. When Congress considered the matter in 1935, it was clear that blunders and frauds on a grand scale had been perpetrated in some systems and that some others were not in strong condition financially. Political considerations at the time called for reforms to be effected in a harsh manner, and the act was so written. Briefly, its provisions are these:

1. Every operating electric or retail gas utility which was a subsidiary of a holding company operating interstate, and every holding company controlling such subsidiary directly or indirectly, was required to "register" with the SEC. Subsidiary or holding company status was measured by the ownership of 10 per cent or more of the voting stock, regardless of the factor of control.

2. Registrants came immediately under the regulatory authority of the SEC on matters relating to capital structure, issuance of securities, expansion, dividends, intercompany loans and investments, intercompany contracts, business methods, and accounting.

3. Every holding company system was required to be reduced to a single geographically integrated and unified system of a size not so large as to "impair the advantages of localized management, efficient operation, or the effectiveness of regulation." In certain cases an additional system or incidental business might be retained.

4. Simplification of the corporate systems and capital structures was required, to assure sound financing, to distribute voting power equitably, to eliminate unnecessary corporations, and to reduce the "corporate layers" to not more than three—operating companies, intermediate holding companies, and top holding company.

This act applied to dozens of systems and to total assets in excess of 15 billion dollars. Its terms have required the transfer to other owners of securities and property amounting to nearly 12 billion dollars. Scores of companies have been merged, liquidated, or recapitalized, with all the inevitable accompanying processes of exchanging and refinancing securities. The delay, uncertainty, and controversy arising out of these procedures can easily be imagined. A few remnants of the readjustments required by the law remain to be completed in 1954 and subsequent years, but the major part of the job is done, and with it the great volume of speculative opportunities arising out of the uncertainties of the reorganization processes.

Maloney Act of 1938

This measure, an amendment to the Securities Exchange Act of
1934, authorizes the formation of national associations of brokers
and dealers for the purposes of establishing fair trade practice rules
and maintaining self-discipline. Such associations must register with
the SEC and accept its regulatory supervision, but they enjoy special
privileges also. Only one such organization, the National Association
of Securities Dealers, has been formed. It has as members about
3,000 of the nation's 4,000 registered securities firms, including most
of the large ones. It maintains its authority by means of a rule which
forbids any member to allow a dealer's concession to (or to receive
one from) any nonmember firm, on any new issue or secondary offering. Since these transactions are vital to most firms' existence, their
memberships must be kept in good standing.

The NASD functions principally along five lines. First, it has
developed a written code of fair practices, dealing with such matters
as the fairness of prices quoted to customers, the profits or commissions taken in no-risk transactions, the disclosure of status when acting as principal, and deceptive or manipulative practices. Second, it
has promulgated standard procedures in transactions between members, covering such matters as nominal and firm quotations, deliveries
and settlements, interest computation, dividend adjustments, and
the like. Third, it is attempting to organize the over-the-counter
market for better service to the public. Employees of member firms
are required to become "registered representatives" by filing personal data sheets, including a statement accepting the NASD rules
of fair practice. Member firms must also accept all rules and are
under pressure to finance themselves conservatively. The NASD also
seeks greater publicity for over-the-counter quotations. Fourth, the
NASD undertakes to investigate and arbitrate disputes between
members or between members and the public and to take discipli-
nary measures when justified. Fifth, the NASD undertakes, along
with the Investment Bankers Association and other industry groups,
to study and make recommendations on pending legislation in the
securities field, and on procedures being considered by the SEC
and other public and private groups.

The NASD seems to be making progress. It is championed by im portant people in the securities business, its meetings and conventions are well attended, and its rulings are obeyed by its members. It has an important function to perform for the protection of the public, in developing ethics and procedures on over-the-counter transactions and in obtaining greater publicity for over-the-counter quotations. This is the area in the securities business where the greatest need for improvement still exists. There is also need to press for better standards of corporate practice on such matters as audits, adequate financial statements, proxies, information about the business, use of registrars, and the like by corporations whose securities are not listed; but this does not seem to be a major objective of the NASD at the moment. Much of the association's energies are directed at systematizing relationships between securities firms and between securities firms and corporations. These are not always harmonious, as witness the 1948 fracas between Otis and Company and the Kaiser-Frazer Corporation over a stock-underwriting transaction. The NASD has been sharply criticized by many firms, both member and nonmember, for an alleged tendency to establish rules of conduct which make transactions in little-known or speculative securities unprofitable and for its rule which discourages transactions between members and nonmembers by forbidding the members to allow dealers' concessions to nonmembers. However, these and other conflicts which developed in the earlier years seem to be less sharply debated as time goes on, and the major work of the NASD remains noncontroversial.

Bankruptcy Act of 1938

The Bankruptcy Act of 1938 made a general revision of Federal bankruptcy laws as they related to the reorganization of general corporations. One portion of this act placed upon the SEC the task of advising the court on reorganization plans in all cases in which the scheduled liabilities exceed $3,000,000 and in other cases when invited by the court. The SEC's statutory task is the rendering of an advisory report on the fairness and soundness of a proposed reorganization plan. Actually, it offers its advice on the preparation of the plan, on the selection of trustees and their counsel, on fee allowances to parties involved, and on matters pertaining to administration of the property pending reorganization.

The introduction of the SEC into bankruptcy reorganizations appears to have improved both the soundness and fairness of reorganization plans. Such plans have often tended to replace failed corporations with successors whose burden of debt has also been excessive or whose capital structures have been too complex. The SEC has persistently fought to obtain more severe and realistic reorganizations. It has also demanded and obtained more equitable plans than might otherwise have been developed.

Trust Indenture Act of 1939

This act regulates indentures and trustees of bond issues exceeding $1,000,000 in amount which are to be registered under the Securities Act of 1933. Indentures effective prior to 1940 are not affected. The objectives of the act were to assure that the trustee served the bondholders, not the corporation; to assure the competence of the trustee; and to require the inclusion of certain safeguards in all new bond indentures. The principal provisions of the act include the following:

1. The corporate trustee must have a capital and surplus of at least $150,000 and must not be affiliated with issuer or underwriter. If in the future any close relations exist between issuer and trustee, the trustee must resign or suffer removal.

2. The trustee must maintain a list of bondholders. It must report to the bondholders annually on several matters pertinent to its trust. It must notify them of all defaults within 90 days.

3. The indenture must contain provisions intended to assure vigilance and necessary action on the part of the trustee, and certain other protective features must be included.

This also is a sound law. A sharply literal interpretation of the requirement that no close relationships exist between a corporate issuer and a trustee at first made it difficult for large national corporations to find large banks eligible to serve as trustees, but this problem has been solved. Because additional and more expensive duties are required of trustees under this law, large corporations with pre-1940 open indentures have tended to continue them in service, rather than to retire them and register new ones.

Investment Company Act of 1940

This act was passed by Congress in an attempt to prevent any repetition of the losses incurred by investors in investment company securities between 1929 and 1935. These losses were in part due to the depression and market slump, but in part they were due to bad management and outright dishonesty. No stigma attaches to most of the larger and stronger surviving companies, but a considerable number of others have less creditable records. Many investment companies were organized between 1925 and 1930 with unsound capital structures and no sensibly planned investment policies. Excessive debt and preferred stock financing left them vulnerable to business depression. Investment in speculative securities led to losses. Investment bankers controlling the companies abused their privileges by selling their own ill-advised investments into the investment companies. Excessive salaries and fees were paid. These and other bad practices added up to a situation which called for corrective legislation.

The Investment Company Act is a highly detailed statute which requires many sound procedures, forbids many unsound ones, and authorizes regulation by the SEC on a number of matters. The purpose of the Congress was evidently to make the investment companies, which can offer diversification and skilled management together in a single low-cost commitment, a safe place for the savings of small investors. The act is sane and sensible in view of its purpose and is firmly supported by the leading investment companies. Significant provisions include the following:

1. Directors must be elected by vote of the stockholders, except that Massachusetts trusts existing prior to the act may continue undisturbed, subject to power in the stockholders to remove trustees. Elected directorates must include persons who are neither officers nor employees, and only a minority may be investment bankers.

2. Officers, directors, and other insiders are closely limited in dealing with the company, employing its funds, or using its credit. Insider trading in company stock is restricted, and they may not sell it short.

3. Stockholders must approve management contracts, selection of independent auditors, and company policy on diversification, specialization, participation in underwriting, and other important matters. These latter policies may not be changed without stockholder consent.

4. Company securities and cash must be deposited in the care of a bank or stock exchange firm or kept safe as the SEC may require. The SEC may require any necessary fidelity or surety bonds.

5. The SEC has general supervision over accounting methods, semiannual reports to stockholders, use of proxies, selling methods, prospectuses, and other business methods.

6. Except for refunding issues, no new bonds may be sold unless covered by three times their amount in assets and no preferred stock unless covered twice on the over-all basis. New bonds and preferred stocks must have contingent voting rights and be protected by restrictions on common stock dividends and repurchases. New open-end funds may not have bonds or preferred stock outstanding.

7. Detailed regulations applicable to open-end companies, periodic payment plans, and face amount certificate companies are provided.

Investment Advisers Act of 1940

To protect the general public against investment advisers who might hire themselves out as expert counselors and then abuse the faith placed in them, the Congress passed the Investment Advisers Act of 1940. The act applies only to advisers who serve the general public professionally as investment advisers, hence exempts lawyers, accountants, and others whose investment advice is incidental and professional advisers who serve only institutions or a limited clientele of less than fifteen persons. Investment advisers subject to the act are required to register with the SEC, file data about themselves, and file reports about their business twice yearly. At June 30, 1953, there were 1,183 registrants. The SEC may not reject or revoke an adviser's registration because of incompetence or error; only ethical or legal infractions are punishable. Specific provisions of the act include:

1. Advisers must not be compensated by a share of market appreciation or realized profits; some other basis must be used.

2. Advisers must not defraud their clients in any way or conceal material facts from them. Advisers must not trade as principals with their clients, or trade with their clients as the agent of another, without the clients' specific permission.

3. Advisers may not assign their contracts with clients.

4. The SEC may require information from any adviser and subpoena records if needed.

This is not a severe statute. There is relatively little regulation of the nature of services undertaken or methods of performing them and none with respect to the advisers' financial standing or their competence. Some of the state laws are more exacting. However, none of the laws shows any disposition to examine advisers' competence; this will no doubt be attempted in due time by voluntary associations of advisers, but probably not in any manner related to the law.

QUESTIONS AND PROBLEMS

1. Is it a proper function of government to deny promoters the right to sell stock in a new corporation because the "inside" group is to receive half the stock in return for a patent? Would it make any difference if the state corporation commissioner thought the patent would not work? Suppose the stock was hard to sell and selling costs took 40 per cent of the proceeds?

2. How would you check up on the reputation of a firm whose salesman wanted you to sell your Union Pacific stock and buy promotional shares which he was offering?

3. What is a better business bureau?

4. How do stock exchanges protect the public from frauds? How can they compel their member firms to obey their rules?

5. What are blue-sky laws? What sort of law does your state have? (Note: Look it up in the *Corporation Manual*.)

6. Why are the blue-sky laws more potent now than in 1930?

7. Is the securities business hostile to the Federal securities acts?

8. Should all of the types of securities now exempt from the Securities Act of 1933 continue to be exempt?

9. Obtain and examine a prospectus. What is in it? Is it too long and dry to achieve its purpose? Should a two-page "opinion of quality and value" by a dispassionate analyst be appended to it?

10. Why did the Securities Act of 1934 impose requirements on corporations having listed securities which are not demanded of those whose securities are actively traded unlisted?

11. What events brought about the Holding Company Act of 1935? What are its main provisions?

12. Should a director who is well acquainted with the true value of his company's stock be discouraged from buying it when it is too low and selling it when it is too high? Would it be legal for the company to do this, to stabilize the market at a "proper" level?

13. Would you expect the NASD to interest itself in stock exchange transactions? What does it do? Would stock exchange member firms belong to the NASD?

14. What does the SEC do in connection with bankruptcy reorganizations? Why would it have to "fight for more severe and realistic" reorganization plans? Would the once-burned old securityholders want to set up another top-heavy corporation?

15. Does the Trust Indenture Act of 1939 apply to all bond indentures now outstanding? Would it apply to railroad bonds? Should it?

16. What bad experiences with investment companies led to the Investment Company Act of 1940? Are recurrences of these bad experiences adequately guarded against in the act?

17. What are the principal features of the Investment Advisers Act of 1940? What else should it do?

REFERENCES

Bellemore, Douglas H.: *Investments Principles and Practices,* B. C. Forbes and Sons Publishing Co., Inc., New York, 1953, Chaps. 9, 12.

Dice, Charles A., and Wilford J. Eiteman: *The Stock Market,* McGraw-Hill Book Company, Inc., New York, 1952, Chap. 22.

Dowrie, George W., and Douglas R. Fuller: *Investments,* John Wiley & Sons, Inc., New York, 1950, Chap. 5.

Investment Bankers Association of America: *Fundamentals of Investment Banking,* Prentice-Hall, Inc., New York, 1949, Chaps. 21, 22.

Leffler, George L.: *The Stock Market,* The Ronald Press Company, New York, 1951, Chaps. 20, 21.

Securities and Exchange Commission: *Annual Reports.*

Shultz, Birl E.: *The Securities Market and How It Works,* Harper & Brothers, New York, 1946, Chap. 20.

Chapter 13: AN APPROACH TO
INVESTMENT ANALYSIS

Investment analysis means the detailed study of the characteristics, quality, prospects, and value of a particular security. It usually also means a comparative study, for such attributes as quality and value are too abstract to be interpreted clearly except in comparison with other somewhat similar securities. Good investment analysis thus becomes a task of estimating and comparing, involving a review of one or more industries, firms, and individual securities in each case.

Investors generally undertake the analysis of a security after casual inquiry has indicated that it is suitable for purchase or that it should be sold from their portfolios. This is a practical approach, for it means that the investigator knows what he is looking for; he wants a security with particular characteristics of safety, price stability, growth, or other features, and the investigation can be pointed to test for the desired features. Every analytical study will also be a general "fishing expedition" designed to uncover unsuspected attributes in the securities studied, if any exist.

Any investment analysis is a forward-looking inquiry. The main issues to be resolved deal with the earnings and payments the investment can make in the future, the probable future behavior of its price, and the degree of certainty which attaches to these forecasts. All of the investment features considered in the analysis are therefore to be examined chiefly for their prophetic value, and the analysis itself will conclude by making estimates as to these items in the future. In fact, it has no other purpose.

Investment analysis is not a process exclusively devoted to the study of high-grade securities. Good analytical work is of course done by most institutional buyers of bonds, to make sure that their bonds are suitable and that they choose the best available for their purposes, price considered; but even more extensive analysis is done by stock buyers, especially on speculative issues. After all, the need for analysis is greatest in speculative issues, where success may be very profitable and error very expensive.

Procedure in Investment Analysis

Because the objectives sought by investors vary greatly, and because the types of investments are so distinctive in nature, it is not possible to suggest a few easy ratios which will provide a measure of value for all securities. However, it does seem feasible to suggest a five-part outline for investment analysis which may help to organize the information ordinarily available on corporate securities. The five parts are as follows:

First, the analysis will set forth the basic indications of value which are almost universally used for the quick appraisal of a security. These will be such things as earnings per share, price-earnings ratios, yields, over-all coverage of interest requirements, and recent price ranges, with the exact items depending, of course, on whether the security being tested is a common stock, a preferred stock, or a bond. These basic indications give a preliminary measure of the quality of a security and of the highness or reasonableness of its price. Since the purpose of the analysis is the anticipation of future values, any tendency of these basic indicators to trend up or down will be especially important.

Second, the analysis will study the industry represented by the subject security, to determine its immediate and long-run characteristics. Third, the analysis must review the firm which issues the security, to determine its strength, position, and future prospects. Fourth, the security itself must be studied, to obtain all pertinent data on its legal rights, market position, and financial strength. Finally, the analysis must reach summary conclusions on the probable future trends of earnings, payments, quality, price-earnings ratios, yields, and price.

The detailed items most commonly considered in making an analysis such as this are presented in outline form on the accompanying pages. Obviously, the outline should be adapted to fit the individual case, since industries are not all alike—banks, for example, do not have the same features as flour milling companies—but the adaptation will not be difficult. The analyst will need to be reasonably familiar with the key characteristics of each industry which he studies, however, for lack of such background information could lead to grievous errors.

In presenting an outline for investment analysis this chapter does not intend to suggest that each individual investor should start with primary statistical data and do his own analytical work, ignoring the mass of interpretive studies published by the financial services and brokers. To do so would be wasteful and foolish. But much that is done by these agencies is incomplete, and more than a little of it reaches hasty conclusions. The investor who has his own outline of procedure in mind can borrow facts from many sources, supplement them with calculations of his own, and test his own final conclusions against those of the experts.

OUTLINE FOR INVESTMENT ANALYSIS

I. Determination of type of investment desired
   1. General type (bond, preferred, common)
   2. Acceptable industries
   3. Quality and characteristics
II. Basic (preliminary) indications

Common Stocks	*Preferred Stocks*	*Bonds*
1. Earnings per share: Recent Average Future	1. Dividend coverage, over-all	1. Interest coverage
2. Dividends	2. Yield	2. Yield
3. P-E ratio, yield	3. Call price, cumulation, conversion	3. Call price, conversion
4. Leverage	4. Asset coverage	4. Asset coverage
5. Book value	5. Market price record	5. Market price record
6. Market price record	6. Reputation	6. Reputation
7. Reputation		

III. Industry analysis
   1. Permanence of the industry
   2. Growth of the industry
   3. Stability of sales and earnings
   4. Competitive conditions

     5. Labor relations
     6. Governmental attitudes
     7. Immediate outlook for sales and earnings
IV. Analysis of the firm
     1. Size, leadership, dominance
     2. Growth
     3. Prestige, established position
     4. Brands, patents, good will
     5. Diversification
     6. Assets and operating situation
     7. Sales outlook
     8. Costs, overhead, profit margins
     9. Earnings estimates
    10. Stability of sales and earnings
    11. Working capital position
    12. Dividend estimates
    13. Capital structure
    14. Management
    15. Stockholder position
 V. The individual security
     1. Its legal rights
     2. Its market position
       a. Number of holders
       b. Popularity of type
       c. Eligibility
       d. Additional issue or secondary offerings
       e. Market history
     3. Financial position in capital structure, improvement or weakening
VI. Conclusions
     1. Future earnings
     2. Future payments
     3. Quality and characteristics
     4. Future price

The Basic Indications

Little explanation of the "basic indications" of investment value is now needed, in view of what has been said in previous chapters. These items are clearly the ones most commonly quoted in investment studies and whose trends are most eagerly noted. Indeed, the entire analysis is little more than an extension and verification of them.

Because of the common use of these basic factors, it is seldom necessary for the investor to compute them himself. Earnings, dividends paid, market price ranges, capital structures, and the like are commonly tabulated in reference manuals and leaflets such as the *Standard Stock Report* on Montgomery Ward & Co., which is reproduced in Charts 11 and 12. All the investor needs to do is to note the figures shown and their trend, in order to have preliminary indications of the values he must test.

The investor who stops collecting information at this point must either make a crude guess as to the future of his securities from the evidence of the past, or he must trust the verdict of others who may have looked farther. This latter is not an unsound procedure; one who has not the time or the experience to study his own investments may reasonably follow the suggestions made in Chapters 4 and 11 for dependence upon others. But if the investor decides to make additional studies himself, he usually finds it necessary to undertake detailed surveys of the industry, the firm, and the security itself, before he reaches his final conclusions.

Industry Features Are Always Important

The detailed work in the analysis of any corporate security logically begins with the industry. Most industries have important unique characteristics which affect the values of their securities, and the analyst must review these carefully. In fact, industry features are so important that much of the space in investment books—including this one—is given over to describing them.

There are at least seven industry features which investment analysts are likely to consider in appraising a stock or a bond. These are:

1. Permanence of the industry. There are many lines of business which are subject to displacement or loss as a result of technological development, change in demand, or change in the law. Examples in recent years would include streetcar companies, makers of farm wagons, and grocery and dry-goods wholesalers. Since industries on the downgrade are likely to be depressed, it seems best to avoid them

M¹   # Montgomery Ward   **678**

Stock—	Approx. Price	Dividend	Yield
COMMON	60¾	²$3.50	²5.8%
$7 CLASS A	178	7.00	3.9

RECOMMENDATION: The well-known conservative policies of the management have made this issue unpopular with many investors. Among the professionals, however, it has a considerable following on the ground that the company is firmly situated, has excellent finances, and that the shares have a high equity value and defensive qualities. For those willing to exercise patience and hold for the pull, commitments in the COMMON should work out well. The CLASS A is a high quality investment issue.

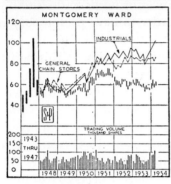

COMMON SHARE EARNINGS ($)

Quarter—	1953-4	1952-3	1951-2	1950-1	1949-50
April	0.96	0.97	1.84	1.40	1.42
July	1.35	1.37	1.72	2.01	0.70
Oct.	1.51	1.84	2.01	3.04	2.17
Jan.	2.30	3.23	2.57	4.73	2.84

In the fiscal year ended January 31, 1954 sales were 7.9% below those a year earlier; the final-half decline was 12.3%. Gross margins improved fractionally, but with expenses cut only about 6%, operating profits declined 10.7%. Taxable income fell 12.1% and in the absence of prior year credits equal to about $0.75 a share, net income was off 17%.

Sales for the two months through March, 1954 were 19.4% below those in the corresponding year earlier period.

⁸SALES (Million $)

Quarter—	1953-4	1952-3	1951-2	1950-1	1949-50
April	240	241	268	244	259
July	267	277	273	299	268
Oct.	281	322	317	339	315
Jan.	291	326	332	376	327

PROSPECTS

Earnings in the fiscal year ended January 31, 1954 were $6.12 a common share, compared with $7.41 in the preceding year, which included a tax credit of about $0.75. Profits for the current fiscal half are likely to be lower, but improvement is possible during the final half. The $0.50 quarterly dividend may again be supplemented by a year-end extra of $1.50.

Demand for soft goods should be well maintained over the near future aided by attractive values. However, volume is expected to be lower for appliances and other big ticket items. Rural business is also likely to be off from a year ago. A lower level of sales is in prospect.

While further upgrading of merchandise lines, probable closing of less profitable stores, and other economies will be beneficial, competitive pricing and probable wage increases may reduce profit margins moderately. Lower first half profits are expected; final half gains are possible.

RECENT DEVELOPMENTS

The greatest sales decline in 1953 occurred in the higher priced items which are generally sold on time payment terms, but the company continued to follow a conservative policy in granting credit and maintained repayment terms on a sound basis. Year-end merchandise on hand and on order was 19% less than the previous year.

DIVIDEND DATA

There are no restrictions. Common payments in calendar 1953 were as follows:

Amt. of Divd. $	Date Decl.	Ex-divd. Date	Stock of Record	Payment Date
0.50	Nov. 28	Dec. 3	Dec. 8	Jan. 15
1.00 Ext.	Dec. 19	Dec. 26	Dec. 31	Jan. 30
0.50	Feb. 27	Mar. 4	Mar. 9	Apr. 15
0.50	May 22	Jun. 2	Jun. 5	Jul. 15
0.50	Sep. 9	Sep. 15	Sep. 19	Oct. 15

¹Common listed New York and Midwest S. Es. and traded Boston, Los Angeles. Phila.-Balt., Cincinnati, Detroit and San Francisco S. Es. Class A traded American S. E. and listed Midwest S. E. ²Indicated rate, including $1.50 extra in January, 1954. ³Based on monthly figures.

STANDARD LISTED STOCK REPORTS
STANDARD & POOR'S CORPORATION
Published at Orange, Conn. Editorial & Executive Offices, 345 Hudson St., New York 14, N. Y.

Vol. 21, No. 79   Tuesday, April 27, 1954   Sec. 15

CHART 11. Standard listed stock report, title side.

678 MONTGOMERY WARD & CO., INCORPORATED

INCOME STATISTIOS (Million $) AND PER SHARE ($) DATA

[1]Year Ended Jan. 31	Net Sales	% Oper. Inc. of Sales	Ratio of Sales to Invent.	Income Taxes	[5]Net Income	Class A Earns.	Class A Divs. Paid	Common [5]Earns.	Common Divs. Paid	[2]Price Range Class A	[2]Price Range Common
1954	----	----	----	----	----	----	[7]1.75	----	[6]0.50	180 -172½	64½ - 56
1953	999.1	8.7	4.7-1	42.88	41.20	204.39	7.00	6.12	3.50	176 -157	65½ - 53⅝
1952	1,084.6	9.1	4.5-1	46.12	49.59	246.05	7.00	7.41	3.00	176 -168	67⅛ - 55⅛
1951	1,106.2	10.4	4.5-1	58.09	54.34	269.62	7.00	7.41	3.00	185⅛-164⅛	75⅝ - 64
1950	1,170.5	12.2	4.7-1	65.14	74.16	367.94	7.00	11.19	4.00	186 -176½	67¼ - 49⅛
1949	1,084.4	7.8	4.8-1	81.64	47.79	237.10	7.00	7.13	3.00	185½-167½	69⅝ - 47⅝
1948	1,212.0	9.7	4.7-1	46.42	68.28	338.53	7.00	10.28	3.00	178¾-162	65 - 47½
1947	1,158.7	9.1	4.2-1	48.15	59.05	292.97	7.00	8.86	3.00	194 -173	64⅝ - 49
1946	974.3	9.6	4.1-1	37.62	42.28	209.78	7.00	6.29	2.00	210¼-180	104¼ - 57¼
1945	654.8	9.4	4.8-1	85.89	22.98	113.78	7.00	4.12	2.00	197¾-179	76 - 47⅞
1944	621.0	3.5	5.3-1	27.78	21.29	105.61	7.00	3.81	3.00	188 165	54 - 41⅝
1943	696.9	6.0	4.8-1	11.90	20.68	102.59	7.00	3.69	2.00	180 -163	50 - 33¼
1939	474.9	8.0	4.9-1	7.30	27.01	134.01	7.00	4.91	2.00	172½-147	57¾ - 40⅛
1938	414.0	6.6	5.1-1	4.40	19.64	97.47	7.00	3.50	1.50	163¾-122	54¼ - 25
1937	414.1	6.9	5.4-1	5.90	19.21	95.31	7.00	3.41	2.00	157 -120⅛	69 - 30
[3]1932	176.5	def.	4.3-1	----	d5.69	d23.27	3.50	d1.59	Nil	78 - 22	16⅛ - 8⅛
[3]1929	267.3	6.1	4.0-1	1.07	13.43	65.54	7.00	2.60	2.62½	135 -105	156⅞ - 42⅝

PERTINENT BALANCE SHEET STATISTICS (Million $)

[1]Jan. 31	Total Assets	Cash Items	Inventories	Receivables	Current Assets	Current [4]Liabs.	Net Workg. Cap.	Current Ratio Assets to Liabs.	Current Ratio Cash to Liabs.	% Inv. of Cur. Assets	($) Book Val. Com. Sh.
1953	717.6	293.1	214.8	161.0	668.9	96.9	572.0	6.9-1	3.0-1	32.1	92.37
1952	717.3	253.7	239.5	173.3	666.5	113.5	553.0	5.9-1	2.2-1	35.9	89.75
1951	696.6	245.7	243.9	153.3	642.9	121.6	521.3	5.3-1	2.0-1	37.9	85.34
1950	677.0	195.6	249.5	178.7	623.8	136.2	487.6	4.6-1	1.4-1	40.0	80.20
1949	589.1	130.2	227.2	178.8	535.7	94.2	441.5	5.7-1	1.4-1	42.4	78.01
1948	578.9	88.1	259.8	172.3	519.7	106.8	412.9	4.9-1	0.8-1	49.9	69.50
1947	530.6	51.1	277.3	144.1	472.5	105.9	366.6	4.5-1	0.5-1	58.7	62.13
1946	441.7	64.7	237.9	86.4	389.0	55.9	333.1	7.0-1	1.2-1	61.1	56.27
1945	333.2	98.9	127.6	48.6	285.1	44.5	240.6	6.4-1	2.2-1	48.8	51.47
1944	316.8	95.5	117.5	48.7	261.7	39.6	222.1	6.6-1	2.4-1	44.9	49.26
1943	299.6	77.2	124.6	42.1	248.9	31.8	212.0	7.7-1	2.4-1	51.1	47.47

[1]Of the following calendar year. [2]Calendar year. [3]13 months ended Jan. 31, 1933. [4]After deducting U. S. Treasury tax notes. [5]After special reserves of $1.15 a share (net) in 1942 and $1.54 in 1946. [6]On Apr. 15. [7]One regular quarterly. d Deficit.

Fundamental Position

Montgomery Ward is the second largest mail order enterprise and one of the largest retail distributors of general merchandise. About two-thirds of sales is obtained from 590 stores located in 46 states. The mail order division, with 258 sales units in 39 states, accounts for the remainder.

Both divisions handle virtually the same lines of merchandise. Soft lines account for about 38% of sales, household furnishings 25%, and hard goods 37%. About 25% of sales is made on the instalment basis.

Retail units are generally of a medium sized style of department store, and the majority occupy three floors. Largest concentration of stores is in California (52), Illinois (47), Indiana (27), Iowa (31), Kansas (28), Michigan (36), and Ohio (30).

Three factories are owned which make paints, fencing, and farm equipment. Nine mail order houses are owned. Twenty-five stores are in owned buildings, with the remainder on leased premises. Total rents in 1953 were $11,253,304.

Employees: 53,000. Stockholders: 67,055.

Earnings-Dividends

Sales rose sharply after the early 1930's, aided by agressive expansion which materially enlarged the earnings base. However, with expansion limited, sales have leveled off since the mid-1940's, although costs and expenses have been under close control.

Dividends have been paid regularly since 1936, mostly on a conservative basis.

Finances

Conservative dividends and capital expenditures have resulted in a substantial rise in liquid funds since the mid-1940's. Cash items alone at January 31, 1954 were about three times current liabilities, and working capital approximated $85 a common share. Receivables were after reserves of $25,209,135.

CAPITALIZATION

Funded Debt: None.
$7 Cum. Class A Stock: 201,554 shares (no par); non-redeemable.
Common Stock: 6,502,378 shares (no par).

Incorporated in Illinois in 1919. **Office**—619 W. Chicago Ave., Chicago 7. **President**—E. A. Krider. **VP**—J. A. Webber. **Treasurer**—H. S. Kambestad. **Secretary**—J. A. Barr. **Directors**—S. L. Avery (Chrm.), J. A. Barr, P. R. Clarke, D. A. Crawford, G. E. Eastwood, P. B. Eckhart, E. A. Krider, C. H. Shaver, S. A. Smith. **Transfer Agents**—Northern Trust Co., Chicago; J. P. Morgan & Co., Inc., N. Y. C. **Registrars**—Bankers Trust Co., N. Y. C.; The First National Bank of Chicago.

CHART 12. Standard listed stock report, reverse side.

in most cases. On the other hand, an industry for which there is no foreseeable substitute, such as meat packing or steel production, is in a relatively strong position. Investors who read the financial periodicals regularly are usually aware of trends toward obsolescence, but studies of industry sales and profit statistics, plus articles on the uses for products and possible substitutes for them, are readily available when definite information is desired.

2. Growth of the industry. It has long been known that an industry which is growing vigorously has three advantages over less dynamic ones: First, there is little occasion for cutthroat competitive tactics, and profits are usually satisfactory. Second, there is opportunity for stockholders to add profitably to their investments from time to time. Third, there is opportunity for early arrivals in a growing industry to develop specialty products, trade names, and customer connections against a day when competitive advantage may be needed. "Growth industries" are much discussed in financial literature, and their popularity among investors sometimes causes their securities to sell higher than they should. This is a hazard to be avoided. Information about growing industries and their products can be obtained in all the usual sources—financial services, periodical articles, brokers' literature, and government and trade association statistics.

3. Stability of sales and earnings. While it is not imperative that every industry show as steady sales volume as the electric power companies, it must be conceded that the extreme irregularity shown during the past 20 years by railway equipment makers or copper mining companies, for example, makes it difficult for stocks in these industries to promise stability in earnings or dividends, though their average earning capacity may be good. Such concerns attempt to avoid fixed charges and to reduce expenses in dull periods, but the maintenance of even moderate dividend stability is a difficult problem. The investor who contemplates commitments in any industry whose behavior and outlook are not familiar to him will do well to study the history of sales, prices, profits, and dividends in the industry and to compare past situations with the present one, before he makes his decision. Data may be found in the financial services, in periodical articles, and in government reports.

4. Competitive conditions. Some industries, such as retailing, are inherently sharply competitive. Others, such as the rubber companies in the thirties, become overbuilt and engage in cutthroat practices. While it is not possible to foretell accurately the progress of competitive conditions into the distant future, investors do well to examine the conditions of supply and demand, price leadership, and competitive tactics in industries they are considering. A complete lack of effective competition would probably betoken a dangerously unstable condition, but a stable marketing and pricing situation permitting reasonable profit margins is definitely to be sought. Competition from without as well as within the industry merits consideration—the cotton goods industry, for example, is keenly affected by the competition of rayon.

5. Labor relations. An industry which is effectively dominated by aggressive unions, as the coal mining and ocean shipping industries are, is often a relatively insecure place for investors' money. This is particularly true if other industries or foreign interests can compete in the field, even though the government is currently attempting, by subvention or otherwise, to assist American-owned enterprise. The best industries from the investor standpoint are those in which (a) unionism is weak and seems likely to remain so, or (b) labor costs represent only a small portion of the costs of operation, or (c) labor has a tradition of reasonable attitudes, or (d) mechanization provides a feasible alternative.

6. Governmental attitudes. Industries in which there is a pronounced trend toward government participation or extensive regulation should be approached with caution. In the prosperous war and postwar years the government has seemed reasonably friendly toward business, but the troubles of the electric power industry in the thirties under the twin afflictions of the public power mania and the Public Utility Holding Company Act of 1935 should not be forgotten by investors. In 1948 and 1949 a renewal of Federal interest in public power projects, public housing, and antitrust proceedings served notice that political factors still bulked large among investment hazards. Another aspect of governmental intervention is of major import to investors: a number of industries, such as air transport, sugar production, and fluid milk distribution, are organized around government subsidies or marketing restrictions. Removal or alteration of the government's policies would cause drastic changes in the industries.

7. Immediate outlook for sales and earnings. Even if business and competitive conditions appear completely sound in the long run, it is not desirable to overlook the market hazards of investment in industries which are facing sales or earnings difficulties in the immediate future. Such difficulties may spring from excess inventories, temporary demand peculiarities, labor troubles, or other sources, but in any case they may cause declines in the prices of the affected securities. If sales and earnings prospects are bright, however, there is a corresponding strong chance for price advances.

Investment Factors in the Individual Firm

Even though an industry operates under favorable conditions, the promise of an investment in it will still depend heavily on the position of the firm. An unstable or poorly managed firm often does poorly under excellent conditions, even as a strong firm sometimes does well in a faltering industry. The factors which most often measure the strength and promise in an individual firm are:

1. Size, leadership, dominance. Unless they have palpably "gone to seed," the larger firms in an industry are likely to afford the best quality opportunities for security investments. Such firms will have diversification of lines, production facilities, and sales outlets, as well as great resources. As examples, General Motors, U.S. Steel, General Electric, Goodyear Tire and Rubber, and Standard Oil of New Jersey might be mentioned. If a large firm has price, design, and research leadership, and if it is maintaining its reputation and strength, there is reason to regard it as a sound and conservative choice. Smaller firms, even promising ones, are likely to be a little more speculative in nature, though for the same reason they may have more dynamic possibilities.

2. Growth. The firm whose recent history and current experience emphasize growth is usually a good one to invest in. There is nearly always a reason for growth—good management, good products, good service to customers—and the securityholders are likely to be beneficiaries. As outstanding examples, attention is called to the growth of Sears Roebuck, Continental Oil, and Monsanto Chemical during the past twenty-five years. However, the growth which will have meaning for the present investor is that of the coming years.

3. Prestige, established position. Regardless of size or growth, the firm which has an established reputation and an established clientele of long standing, and holds firmly to its position, is likely to be a money-maker for its investors.

4. Brands, patents, good will. Among the most important assets of American corporations are the intangibles upon which they depend for leadership. General Foods Corporation assiduously develops interest in its brand names, which include Jell-O, Post's cereals, Maxwell House tea and coffee, Sanka, Minute Tapioca, Baker's Cocoa, and Birds Eye Frozen Foods. Radio Corporation of America pins its faith on a great collection of patents and a determined research program. Sears Roebuck has its mailing list, its thousands of steady customers, and its reputation for selling a great variety of articles at low prices. These are all intangible assets, but they are strong bulwarks for the investor's hopes.

5. Diversification. Other things being equal, a firm is often better off from the investor's point of view if it makes a diversified line of products, in diversified locations, from varied types of raw materials, intended for customers in various lines of business, who live in different parts of the country. Under such conditions the loss of a single contract or the deterioration of a single market will not be a completely devastating blow. However, it must be conceded that many firms making a few items for a very few customers—for example, automobile parts manufacturers supplying only three or four automobile makers—have had long and stable relations with these customers.

6. Assets and operating situation. Where fixed assets such as buildings, machinery, and equipment are very important to the corporation, the investor would usually like assurance that they are adequate, modern, adaptable, and reasonably well located with reference to supplies, labor, and markets. The appraisal of fixed assets from these viewpoints is not usually easy, for neither time of construction nor cost is positive evidence of value. Financial services and periodical articles frequently express opinions, which may or may not be fully reliable. It is a familiar axiom of finance that a well-integrated concern with ample raw material and fixed asset resources is strongly fortified in hard times, for it is able to operate with a minimum of cash payments to outsiders, thus conserving its liquid resources. Contrariwise, a concern which buys its supplies and leases the premises it occupies may feel the pressure on its cash resources when business is bad.

7. Sales outlook. There is no more vital determinant of a firm's future prosperity than its sales outlook. Investors usually believe, and with some justification, that a firm which can make sales will somehow control its costs and operate profitably. Consequently, they devise many ways of estimating future sales, both in the near term and for the distant future. For example, long-term average future sales are often estimated by projecting past sales trends, possibly with adjustments made to allow for commodity price level changes; or estimates may be made as percentages of national income, or per capita in the territory served, or as a share in an industry total which has been projected. For shorter term estimates percentages over or under the previous year are often used. When price levels have been unsettled, it is often desirable to gauge sales trends by some measure of unit volume, such as barrels of petroleum products sold, or number of automobiles sold, or store sales deflated for price changes. Also, it may be desirable in estimating sales trends to disregard war volumes or other fortuitous and nonrecurring experiences, as they give little indication of future peacetime expectations.

8. Costs, overhead, profit margins. Important portions of most security analyses deal with the study of costs and profit margins. The trends of individual cost items, their amounts as percentages of sales and of total costs, the amounts of cost which represent inflexible overhead, the percentage of profit margin to sales under various assumptions of total sales volume, and the "break-even point" [1] are all subjects for statistical investigation. A study of these detailed items and their trends will often lead to very accurate estimates of future earnings.

---

[1] The "break-even point" is a much-discussed figure in industries with high fixed costs and fluctuating sales volume, such as railroading and steel production. It refers to the volume of sales necessary to cover all expenses including taxes, and thus to avoid a loss. It is difficult to compute because unit selling prices and the unit prices of cost items are unstable, being affected by the same economic forces which influence sales volume; and, for that matter, overhead costs are not totally fixed nor are variable ones totally variable. But, despite the difficulties, break-even-point estimates are a fascinating topic. The same techniques used to compute the break-even point may also be used to compute the probable size of the profit or loss at any given rate of output.

9. Earnings estimates. Estimates of future earnings are made in many ways. Crude estimates may be made by projecting the trend of past per share earnings, possibly with allowances for changes in price levels or sales volume. More accurate estimates are possible by making estimates of future sales and deducting projected percentages for various costs and taxes. If earnings before income taxes bear a reasonably constant ratio to sales, this may be a simple basis for estimate. If near term earnings rather than average future earnings are to be estimated, known factors such as inventory gains or losses or other temporary phenomena must be allowed for, and estimates based on increases or decreases in the previous year's incomes and expenses may be most significant.

10. Stability of sales and earnings. Even when the industry displays definite characteristics of stability or instability, the analyst usually finds it desirable to investigate the position of each firm separately. The possession or lack of certain contracts, sales outlets, or special incomes may make enormous differences in these matters. For example, the New York Central Railroad receives annual rentals and dividends of over twenty million dollars; this income does much to stabilize the Central's somewhat erratic earning power. Information of this sort can be had from annual reports, prospectuses, and all the other usual published sources.

11. Working capital position. Working capital is usually measured as the excess of cash, short-term cash investments, receivables, and inventory over the total of accounts payable, short-term bank loans, and taxes payable. A firm is said to be in a sound working capital position if it has enough resources to buy the inventory it needs and extend its customers the credit they need, without ever being embarrassed for cash or forced into abnormal indebtedness itself. To remain in a sound working capital position, a firm must not only conduct its ordinary business with discretion, but must also be prepared to finance all impending bond and mortgage maturities, expansion plans, and seasonal requirements without strain. A poor working capital position is not necessarily a harbinger of trouble when business is good, but it is very difficult to correct under adverse conditions. A sound working capital position is therefore essential before the securities of a firm can be called good in quality. Investors usually investigate a firm's working capital position by studying its most recent balance sheet in conjunction with past balance sheets and its impending cash needs for expansion, debt repayment, and other uses. A number of balance sheet ratios are commonly used in studying working capital position; these will be discussed in the next chapter.

12. Dividend estimates. Long-range dividend estimates for common stocks are usually made with reference to estimated earnings. Inspection of past policies will indicate whether any typical percentage of earnings is normally distributed and whether regular or irregular distributions are likely. Working capital position, expansion needs, needs for debt retirement, and the expressed ideas of the management will all assist in making the estimates. Dividend estimates are very important to the investor; the rate of payments to be made in the future will be one of the important factors controlling the market price of the stock. For the near term, any increase or decrease in the dividend rate will be significant because it is almost certain to cause a sharp change in the price of the stock.

13. Capital structure. The term capital structure refers to the *proportions* of a corporation's resources furnished by the various groups of its creditors and stockholders.[2] Thus Simmons Company at year-end 1953 reported that its net resources came 17 per cent from short-term creditors, 5 per cent from long-term lenders, 14 per cent from preferred stockholders, and 59 per cent from common stockholders. A sound capital structure is one in which debt and preferred stock are sufficiently limited so the corporation can in most years earn enough to discharge its obligations to them and can at all reasonable times sell new securities in normal financial operations. A capital structure characterized by excessive debt or by non-callable bonds and preferred stocks with onerous privileges is not good for common stockholders, nor for other securityholders if the firm needs to do new financing or refunding. A capital structure including a large percentage of common stock—in other words, a low-leverage situation—might well suggest that all the securities are good quality. The nature of a firm's capital structure may reasonably vary with the type of the firm and the industry—stable earnings, well-established position, and large size will justify a greater percentage of debt and preferred stock than a new or small firm should have.

---

[2] The orthodox definition of capital structure refers to the proportioning of long-term debt, preferred stock, and common stock, leaving current debt out of the calculation. The author believes his suggested calculation to be more significant.

14. Management. A management which is able, vigorous, and possessed of good commercial and financial connections is of great advantage to the firm. Such managements inspire cooperation and confidence, obtain internal efficiency, and also secure advantageous purchase, sales, and credit terms for the firm. Incompetent and indifferent managements are an obvious disadvantage, as are those racked by dissent. Over the longer range, one-man organizations are also of doubtful attractiveness because of the obvious hazard if the key man is lost. It is difficult for an investor to appraise a corporate management from published reports. The list of directors may be examined to note their other corporate connections, and the occasional public-relations-inspired biographical letters "about our executives" may be read, but these are of limited value. More illuminating facts are gleaned from news reports when an executive is chosen for distinguished public service or when a conspicuous controversy such as the Montgomery Ward episode of 1949 breaks into the headlines.[3] Mostly the investor must judge the management by results.

15. Stockholder position. A corporation is usually in a better financial position if its stock is widely held, if its stockholders are familiar with it from long experience, and if its important stockholders include some groups of financial experience and power. A wide distribution of stock facilitates new financing among the stockholders and promotes price stability, especially if the stockholders know the company well. Financial experience and power among the stockholders means that competent groups will watch the company's progress, possibly contribute to the management, and sponsor the company in transactions with financial institutions. The best evidence of wide distribution of stock will be in the published data on the number of stockholders and the number of holdings of various size blocks. Important stockholding groups may be identified if they are represented on the board of directors or if large holders have been named for other reasons.

---

[3] Over a 12-month period ending in April, 1949, Montgomery Ward lost six directors, its president, and twelve vice-presidents by resignation, because of internal dissension. See the *Wall Street Journal*, Apr. 14, 1949, p. 1. During the ensuing five years a number of other officers, including some men promoted or employed to replace the 1948–1949 dissenters, have left for substantially the same reasons. A nonmanagement group solicited proxies in an attempt to change the management at the 1955 stockholders' meeting, but their attempt failed.

The Security Investigation

The portion of an investment analysis which deals with the position of the individual security, as distinct from the study of the industry and the firm, has usually to do with three elements—its legal rights, its market position, and its financial strength. The legal position of a security is determined by its statutory, (bond) indenture, and charter rights—such matters as mortgage security, call prices, voting rights, etc. These have been reviewed in earlier chapters; so the reader will have no difficulty in listing the ones which will be most pertinent in considering any particular stock or bond.

The market position deals mainly with factors previously considered in studying the markets for stocks and bonds—the number of holders, the volume of trading in the issue, whether dealers and brokers sponsor the issue, where it is traded, whether it is seasoned and well known to the public, the popularity of such issues with the public, eligibility (of bonds) for institutional purchase, possibility of new offerings or secondary distributions, and the market price history of the issue. The problem here is to determine whether the stock or bond being studied will be considered by enough potential buyers and sellers so that its merit will be properly reflected in its price and to determine whether the market is broad enough to absorb any probable selling or buying without radical price fluctuations. Clearly, it would be unprofitable to buy a security for price appreciation if the issue had no broad market and if several large blocks were known to be awaiting sale at the earliest opportunity; nor would one be willing to buy a stock on a normal price-earnings basis if it were evident from recent price ranges that the price frequently fluctuated far below a normal range. One of the more objective items to be noted with reference to a security's market position is the history of its price-earnings ratios and yields; if a stock has consistently sold at a higher than average price-earnings ratio or if its price-earnings ratio (in terms of year-by-year prices and earnings) is trending upward, some presumption of a strong market position may be entertained; and if a stock or bond customarily sells on a low yield basis or has been rising in price with a consequent declining yield tendency, the same presumption of strong market position may be deduced.

The financial position of an issue has chiefly to do with its place in the capital structure and the improvement or weakening of that place as time goes on. The best evidence of improving financial position for a bond would be a steadily increasing earnings coverage for its interest and asset coverage for its principal; the best evidence for a stock would be that an increasing percentage of operating earnings remained as "earnings for common" after all senior claims and that the common stock equity represented an ever-increasing percentage of the balance sheet total.

Conclusions

Supplied with the plethora of facts and estimates as thus outlined, an investment analyst would be able to judge the quality, characteristics, and future of the securities before him as well as any man could hope to do. He could not hope to be right all of the time, for the unforeseeable facts of new discoveries, political events, wars, and human imponderables would often confound his estimates, but he should be right more often than not, and proper diversification would then care for his errors. The specific function of these "conclusions" is to make a final summary of future earnings, dividends, investment features, quality, price-earnings ratios, and yields and to translate these into probable future market values. Many of the techniques which may help in doing this have already been suggested, and others will suggest themselves in individual cases. However, the task is fundamentally one of exercising an informed judgment.

Sources of Data

Investment analysis obviously makes use of all the standard sources of investment information and, in addition, has extensive use for general statistical data such as national income figures, commodity price indexes, and indexes of physical production such as carloadings or electric power production. Much of the descriptive material necessary in a good analysis can be drawn from reference manuals, annual reports, and similar documents with little effort. Other desired information, such as (for example) the percentage of a given concern's sales to the national income or to the total for its industry,

320 INTRODUCTION TO INVESTMENTS

will require calculations based upon data drawn from government sources, trade associations, and other research agencies.

But the one major source of statistical data for investment analysis continues to be the financial statements of the corporations. Because these are fundamental in importance and very widely used, the next chapter is reserved to discuss them.

QUESTIONS AND PROBLEMS

1. Why is investment analysis usually made a comparative study? Could you not determine whether Southern Pacific debentures were satisfactory just by studying them?

2. Would investment analyses be needed on United States government bonds? On telephone bonds?

3. Would the Outline for Investment Analysis as presented on page 305 give you the information you needed to study the stock of the Iron Fireman Manufacturing Company, which makes automatic coal stokers, and has recently added a line of oil and gas heaters and furnaces as well? Is anything missing?

4. As a practical matter, should middle-class professional men such as professors and lawyers make their own investment analyses, or should they rely on others?

5. Does the *Standard Stock Report* on Montgomery Ward stress the right things, for a condensed report? What vital things are omitted, if any?

6. Investigate the rapidly growing paper box industry, and decide whether Container Corporation has reaped the alleged benefits of industry growth.

7. What faith do you have in a fruit and vegetable canner such as California Packing Corporation (producer of Del Monte products), in this day of frozen foods, rapid transportation of fresh products, and improvement of paper-packaged dehydrated foods? How would you check on these hazards?

8. Make an investment analysis of Montgomery Ward & Co. common stock, and compare it with R. H. Macy & Co.

9. If you had all the necessary data with which to work, how would you go about estimating Montgomery Ward's probable sales for the next two or three years?

10. How would you estimate Ward's earnings for the same period? The probable dividend rate?

11. How would a reduction in its product prices, with no changes in its principal costs, affect a concern's break-even point?

12. Why are investors concerned about the proportion of a concern's expenses which consists of "inflexible overhead" costs?

13. Define working capital. Why is it so important? Would it be as important a factor to an established, low-leverage concern as to a new, high-leverage competitor in the same industry? Explain.

14. As this is written, the fire insurance companies are earning well but, on the whole, paying only moderate dividends. Would dividend increases affect the prices of the stocks?

15. How would you identify a sound capital structure? An unsound one? Would a high-leverage structure necessarily be a risky one?

16. Do you approve of a management which demonstrates as much dissension as that of Montgomery Ward? Does it change your mind to be told that the victor in the controversy was the autocratic chairman of the board of directors, who is credited with restoring the company to vigor after serious losses in 1930–1932, with preventing high-cost expansion in 1946–1948, with reducing inventories without loss in 1948, and with improving working capital greatly in 1946–1954?

17. Summarize the principal market factors you would want to know about if you were considering long-term investment in the stock of Celotex Corporation. Would your emphasis be changed if you were contemplating a short-term speculation because the stock appeared to be low in relation to earnings and dividends?

18. Will careful investment analysis eliminate errors? Then why bother?

REFERENCES

Badger, Ralph E., and Harry G. Guthmann: *Investment Principles and Practices,* Prentice-Hall, Inc., New York, 1951, Chap. 7.

Dice, Charles A., and Wilford J. Eiteman: *The Stock Market,* McGraw-Hill Book Company, Inc., New York, 1952, Chap. 28.

Dowrie, George W., and Douglas R. Fuller: *Investments,* John Wiley & Sons, Inc., New York, 1950, Chap. 17.

Grodinsky, Julius: *Investments,* The Ronald Press Company, New York, 1953, Chaps. 3, 4, 5, 6.

Mead, Edward S., and Julius Grodinsky: *The Ebb and Flow of Investment Values,* Appleton-Century-Crofts, Inc., New York, 1939.

Pickett, Ralph R., and Marshall D. Ketchum: *Investment Principles and Policy,* Harper & Brothers, New York, 1954, Chap. 8.

Chapter 14: MAKING USE OF FINANCIAL REPORTS

Most investors are familiar with the balance sheets and income statements which are published annually or at more frequent intervals by nearly every important business corporation. These statements are the source of data for the most basic of investment calculations, such as those of earnings per share or the leverage factor, and also figure importantly in much of the more detailed work of investment analysis. They contain so much of the fundamental information on working capital position, capital structure, sales, expenses, and earnings that no investor can afford to ignore them; yet they are technical enough to require an understanding of accounting assumptions and techniques for their proper interpretation.

It is clearly beyond the scope of the present volume to discuss the art of accounting. An attempt has been made in an earlier chapter to define the difference between a consolidated and a corporate statement. Assuming that this distinction is already clear to the reader, the functions of the present chapter must be reduced to three: First, it seems desirable to review the items typically found on financial statements and define their meanings from the investor's point of view. Second, a brief study of the most important financial ratios used in investment analysis will be in order. Third, an example of a special survey to test some phase of the investment attractiveness of an important stock will be presented.

In order to lend objectivity to a topic which is necessarily somewhat abstract, the presentation of this chapter will be built around the financial statements which appeared in the 1953–1954 annual report of Montgomery Ward & Co. While these Ward statements are reasonably typical, it must be remembered that every industry has its own peculiar business and accounting problems and that even concerns in the same industry may differ considerably. Most of the general principles suggested here are broadly applicable, but routine calculations based on financial statements are no substitute for clear understanding and careful thinking.

The Balance Sheet

Table 20 presents the balance sheet of Montgomery Ward & Co. as it appeared in the company's 1953–1954 annual report. This balance sheet is somewhat less detailed than the typical annual report statement and is not accompanied by any footnotes elaborating on the accounts. However, it is adequate to give the analyst many useful facts about the company's financial position.

As is usual with American corporate balance sheets, the statement is divided into an Assets, or left-hand, side and a Liabilities, or right-hand, side. The assets side consists of an enumeration of all of the property in the possession of the business, assigning dollar values to each item. The liabilities side shows all of the debts of the business and also all of the net worth or stockholders' interest in the business. Obviously, the total assets must equal the total of the business' debts plus the total of the owners' interest in the business; hence the balance sheet achieves an automatic balance.[1]

It has become customary to "classify" the items appearing on most balance sheets, that is, to group certain items together and show a subtotal of values for each group. On the assets side the most commonly used groupings are the Current Assets and the Fixed Assets, although other groupings labeled Investments and Deferred Charges are often found, and many others are occasionally used. On the liabilities side the groupings usually include Current Liabilities, Long-term Liabilities, Reserves, and Net Worth. These group headings will be defined in proper order.

The Current Assets grouping on Ward's balance sheet includes all of the assets which the management regards as cash, cashable, or likely to be sold for cash or collected in cash within a year's time in the ordinary course of business operations. This logically includes all cash, highly salable securities, receivables, and inventory. These assets constitute the company's active trading capital and measure its

[1] A number of corporations now use a subtractive form of statement, in which liabilities are subtracted from assets to measure net worth. All the usual statement items appear, but in different arrangement. This form of balance sheet is used by General Foods Corporation, Caterpillar Tractor Company, and a considerable number of others.

Table 20. Montgomery Ward & Co. Balance Sheet, January 31, 1954

Assets

Current Assets:

Cash		$ 23,155,063
U.S. Government securities (short term)		269,987,032

Receivables:

Time payment accounts	$177,195,098	
Other accounts	9,015,190	
	$186,210,288	
Less—Reserves for doubtful accounts and collection expense	25,209,135	161,001,153
Merchandise inventories (priced at the lower of cost or market)		214,774,864
Supply inventories and prepaid catolog.... costs		15,556,397

Total current assets		$684,474,509

Properties and Equipment (at cost):

Land		$ 6,849,461	
Buildings, fixtures and equipment	$ 67,597,176		
Less—Depreciation reserves	43,357,301	24,239,875	
Leasehold improvements (less amortization)		2,082,639	33,171,975
			$717,646,484

Liabilities and Stockholders' Investment

Current Liabilities:

Accounts payable	$ 31,357,065	
Due customers	7,757,527	
Accrued expenses and insurance reserve	15,336,920	
Federal taxes on income	42,430,483	
Total current liabilities		$ 96,881,995

Stockholders' Investment:

Class "A" stock—Authorized 205,000 shares of no par value, non-callable, $7.00 per share cumulative dividends; issued 201,554 shares, stated at liquidating value	$ 20,155,400	
Common stock—Authorized 10,000,000 shares of no par value; issued 6,502,378 shares, at stated value	211,231,385	
Earned Surplus—representing earnings reinvested in the business	389,377,704	620,764,489
		$717,646,484

capacity to do business, pay its bills, and possibly spare a few occasional millions for dividends. Because a company's current assets are very important to their welfare, investors usually scan the items critically, trying to make sure that all are actually current and that they are accurately valued. In addition to the cash or cash-producing items, it is now becoming standard practice to include among the current assets any important prepayments such as Montgomery Ward's catalogue outlay, on the theory that a prepayment in such case is just as good as the cash to meet an unpaid bill would be.

The Cash item on the balance sheet is a reasonably exact total of all company cash and bank deposit holdings at the close of business on the date of the statement. The second current asset item, U.S. Government securities (short term), probably reflects the cost of these securities rather than their market value. Corporation balance sheets usually show securities investments in nonsubsidiaries at cost, regardless of whether the investments are regarded as current assets or long-term holdings.[2] If the market value of the securities deviates far from cost, a footnote should be used to disclose the market value. In the case of Montgomery Ward the statement indicates that the securities are short-term governments, which assures that their value will not fluctuate significantly.

The Receivables on Ward's statement are shown at their total value on the books, "Less—Reserves for doubtful accounts and collection expense." These Reserves are simply an estimated $25,209,-135 of the receivables which will be lost because not collectible or which will be absorbed in collection expenses. The statement does not indicate how many overage accounts remain on Ward's books or how many are currently "going bad." Not infrequently a company's estimate of bad debts is in error, in which case the net asset may be undervalued or overvalued. One of the constantly interesting problems in statement analysis is that of estimating what the net receivables are really worth.

Merchandise inventories on this Ward statement are "priced at the lower of cost or market." Since this pricing method usually applies to each inventory item separately, the total inventory is undoubtedly valued at prices below market (*i.e.,* replacement cost).

---

[2] Fire and casualty insurance company and some investment company statements reverse this rule, showing market values in the statement and cost figures in appended footnotes.

Investors need to watch methods of inventory valuation carefully; many firms are now using the LIFO (last-in first-out) method of inventory valuation, which appraises important portions of the inventory at prices prevailing at earlier dates, often as far back as 1941. The LIFO method therefore tends to undervalue inventories, in view of postwar price levels. Most balance sheets indicate the method of inventory valuation used.

The last item in Ward's list of Current Assets is labeled "Supply inventories and prepaid catalog costs." Some of this $15,556,397 item doubtless represents shipping cartons, wrapping paper, and the like, but the bulk of it consists of the company's outlay on its new 1954 spring and summer catalogue, which was about ready to mail at the date of this balance sheet. This large catalogue item will be removed from the assets and regarded as an expense when the 6 months' life of the catalogue has expired.

Ward's next major balance sheet grouping is labeled Properties and Equipment instead of the conventional Fixed Assets, but the items included are typical. They consist of the long-term tangible assets, such as buildings, fixtures, and equipment, which are owned by the firm. They are shown on the statement at original cost plus the cost of subsequent improvements minus the Reserves for Depreciation. The reserves for depreciation are in no sense replacement funds or any kind of property; they are merely estimates of accumulated wear and tear. Reserves for depreciation, like the assets whose values they modify, are usually based on the cost of the assets. Ward's statement therefore shows net fixed asset values based on the prices which existed at the time the assets were acquired. There are three reasons why these net figures may be far removed from present market values. First, changes in general price levels may have made the basic cost figures obsolete. Second, the estimates of total accumulated depreciation may be too large or too small, resulting in inaccurate net values. Third, the economic usefulness of a fixed asset is not necessarily measured by its cost; some are well-chosen and profitable, others may be white elephants.

Montgomery Ward does not show a Deferred Charges grouping on its balance sheet. Deferred Charges, which appear as the final group of assets on many such statements, may include certain prepayments such as insurance, may show certain irrecoverable past outlays such as costs incurred in marketing the firm's securities, and may also include values for patents, good will, and other intangibles. The real value of many deferred charge items is doubtful, but many obviously have very great value. Because this final grouping of intangible assets often contains items which are not deferred charges in the technical sense, other labels such as Intangible Assets are often used.

The first grouping on the liabilities side is usually the Current Liabilities, which may be defined as items due to be paid in cash within a year. Short-term bank loans, trade and other accounts payable, and accrued expenses and taxes are usually the major items in this category. Montgomery Ward's current liabilities are typical, for short-term bank loans are not usually present on corporate statements at the end of a fiscal year. The reason is that most concerns adopt a fiscal (accounting) year which ends between busy seasons, at a time when inventories are sold off, receivables collected, and current liabilities paid down to a minimum.

The second important liability grouping on the typical balance sheet, the Long-term Liabilities, does not appear on the Ward statement, since the company has no such debt. Bonds, mortgages payable, and long-term bank loans are the most common types.

Although this Ward balance sheet does not have a section labeled Reserves, previous Ward statements have had one and they are not uncommon on corporate statements. Several years ago Ward's statement showed a "Reserve for possible future inventory price decline," indicating a sum which the management felt might be lost if prices collapsed in a depression. The same statement showed as a "Reserve for self-insurance and contingencies" an amount which might be lost if uninsured accidents occurred, if lawsuits turned out adversely, etc. Such reserves may be careful estimates of potential losses, or they may be entirely arbitrary. These reserves are in no sense cash funds. Any cash or other current resources would be shown on the assets side of the statement; the reserves are simply segregated portions of the present apparent net worth of the company.

The Capital Stock and Surplus section indicates the stockholders' net worth in Montgomery Ward & Co., assuming the asset values to be accurate, the liabilities to be correct, and the reserves to be exact estimates of pending losses. The Class A stock, which is a high-grade preferred, is carried at its liquidation value. The remainder of the net worth is divided between the common stock account and the surplus, which together presumably represent the common stockholders' equity in the business.

It has been noted that Montgomery Ward's balance sheet contains no asset items representing good will, mailing lists, trade names, going-concern value, or any other such intangibles. Yet it is hardly conceivable that a Montgomery Ward with the present holdings of cash, receivables, inventory, catalogues, and fixed assets would earn as much as the present firm, without the firm's reputation, established customer relationships, and personnel. But neither asset accounts nor net worth section reflect these values. Corporate accounting policies respecting the inclusion of intangibles are varied, but Ward's policy of omitting them entirely is one which is widely followed in conservative circles.

The Income Statement

Income statements are searched and interpreted by investors with even more eager attention than balance sheets receive. After all, earnings constitute the prime prerequisite to the investor's twin objectives of dividends and capital appreciation, and the income statement is the basic source of information about earnings. Because the Montgomery Ward income accounts shown in Table 21 are unusually brief, a more detailed illustrative form is shown alongside to elaborate the meaning of the Ward figures. For example, the initial figure on the Ward statement, that for net sales, is doubtless arrived at by deducting sales returns and allowances for damaged merchandise from a total sales figure. The illustrative form shows how this would appear in a more complete statement. Investors would no doubt like to see such details; they provide a clue to the efficiency of operation.

The second section on the Ward income statement shows the cost of merchandise sold and five important categories of operating expenses. These figures are intended to show investors the relative importance of the various expenses, and to permit the comparison of these costs (in total size and as a percentage of sales) with those of other firms and with the Ward statements of other years. Such comparisons would give an excellent idea of the trends of costs and the possibilities of future improvement.

The second section of many corporate income statements is used to show the cost of merchandise sold subtracted from net sales and the resulting gross profit on sales. This would be of interest if it

Table 21. Montgomery Ward & Co., Statement of Earnings, Year Ended January 31, 1953

	As Published by the Company	As a More Detailed Report Might Appear
Gross sales...		xxxx
Less returns and allowances........................		x
Net sales...	$999,123,379	xxxx
Cost of merchandise sold..........................	$680,099,705	xxx
Gross profit on sales.............................		xxx
Wages and salaries................................	167,623,064	xxx
Allowances for bad debts..........................		x
Other expenses—net...............................	41,011,483	xx
Rents...	11,253,304	x
Depreciation on buildings and equipment............	3,178,987	x
Property, social security, and state taxes.............	11,881,663	x
Total (costs) and expenses........................	$915,048,206	xxx
Net earnings from operations......................		xxx
Other income.....................................		x
Other deductions.................................		x
Available for bond interest........................		xxx
Bond interest, etc................................		x
Earnings before taxes on income...................	$ 84,075,173	xxx
Provision for federal taxes on income...............	42,880,000	xx
Net earnings.....................................	$ 41,195,173	xx

were done on the Montgomery Ward statement, because it would show how high a markup Montgomery Ward was able to get on the merchandise which it sold. The cost of goods sold is a critically important item whose measurement often depends on inventory accounting methods. For example, a firm using conventional "cost or market" methods (the so-called first-in first-out methods) of evaluating its inventories, as Montgomery Ward does, tends to compute the "cost" of goods sold in any fiscal period at a figure close to their actual purchase cost. Thus the reported cost of goods sold in any year will tend to be the actual costs paid in the early part of the year or a previous year; and in a period of rising commodity prices the generous selling prices obtained will make profits look good indeed. When commodity prices are falling, this combination of early purchase costs and later sales prices will make profits look small. But if the LIFO (last-in first-out) or a "base stock" method of inventory valuation is followed, the computed cost of goods sold in any year tends to approach the cost of replacement goods bought as each item of inventory is sold and replaced. Under this system current sales are compared with current replacement costs, and changing price levels have relatively little effect upon the profit computations. From the investor's viewpoint the LIFO system appears to give a more realistic view of profit margins and earnings than does either a first-in first-out or a base stock system.

If a separate section of the income statement was devoted to cost of goods sold and the gross profit, the following section would deal with operating expenses. The items in this section would consist of the selling expenses and general operating expenses, which would include between them all outlays for wages, salaries, rent, maintenance, supplies, general taxes, costs of operation, and an allowance for losses on uncollectible accounts. The size of these various expenses often discloses important features of the business. For example, Montgomery Ward's rent expenses of over 11 million dollars indicate that Ward stores operate in many cases in rented instead of owned premises. The Ward statement does not disclose what amount, if any, was included as an allowance for bad debts. Presumably such an amount is included, along with advertising, insurance, and other things, in "Other Expenses." The allowance for bad debts is an expense because it is impossible to do a credit business without losing some money on bad credits and collection expenses. Most firms anticipate such losses by recording as an expense the expected loss on each year's business. The amounts so charged appear on the balance sheet as reserves for doubtful accounts and collection expense and are usually subtracted from the accounts receivable to show the "net" value of the receivables. Obviously, if these reserves are being built up faster than bad credits are being extended, the expense (allowance for bad debts) is being overstated and profits understated. The large accumulated (unused) reserves on the balance sheet suggest that this may be happening at Ward's.

Depreciation on buildings and equipment is simply the proportion of the cost of Ward's fixed assets which is charged to expense this year because that proportion of the useful life of the assets was consumed during the year. This annual expense is an estimate based on experience, engineering estimates, and simple opinion. Usually it is passably accurate, but analysts check to see if it appears reasonable in comparison with the charges made by other firms and by the given firm in other years. Many companies publish the percentage rates of annual depreciation applied to various types of assets; for the others, depreciation charges may be gauged as a percentage of the total cost of fixed assets or as a percentage of sales. After any radical change in price levels, depreciation charges lose much of their meaning. The annual cost of using a machine costing $1,000 and good for 10 years' service would seem to be $100, but if price-level inflation makes the replacement cost $2,000 the owner is not very bright if he prices the machine's output on the theory that the annual cost of its services is $100. However, depreciation charges based on cost are standard accounting practice; it is up to the securities analyst to guess at what the profits would be if depreciation charges were adequate to provide for actual replacement of deteriorated equipment.[3]

General Taxes is the last significant main group in this cost-of-sales and expense section. This item is important because of its constantly growing size. Income taxes are not included at this point in

[3] For a striking analysis of this and related points see Ralph C. Jones, "Effect of Inflation on Capital and Profits: The Record of Nine Steel Companies," *Journal of Accountancy,* January, 1949, p. 9.

In the years 1951–1960 depreciation allowances and income tax costs are greatly confused by special tax legislation. In these years certain "defense-certificated facilities" —important portions of new steel mills, railroad equipment, electric generating equipment, and the like—may be charged off at 20 per cent per year in computing taxable income. All important fixed assets installed after January 1, 1954, whether defense-certificated or not, may in tax computations be written off at rapid rates in early years and slower rates in later years. And the depreciation charges used in the corporate financial statements may or may not be the same as those used in computing income tax liability. Clearly, the reported figures on depreciation expense, income tax costs, net income, book values of assets, and net worth are all subject to drastic distortion.

theoretically accurate statements, for income taxes are properly a
share in net income, not a cost which must be met in the attempt to
earn that income.

When the operating expense total is deducted from the gross profit
on sales, the remainder may be called the net earnings from operations. To this must next be added any nonoperating income such
as dividends and rents received on investments, to determine the
amount available for bond interest. After bond interest and other
fixed charges have been deducted, the remainder can properly be
called earnings before income taxes. In the case of Montgomery
Ward the company had no significant nonoperating income and no
bond interest to pay; so the net profit from operations is also the net
profit before income taxes. Deduction of provision for income taxes
leaves the net earnings for the year.

Problems in Statement Analysis

Many of the errors made by investors in their attempts to interpret
financial statements can be credited to the failure of the investors to
understand the ordinary principles of accounting, such as those
which underlie depreciation estimates or inventory valuation. This
is not a problem for accountants, nor even for writers of texts on investments; those who wish to catch the nuances in financial statements must go to an appropriate authority and learn how. A second
source of investors' errors appears to be lack of alertness or laziness,
as reflected in failure to realize the exact implications of statement
titles, footnotes, and accompanying "schedules" of supplementary
data. These would not be phrased so carefully or even published if
they did not have significant meaning. A third source of error centers around the fact that accounting practices and definitions are far
from uniform. Despite valiant efforts by the SEC, various public
utility regulatory agencies, and leading accounting associations, there
are important differences in accounting techniques which may cause
condensed statements to deceive even the accountants themselves.
Obviously, this panorama of confusion is not the province of an investments text; only occasional examples of differences due to techniques may be noted here.

In considerable part, investors' troubles with financial statements
are due to the intricacies of consolidated statements. In Chapter 3

a consolidated statement was defined as one which combined the accounts of a parent company and its subsidiaries into a single statement, just as though they were one unified concern. But as a matter of fact, many parent companies only "consolidate" the accounts of domestic subsidiaries and sometimes only those in which they have almost complete ownership; the "consolidated" statements in such cases will omit the detailed assets, liabilities, sales, and expenses of the nonconsolidated subsidiaries and include only the parent company's equity in the nonconsolidated subsidiaries' net worth and earnings, respectively. Alternatively, instead of including in consolidated statements the parent company's entire equity in nonconsolidated subsidiaries' net worth and earnings, some accountants include only the cost of the parent company's investment in such subsidiaries in the consolidated balance sheet and only dividends received by the parent company in the consolidated income statement. In either of these cases the consolidated statements may give a false impression of the consolidated system's assets, liabilities, sales, and expenses, unless the reader understands exactly what is being done. There are other distortions which may creep into consolidated statements; some of these are often commented upon under the heading Principles of Consolidation in footnotes to the statements themselves; but they are too intricate for the present discussion.

Another source of error for casual statement readers is found in the fact that many companies have important foreign branches, whose accounts are properly to be included in the financial statements. But earnings and assets in foreign countries must be evaluated in dollars, even when foreign assets are hard to convert into dollars. Are nonavailable foreign earnings truly earnings from the American securityholder's standpoint? Are foreign current assets really current from the American point of view? The most common accounting technique is to evaluate foreign earnings and foreign current assets at current quoted rates of exchange, but to show foreign fixed assets at the dollar values they represented at the time of construction, less regular depreciation allowances. This obviously does not reach ideal conclusions, and it is by no means a universal procedure. The investor must discover the procedures used in each individual case and then decide whether the financial statements are truly meaningful.

A third common pitfall for the hasty reader is his tendency to regard the net profit shown at the bottom of an income statement as an indication of the firm's normal earning capacity. Actually, there are many nonrecurring factors which may distort any year's income, as well as many accounting techniques which may affect the figures. For example, large capital assets such as buildings or securities investments may be sold at a profit or at a loss; nonconsolidated subsidiaries may pay abnormally large special dividends or fail to pay normal ones; income tax adjustments on account of prior years, or other special tax considerations, may affect the present year's tax charges; or the present year's figures may be affected by abnormal developmental costs or commodity price changes or other temporary factors. Some of these nonrecurring factors, such as gains on sale of capital assets, are likely to be explained clearly in the statement or its footnotes; but others, such as temporarily increased costs due to a developmental advertising program, may not even be noted as separate items on the statement. The investor's general knowledge of the business plus the information he may obtain elsewhere must be applied in interpreting the figures before him. As illustrations of the significance of accounting methods the following instances may be cited:

1. International Harvester Company has a number of wholly owned subsidiaries, mostly located in foreign countries, whose earnings are not consolidated with those of the parent company. Since most of the subsidiaries' earnings are kept in the subsidiaries to finance their growth, these earnings are not included in Harvester's income. If they had been consolidated in 1952–1953 the reported earnings would have been nearly 50 per cent larger. Furthermore, Harvester showed these subsidiaries on its balance sheet at about $125,000,000 less than their book value, thus reducing the book value of its own stock by about 15 per cent.

2. United States Steel has extensive defense-certificated facilities which are being in part depreciated at the 20 per cent rate permitted by the Defense Production Act. This reduces both earnings and income taxes. In 1954 posttax net earnings were being reduced about 15 per cent by this factor. After these facilities are fully depreciated no more depreciation expense can be charged, and net income and income taxes will both rise. The railroads, on the other hand, are charging accelerated depreciation rates on their certificated facilities in their income tax calculations, thus obtaining lower taxes, but they are using normal depreciation rates in their published financial statements. Their reported posttax

net income is therefore larger now, because of lower taxes, but will decline in the future.

3. Chrysler Corporation in 1952 and 1953 chose to charge depreciation rates on fixed assets in excess of those deemed proper by the income tax authorities. The result was a very substantial reduction in Chrysler's reported earnings, value of assets, and net worth.

4. Endicott-Johnson Corporation, a large shoe manufacturer, agreed in 1945 to provide pensions to employees based on both past and future years in company service. The sum required to finance the past-service pensions was very large, but the company undertook to accumulate it in ten years in addition to the sums needed for current-service funding, out of current income. The past-service charges alone in the years 1950– 1953 amounted to about as much as the reported earnings on the common stock.

5. Most oil companies charge the cost of drilling and equipping a successful oil well to an asset account, and then charge the expense accounts with depreciation on it over the life of the well. However, some companies, of which Continental Oil Company is a conspicuous example, charge the cost of drilling wells immediately to expense. As long as the company continues to grow its drilling costs are far greater than depreciation charges on old wells would be; hence it is clear that this practice reduces the reported net income as well as the balance sheet assets and net worth.

Techniques in Interpreting Financial Statements

In examining financial statements there are three ways of using the available figures. First, one may look at the figures themselves and try to judge whether they indicate strength or weakness. For example, the 1954 Montgomery Ward annual report indicated that sales volume had declined over 17 per cent between 1949 and 1954 but that cash and government bond holdings at January 31, 1954, had reached the impressive total of $293,142,395. Second, one may test the soundness of the situation by the use of significant ratios; thus, the adequacy of Montgomery Ward's 684 million dollars in current assets may be tested by comparing it with the 97 million dollars in current liabilities; the ratio of 7.1 to 1 suggests a highly liquid position for this type of business. Third, the statement figures may be tested by ratios between themselves and external or nonfinancial data; for example, estimates of changes in the physical size of Montgomery Ward's inventory might be made by dividing the dollar values reported on the successive balance sheets by wisely chosen price indexes.

Reaching sound conclusions based on examination of figures or ratios is a task which requires a modicum of work. Experience and good judgment might enable one to decide by direct inspection whether Ward's government bond holdings were sufficient as a cash backlog, or whether the current ratio (ratio of current assets to current liabilities) was adequate, but most analysts would also try historical comparison and comparison with other firms. That is, they would check to see what current ratio Ward's had had in past years, and also what Sears Roebuck, J. C. Penney Co., and similar firms had now. A figure or a ratio may depart sharply from the normal for good reason, but the careful investor will want to discover both the departure and the reason.

Users of financial data must be always careful to avoid comparing unlike things and to escape illogical deductions. For example, the cash, inventories, accounts payable, and bank debt of Libby, McNeill & Libby all vary enormously through the canning and selling season as their annual pack of food products is processed and sold. Their current ratio on September 1 would not bear comparison with the one they would show on February 1; yet comparison of the ratio on any given date with those existing on similar dates in previous years should give significant results. Another illustration of illogical comparison is found in the attempt to measure the "efficiency" of use of corporate assets by retailers, by dividing annual sales into total assets. If the "asset turnover" is fast—that is, if it takes only a few months for sales to equal total assets—the firm is presumably making efficient use of its assets. So far, so good. But to compare the asset turnover of a retailer whose assets consist of fixtures plus inventory and who does a cash-and-carry business in a rented building with that of a competitor who sells on credit and also owns his building is to achieve the heights of absurdity. The second firm could be twice as efficient and twice as profitable as the first and still require three times as long for a complete "asset turnover."

Financial Ratios

There are a number of commonly used financial ratios and calculations which are both important and significant in many industries. While all ratios are subject to the weaknesses noted in the preceding section and must be used with discretion, these are widely applicable. They are not the only useful ratios; many others are used to bring out details in various situations, and still others have special applications in specific industries. Also, this list is limited to ratios developed from financial statement data and, therefore, does not include calculations which make use of nonfinancial data such as price indexes, measures of physical volume, or national income figures.

1. Current ratio. The ratio of total current assets to total current liabilities is used to measure the adequacy of the current assets to meet all early obligations. This is the best known of all the ratios. Traditionally a 2-to-1 (200 per cent) ratio is said to be the dividing line between adequacy and inadequacy, but this universal rule is not sound; utilities and railroads hardly need a 2-to-1 ratio, but manufacturers and retailers who must carry inventories and receivables usually need a higher one. Firms which do a heavily seasonal business are likely to have high ratios in the dull seasons but low ones in the busy seasons when large operations are being financed on credit. Note that all figures which include inventories may be distorted if LIFO valuations are used.

2. Net current assets. This is not a ratio, but the simple excess of current assets over current liabilities, often referred to as net working capital. It measures the amount of current assets provided to the firm by its permanent investors. Any tendency of net working capital to increase or decrease is very important to investors, as an indication of the financial health of the business and of its capacity to pay dividends.

3. "Acid test." This is a ratio of the most liquid current assets to the current liabilities, often defined as the ratio of all current assets except inventory to the current liabilities. A ratio of 1 to 1 is said to be usually adequate. The test supplements the current ratio, to indicate whether the business is truly in a liquid condition.

4. Percentage of net current assets to sales. This ratio is an attempt to measure the adequacy of the net working capital to handle the existing volume of sales. No typical ratio applicable to all industries can be suggested, but comparison of a present ratio with that of prior years and with that shown by competitors is often illuminating.

5. Percentage of net receivables to sales. This ratio is used to gauge the success of collection efforts. A rising ratio of receivables might indicate that collections were slowing down or that bad receivables had accumulated on the books, though it might merely indicate an increasing percentage of credit and installment sales. Between 1945 and 1952 the increasing sale of consumer durables on the installment plan caused this ratio to rise in many lines of business.

6. Percentage of inventory to sales (or better, inventory to cost of goods sold). This measures the soundness of an inventory investment. If inventory is large in relation to sales, it may be excessive in amount, ill-selected and not effectively salable, or purchased at a too high price. This ratio is of little use when LIFO inventory values are the only ones available.

7. Asset turnover. This is the ratio of total net assets to sales and is designed to measure the effectiveness of the use of assets by seeing how active they are in producing gross income. This ratio is subject to manifold distortions, including the effect of comparing prewar cost valuations of fixed assets with postwar sales values.

8. Total debt to net tangible assets. This is a measure of total current and long-term debt compared with total assets, excluding such intangibles as good will, patents, and bond discount. The strength of the firm is obviously greater when the debt ratio is small, though it is always necessary to remember that the book value of assets does not necessarily measure either their market value or earning power.

9. Net worth to net tangible assets. This is the obvious complement to item 8 and a measure of leverage as it affects the stockholders.

10. Gross profit to sales. This comparison is usually expressed as the percentage of gross profit to net sales. The figure is important in merchandising operations as an indicator of competitive pressure and the amount of markup obtainable. It varies more in response to price-level changes when cost-or-market inventory values are used than when LIFO methods are followed.

11. Operating ratio. This very important calculation, computed as the percentage of operating expenses to sales, varies somewhat in customary content from one industry to the next. The general idea is to gauge the percentage of sales revenue absorbed in the wage, salary, material, and general (not income) tax cost of conducting the business. The higher the ratio, the more dangerous is an increase in expenses. A low ratio suggests security and relatively stable earnings. The operating ratio is used more in analysis of securities in service industries—for example, utilities, railroads, and banks—than in merchandising or manufacturing industries.

12. Percentage of depreciation to cost of fixed assets. The annual depreciation (expense) allowance to spread the cost of fixed assets over the estimated life of the assets is one of the operating expenses. One way for an ineffective management to make a good impression on stockholders is to increase profits by underestimating depreciation. This ratio enables the stockholder to compare this year's depreciation rate with the depreciation rates of other years and other concerns.

13. Percentage of depreciation plus maintenance to cost of fixed assets. Some industries, notably utilities and railroads, can reduce actual depreciation to small amounts by constant maintenance and replacement. In such cases the total of the two items, both of which are operating expenses, makes a better indication of proper accounting than would either separately.

14. Percentage of depreciation plus maintenance to sales. Because depreciation and maintenance are both related to the amount of use imposed on the assets, it sometimes seems better to compare them with sales than with asset costs. This is especially true of utility and railroad statements. A low ratio suggests understatement of expenses and overstatement of profits; a high ratio, the opposite.

15. Percentage of bad debts allowance to sales. The portion of the annual sales which will be lost because the resulting receivables cannot be collected must be estimated and the amount included in the year's operating expenses. This ratio is important in merchandising operations but even more important in the case of banks, finance companies, and other lenders. If the allowance is too small, the earnings will be overstated, and vice versa. However, conclusions must not be reached hastily; a high bad debts allowance may mean poor credit management, or the deliberate assumption of credit risks to gain higher profits through more sales, or simply bad debt allowances in excess of actual losses.

16. Percentage of operating earnings to sales. This is an important measure of the concern's capacity to retain a percentage of its gross revenue as earnings available for its securityholders. A decline in the ratio suggests a decline in the quality of the earnings, even though their amount does not decline. This ratio is of course the complement of the operating ratio.

17. Earnings available for fixed charges to fixed charges. This measures the adequacy of operating earnings plus other income to meet bond interest and other fixed charges such as lease rentals. Earnings available for fixed charges should ordinarily be computed before deductions for income taxes. A ratio of 2 to 1 is sometimes said to be satisfactory when earnings are stable, but 3 to 1 would seem to be a safer minimum. When income taxes are deducted before arriving at income available for fixed charges, a lower ratio would be tolerable. In industries with unstable earnings the minimum average ratio must be much higher than 3 to 1.

18. Net profit to net worth. Expressed as a percentage, this ratio appears to be an excellent indication of the soundness of the stockholders' equity. Its accuracy is of course subject to the accuracy of both the net profit and net worth figures, which are in turn dependent upon many elements of accounting policy and procedure.

In addition to the foregoing ratios, securities analysts make constant use of a number of calculations involving earnings per share, over-all interest or dividend coverage, asset coverage, capital structure, leverage, and book values. These have been discussed in earlier chapters and will not be repeated here, though their relationship to these techniques of statement analysis is obvious.

Standard Ratios

Investors often like to compare the financial ratios of their companies with average ratios representing large groups of companies in the same industry. Such average or typical ratios are often termed standard ratios. Standard ratios are available for investor comparison in the *Standard Industry Surveys,* in the *Special Features* sections of the Moody investment manuals, and in a number of other financial services. More detailed ratio studies for particular industries are made by several trade associations, and the Graduate School of Business Administration of Harvard University has made a number of such studies. Dun and Bradstreet, Inc., and the Robert Morris Associates have made extensive ratio studies from the point of view of credit men.

A Special Analytical Survey

In Chapter 11 a suggested outline for a general analysis of a stock or bond was presented. This outline is intended to provide an introduction to almost any topic an investor might wish to explore, and might, in fact, remind him of topics which needed to be explored. However, there are many cases in which an investor may feel that two or three of the topics in the outline contain the key to the entire situation. In such a case he may wish to make a study of these topics alone, relying on his general knowledge of the industry and the company to supply the basis for a final judgment.

As an illustration of such a study, the following pages will review certain phases of the situation of Montgomery Ward & Co. stock in the summer of 1954.

Montgomery Ward Example

In the first half of 1954 the monthly reports released by Montgomery Ward & Co. indicated that sales volume was falling about 12 per cent below the previous year. Because Ward's sales had been tending downward ever since 1948 in a period of generally rising business activity, many stockholders felt some concern about the future of the company's earnings and dividends.

Ward's general position as the nation's second largest mail-order concern and operator of 590 medium-sized department stores was well known to investors. Every financial service—for example, the Standard Stock Report reproduced as Charts 11 and 12 in Chapter 13—provided a satisfactory basic description. Investors were also well aware that Ward's elderly chief executive, Sewell Avery, expected the postwar boom to end in a substantial business recession and believed that the situation called for minimum inventories, careful control of expenses, postponement of all outlays for expansion or improvement, and accumulation of cash resources. Because this policy was inaugurated about 1947, Ward's had made no important postwar improvements, had not shared in postwar business growth, had suffered some internal dissension and the loss of many ambitious executives and other personnel, but had accumulated cash.

Despite the no-expansion policy, and perhaps because of rigorous expense control, Ward's had had substantial profits in the years 1946–1953. However, the policy of accumulating cash had resulted in severe limitations of dividends, and this coupled with the no-expansion policy had reduced investor interest and caused the price of the stock to remain low in relation to earnings and asset value. On the other hand, a considerable group of professional investors, including many investment companies, held the stock because they felt that the company was too strong to deteriorate quickly and that the strong cash position would permit vigorous expansion when the time appeared right.

In the summer of 1954, with the price of the stock at about $65 per share, barely 10 times the average earnings of 1952–1953 and only 70 per cent of book value, it seemed obvious that only a drastic change in top management or a drastic change in economic conditions would alter the company's basic policies. Neither change seemed imminent, so investors needed to know how a continuation of present policies would affect sales volume, earnings, dividends and long-range future opportunities.[4] Tables 22, 23, and 24 present some of the quantitative evidence on these matters.

Table 22 contains some of the basic data needed in exploring the Ward situation. Most of the figures seem to show great growth, but it must be remembered that much of the growth in sales, net income, and net worth between 1940 and 1953 is the result of the doubling of the commodity price level; it is probable, for example, that the physical volume of Ward's sales in 1953 did not exceed that of 1940. The net worth figures are of course greatly augmented by retained earnings as well as price-level change. But the greatest change in the

[4] In September, 1954, certain interests not previously connected with the Ward enterprise announced an intention to buy some of the stock and attempt to gain control by ousting Avery at the next stockholders' meeting. This group was headed by Louis E. Wolfson, who promised extensive policy changes if elected. After a spectacular proxy battle the Avery management was reelected in April, 1955.

Ward situation over these years is in the cash and government bond holdings and the net working capital in which they are included. The immense size of the cash and government bond holding is attested by the fact that the January 31, 1949, position was larger in relation to sales than any prewar position shown in the table, yet

Table 22. Selected Items from Montgomery Ward Financial Statements, 1937–1954

(In millions of dollars)

Year ended January 31	Net sales	Net income	Net fixed assets	Cash and government bonds	Net working capital	Total net worth	Book value per common share *
1937	$ 361	$20.2	$44.9	$ 17.1	$118.8	$176.8	$29.98
1938	414	19.2	46.9	18.5	125.5	185.5	31.48
1939	414	19.6	46.7	24.4	136.6	195.9	33.48
1940	475	27.0	49.8	14.4	148.9	211.1	36.38
1941	516	23.0	49.6	16.4	163.4	222.3	38.53
1942	633	27.4	49.0	16.0	178.9	239.1	41.50
1947	974	52.3	39.4	101.4	343.2	382.5	55.74
1948	1,159	59.1	40.3	51.1	380.5	420.7	61.60
1949	1,212	68.2	39.9	88.1	428.2	468.0	68.88
1950	1,084	47.8	38.4	130.2	456.5	494.9	73.01
1951	1,170	74.2	37.4	195.6	504.2	541.6	80.20
1952	1,106	54.3	35.9	245.7	539.2	575.1	85.34
1953	1,085	49.6	35.1	253.7	568.7	603.7	89.75
1954	999	41.2	33.2	293.1	587.6	620.8	92.37

* In dollars per share.

sales by 1954 had dropped 17 per cent while cash and governments were up 200 per cent over 1949!

Table 23 compares Ward's sales record with six related sets of figures. The first two columns compare the sales with net worth and working capital, and indicate that in the years following 1948 and 1949 the sales failed to increase to make proper use of the growing net worth and working capital. However, when sales are compared with the net worth and working capital actually useful to the business, excluding the excessive hoard of idle government bonds, the sales drop becomes impressive only in 1953 and 1954. In comparison with aggressively managed Sears Roebuck the entire postwar sales record is a drab one.

Table 24 undertakes to evaluate the Ward profit and dividend record. The first column indicates that profits as a percentage of

Table 23. Analysis of Montgomery Ward's Sales Record, 1937–1954

| Year ended January 31 | Ward's sales as percentages of | | | | |
	Ward's net worth	Ward's working capital	Ward's active net worth *	Ward's active working capital *	Sears Roebuck sales
1937	208	308	...	...	72.9
1938	223	330	...	...	76.7
1939	211	306	...	...	82.1
1940	225	319	...	...	77.0
1941	232	315	...	...	73.3
1942	265	354	...	...	69.2
1947	254	284	273	307	60.4
1948	276	305	276	305	58.6
1949	259	283	267	292	52.7
1950	219	238	247	270	50.0
1951	216	230	278	305	45.8
1952	193	205	274	303	41.5
1953	180	191	256	278	37.0
1954	161	170	248	270	32.0

* Active net worth and active working capital are measured by excluding holdings of cash plus government bonds in excess of $75,000,000.

sales dropped sharply from 1951 to 1954. However, it must be remembered that the postwar margins up through 1952 were aided by inflationary price changes, and that only those of 1950, 1953, and 1954 are comparable with prewar years. By this test, net income as a percentage of sales seems passably satisfactory even in 1954. Net income as a percentage of net worth shows a sad decline from 1949 to 1954, but in ratio to net worth actively used in the business even the final year falls only a little short of prewar standards. The Sears Roebuck profit record as a percentage of sales is certainly no better in the postwar years than Ward's, but it must be remembered that Sears's profits were made after promotional expense outlays which helped to increase Sears's sales steadily; and it will be observed that Sears's profits as a percentage of net worth are decidedly better than Ward's.

Table 24. Analysis and Comparison of Montgomery Ward's Earnings-Dividend Record, 1937–1954

Year ended January 31	Ward's net income as a percentage of			Ward's earnings per share	Ward's dividend per share	Sears Roebuck net income as a percentage of	
	Sales	Net worth	Active net worth			Sales	Net worth
1937	5.6	11.4	....	$ 4.12	$4.00	6.2	12.9
1938	4.6	10.4	....	3.41	2.00	5.7	12.8
1939	4.7	10.0	....	3.50	1.50	4.6	9.6
1940	5.7	12.8	....	4.91	2.00	6.1	13.9
1941	4.5	10.4	....	4.14	2.00	5.1	12.9
1942	4.3	11.5	....	4.97	2.00	4.0	12.5
1947	5.4	13.7	14.7	7.83	3.00	6.2	24.1
1948	5.1	14.0	14.0	8.86	3.00	5.4	22.1
1949	5.6	14.6	15.0	10.28	3.00	6.0	24.0
1950	4.4	9.7	10.9	7.13	3.00	5.0	17.2
1951	6.3	13.7	17.6	11.19	4.00	5.6	20.3
1952	4.9	9.4	13.4	8.14	3.00	4.2	14.8
1953	4.6	8.2	11.7	7.41	3.00	3.8	13.5
1954	4.1	6.6	10.2	6.12	3.50	3.8	13.6

These data suggest and nonquantitative information confirms the idea that the postwar Ward program has not only refrained from expansion but has also omitted the improvement and promotional and service expenditures which might have increased the sales of existing Ward establishments. The profit ratios seemingly have been sustained at the cost of falling sales and competitive effectiveness. But the figures do not indicate that the deterioration has gone far. The sales decline is the most serious; even the reduced incomes of farmers and the market glut in household appliances do not explain away a 17 per cent five-year sales decline when the principal competitor was growing at 7 per cent per annum. The profit ratios show only a little weakness, and only in the one or two most recent years. Apparently there would still be time for sales-promotional and organization-building efforts to control this phase of the situation, for there is as yet no vicious circle of low sales–high overhead–enforced economies–further sales decline to drag the company down.

The tables therefore support the idea that Ward is a sound and well-entrenched retail system, in need of aggressive upbuilding but not in trouble. And Table 22 indicates that all the resources needed for upbuilding are ready and waiting. Comparison of Ward's cash and government bond holdings with the sales figures prior to 1950 indicate that 65 to 75 million dollars in cash and governments would have been ample at January 31, 1954. That suggests that at least 37 per cent of Ward's net worth was virtually idle, contributing in government bond interest no more than 4 per cent of total earnings in 1953–1954. The possibilities for earnings improvement here are impressive.

Finally, Table 24 contains a hint on dividend policy which is intriguing. A comparison of Ward's postwar earnings per share with the dividend payments discloses that until 1953 (the year ended January 31, 1954) the dividends had averaged close to 40 per cent of earnings. In 1953 an unprecedented 57 per cent was paid out, and Avery's annual report stated that the earnings plus the strong financial position of the company permitted the increase. No more was said, but if the 1953 action implies that the cash-accumulation objectives of the management have been reached, the continuation of dividends at a $3 or $3.50 rate for a reasonable time seems assured, even if lower sales in 1954–1955 result in another decline in profits.[5]

In summary, therefore, this 1954 survey finds (1) that the Ward sales and profit situation is deteriorating, (2) that the deterioration has not progressed to a serious degree, (3) that Ward's possesses tremendous cash resources with which to restore its position, (4) that 37 per cent of Ward's resources are virtually idle and might add greatly to earnings if effectively employed, and (5) that the dividend rate may be secure against any probable early earnings decline. In view of these findings, the general situation seems to justify

---

[5] The 1955 fiscal year (ended January 31, 1955) did show a decline in earnings to $5.20 per share, but the Ward dividends for the period totaled $4.00 per share, or 77 per cent of earnings.

acquisition of the stock in the hope of reasonable dividend income and substantial ultimate profit when Ward's great idle resources are put to work.

QUESTIONS AND PROBLEMS

1. Would it be reasonable to set certain "minimum standards" for statement ratios—for example, the current ratio and the operating ratio—and say that all concerns falling below the standards were in poor condition and all rising far above were in good state? Explain.

2. If the firm's current assets contained a large item labeled Miscellaneous Stocks and Bonds, what would you need to know about it in order to assure yourself of the firm's true working capital position?

3. Explain the difference between inventory valuation on a "cost-or-market" basis and on a LIFO basis. Which would make a company's surplus account the largest, after a long period of declining price levels? Which gives the most accurate portrayal of net working capital?

4. What will a LIFO inventory system do to a company's reported profits during a period of rising prices? Of falling prices? Will the company's income taxes be affected? Are profits computed this way realistic?

5. Explain why net fixed assets as shown on a balance sheet may not accurately reflect the earning power in which the investor is chiefly interested. Would you therefore disregard the stated assets? Explain.

6. What are "deferred charges"? Are they of any real value to investors?

7. Explain the nature of "reserves." Are these in cash?

8. How would you decide whether Montgomery Ward's depreciation allowances were adequate? How would you define an adequate allowance?

9. Should income taxes be included among operating expenses, such as advertising and depreciation, in an income statement? Does this show the earnings coverage for bond interest properly?

10. Why are financial statement titles and footnotes important? What kind of thing would they show?

11. Explain the different ways of including an 80 per cent owned subsidiary in a "consolidated" balance sheet or income statement, assuming that other wholly owned subsidiaries are also included. Then look up the annual reports of American Telephone and Telegraph, Chrysler Corporation, and Westinghouse Electric, and see how they do it. Watch the statement titles carefully.

12. Armour and Company, which does 15 per cent of its business from its plants in South America, combines domestic and foreign operations in a single statement. What problems does this pose for the in-

vestor? (Note: Armour furnishes the necessary additional data in its annual reports.)

13. If you had Armour's last annual report, how could you judge the soundness of its working capital position?

14. Why does the current ratio fluctuate with the seasons in many concerns? Would net working capital fluctuate similarly?

15. What is the operating ratio? Would it be significant to subdivide the operating ratio and study the trend of each of the operating expenses separately in relation to sales?

16. In the Montgomery Ward example, how were the amounts of active net worth and active working capital estimated? Is it reasonable to believe that a successful expansion program could invest the idle cash resources so successfully that they could earn 10 per cent after taxes?

17. In evaluating Ward's stock, it would be desirable to have an estimate of average earnings per share over the next several years. Can you outline a method for making such an estimate?

18. Obtain a copy of the Jones & Laughlin Steel Corporation's 1954 annual report and study the effect of the change in their depreciation accounting methods on their 1954 earnings. Why did they make this change?

REFERENCES

Badger, Ralph E., and Harry G. Guthmann: *Investment Principles and Practices,* Prentice-Hall, Inc., New York, 1951, Chap. 7.

Dowrie, George W., and Douglas R. Fuller: *Investments,* John Wiley & Sons, Inc., New York, 1950, Chaps. 19, 20.

Financial Handbook, The Ronald Press Company, New York, 1948, pp. 212–260.

Foulke, Roy A.: *Practical Financial Statement Analysis,* McGraw-Hill Book Company, Inc., New York, 1950.

Graham, Benjamin, and David L. Dodd: *Security Analysis,* McGraw-Hill Book Company, Inc., New York, 1951, Part II.

Grodinsky, Julius: *Investments,* The Ronald Press Company, New York, 1953, Chaps. 9–11.

McLaren, N. Loyall: *Annual Reports to Stockholders,* The Ronald Press Company, New York, 1947.

Robbins, Sidney M.: *Managing Securities,* Houghton Mifflin Company, Boston, 1954, Chaps. 22–24.

Shultz, Birl E.: *The Securities Market and How It Works,* Harper & Brothers, New York, 1946, Chap. 21.

Chapter 15: RAILROAD SECURITIES

The railroad industry offers investors almost every type and quality of security. There are serial bonds, mortgage bonds, debentures, income bonds, preferred stocks, common stocks, guaranteed securities, long maturities, short maturities, superb quality investments, and hazardous speculations. The issuers are the 132 Class I railroads —those having annual revenues of $1,000,000 or more—and a considerable number of small railroads, terminal companies, and property-owning lessor companies.

Railroad operations are enormous and vital in scope. The American railroads in 1953 earned transportation revenues amounting to 2.91 per cent of the entire gross national product for the year. They employed 1,206,000 people, or about 1.95 per cent of those gainfully employed. They produced nearly 55 per cent of the ton-mileage of commercial freight transportation in the country. They represented a capital investment of 24 billion dollars and earned more than a billion for their creditors and owners.

Because the depression years 1931–1935 resulted in net losses for most railroads and bankruptcies for many, there is a widespread belief that railroad earning power is undependable. Such is not the case. Though railroad earnings do tend to decline sharply when depressions reduce the traffic volume, there are few years when railroad operations do not earn something. For example, in the worst depression year, 1932, the railroads as a group earned 1.38 per cent on their capital investment. It was not enough to pay bond interest and lease rentals in most instances, so the stockholders' earnings became deficits, but the bankruptcies of the depression period should be blamed on excessively bonded capital structures, not on inherent weakness in the industry. Railroads whose capital structures were suited to present-day conditions in the industry survived the 1931–1935 ordeal satisfactorily.

The railroad business has for many years been classed as "affected with a public interest"; hence it is subject to public regulation on matters of rates, service, and capital structure. Regulatory authority

is divided between Federal and state commissions, but the Federal
Interstate Commerce Commission has established dominance in both
policy and procedure. The purpose of regulation is to assure the
public of adequate service at reasonable rates and to assist the railroads in obtaining a fair return without the burdens of rebating and
rate cutting.

Economic Position of the Industry

Prior to 1920 the railroads had a near-monopoly of transportation
in the United States. There was some competition between railroads, to be sure, but trucks, busses, private automobiles, pipe lines,
and airplanes were relatively unimportant. And transportation services were urgently needed. The nation's industries were highly cen-
tralized in specialized regions, each of which shipped in supplies and
shipped out its special products. Under such conditions a prospering
railroad system required only the establishment of adequate rates.

With the advent of competing forms of transportation after 1920,
and with the concurrent tendency toward industrial decentralization,
new problems developed. Trucks made great inroads on short-haul
and package freight, especially on items which were not bulky or
heavy. Pipe lines invaded the field of petroleum transportation. Private automobiles and busses captured more than half of the passenger business, especially the short hauls. Airplanes began to share the
long-haul passenger and mail business. The railroads found themselves in a hotly competitive arena, in which the volume of traffic
needed to assure low operating costs could be obtained only by
charging moderate rates.

Traffic volume is very important to the railroads, for their earnings
tend to increase in much greater ratio when volume increases and to
decline in greater ratio when volume declines. The reason for this
tendency is to be found in the relatively large percentage of fixed
and semifixed expenses borne by the railroads. Their costs for maintenance and depreciation of track, bridges, and buildings, their outlays for station and office crews, and their property taxes are heavy
items which vary only moderately with changes in traffic volume. An
increase in volume therefore adds only a moderate amount to expenses, mostly in the categories connected with train operations, and

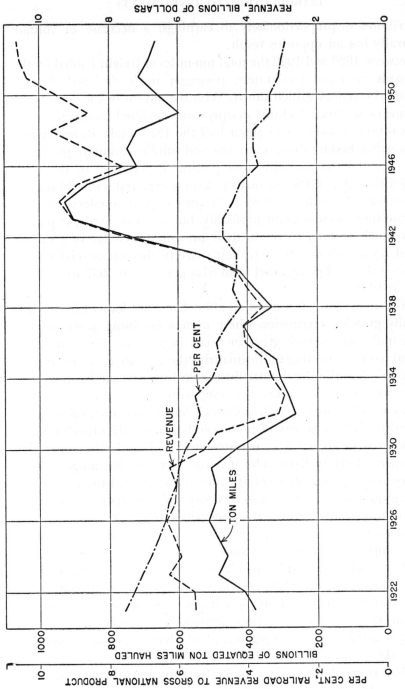

CHART 13. Railroad traffic volume and revenues, 1921–1953, all Class I railroads. Traffic volume in equated ton-miles, revenue in billions of dollars and in per cent of gross national product. (Data adapted from Standard Industry Surveys, Moody's Transportation Companies, and U.S. Department of Commerce.)

351

contributes disproportionately to earnings; a decrease in volume naturally has an opposite result.

Between 1920 and 1929 the total ton-miles of freight hauled by the railroads increased moderately, passenger traffic declined sharply, and total revenues gained slowly. With the advent of the depression, volume of all kinds declined sharply, rates declined moderately, and gross revenues dropped to about half the 1929 totals. Recovery and the wartime boom subsequently restored volume and more profitable operations to the railroads, and postwar experiences in the years 1946–1954 have been reasonably satisfactory, but two things are made clear: the railroads have sufficient competitive effectiveness to operate their present plant profitably, but they can hardly expect to grow much or even to retain their present percentage of total national traffic volume. In fact, their share of the commercial freight traffic of the nation declined from 61.8 per cent in 1937 to 54.9 per cent in 1952.

Of course, railroads are not all alike. Some are located in or serve rapidly growing territories, where even a declining percentage of total traffic will permit great increases in volume. The transcontinental roads connecting California with the East are examples of this. Others such as the Pocahontas district coal carriers are located in regions where heavy, bulky, and long-haul freight traffic abounds; trucks are often unable to handle such business economically, hence the railroads have plenty of profitable business. Still other railroads are located in areas where maintenance, fuel, and other operating costs are relatively light. The investor therefore has ample opportunity to find profitable commitments in the railroad industry. However, some roads are located in territory which offers few advantages in the foreseeable future; their securities make acceptable investments only at prices which discount the considerable risks incident to a competitive struggle in a nongrowing industry.

The principal railroad expenditures are those for labor, fuel, supplies and repair materials, and taxes. Although the percentage of gross revenues disbursed on these items varies somewhat from year to year, the first three show no striking long-term trends; labor costs seem to average about 50 per cent, fuel about 5 per cent, and supplies about 12 per cent. Taxes, however, are increasing, having climbed from about 6 per cent in 1929 to more than 11 per cent in 1953. In general, it appears that railroad operating costs other than labor and taxes are not threats to the investor's position. Labor costs are important because of the relative importance of the item among railroad expenses. Since 1940 the improved efficiency of the railroads has assisted in absorbing general cost increases, but earnings have remained modest because a combination of public regulation and rate competition from other forms of transportation has kept rate increases from keeping pace with increases in the cost of labor, supplies, and taxes.

Railroad Rates

Though shippers, chambers of commerce, cities, and even states are always ready to clamor for lower railroad rates, it is probably

Table 25. *Percentages Earned by Class I Railroads on Their Net Property Investment, 1929–1953*

1929	5.24	1938	1.62	1947	3.41
1930	3.59	1939	2.56	1948	4.24
1931	2.20	1940	2.94	1949	2.86
1932	1.38	1941	4.28	1950	4.23
1933	2.03	1942	6.34	1951	3.69
1934	1.99	1943	5.75	1952	4.16
1935	2.16	1944	4.73	1953	4.18
1936	2.88	1945	3.77		
1937	2.56	1946	2.75		

Source: Standard & Poor's *Industry Surveys.*

fair to say that the regulatory authorities are friendly to the roads. Rates are not adjusted upward so often or so promptly as some rail managements desire, but a sincere effort to do the proper thing is evident. There is no statutory instruction to the ICC to establish rates which will cause earnings of 5½ per cent or any other definite percentage on railroad investment, but the commission is instructed to prescribe rates which will enable carriers to provide "adequate and efficient service." It is unlikely that rates could be set high enough to average 5½ per cent return on the railroads' investment without driving necessary volume to competitors. Consequently, the railroads have had to content themselves with rather low rates of return, as shown in Table 25.

In establishing railroad rates it was clear from the beginning that high-value items such as clothing, processed foods, and manufactured articles would have to pay higher freight rates per ton than heavy items such as coal, lumber, and building stone. Not only did the small and valuable items cost more to handle; the heavy, less valuable items would be driven off the road if they were charged a prorata share of the railroad's expenses and desired profits. The only feasible rate-making principle was that of charging what the traffic would bear, making sure that no item was charged less than the out-of-pocket cost of handling it nor so much that desirable business was lost. Railroad rate systems thus became patterns of rates, under which each item of traffic was presumably charged what it could afford to pay.

Because handling costs at terminal points are a large percentage of a railroad's total costs, most rates per ton-mile are far lower on a long haul than on a short one. However, trucks and other competitors can compete more effectively on short hauls than on long ones. Railroads therefore often find it necessary to accept lower earnings margins on short hauls than on long ones.

Competition between railroads would result in rate-making confusion if the roads were permitted to establish competitive rates where competition existed and to charge what the traffic would bear where no competitors were operating. Consequently, regulating agencies have insisted on compensatory competitive rates and reasonably related rates to noncompetitive points. This has led to the development of regional levels of rates—rate formulas and patterns which are reasonably uniform for like services on different railroads and over whole groups of states. As a result, well-located railroads with heavy traffic and moderate costs do well in regions where poorly located competitors are hard pressed to pay expenses.

Transportation costs are a significant portion of the expenses of many industries. Consequently, such industries tend to locate their plants with reference to raw materials sources and markets. Having done so, they have a vested interest in the maintenance of the existing system of railroad rates. New England manufacturers, for example, would be bitterly opposed to increases in freight rates east of the Mississippi and north of the Ohio, if the result would be an increased competitive advantage for Chicago, St. Louis, Cincinnati, and other such cities. And California orange growers are definitely opposed to lower rates from Florida to New York and Chicago unless rates from the Pacific Coast are correspondingly lowered. Thus a nationwide collection of vested interests resists change in the pattern of railroad rates and makes blanket percentage increases or decreases easier to impose than regional or specific adjustments. This fact makes local trends in traffic volume, competition, and expenses very important matters to railroad securityholders. With rates tending to be established on a nationwide and a regional basis, much of the gain or loss from local changes in traffic volume and expenses accrues to the railroad and its investors.

During the war and inflation period from 1940 to 1953 the general price level rose about 100 per cent, and the cost of the labor, fuel, and other materials purchased by the railroads rose more than proportionately. Because traffic volume also rose enormously, railroad rates had to be increased only about 58 per cent in order to maintain normal earnings. However, the 1953 earnings of 4.18 per cent on invested capital did not permit the average railroad to share generously in the boom, and railroad investors generally feared that the end of the boom would produce declines in traffic volume which would reduce earnings drastically. During the period 1946–1953 the regulating commissions authorized general rate increases which averaged 78.9 per cent on all freight traffic, but competition from trucks and other carriers forced the railroads to limit their actual increases to an average of about 58 per cent.

Efficiency

The railroads are often alleged to be laggard in developing new ideas, new methods, and efficiency in general. In their defense they point to the steady improvement in their services—faster trains, more economical locomotives, door-to-door delivery of freight, larger freight cars, air-conditioned passenger equipment, safety features—as well as to their marvelous records of performance during the war. And it must be conceded that innovations often meet the resistance of shippers, regulatory authorities, and labor organizations. Many people are unwilling to relinquish any advantages which outmoded services and obsolete methods hold for themselves.

From 1922 to 1941 the average speed of freight trains increased 48 per cent, tonnage per train increased 35 per cent, and gross ton-miles per train hour more than doubled. Fuel consumption per ton-mile declined 32 per cent, and ton-miles per labor hour increased 102 per cent. Some of these gains could not be held during the war, when traffic congestion and emergency use of obsolete equipment caused loss of efficiency, but since 1946 rapid progress has again been made. In the seven years from 1946 to 1953 freight-train speeds increased an average of 14 per cent, ton-miles per train hour 35 per cent, and ton-miles per employee hour 28 per cent. The new diesel locomotives have decreased fuel and maintenance costs, and new methods generally are helping to control costs and improve the service. These changes offer the railroad investor some hope of stabilized or improved earnings in the future, even if the end of the postwar boom brings some decline in traffic volume.

Other Income

Many railroads own securities and property investments other than those used in their transportation business. Most of these are developments on terminal property acquired in the early days of the roads, or stock interests in affiliated railroads, or incidental developments on land donated by the government when the railroads were built. The New York Central Railroad has real estate and securities investments which bring in close to 25 million dollars annually, or half enough to pay the railroad's fixed charges. The Pennsylvania Railroad has enormous securities holdings. The Union Pacific owns securities, operates real estate projects such as the resort hotel at Sun Valley, Idaho, and is also one of the country's major producers of crude oil. Other railroads have heavy interests in coal, lumber, and other projects.

The dividend, interest, and rental incomes which these investments produce are important to many railroads because of the large amounts involved. However, their significance is also affected by their dependability and by the source of the incomes. For example, the New York Central's rental income is very steady and has been of great assistance in meeting interest charges in several years when transportation earnings were uncomfortably low. The Pennsylvania's bond and stock holdings include large investments in the bonds and stocks of companies whose properties the Pennsylvania operates under long-term leases; the railroad therefore includes among its fixed charges fairly large sums in rentals which come back to it as interest and dividends. On the other hand, the stock investments owned by some railroads are very uncertain sources of income, because of the irregularity of dividend payments.

Financial Situation

Many railroads entered the depression period after 1929 with capital structures top-heavy with bonded debt. Such capital structures had seemed all right when the railroads were prosperous and growing transportation monopolies, but they became very burdensome when traffic volume declined in 1930–1933 and competition forced rate reductions. Several big railroad systems, including the Chicago and North Western, the Chicago, Milwaukee, St. Paul and Pacific, the Chicago, Rock Island & Pacific, the Missouri Pacific, the Denver and Rio Grande Western, and the Wabash, were forced into bankruptcy. Others struggled through the depression but seized the subsequent wartime earnings opportunity as a means of paying down debt.

At the present time most of the railroads appear to be able to manage their fixed charges, though some will have difficulty during depressions. Nearly all of the recently reorganized roads have fixed charges which are well within their means. However, most railroads still have fixed and contingent (income bond) charges which absorb so much of their earning power that their stocks are distinctly speculative. There are a few exceptions—the Union Pacific, Chesapeake and Ohio, Norfolk & Western, Louisville & Nashville, Atchison, Topeka & Santa Fe, and a few others have moderate debt burdens— but the majority of stocks do not appear to be of investment quality because heavy prior charges make the net profits unstable.

Because the railroad companies are not extending their lines significantly, their operations do not require much new capital financing. New rolling stock can be financed by equipment issues, and capital improvements can be paid for from depreciation allowances and retained earnings. Refunding of maturing bond issues is the main financial task for the heavily bonded roads; in fact, one of the essential items in analyzing the securities of such roads is a check to see if any bond issues mature within the next decade. While maturing issues can usually be refunded or extended if interest payments are reasonably assured, an impending maturity is always a hazard until finally cared for.

A railroad's working capital position can be called satisfactory if the ratio of current assets to current liabilities is 1½ to 1, if the net working capital amounts to 10 per cent or more of annual operating revenues, and if no unusual drains upon working capital are in immediate prospect. A strong working capital position is advantageous for any business, but on the whole it is less imperative for a railroad or a utility than for other forms of business, if fixed charges are comfortably covered by earnings.

Incomes and Expenses

Postwar operating revenues on the average railroad are averaging about 83 per cent freight, 8 per cent passenger, and 9 per cent mail, express, and miscellaneous receipts. The freight business is the main source of earnings for practically all the roads, as it has always been. The passenger business may be mildly profitable for a few lines doing a commuter business and for a few others blessed with long hauls, but for most railroads it barely pays for itself. Mail and express business has been profitable in times past, but since the war has been unsatisfactory.

The *operating expenses* of a railroad consist of five categories— maintenance of way (roadbed) and structures, maintenance of equipment, transportation, traffic, and miscellaneous. The maintenance items include all labor and materials costs involved in the upkeep of properties, plus depreciation allowances as required. Investors expect maintenance of way to average about 13 per cent of revenues and maintenance of equipment about 19 per cent, though these figures vary between roads and from time to time. The railroads keep these maintenance percentages from rising greatly when business is slack, by skimping maintenance at such times. Transportation expense includes train and station labor, train and station supplies, and fuel. This item in prewar years absorbed about 35 per cent of revenues, but higher labor and materials costs caused it to rise to an average of 38 per cent in the years 1950–1953. The other two categories of operating expenses are small, aggregating about 6 per cent. The total operating expenses in prewar years averaged about

72 per cent of operating revenues, as compared with 76 per cent in 1952–1953. This percentage is known as the *operating ratio.*

Railroad earnings statements subtract the total operating expense from the total operating revenue and label the difference *net railway operating revenue.* From this sum is next deducted the road's property and income taxes and the net rents (this item may be an addition if the road owns excess equipment which is used by others) paid for the use of rolling stock, terminals, bridges, etc. This determines the *net railway operating income,* the final measure of the earning power of the railroad as a transportation agency.[1]

Since many railroads own securities or businesses apart from their railroad operations, it is next necessary to add in the *other income* and subtract out the *miscellaneous deductions.* The other income item is often very important, sometimes equaling the net railway operating income. This summation of operating income and vested income produces a total which is called *income available for fixed charges.*

Fixed charges include bond interest, amortization of bond discount and expense, and rentals paid for leased trackage and other property. If some of the bonds are income bonds, their interest is usually shown separately under the heading *contingent charges.* When all fixed and contingent charges are deducted from the income available for fixed charges, the remainder is the *net income.*

This summary of railroad income accounting follows the standard ICC form as used by all the railroads and is illustrated in Table 26. However, a special form is submitted annually by some of the recently reorganized railroads which have income bonds outstanding. These roads are required by their bond indentures to set apart certain portions of their remaining income after payment of bond interest and additional portions after payment of income bond interest to be used for bond retirements or capital improvements on the railroad. Since these sums are not available for income bond interest or

[1] In the years 1950–1954 many railroads invested large sums in new facilities under the rapid amortization provisions of the Defense Production Act. Railroad accounting provides for normal depreciation charges on these facilities but writes them off at 20 per cent per year for income tax purposes. The result is a major reduction in income tax burden for the moment, with a corresponding prospect for increased taxes later. Net railway operating income is thus increased until about 1959 and will be burdened after that.

Table 26. Class I Railways of the United States Combined Income Statements, 1940 and 1953 *

	Millions of dollars		Per cent of total operating revenue	
	1940	*1953*	*1940*	*1953*
Freight Revenues..........................	$3,537	$ 8,951	82.1	83.9
Passenger Revenues.......................	417	842	9.7	7.9
Total railway operating revenues.........	4,297	10,664	100.0	100.0
Maintenance of Way......................	497	1,584	11.6	14.9
Maintenance of Equipment................	819	1,982	19.1	18.6
Transportation Expenses..................	1,501	3,872	34.9	36.3
Total railway operating expenses.........	3,089	8,135	71.9	76.3
Operating ratio..........................	71.9%	76.3%	71.9	76.3
Net railway operating revenue............	1,207	2,529	28.1	23.7
Federal Income Taxes.....................	60	535	1.4	5.0
All Other Taxes..........................	337	651	7.8	6.1
Hire of Equipment (net dr.)...............	96	192	2.2	1.8
Joint Facility Rents (net dr.)..............	33	42	.8	.4
Net railway operating income............	682	1,109	15.9	10.4
Other Income............................	169	278	3.9	2.6
Miscellaneous Deductions (dr.)............	28	63	.6	.6
Income available for fixed charges........	824	1,325	19.2	12.4
Rentals on Leased Property...............	147	76	3.4	.7
Fixed Interest on Bonds..................	444	321	10.3	3.0
Total fixed charges......................	609	405	14.2	3.8
Income after fixed charges...............	215	920	5.0	8.6
Contingent Interest Charges..............	26	27	.6	.3
Net income.............................	189	893	4.4	8.4

* Condensed statements. Certain accounts are omitted, and dollar figures are rounded in millions.

Source: Moody's *Transportation*, 1954.

dividends, it is necessary to compile a special form of financial (income) statement to show clearly what earnings may be used for these purposes.

Important Investment Factors: Summary

While the outline for investment analysis suggested in Chapter 13 is as readily applicable to railroads as to other industries, there are certain peculiar features in railroading which deserve special emphasis. Eight of these features will be noted here.

An investor who is interested in the securities of a railroad will often start his investigation with a careful scrutiny of the earnings available for fixed charges. He will need to determine their adequacy, their stability, and the trend of growth or decline. Perhaps the best way to study these matters is to consider the record of the road's earnings in the peacetime years since about 1935, compared with the charges and dividend requirements as they exist at the present time. Chart 14 suggests a way to begin this task. The reader will observe that this is evaluation in retrospect, rather than by looking forward at the more important future. However, it is important to note that a railroad is usually a very large business, rendering diverse service to many people in many communities. Its economic position is unlikely to suffer permanent change of an extreme nature very quickly. Past records of earnings are therefore significant, and their trend over a period of years is doubly significant, in evaluating the future.

The second subject for investor study deals with operating revenues, operating expenses, and the operating ratio. The trends of freight revenues, passenger revenues, and other revenues should be inspected separately and in the aggregate. Operating expenses are studied both in dollar amounts and as percentages of gross revenue. A low or declining transportation ratio (ratio of transportation expense to gross revenue) is a good sign, for it presumably denotes efficiency or increasing efficiency. Abnormally small maintenance ratios are not necessarily good signs, however; they might indicate inadequate maintenance expenditures and consequent deterioration of property. In general, a low or declining operating ratio is favorably regarded, for it indicates a wide earnings margin which could not easily become a deficit if expenses increased or revenues de-

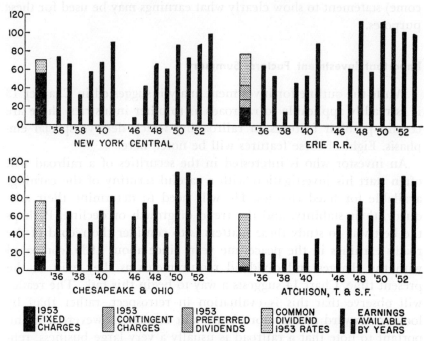

CHART 14. Earnings available for securityholders of four major railroads in peacetime years 1936–1953 compared to 1953 interest and dividend payments.

Note: All figures in each case are expressed as percentages of earnings available in 1953. Earnings available as shown in the narrow bars consist of Income Available for Fixed Charges as ordinarily reported plus amounts allowed for income taxes; this is based on the assumption that all earnings are first subject to fixed charges and that income taxes are a share in net income after fixed charges.

The amounts shown in the broad bars for fixed charges and income bond interest are the amounts actually paid in 1953. The amounts shown for preferred and common dividends include in each case the income taxes (at the 1953 rate of 52 per cent) which must also be paid if these dividend requirements are earned. The common dividend segments show the earnings required to pay the 1953 common dividends of $7 on the Atchison, $3 on the C & O, $1.75 on the Erie, and $1 on the New York Central. The Atchison's small Contingent Charges are included in the amount shown as Fixed Charges.

In April, 1955, the Erie was exchanging a new issue of junior-ranking income bonds for the preferred stock shown here.

clined. Operating revenues are regarded as of good *quality* if the operating ratio is low; and this is especially true if the operating ratio is low because the transportation expenses are low.

A third item is the financial position, as measured by impending bond maturities, the need for additional financing, the current ratio, and net working capital.

Fourth, the amount and quality of other income must be considered. Other income is of high quality if it comes from dependable, long-lasting sources and is not likely to be affected by adverse business conditions. On the other hand, other income drawn from such investments as coal mines, standing timber, and stockholdings in other railroads has often been intermittent in nature.

Fifth, traffic volume and its future prospects must be studied. A railroad which has heavy annual gross revenues and ton-mileage per mile of track operated should do well. Such high "traffic density" usually occurs when the railroad serves a populous area and a prosperous one. It also occurs when the railroad connects vital traffic centers such as New York and Chicago, when it serves as a link in important long-haul chains (for example, between Chicago and San Francisco), and when it operates in a teeming industrial area such as the North Central states. Growth of the area served, in terms of population, industrialization, and general prosperity, is a vital factor which tends to increase total available traffic. An indication of a railroad's competitive efficiency in obtaining traffic is afforded in ICC statistics which show each road's proportion of total rail traffic in its region and in the nation.

Sixth, the nature of the traffic is important. Noncompetitive business, which can usually be obtained at compensatory rates, is more profitable than competitive business on which little is earned. This type of business is also more durable than others; competitors cannot attract it away. Long-haul business, carload-lot business, and items like coal which can be loaded mechanically have lower handling costs and are more profitable than packages or passengers. The railroads north of the Ohio and east of the Mississippi normally have a heavy volume of short-haul, package, and passenger business; this has resulted in burdensomely high operating ratios in the postwar period. Detailed statistics on the types of business done by each railroad are available in the investment reference sources.

Seventh, operating problems or advantages inherent in the route demand consideration. These include mountain grades, areas subject to flood, availability of fuel, and the obstacles imposed by weather. The New York Central has a great advantage in its mountain-free route between New York and Chicago; the Denver and Rio Grande Western has both grade and weather problems in the Colorado mountains. The Southern Pacific finds great fuel economy in the oil-rich territory it serves.

Eighth, the condition of a railroad's property and equipment is a factor in its position. The probable level of maintenance on a railroad can be tested by comparing its maintenance ratios with those of other railroads and by comparing maintenance of way expenditures per mile of track with those of other roads. Also, the ages of its locomotives and other rolling stock can be compared with those of other railroads, and the published statistics on bad-order rolling stock awaiting repairs will give indication of the need for maintenance work.

Fixed-interest Bonds

Any truly first-class corporate bond must be the obligation of a financially strong debtor and will usually either have adequate property security or be protected by indenture provisions which assure the bond of priority in case of trouble. Railroads have generally mortgaged their property to secure their bonds.

A railroad whose earnings available for fixed charges have averaged two and one-half times its present fixed charges in the peacetime years since 1935 and have never fallen below present fixed charges in that period has prima facie proved itself to be a financially strong debtor. A better measure of quality would be obtained by adding income taxes paid to the officially reported earnings available for fixed charges and measuring the adequacy of this sum to cover fixed charges. On this basis the charges should be covered, on the average, three times over. The bars of Chart 14 are charted on this basis.

Even when earnings and other criteria prove a railroad to be financially sound, the protection provided by lien security must also be considered. In addition to examining the indenture terms to make sure that they are acceptable, investors usually attempt to gauge the importance of the mortgaged property and its adequacy in amount. Main-line track is usually better security than branch lines, and major bridges, terminals, and repair shops are highly regarded. It is sometimes said that a first lien on mingled branch and main-line mileage can provide good security at $25,000 to $75,000 per mile on a railroad whose operation is reasonably profitable. This is an almost completely indefinite criterion, depending as it must upon traffic density, cost of operation, and the presence of terminals, shops, and other facilities along the line, but it may serve as a rough guide for comparison. If a junior mortgage or debenture bond is under consideration, debt per mile is computed by adding senior and junior debt and dividing by the appropriate mileage figure.

High-class railroad bonds are as readily accepted for institutional and other conservative investment as utility or industrial bonds. However, the railroad industry still has outstanding many millions of bonds which grade down from almost high class to frankly hazardous. The market prices on the lower quality bonds are low and unstable, reflecting the possibility of long delay without interest payments and compulsory conversion into income bonds or stock if bankruptcy reorganization should become necessary. This is a serious hazard; most of the railroads which became unable to meet their interest obligations in 1930–1935 were in bankruptcy for 5 to 12 years; during most of such period the junior bonds received no interest payments, and it was difficult to judge when a bankruptcy would be terminated or the types or amounts of new securities which each claimant would ultimately receive. A 1948 bankruptcy act amendment undertakes to provide a faster way for embarrassed railroads to adjust their financial troubles, by means of a recapitalization plan which becomes binding upon all affected securityholders if approved by 75 per cent of each class and the ICC.[2] Bond prices indicate that the investing public is not much impressed by the change.

The most highly regarded railroad securities are their equipment obligations, which are discussed in Chapter 6. These are usually issued in sums not to exceed 80 per cent of the value of newly purchased equipment and mature serially over a 10- to 18-year period. The maturities occur somewhat faster than the equipment depreciates, and the equipment itself is vital to the railroad and presumably salable if repossessed. Defaults on equipment obligations prac-

[2] See review of railroad bankruptcy legislation in Chap. 7.

tically never occur. Because of these factors the yields are usually less than on mortgage bonds.

Income Bonds

Few railroad income bonds are well enough protected by income and mortgage lien to be called high grade, but many of them are preceded in rank by relatively small fixed-interest claims, hence are practically certain of some income every year. When income bonds are assured of full payment in most years and of reasonably early payment of occasional omissions, they have definite elements of quality.

Most of the railroad income bond issues now on the market are the obligations of railroads which underwent bankruptcy reorganizations in the period 1933–1948. In such cases the interest-bearing debt was usually reduced to an amount on which the interest could be earned in all but very poor years. Unearned interest on income bonds need not be paid, but unpaid amounts usually cumulate to the extent of 3 full years' interest, and both current interest and arrears must be paid to the full extent earned in any year. Fairly heavy sinking funds for debt retirement and property improvement are required in many cases, but the sinking fund requirements are mainly junior to income bond interest, not senior to it. Few of the reorganized railroads have any early bond maturities of significant size, nor do they have extensive expansion programs to finance.

Everything considered, it would appear that well-selected railroad income bonds should be satisfactory income-producing investments. At present they are unstable in price, perhaps because they are unseasoned, but a good record of payments for a few years should overcome investor suspicion of them. Chart 14 and Table 27 illustrate the quality position and price ranges of some of these bonds.

Railroad Stocks

The weakness of the railroad industry in the years following 1929 lost the railroad stocks much of the prestige which they had previously enjoyed. Even in 1954, after 14 years of relative prosperity, railroad stocks sold at lower price-earnings ratios and yielded more than utility or industrial stocks of apparently comparable quality.

There is reason for this. The great economic upheavals caused by war and inflation have not yet run their course, and it is difficult to be sure just what the long-run postwar earnings situation will be.

Table 27. Price Ranges of Selected Railroad Securities

Security and 1953 dividend	Lien position	Railroad operating ratio		Price range			
				1936–1945		1952–1953	
		1940	1953	High	Low	High	Low
New York Central 3½s, 1997.....	Senior	75.2	82.8	108	67	78½	69
New York Central 5s, 2013.......	Junior	....	....	103½	42	86	71¼
New York Central Stock ($1).....	.....	....	....	55¼	6½	25½	17
Erie First G 3⅛s, 2000..........	Senior	71.2	75.1	102¼	96½	87	76
Erie Income 4½s, 2015..........	Junior	....	....	102¾	45¼	84½	70
Erie $5 Preferred ($5)...........	.....	....	....	86	30½	74¼	62½
Erie Common ($1.75)...........	.....	....	....	20½	4½	23½	16
Chesapeake & Ohio Ref. D 3½s, 1996......................	Junior	55.9	72.2	109½	85½	101	89
Chesapeake & Ohio Common ($3).	.....	....	....	77¾	22	41½	32¾
Chicago & North Western First 3s, 1989.....................	Senior	78.8	85.9	104½	101	80½	71
Chicago & North Western Income 4½s, 1999...................	Junior	....	....	95	63¼	64	52¾
Chicago & North Western $5 Pfd. ($3.25)......................	.....	....	....	76¾	43½	44	30½
Chicago & North Western Common (none)...................	.....	....	....	49½	21½	21½	10
Southern Pacific 4½s, 1981.......	Junior	73.0	76.0	106½	30	104	92½
Southern Pacific Common ($3)....	.....	....	....	32¾	3½	49¾	30½
Atchison, T. & S.F. 4s, 1995......	Senior	76.3	71.9	133¾	98½	121	106
Atchison, T. & S.F. Income 4s, 1995........................	Junior	....	....	125	75	114	100½
Atchison, T. & S.F. $5 Pfd. ($2.50)	.....	....	....	60	19¾	58	50¼
Atchison, T. & S.F. Common ($7)..	.....	....	....	56¾	6½	104¾	73½

The New York Central and the Pennsylvania will, for example, have high traffic density and high gross revenues, but no one can be sure what they will earn for their stockholders. The Chesapeake and Ohio and the Louisville and Nashville will continue to haul a heavy volume of coal and other freight, but whether volume will stay up and expenses down sufficiently to permit stable or increased dividends is not yet sure. The Atchison and the Southern Pacific will continue to benefit from the growth of their territory, but whether good volume and well-controlled costs will permit them to hold or increase their magnificent 1952–1953 earnings cannot yet be ascertained.

Because of the leverage which exists in almost every railroad financial structure, the position of the stocks is far more speculative than that of the business as a whole. Obviously, the railroad stocks which have the greatest investment quality are those like the Atchison and the Chesapeake and Ohio, with their relatively low fixed charges. More drastic speculative possibilities are found in the Pennsylvania and the New York Central, where high leverage combined with possible changes in operating earnings could make for great gains or losses to stockholders. But in these cases the stockholders' future is so uncertain that stock prices fluctuate far more than the average, marketwise. The well-known sensitiveness of rail earnings to the volume of traffic, which is obviously affected by general business conditions, is a factor in causing fluctuations in rail stocks.

Guaranteed Securities

The railroad industry is the source of most of the guaranteed stocks and bonds which are available to American investors. Although a considerable number of such issues exist, only the ones whose guarantees relate to lease contracts and similar arrangements pose any peculiar problems. Since such problems were reviewed in Chapters 5 and 6, no further comment will be made here.

Sources of Information

The amount of information available about railroad operations is almost unbelievable. Not only are very complete financial reports of all kinds at hand, but statistics on traffic, operations, facilities, equipment, maintenance, and personnel matters abound. Many of these figures are compiled on track-mile, ton-mile, or train-mile bases, to facilitate study and comparison.

The most useful figures can be found in the Moody or Standard &

Poor's reference services, but some are available only in the annual reports of the railroads, reports of the ICC, or publications of the Association of American Railroads. All of the usual supplementary sources, such as brokerage house studies and financial magazine articles, contribute to the general literature on the subject. In addition, there are several valuable though expensive services which attempt to inform bond investors in detail of the exact nature of the property covered by their liens and of the traffic density upon this property.

Markets

As has been noted, railroad equipment obligations and well-secured bonds are held by institutions and conservative investors. Less amply secured bonds, the income bonds, and the stocks are widely held by the public.

The equipment obligations, small bond issues, and the guaranteed stocks and bonds are traded over the counter. These markets do not appear to be very active, but because of the considerable numbers of such issues outstanding there is always a market for them. The large bond issues, income bonds, and large stock issues are mostly listed on the New York Stock Exchange, and many of the stocks are on regional exchanges as well. As a rule, their markets are broad and fairly active.

QUESTIONS AND PROBLEMS

1. Are railroads declining in importance as economic institutions in the United States? Is the industry declining sufficiently to place its securities in the speculative category?

2. Why does railroad "net railway operating revenue" fluctuate more sharply than "total railway operating revenue"?

3. What general type of business provides the bulk of railroad revenues? Of railroad earnings?

4. What types of freight business are most advantageous, competitively, for the railroads? Why?

5. Why is a populous and prosperous territory important to a railroad? How do you account for the fact that the Atchison, Topeka & Santa Fe, which connects Chicago and California via New Mexico and Arizona, is prosperous?

6. Explain the general system of railroad rate making. Why do the

railroads not demand rates high enough to permit 6 per cent earnings on their investment?

7. Do you believe that the railroads can honestly claim to have attempted real competitive efficiency?

8. Explain why the "quality" of a railroad's "other income" is important to its investors. What kinds of "other income" do railroads have?

9. Look up the "other income" of the Northern Pacific Railway. Would you call it good quality? Is the stock of the Northern Pacific of investment caliber? Give your reasons.

10. Which appears to be the best quality investment, the junior bonds of the New York Central or the common stock of the Chesapeake and Ohio? (Refer to Chart 14 for an indication.) Would it affect your decision if you learned that the NYC had a much higher operating ratio than the C & O?

11. Why are maintenance and transportation expenses often expressed as percentages of total railway operating revenue? Would high ratios ever be a good sign? Would declining ratios be good?

12. What items are included in railroad fixed charges?

13. Why does a standard railroad income statement not always indicate correctly the amount of earnings available for dividends?

14. Which is a borrowing railroad more likely to sell, mortgage bonds or debentures? Why?

15. How would you judge the quality of a railroad first mortgage bond? Would you like a well-secured first mortgage bond on a road which had an excessive amount of fixed-interest junior debt? Would it be better if the junior debt consisted of income bonds?

16. Investigate the Erie Income 4½s of 2015. (Begin with Chart 14.) Are they acceptable as a medium-risk investment? Are they as good quality as the average good industrial stock? Do you think life insurance companies would buy them? Should they? Would they be satisfactory speculations for market profit?

17. Why did the Pennsylvania and the New York Central have poor earnings in the boom years 1946–1954? Is this trouble permanent?

18. In April, 1955, the Erie Railroad was exchanging new 5 per cent income bonds due in 2020 for its outstanding 5 per cent preferred stock, in order to retire the latter. The new income bonds were junior in rank to and matured subsequent to all other Erie bonds. How will this change affect (a) the Erie's income taxes, (b) the quality of the Erie's other bonds, (c) the position of the preferred stockholders who accept the new bonds, and (d) the position of the common stockholders?

REFERENCES

Badger, Ralph E., and Harry G. Guthmann: *Investment Principles and Practices,* Prentice-Hall, Inc., New York, 1951, Chaps. 13, 14.

Financial Handbook, The Ronald Press Company, New York, 1948, pp. 272–281.

Investment Bankers Association of America: *Fundamentals of Investment Banking,* Prentice-Hall, Inc., New York, 1949, Chaps. 7, 8.

Jordan, David F., and Herbert E. Dougall: *Investments,* Prentice-Hall, Inc., New York, 1952, Chap. 24.

Pickett, Ralph R., and Marshall D. Ketchum: *Investment Principles and Policy,* Harper & Brothers, New York, 1954, Chap. 22.

Plum, Lester V., and Joseph H. Humphrey: *Investment Analysis and Management,* Richard D. Irwin, Inc., Homewood, Ill., 1951, Chaps. 11, 12.

Robbins, Sidney M.: *Managing Securities,* Houghton Mifflin Company, Boston, 1954, Chaps. 29, 30.

Chapter 16: PUBLIC UTILITY SECURITIES

The public utilities—telephone, electricity, gas, water, telegraph, and local transit companies—probably provide securities investments for more people than any other industry group. The utility business offers a wide assortment of securities, including bonds, preferred stocks, and common stocks, and affords a considerable variety of qualities in each. Needless to say, the utilities in the United States represent a very large aggregate investment. As of December 31, 1953, their total invested capital exceeded 50 billion dollars.[1]

The utility industries which are of greatest interest to investors are typically characterized by rapid growth, monopoly franchises in their service areas, dependable earnings, capital structures employing large percentages of bonds and preferred stocks, and extensive public regulation of operations and earnings. Each of these characteristics has an important bearing on the investment qualities of the securities and must therefore be examined in some detail.

The Utility Industries

The various utility industries do not by any means exhibit the same economic characteristics. The three largest, electric power, telephone, and natural gas, are growing with extraordinary speed and appear likely to continue to do so for some time. They do not have serious competition from either similar or substitute products, and consequently their earnings can be made large or small simply by adjusting their rates. Their sales volumes are not acutely affected by economic fluctuations, and their earnings are highly dependable. These are the utility industries in which the greatest investor interest exists and with which this chapter is chiefly concerned.

The electric power business is by far the largest of the utility industries. It is probably also the most depression-resistant, for its

---

[1] Other industries sometimes classed as utilities, but which are not discussed in this chapter, include oil pipe lines, motor freight lines, bus lines, air lines, stockyards, grain elevators, storage warehouses, and radio stations.

sales volume dropped less than 15 per cent and its earnings from operations less than 20 per cent between 1929 and 1933. The 1938 recession hardly made an impression on its sales or earnings. The reasons for this fine record lie in the rapid growth of the industry, which means that a depression causes a halt rather than a retrogression in sales volume, and in the fact that most of the industry's revenue comes from residential and commercial use, which is very stable. Some differences appear at times between companies which have varying percentages of rural, urban, and industrial load and between companies which depend on steam power, hydroelectric generation, and purchased power. Steam plants are subject to fuel costs, hydroelectric plants are subject to drought, and purchased power is subject to whatever terms occur in the purchase contract. However, these factors are usually secondary rather than fundamental in importance.

Telephone operations are less stable than electric power. Between 1929 and 1933 the Class A telephone systems showed a decline of nearly 35 per cent in net operating earnings, and an 8 per cent drop was experienced from 1937 to 1938. The shrinkage was somewhat greater in toll business than in local exchange operation, but both suffered. The telephone business is also more sensitive to changes in labor and materials costs, such as occurred in 1945–1953, than is the power business. Most telephone companies needed two or three rate increases during this period, but relatively few power companies had asked for more than one. Nevertheless, the telephone industry has proved itself to be a dependable outlet for investors' funds. It seems to be relatively free of public competition and seldom encounters regulatory hostility or franchise fights. The telephone business in the United States is dominated by the great American Telephone and Telegraph Company system, which handles well over 80 per cent of the nation's telephone business. The system is conservatively financed and ably managed. The second largest system, comprising General Telephone Corporation and its subsidiaries, does about 3 per cent of the nation's telephone business.

Natural gas companies divide themselves into two types, pipe line operators and retailers. Some companies are both. The pipe line companies buy gas from the oil fields under long-term contracts, or produce it themselves, and transport it in pipe lines to towns and cities where it is sold to the local gas companies. The local companies send the gas through their city mains to subscribers' homes and business establishments. It is probable that both pipe line transmission and retailing of natural gas will prove to be steady and profitable. Though this business has developed on a large scale since the war, it seems to have established itself solidly. Long-range problems of gas supply, some unsettled regulatory problems, and the highly conjectural possibilities of future competition from electrically powered heating devices, are the chief hazards.

Water service systems are municipally owned in most places, but several major companies and a number of minor ones operate as private enterprises. Generally speaking, the water companies grow about in proportion to the populations in the areas served. Their earning power is extremely stable, and because of this factor most companies employ a high percentage of senior capital in their financing. The American Water Works Company system, largest of the privately owned water supply organizations, is typical of the operating experience of the industry.

The telegraph business consists of the Western Union Telegraph Company, several property-owning companies whose properties are leased to Western Union, and a scattered few radio and cable companies. Western Union is an aggressively managed organization whose expansion into such fields as money transmittal, stock ticker and quotation services, private teletype service, and other activities has scarcely managed to compensate for the inroads made by air mail and telephone competition into its message business. A large part of the operating cost of the telegraph business has always been labor cost, and although mechanization is increasingly possible, high labor costs have been unavoidable as the value of labor time has risen. Western Union bonds have dropped in 20 years from top quality to medium grade, and the stock has slipped from investment to speculative quality, but the business is still capable of substantial earnings and possible renascence.

Companies selling manufactured gas are also under competitive pressure from the modern and increasingly efficient electric power industry. Manufactured gas is usually too expensive to use for space heating in homes or business buildings but has been extensively used in light manufacturing, for cooking purposes, and for water heating. The development of efficient electric appliances for these purposes has coincided in recent years with higher costs for the coal and oil used in gas manufacture. In areas where electricity is cheap, this competition has been devastating; in all areas it is substantial. Many manufactured gas utilities have been saved from virtual obsolescence by the arrival of natural gas pipe lines, which have sold them cheap and efficient natural gas piped from the oil fields. This has enabled the local gas companies to cut rates, take on space-heating loads, and earn profits beyond their fondest previous hopes.

Local bus and transit lines are generally speculative. Their costs for labor, fuel, and maintenance absorb a high percentage of operating revenues and are by no means stable. Operating revenues themselves are highly cyclical, and rates are held down by automobile competition and by determined public and political pressure. However, some companies seem to do very well most of the time. Others are in constant difficulty.

Regulation and Franchises

The public utility industries are all subject to extensive regulatory control by municipal, state, or Federal authority. The extent of municipal authority is generally limited to powers expressly delegated by the states, which may be minor or very far-reaching, depending on the policy of the state. The state power over intrastate utilities extends to regulate the area served, the quality of service, the capital structure of the utility, the accounting practices followed, the rate structure, and the general level of rates for the purpose of limiting the utility's earnings. Federal authority is theoretically effective only as it affects interstate commerce and the use of streams supplying navigable waters but under Federal laws relating to holding companies, interstate transmission of natural gas, and water power, the Federal government has been able to extend its influence far beyond the nominal limits of its powers.

A long line of court decisions beginning shortly after the Civil War and extending down to the present time outlines the justification for and the guiding principles of utility regulation. The monopolistic features of the business plus its importance to the public justify regulation in the public interest. Use of the public streets and the need for eminent-domain powers are added occasion for control. It is commonly said that utility regulation extends only to regulation of *what* is done and does not enter the management province of determining *how* it is done. However, the increasing scope and detail of regulation seem constantly to narrow the field of management authority and increase that of the regulating commissions. Such matters as a decision to build a new generating plant, a plan for refunding a bond issue, or even the accounting treatment of the cost of floating a bond issue are as much subject to commission decision as to the judgment of management.

Most utilities operate in the communities they serve and use the public streets under long-term permits known as franchises. In many instances the franchises are contractual in nature, assuring the utilities of certain privileges and in return obligating them to pay certain taxes, maintain certain standards of service, and accept specified rates of return. Usually the franchises assure a monopoly during their term. Sometimes they contain options permitting the municipality to buy the property at stated times and prices. Franchise policies vary greatly from state to state and from municipality to municipality, but they are important enough so that no utility security should ever be bought without first investigating the company's franchise position. Investment reference manuals and new-issue prospectuses generally review franchise matters.

Public Ownership and Public Competition

Municipalities have for many years ventured into utility ownership as a means of obtaining certain desired services at low cost. Municipally owned water systems operate in thousands of cities and towns. New York City owns its subway system; San Francisco and many other cities own streetcar and bus systems; Los Angeles, Seattle, Omaha, Chattanooga, and dozens of other cities and towns own electric power systems. Gas, telephone, and telegraph properties are seldom municipally operated.

The Federal government in the past twenty-five years has engaged in a number of water power developments which were too large to be attractive to private enterprise, or which were financially possible only when land reclamation, flood control, and navigation were combined with power operation. These projects included the Tennessee Valley Authority, the Grand Coulee development in Washington, Hoover Dam on the Colorado River, Shasta Dam on the Sacramento River, Bonneville Dam on the Columbia River, and other less ambitious undertakings in the Mississippi basin and on the Atlantic

seaboard. Comparatively few of these projects would pay for themselves as power developments, even when completely exempt from
taxation and financed with 2½ per cent money provided by the government. However, the sale of power by these ventures at the best
prices obtainable is justifiable business, if the venture as a whole
is to be undertaken.

Federal policy toward private enterprise in the electric power field
has been an unstable one. Prior to 1933 it was customary to sell
power generated at Federal dams to municipal or private utilities
without discrimination; for example, Los Angeles' Bureau of Water
and Power and the Southern California Edison Company obtained
power at Hoover Dam on similar terms. Between 1933 and 1941 the
Federal policy was hostile to private enterprise. Not only were private companies often denied access to Federal power, but in many instances Federal loans and gifts were made to induce municipalities
to construct retail power lines to distribute power in competition
with existing private facilities, franchises permitting. During the war
and subsequently the Federal attitude has been more moderate, but
it is probably wise for investors to study the circumstances surrounding proposed public projects before investing in utilities operating
nearby.

In the absence of Federal intervention the development of municipal utility enterprises has not usually been destructive to honest
private investment. Duplication of private facilities by a municipality is not likely if the project must pay for itself. It is better to buy
out the private company. Negotiations for municipal purchase of a
private plant are often accompanied by some rancor and name calling, but passably equitable results are usually achieved. Investors are
of course wise to seek out utilities with sound public relations as well
as sound franchise position; this may avoid ultimate loss as well as
occasional nerve-racking episodes.

Rates and Earnings

From the investor's viewpoint the most important aspect of utility
regulation is the one relating to rates and earnings. In almost all
jurisdictions at present the regulating authority has the right to prescribe or control the rates charged by the utilities. Since the earnings of the utilities depend very closely upon the rates permitted by

the regulating authority, the attitude and promptness of that authority become of paramount importance. A utility is legally entitled to "reasonable" earnings under the "due process" clauses of the Federal constitution, and the courts will intervene on behalf of one which is unfairly treated, but investors will do well to investigate the reputation of a regulatory commission before investing heavily under its jurisdiction.

The classic objective of rate making is to permit "a fair return on a fair valuation of the property used and useful in the public service." That is, rates are to be set at a level which will allow the utility to earn a fair percentage on its investment after deducting all costs including income taxes. The fair percentage in most jurisdictions is to be earned on the total investment in necessary property—fixed assets, equipment and supplies, accounts receivable, cash, and all other operating essentials [2]—regardless of whether the assets represent stockholders' or borrowed capital. Out of the permitted earnings the stockholders must pay interest on borrowed funds at whatever rate they have contracted to pay. The rest is profit.

A second objective of rate-making authority is that of allowing earnings sufficient to "maintain the company's credit standing and attract capital." In recent commission and Supreme Court decisions, notably in the Hope Natural Gas case [3] and in the Northern Natural Gas case,[4] this objective has received close attention. These cases have established the idea that an over-all fair rate of return on the company's assets can reasonably be established by computing a weighted average of (1) the cost of borrowed money to the company, (2) the dividend rates paid on its preferred stock, and (3) the percentage of earnings needed on the common stock net worth to keep the market price of the stock slightly above [5] its net worth (recognized book value) most of the time. Thus, if a company's capital structure consisted of 50 per cent debt costing 3.5 per cent interest, and 20 per cent preferred stock paying 5 per cent dividends, and 30 per cent

---

[2] In instances where rate of return is allowed on fixed assets only, or on some other partial tabulation of used and useful property, the rate is simply made high enough to allow adequate total earnings. The valuation upon which the fair return is allowed is technically known as the "rate base."

[3] *Federal Power Commission v. Hope Natural Gas Company*, 320 U.S. 591 (1944).

[4] *Northern Natural Gas Co. v. Federal Power Commission*, 1 P.U.R.3d 310 (1954) or 206 F.2d 690 (1953).

[5] If the price is slightly above book value the company can sell new stock and pay the costs of sale without diluting the existing book value.

common stock equity whose shares would sell slightly above book value most of the time if they earned 10 per cent on book value, the necessary over-all average rate of return would be 5.75 per cent. It is clear that the over-all rate of return needed under this formula will be affected by the capital structure of the company as well as by the cost of money. In a few instances ultraconservative companies have been urged by the regulating commissions to use more low-cost borrowed money and less high-cost common stock equity, but this has not often been a seriously disputed point.

A fair percentage rate of return is theoretically a substitute for the average rate which might be earned with equal risk in competitive industry. It should therefore be set with reference to average interest rates on borrowed money and average profit rates in stable industries. Also, as the preceding paragraph noted, it should be set at a level which will attract necessary equity capital into the utility field. The Federal Power Commission at one time indicated a belief that 5 to 5½ per cent was enough for most electric power companies, but that 6 to 6½ per cent might be more appropriate in the natural gas business. The state commissions have for the past 15 years regarded 5 to 7 per cent as acceptable for electric power, telephone, and natural gas companies. Strong companies in safe areas are usually allowed less than weaker concerns which need high earnings in order to attract investors' money. Since World War II many commissions have been inclined to tolerate fairly good earnings, averaging 5¾ per cent or better, because this helps the companies to raise the huge sums needed for expansion. It seems probable that the average return to strong companies will recede toward 5½ per cent when the utilities catch up with their construction programs, especially if interest rates remain low.

When a fair percentage rate of return has been determined upon, it is still necessary to establish a valuation (a rate base) for the property employed by the utility. It is generally conceded that this valuation should be a net figure after allowance for depreciation. However, the basic theory for valuation of utility property for rate-making purposes has been much disputed. Some experts hold that the prudently invested historical cost of construction is the proper beginning point; others insist that cost of reproduction at current prices is more logical; and there are several variations of each approach. The Federal Power Commission, the SEC, and a number of influential state commissions are known to regard the actual historical prudent cost of construction as the proper beginning point. Statutes and court decisions are often slightly evasive, declaring in favor of a "fair" valuation arrived at after considering all possible methods, but it appears that the historical-prudent-cost method is dominant and becoming more so.[6]

The investor who wishes to test the current earnings of a utility for reasonableness, to determine whether future rates will probably permit the same or smaller or larger earnings, can do so by computing the percentage of present earnings to an estimated property valuation.[7] If the earnings exceed $6\frac{1}{2}$ per cent on an electric power, telephone, or gas utility, a rate reduction is likely. If earnings are below 5 to $5\frac{1}{2}$ per cent, some improvement is possible. The conclusions which can be drawn from a process of this sort are little better than informed guesses, because of uncertainties in both regulatory policy and in the available accounting records, but an informed guess is certainly better than total ignorance.

It should be noted at this point that utility rate adjustments are not usually made on a month-to-month basis, to keep the utilities' earnings always at the same rate. Rather, adjustments are made on a long-range basis, in response to permanent changes in costs or values. For example, a system depending on hydroelectric plants would have to bear the temporary losses which might result from a drought and could keep the high profits occurring in a year when water was abundant; but the effects of a permanent change in wage rates would sooner or later be compensated by a change in power rates.

In contrast to the regional plan used in establishing rate levels for the railroads, the level of utility rates is usually set separately for each utility operating company. A company which serves sparsely settled territory or finds its fuel costs higher by reason of its location is therefore not penalized. It is allowed rates high enough to pay its

[6] The study of utility valuation is extensive and complex. Interested readers are referred to any good book on utility regulation (for example, E. W. Clemens, *Economics and Public Utilities*, 1950) and to a line of Supreme Court decisions culminating in and cited in *Federal Power Commission v. Hope Natural Gas Company*, 320 U.S. 591 (1944).

[7] The earnings of any year must be compared with the average value of property in service during the year, not with the value at the end of the year. Because of the rapid rate of utility growth, the difference is often important.

justifiable costs plus a fair return on its investment. Of course, a poorly managed or inefficient utility would probably not be allowed rates higher than those charged by well-managed neighboring concerns. For this reason investors commonly compare a given utility's rates with those charged by neighboring companies, before buying its stock.

Estimating Reasonable Earnings

Investors are always interested in the probable future earnings of a company whose securities they are considering. In addition to the familiar techniques of projecting past earnings trends, making estimates from sales and cost trends, etc., it is possible in the case of utilities to estimate average future earnings by applying an average rate of return to an estimated rate base. The probable rate of return may be determined by an investigation of the practices of the regulatory commission having jurisdiction—these will be shown in its published decisions and in articles which treat of its decisions, as well as by statements in the investment reference manuals—and the company's rate base may be estimated from the same sources and to some extent from its published financial statements.

Modern utility balance sheets usually indicate reasonably well the nature of the assets held and the methods used in evaluating them. Even consolidated statements are usually clear on these points. Footnotes to the statements interpret items which are not clear on the statements themselves. It is therefore reasonable, in cases in which a rate base figure is not conveniently available, to make a rough estimate of rate base valuation—that is, value for rate-making purposes —from the balance sheet as shown in a prospectus or in the company's annual report. An investor who uses this method must guard carefully against errors, to the extent of making sure that he understands what is included and what is excluded from the balance sheet, that he knows what types of utility service are included (local transit systems, for example, may not be capable of earning a fair return), and that he is aware of any original cost or extent-of-depreciation disputes which may impair the validity of the balance sheet figures.

Table 28 shows a condensed version of the consolidated balance sheet of the New England Electric System's 1953 annual report. According to this statement the company valued its assets at $436,-

Table 28. New England Electric System and Subsidiaries Consolidated Balance Sheet * at December 31, 1953

Assets

Property, plant and equipment, including intangibles:

Electric plant....................................	$402,092,514
Electric plant acquisition adjustments.............	3,884,119
Gas plant.......................................	41,134,543
Construction work in progress....................	36,740,282
Other..	1,012,766
Total.......................................	$484,864,224
Less reserves for depreciation...................	93,327,234
	$391,536,990

Current assets:

Cash..	9,289,787
Accounts receivable less reserves..................	14,598,964
Materials, fuel, general supplies, and merchandise...	13,295,183
Total current assets...........................	$ 37,183,934
Miscellaneous investments........................	1,922,144
Cash in sinking funds and other restricted deposits....	133,722
Unamortized costs for conversion to natural gas......	4,637,065
Capital stock expense............................	822,988
Prepaid expenses and other deferred charges........	252,052
	$436,488,895

Liabilities

Common shares, par value $1 per share.............	$ 9,108,824
Paid-in surplus.................................	95,430,765
Capital surplus..................................	10,889,427
Premium on preferred stocks of subsidiaries.........	68,175
Consolidated earned surplus.......................	11,277,254
Total common share equity....................	$126,774,445

Shares of subsidiaries held by the public:

Preferred stocks (see accompanying statement).....	40,028,000
Common stock equity...........................	6,666,075
	$ 46,694,075
Long-term debt of company and subsidiaries........	213,699,000

Current liabilities:

Notes payable and sinking fund installments.......	26,670,000
Accounts payable...............................	5,463,866
Accrued taxes..................................	10,025,404
Other current liabilities.........................	3,031,970
Total current liabilities.......................	$ 45,191,240
Reserve re tax allocation.........................	1,326,614
Other reserves and deferred credits.................	2,803,521
	$436,488,895

* This balance sheet has been condensed for textbook purposes. It omits details and explanatory notes carried in the System's 1953 Annual Report, from which it is taken.

488,895, after making appropriate deductions for depreciation and bad debts. But there are four assets shown on the balance sheet on which the regulating commissions would probably allow no earnings and three others which must be accepted with reservations. First, there is a $3,884,119 item entitled "Electric plant acquisition adjustments." This represents the purchase cost of certain properties over and above what the regulating commissions regard as an acceptable rate base value. This $3,884,119 is now being written off against income, and will probably not be included in the rate base. Next, there is a small item of $133,722 of "Cash in sinking funds and other restricted deposits," which represents assets withdrawn from the business to be used for debt retirement. Third, the $4,637,-065 of "Unamortized costs for conversion to natural gas" may be excluded from the rate base, though we cannot be sure of this. Fourth, the "Capital stock expense" of $822,988 is strictly a contra net worth item, and certainly does not represent an asset used in producing electricity. Fifth, the $1,922,144 item entitled "Miscellaneous investments" is probably not an asset in utility operations. It is not clear in the report just what is in this item, but if it earns reasonably on its stated value it will not distort the result very much if it is assumed to be part of the rate base. Sixth, the balance sheet shows an investment of $41,134,543 in "Gas plant," and it must be assumed that a part of the company's current assets is also invested in the gas business. The annual report states that the gas business in 1953 had earned only 3.7 per cent on its resources, but that the recent conversion to natural gas was expected to make improved earnings possible. Finally, the item of $36,740,282 of "Construction work in progress" will earn nothing until completed and placed in service. However, about 3 per cent per annum of the investment in construction in progress is usually capitalized and added to the rate base value of the assets (the accounting credit goes to the interest cost account), so the net effect on the utility's earnings is not excessive. Since many financial statements do not distinguish between assets in service and those under construction, it seems best in a rough calculation to assume that all assets under construction are already in service. This will result in overestimating the typical utility's per share earning power by 3 per cent to 7 per cent, but seldom by much more.

If the first four questionable assets totaling $9,477,894 are removed from the asset total of $436,488,495, a remainder of $427,-010,601 is found. If the "Miscellaneous investments," the "Gas plant" valuation, and the "Construction work in progress" figures are accepted as they stand, and if there are no other assets whose values the commissions might reject (the annual report implied that some might be questioned but that no large revisions were expected), the $427,010,601 figure can be used as a possible basis for estimating future earnings.

Under normal conditions New England Electric System could expect to earn between 5 and 6½ per cent on its rate base, or roughly between $21,300,000 and $27,700,000 on $427,010,601. This represents total earning power available to service the securities outstanding at year-end 1953, after deducting all other expenses and taxes. (Actual 1953 earnings, which were based on average, not year-end, assets and included the poor results on the gas business, amounted to $20,153,190.) Examination of the System's outstanding securities at year-end 1953 indicated that annual interest requirements were then running at the rate of about $7,800,000 per annum and that preferred dividends and minority interests amounted to $2,500,000. These claims total $10,300,000. If this sum is subtracted from the estimated $21,300,000 to $27,700,000 of normal operating earnings, there will remain $11,000,000 to $17,400,000 for the 9,108,824 common shares. This would mean annual earnings of $1.21 to $1.91 per common share, with the exact figure depending on the percentage return obtained. (Remember, these figures are slightly overstated because they assume that all plant investments are already in service.)

New England Electric System's actual per share earnings were $1.18 in 1953 and $1.24 in 1954.

The investor who uses this method of testing a company's normal earning power must realize that his balance sheet computations attempt to establish the rate base as of the exact date of the balance sheet. Application of a fair percentage rate to this computed rate base will produce an earnings figure which is normal only for the assets held and the securities outstanding at the date of the balance sheet. Deduction of amounts required as of that date for interest charges, preferred dividends, and minority claims will indicate the total normal earning power for the common shares outstanding.

However, if the company maintains a fairly constant proportioning of bonds, preferred stock, and common stock equity as it grows, this sort of estimate may give a fairly durable indication of its position.

It must also be conceded that the process here suggested is an extremely crude one, a rough-and-ready method of estimating. For example, in a large utility system it lumps together different subsidiary companies which may be rendering different types of service under different regulatory jurisdictions. Second, it includes the "investments," which in a utility are most likely to consist of securities in partially owned affiliated companies, in some cases not even in the utility business, as part of the estimated rate base; this is excusable only if the item is small. Yet an estimate of this type is worth making; if, for example, the investor discovers that a stock which he is considering has attractive earnings per share only because the company is earning 7 per cent on its apparent rate base, he is warned to proceed with caution.

Utility Capital Structures

Because of the high degree of stability inherent in utility earnings, it has become customary to use large amounts of senior capital in utility financing. A typical capital structure might consist of 50 per cent debt, 15 per cent preferred stock, and 35 per cent common stock equity. Even less conservative structures are used, though regulating commissions usually advocate a debt maximum not much over 50 per cent and a common stock equity not much under 25 per cent.

Many managements attempt to introduce the maximum feasible leverage into their capital structures, in order to maximize earnings on the common stockholders' investment. They observe that a 50–25–25 structure can usually be financed with $3\frac{1}{4}$ per cent bonds and $4\frac{1}{2}$ per cent preferred stock. If a $5\frac{1}{2}$ per cent rate of return were permitted, $5.50 would be earned annually on every $100 of company investment. Of every $100 invested, $50 would be provided by the bondholders at an interest cost of $1.625 and $25 by preferred stockholders at a dividend outlay of $1.125; the other $2.75 of earnings would remain for the common stockholders, as an 11 per cent net profit on their $25 investment. Earnings of this magnitude would probably permit the payment of a $2 annual dividend on every $25 of common stock investment.[8] It is true that the common stockholders must bear the risk and absorb any losses which occur, but the generous returns which accrue to this kind of risk bearing make it undeservedly popular.

Table 29. Consolidated Capital Structures of Representative Utility Systems, December 31, 1953

System	Percentage of resources * represented by		
	Bonds plus current debt	Preferred stocks and minority interests	Common stock equity
American Telephone and Telegraph....	46	2	52
General Telephone...................	53	18	29
Boston Edison......................	48	0	52
Consolidated Edison of New York......	48	12	40
General Public Utilities..............	51	13	36
Detroit Edison......................	57	0	43
Commonwealth Edison..............	55	4	41
Pacific Gas and Electric..............	50	18	32
Southern California Edison...........	51	18	31
Columbia Gas System................	59	0	41
Southern Natural Gas...............	74	0	26
Pacific Lighting....................	48	16	36

* Without deduction for intangibles or other valuation adjustments, and including investments in nonconsolidated subsidiaries as net assets.

Table 29 indicates the proportioning of debt and stock interests in several important utility systems as shown in their consolidated balance sheets dated December 31, 1953. These figures may show a slightly larger percentage of debt than the utilities' ultimate plans contemplate, for the postwar years 1946–1953 required expansion at an unprecedented rate, and borrowing was necessary because stock sales of adequate proportions did not seem feasible. Stock sales and

[8] A common share representing a prudently invested $25, on which the per share earnings averaged $2.75, and which paid a $2 dividend, would normally sell between $30 and $40.

conversion of convertible bonds into stock may ultimately increase the common stock equities.

Some students of finance believe that it is safe for a growing and monopolistic utility to use a 50–25–25 capital structure, because little chance of damaging financial reverses seems to exist. However, railroads, streetcar companies, and manufactured gas companies once regarded their positions as financially impregnable, and many of them used high-leverage capital structures just as some growing utilities do now. The result was financial confusion and in many cases bankruptcy when growth ceased and competing industries forced limitation of rates. It would seem that many utilities are disregarding the lesson of history in planning their capital structures.

Because sales and cost stability and growth rates differ it is not proper to set down universal rules to define a sound consolidated capital structure for a growing utility. If a rough-and-ready rule is required, the following seems reasonable: Determine first the total net good assets, after deducting depreciation reserves and all questionable (non-rate-base) assets. Second, determine a typical or average earning power after allowing for income taxes but before deducting for interest. The structure meets accepted standards: (1) if total current and bonded debt is less than 60 per cent of asset value and if interest charges are covered three times over after tax allowances; and (2) if debts plus preferred stocks plus minority interests do not exceed 75 per cent of the net assets and do not absorb over 60 per cent of the posttax earnings.

The foregoing implies that a common stock equity having a 25 per cent interest in net good assets and a 40 per cent equity in average earnings is acceptable in quality, if no other weaknesses appear. An equity of this grade is doubtless fortified against early obliteration in a depression or a cost inflation, but it cannot be said to be immune to a long-term market revolution such as the railroads encountered between 1920 and 1940. A really high-quality utility common stock should have a 40 per cent or better equity in net good assets and a 60 per cent equity in posttax earnings. Such a stock could bear the loss which a lowered rate of return would impose, regardless of whether the lower return stemmed from economic change or from adverse regulatory policy.

Operating Revenues and Expenses

Monopoly position, dependable sales, and persistent growth relieve the utilities of many of the problems which beset ordinary competitive businesses. Another factor, that of constantly increasing technical efficiency, has held down or lowered operating costs for many years. Aside from harassment of a political or regulatory nature, therefore, the utility industries have had relatively few serious operating problems. Sharply rising price levels have been the most burdensome; these have at times caused increases in labor, fuel, and materials costs at a speed which mounting efficiency plus occasional rate increases by slow-acting commissions could not always match. Tax increases during the past ten years and especially during the war have imposed heavy burdens. Finally, occasional impairment of earnings due to drought affects companies dependent on hydroelectric installations.

The utilities which were affected first in the price inflation of 1946–1953 were the telephone companies, whose relatively heavy labor and materials costs increased sharply. Natural gas companies felt the cost increases a little later, especially as their costly expansion programs developed. The electric power companies during this period had unusual advantages in cost-saving technological developments and in increased sales per customer, which shielded them from part but not all of the impact of the inflation. In the latter part of this period a new aspect of the inflation was presenting itself: a large part of the utilities' installed facilities now consists of postwar construction, and as prewar facilities wear out and are replaced, this percentage increases. But the unit cost of postwar facilities is much greater than the older ones, hence depreciation charges and the fair return on capital may require increasing rates even if no further inflation occurs. Many utility executives wonder if increased rates will be politically expedient, if the price level ceases to rise.

Working Capital Position

Except when important construction or refunding programs are under way, the utilities are not likely to possess large amounts of working capital. Current assets amounting to 10 per cent of total assets would usually be sufficient, and of these two-thirds might well be offset by current liabilities. Steady and dependable earnings make small amounts of net working capital and a low current ratio tolerable.

Because most of their assets are permanently employed in fixed capital the utilities are not likely to employ serial bonds, serial bank loans, or any bank loans at all except those incurred temporarily pending sale of securities.

Dividend Policies

Steady and dependable earnings make it possible for a utility to pay regular dividends which amount to a fairly high percentage of average earnings, possibly 75 per cent or more. This is the common practice, except for a few companies urgently in need of small amounts of additional capital which can be drawn from earnings, and a few whose managements have unique ideas about dividend policies.

The precedents for the industry are set by such conspicuous concerns as the American Telephone and Telegraph Company, whose quarterly payments have been unchanged at the $9 per annum rate since 1922 and whose uninterrupted dividend record goes back to 1881. Other leading utilities have similar long records of uninterrupted payments, including Boston Edison Company since 1897, Consolidated Edison Company of New York since 1893, Commonwealth Edison Company (Chicago) since 1890, and Pacific Lighting Corporation (California) since 1909. These are outstanding rather than average records, of course, but they illustrate the capacity of the industry as well as the precedents which are now generally recognized to be appropriate.

Generous regular dividends are usually popular with stockholders. They are good business for companies whose growth is so rapid that large sums must be raised by selling new stock. The stockholder who gets a satisfactory dividend is usually willing to buy new stock when the company needs extra money; the company can get back its dividend money and more too if it needs it, and at very low cost. Utility managements are well aware of these facts, and generous dividend policies are coupled in most companies with frequent common stock sales to stockholders on a "rights" basis.

Financing Policies

Most utility bonds are now of investment grade, suitable for institutions and trust funds. Consequently, a large percentage of utility bonds in recent years has been sold to institutional buyers and conservative accounts at interest rates ranging between 2¾ and 3½ per cent. They have not been widely distributed. Occasional exceptions must be noted: the American Telephone and Telegraph Company has sold very large issues of convertible debentures to its stockholders, Consolidated Edison has sold an issue of convertible 3s to its stockholders, and a few other similar instances have occurred. The companies of course expect these bonds to be converted within a few years.

Preferred stocks offered by the utilities in recent years have also been mostly good grade. Yields have ranged between 3¾ and 5½ per cent, with most issues paying between 4 and 5 per cent. A number of these issues have been distributed in refunding operations to retire older stocks paying 5 to 6 per cent. The new preferred stocks have gone into both institutional and personal holdings, but it appears that they are not being scattered into the large numbers of small holdings which characterized utility preferred issues of 30 years ago. At that time relative stability plus good yield attracted thousands of small stockholders, especially among the utility's customers. In fact, many companies then made persistent efforts to sell their preferred stocks to their customers; they even sold them on the installment plan, billing the customer monthly along with his power bill.

New common stock financing by utility companies is mostly obtained by offering new stock to existing stockholders, though the stronger stock market since 1950 has induced many companies to sell their shares outright to investment bankers for resale to the general public. When large sums are needed and it appears that large stock offerings would be hard to sell, convertible bonds or preferred stocks are used. Usually the convertibles are offered to existing stockholders, but not always: General Telephone Corporation, for example, offered new common stock directly to its stockholders but sold an issue of 4.4 per cent convertible preferred stock to underwriters for general distribution. The companies usually seek a wide distribution for their stocks because it makes additional stock financing easy and because numerous stockholders represent good public relations and political strength.

Utility common stocks still vary in quality from the superb to the moderately speculative. One of the avowed objectives of modern utility regulation is to plan the new financing of the utility companies along lines calculated to make all utility securities reasonably good in quality. This will require a considerable increase in the proportion of common stocks in many capital structures.

Most good utilities have large numbers of common stockholders, especially small stockholders. Large numbers of investors are attracted by earnings stability and generous dividends; the utility stocks are commonly used in portfolios in which regular cash dividends must be maximized. Utility stocks are also regarded as "defensive" stock investments, havens for investors who fear that depression may shortly reduce the dividends from industrial stocks but who do not wish to accept the low incomes paid by bonds.

Markets and Market Behavior

Most of the more important utility stocks and bonds are listed on the stock exchanges. Smaller issues are traded over the counter. Bonds and preferred stocks of good quality are usually very stable in price, fluctuating only with money-rate conditions and other general factors which affect all good-grade low-yield securities.

The medium-grade preferreds and the common stocks of utility companies seem to behave on the markets just about as industrial stocks do, though their fluctuations are a little less extreme, probably because of the relative stability of their earnings and dividends. Under ordinary conditions utility and industrial stocks fluctuate together, following the primary and secondary swings of the market to about the same degree and at about the same time. However, there are two points of difference, especially as respects common shares: first, utility stocks are not so sharply affected by permanent changes in the price levels as are some industrials, for price-level changes do not directly alter their original cost rate base values and consequent long-term earning power, whereas industrial stocks may be sharply affected. Second, the utilities are a homogeneous enough group so that either favorable or adverse circumstances might cause their stock prices as a group to deviate from the market pattern. This was especially manifested in the period 1933–1941, when they were under political attack, and in the period 1946–1948, when heavy financing by utility companies temporarily sated the market for utility stock.

Because most utility common stocks pay higher percentages of their earnings in dividends than the average industrial stock does, they usually yield a little more than industrials of similar quality. For the same reason, they ordinarily will command slightly higher price-earnings ratios.

Testing Utility Securities

The plan of analysis outlined in Chapter 13 is definitely appropriate for utility securities. Because utility accounting is reasonably well standardized and because utilities of similar types are much alike in their methods of operation, analysis by means of financial ratios is more than usually significant.

In studying utility securities there are 10 topics which analysts invariably check. Most of these have already been mentioned, but some repetition in summary may perhaps be justified.

1. A reasonably stable and prosperous territory is desirable, in which volume can grow enough to keep present plant occupied and to permit addition of new and more efficient plant from time to time.

2. If the utility's sales volume is from mixed services, a maximum percentage of electric power, telephone, natural gas, or water sales is preferable; manufactured gas or transportation service is less desirable. Residential, commercial, farm, and industrial load is stable and profitable in descending order, hence preferable in that order.

3. Public competition is to be avoided. Neighboring Federal power projects, local municipal ownership enthusiasm, unsound franchise situations, and bad public relations are warnings to the investor.

4. The attitudes and policies of regulatory commissions are important, particularly on matters dealing with rate base and fair return, holding company structures, and dividend policy.

5. The company's rates should be compared with those of similarly situated companies, to make sure that inefficiency does not make high rates necessary in order to earn a profit.

6. The company's reasonable rate base and normal earning power should be checked.

7. The capital structure and earnings coverage should be tested, to make sure that debt is not excessive and that the common stock has a reasonable equity in assets and earnings.

8. The operating ratio and other cost ratios should be checked. Operating ratios for most utilities have risen in late years, as a result of increases in the cost of labor and supplies. Utility earnings have consequently tended to deteriorate in quality, though increased volume and occasional rate increases have maintained their per share amounts.

9. Depreciation and maintenance (combined) should be checked. These items usually total about 14 or 15 per cent of gross sales for a power or gas company and twice that for a telephone company.

10. In the case of power companies, it is important to note the proportions of hydroelectric and steam generation, the modernness of the installations, and the dependability of hydroelectric power, if any.

QUESTIONS AND PROBLEMS

1. What economic characteristics in the electric power, telephone, and natural gas industries are most significant to investors?

2. Why is the telephone business more sensitive to cost increases than is the electric power business?

3. Are water companies satisfactory investments? Is this a big field for private enterprise?

4. What subjects are covered by public utility regulation? Which are most important to investors?

5. What are franchises? In what ways are they important to investors?

6. Why are Federal hydroelectric projects dangerous to investors in neighboring power companies? Can you imagine why the private power companies fought so vigorously in 1949 to keep the Federal government from building its first steam generating plant in connection with its TVA development?

7. Explain the concept of a "fair return on a fair valuation." How has the doctrine of the Hope Natural Gas case affected the "fair return" idea?

8. What difference does it make in 1954, after a great inflation in the price level has occurred, whether historical prudent cost or cost of reproduction is used in evaluating a utility for rate-making purposes?

9. Why were the utilities glad to see prices stop rising in 1953?

10. At December 31, 1953, the Hotwire Electric Company had $4,000,-000 of current assets and $46,000,000 of net fixed assets after deducting depreciation reserves. The assets appear to be properly valued. At December 31 the company owed $2,000,000 in outstanding accounts, $20,-000,000 in 3 per cent bonds, and had outstanding $14,000,000 in 5 per

cent preferred and 1,000,000 shares of common stock. In 1953 the common stock earned $1.45 per share and paid $1 in dividends. Can these rates of earning and payment be continued?

11. Is this common stock good grade? What would it sell for on the market?

12. Are the bonds good grade? What would they sell for?

13. Look up the last balance sheet of the Pacific Gas and Electric Company, and determine what rate of return would be necessary in order to permit the common stock to earn $3 per share. What would be a reasonable per share earnings figure? What does the company actually earn? Is Pacific Gas common a good stock?

14. Try the techniques of question 13 on the consolidated balance sheet of American Telephone and Telegraph, with $11 per share as the earnings objective.

15. Why is working capital position not of outstanding importance in utility security analysis?

16. Investigate the utilities listed in Table 29, to determine whether they follow the policy of paying 75 per cent or more of their earnings in dividends.

17. Would utility common stocks be as attractive to a high-salaried executive as to a retired person? Why?

18. Do the stable earnings and dividends of the utilities exempt their stocks from market fluctuations? What are "defensive stocks"?

REFERENCES

Badger, Ralph E., and Harry G. Guthmann: *Investment Principles and Practices,* Prentice-Hall, Inc., New York, 1951, Chaps. 10–12.

Financial Handbook, The Ronald Press Company, New York, 1948, pp. 282–290.

Graham, Benjamin, and David L. Dodd: *Security Analysis,* McGraw-Hill Book Company, Inc., New York, 1951, Chaps. 20, 21, 39, 40.

Investment Bankers Association of America: *Fundamentals of Investment Banking,* Prentice-Hall, Inc., New York, 1949, Chap. 6.

Jordan, David F., and Herbert E. Dougall: *Investments,* Prentice-Hall, Inc., New York, 1952, Chap. 25.

Pickett, Ralph R., and Marshall D. Ketchum: *Investment Principles and Policy,* Harper & Brothers, New York, 1954, Chaps. 23, 24.

Plum, Lester V., and Joseph H. Humphrey: *Investment Analysis and Management,* Richard D. Irwin, Inc., Homewood, Ill., 1951, Chaps. 13, 14.

Robbins, Sidney M.: *Managing Securities,* Houghton Mifflin Company, Boston, 1954, Chaps. 27, 28.

Chapter 17: INDUSTRIAL SECURITIES

In securities market parlance the term "industrial" applies to almost any manufacturing, extractive, or merchandising concern. Railroads, public utilities, and financial institutions are not industrials, but steel companies, motor companies, meat packers, oil companies, shoe manufacturers, department stores, retail drug chains, and a host of others all belong in the industrial category. Obviously, such a diverse group of industries will not be alike or even similar in their investment characteristics. The investor is forewarned, therefore, that the discussions in this chapter will be largely generalizations and that explicit knowledge of the behavior of individual industries must be obtained elsewhere.[1]

From the investor's point of view the outstanding features of the industrial category are general freedom from government regulation and the prevalence of competition. These features lead immediately to the great emphasis upon sales and selling, intangible assets, cost control, and other variables with which this chapter is mostly concerned. Industrials are typically involved in a rough-and-tumble competitive scramble in which weakness may be disastrous, but in which strength and skill may be richly rewarded. The securities of strong industrial concerns are unquestionably of investment grade, but those of some of the weaker concerns can hardly even qualify as intelligent speculations. This competitive scramble is a never-ending affair; although the great entrenched concerns may maintain a relatively stable position in it, many of the weaker ones are alternately very prosperous and drably unprofitable, as their operations proceed. Consequently, individual industrial stocks often rise or fall in marked degree, as their prospects appear to wax or wane.

The Price-level Factor

The prices charged and paid in an unregulated, competitive, cost-conscious industry have a general tendency to follow the average

[1] The most convenient source is probably the *Industry Surveys* section of the *Standard Trade and Securities Service,* which is reviewed in Chap. 11.

trends of commodity prices. This is not a universal rule, and certainly there is no dependable proportionality between the prices in an individual industry and the level of all commodity prices, but the tendency is marked enough to be important to investors. If prices rise, an industry's inventories and fixed assets theoretically tend to appreciate in proportion to the increase in replacement costs, and normal profit percentages should produce a corresponding increase in dollar earnings. Price declines would of course induce a contrary effect. Actual tendencies for individual stock prices, earnings, and dividends to follow commodity price changes were noted in Chapter 4.

Industrial securities thus seem to offer the investor a rather promising opportunity to hedge his income and property values against changes in the general price level. This is particularly true if the investor avails himself of the diversification possible through participation in a number of the different industries in the industrial category. Any single industry might be an exception to the general rule, to the discomfiture of its investors. After all, price-level changes are often accompanied by working capital problems, changes in operating costs, changes in consumer demands, changes in competitive pressure, and disturbed securities markets, any of which may upset the most logical investment calculations; but a diversified position should assure its holder of reasonably typical results.

It is not to be expected that industrial bonds, preferred stocks, and common stocks will all be affected in similar fashion by price-level changes. Like all senior securities, industrial bonds and preferreds have limited claims to income and assets, while common stockholders occupy a residual position. Price-level increases which cause the corporate earnings to consist of a larger number of less valuable dollars will make the senior securities' income more secure, while debasing its buying power. This might actually be an advantage to a medium- or speculative-grade bond or preferred, for an increase in quality might cause its price to rise, but the holder of a good bond or preferred would suffer a decline in the buying power of his income with no compensating capital gain. Common stockholders in a company which had senior securities outstanding would presumably have disproportionately larger per share earnings as a result of price-level inflation. Deflation would present all these tendencies in reverse.

Sales Outlook

Since the profitableness of an industrial concern is first of all contingent upon a satisfactory sales volume, the investor must always investigate the sales prospects of a firm in which he is interested. The problem has a threefold aspect, for conclusions are needed with respect to long-run probabilities, near-term prospects, and the degree of stability which can be expected.

The long-run outlook for a company's sales volume is first of all concerned with the sales volume available to the industry. If the industry is a growing one, if it is essential to the nation's future, if there are no developing substitutes for its product, then there will undoubtedly be a market for the company's output. In the foreseeable future there can be few doubts as to the market for steel, industrial chemicals, or meat products; but there are new products which may successfully challenge the market for woolen cloth. Second, diversification of product may be assurance of continuing long-run sales volume; the fluid milk business alone might not adequately assure the future for National Dairy Products Corporation, but its extensive diversification into cheese, mayonnaise, salad dressing, margarine, cooking oil, ice cream, and candy products affords multiple opportunities for sales expansion. Third, a concern's competitive position is often indicative of its long-run prospects; possession of good will, established sales outlets, reputation, brand names, patents, and management connections may mean much.

The immediate sales outlook for a company is likely to be compounded of the customers' needs for the product, their capacity to buy, and the company's own competitive position. In 1954, for example, there was still substantial need in the United States for new refrigerators, ranges, and other household appliances, and the capacity of consumers to buy was still considerable; but the wartime shortage of these products was over, and the sales volume was going increasingly to the concerns occupying the better competitive positions. These were the companies with the best brand names, the best new models, and the best sales outlets.

Concerns dependent on consumer demand seem to have a more stable market for their wares than those making producers' goods, and ordinary consumption goods sell more steadily than consumers' durable goods. Sellers of producers' goods who supply the suppliers of consumption goods—for example, those who furnish materials to the electric utilities or to the oil companies—find more regular sales demand than those who supply building materials or machinery to other industries. However, the sellers of producers' goods may prosper just as much in the long run as those who sell consumers' goods, even though their sales volume and profits fluctuate more. To the investor, the less stable performance of certain producer goods industries is not only a warning of undependable dividends and stock prices, but a promise of profits in stocks which are bought at the right time.

Diversification of products and markets usually tends to stabilize sales volume and profits. Thus, the Glidden Company is a well-known maker of paints, but its vegetable oil business includes the manufacture of the famous Durkee line of pickles, salad oil, margarine, and other products, and a third department produces a line of plastics. Again, the Borg-Warner Corporation, which is a major supplier of automotive parts, has diversified itself by producing the important Norge line of refrigerators and other household appliances, as well as an extensive list of other domestic and industrial equipment. Investors' appraisals of sales prospects for such firms as these must necessarily consider all of their operations, not just the best known one. Corporate annual reports, prospectuses, and the securities reference services will provide the necessary information.

Costs, Expenses, Profit Margins

Next only to sales and sales prospects, the investor's constant attention must be given to costs and profit margins. Because of the diversity of industries to be envisaged, little more can be said here than that trends in cost of goods and materials, operating expenses, and final profit margins should all be watched and understood if possible. Such experiences as the sudden disappearance of the Penick and Ford Company's normally stable profits in 1937 are easily explained and of little concern when the investor knows them to be caused by high corn prices resulting from a poor crop, which temporarily made the manufacture of corn syrup and starch unprofitable. Again, the relatively low percentages of sales which General Foods Corporation paid out in selling costs in 1946–1947 could be found not to indicate great economy in the sales department; it merely reflected an abnormal inflationary increase in sales prices caused by an increase in raw materials prices. These and similar interpretations of operating results are vital to sound investment decisions and may also be extremely profitable.

The most important factors affecting operating costs and profit margins are usually volume of business, the relationship between raw materials and product prices, labor conditions, and competition. These factors vary in relative importance from one industry to another.

The steel industry, for example, is acutely sensitive to volume. It has heavy plant investment, heavy maintenance and other overhead expenses, and operates in a market in which competitive pricing appears to reflect long-run rather than current unit costs. Consequently, the industry is unprofitable on light volume and very profitable on large volume. By contrast, many manufacturing industries where materials and hourly wages represent the major costs are able to earn moderate profit rates on almost any reasonable volume, since the expenses vary almost in proportion to the sales.

The margins between raw material and final product prices are vital to most industries. Some, like the meat packing industry, can ordinarily control these margins fairly well. Others, like the fruit and vegetable canning industry, find them very hard to manage. In the canned foods business the size of the annual crop, the size of the pack, and the resulting behavior of product prices on a market where demand is relatively inelastic govern the profit trends. Most food canners pack their annual inventories on a speculative basis, expecting to recover the inventory costs plus a profit during the ensuing selling season. A light or moderate pack usually brings a good price, but a big pack often gluts the market and brings inadequate prices, especially if general employment conditions and consumer demand are poor.

Labor conditions affect the profitableness of industries in many ways. Wage scales higher than those paid elsewhere for similar work, and limitation of output policies by labor organizations, can make a firm's operations unprofitable or less profitable than its competitors'. Rubber companies found their operations in the Akron area burdened in this way before the war; New England textile mills encountered similar problems after the war. Repeated interruptions of operations by strikes may reduce volume, lose customers who demand a steady source of supply, and alienate important agencies and sales outlets. Because of the aggressiveness and great bargaining power of labor in recent years many investors prefer industries in which labor cost is a relatively small proportion of the final value of the product. However, this is not necessarily a sound conclusion, for labor costs are usually variable costs, and variable costs are often less burdensome than fixed costs. The important thing is to be sure that the labor factor is not adversely affecting the earning power of the firm or the industry.

The severity of competition is the fourth of the important factors determining average earning power and, particularly, determining the stability of earning power. There are many industries—for examples, automobile manufacturing, farm machinery manufacturing, and petroleum—in which vigorous competition seems to stabilize earning power, and even to prevent earnings for inefficient firms, without ever seriously threatening the earnings of the leaders. There are other industries, among them meat packing, flour milling, and cotton goods manufacturing, in which competitive pressure is so constant and vicious that earnings margins are usually narrow and often nonexistent for many firms. The severity of competition seems to be greatest (1) in industries in which large numbers of firms operate, so that some are always struggling to enlarge their volumes, raise cash, or introduce new brands; (2) in industries in which brands, firm names, and distribution channels are not dominant factors, but where products are sold mainly by technical description or simple display; (3) in industries where patents and patented processes are not of paramount importance; (4) in industries where surplus capacity exists and where markets are not growing rapidly; and (5) in industries where close competitive pricing is traditional, or in which certain leading firms consistently practice it.

Previous chapters have called attention to the important effects which accounting methods may have on the determination of reported profits, especially when price-level changes influence inventory and fixed asset values. An additional accounting factor may have an important effect on oil and mining company profits; it is customary in these industries to charge certain exploration and developmental costs to expense in the year incurred, despite the fact that the benefits of such outlays will be reaped chiefly in future years.[2] As a result, the earnings of a particular year may depend to a considerable extent on how much developmental work was done in the year. Unless investors have the time and opportunity to unravel these variables, their impressions of earnings are likely to be general indeed.

Inventories

Many industrial concerns are compelled by the nature of their business to carry very large merchandise or materials inventories and to contract in advance for large additional quantities. In times when price levels are changing, this situation is both opportunity and hazard. Substantial accumulation before a price rise will naturally augment the firm's earnings, but a heavy inventory may be a source of severe loss if prices fall. Furthermore, an unsalable inventory will be a source of loss in any case; whatever happens to prices, it is desirable to keep the inventory and purchase commitments within reasonable bounds by anticipating sales volume and by purchasing or producing only what is needed.

As might be expected, the inventory problem is different in different industries. In the clothing industry, for example, the problem of proper quantity to buy and the concern about price are further complicated by seasonal demand changes and styles. In the meat packing industry, the necessity of carrying a very large tonnage of inventory at all times, despite the great volatility of meat prices, combines a delicate profit or loss problem with a need for huge variations in working capital supply as prices change. The flour milling business is a little better off than the meat packers; large inventories are unavoidable, but the price hazard can be hedged on the speculative wheat markets, if desired. The motion picture companies have a peculiar variant to their inventory problem; their pictures, when marketed competitively, command the public's interest roughly in

---

[2] The extent to which this is done is also a factor. While most leading oil companies charge the costs of exploratory work and the cost of drilling dry holes (unsuccessful oil wells) to expense in the year done, the Continental Oil Company goes farther and charges the entire cost of drilling successful oil wells to current expense. Only the costs of well liners, pumps, and other installed equipment are regarded as capital outlays. Continental's annual earnings statements thus carry heavy charges for current drilling, but no amortization of past drilling costs, and its balance sheet assets do not include its very large investment in active oil wells.

proportion to their quality, which is in considerable degree proportionate to their cost. The picture companies must therefore invest in their inventories a sum sufficient to equal or better their competitors', but not more than is recoverable from the public.

The investor's interest in the inventory position of his company can be summed up in inquiries as to its salability and as to the potential gain or loss in it. Purchase commitments not as yet included in inventory must be regarded as part of it, for this purpose, and fixed-price contracts in which part of the inventory will be used may reasonably be allowed for. There is no definite rule by which the investor's appraisal of the inventory situation is made easily. He needs to know the position and outlook for the industry, the normal needs and the present situation of his company, and the inventory accounting policies employed. Company annual reports and the better grade financial services are probably the best sources of information.

It should be noted that the use of LIFO or similar accounting devices may minimize the effect of inventory value fluctuations on reported incomes and stabilize the values as reported on balance sheets, but they will not solve working capital problems, nor will they avoid the reality of loss if large inventories are bought just before a price decline. Inventory problems are real, no matter how recorded on the books.

Assets and Asset Valuation

Substantial assets are no guarantee of earning power to an industrial concern. All industries in this category are competitive, and comparatively few concerns can report satisfactory earnings without good products, good organization, good management, and an established position. Assuming these latter attributes to be at hand, however, the properties and equipment with which the concern must work will naturally be a factor in its success. Efficiency and suitability of the assets are highly important to low-cost operations; their completeness, which could make possible a thoroughly integrated operation free of rental payments and service charges to others, is important in reducing overhead and widening the normal profit margin.

But industrial assets cannot be measured with complete accuracy on the basis of book valuations. Book valuations are based on cost less estimated depreciation to date; they do not testify regarding obsolescence, condition, replacement cost, or suitability for present purposes. However, some indication of a company's asset position can be had by investigating the nature of the assets, the date of construction or acquisition, and the accounting methods followed. Such data are available in securities reference books, new-issue prospectuses, and annual reports.

Since the great advantage in owning business assets lies in the operating economies they make possible—in the avoidance of rents, service charges, special contract charges and other costs which any competitor must similarly avoid or pay—the investor's interest in them may well be centered on their contribution in this regard. If a firm's asset position indicates that a very limited capital outlay would enable a competitor to enter its markets on equal terms, its own earning power is vulnerable indeed; but if a challenging competitor must invest heavily in expensive equipment or pay higher operating costs, the original firm is sheltered from excessive numbers of competitors at least, and its earning power is to some extent protected.

Investors in bonds and preferred stocks are particularly likely to appreciate the long-term stability which substantial integration and extensive ownership of fixed assets give to an industrial concern. Even a clumsy business organization should earn enough to pay reasonable bond interest and preferred dividends, if it has the advantage of integration and large fixed resources. Furthermore, the possession of ample fixed assets provides a durable advantage which errors in administering working capital should not quickly dissipate; they therefore have a special appeal to senior securityholders who are not interested in risk bearing or participation in management.

Working Capital Position

Though conditions vary greatly in different industries, it is reasonable to generalize that most firms in the industrial category need a substantial supply of working capital. They must usually finance inventories and receivables, and their earnings are often irregular enough to require occasional dividend payments and even losses to be met out of working capital. This calls for a very comfortable excess of current assets over current liabilities at all times and for a current ratio ranging between 2 to 1 and 6 to 1 (200 to 600 per cent) at the fiscal year end. Industrial concerns which do not habitually maintain a strong working capital position are always vulnerable to financial strain, loss of cash discounts and other opportunities, and dividend omissions, when business conditions become adverse.

Many industrial concerns are engaged in businesses which are seasonal in nature, and others occasionally undertake large contracts which require more than normal amounts of working capital. These operations are usually financed by bank loans, arranged on terms which permit the borrowings in the amount and for the time needed. This use of bank credit is proper and economical. However, it is not often good practice for a concern whose seasonal operations require short-term borrowings to allow them to be unpaid from one year to the next; an annual "cleanup" at the business low point of the year (usually at the end of the fiscal year) will be possible unless the concern is abnormally short of working capital. Short-term bank loans outstanding at the end of a fiscal year are therefore to be regarded as a warning to the investor; they may not be a danger signal, but they deserve scrutiny. Since corporate annual reports usually carry financial statements dated as of the end of the fiscal year, they offer an excellent opportunity to check for excessive dependence on banks.

It is well to note in passing that seasonal dependence on banks makes desirable a capital structure so strong that the banks will be glad to advance seasonal loans even in bad years.

Examination of the working capital position of an industrial concern requires an inspection of the quality of the current assets and, to some extent, of the nature of the current liabilities. Unsalable inventories and uncollectible receivables are not good current assets; past-due accounts payable are more burdensome than accrued payables which are not yet due. Information on these matters is not easy for an investor to obtain. Hints may be found in annual reports and the gossip columns of financial newspapers, which may be sufficient to put a careful investor on his guard.

Working capital seems to have a persistent tendency to disappear into fixed assets. Most businesses tend always to grow, to add departments, add equipment, add buildings, as time passes. Funds represented by depreciation allowances, undistributed earnings, and new financing pay for these additions, and if these sources are not sufficient a reasonable amount from working capital will make up the difference. Since contracts for new fixed assets are made months in advance of delivery and payment, it is not unusual for working capital to have to make up shortages in expected earnings or in the proceeds of new financing. For this reason, investors are usually much interested in their companies' construction plans and in the plans for financing them.

Though the general tendency under adverse conditions is for working capital positions to weaken, the opposite is sometimes the case. During the early 1930s U.S. Steel Corporation spent less on new plant and replacements than the depreciation and depletion allowances on its huge integrated plants. It also sold down its inventory and collected down its receivables as the depression deepened. As a result U.S. Steel was able to meet operating losses, pay part of the dividend on its preferred stock, pay down its current liabilities, and actually improve its cash position and its current ratio.

Capital Structures

It is almost traditional for industrial corporations to choose conservative capital structures. Bonds and preferred stocks have been regarded as convenient means of financing when stock market conditions were adverse, and modest amounts of senior securities are a permanent part of the financing of many corporations, but standard practice in recent decades has favored a heavy emphasis on common stock financing. This policy was given impetus by the stock boom of 1927–1929, which enabled many firms to sell stock to obtain money to retire their bonds, and it received still greater impetus during the depression of 1930–1939, when industrial leaders observed the great convenience of freedom from heavy senior charges.

However, it must be admitted that corporate structures were not so free of senior securities in 1954 as they were in 1945. Heavy postwar cash requirements for new fixed assets and enlarged working capital exceeded the capacity of the postwar stock market, and the corporations were forced to sell bonds and preferred stocks in huge amounts. Such debt-free citadels as Borden Co., General Motors, General Electric, and Goodyear borrowed heavily, and many others incurred or greatly enlarged their senior obligations. No pattern of action has yet been established by which one may judge whether future policies will work toward retirement of these senior securities or whether a reversal of the trend of the preceding 20 years has taken place.

Many industries in the industrial category have earnings records which are irregular, showing dependence on business conditions or other unsettling circumstances. Such industries obviously should avoid bond financing and keep preferred stock financing at a minimum. However, industrial concerns such as Borden, General Motors, General Electric, General Foods, International Shoe, J. C. Penney, Sears Roebuck, F. W. Woolworth, and many others have shown a stability of earnings which clearly justifies senior financing. It is perhaps fair to state that the firms best able to service senior securities are least likely to have them, but certainly there is no reason to hold that all industrials should refrain.

Importance of Intangibles

In open competitive operations the intangible assets of prestige, brand names, good will, management "connections," established sales outlets, experienced personnel, and patent rights are among the most important property an industrial concern may have. Sometimes these properties are assigned values on corporate balance sheets, and sometimes they are omitted entirely. Regardless of balance sheet valuations, however, it is obvious that these intangibles must be considered and compared with those of competitors, before any accurate appraisal of a concern's future may be made. General Electric Company is a major manufacturing establishment, but its great earning power rests also on its preeminence as a holder of patents and a leader in research. The investor in industrial securities is seeking earnings in competitive markets where intangible factors often make the difference between success and failure.

Competitive Advantage and the Antitrust Acts

For many years investors have tended to regard corporations enjoying positions of competitive advantage as particularly safe and desirable investment outlets. Advantages due to size, complete integration from raw material production to sale of finished product, patents, research and prestige leadership, brand names, and possession of well-organized sales distribution systems have always been reckoned as valuable assets. They must still be so reckoned. However, court decisions and antitrust actions brought by the attorney general's office since 1940 give warning to investors that the antitrust laws may threaten the legality of any competitive superiority great enough to promise substantial investment security.

In the "rule of reason" cases against the United States Steel Corporation and International Harvester Company in the early 1920s the decisions clearly indicated that size, superiority in research, and superiority in distribution were not illegal if no overt efforts were made to destroy or thwart competitors. This is still nominally the law, but it appears that vigorous and successful business methods are very likely to be assailed as illegal if they establish effective competitive advantages.[3] The courts do not sustain all the antitrust prosecutions undertaken by the energetic (and sometimes politically inspired) government attorneys, but the inconvenience and expense of defending the suits is often a burden.

Political Problems

Many industries are acutely subject to political and governmental policies of one sort or another. Some are chiefly affected as suppliers of goods or services to the government; among these are the aircraft manufacturers, who have little chance of steady profitable operation except with the help of military orders, and the air and ocean transport companies, whose mail service contracts are often frankly subsidies. Others are deeply concerned over tariffs, import quotas, and export financing policies; cigar manufacturers need tariffs on foreign cigars and sugar producers need import quotas on Cuban and other foreign sugar, if they are to continue to prosper in high-priced American markets; exporters of agricultural machinery, American flour, and many other products flourish or suffer in accordance with the volume of sales made possible to them under the terms of government gifts and loans to foreign countries.

Nearly all industries would be disturbed greatly by excess profits taxes, price controls, raw materials allocations, and the like, if these devices should become a part of American peacetime economic

---

[3] See A. D. H. Kaplan, *Big Enterprise in a Competitive System*, Brookings Institution, Washington, 1954, especially pp. 32–38.

policy. Tradition would suggest that such measures are likely to decline in interest and portent if the postwar world disturbances abate, but there are indications that the nation may enter into an era in which traditions will be broken. In that case investors might well wonder whether future successful research and pioneering would pay off in dividends or merely in excess profits taxes to the government. No one can be sure how the excess profits taxes of the future might be levied, but it seems likely that the possession of large and costly tangible assets would be a shield of sorts, for surely a reasonable return on tangible assets would not be confiscated as "excess profits." The usefulness of such valuable intangible assets as good will, brand names, and patents for this purpose might be doubted.

As respects price controls and materials allocations, they would seem most likely to affect the basic essential commodities, such as foodstuffs, clothing, and widely used raw materials. These are precisely the commodities whose production would normally afford secure and reliable investment opportunity. Obviously, price regulation and output control would make earnings less certain and investment opportunity subject to increased political as well as economic hazards.

Value of Industrial Securities

Quality considered, it would appear that industrial securities are usually at least as popular with investors as either utility or railroad issues. Certainly their typical price-earnings ratios are as high and their average yields as low as those of any other major group.

Industrial corporation bonds and high-grade preferred stocks are indicative of this situation. Such bonds as the American Tobacco 3s of 1969, Bethlehem Steel 2¾s of 1970, United Biscuit 2¾s of 1966, and Swift & Co. 2⅝s of 1972 commonly yield as little as the very best utility bonds. High-grade industrial preferred stocks are equally well regarded; such issues as Continental Can Company $3.75 preferred, du Pont $3.50 preferred, General Motors $3.75 preferred, General Foods $3.50 preferred, and Westinghouse Electric 3.8% preferred all sold in 1954 markets on a 4 per cent or lower yield basis. To some extent the popularity of high-grade industrial bonds and preferreds must be ascribed to the desire of investors for diversification. The varied nature of the industries responsible for these securities enables many industrials to be held in a portfolio without undue concentration in any single industry.

Industrial common stocks and the speculative grades of bonds and preferreds are equally well regarded. High-quality common stocks such as American Can, Dow Chemical, General Electric, Eastman Kodak, and Sears Roebuck seem preeminently sound for long-term investment and offer a high degree of stability as well. And almost all common stocks and speculative senior securities of industrial concerns are at times attractive for the possibility of extensive appreciation.

It is possible that the prices of industrial common stocks will be somewhat less stable in the ensuing few years than those of good-grade rail and utility issues. This has not been true of the past two decades, when railroad earnings were unstable in depression and war and utility fortunes were subject to both economic affairs and politics. But if price-level unsettlement, political policies, and a varying burden of taxation should affect the industrials' efforts during these coming years, it is not unlikely that their stock values will fluctuate as their prospects appear to vary.

Markets for Industrial Securities

Industrial securities are bought and sold in all the customary markets. Because of the great number of large industrial stock issues outstanding, such stocks appear to concentrate heavily on the stock exchanges; but great numbers of smaller industrial stock issues are traded over the counter as well. Large issues of industrial bonds are often listed, but the smaller ones are more often traded unlisted. In recent years many issues of bonds and high-grade preferred stocks have been placed privately with insurance companies, especially when the issues were serial ones or contemplated heavy sinking fund payments. These issues seldom find their way to the open markets.

QUESTIONS AND PROBLEMS

1. Explain what is meant by an "industrial." Are industrials as homogeneous a group as utilities?

2. Explain how working capital problems, changes in operating costs, changes in consumer demands, and changes in competitive pressure may

operate to prevent an industrial's earnings and dividends from following price-level changes closely.

3. How could medium-grade industrial preferreds profit from a price-level inflation? Could they profit from a deflation also?

4. Investigate and comment on the sales outlook for Kelsey-Hayes Wheel Corporation, Hunt Foods Company, Scovill Manufacturing Company, and Blaw-Knox Company. Which has the best immediate prospects? Long-run prospects? Why?

5. Would the break-even point be relatively high for a company with high fixed costs as compared with one having chiefly variable costs?

6. What features characterize industries in which competition is the most severe?

7. Explain how the amount of exploration work done by an oil company can affect its reported profit for the year. Would this be true of the research work done by General Electric or Radio Corporation of America or of a big sales-promotion campaign by a cigarette maker?

8. Other things being equal, which is the most conservative investment, stock in a department store chain which owns its own buildings, or that of a chain which leases its buildings? Would this conclusion hold good of an integrated producing-refining-marketing oil company, as compared with one which buys, refines, and markets? Could there be a disadvantage in integration, in that it compels a top management to try to understand too many things?

9. Why do bond buyers prefer concerns with substantial fixed assets?

10. What kind of capital structure should be employed by a fruit and vegetable canner who must build up a huge inventory during the canning season and sell it all out during the next few months? Do California Packing, Stokely-Van Camp, and Libby, McNeill & Libby do as you think best?

11. Do you regard the sugar companies, whose profits are profoundly affected by the government's sugar import quota system, as stable investments? Are the air lines any better off? Why?

12. What was the nature of the excess profits tax of 1942–1946? Would such a tax in peacetime be bad for investors, necessarily?

13. Look up the income sources of the following concerns, and identify their points of strength: General Mills, Cluett Peabody, International Business Machines, Chesebrough Manufacturing, General Motors, Procter and Gamble.

14. Review the factors which led to dividend omissions in 1949 by Armour and Company and Cudahy Packing. Why did Swift escape this?

REFERENCES

Badger, Ralph E., and Harry G. Guthmann: *Investment Principles and Practices,* Prentice-Hall, Inc., New York, 1951, Chaps. 8, 9.

Financial Handbook, The Ronald Press Company, New York, 1948, pp. 290–295.

Investment Bankers Association of America: *Fundamentals of Investment Banking,* Prentice-Hall, Inc., New York, 1949, Chap. 9.

Jordan, David F., and Herbert E. Dougall: *Investments,* Prentice-Hall, Inc., New York, 1952, Chap. 26.

Pickett, Ralph R., and Marshall D. Ketchum: *Investment Principles and Policy,* Harper & Brothers, New York, 1954, Chaps. 19–21.

Plum, Lester V., and Joseph H. Humphrey: *Investment Analysis and Management,* Richard D. Irwin, Inc., Homewood, Ill., 1951, Chaps. 9, 10.

Robbins, Sidney M.: *Managing Securities,* Houghton Mifflin Company, Boston, 1954, Chap. 26.

Chapter 18: BANK STOCKS

The stockholders of the 14,000 American commercial banks have nearly 14 billion dollars invested in the business. This sum alone is sufficient to place banking among the nation's major industries, even without consideration of the immensely larger amounts handled as deposits and in trust departments.

The stocks of well-managed banks have always been regarded as secure and stable income producers. The business is one in which both incomes and expenses are fairly steady, making reasonable earnings possible for most institutions in most years and enabling good banks to maintain steady dividend payments. However, the record of the banking business has been marred at times by fantastic speculation in bank stocks and by losses due to bad management in many banks. Although these are problems which the investor meets everywhere, their appearance in bank stocks is a particular warning against speculative enthusiasm and carelessness. No matter how stable the industry, care must be taken to avoid paying too much for a stock, and the soundness of a business and its management must always be verified.

American banks range in size from small local institutions with a very few stockholders to the huge metropolitan and branch banks with many thousands of stockholders. Though the larger banks presumably have the advantage of greater diversification in sources of income, it is not possible to say that either is preferable as an investment. Thousands of small local institutions have proved their worth for many years. However, the opportunity for investment in the small banks is available only infrequently to most people, while the larger banks' stocks are always purchasable as desired. This chapter will accordingly deal chiefly with large banks.

The Business

Banks obtain the bulk of their resources by accepting deposits of money from their customers. The deposit agreements obligate the

banks to return the money on demand or after a relatively short period of notice but permit them to use it while it remains on deposit
with them. In return for the use of the money the banks give their
depositors checking services and other banking facilities free or at
nominal cost and, in addition, pay interest on time and savings deposits. Banks also operate incidental services such as trust departments and safe-deposit vaults.

Because of the obligation to return their deposits on demand or
at short notice the banks find it desirable to keep a substantial percentage of their resources in cash or on deposit with other banks and
another substantial percentage invested in short-term loans or securities of very high quality. The short-term high-quality holdings are
termed secondary reserves; they are sold or collected to replenish the
bank's cash position if any large withdrawals of deposits occur. Secondary reserves usually consist of short-term government obligations,
although some banks also use call loans, bankers' acceptances, and
commercial paper, all of which can be classified as satisfactory holdings for this purpose.

Secondary reserves are not usually very profitable holdings for
banks. From 1935 through 1947 their average yield was close to 1
per cent. Even the temporary money stringency in mid-1953 did not
lift this average much above 2 per cent, and a few months later it
had returned to the 1½ per cent area. These low yields have induced
some banks to limit their holdings of short-term items and substitute
medium-term government bonds on which yields of up to 2 or 2½
per cent are sometimes available. Although the Federal Reserve
System obviously intends to stabilize the prices of medium- and long-
term government bonds to a reasonable extent, it must be assumed
that economic conditions affecting the demand for borrowed money
will affect the yields and the prices of such bonds, and that a bank
which invests its secondary reserves in them is taking the risk of
having to sell them on an adverse market, if it needs to raise cash.

Cash and secondary reserves in 1954 probably occupy about 35
per cent of the average bank's assets. Another 20 per cent is usually
invested in long-term government bonds, leaving the final 45 per
cent for loans and miscellaneous investments. The importance of
the final 45 per cent is attested by the fact that the insured commercial banks obtain more interest income from loans than from
all the rest of their resources combined. Of this final 45 per cent,

about 35 per cent will probably be loans, and most of the remainder will be state or municipal bonds. Corporate bonds are of minor importance as bank investments, and bank real estate and facilities usually amount to less than 1 per cent of total resources. Of course, banks vary greatly as to the distribution of their total resources, as Table 32 (on page 428) shows.

Table 30. Assets and Liabilities of All Insured Commercial Banks, December 31, 1942 and 1953

(In millions of dollars)

	1942	1953
Assets		
Cash and cash items...........	$27,593	$ 44,478
U.S. government obligations....	40,712	62,473
Other securities................	6,632	14,379
Loans and discounts...........	18,907	67,266
Bank premises.................	1,048	1,520
Other assets...................	567	946
Total......................	$95,459	$191,063
Liabilities		
Deposits......................	$87,820	$175,083
Other liabilities...............	583	2,566
Capital, surplus, etc...........	7,056	13,264
Total......................	$95,459	$191,063

Source: Data from *Annual Reports* of the FDIC.

Table 30 presents a comparative summary of banking resources and liabilities in the United States in 1942 and in 1953. Like most bank statements, the table does not distinguish clearly between secondary reserve items and other assets—for example, short-term and long-term government obligations are grouped together and certain other secondary reserve items are included as loans and discounts—but it indicates the general structure of the banking system.

The combined earnings report of all insured banks for 1942 and 1953 is presented in Table 31. These figures are similar in outline to those reported to their stockholders by the banks, but they may not be comparable in all respects, particularly on the subject of charge-offs and losses. Bank earnings statements are not standardized in form, and many banks do not provide enough detail to permit accurate analysis of their operations.

Table 31. Earnings and Expenses of All Insured Commercial Banks, 1942 and 1953

(In thousands of dollars)

	1942	1953
Current operating earnings:		
Interest on bonds	$ 610,298	$1,504,704
Interest on loans	804,717	3,107,885
Fees and charges	375,677	871,369
Total	$1,790,692	$5,483,954
Current operating expenses:		
Salaries and wages	$ 564,100	$1,686,886
Interest paid	175,010	534,493
Other	483,047	1,154,176
Total	$1,222,157	$3,375,555
Net current operating earnings	$ 568,535	$2,108,398
Profits on securities sold	66,457	38,865
Recoveries on assets charged off, etc...	156,318	113,508
Losses and charge-offs	271,118	448,323
Net profit before income taxes	$ 520,192	$1,812,451
Income taxes	79,541	786,490
Net profit	$ 440,651	$1,025,963

Source: Data from *Annual Reports* of the FDIC.

Leverage

A comparison of Tables 30 and 31 will indicate that the banks' gross revenues from all sources amounted to only 1.88 per cent of total resources in 1942 and 2.87 per cent in 1953 and that the final net profit amounted to only about one-half of one per cent of total resources in each year. Clearly, bankers do not earn their profits by employing their own funds. They earn them by employing the much larger amounts of other people's money which are left on deposit with them. The capacity of a bank to earn a good return on its capital funds depends in large part on its ability to attract and hold deposits.

It is generally said that under present-day conditions a bank whose capital funds exceed 10 per cent of its total resources will not easily earn a fair return. With equal truth it might be said that a bank whose capital funds amount to less than 5 per cent of total resources may not have enough capital, for losses or even temporary shrinkages in the value of its investments could impair its position very quickly. At the end of 1953 the average bank in the United States had capital funds (including contingency reserves) amounting to about 6.9 per cent of total resources. Banks in the Northeast section of the country averaged about 8.5 per cent, while those in the West and South averaged about 6 per cent. However, the banks' capital funds are being increased steadily out of earnings and will doubtless rise in ratio to total assets in any year in which inflationary expansion of bank assets does not occur.

The nature of a bank's assets also influences the amount of capital needed. If the resources were all in government bonds and cash, it might be argued that 2 or 3 per cent would be enough capital. On the other hand, a bank whose assets are predominantly employed in loans should have a high percentage of capital, to absorb any possible losses. Analysts usually consider this risk factor in relation to capital funds by computing the percentage of capital funds to *assets at risk*. It is assumed that cash and government bonds are risk-free. Therefore, the ratio becomes the percentage of capital funds to assets other than cash and government obligations. Table 30 indicates that the combined ratio for all insured banks was 26 per cent in 1942 and 16 per cent in 1953.

It is probably fair to conclude that a bank whose capital funds amount to less than 5 per cent of total assets or 15 per cent of assets at risk should seek more capital, for depression losses might cut deeply into an equity as small as this. Of course, it might be reasonable for one of these ratios to be low if the other was relatively high. Also, consideration can be given to the quality of the bank's assets and its reputation for conservatism or lack of it in bookkeeping procedures, when appraising these ratios.

Though the most important effects of the capital position of a bank are those concerned with earnings and degree of risk, the dividend rate and market price of the stock may also be affected. If the capital is inadequate, the directors will be very likely to limit dividends in an effort to increase the capital out of earnings. They may also plan to offer additional stock for sale, which may depress the market because of the dilution of per share earnings which would follow.

Growth of Deposits

Since a bank's earning power depends on its ability to obtain and hold deposits, the investor must consider this phase of its operations. Even when a bank is short of capital it must usually compete actively for new business, for a stagnant institution is not likely to retain the business it has. In general, the growth of deposits depends on the growth and prosperity of the community served, on the type of customers and industries the bank ordinarily serves, and on the competitive success of the bank.

Banks in areas which have developed greatly during the years 1941–1954 have received a phenomenal influx of new deposits. In many cases these deposits were held for a time in cash and short-term government securities, since the banks wished to be prepared to return the money if the new depositors did not remain in their communities. But many of these great industry and deposit shifts now appear to be permanent, indicating that some banks have sustained a loss of depositors, while others in the growing communities have gained greatly. Community prosperity is another factor which brings earning power to a bank. For example, banks located in farming regions received large amounts of deposits from their prospering clientele during the period 1942–1951. As long as these depositors remain prosperous their accounts will remain large, and the banks will have the use of large sums.

Banks which are closely affiliated with particular industries or types of business find their customers' affairs reflected in their own deposit totals. For example, banks with a preponderance of big business accounts lost deposits between 1945 and 1948, for big business in these years had much less than its normal proportion of the nation's money supply. Banks which operated neighborhood branches and catered to small personal accounts had a larger than normal share of deposits during this period.

The ability of a bank to give customers the services and accommodations they desire is a major factor in attracting and holding their deposits. The great Bank of America, in California, grew much faster than some of its competitors during the period 1937–1954 by convincing depositors that it would provide any type of banking services they needed whenever the need arose.

Finally, it should be noted that deposit growth for all banks is closely related to general economic conditions. During a boom or a wartime expansion the banks are able to accept customers' notes and newly printed government bonds as assets in return for newly created deposits credited to these borrowers on their books. In periods of business deflation or government fiscal surplus the borrowers obtain title to existing bank deposits and pay off their notes or bonds by canceling the deposits against them. This familiar banking process affects very greatly the total deposit supply of the nation and the total volume of earning assets which the banks hold. Because of its very obvious effect on prosperity and price levels, the banks' right to increase the supply of deposit money is regulated by the Federal Reserve System through the imposition of "reserve requirements"; but this is a complex topic beyond the scope of this book.

Growth of Loans

The importance of loans to the banks is attested by the fact that in 1953 the average income on loan funds was 4.84 per cent, while securities holdings earned only 2.01 per cent. Banks make business loans, mortgage loans, personal loans, and various other types of loans in the quantities which their banking policies and business opportunities make possible.

The most important element in lending policy is the willingness of the bank to take necessary risks and to adapt its procedures to the borrowers' needs. One of the reasons for the spectacular earnings of the Bank of America is its willingness to do these things. This bank expects to take occasional losses, but the large revenue from its loans provides a generous reserve to absorb the losses. By contrast, some banks limit their loans to routine and ultrasecure cases, take few losses, and content themselves with moderate earnings and security.

Obviously, the loan opportunities which come to the banks depend on their locations and clientele. Thus, personal installment loans and mortgage loans are available chiefly to small or branch-banking institutions with numbers of personal accounts. Medium-size business loans in large volume are obtained mostly in growing communities. Big business loans are available only to the big banks, and then mainly when big business is engaged in expansion, as it was in 1946–1954. In all cases, institutions serving growing communities or industries are likely to find more and better loan opportunities than those in static areas. Between 1945 and 1954 most banks were able to find record quantities of loans. Whether the same opportunities will be available in the next few years is a question of major importance to the banks.

Liquidity

A bank is said to be in a liquid condition when it has ample holdings of cash and secondary reserves. This is important, for two reasons: a liquid bank can readily provide funds for withdrawals, and it can also provide funds for additional loans or bond investment if it desires to increase its gross income. By contrast, a nonliquid bank cannot increase its gross income by making more loans, and it might even have to decrease gross income by reducing loans or selling bonds, if withdrawals took place. Other things being equal, an investor should always prefer a liquid bank over a nonliquid one.

Liquidity is usually measured in two ways: by the ratio of cash and government bonds to total assets and by the ratio of cash plus government bonds maturing in one year or less to total assets. The second of these calculations cannot always be made, since the banks do not all publish maturity data on their bonds, but it is usually possible to get some fragments of information about them. Many banks state the average time to maturity of all their government obligations. This provides a measure of relative liquidity.

Current Operations

As in other forms of business, investors in banks are keenly interested in the trend of gross income, the trend of expenses, and the ratio of expenses to gross income.

The importance of deposit volume and loan volume have already been noted. The other major factor helping to determine gross earnings is the rate of interest earned. This factor is largely determined by business conditions, competition, and Federal Reserve policy in so far as secondary reserve items and loans to big business are concerned. These competitive rates are subject to considerable fluctuation. The yield on long-term bonds and on mortgage, small business, and personal loans is more stable, for various reasons, and tends to lend relative stability to the gross revenues of the smaller banks. A factor adding some stability to the larger banks' receipts is the volume of fee earnings from trust departments and miscellaneous services, which may amount to as much as 15 to 25 per cent of total gross revenues.

About 31 per cent of the average bank's gross revenues is paid to employees in salaries. Another 10 per cent is paid as interest on deposits, 3 per cent goes for property taxes, and about 18 per cent goes to cover costs of materials, services, rent, depreciation, and miscellaneous items. The total of these items for all insured banks amounted to 62 per cent of gross revenue in 1953, as compared to 68 per cent in 1942. This ratio of operating expenses to gross revenue is called the operating ratio.[1] A low operating ratio is regarded as a point of strength, for it indicates that a sizable percentage decrease in gross revenue or increase in expenses could be absorbed without incurring a deficit.

In general it appears that big banks which specialize in large business accounts have lower operating ratios than the branch banks or small banks which handle smaller accounts. For example, the First National Bank of New York, which catered to big business exclusively, had a 1954 operating ratio of only 56 per cent. The Bank

[1] The 61 and 68 per cent ratios quoted here are based on figures of Table 31, which correctly classify income taxes as shares in net profit, not as operating expense. Many commercial bank statements include income taxes with operating expenses, and security analysts compute operating ratios on that basis, in order to be able to make comparisons. The operating ratios of Table 32 and those mentioned in the next paragraph are computed to include income taxes with the operating expenses.

of America, which operated 548 branches and has many small accounts, had a 1954 ratio of 79 per cent despite an extraordinarily large gross income. However, the low operating ratios of the big-business banks do not mean that they make more money. The small-account banks will generally get higher interest rates on loans and a larger gross revenue per dollar handled and can therefore earn a good profit after meeting their higher expense ratios.

Net Operating Earnings and Net Profit

Although bank income statements do not follow any definite standard form, most of them resemble the Citizens National Bank statement shown on page 422 in computing two kinds of net earnings figures, the *net operating earnings* and the *net profit*. The statements usually begin by reporting the current operating earnings, which consist of interest and fee receipts. Current operating earnings ordinarily do not include any profits from sale of securities or other assets which the bank may have owned. From the current operating earnings the statement deducts as current operating expenses all salary costs, interest payments, taxes, rent, depreciation, insurance, and similar items; income taxes are usually included with these items, but strangely, provisions for loan and investment losses are not included. This subtraction of current operating expenses and taxes from operating earnings determines the net operating earnings.

In computing net profits the typical bank adds to its net operating earnings its profits on sale of securities and its recoveries on assets previously written down and subtracts its provisions for current and future losses. In most banks these computations usually result in a net deduction, making net profits smaller than net operating earnings. However, some of the large banks do an important business as dealers in government and municipal bonds, and these banks often earn enough security profits to offset their loan losses, making it possible for net profits to equal or exceed net operating earnings. The trend of bond prices will of course affect securities profits or losses for all banks.

The net profits figure as reported by banks is often affected by bank bookkeeping policies. Provisions for future losses are sometimes made sporadically, as the management happens to feel optimistic or pessimistic. Some banks make excessive provision for losses, write down assets drastically, and as a result have large recoveries as the written-down assets are collected or sold. A change in Federal income tax policy in 1947 caused many banks to increase provisions for loan losses greatly in the years 1947 to 1951. The new income tax policy permitted banks to deduct from taxable incomes a pro-

Citizens National Trust & Savings Bank of Los Angeles
Comparative Statement of Earnings

	1954	1953
Operating Earnings:		
Interest and discount on loans.........................	$ 5,817,838	$ 5,626,325
Interest and dividends on securities...................	3,953,888	3,921,151
Other operating earnings.............................	2,929,672	2,531,034
Total...	$12,701,398	$12,078,510
Operating Expenses:		
Salaries and wages.................................	$ 5,249,217	$ 4,983,918
Assessments and taxes (other than on income)..........	320,948	283,785
Interest expense...................................	1,053,200	1,021,985
Other operating expenses............................	2,346,831	2,229,397
Total...	$ 8,970,196	$ 8,519,085
Net operating earnings before income taxes..............	$ 3,731,202	$ 3,559,425
Provision for Federal and State taxes on operating earnings	1,623,000	1,722,000
Net operating earnings after income taxes................	$ 2,108,202	$ 1,837,425
Net operating earnings per share..................	$ 8.43	$ 7.35
Add Other Income:		
Profits and recoveries on sales of securities.............	$ 1,003,963	$ 76,897
Other profits and recoveries.........................	37,037	159,072
Total...	$ 1,041,000	$ 235,969
Less Other Deductions:		
Write-downs of premiums on U.S. securities...........	$ 905,000	$ 303,380
Other write-downs, losses and transfers to reserves......	158,562	129,612
Provision for Federal and State taxes on other income and deductions.....................................	303,000	14,000
Total...	$ 1,366,562	$ 446,992
Net Profit...	$ 1,782,640	$ 1,626,402
Net Profit per share...........................	$ 7.13	$ 6.51

Source: *Annual Report, 1954.*

vision for losses equal to the average percentage loss rate sustained during the preceding 20 years, even though no losses were currently sustained; such loss provisions could be repeated annually until loss reserves equal to 3 years' average losses were accumulated. Actual losses each year are charged against this reserve, which may then be restored by another tax-deductible charge against earnings. Since the 20-year period included the disastrous depression years, these reserve provisions were very large; but the banks were willing to make them because of the income tax advantage in doing so. Another odd factor affected net profits and to a lesser extent current operating earnings in 1953; in that year a temporary decline in bond prices induced many banks to sell depreciated long-term bonds and replace them with other similar ones; the "loss" on the sold bonds reduced the 1953 net profits but permitted an important income tax saving. Another example of unusual factors in net profit computation is shown in the accompanying Citizens National Bank statement; in 1954 the bank sold certain securities at a large profit, bought others at a premium above their par value, and wrote this premium off by a $905,000 charge against net profit.

Because the net profits computations are likely to be distorted by these irregular influences, most securities analysts emphasize net operating earnings in their appraisals of bank stocks, despite the fact that neither bond profits nor provisions for losses are included in the figure. Net operating earnings are usually implied when earnings per share are discussed and when price-earnings ratios are quoted. However, no bank earnings figure may be taken for granted, for uniformity in definition does not exist. For example, the Bank of America in its annual reports ordinarily includes profits or losses on bond transactions in its computation of net operating earnings. Since the bank operates an important bond trading department, this practice has a significant effect on the reported net operating earnings. In this instance no one who reads the annual report carefully can be misled, for the report is detailed and thorough, but the instance illustrates the need for care in reading bank earnings statements, and especially in making comparisons between banks.

Because some banks do not publish earnings statements except annually, securities analysts try to gauge their earnings progress by computing *indicated earnings* from the published condition statements. This is done by the formula: indicated earnings for any fiscal period are equal to total capital, surplus, and undivided profits at the end of the period plus dividends paid during the period minus total capital, surplus, and undivided profits at the beginning of the period. This formula will compute a net profits figure provided each condition statement used reflects an accurate accounting for all incomes and expenses to date and proper adjustments for depreciation, taxes, recoveries, losses, and similar items. Unfortunately, banks' interim condition statements are not always so elaborately constructed, and the indicated earnings are therefore occasionally somewhat inaccurate.

Capital Accounts

Bank capital is ordinarily supplied by a single class of common stock, although a few institutions also have preferred stock outstanding. The traditional plan of bank financing calls for common stock only, but the banking laws were amended in 1933 to authorize the use of preferred stock or capital notes (subordinated debentures), when legislatures feared that depression losses would require emergency financing. A considerable number of banks issued preferred stocks or capital notes in 1934, but nearly all of these were retired within a few years.

Banks ordinarily show their capital accounts on their statements of condition under three headings: capital stock, surplus, and undivided profits. The capital stock and surplus items are regarded as permanent capital, while the undivided profits item is available for dividend purposes. In addition, some banks show "reserves for contingencies" on the credit side of their statements of condition. A reserve for contingencies is usually a portion of the bank's provision for future losses which has not yet been used to write down doubtful assets. Since losses requiring the use of the reserve have presumably not occurred, most analysts regard a reserve for contingencies as a type of surplus account and include it in their computations of a bank's net worth.

Some banks do not show their reserves for contingencies on their statements, but, instead, deduct them in lump sums from their various assets before compiling their statements. If the contingency reserves are larger than the losses which might normally be expected among the assets, it is clear that this practice will understate both the assets and the stockholders' equity in a bank. Other banks follow a somewhat similar practice in providing large reserves for contingencies and then using them at once to make drastic writedowns of good assets. This results in low asset totals and low apparent net worth and also causes large annual recoveries as the written-down assets are sold or collected. The banks then repeat the process by providing new reserves and writing down other assets.

The Citizens National Bank, whose condensed statement appears on page 426 illustrates at least two of these practices. There is no reserve for contingencies shown on the statement of condition, but the text of the annual report states that at December 31, 1954, the bank had a Reserve for Possible Future Loan Losses amounting to $1,782,322. This reserve was deducted from the actual total of active loans in order to arrive at the $120,497,322 of loans shown on the condition statement. All known losses were already charged off before these figures were compiled. Finally, this bank reports that its securities holdings have in certain cases been written down so that all United States government securities are now carried on the books at par or below and all securities combined are carried at less than their market prices.

It would appear that asset values and net worth accounts as reported by banks are acutely subject to bank accounting policy. Because of lack of disclosure of details about reserves, writedowns, and asset valuations, it is often necessary to depend on casual information and the bank's general reputation in such matters. As a group, the stronger banks may be suspected of understating assets and net worth.

When investment analysts compute net assets per share, they usually regard a reserve for contingencies as a surplus item, not as a valuation reserve, hence include it with the net worth of the bank. If unused reserves are known to have been deducted from the asset totals in preparing the statement of condition, as is the practice of the Citizens National and many others, these are also regarded as a part of the net worth, if the bank will disclose the amount. The net asset or book value per share is not so important to investors as many other figures concerned with a bank's operations, but it serves to indicate the amount of capital committed to support each share of stock and to provide, in comparison with other banks, a measure of the earnings and dividend performance which the stockholder has

Citizens National Trust & Savings Bank of Los Angeles
Condensed Statement of Condition at Close of Business, December 31, 1954

Resources

Cash and Due from Banks	$ 98,807,100.56
United States Government Securities	184,010,046.03
State, County and Municipal Bonds	15,819,238.71
Other Bonds	50,001.00
Loans and Discounts	120,497,322.22
Federal Reserve Bank Stock	450,000.00
Stock in Commercial Fireproof Building Co.—Head Office Building	348,500.00
Bank Premises, Furniture and Fixtures, and Safe Deposit Vaults (Including Branches)	3,978,202.81
Other Real Estate Owned	16,713.72
Customers' Liability under Letters of Credit and Acceptances	816,410.37
Earned Interest Receivable	1,359,269.61
Other Resources	145,921.52
Total	$426,298,726.55

Liabilities

Capital Stock	$ 5,000,000.00
Surplus	10,000,000.00
Undivided Profits	5,367,262.82 $ 20,367,262.82
Reserves for Interest, Taxes, and Expenses	2,325,412.96
Discount Collected—Unearned	1,541,313.99
Letters of Credit and Acceptances	816,410.37
Other Liabilities	427,857.38
Time Deposits	118,631,776.00
Demand Deposits	282,188,693.03
Total	$426,298,726.55

Source: *Annual Report, 1954.*

a right to expect in the long run from his own bank. As Table 32 indicates, bank stock prices since the war have fluctuated above and below their net asset values.

Dividends

Bank dividend policies usually incline toward regularity and stability. Most payments are made on a regular quarterly or semi-annual basis, with infrequent changes in rate, though a few institutions supplement their regular disbursements with year-end extras when circumstances warrant. Although banks are reputedly conservative in dividend matters, it appears that most of the large ones are fully as generous as leading industrial concerns; before the war their dividends averaged more than two-thirds of operating earnings, and in the period 1951–1953 they averaged more than half such earnings. However, a majority of the medium-sized and smaller banks pay out less than half of their earnings.

There is, of course, considerable difference between banks. Banks whose capital funds amount to less than 6 per cent of total resources or to less than 15 per cent of assets at risk, or which operate in growing communities where larger capital resources may soon be needed, should obviously either limit dividends or plan to sell additional stock. Many of the Southern and Pacific Coast banks are in this category. On the other hand, most banks in the Northeastern areas have plenty of capital and are able to pay out large percentages of their earnings; this is true, for example, of the First National Bank, the Irving Trust Company, and the Guaranty Trust Company, all of New York, which in 1954 distributed 95 per cent, 72 per cent, and 83 per cent, respectively, of their operating earnings. These institutions are typical among banks in having unbroken dividend records extending back for 92 years, 49 years, and 64 years, respectively.

Prices and Markets

Bank stocks are highly regarded by conservative investors. Although there seem to be many large blocks of bank shares in the hands of wealthy holders, there are also many small stockholders in most of the large banks. Bank stocks are also favorite investments for fire insurance companies, trust funds, and endowments.

Most bank stocks are traded over the counter, although a few, such as the Anglo-California National in San Francisco and the Farmers

Table 32. Comparative per Share Data on Leading Bank Stocks

Per share values and ratios	National City, New York	Guaranty Trust, New York	Conti- nental Illinois, Chicago	Bank of America, Cali- fornia	Security- First National, Los Angeles
Price per share, 2/16/55............	58	81	98	38	55
Price range, 1953–1954.............	59–46	75–62	101–81	39–29	57–38
Dividend rate, 2/16/55............	2.40	3.55	4.00	1.60	1.60
Yield, 2/16/55....................	4.1%	4.4%	4.1%	4.2%	2.9%
Net operating earnings, 1954........	3.38	4.30	7.21	2.64	3.38
Price-earnings ratio, 2/16/55........	17.1	18.8	13.6	14.4	16.2
Net profit, 1954...................	4.17	5.54	8.06	2.65	3.77
Net worth, 12/31/54...............	63.47	82.07	104.52	22.05	34.86
Ratio net worth to total assets, 12/31/54......................	9.8%	13.2%	8.7%	5.8%	6.6%
Ratio net worth to assets at risk, 12/31/54......................	18.3%	25.8%	25.2%	11.4%	20.9%
Ratio cash and U.S. securities to total assets, 12/31/54.................	50.5%	49.7%	68.5%	42.2%	69.9%
Average term to maturity of U.S. se- curities, 12/31/54...............	4.7 yr.	4.5 yr.	No data	4.5 yr.	6.0 yr.
Ratio loans to total assets, 12/31/54..	36.2%	44.2%	25.2%	44.1%	25.2%
Operating ratio, 1954..............	76.9%	69.1%	70.2%	79.5%	79.0%
Number of domestic branch banking offices, 12/31/54.................	71	3	0	548	141
Increase in deposits, 1944–1954......	31.6%	−24.4%	1.2%	90.1%	45.3%

Note: Although the net worth figures include certain known reserves held by each of these banks, the data on these may not be complete. Where the banks' own reports used unorthodox groupings of assets, liabilities, incomes, or expenses, such items have been regrouped on a uniform basis. Data for this table are primarily from the *Bank Stock Analyzer* by Blair & Co., and are adjusted to reflect stock splits and stock dividends down to February 16, 1955. In March, 1955, the National City Bank purchased the business of the First National Bank of New York and changed its own name to First National City Bank of New York.

and Merchants National in Los Angeles, are listed on the regional exchanges. The markets are usually steady on a day-to-day basis, but the prices participate in both primary and secondary market movements, fluctuating about as widely as high-grade industrial or utility shares. The general level of bank stock prices seems comparable to that of high-grade industrials; their price-earnings ratios are similar, and their yields average only slightly lower. There seems to be some provincialism in the pricing of bank stocks; the shares of the Eastern banks generally bring higher price-earnings ratios and lower yields than those of the South and West. Table 32 indicates something of bank stocks and their prices in the years 1952–1954.

Sources of Information

All of the usual sources of information provide data about bank stocks. In addition, dealers in bank stocks compile excellent comparative statistical sheets which enable a reader to appraise relative values and choose between the advantages offered in various banks. Table 32 suggests the nature of some of these dealers' compilations. Three of the leading statistical compilations are *Banks and Bank Shares,* published by Blyth & Co.; the *Bank Stock Analyzer,* published by Blair & Co.; and the *Bank Stock Guide,* published by American Bureau for Financial Research, Inc.

Inflation and the Banks

The extensive government bank borrowings during the depression and the war, plus the private borrowings after the war, played an important part in the price-level inflation of 1941–1953. During this period the volume of bank deposits increased from 65 billion to 177 billion dollars, or almost threefold. Though the steady inflation of the money supply kept interest rates much lower than they would have been otherwise, the great increase in deposit volume enabled the banks to triple their gross incomes and to increase their net operating earnings almost proportionately. Because capital funds increased less than 100 per cent during the period and because more than half of this increase came from reinvested earnings, the per share earnings of the banks showed very substantial gains.

There seems little chance that price levels and bank deposit volumes will return to prewar levels or even decline greatly from their 1953 levels. Consequently, the banks should be able to retain their increased per share earnings. Interest rates through the period 1945–1954 were at low levels, and any long-term changes which occur are not likely to be downward. A renewed inflation, on the other hand, could be harmful, for operating expenses would increase almost as fast as gross income and additional deposits should no longer be accepted without proportional increases in capital.

Government Regulation

Although statutory authority to regulate the banking business is scattered in irregular fashion among a number of state and Federal agencies, a fairly consistent pattern of regulation has emerged. Regulatory activities may be classified into three groups. First, banks are regulated as public service enterprises, to guard against duplication of facilities, cutthroat practices, and the like. New banks or branches must have certificates of convenience and necessity from the proper officials, interest payments to depositors must not exceed prescribed maximums, and standard minimum capital requirements are imposed. Second, banks are subjected to rules and supervision to assure the public of their solvency. Their bondholdings are restricted as to quality, their real estate loans are controlled as to both quality and quantity, stock investments are forbidden, all assets are reviewed by bank examiners, and deposit insurance is made virtually mandatory. Third, the banks are subjected to credit controls imposed for the good of the general public. They are compelled to hold varying portions of their deposits in cash reserve accounts, and their loans are often limited by law or regulatory pressure.

The general effect of these restrictions is not excessively burdensome. Limitations on competitive pressure are helpful, quality restrictions on loans and investments are desirable, and any effective Federal Reserve limitations on total lending power are likely to be compensated by higher interest rates on available funds. The cost of deposit insurance is considerable—at 1954 rates it absorbs about 3 per cent of the average bank's profits after taxes—and some earnings are lost as a result of personal and securities credit restrictions, but profitable banking is unquestionably possible. The regulations do not limit either earnings or dividends, except to discourage reckless lending and operations with inadequate capital.

Some of the intensified regulation which has developed since 1933 has greatly reduced the risks borne by bank stockholders. Deposit insurance has practically eliminated the hazard of "runs," which sometimes forced the sale of bonds and mortgages at a loss. Double liability, that is, the liability of a stockholder to pay assessments if his bank failed, has been eliminated from most banks. The Federal Reserve Act has been liberalized in ways which almost assure that hard-pressed solvent banks can obtain loans when they need them and that currency scarcities will not again be a hazard. Bank bond and loan portfolios will be scrutinized continuously by examiners to prevent unsound positions, but banks will not be closed during depressions because their sound holdings are temporarily depressed in price.

Competition

Practically every type of loan or investment made by banks is subject to competition. Insurance companies, finance companies, savings and loan associations, and government agencies all make loans or buy good bonds. There is nothing new in this situation, and some of the competition has been advantageous. In fact, the development of government-insured long-term loans to business firms, real estate owners, farmers, and veterans has enabled the banks to compete for business which would not otherwise be available to them.

Government lending has declined materially since 1940 in all fields including that of mortgage loans to farmers. The present political trend is toward government guaranties or subsidies to enable politically favored groups to get private loans, rather than toward a renewal of government lending. No one can predict the future of politico-economic affairs, but at least at present there seems to be no tendency to impair the position of the banks.

Summary

The investor who elects to invest in bank stocks has a number of additional decisions to make. He must decide whether he prefers a high-leverage institution with attendant risks and earning power or a conservative low-leverage one. He must choose between one with a vigorous lending policy or one which takes no chances. He must choose a branch bank or a big-office type, a big-business bank or a diversified one, a growing community or a mature one, a bank with a high operating ratio or a low one. The bank's dividend policy will be a factor; the type of industries served may be important; and always, the reputation of the bank and its management must be studied. All of these things must be considered in the light of bank stock prices; after all, price-earnings ratios and yields are the very proof of value.

It will be apparent at once that the investor who makes the above decisions after a correct forecast of coming events can choose to his own advantage. For example, if big business does not borrow heavily during the coming decade, and if government bond yields remain low, the New York banks may have only moderate earnings; but if the Pacific Coast continues to grow in population and industry, its banks will be very prosperous. Well-established banks are stable enough so that an investor takes less than the average stockholder risk in buying them, but there can be a great difference even here between buying with sagacity and merely buying.

QUESTIONS AND PROBLEMS

1. Would you call the Wells-Fargo Bank of San Francisco, which in 1953 had total capital funds amounting to 4.8 per cent of total resources, but whose cash and government bonds totaled 70 per cent of resources, a high-leverage bank?

2. Would you expect a generous dividend policy in this bank?

3. Why would a branch banking system have a high operating ratio? How could it be profitable?

4. Would the net asset value (book value) of a bank stock be of any importance to investors? Explain.

5. If a bank had a very high capital ratio and a price-level inflation caused its assets to double without requiring it to obtain additional capital, what would happen to its earnings per share?

6. If a bank with $95 million of deposits and $5 million of capital funds sold 20 per cent more shares for $1 million, what would happen to its earnings per share? To the value of its stock?

7. Why would a statistical tabulation similar to Table 32, but covering 20 or 25 leading banks, be important to an investor in bank stocks? Are such tabulations available?

8. Compute the net asset value and the earnings per share of Citizens National Bank from the statements given in this chapter. The bank had 250,000 shares outstanding on December 31, 1954. Its dividend rate was $3 per share per year. The stock then sold for $80 per share. Does this figure seem reasonable?

9. Judging by the statement presented in this chapter, and comparing

the statement with the statistics given in Table 32 for Bank of America and Security-First National Bank, would you call the Citizens National a conservative bank? Is it liquid? Should it seek more loans in an effort to increase its earnings? Is its $3 annual dividend, which was established in 1954, a reasonable one? Early in 1955 this bank split its stock 2 for 1, and subsequently offered its stockholders the privilege of buying 200,000 additional new shares at $33 each. Did the bank need this additional net worth? How much per share can it earn on 700,000 shares? Can it pay a $1.50 dividend on them? Would you now expect a change in the bank's loan or investment policies?

10. Which offers the most promise at present, investment in the stock of the big New York banks or in those of outlying cities? Why?

11. Explain why a bank's deposits grow when the surrounding community is prosperous.

12. Which would need the largest secondary reserves, a bank in a copper-mining community or one in a diversified city such as St. Louis? Why?

13. Does the present trend of political and economic affairs appear to be strengthening or weakening the position of the banks? Cite evidence.

14. Would bank stocks be suitable "defensive" holdings for investors who fear possible business depression? Explain.

15. Why have trustees, endowment funds, and fire insurance companies favored bank stocks as investments?

REFERENCES

Badger, Ralph E., and Harry G. Guthmann: *Investment Principles and Practices,* Prentice-Hall, Inc., New York, 1951, Chap. 15.

Comptroller of the Currency: *Annual Report,* Washington, D.C., 1935–date.

Federal Deposit Insurance Corporation: *Annual Report,* Washington, D.C., 1935–date.

Jordan, David F., and Herbert E. Dougall: *Investments,* Prentice-Hall, Inc., New York, 1952, Chap. 27.

Robbins, Sidney M.: *Managing Securities,* Houghton Mifflin Company, Boston, 1954, Chap. 31.

Chapter 19: INVESTMENT COMPANIES

Investment companies are variously known as investment companies, investment funds, or investment trusts. They offer the investing public nearly 300 securities issues, representing 200 different issuers, having over 1,800,000 investors, with total assets exceeding $5,000,000,000.[1]

The basic function of an investment company is to offer an investor the security of diversification plus some degree of management supervision in a single investment. It does this by selling its own securities to the public and investing the proceeds in a diversified list of stocks and bonds. Subsequently these investment holdings may be sold and replaced by others as circumstances warrant. The objectives of the investment company, its method of operation, the types of investment it will make, and the degree of risk it will assume are all matters for decision by the individual company. The investor chooses the investment company and the type of security in it which meet his needs and his tastes but delegates the burden of studying business corporations, industry trends, and market conditions to the management of his company.

It is clear that an investment company will have certain operating expenses to pay and that these expenses must necessarily be interposed between the investor and the underlying securities which are the source of his income. This means that an investment company security is a wise choice only if the diversification and management advantages which it offers are worth the added cost. The added annual costs typically amount to .50 per cent to .75 per cent of the principal sums managed by the companies;[2] but in the opinion of the author this is more than compensated to the average unskilled investor by the advantages offered.

Investment companies in the United States are a relatively recent development, most of them having been founded since the early twenties. The idea is allegedly borrowed from the British, who have

[1] *Investment Companies, 1953,* Arthur Wiesenberger & Co., New York, pp. 21, 25.
[2] See Table 33.

operated investment companies extensively, but on the whole con-servatively, for many years. The American investment company movement did not have a conservative early history; much of its early experience was gained during the boom of 1927–1929 and the depression which followed and is replete with error, fraud, and losses.[3] This era of confusion may be said to have closed with 1940, for in that year the sound and constructive Investment Company Act imposed upon the whole industry the high standards which the best companies had developed through experience.[4] It cannot be said that investment companies are now immune to losses due to management error, but it is fair to say that they are in nearly all cases operated openly, honestly, and in the interests of their security-holders.

Form of Organization

Investment companies are usually either corporations or Massa-chusetts trusts. Directors or trustees may be elected, or a board of trustees may be self-perpetuating, as in the case of some of the older Massachusetts trusts. Directors or trustees establish the company's policies within the scope of the charter or trust indenture, supervise the investment portfolio, and choose the investment advisers and company managers. Although the Investment Company Act pro-hibits any single investment banking firm from furnishing a major-ity of the directors for an investment company, many companies are regarded as closely allied to investment firms: for example, Tri-Continental Corporation is identified with J. & W. Seligman & Co., Lehman Corporation with Lehman Brothers Co., and Century Shares Trust with Brown Brothers Harriman & Co. Investment counsel firms whose chief function is the sale of research service to investment companies, and securities distributors whose main func-tion is the selling of investment company shares to the public, are identified as dominant in the affairs of other investment companies. For example, the Calvin Bullock organization sponsors six com-panies with total assets at year-end 1953 of 237 million dollars. Other investment companies, such as Adams Express Company, Massa-

[3] See Securities and Exchange Commission, *Report on Investment Funds and Investment Companies,* Washington, 1939–1940.

[4] The act is reviewed in Chap. 12.

chusetts Investors Trust, and Wellington Fund, are regarded as independent of professional external control, though they of course have directors who are in the securities business.

Though final decisions on investment policy and the purchase or sale of individual investments will be the province of directors or trustees, an investment company must either maintain or employ a research organization of considerable scope to provide information and advice. This work is done by investment company employees in a substantial number of cases, but in many instances it is done on a contract basis by investment counsel firms. In a number of such instances the investment counsel firms organized the investment companies, with the marketing of their services as a chief objective. A third method of providing adequate research and advice is that of maintaining a research agency jointly with others. The Tri-Continental group of four investment companies find this convenient.

When investment counsel is contracted for and all investments are kept in securities, there is little occasion for an investment company to maintain an employee organization. Consequently, the entire management of an investment company is often contracted for, except for policy matters on which instructions can be issued to the contracting firm by directors or officers. Even the securities owned by an investment company are usually in the safekeeping of a bank, trust company, or investment house. These devices help to keep down investment company expenses.

Types of Investment Companies

In a very broad sense there are four types of investment companies: the closed-end company, the open-end company, the fixed trust, and the face-amount certificate company. Only the first two are of importance at present, and 80 per cent of all investment company resources in 1954 was in the open-end companies.

A closed-end investment company is an ordinary business concern whose securities are similar to those of any business corporation. It is unusual only because its corporate business consists largely of investing its funds in the securities of other corporations and managing these investment holdings for income and profit. The stockholders and bondholders in a closed-end company are perfectly free to sell their holdings on the securities markets for whatever they will bring or to buy more from others if they are so minded. However, they have no right to ask the investment company to redeem their shares or to sell them more. The company functions as an ordinary business corporation, earning what it can from dividend receipts and market profits and paying dividends when it can. If its operations are extraordinarily successful or promising, the market price of its stock may rise above the net asset value per share of its investment holdings. If it does not do well, the market price is certain to drop below the net asset value. Most closed-end investment companies are corporations, but the group includes a number of Massachusetts trusts, such as Amoskeag Company and Boston Personal Property Trust, and at least one joint stock company, the Adams Express Company.

An open-end investment company is one which continuously offers new shares for sale and which stands always ready to redeem existing shares in cash at the request of any stockholder. Meanwhile, the resources in the possession of the company are invested in securities, and periodic dividends are paid to stockholders as earnings warrant. Although stockholders are free to sell their stock to others or to buy more from others, it is clear that market prices can never deviate far from the sale and redemption prices set by the company. Most open-end companies sell new shares at net asset value (total market value of asset holdings minus liabilities divided by number of outstanding shares) plus a "loading" or marketing fee, and redeem shares approximately at net asset value.[5] This keeps any possible resale price between these two limits. Open-end companies are usually either Massachusetts trusts or corporations. In recent years the trade literature has mostly referred to the open-end companies as *mutual funds*.

Since the open-end shares must constantly be sold on a nationwide basis, most companies have sales "distributors" to carry on this task. The distributor is usually an established securities firm or a selling firm organized for the purpose, which has an exclusive franchise to buy all new shares issued by the investment company. The distributor organizes a selling group consisting of practically all

[5] Values for sales purposes will be computed at least twice daily and for redemption purposes at least once daily, in order to keep abreast of changing stock market prices. The value of any open-end share thus changes daily, in proportion to the changing values of the investments held by the company.

NASD members who are willing to sign the selling group agreement. These selling group members may then get new shares from the distributor at a concession from the public offering price for sale to their customers. The public offering price per share must usually be high enough to (1) add a sum equal to the net asset value of existing shares to the company's resources, (2) pay the clerical costs of recording the new share, (3) pay the distributor, and (4) pay the selling group member. Most open-end companies make the public offering price 107 to 109 per cent of net asset value [6] for investments under $25,000, a figure which compares reasonably with the cost of marketing common stocks in ordinary corporations. However, at least three companies, the Loomis-Sayles Mutual Fund, Inc., and the two Scudder, Stevens & Clark funds, make neither a selling markup nor a surrender charge. These funds are operated by investment advisers who sell only on application to their own organizations. There is an over-the-counter market in the shares of some of the larger open-end investment companies, through which an investor might sell for a little more than net asset value or buy for a little less than the public offering price. However, it is not a well-publicized market, for members of the selling group do not participate in it, and many dealers regard such activities as slightly unethical when the selling group is maintaining fixed price schedules.

Capital Structure and Leverage

Investment company shares can be given a speculative quality akin to leverage in at least three ways. First, the investment company itself could be financed on a leverage basis by sale of bonds and preferred stock as well as common. Second, the investment company might invest in the common stocks of high-leverage corporations. Third, the investment company might make its investments in frankly hazardous industries or concerns, whether leverage existed or not. If conservatism is preferred to leverage and speculation, the investment company may follow exactly the reverse of these leverage policies. It may avoid leverage itself by selling only common stock, it may avoid speculative investment by refusing to buy high-leverage or speculative stocks, or it may even invest in high-quality preferred

[6] Funds investing chiefly in bonds often sell at 104 or 105 per cent of net asset value.

stocks or bonds, thus making its stockholders actually senior security-holders. Various investment companies do each of these things.

With one significant exception, all the investment companies which use leverage through their own capital structures are closed-end companies. Not all closed-end companies have senior securities outstanding—in fact, over half of them have not—but those which have provide both conservative and speculative investment opportunity. A few bonds are available, such as the Tri-Continental Corporation 2⅞s of 1961. These are moderately well protected and yielded 3¼ to 3½ per cent in 1954 markets. Preferred stocks are numerous and range from good-quality issues yielding about 4.5 per cent in 1954 markets to slimly covered issues yielding 7 per cent or more. There are also preferred stocks whose claims to assets and income exceed the total available company resources. The common stocks of the closed-end companies must therefore range from debt-free ownership in the nonleverage companies to moderate-leverage, high-leverage, and negative-equity situations. Strange as it may seem, investment company common stocks subject to very high leverage sometimes bring a significant price even when they have a negligible equity in earnings or assets, because of their dynamic possibilities in a stock market boom.

Investment and Operating Policy

An investment company must make four basic decisions with respect to its investment policy. First, it must decide whether it is to be strictly a diversified investment company, or whether it wishes to invest substantial sums in "special situations" where it may have an important voice in the management. The open-end investment companies are mostly diversified, meaning that as a rule they neither place more than 5 per cent of their assets in any one stock or bond, nor own over 10 per cent of the stock of any corporation. However, a number of closed-end companies make a business of buying large or controlling interests, developing the corporations involved, and possibly attempting to sell the whole commitment later. For example, Atlas Corporation in 1947 acquired 8.4 per cent of the common stock of Consolidated Vultee Aircraft Corporation and made its president the chairman of Consolidated Vultee's directorate. After

several years on this basis, Atlas was able to sell its entire commitment to purchasers desiring to gain control of Consolidated Vultee.
This type of transaction is a regular phase of Atlas's operation.

Second, the investment company must decide whether to operate
as a balanced fund, a bond fund, a preferred stock fund, a general
common stock fund, or a specialized industry fund. A *balanced fund*
is one which undertakes to maintain a portfolio of securities of all
types, including always the proportion of bonds and stocks which a
well-balanced individual portfolio would have at the time. The proportioning naturally changes as conditions change. The balanced
fund is the most completely managed diversified investment available, since the management decides on both portfolio tactics and
choice of securities. *Bond* or *preferred stock funds* are those committed to investment largely or exclusively in these types of securities. On the whole they have not been outstandingly popular,
though they make it possible through diversification for medium-
grade securities to afford the investor a fair degree of safety. Most investment companies are intended chiefly as *general common stock
funds.* Any general common stock fund may on occasion retire from
the stock market and hold large amounts of cash or government
bonds, but its major functions are investment and speculation in
common stocks, and it will be "out of the market" only until attractive common stock opportunities become available. The investor in
a common stock fund regards it as a diversified and managed common stock investment; other elements in his portfolio can be provided by other investments. An interesting variation in common
stock funds is provided by *specialized industry funds,* in which the
investment is confined to single industries and the management's
function is limited to choosing the stocks in which the available
resources are to be kept. The investor in a specialized industry fund
procures a prorata interest in a group of selected steel stocks or oil
stocks or utility stocks or whatever industry he chooses. Within the
industry chosen by himself he obtains diversification and professional selection.

The third basic decision on investment company policy is whether
to participate in underwriting securities offerings. Investment companies with several millions in resources are frequently able to earn
underwriting fees simply by agreeing to buy the unsold portions of
new or secondary offerings if the planned sales effort fails. Closed-end

companies frequently do this, usually operating through a subsidiary which is regularly in the investment banking business.

The fourth decision on investment policy involves a choice of objectives. Shall the company spend heavily on study and research, in the hope of earning market profits, or shall it invest conservatively, operate economically, and offer its stockholders a stable dividend income? If it chooses to try for market profits, shall the effort be made in good-grade stocks, or will it be better to use risky ones and depend on diversification for security? In seeking market profits, is the policy to be one of selecting promising stocks and holding them until they develop, or is it to be one of attempting to "beat the market" by a constant process of buying low and selling high? While investment company policies are not always consistent on these points, it will be possible to determine where the emphasis lies by studying their portfolios and their records.

The Investment Company Act of 1940 requires that each investment company state its general investment and operating policies clearly and thereafter change only after stockholder approval. These statements may be found in the prospectuses of the open-end companies, and the financial services summarize them in their descriptions of all companies. The investor may therefore select an investment company whose policies conform to his needs and tastes.

Specialized Open-end Groups

A novel opportunity for diversified speculation is afforded by Group Securities, Inc., Keystone Custodian Funds, National Securities Series, and certain other *groups* of open-end companies. An investor entering one of these groups has a choice of specialized investment companies, perhaps including one which owns only bonds, one owning only preferreds, one owning very high-grade common stocks, one owning very volatile common stocks, or one each in several specialized industries, such as steel, oil, or utilities. After he makes his initial choice he is furnished with data on the economic outlook for all of the specialized companies and is permitted to surrender the shares he holds in exchange for shares in one of the other specialized companies, if he wishes. There is usually some cost to this shift, possibly about 4 per cent of the sum involved. However, it provides a convenient way for a small-time speculator to shift from one industry to another or from stocks to bonds, or vice versa, with the constant advantage of diversification, professional stock selection, and market letter advice, at a cost not greatly in excess of brokerage fees plus odd-lot differentials.

Investment Companies and Income Taxes

An investment company operating as a corporation, joint stock company, or Massachusetts trust is basically subject to the same income taxes which any business corporation would pay, and its dividends are taxable to its stockholders just as any corporate dividends would be. However, the income tax laws for some years have provided special tax advantages for "regulated investment companies" which follow prescribed diversification and dividend procedures. The distinction may be important for investors attempting to limit their tax burdens.

An investment company being taxed as an ordinary corporation has two general types of taxable income. The first, which may be called *taxable investment income,* consists of 100 per cent of taxable interest received plus (approximately) 15 per cent of dividends received, minus all operating expenses and general taxes. This is taxable at the (1954) regular corporate rate of 52 per cent. The second type, *capital gains,* consists of profits realized on sale of investments. Net short-term capital gains (those on assets owned less than 6 months) are taxable at 52 per cent and net long-term capital gains at 26 per cent. When an investment company in this tax category pays dividends to its stockholders, the dividends are usually also taxable income to the stockholders. However, there may be an exception in some cases; if the investment company has sustained severe investment losses in the past and thus has a surplus deficit, the dividends which it pays out of current dividend and interest receipts may be technically a return of capital to its stockholders, hence not taxable income to the stockholders. Investment companies able to pay tax-free cash dividends are obviously interesting to high-bracket taxpayers. Examples of this sort of thing may be found in the histories of Adams Express Company, Atlas Corporation, Equity Corporation, Pennroad Corporation, and others.

An investment company may at its own request cease to be taxed as an ordinary corporation and instead become a *regulated invest-*

ment company for tax purposes, if it (1) obtains at least 90 per cent of its gross income from interest, dividends, and securities profits, with less than 30 per cent from short-term profits; (2) maintains a substantial degree of diversification, as defined in the law; and (3) pays out in dividends at least 90 per cent of its net investment income. A regulated investment company pays no income tax on any of its income or capital gains which it distributes to its stockholders in dividends. On the undistributed portion it pays the regular corporation rates. The stockholders of a regulated investment company must be notified as to whether their dividend receipts originate in investment income plus short-term capital gains or in long-term capital gains. The stockholders must record the former as ordinary taxable dividend income, but the latter they may count as their own personal long-term capital gains, to be taxed at the favorable capital gains rates.

If an investment company is willing to distribute both net investment income and capital gains in dividends to its stockholders, its tax saving as a regulated investment company may be fairly substantial. It will be large if the investment company draws a large share of its income from bond interest or market profits. On the other hand, a company which wishes to limit its dividends to the amount of its net investment income will be fully taxed on its capital gains and will probably save only a little by becoming a regulated company. The desire to limit dividends usually arises when a company with bonds or preferred stock outstanding is obligated to do so because of indenture or charter provisions, or when conservative managements believe that market profits should be retained in surplus as a protection against possible future losses. There is one other deterrent to accepting status as a regulated company: regulated companies' dividends may never be tax-free to their stockholders except in actual liquidation. Companies with surplus deficits therefore do not usually become regulated investment companies. However, nearly all the open-end companies and most of the diversified closed-end ones are now regulated.

Financial Reports

Investment companies usually furnish thorough and informative financial reports to their stockholders. The year-end annual reports are supplemented by semiannual or quarterly mid-period reports, and additional data can usually be had in the financial reporting services if desired. The reports to stockholders usually contain a balance sheet, an income statement, a list of securities held, and various analytical summaries classifying the company's securities,

Tri-Continental Corporation Balance Sheet, December 31, 1954

Assets

Cash in banks..		$ 2,935,533
Investments in U.S. Government securities—at cost (note 1)		500,000
Investments in other securities—at cost (note 1):		
Securities of and advances to majority owned subsidiary corporations.......................................	$ 2,140,860	
Securities of other corporations.........................	122,039,275	
		124,180,135
Receivable for dividends and interest.....................		606,804
		$128,222,472

Liabilities, Capital Stock, and Surplus

Interest accrued and dividends payable....................		$ 745,305
Payable for securities loaned for cash......................		153,300
Payable for securities purchased...........................		1,095,656
Accrued expenses and taxes...............................		1,503,159
Funded debt...		18,060,000
Capital Stock:		
$2.70 Cumulative Preferred Stock, $50 par value........	$40,537,000	
Common Stock, $1 par value (note 5).................	4,185,881	
	$44,722,881	
Surplus (note 1)...	61,942,171	
		106,665,052
		$128,222,472

Excerpts from Balance Sheet Notes

1. Investments at value as at December 31, 1954, amounted to $236,119,372 ($111,439,237 more than cost) before deducting $26,189,000 for possible Federal income tax payable if net unrealized appreciation of investments were realized. The aggregate cost of investments for Federal income tax purposes, as calculated by the Corporation from its tax records, without audit, amounted to $119,757,952.
5. There are reserved for issuance 4,142,706 shares of Common Stock for exercise of 3,261,974 Warrants, each of which entitles the holder to purchase 1.27 shares of Common Stock at any time at $17.76 per share.

analyzing its surplus account, explaining its position with respect to unrealized profits and losses, etc.

The balance sheet of an investment company may list its securities investments either at cost prices or current market values. The accompanying Tri-Continental Corporation balance sheet shows the

Tri-Continental Corporation Summary of Assets, December 31, 1954

Based on market or fair value

Cash and receivables.	$ 3,542,337
Investments in U.S. Government securities.	497,188
Investments in other securities.	235,622,184
Gross assets.	$239,661,709
Current liabilities.	3,497,420
Net investment assets.	$236,164,289
Provision for possible Federal income tax on net unrealized appreciation of investments.	26,189,000
Net assets before deducting funded debt.	$209,975,289

Asset Coverages and Asset Value

Debentures—asset coverage per $1,000 of $18,060,000 principal amount.	$11,626
$2.70 Preferred Stock—asset coverage per share of 810,740 shares.	236.71
Common Stock—asset value per share of 4,185,881 shares.	36.16

Asset coverage for the Preferred Stock is after deducting the principal amount of Debentures. Asset value for the Common Stock is after the Preferred Stock at $50 per share, which is the value in liquidation; the redemption value of the Preferred Stock is $55 per share and accrued dividends.

If all the outstanding Warrants had been exercised as of December 31, 1954, and the Corporation had received the aggregate purchase price of $73,574,464 therefor, the asset value of the Common Stock would have been equal to $27.00 per share.

securities at cost, but appends a footnote stating their market value. In computing a net asset value per share from this type of balance sheet, it is customary to substitute market values for the cost values in the statement, thus basing the net asset value on market price rather than cost.

Tri-Continental's *summary of assets,* which accompanies the balance sheet in all of this company's published reports, compares the market values of the company's assets with the claims represented by the outstanding debts and shares. This statement is not a conventional form such as a balance sheet, but it illustrates the calculations common to all leverage types of investment companies. However, it contains one controversial feature; in computing the asset values available for bondholders and shareholders, the company has deducted $26,189,000, or over 12 per cent of its total assets, which would be payable as capital gains taxes if the company sold all its assets, realized the available market profits thereon, and then failed

Massachusetts Investors Trust Income and Expense, Year Ended December 31, 1954

Income

Cash dividends received.....................................	$29,304,014
Dividends in stocks of other than paying companies..............	393,144
Discount earned on short-term bills and notes...................	108,659
	$29,805,817

Expense

Compensation of Trustees and Advisory Board including amounts for retired Trustees......................................	$771,179	
Research department and general office.......................	406,923	
Fees paid State Street Trust Company:		
As custodian and agent..................................	42,250	
As transfer and dividend paying agent......................	176,254	
Legal fees..	16,000	
Auditors' services..	9,900	
Federal tax on issue of Trust's shares and other taxes...........	13,650	
Securities Act registration fee..............................	4,023	
Printing and postage......................................	105,042	
Miscellaneous..	88,237	1,633,458
Net (Investment) Income................................		$28,172,359

to distribute these profits as capital gains dividends. It does not seem likely that the company will do things which would subject it to this huge tax, and if it does not the resources will remain available to its securityholders. Consequently, the net asset value of $36.16 per share reported here is an extremely conservative understatement. Most investment companies have substantial unrealized profits in their security holdings because of the postwar rise in the stock market, so investors should be careful to note whether the net asset values reported to them have been reduced by provisions for possible but unlikely taxes.

The statement of income is a financial report which shows the investment company's interest and dividend income, its normal running expenses, and the resulting *net investment income*. If the company engages in underwriting operations, the income from these will be included. The normal running expenses include management expenses, investment research costs, and ordinary taxes. However, gains or losses from securities transactions and brokerage fees and taxes connected with securities transactions are not usually included, for these are not regarded as regularly recurring incomes and expenses. The Massachusetts Investors Trust income statement which appears on page 446 is a typical one. This company is one of the very large diversified open-end funds.

The net investment income per share is the figure usually tabulated for investment companies in pocket manuals and other compilations in which per share earnings are shown. This may often be a deceptively small figure, for it obviously does not include an investment company's realized or unrealized securities profits, nor does it in any way recognize the value of the undistributed earnings of the corporations whose stocks are owned, yet it does include the expenses involved in selecting and watching the securities on which profits are expected.

Massachusetts Investors Trust's *statement of changes in net assets* (page 448) is a form used by many open-end funds to summarize their financial experience for the year. It compares the net investment income with the ordinary dividends paid from it (note that the payout was practically 100 per cent), it reports the profits on sale of securities (note that the capital gains dividend approximately equals this profit computed on a tax basis), it reports the change in unrealized profits due to stock market fluctuation, and it reports the sales of new shares and redemption of old ones during the year.

Both this statement and the Tri-Continental balance sheet on page 444 point up a tax problem which bothers many investment company managements. The unrealized profits on securities purchased early in the postwar period are very large. Like all others, these securities should be sold if their prices become too high or if money is needed for other opportunities—yet each sale would realize a large capital gain which must either be distributed as a taxable dividend to the recipient or retained as a taxable profit in the investment company. Either outcome is unfair to a new shareholder in the investment company who has just paid net asset value plus a loading charge for his shares, and even an old shareholder is re-

Massachusetts Investors Trust Changes in Net Assets, Year Ended December 31, 1954

Net Assets December 31, 1953:

Principal...		$522,188,718	
Undistributed net income.............................		179,680	$522,368,398

Income:

Net income for the year as per statement................		$ 28,172,359	
Add—net amount for participation in undistributed net income included in the price of shares issued and repurchased		228,320	
		$ 28,400,679	
Deduct—ordinary dividends ($1.02 per share).............		28,412,613	
Decrease in undistributed income.....................			(11,934)

Principal:

Gains and Losses on Investments—based on average cost:

Realized Net Gain (on federal income tax basis $8,191,378)	$ 8,416,050		
Deduct—special distribution (29¢ per share) from net gain on investments realized in 1954, payable February 18, 1955, to shareholders of record December 31, 1954....	8,197,548		
	$ 218,502		
Increase in Unrealized Appreciation *.................	241,492,217		241,710,719
Special distribution (24¢ per share) from net gain on investments realized in 1953, paid February 19, 1954, to shareholders of record January 4, 1954..............			(6,423,645)

Trust Shares Issued and Repurchased—exclusive of amounts allocated to income above:

Receipts for 2,531,709 shares sold.....................	$ 57,749,253		
Asset value of 224,568.8 shares issued in special distribution February 19, 1954..........................	4,311,720		
Deduct—cost of 1,241,800.1 shares repurchased and retired	(28,630,651)		33,430,322

Net Assets December 31, 1954:

Principal...		$790,906,114	
Undistributed Net Income.............................		167,746	$791,073,860

* Total unrealized appreciation of investments at December 31, 1954, amounted to $423,-563,014, or 53 per cent of total assets.

luctant to have his net asset value depleted by taxes. Consequently, investment company managements are reluctant to "manage" their resources as effectively as they might if tax depletion was not a factor.

Operating Results

The efficiency of management in investment companies is commonly measured in two ways: by test of the statement of income and by a long-term measure of *performance*. Neither is a perfect check, because neither allows for the degree of security which has been

Table 33. 1953 Income and Expense Ratios of Certain Investment Companies

Company	Total dividend and interest income as per cent of average assets	Expenses as per cent of average assets	Expenses as per cent of total income	Net investment income as per cent of average assets
Adams Express..............	4.6	.56	12.2	4.0
Atlas......................	4.4	1.83	41.9	2.6
Lehman....................	3.5	.56	16.1	2.9
Tri-Continental..............	4.7	.38	8.2	4.3
27 Closed-end companies.....	4.6	.69	14.8	3.9
Broad Street Investing.......	5.2	.44	8.5	4.8
Bullock Fund...............	4.7	.55	11.7	4.2
Mass. Investors Trust........	4.8	.27	5.5	4.5
Wellington Fund............	4.1	.50	12.2	3.6
69 Open-end companies.......	4.5	.73	16.1	3.8
S & P 90-stock Index........	5.9			

Note: Expenses do not include bond interest or income taxes.
Source: Data adapted from *Investment Companies, 1953*, by Arthur Wiesenberger & Co.

afforded by conservative handling of the assets. Income statement analysis has the further defect of failing to allow for deliberate choice of low-dividend or nondividend stocks which appear likely to rise in price or for high research expenses incurred in a search for profit opportunities.

In the statement of income the three essential figures are the total income, the total operating expenses, and the net investment income. The ability of management to keep the gross and net income high and the expenses low is a measure of efficiency. All of these items may properly be shown as percentages of the average value of assets held, though the percentages must be expected to vary from year to year because of fluctuations in the market value of the assets. Expenses are also shown as percentages of total income. Table 33 shows percentages compiled from 1953 company reports.

An *index of performance* is a percentage measure of total gain or loss in an investment fund between two dates. For example, if a non-leverage fund had a net asset value per share of $10 at the beginning of a year, paid a $1 dividend during the year, and ended the year with a net asset value of $11, it is clear that the performance gain for the year was $2, or 20 per cent of the initial $10 value. An index of performance might cover only a single year, or it might be measured over a long period, such as 10 years. The purpose of an index of performance is to measure the actual total success of an investment company management, whether that success is achieved in obtaining large dividend income or market profits. The index will also enable stockholders to compare the results of different investment companies, if the comparison covers a long enough period for accidental variations to be averaged out and if due allowance is made for differences in safety. To be most significant, a long-period measure of performance must begin and end at dates when the stock market is neither very high nor very low, for investment company assets invariably reflect general market trends, and a measure of performance which merely records a market cycle will be misleading.

Different analysts compute indexes of performance in slightly different ways, though the general theory remains the same. The simplest method, that illustrated in the preceding paragraph, is applicable to investment company common stocks only. This method measures the total gain per share for the period by adding up dividends paid plus increase in net asset value per share (or decrease if a shrinkage has occurred) plus the value of rights or stock dividends paid and expresses this total gain as a percentage of the net asset value on the beginning date.

If it is desired to measure the performance of the *total assets* of an investment company, instead of just the net asset value of the common stock, the calculations become complicated because of changes in capital structure of the leverage companies. However, some of the financial services do excellent jobs in computing such indexes. The technical differences in methods used make it necessary for the reader to consider the method followed in order to understand the figures.

Table 34 shows the year-by-year performance records of a number of investment companies over an 8-year period. The comparative performance of an imaginary fund having no expenses, holding no cash or bonds, and invested continuously in the stocks comprising the Standard & Poor's 90-stock index of stock prices is shown for comparison. No attempt has been made in this table to cumulate these annual figures into an 8-year total; perhaps a measure of average performance for these years could best be attempted here by

Table 34. Performance of Investment Company Portfolios: Percentage Gains and Losses during Selected Years

Company	1946	1947	1948	1949	1950	1951	1952	1953
Adams Express................	−6	+5	0	+10	+26	+22	+7	−5
Carriers & General............	0	−1	+1	+20	+21	+15	+16	+2
Consolidated Investment Trust..	−7	+3	0	+22	+30	+26	+10	−2
Lehman......................	+2	+2	+2	+22	+20	+29	+11	−1
Tri-Continental...............	−9	0	+4	+22	+23	+21	+15	+2
Affiliated Fund...............	−15	−1	0	+22	+22	+17	+13	+2
Broad Street Investing.........	−1	−2	−1	+17	+25	+22	+13	+2
Fundamental Investors.........	−9	+1	+2	+19	+26	+19	+12	−3
Mass. Investors Trust..........	−5	+2	+1	+20	+27	+22	+14	0
Wellington Fund..............	−2	−3	+4	+16	+12	+12	+11	+2
S & P 90-stock Index..........	−8	+6	+6	+18	+30	+23	+18	−1

Source: Data adapted from *Investment Companies, 1953*, by Arthur Wiesenberger & Co.

computing an arithmetic average of the annual performance percentages for each company. But it must be remembered that this postwar period has been characterized by a strongly rising stock market, which would tend to increase the percentage gains for all investment companies and especially the least conservative ones. In fact, the table shows a relatively weak performance for the Wellington Fund, which is a conservative and stable balanced fund, and a strong performance by the 90-stock average, which is probably lower in average quality than any investment company listed in the table. The general impression gained by inspection of Table 34 and other more detailed similar records is that the managements of investment companies can provide diversification and a fair degree of security, but that they cannot in normal good years invest mostly in superior securities and pay their operating expenses and still equal the expense-free "performance" of a collection of good-grade stocks such as those included in the 90-stock average.

The principal reasons why the professionally managed investment companies do not exceed the averages in performance are probably found in the following three circumstances: (1) The investment companies (especially the open-end ones) usually have a small percentage of their assets idle in cash at all times, because of sales of new shares, redemption of old ones, and investment sales and purchases in process; this inevitably reduces the income as compared to the assumed fully invested market average. (2) The market averages are assumed to be expense-free, whereas the investment companies (and for that matter, investors in individual stocks) encounter brokerage charges, taxes, clerical costs, and other operating expenses. (3) Most of the investment companies probably hold higher grade average investments than those represented by the market averages, which means a lower rate of dividend and interest income. This is especially true of balanced funds, preferred stock funds, and bond funds.

Dividends and Yields

Because of the income tax advantages inherent in the practice most investment companies consistently distribute both net investment income and net realized capital gains in dividends to their shareholders. As Table 33 shows, the net investment income is likely to average about 4 per cent of net asset value in the typical company, but may be less than 3 or as much as 5 per cent in some cases. If an investor pays more than net asset value for his stock his yield will be correspondingly less, but if he buys for less than net asset value his yield will be greater. Because of the regularity of interest and dividend income in a diversified portfolio the net investment income in most investment companies is reasonably stable, but the yield rate as a percentage of market price will vary as the market price level varies.

Capital gains are paid out in dividends by most investment companies but not by all. Some companies prefer to retain capital gains on the theory that they are mostly the nonrecurring results of a rising market and should be held to absorb the probable losses in some future falling market. In most companies capital gains will occur irregularly as sound policy dictates the sale of appreciated assets, though managements will doubtless consider the effect on dividends and taxes each time a sale at either a profit or a loss is contemplated. Investors in most cases can count on capital gains dividends now and then, but they can hardly be expected to continue at the generous rates characteristic of the years 1948–1954, nor can they be expected in years of serious market decline. Investors should therefore regard their dividends from investment income as their basic regular dividend income, and regard the capital gains dividends in the main as extra payments dependent on good times.

Table 35. Discounts on Closed-end Common Stocks at Various Dates

Company	12/31/53	12/31/50	12/31/47	12/31/44	12/31/41
Adams Express..............	27%	28%	35%	31%	32%
Atlas......................	27	26	25	30	41
Lehman....................	3	0	0	14	24
Niagara Share..............	33	33	49	40	65
Average of 24 stocks..........	22	22	30	29	39

Source: Data adapted from *Investment Companies, 1953,* by Arthur Wiesenberger & Co.

In order to permit investors to accumulate larger holdings conveniently many open-end investment companies offer their shareholders the option of reinvesting their dividends in additional shares in the company. In the case of capital gains dividends the reinvestment is often permitted at a price equal to net asset value, without payment of the customary loading charge. This is a valuable privilege, since it is equal to the privilege of making a diversified stock investment without any brokerage expense whatever.

The stocks of the larger closed-end companies are traded on the stock exchanges, and the smaller ones usually have good over-the-counter markets. Strange as it may seem, the closed-end company shares usually sell far below net asset value, often by 25 or 30 per cent. The discounts on stocks with poor records tend to be larger than the others, but all seem to fluctuate irregularly. Discounts are usually larger in weak markets than in bullish ones. Because of the discounts, a closed-end stock can usually be purchased at a price on which the dividend yield will be considerably more than can be had on an open-end stock of similar quality. In fact, the discount is usually large enough so that the investor's yield on dividends out of net investment income is as great as the company's gross dividend and interest yield on the value of its holdings. In other words, the discount endows the management costs. The market prices of closed-end common stocks fluctuate in sympathy with the general market.

Table 36. Investment Company Preferred Stocks

Company	An-nual divi-dend	Call price	Price, 12/31/53	Price range, 1953	Safety factor *	Over-all income coverage,† 1953
Central-Illinois Securities.....	$1.50	32½	27½	29¾–26	178%	145%
General American Investors...	4.50	105	103½	104¾–98	750	460
North American Investment..	1.50	N.C.	20½	22–20½	176	117
Pacific-American Investors....	1.50	26¼	25	25½–24½	202	159
U.S. & International Securities	5.00	105	88	96¼–86	348	188

* Ratio of total assets to all prior claims plus market value of this stock.
† Based on net investment income only.
Source: Data adapted from *Investment Companies, 1953*, by Arthur Wiesenberger & Co.

Closed-end company preferred stocks present another anomalous price situation. They usually sell at prices which afford a very generous yield, quality considered, and their cash yield often equals the performance records of investment company common stocks. Except for the very best issues these preferreds are volatile marketwise, and it is often possible to buy them at prices which may add a market profit to a generous yield. Table 36 illustrates.

Fixed or Unit Type of Trusts

Between 1928 and 1933 the fixed or unit type of investment trust enjoyed a vogue in the United States, and scores of millions of dollars were invested in them. Subsequently the idea lost favor, but many trust certificates remain in circulation. Briefly, the plan was this: an investment firm desiring to sponsor a new trust would plan an ideal stock portfolio of 30 to 40 issues, worth at market prices about $10,000 to $15,000. This portfolio would constitute a *unit*, to be deposited in the care of a bank or trust company for a period of 20 or 30 years. As many units would be deposited as the sponsor could sell. Participation shares in each unit (possibly 1,000 shares per unit) would then be sold to the public at a price sufficient to pay for the deposited stock, prepay the trustee's fee in its entirety, and pay the sponsor's selling costs plus a profit. The participation shares were usually evidenced by bearer certificates issued in 10-, 50-, 100-, and 1,000-share denominations. These certificates were salable, transferable by delivery, and bore semiannual dividend coupons. The trustee collected all dividends on the trusteed stocks and on each semiannual dividend date paid the money out pro rata on the dividend coupons. At the expiration of the trust period the trustee was obliged to sell the trusteed stocks and redeem the participation shares pro rata with the proceeds. Prior to the expiration date any holders who wished to sell their participation shares had the right to ask the trustee to redeem them; this the trustee would do by selling out one unit at a time and using the proceeds for redemption purposes, at net asset value for the shares.

The fixed trusts differ from the modern management companies in two important respects. First, there is little or no management involved, since the portfolio usually does not change greatly during the life of the trust. Secondly, there are no recurring management costs, since the trustee is paid in full in advance.

The remaining fixed trust shares may be bought over the counter at prices very little above current net asset value.

Installment Plans

Many of the open-end investment companies now operate installment sales plans under which an investor may make periodic or even irregular small investments in the company over a span of years. The investor's "account" is usually placed in trust with a well-known bank, to which he remits his payments. Each payment is invested in trust shares when received, at net asset value plus a loading charge of about 9 per cent. The investment company usually sells fractional shares to these installment accounts, so that the funds are always fully invested. Dividends on the shares held may be added to the new payments to buy additional shares. Sometimes, for a small additional cost, the investor may buy life insurance covering the period of his investment contract, to assure that his saving program will be completed even in the event of premature death. If the investor wishes to drop his program or withdraw his paid-for shares before completion of the contract he may usually do so without penalty.

These plans are attractive to many people. The loading cost is high but not excessive, and the advantages of dollar averaging may offset the loading costs in part. Coupling the program with insurance may also suit many investors' needs. However, the formality of an installment contract is in most cases unnecessary, for the open-end companies are willing to sell new shares in very small quantities at any time without any prearranged plan.

Conclusions

It is clear that investment company shares are varied in nature and function. They probably have a place in most portfolios and perhaps should constitute the principal common stock holdings of many small investors, but an inappropriate selection will obviously limit the usefulness of even these investments. A proper choice must consider (1) the degree of marketability desired, (2) the amount of risk which may be borne, (3) whether specialization is desirable, (4) the desire for speculative trading opportunity, (5) the dividend policy, (6) the performance record, and (7) the price. Since consideration of all these factors requires a mastery of the subject far beyond the scope of most investors, it is probable that investment company opportunities are not fully utilized.

Many pronounced opinions about investment companies are held by individual investors and by securities dealers, most of which are founded on individual tastes as well as factual background. Some of the more important of these are as follows:

1. Open-end shares are preferable to closed-end shares because (a) the sales loading pays for full explanations by salesmen and in the sales literature; (b) the sales loading is not much greater than brokerage commissions plus odd-lot differentials on a diversified portfolio would cost the average investor; (c) the assurance of a redemption price based on net asset value is an important safeguard to a small investor; and

(d) the opportunity to dollar-average by buying small quantities periodically or on an installment contract is profitable.

2. Closed-end shares are preferable to open-end ones because (a) the shares may often be bought far below net asset value, hence their dividends and market gains based on their own assets may be large compared to the investor's purchase price; (b) the brokerage charge of 1 or 2 per cent does not deplete the investor's principal as much as an 8 per cent loading; (c) brokerage charges are low enough to make speculative buying and selling possible; and (d) market price fluctuations make trading profits possible.

3. Balanced funds are preferable to common stock funds because (a) they provide a balanced assortment of securities, not just stocks; and (b) they contain bonds and preferred stocks, hence are relatively safe and stable in price.

4. Common stock funds are preferable to balanced funds because (a) they earn more; (b) management costs and loading fees pay for management service on common stock money, where it is needed, not on bonds and savings account money where it is not needed; and (c) bonds and savings accounts can be kept separate, hence available in emergencies without the necessity of surrendering any stocks (the stock portion of a balanced fund share) at a possible loss.

5. A very large investment fund is preferable to a small one, because (a) it can be more widely diversified; (b) it can afford the research costs necessary to sound portfolio management; and (c) its cash operations re sale and redemption of shares (in an open-end fund) are likely to be more stable, hence to permit a more stable investment policy than would be possible in a small fund.

6. A small fund is preferable, because it can make investment shifts, selling one holding and buying another, without a large impact on the market price of the stocks, whereas large-volume trades by large funds drive the market down as they sell or up as they buy.

Information about investment companies is easy to obtain. Perhaps the most comprehensive source is the annual issue of *Investment Companies,* published by Arthur Wiesenberger & Co., and available in most libraries and securities houses. This book is replete with information and statistics about investment companies in general and all of the important American management companies individually. A second important source is the *Standard Industry Surveys;* this contains a survey of the business and comparative data on leading companies. Other financial services also cover this important field.

INTRODUCTION TO INVESTMENTS

Many investment periodicals, notably *Barron's,* cover this field frequently and are especially faithful in studying incomes, expenses, and performance records at quarterly or semiannual intervals. The investment reference manuals cover investment companies as thoroughly as they do other types of investments.

The interest of the securities business as it relates to investment companies is heavily concentrated in the open-end companies. The sales loading on these shares is great enough to finance a vigorous sales effort supported by advertising and quantities of sales literature, and the real merit of most of the shares supplies any other needed incentive to the trade. The closed-end companies, on the other hand, usually have little market sponsorship. The stocks of the larger closed-end companies, such as Adams Express, Lehman Corporation, and Tri-Continental Corporation, are listed on the stock exchanges; those of the smaller companies are traded over the counter.

QUESTIONS AND PROBLEMS

1. What is the basic purpose of an investment company? In your opinion, is this worth its cost?

2. Do you think that many investors who use investment companies select them "in accordance with their needs and tastes"? Is an informed selection really of paramount importance?

3. Would you recommend a balanced fund or a diversified stock fund plus an independent holding of government bonds, for a general portfolio? Which would provide the necessary element of liquidity in the investor's holdings to best advantage?

4. Would you prefer open-end companies or closed-end companies for your own purposes? Review the advantages and disadvantages of each. Would your choice be the same if you were advising a widowed aunt who knew little of business?

5. What practical use could an investor who is not a speculator make of high-leverage investment company common stocks?

6. Does the preferred stock of an investment company which owns mostly common stocks really have a senior position, or is it just common stock in quality without the customary common stock advantages?

7. The tax privileges granted to regulated investment companies were passed by Congress in order to permit investors to obtain investment company advantages without bearing an extra tax burden. Explain how this is accomplished. Is the arrangement unfair to the government?

8. Explain the nature of net investment income. Is net investment

income per share comparable with the earnings per share of ordinary business corporations?

9. Would the net investment income and the long-term performance record of a conservative balanced fund be comparable with those of a common stock fund? Explain the difference.

10. Explain the fixed trust idea. Would their shares be satisfactory investments at present if one could buy them at or close to net asset value? Would you hesitate to use them? Why?

11. Why does the securities business favor the open-end funds over the closed-end ones?

12. How would you go about choosing an investment company stock for your own use? Plan a definite procedure, considering the decisions you would have to make and the sources of information you would probably use.

13. Would investment company shares be good investments for a dollar averaging program? For a constant ratio type of formula planning?

REFERENCES

Badger, Ralph E., and Harry G. Guthmann: *Investment Principles and Practices,* Prentice-Hall, Inc., New York, 1951, Chap. 16.

Financial Handbook, The Ronald Press Company, New York, 1948, pp. 323–339.

Hoagland, Henry E.: *Corporation Finance,* McGraw-Hill Book Company, Inc., New York, 1947, Chap. 39.

Investment Bankers Association of America: *Fundamentals of Investment Banking,* Prentice-Hall, Inc., New York, 1949, Chap. 25.

Investment Companies, Arthur Wiesenberger & Co., New York, annual.

Jordan, David F., and Herbert E. Dougall: *Investments,* Prentice-Hall, Inc., New York, 1952, Chap. 29.

Plum, Lester V., and Joseph H. Humphrey: *Investment Analysis and Management,* Richard D. Irwin, Inc., Homewood, Ill., 1951, Chap. 19.

Robbins, Sidney M.: *Managing Securities,* Houghton Mifflin Company, Boston, 1954, Chaps. 33, 34.

Ryals, Stanley D., and David F. Cox: *Investment Trusts and Funds from the Investor's Point of View,* American Institute for Economic Research, Great Barrington, Mass., revised annually.

Securities and Exchange Commission: *Report on Investment Trusts and Investment Companies,* Washington, 1939–1940.

Weissman, Rudolph L.: *The Investment Company and the Investor,* Harper & Brothers, New York, 1951.

Chapter 20: FIRE AND CASUALTY INSURANCE STOCKS

The stocks of fire and casualty insurance companies are generally regarded as conservative investments, suitable as long-run holdings for endowed institutions, trustees, and small investors. There are exceptions, of course, for every line of business has its weak and poorly managed units, but the industry is basically stable. Most of the companies issue only common stocks, though a very few preferreds exist.

It is often said that a fire or casualty company is really a mixture of closed-end investment company and insurance carrier. The stockholders invest their funds in the capital and surplus of the insurance company, which in turn invests the money in good income-producing stocks and bonds. These holdings constitute a guarantee fund on which the company may draw if its insurance business sustains unexpected losses, but their principal function is to contribute interest, dividends, and possibly an occasional capital gain to the company's earnings. The insurance underwriting activities also contribute to earnings; the underwriting departments usually expect their expenses and insured losses to absorb only 94 to 98 per cent of the premiums paid in by policyholders, thus leaving 6 to 2 per cent for profit to the company. In addition, the practice of collecting premiums in advance gives the insurance companies custody of large amounts of policyholders' money at all times; this money is mostly invested in bonds, thus adding to the companies' interest income. The typical company probably obtains about 60 per cent of its net earnings from its investments and the other 40 per cent from insurance profits.

Insurance companies vary greatly in size. The Hartford Fire Insurance Company reported consolidated assets of $629,548,786 at year-end 1953 and collected $335,232,997 in premiums during the year. By contrast, the competing Jersey Insurance Company had $11,585,628 in assets and collected $5,669,683 in premiums. It is probable that the Jersey Insurance Company acting alone is too small to operate economically, but small insurance companies commonly affiliate themselves in groups which use common facilities and supervisory staffs and reinsure each other's business. The Jersey is affiliated with two other companies in a group whose combined resources exceeded $50,000,000 at year-end 1953.

Like the banking business, insurance companies are subject to regulation in the public interest. This regulation is administered by the states and extends to examinations to assure solvency, supervision of policy forms to assure soundness and fairness and to control of rates. State regulation is not detailed or aggressive, but it seems generally adequate. The insurance business is vigorously competitive, and regulatory control of rates has been exercised as often to keep them up as to bring them down, since the solvency of the companies is a matter of great importance. Federal intervention in the regulatory field is legally possible, but Congress has thus far left the task to the states.

The volume of insurance underwriting varies with the nation's population, the level of business activity, and the fluctuation of commodity prices. Business booms usually mean more business firms, more new homes and automobiles, bigger business inventories, higher insurable values because of higher prices, and a population able to pay for the insurance it needs. Depressions mean the reverse. While the growth of the country suggests that insurance volume will always tend to increase, it should be noted that fire volume dropped 40 per cent and casualty volume 32 per cent, between 1929 and 1933. This loss was recovered by 1940, and all previous records have been far surpassed in recent years, as a result of the postwar boom and price-level inflation.

Types of Business

Investors usually classify insurance companies as fire companies, casualty companies, mixed companies, and reinsurance companies. The *fire* companies write fire insurance, extended coverage (*i.e.*, windstorm, explosion, water damage, and other supplements to the fire policy), marine, inland marine, automobile fire and collision, and various other lines. The bulk of this business is in fire insurance, though different companies have different proportions of the various lines. The *casualty* business includes workmen's compensation, general liability, automobile liability, automobile collision, accident and health, and a great variety of less important types. Individual casualty types have been less stable in times past than fire insurance, but the diversity of the casualty business enables a company to protect itself by carrying unrelated types of risk. *Mixed* companies are those which carry both fire and casualty insurance risks. Many of the larger companies are mixed carriers in their own operations, and in other cases large fire insurance companies have subsidiaries which do a casualty insurance business. In the latter cases the investor in the parent company is indirectly an investor in the subsidiary also, and from his standpoint the business is a mixed one. The additional diversification obtained when both fire and casualty insurance is written adds further stability to operations, and the convenience of combined operations through the same sales offices and agencies is economical.

Reinsurance companies are companies which agree to share the risks on policies written by other companies. Insurance companies do not like to carry policies of large size, so they contract in advance with other companies to share the premiums and the losses on large risks. These reinsurance arrangements are often made by direct writing companies among themselves, but there are a number of companies which do nothing but a reinsurance business. On the whole, it appears that reinsurance companies have a more unstable record, both as to volume of business and earnings, than the direct writing companies, but the average experience of well-managed concerns is very satisfactory.

Though one of these four classifications will indicate the general type of business in which any company is engaged, it is possible for an investor to select a company whose operations are diversified or highly specialized, as he chooses. For example, the Fireman's Fund Insurance Company in 1953 had its insurance underwriting widely scattered in both fire and casualty lines, while the Republic Insurance Company had 88 per cent of its business in fire and extended coverage. Wide diversification offers the probability of stable earnings experience, but investment in specialized companies gives a close student of loss trends an opportunity to select stocks whose earnings appear likely to improve.

Investment Policy

The state regulations imposed on fire and casualty company investments usually require a minimum amount of cash or high-grade bonds, but leave the companies free to allocate the major part of their investments as they see fit. In general the fire and casualty companies have confined their investments to stocks and bonds. Some of them own their home office buildings and a few make mortgage loans, but investments of this type are neither common nor extensive.

In planning the investment of their funds the companies must keep three fundamental facts in mind: First, between one-third and two-thirds of their resources consist of premiums collected in advance and held available to pay future losses and expenses. Such funds must be kept safe. The companies therefore plan their investments so that cash on hand plus premiums in course of collection plus holdings of high-class bonds will equal all probable obligations. Second, about 15 per cent of resources will always consist of premiums in course of collection and cash balances actively used in the business. These are regarded as safe assets. Third, incoming cash premiums will usually be more than enough to pay all current expenses and losses, so all resources except the 15 per cent in cash and receivables can be kept continuously invested. Typical investment policy therefore requires (1) maintenance of a maximum invested position, employing all funds not needed in cash and receivables; (2) investing policyholders' and creditors' money only in bonds; and (3) investing the stockholders' equity in bonds, preferred stocks, or common stocks. Usually only a portion of the stockholders' equity will be invested in stocks. This portion can be relatively large without sacrifice of safety if the stockholders' equity represents a large percentage of the company's assets.

Table 37 indicates a wide divergence of company policy in the choice of investments. Four of these ten companies hold relatively few stocks, preferring to invest even their stockholders' capital funds chiefly in bonds. Four others invest three-fourths or more of their stockholders' equity in stocks; of this, one-fifth to one-half is in preferred stocks, the balance in common. Two other companies divide their stockholders' money more evenly between bonds and stocks. These variations are typical; the investor in insurance company stocks may choose one whose policy pleases him. Almost without exception insurance company investment policy is aimed at steady income and value stability rather than capital appreciation. The bonds held are usually high grade, often including a large proportion of

Table 37. Capital Structures and Investment Holdings of Leading Insurance Companies, December 31, 1953

(Consolidated figures)

Company	*Per cent stockholder equity to total assets*	*Per cent of total assets in*			
		Bonds	*Preferred stocks*	*Common stocks*	*Cash and all other*
Aetna Casualty & Surety........	35	66	7	14	13
Aetna Insurance................	42	66	1	13	20
Continental Insurance..........	61	38	4	44	14
Fireman's Fund Insurance........	45	66	2	18	14
Firemen's Insurance............	36 *	37	16	28	19
Glens Falls Insurance...........	41	60	8	12	20
Great American Insurance........	54	37	13	35	15
Hartford Fire Insurance..........	45	52	14	15	19
Home Insurance................	54	46	5	32	17
Insurance Co. of North America..	55	35	12	37	16

* Not including 1 per cent of preferred stock equity.
Source: Data adapted from *Insurance Stock Analyzer, 1953*, by Geyer & Co.

government obligations. The stocks are likely to be conservative, featuring bank, public utility, and seasoned industrial issues.

Insurance companies which confine their investments largely to bonds do so to assure stability of income, freedom from the effects of stock market fluctuations, and the sure availability of their resources if a big loss occurs. Other companies resort to stock investments to obtain a larger dividend income, to reduce income tax liability, and possibly in the hope of long-term price appreciation. Assuming equally adept managements, there is no doubt greater security in the bond-owning companies. However, major catastrophes are rare in modern times, and well-managed companies seldom find their stockholdings depressed to the point of disaster. Since the stocks produce at least twice as much net income per invested dollar as bonds, there is reason to make use of them.

Underwriting Policy

Underwriting policy has many aspects, but the investor needs to be keenly interested in two—the amount of insurance written and the degree of selectivity attempted. A large volume of insurance is advantageous because the policyholders' premium money can earn interest for the company, because large volume is economical from a clerical standpoint, and because total underwriting profits may be larger on larger volume. It is disadvantageous in that the possibility of disastrous losses is cumulated with increased volume, and the company's investments must therefore be kept to a greater degree in stable but low-yielding bonds. An average company writes net premiums amounting to about 55 per cent of its total assets annually and has a stockholders' equity equal to about 45 per cent of its total assets, but company policies vary on this point, as Table 37 shows.

Insurance companies usually attempt to control their losses by accepting good risks and rejecting poor ones. However, excessive caution would be poor business, for it would alienate both insureds and selling agents. Good loss control therefore becomes a long-run problem of developing a relatively low-risk clientele. Some companies have been able to do this to an outstanding degree—the Continental Insurance Company, the Glens Falls Insurance Company, the Hartford Fire Insurance Company, and the St. Paul Fire and Marine Insurance Company are conspicuous examples—while others have had to accept less desirable business. From the standpoint of investment in insurance stocks these successful companies are always attractive. However, their success is well known and is reflected in relatively high prices for their stocks. The investor can usually find equally attractive price-earnings ratios and yields in companies with less effective loss control.

The stock fire and casualty insurance companies compete for business with a considerable number of mutual, reciprocal, and state-owned companies of various kinds. This competition obtains about one-sixth of the fire insurance business and about one-third of the casualty business. Its share of the fire business has not changed appreciably in many years, but its portion of the casualty field increased from 25 to 32 per cent in the decade 1937–1946. However, the stock companies' business in all lines has increased greatly because of business expansion and inflation in 1941–1953, and as a result most stock companies in 1954 were carrying about as large a volume of insurance risks as their capital funds would justify. It therefore seems unlikely that any shortage of volume will concern them in the near future. For the same reason, it seems unlikely that competitive pressure will force damaging rate reduction or relaxation of present policies of rejecting poor risks.

Underwriting Ratios

Investment analysts measure the profitableness of underwriting operations by the use of the loss ratio, the expense ratio, the loss-and-expense ratio, and the underwriting profit margin.

The loss ratio is the ratio of losses incurred to premiums earned. The losses incurred are those which occur during the fiscal period in question. The premiums earned are the portions of premiums previously and currently collected which apply to the months of the fiscal period being studied. (The premiums currently being collected apply mostly to future fiscal periods.) The loss ratio as here defined shows the percentage of losses to the corresponding premiums earned.

The expense ratio is the ratio of selling and operating expenses to new premiums collected. More than three-fourths of an insurance company's expenses consist of advertising, sales commissions, premium taxes, and other items related to the acquisition of new business. It is consequently reasonable to relate expenses to new premiums collected rather than to premiums earned.

The loss-and-expense ratio is the total of the separately computed loss and expense ratios. It seems reasonable to state, for example, that if losses absorb 54 per cent of premiums earned and expenses take 42 per cent of premiums written, losses and expenses combined are tending to amount to 96 per cent of premium revenues.

The underwriting profit margin is the percentage of a company's premium earnings which is remaining as underwriting profit. It is computed by subtracting the loss-and-expense ratio from 100 per cent. It is obvious that each of these four ratios is of high importance to investors. Not only is it important to know the size of each ratio in the most recent year; any recent trends up or down, and the reasons for the changes, may be of great investment significance. Company annual reports do not always include the needed details, but much more information, including the loss experience on different types of insurance, can be found in the reference manuals.

Table 38. Underwriting Experience of Leading Fire Insurance Companies in the Five Years 1949–1953

Company	Loss ratio	Expense ratio	Loss-and-expense ratio	Underwriting profit margin
Aetna Insurance...................	53.6%	42.1%	95.7%	4.3%
Continental Insurance..............	55.1	38.4	93.5	6.5
Fireman's Fund Insurance..........	54.1	39.7	93.8	6.2
Firemen's Insurance...............	59.7	37.1	96.8	3.2
Glens Falls Insurance..............	54.6	39.7	94.3	5.7
Great American Insurance..........	55.5	40.2	95.7	4.3
Hartford Fire Insurance............	56.4	36.8	93.2	6.8
Home Insurance...................	53.2	41.9	95.1	4.9
Insurance Co. of North America......	53.4	38.2	91.6	8.4
St. Paul Fire and Marine Insurance...	55.2	37.4	92.6	7.4

Source: Data from *Insurance Stocks, 1954 Issue*, by Blyth & Co., Inc.

Table 38 indicates the ratios reported by leading fire insurance companies on their total business during a 5-year period. This table covers a turbulent period of boom and inflation, but the average figures shown are at least reasonably typical. It will be noted that the different companies have varying success in keeping their loss-and-expense ratios down and that the largest underwriting profit margin shown in the table is more than 2½ times as great as the lowest. Yet these are all large and successful companies.

Financial Statements

Since the computation of earnings per share and net asset value per share becomes rather complicated when insurance companies are holding companies controlling other insurance companies and when the insurance business extends to both fire and casualty lines, the analysis of insurance stocks is usually done by experts. However, some of the fundamentals in the process should be understood by all investors. The accompanying simplified illustration uses consolidated financial statements published by the Aetna Insurance Company, whose subsidiaries are wholly owned. These companies do a diversified insurance business, about two-thirds in fire and

Aetna Insurance Company and Subsidiaries
Consolidated Statement of Income, 1953

Net Premiums Written....	$127,761,741	
Increase in Unearned Premium Reserve.....	4,327,902	
Net Premiums Earned.....		$123,433,839
Net Losses Incurred.....	$ 61,047,178	
Loss Expenses Incurred.....	7,760,648	
Underwriting Expenses Incurred.....	50,076,917	
General Taxes Incurred.....	4,007,652	122,892,395
Underwriting Profit.....		$ 541,444
Net Interest, Dividends, and Rents Earned..	$ 4,789,555	
Loss on Sale of Securities.....	39,070	4,750,485
Net Income before Taxes.....		$ 5,291,929
Federal Income Taxes Incurred.....		1,680,925
Net Income.....		$ 3,611,004

marine lines and one-third in casualty lines. The Aetna statements are conventional and typical.

The 1953 income statement begins with the computation of net premiums earned as the difference between net premiums written and the increase in unearned (prepaid) premiums remaining on the books. Net premiums earned thus becomes the basic item of underwriting income. From this premiums-earned figure are next deducted the losses and operating expenses incurred during the year, to obtain the underwriting profit (or loss) for the year. This figure is commonly referred to as the *statutory underwriting profit (or loss)*, because this computation is recognized by the regulatory and income tax authorities. However, the computation is not a very logical one, for it charges all the expenses incurred in obtaining a large amount of new business (note the large increase in unearned premiums during the year) to the operations of 1953, whereas the premium income resulting from this business will be spread over the entire period covered by the policies. The result is that the statutory underwriting profit sometimes appears as a loss in a year when the company has obtained a large amount of attractive new business, because of the heavy acquisition costs charged to current expenses. Likewise, a very bad loss year might show a statutory underwriting profit if new business declined greatly so that sales commissions and other acquisition costs were lower for the year.

To the statutory underwriting profit of $541,444 the Aetna statement next adds the investment department's income, consisting of interest, dividend, and rent income (net after investment department expenses) and the profit (in this case, loss) on sale of securities. This produces the total operating income figure of $5,291,929, which is subject to income tax charges of $1,680,925, leaving $3,-611,004 as the official net income for the year. This would be $3.61 per share on the Aetna's 1,000,000 shares.

Investment analysts do not accept the view that a net income of $3,611,004 correctly represents this company's earnings for the year. They would point out that the company during the year prepaid the acquisition costs on $4,327,902 of new business which contributed nothing to the year's premium income. If the year's expenses were adjusted to defer these acquisition costs (with the purpose of adding them into future expenses proportionally as the related premiums come into the earnings), the statutory underwriting profit would be corrected to a more realistic figure. Investment analysts usually make a correction by adding back 40 per cent of the increase in unearned fire insurance premiums and 35 per cent of the increase in unearned casualty premiums to the statutory underwriting profit or loss.[1] These percentages are supposed to be normal acquisition

[1] This has been the conventional view. However, analysts since 1950 have been making changes in their methods of computing both adjusted underwriting profits and the stockholders' equity (net worth) in insurance companies. Since the new procedures have not become standard, it is only possible here to note three which seem to gain some favor. First, some analysts hold that the conventional 40 and 35 per cent figures for acquisition costs (and stockholders' equity in the unearned premium reserve) are too high, and that 30 and 28 per cent, or a figure based on each company's actual costs, should be substituted. Second, it is argued that because acquisition costs are expenses for income tax purposes in the year incurred, they automatically cause a deferral of taxes equal to 52 per cent (the present corporate rate) of themselves; therefore, the adjustment percentages to income and net worth should be 48 per cent of the "de-

costs. Adding back this correction produces an *adjusted underwriting profit* which is allegedly representative of actual results. If the unearned premiums declined instead of rising, the correction would be a corresponding subtraction from the statutory underwriting profit. One further unrelated adjustment would be made by analysts computing earnings per share in this case. They would not regard securities profits or losses as a part of the regular operations of the company, hence would not include the $39,070 Loss on Sale of Securities in their adjusted earnings figures.

Aetna Insurance Company and Subsidiaries
Consolidated Balance Sheet, December 31, 1953

Assets		Liabilities	
Bonds	$151,786,840	Unearned premiums	$113,234,839
Preferred stocks	1,686,023	Unpaid losses and expenses	44,222,605
Common stocks	29,376,898	Other liabilities	11,558,426
Real estate	4,242,206	Capital stock	10,000,000
Cash	19,163,915	Security valuation reserve	10,916,986
Receivables	19,591,212	Surplus	38,329,038
Other assets	2,414,800		
Total assets	$228,261,894	Total liabilities	$228,261,894

In the case of the Aetna Insurance Company's 1953 income statement, the $4,327,902 of Increase in Unearned Premium Reserve for the year suggests that 37½ per cent [2] of this amount, or $1,622,963, of expenses should be deferred to later years. Adding this sum to the statutory underwriting profit of $541,444 produces an adjusted underwriting profit of $2,164,407. When the net interest, dividend, and rent receipts of $4,789,555 are added to this the pretax net profit becomes $6,953,962, and after deducting $1,680,925 for income taxes the final income figure is $5,273,037. On a per share basis

ferred" acquisition costs, not 100 per cent of them. Third, it is argued that the stockholders' net worth should be computed after deduction for income taxes on securities profits which would be incurred if the companies sold their securities.

The SEC now demands the inclusion in insurance stock prospectuses of figures based on the second and third of these new procedures. The author of this text believes that the first proposal is probably valid, that the second is debatable, and that the third has little logical merit.

[2] This is a guess, since the company has more fire than casualty business but the latter is a more rapidly growing field. We assume here that the increase is half fire (40 per cent adjustment) and half casualty (35 per cent adjustment).

(there are 1,000,000 shares) an analyst would report: statutory underwriting profit $.54, acquisition expense adjustment $1.62, adjusted underwriting profit $2.16, investment income $4.79, taxes $1.68, computed net earnings $5.27.

It is customary for insurance companies to publish balance sheets or statements of condition showing their stockholdings at market values and their bonds at amortized cost. Footnotes to the statements usually explain fully when further explanations are needed. Consequently, the analyst has little difficulty in obtaining the information he needs.

There is one adjustment which must be made in interpreting an insurance company balance sheet. The unearned premiums item shown on the liabilities side represents the entire amount of premiums collected but as yet unearned. However, the company has already paid the acquisition costs on these policies, in amounts approximating 40 per cent on fire policies and 35 per cent on casualty policies, and the losses and remaining expenses should not exceed 60 or 65 per cent of the premiums. It is therefore customary to assume that the stockholders' equity in an insurance company includes 40 per cent of the unearned fire premiums and 35 per cent of the unearned casualty premiums. In the foregoing statement the stockholders' equity consists of the $10,000,000 capital stock item plus the $10,916,986 security valuation reserve (excess of market value of stocks over cost) plus the $38,329,038 of surplus plus about 37½ per cent of the $113,234,839 of unearned premiums, or $42,463,-065. The total stockholders' equity is therefore $101,709,089, or $101.71 per share on 1,000,000 shares.

The net asset value per share is a reasonably important figure to insurance stock investors, for it measures the maximum amount which normally should be invested in stocks, as well as the basic sum of earning assets which will remain in the investment account even if the volume of insurance underwriting declines drastically.

The foregoing examples should convince the reader that all per share earnings and net asset value figures for insurance stocks are inevitably estimates, even when reported by the companies themselves. It will always be important to know whether such figures are statutory or adjusted, and if adjusted, what adjustment methods were used. Also, since many important insurance companies are holding companies, it is essential to know whether the per share figures are based on consolidated statements. Not all companies furnish consolidated statements, but security analysts customarily work out consolidated per share estimates in such cases by combining separate company figures.

Corporate Income Taxes

Fire and casualty insurance companies do not have any special income tax privileges. Their operating profits and capital gains are subject to the regular corporate income taxes, and their dividends are taxable income to their stockholders. However, there is one peculiar feature about the computation of insurance company income taxes: their taxable income is based upon their statutory underwriting profits, not on the more accurate adjusted underwriting profits. Except for the relatively minor sums paid on investment capital gains, insurance companies' taxable corporate incomes are roughly measured by the following formula: taxable income equals premiums earned minus losses incurred minus expenses paid plus interest earned plus approximately 15 per cent of dividends received. Consideration of this formula will indicate that a steady growth of premium sales would minimize taxation, while a decline would increase it. Statutory underwriting profits and interest income are fully taxed, whereas only about 15 per cent of dividend income is included in the tax base.

Corporate income taxes are usually not included in the expenses used to compute the expense ratio, nor are they included in the customary computations of underwriting profits per share or invested income per share. They are deducted separately on a per share basis after these computations are made, as shown in Table 40.

Underwriting Experience

Insurance companies are accustomed to commit themselves on policies which run from 1 to 5 years into the future. The premiums charged on these policies are based on loss experience data gathered chiefly over the preceding few years. It is natural that there should be a lag between current loss experience and the premiums charged by the companies. Sometimes the lag will favor the companies, and sometimes the opposite will be true. It is often said that underwriting profits follow a cycle of 10 or 12 years' duration, alternating periods of profitable years with periods of poor ones.

Whether the cycle theory is accepted or not, it is clear that fire loss ratios tend to rise (1) when price levels rise rapidly, magnifying repair costs; (2) when inexperience and haste in industrial operations induce carelessness, as in wartime and boomtime; (3) when fire-fighting equipment and organizations deteriorate, as in wartime or depressions; and (4) when concentrations of values magnify individual losses, which occurs when large inventories are accumulated in single locations during booms. Automobile losses are affected by similar factors, as are most other forms of risks. Favorable trends in loss experience also occur; in fact, the long-term history of most fire and marine lines shows a steady decline in losses and premium rates. The acceptance of business and the selection of risks at prevailing premium rates is thus an important responsibility for insurance company managers.

Performance Record

Because market gains or losses on investments which are still held are not included in insurance company income reports, it is sometimes difficult to appraise the total success of a company's investment and insurance operations. This is especially true in periods of fluctuating business conditions, when both investment values and underwriting profits are likely to be unstable. It therefore seems reasonable to consider a total performance record by computing a performance index similar to that employed in testing investment company results. Such a test is entirely retrospective, but the stable nature of insurance operations seem to justify placing considerable emphasis on past records.

Table 39 suggests a rough means of gauging the total performance of insurance stock equities. It shows that the increases in per share net asset values plus the dividend distributions of these companies make total performance gains which compare favorably with those of the investment companies considered in Chapter 19. This indicates that insurance stocks may well be considered by investors who seek reasonable asset growth as well as diversification, safety, and steady income. Column F has been included in Table 39 to show the amount of the 8-year gain which is attributable to investment income and insurance profits; the balance of the gain shown in Column D is presumably due to securities market appreciation. While market gains are very acceptable, ordinary investment incomes and insurance profits are doubtless more certain to recur in the future, so the investor is perhaps wise to place greater emphasis on these than on market gains.

Table 39. Total Performance of Selected Insurance Share Equities, Consolidated per Share Basis, 1945–1953

Stock	A Net asset value, 12/31/45	B Net asset value, 12/31/53	C Dividends paid, 1946–1953	D Total gain (B+C)−A	E Per cent gain D over A	F Total income from investment plus underwriting
Aetna Casualty & Surety...........	$93.24	$155.40	$24.20	$86.36	93%	$53.07
Aetna Insurance....	78.71	101.71	16.75	49.35*	62	46.17
Continental Insurance............	54.54	97.35	18.51	61.32	112	42.73
Great American Insurance..........	29.07	47.87	7.74	26.54	91	21.05
Hartford Fire Insurance............	82.25	150.42	15.60	83.77	102	76.99
Home Insurance....	38.90	61.54	12.60	35.24	90	27.99
Moody's 125 industrial stocks (for comparison)......	49.30	77.06	26.74	54.50	111	

* Includes $9.60 as book value of stock rights.

Dividend Policy

Insurance companies have long held to a curious tradition that underwriting profits are a public trust, to be retained to strengthen the finances of the company, and that their dividends must therefore be paid out of interest and dividend income. While the tradition is unclear as to whether the investment income available for dividends is measured before or after income taxes, and despite the fact that the tradition is not recognized in law, most companies keep their dividend disbursements well below their investment incomes. Only in the long run do stockholders benefit from underwriting profits, when these profits have been invested in income-producing securities which add to the company's investment income. However, there is one advantage to the stockholders in the tradition which sets the investment income apart as the source of their dividends. The investment income is sure and steady, and the tradition justifies dividends from it even when underwriting losses are experienced, unless the losses are very severe. As a result, insurance company dividends are incomparably dependable; most of the leading companies have unbroken dividend records extending back 50 to 100 years.

Insurance company dividends in 1954 were averaging between 50 and 60 per cent of pretax investment income, and between 30 and 40 per cent of posttax earnings from investments and underwriting combined. This compares with a prewar payout of 75 to 80 per cent of pretax investment income. However, most of the companies had a higher ratio of net worth to premium volume in the prewar years than they have had in the years 1945–1954; in fact, in the postwar period many companies felt that their net worth was inadequate to justify the volume of insurance business which they were obtaining. Consequently, they kept dividends low in order to augment net worth out of retained earnings. Although most insurance companies' dividend rates in 1954 are substantially higher than they were in 1941, further increases do not seem impossible when the inflation and postwar boom are over and insurance volume grows at more normal rates.

Needless to say, investors watch the companies' investment income and the other factors affecting dividend policy with close attention.

Stock Prices

Insurance stocks fluctuate in value along with the general level of stock prices and to about the same extent as other stocks of similar quality. They also reflect at any time the conditions and prospects of the insurance business. On the whole, price-earnings ratios for insurance stocks seem a little lower than those on industrial stocks of comparable quality. Yields are also somewhat lower, reflecting the conservative dividend policies of the industry. Most insurance stocks sell below net asset value most of the time, usually ranging between 60 and 100 per cent of it, but some sell well above it at times. Naturally, the better grade and more profitable stocks sell for a higher percentage of asset value than the weaker issues.

Table 40. Price Relationships in Insurance Stocks, 1953–1954

Stock	Approximate price range, 1953–1954 *	Consolidated net assets, 12/31/53	Average consolidated earnings per share, 1952–1953				Dividend rate, 1954
			Adjusted underwriting profit	Net investment income	Income tax	Net earned per share	
Aetna Insurance......	66–51	101.71	3.39	4.65	2.15	5.89	2.40
American Insurance...	30–23	38.67	1.56	2.16	1.12	2.60	1.20
Continental Insurance.	91–67	97.35	2.73	5.00	1.61	6.12	3.00
Firemen's Insurance...	34–24	47.90	1.96	3.27	.97	4.26	1.00
Glens Falls Insurance..	69–55	83.31	4.14	3.87	1.64	6.37	2.00
Great American Insurance..............	40–27	47.87	1.24	2.64	.97	2.91	1.50
Hartford Fire Insurance..............	169–118	150.42	8.77	6.76	5.54	9.99	3.00
Home Insurance......	46–37	61.54	1.18	3.02	.76	3.44	2.00
Insurance Co. of North America............	101–77	78.72	3.98	4.17	2.18	5.97	2.50

* To June 30, 1954.

As an illustration of price relationships, Table 40 presents a comparison of prices, dividends, and 1952–1953 earnings of leading insurance stocks. Figures such as these can never be regarded as fully typical—for example, many automobile insurers lost money in 1952 and the fire and windstorm lines were generally disappointing in 1953—but they are not flagrantly abnormal. The dividend rates seemed reasonably stabilized, and the stock prices were influenced by both weak and strong market conditions, during the period covered by the table.

The Market

The market for insurance stocks is almost entirely over the counter. However, the larger companies have many stockholders, and trading in their stocks is moderately active. Dealers maintain close margins; their bid and asked prices are only about 1 per cent apart on the leading stocks and are seldom in excess of 3 per cent apart on any sizable issue. Because of their quality and dependable market, insurance stocks have an excellent rating as bank loan collateral.

Insurance stocks are not so well known to the general public as other leading types of stock investments, and as a result there is a considerable concentration of such stock in large family holdings, trusts, and endowments. However, an increasing number of conservative small stockholders are learning that insurance stocks offer a desirable investment medium, in which the diversification of an investment company is combined with a stable and profitable underwriting business. The number of small stockholdings in insurance companies is therefore increasing.

Special Sources of Information

Because of the specialized nature of the business, detailed information on insurance stocks is best obtained from specialized sources. For reference manuals the leading publications are the annual *Best's Insurance Reports,* which appear in two volumes, the *Fire and Marine Edition* and the *Casualty Edition.* This publisher also offers a condensed annual reference book entitled *Best's Digest of Insurance Stocks* and a leading magazine on insurance finance, *Best's Insurance News, Fire and Casualty Edition.*

Investors will also find important use for the elaborate statistical comparisons of insurance stocks which dealers and brokers prepare. The annual *Insurance Stock Analyzer,* prepared by Blair & Co., insurance and bank stock dealers, is one of the best of these. It shows for each company the size of the company; amount of business done; types of investments held; amount of each type of insurance written; and on a per share basis the net asset value, detailed earnings record, dividend rate, and stock price. Similar annual compilations are made by Blyth & Co., Inc.; John C. Legg & Company; and others.

QUESTIONS AND PROBLEMS

1. What are the sources of net income for fire and casualty insurance companies?

2. Is the stockholders' equity in an insurance company used as working capital in the conduct of the insurance business?

3. How would it be possible for one who is conversant with the trends of premium rates and losses to choose companies whose earnings were likely to increase? Explain.

4. What are the factors controlling the percentage of total assets which a company can safely invest in stocks? Why is it advantageous to invest in stocks?

5. Explain the tradition of insurance company dividend policy. Why do investors watch the investment income so carefully?

6. Would you prefer to invest in a fire company which wrote a small percentage of premiums to capital, or one which did a large amount of insurance business? Explain.

7. Do you think that the process of adding a loss ratio based on earned premiums to an expense ratio based on premiums written, to obtain a combined loss-and-expense ratio, is statistically sound? Why is it done?

8. Explain the difference between statutory underwriting income and adjusted underwriting income. Which is the largest in a year when premiums written decline below those of previous years?

9. Why does an insurance company's income tax tend to increase when its business declines?

10. Explain the computation of the net asset value per share in an insurance company.

11. Why do insurance company underwriting profits tend to be "cyclical"? Would this tendency be less in a company writing many lines of insurance?

12. Does the performance record as measured in Table 39 give any indication of whether the insurance stock being studied has gone up in price? Explain.

13. Bring the data of Table 40 up to date, and determine whether the yields and price-earnings ratios of insurance stocks are comparable with those of bank and utility stocks.

14. Compare the underwriting, investment, and dividend policies of the companies listed in Table 40. Considering present prices and prospects, which would you choose to invest in?

REFERENCES

Badger, Ralph E., and Harry G. Guthmann: *Investment Principles and Practices,* Prentice-Hall, Inc., New York, 1951, Chap. 15.

Best's Digest of Insurance Stocks, Alfred M. Best Company, Inc., New York, annual.

Best's Insurance Reports, 2 vols., *Fire & Marine or Casualty & Surety,* Alfred M. Best Company, Inc., New York, annual.

Jordan, David F., and Herbert E. Dougall: *Investments,* Prentice-Hall, Inc., New York, 1952, Chap. 28.

Robbins, Sidney M.: *Managing Securities,* Houghton Mifflin Company, Boston, 1954, Chap. 32.

Chapter 21: UNITED STATES
GOVERNMENT SECURITIES

The total interest-bearing debt of the United States government in June, 1954, stood at approximately 271 billion dollars. The magnitude of this sum and its importance to investors can be gauged by contrasting it with the total value of all corporation stocks listed on the New York Stock Exchange, which amounted to approximately 138 billion dollars, or the total assets of all American life insurance companies, which amounted to about 80 billion dollars. Not all of the government's debt was available for private investment, since government-operated agencies and trust funds such as the social security reserves, veterans' life insurance reserves, government employees' pension funds, and deposit insurance funds owned about 48 billion dollars, and the Federal Reserve banks held 25 billion dollars more, but the remaining 198 billion dollars still constituted a tidy sum.

Government securities are owned by large numbers of investors. According to the Federal Reserve System's 1948 *Survey of Consumer Finances,* over 48 per cent of American families owned government securities, as compared with 46 per cent which owned savings accounts, 45 per cent which owned real estate, 9 per cent which owned corporate securities, and 78 per cent which owned life insurance.[1] Governments are also important investments for business concerns, insurance companies, banks, endowment funds, and trust funds. At mid-year 1954 the life insurance companies had 12 per cent of their total assets invested in governments, and the banks 34 per cent.

Quality of Government Securities

United States government securities are generally reputed to be about as certain of payment as any obligation known on this troubled

[1] *Federal Reserve Bulletin,* July, 1948.

planet. They are included without question on all lists of securities permitted as investments for banks, trust funds, and insurance reserves, and they yield as little as any securities of comparable maturity and tax position.

It is said that the two prime tests of quality in a sovereign government's obligations are its ability to pay and its willingness to pay. Ability to pay is found in the government's capacity to raise, by taxation or further borrowing, sufficient money to pay the unavoidable costs of government plus the interest and principal on its debts. Willingness to pay is found in the willingness of public officials and citizens to levy taxes and limit public expenditures so that creditors may be given their due without evasion or compromise.

The ability of the United States government to raise money is very great. In the first place, it has access to very productive taxes; the income and excise levies in particular are capable of producing almost astronomical sums, as is demonstrated by their performance since 1942. In the second place, the government's credit is good; individuals, banks, and all other principal lenders trust the Federal bonds and will buy them willingly to finance a refunding operation, a war, or a peacetime deficit. In the third place, the government controls the banking system, and in particular the Federal Reserve banks; even if private investors were not enthusiastic about lending to the Treasury, bank credit and currency expansion could provide any reasonable needed sums. It is therefore logical to conclude that the ability of the Federal government to pay its expenses plus the interest and principal on its debts is not seriously open to question.

The test of a government's willingness to pay is not usually a simple inquiry as to any popular desire to repudiate debts; the real issue is whether or not taxes will be accepted and governmental economy practiced to a degree which makes honest debt service possible. Modern governments often levy taxes to the extent which political and economic expediency makes convenient and spend for general government, defense, and welfare whatever seems desirable. If circumstances cause this formula to produce a deficit, the government will usually borrow the necessary amounts; if borrowing proves impossible, interest or principal payments or both can be defaulted.

In the case of the United States government, the general willingness of the electorate to pay the public debt is firm; there is no bitterness against the bondholders or former public officials which could cause a desire to default. Furthermore, American political leaders are fully aware of the importance of the government bonds to the financial life of the country and are very unlikely to tolerate any suggestions looking toward nonpayment. Third, high taxes are accepted by the American people with gratifying willingness, even

Table 41. Trend of Federal Finances, 1929–1954

Fiscal Years Ended June 30

Year	Revenues, billions	Expenditures, billions	Total interest-bearing debt, billions	Revenues as a per cent of national income
1929	$ 4.03	$ 3.85	$ 16.64	4.6
1933	2.08	4.33	22.16	5.1
1937	4.98	7.76	40.47	7.2
1941	7.23	13.39	54.75	7.8
1945	44.48	98.42	256.77	24.5
1948	41.49	33.07	250.13	20.0
1949	37.70	39.51	250.76	17.1
1950	36.50	39.62	255.21	16.9
1951	47.57	44.06	252.85	18.2
1952	61.39	65.41	256.86	21.8
1953	64.83	74.27	263.95	21.6
1954	64.66	67.77	268.91	21.5

Source: Data for years 1929–1954 are adapted from *Treasury Bulletin* and *Survey of Current Business*. Revenues and Expenditures figures of 1952 and prior years are older series slightly different in composition from subsequent data.

though there are indications that the burden imposes some impediment to prosperity and progress. However, there is one derogatory bit of evidence in the general situation; neither the American people nor American political leaders seem willing to admit that there is need to limit public spending. The high level of postwar expenditures disclosed in Table 41 not only raises no effective demand for economy but actually seems to serve as a precedent for even more extensive spending programs.

It is not feasible to reproduce here the oft-debated evidence of the trend of government budgets, but in 1954 it seems reasonable to conclude that the government's revenue resources will be fully occupied to balance the budget in average peacetime years during the next decade or so. Depressions will produce deficits, and the trend of the public debt seems as likely to be up as down. In view of the government's credit stability and close liaison with the banking system this need not cause anyone to doubt that government obligations will be paid. However, there is reason to admit two possibilities: first, that a degree of credit inflation may at times raise the price level and conversely cheapen the dollars in which government and all other bondholders are paid; and second, that there may be occasions when the public welfare will require some restriction of bondholders' rights. For example, it might some day be necessary to forbid banks to sell their government bonds for a time, or to deny individuals the privilege of cashing their savings bonds, as part of a program of inflation control. This would be no more drastic than the government's repudiation in 1933 of its promise to pay its outstanding bonds in gold coin of stipulated weight and fineness.

But the admission that a government bond is not perfect need not imply that it is a bad risk. There is no security more certain to make ultimate payment. Price-level inflation, if it comes, will affect all other dollar obligations similarly. Restriction of bondholders' rights is unlikely to be seriously damaging. And government securities will nearly always be relatively stable in price, unexcelled as cash resources, readily marketable or cashable, and eligible for every kind of trust or bank investment.

Types of Federal Obligations

The Federal credit is at present involved in assuring payment of three groups of obligations: the direct debt, the fully guaranteed debt, and the nonguaranteed debt of certain so-called Federal instrumentalities. Of these three the direct debt is by far the most important in every way. In 1954 it included 150 billion dollars of marketable public debt, so called because the bonds may be sold by one private citizen to another; 77 billion dollars of nonmarketable debt such as savings bonds and armed forces leave bonds; and 42 billion dollars of special bonds sold to government agencies such as the social security and veterans' life insurance trust funds.

In 1954 the fully guaranteed debt was not of great importance, totaling only 65 million dollars, all obligations of the Federal Housing Administration. As recently as 1941 the fully guaranteed debt exceeded 6 billion dollars, consisting of obligations of the Federal Farm Mortgage Corporation, Home Owners' Loan Corporation, and other federally controlled agencies whose debts Congress had seen fit to guarantee.

The third type of Federal obligation, the bonds of the nonguaranteed Federal instrumentality, is the debt of a federally controlled agency or territorial government whose credit is not guaranteed by the United States, but which is presumably supported because the Federal government's supervisory authority implies the capacity to prevent defaults. The debtor instrumentalities include such agencies as the Federal Land banks, Federal Intermediate Credit banks, and Federal Home Loan banks and such territorial or insular governments as those of Alaska, Hawaii, and Puerto Rico. The total volume of this debt was small in 1954, aggregating well under 2 billion dollars.

Despite the written and much-publicized opinion of an Attorney-General of the United States that "there can be no doubt" that the national government would protect the purchasers of territorial obligations against default,[2] and despite the fact that Congress actually did supply the Federal Land banks with funds when they were embarrassed in the 1930s, the nonguaranteed bonds yield a slightly higher rate than can be had on direct or fully guaranteed obligations. The yields are seldom higher than those of the best similar private obligations, however, and the bonds usually qualify as legal for savings banks and trust funds in most states.

Terms and Features

Instead of the contractual bond indenture which is customary in the issuance of corporation bonds, the usual public obligation follows the terms indicated in the statute authorizing the bonds, with the addition of such details as the statute may leave to the discretion of the supervising officer. The actual terms and features of each issue are summarized in the official announcement offering the bonds. No corporate trustee is used, as the enforcement of the terms

[2] Opinion dated Aug. 11, 1921, in connection with the issuance of the Philippine 5½s of 1921.

of the issue is the obligation of regular public officials, and all payments are made through designated banks or treasury offices.

Significant terms and features which may characterize Federal obligations include the following:

1. Maturity and call dates. Federal obligations run for terms ranging from 60 days to 50 years. Most of the longer issues are callable at par in their last 1 to 5 years; such issues are cited as though they had two maturity dates, as for example the Treasury 2½s of 1967–72, but the earlier date merely indicates the date the bonds become callable at par; the later date is the maturity date. A few issues are callable at any time, and many are non-callable. Call price is always par plus accrued interest, without premium. Savings bonds and a few other issues will be paid off in cash on demand or upon short notice, at the request of the holder.

2. Denomination and form. Denominations vary from $10 to $1,000,000, with most long-term bonds available in units ranging from $500 to $100,000. Most issues are available in either coupon or fully registered form, with either exchangeable for the other, but variations exist. Savings bonds are available only in registered form.

3. Eligibility to own. Most government securities may be owned by anyone, but certain large issues of treasury bonds may not be owned by commercial banks prior to stated dates. Series E savings bonds may be owned only by individuals, and all savings bonds are restricted as to the amounts a single holder may acquire within a year's time.

4. Transferability and collateral value. All of the so-called marketable issues are transferable from one holder to another and, consequently, are useful as collateral for loans. Savings bonds are transferable only upon the death of the holder and in a limited number of other specified situations, hence are not useful as collateral. Issues not eligible for bank ownership may not be used by banks as security for government deposits.

5. Acceptability for taxes. Several large issues of marketable bonds are acceptable at par and accrued interest in payment of estate taxes levied at the owner's death. Nonmarketable treasury savings notes are acceptable for any Federal taxes at the option of the holder.

6. Taxability. All Federal bonds are free of state and local property and income taxes, and territorial bonds are free of Federal income taxes. Federal bonds and agency obligations issued since 1941 are subject to all Federal income taxes; those issued prior to that date have varying degrees of exemption. No bonds have any exemption from Federal or state estate and inheritance taxes.

Marketable Federal Issues

The 150 billion dollars of marketable Federal obligations outstanding in 1954 included 80 billion dollars of treasury bonds, 32 billion dollars of treasury notes, 18 billion dollars of treasury certificates of indebtedness, and 20 billion dollars of treasury bills. Except for 50 million dollars of Panama Canal 3s due in 1961 and a few million dollars of postal savings bonds due 1954–1955, these four classifications included the entire marketable direct government debt.

The treasury bonds consisted of 25 issues maturing between 1954 and 1983, which were originally issued for terms ranging from 6 to 30 years. Interest rates ranged from 2 to 3¼ per cent, reflecting the varying rates which the Treasury had to pay at various times in order to sell its bonds at par. Most but not all issues were available in either coupon or registered form. Minimum denominations available in the various issues were set at $50, $100, and $500, and maximums went as high as $1,000,000. Three of the 25 issues were restricted against bank ownership before certain dates, and eight were acceptable by the government in payment of taxes levied upon the estate of a deceased owner. Twenty-one issues were fully subject to Federal income tax; the other four had partial but not complete exemption. Since all these features affect the usefulness of the bonds to their owners, they also affect the prices of the bonds. It is important, therefore, for an investor interested in treasury bonds to compare the details of the issues and obtain the ones which suit his purposes, price considered.

Treasury notes are obligations whose terms exceed 1 year but do not exceed 5 years. Interest rates on notes issued in the period 1949–1954 ranged between 1⅛ and 2⅞ per cent. The coupon form is generally used, with minimum denominations varying from $100 to $1,000. No restrictions are placed on ownership, transferability, or use as collateral, and no Federal tax exemptions or special tax privileges are usually granted.

Treasury certificates of indebtedness are short-term obligations, usually of 1-year term, though 11- and 13-month issues have been offered on occasion. Certificates are offered for public subscription by the Treasury several times per year, mainly for refunding purposes. Since the offering price is always par the interest rate must reflect market conditions at the time of the offering; during the war it was ⅞ per cent per annum, but in 1953–1954 it varied between 2⅝ and 1⅛ per cent. Certificates are in coupon form, non-callable, minimum denomination $100 or $1,000 unlimited as to ownership, transferable, fully usable as collateral, and subject to all Federal taxes.

Treasury bills are very short-term obligations, usually maturing 90 to 91 days after issuance, which the Treasury offers for subscription about four times per month. Bills do not bear running interest; they mature at face value and are sold initially at a discount below face value. It is the Treasury's practice to invite subscribers to indicate the maximum amount they are willing to pay for the bills; the Treasury then allots bills to the highest bidding subscribers at their own bid prices down to the lowest bid price it finds itself compelled to accept in order to raise the necessary money. Bills are usually available in $1,000 and larger denominations, are unlimited as to ownership, and are salable, pledgeable, and fully subject to Federal taxes. During the war the interest yield on bills remained at ⅜ per cent per annum, but in 1953 it rose for a time to about 2 per cent. Easier money conditions in 1954 caused the yield on bills to decline to a level below three-fourths of 1 per cent for a few weeks. The average for the years 1950–1954 was about 1½ per cent.

Nonmarketable Federal Issues

Nonmarketable (*i.e.*, nonsalable) Federal obligations in public hands in mid-1954 included 58 billion dollars of United States savings bonds, 5 billion dollars of treasury tax and savings notes, 12 billion dollars of convertible (into salable treasury notes) 2¾s due 1980, and smaller amounts of depository bonds, armed forces leave bonds, and miscellaneous others. The United States savings bonds consisted of 36.4 billion dollars of Series E, .9 billion dollars of Series H, .3 billion dollars of Series J, .9 billion dollars of Series K, and 19.5 billion dollars in the Series F and G bonds, whose issuance was discontinued in 1952. Of these latter, 3.4 billions were Series F and 16.1 billions Series G.

Series E savings bonds are continuously offered by post offices, banks, and other financial agencies in denominations ranging from $25 to $10,000 maturity value. The bonds are issued in registered form only and may be registered in the name of one individual, in the names of two individuals either of whom is entitled to payment, or in the name of one individual but payable in case of his death to a second-named individual. Certain categories of personal fiduciaries may also own the bonds. Transfers are not permitted except to an heir in case of the death of the owner(s) and in a limited few other cases; hence, the bonds cannot be resold or used as collateral. The bonds mature 9 years and 8 months from date of issue. They pay no running interest but are sold for 75 per cent of face value; if held to maturity this will allow 3 per cent compound interest on the sum invested. The bonds need not be collected at maturity; the maturity value will earn 3 per cent compound interest through a second decade if the investor simply continues to hold the bond. Until 1948 no investor was permitted to purchase more than $5,000 face value of Series E bonds in any one year, but in subsequent years the limit was raised to $20,000. This limit applies per person; coowners may each buy a full quota. Since the bonds are not salable, an owner is permitted to surrender his Series E bond for cash at any time after 60 days from date of issue; but the cash values are so arranged that the compound interest earned on the investment increases progressively from zero to 3 per cent, depending on the length of time the bond is retained. Interest earned on savings bonds is subject to Federal income tax as ordinary income, not as capital gain, but it may be reported either as it accrues or in the year when it is collected.

Because of the increasing rate of earnings on savings bonds as they grow older, it is important that investors understand the earning power of older issues. Table 42 illustrates the point. If an investor must surrender one of his bonds for cash, it is advantageous for him to choose the one with the most recent issue date. Bonds held over 4 years earn such high rates during their remaining term that few investors can afford to cash them. This is especially true of the Series E bonds sold before May, 1952.

The Series E bonds have two unique advantages which should be mentioned, especially now that their term can be lengthened to 19 years and 8 months. First, an investor may cash them and take the interest income for tax purposes (or report the accumulated

Table 42. Yield Rates on United States Savings Bonds *

Year	Cash value at end of year on $100 bond		Average percentage yield on purchase price from issue date to end of year		Percentage earned on cash value during this year		Average percentage yield on present cash value from end of this year to maturity	
	Series E	Series K	Series E	Series K	Series E	Series K	Series E	Series K
Issue date..	$ 75.00	$100.00	....	....	....	....	3.00%	2.76%
First.......	76.20	98.50	1.59%	1.26%	1.59%	1.25%	3.16	2.92
Second.....	78.20	97.50	2.10	1.52	2.63	1.78	3.23	3.05
Third......	80.20	96.90	2.25	1.75	2.56	2.21	3.34	3.16
Fourth.....	82.20	96.60	2.30	1.94	2.50	2.53	3.49	3.25
Fifth.......	85.00	96.70	2.52	2.13	3.41	2.95	3.51	3.29
Sixth.......	87.80	96.90	2.64	2.27	3.30	3.05	3.58	3.33
Seventh....	90.60	97.20	2.72	2.39	3.19	3.15	3.74	3.37
Eighth.....	93.60	97.60	2.79	2.49	3.31	3.24	4.01	3.41
Ninth......	96.80	98.10	2.86	2.57	3.42	3.33	4.94	3.43
Tenth......	100.00	98.70	3.00	2.65	3.31	3.42	Mature	3.44
Eleventh...	......	99.30	....	2.70	....	3.40	....	3.48
Twelfth....	......	100.00	....	2.76	....	3.48	....	Mature

* Redemption values and yield percentages change at semiannual intervals; this table is not complete.

Source: Data from Treasury Department Circulars Nos. 653 and 906.

accrued interest and shift thereafter to an accrual basis) in any year when lack of income or deductible losses reduce his tax bracket or make his year tax-free. Second, investors over 45 years old may expect to carry their bonds into postretirement years when their incomes will be low and their exemptions greater, thus reducing the tax depletion of the interest earnings.

Series H savings bonds are somewhat similar to Series E except that they pay interest semiannually by check and there is no provision for extending their maturity beyond 9 years and 8 months.

They are issued in denominations ranging from $500 to $10,000. The $20,000 per person annual purchase limit, names in which issued, and transfer limitations are the same as for Series E. However, the Series H bonds are sold at par, not at a discount, and are always cashable at par after one month's notice. The interest payments on this bond are not uniform in amount; in order to provide an incentive to the holder to retain his bond the annual interest payments begin at 1.65 per cent and rise each year, following roughly the annual accruals shown for Series E in the fifth column of Table 42, and averaging 3 per cent for the whole 9 years and 8 months.

Series J savings bonds are similar in general plan to the Series E issue, except that they run for 12 years and are priced at $72 per $100 of maturity value, to yield an average of 2.76 per cent compound interest. Denominations range from $25 to $100,000 maturity value. Bonds may be registered as prescribed for Series E bonds, and in addition ownership is permitted to trustees and other fiduciaries, to owners or custodians of public funds, and to partnerships, associations, corporations, and any other incorporated or unincorporated bodies except commercial banks. Transfers are permitted in only a specified few cases, such as to heirs or business successors, and no collateral values exist. Cash values are arranged so that the yields roughly parallel those of Series K bonds, as illustrated in Table 42. No investor is permitted to purchase more than $200,000 issue price of Series J and Series K bonds combined in any calendar year.[3] Series J bonds are very similar to the Series F bonds sold between 1942 and 1952, except that Series F earned 2.52 per cent instead of 2.76.

Series K savings bonds are unique among the savings bonds in that they are sold at face value and pay semiannual cash interest at the rate of 2.75 per cent per annum to their holders. They are issued for a 12-year term, in registered form only, and in denominations ranging from $500 to $100,000. Ownership eligibility, restrictions on transfer, absence of collateral value, and limitations on annual purchases are the same as for Series J bonds. Like all savings bonds, they are continuously available at post offices and banks and may be

[3] Additional purchases in varying amounts were permitted to each financial institution which applied during the first 15 days of July, 1948, and again in late 1950. These exceptions were part of a program of inflation control then in progress.

cashed at any time after 6 months from date of issuance. The cash values on Series K bonds are continuously below the face value of the bonds until the maturity date, as shown in Table 42; the purpose is to keep the average yield on a bond cashed before maturity below that obtained on one which is held for the entire 12 years, despite the fact that current interest payments are made by check at the full 2.75 per cent rate. There is one exception to this practice of redeeming Series K bonds at a discount; if a holder or a joint holder dies, his estate or his heir may cash his unmatured Series K bonds at face value upon application within 6 months.

The vigorous selling campaigns conducted by the Treasury have made the savings bonds a popular investment medium with individual investors. The selling campaigns have stressed the fact that the bonds can always be "cashed in" upon demand, that their yield to maturity is satisfactory, that they are completely safe, and that they cannot depreciate in selling price. In fact, savings bonds have even been advocated as a means of accumulating money to buy an automobile or make a down payment on a home. It is probably a good thing to have bond savings efforts directed at small income groups, and it is doubtless a good thing to maintain a guaranteed minimum redemption price to assure small savers against bond price declines as severe as those of 1920, but the Treasury's sales arguments have diverted investor attention from two important features of the bonds. First, they have no collateral value, hence may not be used to raise emergency cash except by cashing them in at a sacrifice in yield; yet they are sold to small savers as investments for emergency use. Second, they may not be sold at the holder's convenience, except by cashing them at a sacrifice of yield. The purpose of restricting negotiability in this manner is doubtless to encourage thrift by attaching a penalty to the act of cashing the bonds. No doubt the restriction of transfers also saves the government some clerical costs. But it must be noted here that savings bonds are most profitable to the holder if he expects to hold them quite a long time; though it must be admitted that a Series E bond held for as short a period as two years will earn more than a commercial bank savings or postal savings account.

The government has made every effort to keep the legal technicalities which affect the ownership of savings bonds at a minimum. For example, a savings bond issued to two persons as coowners (John

Doe or Mary Doe) may be cashed before maturity or collected at maturity by either, and the interest checks are cashable by either. Upon the death of one coowner no transfer is required; the survivor has full authority. At the survivor's death the bond is a part of his estate. In the case of bonds issued to an individual but payable at his death to a named beneficiary, the bonds will be cashed or transferred to the name of the beneficiary after the owner's death without waiting for probate orders or other legal details, if the beneficiary obtains possession of the bond and delivers it, with proper proof of the owner's death, to the transfer office. These procedures can be very useful to investors who wish some of their funds available to their heirs without the delay and expense of probate. Other ownership and transfer rules, which may not be included here because of space limitations, are very useful under proper circumstances. Savings bond investors will do well to study them and take advantage of them.

Although the bonds are no longer sold, some mention should be made of the old Series E and the Series F and G bonds sold prior to May, 1952. The old Series E bonds were very similar to the present ones, except that their 10-year yield averaged only 2.9 per cent instead of the present 3 per cent, and their cash redemption values grew very slowly during the first five years and very fast (at an average rate of 4 per cent) during the second five years. It is therefore especially profitable to hold these to maturity after they are four or five years old. The old F and G bonds are close predecessors to the present J and K bonds, except that they yielded an average of 2.50 per cent instead of 2.75, and also had their cash values arranged to penalize the early years and make the later ones highly profitable.

Treasury savings notes are nontransferable but pledgeable 3-year notes sold to individuals and business firms primarily as investments for accumulating tax funds. The notes are sold at par and accrue added value as interest each month until redeemed or until maturity. They may be delivered to the government at face value plus accrued interest in payment of Federal taxes at any time during and after the second calendar month following date of purchase. The interest rate earned on these notes increases with the time held but amounts to normal market rates if the notes are held to maturity. The interest rate offered on new issues of these obligations is adjusted occasionally to conform to prevailing short-term money rates.

Ownership of Federal Obligations

The government's direct obligations are widely scattered among all sorts of owners. At March 31, 1954, the commercial banks held 23 per cent of them, the reserve banks 9 per cent, individuals 24 per cent, insurance companies 6 per cent, mutual savings banks 3 per cent, state and local government agencies 5 per cent, and federally controlled trust funds 18 per cent.

Of the 61 billion dollars held by commercial banks, it appeared that about 39 billion dollars were treasury bonds, 9 billion dollars were treasury notes, 6 billion dollars were treasury certificates, 5 billion dollars were treasury bills, and 2 billion dollars were in various nonmarketable bonds.[4] Comments in various banks' annual reports indicate that the bonds held by the banks are of assorted maturities, and other Federal Reserve statistics indicate that about 40 per cent of them mature within one year and two-thirds within five years. Because several of the largest bond issues are still restricted against bank ownership, the banks have had to concentrate their bondholdings in the remaining issues, with the result that these have at times been priced a little higher than restricted ones.

The Federal Reserve banks are accustomed to adjust the amount and types of their holdings to accomplish their objectives of credit control and bond price stabilization. In March, 1954, they held a total of nearly 25 billion dollars of Federal obligations, of which 4 billion dollars were bonds, 13 billion dollars notes, 6 billion dollars certificates, and 2 billion dollars bills.

Individuals owned 65 billion dollars of obligations in June, 1954, comprised of about 49 billion dollars in savings bonds and 16 billion dollars in treasury bonds, notes, certificates, bills, and miscellaneous items. Three-fourths of the savings bonds were in the Series E issue, which offers the highest yield normally available in any government issue, coupled with reasonably short maturity, complete liquidity, and income tax flexibility. Most of the remaining savings bonds were the old Series G and its successor Series K types, though Series H has also been fairly attractive. The Series G and K bonds have satisfactory 12-year yields, pay a full-rate cash return, and are redeemable

[4] Estimates based on Treasury Department figures regularly presented in the *Federal Reserve Bulletin*.

without discount by the other coowner, an heir, or the executor if an owner dies; hence they have been attractive to people who must plan for estate liquidation and death taxes. It appears that most individuals holding treasury bonds have combined highest yield with estate liquidity by selecting bank-restricted long-term issues which have the privilege of use at par plus accrued interest to pay taxes levied on a deceased owner's estate. These "estate tax privilege" bonds were eagerly bought by many wealthy investors when their prices were down below 95 during the tight money period in 1953.

Insurance companies, savings banks, and government-administered trust funds have chosen mostly long-term treasury and convertible bonds for their government bond portfolios. Obviously, maximum yield was their main consideration. Business corporations, miscellaneous associations, and state and municipal funds seem to have substantial holdings of treasury bonds, but these groups also have large quantities of notes, bills, and certificates, as well as savings bonds and tax notes.

Economic Position of Government Securities

Despite the great variety of ownership interests in government bonds, it seems clear that nearly all these investors choose them because of two characteristics: absolute certainty of payment and a high degree of price stability. Banks want exactly these features, as do individuals, at least in a portion of their investments; business firms, insurance companies, state governments, savings and loan associations, and many others have the same ideas. Low interest rates on government securities are accepted by investors because the safety and stability they need are of paramount importance to them.

From the standpoint of the government the maintenance of low yields on its huge debt is of high importance, for every additional one-fourth of one per cent in average interest charges would add 675 million dollars to its annual interest payments. But there is an even more important reason for the government to exercise great care in satisfying its creditors; the government debt can be paid down only very slowly if at all, and refunding issues averaging nearly 2 billion dollars monthly must be sold during the coming decade to help meet maturing long-term bonds and savings bond cash-ins.

In addition, 38 billion dollars of 90-day and 1-year obligations must be constantly refunded by new sales to short-term holders. Refunding issues must have buyers, and buyers will appear most readily if existing bondholders are obtaining the security and price stability which they seek.

To meet this situation the government has enlisted the cooperation of the Federal Reserve System. The primary function of the Reserve System is to assist the banks of the country in accommodating industry and commerce and maintaining an orderly credit structure. This would be an almost impossible task if the prices and yields on government obligations became unstable or moved in directions not compatible with sound credit conditions. It appears that the Reserve authorities are convinced that an orderly credit structure requires their intervention in the government bond market, for an official spokesman for the System has stated: "The public interest requires a stable market for Government securities. This is the responsibility of the Federal Reserve." [5]

The Reserve System is able to influence money supplies, interest rates, and the prices of government securities in general by open market purchases and sales, by changes in member bank reserve requirements, and by changes in rediscount rates; and it can also affect the relative prices and yields of long-term and short-term government securities to a considerable degree by buying or selling them in unlimited quantities, as the situation requires. Sometimes these price-stabilizing operations are on a huge scale; for example, in the last week of 1947 the System bought 1.1 billion dollars of treasury bonds and sold 500 million dollars of shorter obligations. Needless to say, the Treasury Department cooperates fully in these matters; the purchase or sale of bonds by government trust funds and the nature, timing, and interest rate terms of new government securities offerings all coincide with established policy.

It is not the policy of the Reserve System and the Treasury to attempt to "freeze" the interest yields or the prices on government securities. Instead, the policy is to attempt to control them within a reasonable range, so that a number of objectives may be achieved. These objectives will include low interest costs to the government and reasonably stable prices on long-term bonds for the convenience of investors, as has been noted, but the Reserve System is also in-

[5] Marriner S. Eccles, in the *Federal Reserve Bulletin*, November, 1946, p. 1232.

terested in economic stability, which seems to call for a plentiful money supply and low interest rates when business is dull but for scarce money and higher interest rates when inflationary booms require restraint. The use of money supply powers in the interest of economic stabilization is relatively harmless to the holders of treasury bills and certificates, for even a drastic increase (say, from 1 per cent to 2 per cent) in their yields would affect their market values less than 1 per cent, and even this loss would disappear within the year as they matured. But an increase from 2.50 to 3 per cent in the yield on a 15-year marketable bond will subtract about 7 per cent from its market value, which is a startling loss on a security held for reasons of safety and price stability. (Savings bonds are cashable in accordance with a fixed schedule; these money-market prices do not apply to them.) From 1945 to 1951 the Federal Reserve System attempted to restrain the inflationary boom chiefly by inducing increases in short-term money rates, supplemented by mild increases in long-term rates. These cautious measures were not fully effective, so the System and the Treasury agreed in 1951 to permit greater fluctuations in yield rates and bond prices, if these proved unavoidable in achieving economic stability. The results approached the spectacular. The Treasury 2½s of 1967–1972, which had sold as high as 106.16 under the low interest rate policy in 1946, and which had never sold below par prior to 1951, declined until they reached 89.28 in June, 1953. A few months later the high interest rate policy was reversed in an effort to combat the business recession of 1953–1954, and in mid-1954 the bonds sold at par again. It is not possible to be sure of Federal Reserve attitudes in the future, but it seems reasonable to expect (1) that bond price stabilization will continue to be an objective of the System, (2) that money rates on long-term bonds will be held down so that the long-term 2½s sold during the war will sell at par if possible, but (3) that changes in money rates will be used to counter inflationary or deflationary trends in the economy. This doubtless means that long-term bonds will on occasion fluctuate substantially in price.

It would of course be impossible for government bonds to move in response to money supply and interest rate changes without similar fluctuations in other bond yields and prices. After all, if government bond yields declined because of increased money supplies, people would sell governments and buy high-grade corporates until the two yields were again in a normal relationship. Similarly, yields on treasury bills and bankers' acceptances are related. Table 43 illustrates these tendencies. It is probable that government security prices are a little more stable than high-grade private ones, espe-

Table 43. Percentage Yields on Fully Taxable Government Securities Compared with Private Obligations

	Governments			High-grade corporate bonds	Bankers' acceptances, 90 days
	Bills, 3 months	Certificates, 9 to 12 months	Bonds, over 12 years		
1945 average....	.375	.81	2.37	2.62	.44
1946 average....	.375	.82	2.19	2.53	.61
1947 average....	.604	.88	2.25	2.61	.87
1948 average....	1.040	1.14	2.44	2.82	1.11
1949 average....	1.102	1.14	2.31	2.66	1.12
1950 average....	1.218	1.26	2.32	2.62	1.15
1951 average....	1.552	1.73	2.57	2.86	1.60
1952					
June...........	1.700	1.74	2.61	2.94	1.75
December.......	2.126	2.03	2.75	2.97	1.75
1953					
June...........	2.231	2.46	3.09	3.40	1.88
December.......	1.630	1.61	2.79	3.13	1.88
1954					
June.	.650	.76	2.54	2.90	1.25

Source: *Federal Reserve Bulletin.*

cially in emergency situations in which Federal Reserve influences dominate the market, but the difference is not great.

Market for Government Securities

Though treasury bonds are listed on the New York Stock Exchange, the principal market for all transferable government securities is over the counter. About two dozen large-scale dealers, including the bond departments of several banks, are usually ready to buy or sell any issue of Federal certificates, notes, or bonds, and a number of them make markets in the bills also. Several of these dealers act regularly as brokers or dealers in transactions involving the Reserve System and are known to cooperate in effectuating Reserve System policies. In addition to the large-scale dealers, many of the large banks of the country make dealers' markets in selected issues.

Dealers' markets on government securities are remarkably close; for example, bids and offers on substantial sums in treasury bonds are usually separated by only two thirty-seconds of one percentage point, and on treasury notes this spread is often only one thirty-second. On small quantities the spread is approximately doubled. The dealers' market is not available exclusively to dealers, either; small banks, trust funds, and substantial individual investors can often obtain the inside market price by going directly to the dealers. However, it is more convenient for most individuals to transact their government bond business through their regular brokerage connections; in such cases the brokerage commission is usually one-eighth of one per cent of the par value of the bonds. Most market transactions in government securities are in units of $5,000 to $10,000 or more, because small investors who might deal in lesser sums usually prefer the nonmarketable savings bonds.

As has been previously noted, treasury bonds and notes are quoted in percentages of par value, with fractional percentages expressed in thirty-seconds. For convenience in writing, the unit percentage is placed before and the number of thirty-seconds after a decimal point; thus, 101.5 means 101 and five thirty-seconds, and 101.29 means 101 and twenty-nine thirty-seconds. Certificates and bills are usually quoted in terms of yields; thus the Series H 1¼ per cent certificates due in December, 1949, were quoted in December, 1948, at 1.23 per cent bid, offered at 1.21 per cent.

Sources of Information

Quotations on government securities are found on the usual newspaper financial pages, in financial periodicals, and on dealers' offering sheets. Brief descriptions of all issues are contained in the regular reference services and on circulars and offerings sheets distributed by dealers. In choosing issues for specific purposes, for example, with reference to liquidity for estate tax purposes, it is sometimes desirable to obtain the details about the issue by studying the official announcements at the time of offering. These can be had by request to any Reserve bank, by reference to announcements in financial periodicals dated at the time of issuance, and from the files of dealers or banks.

Investors interested in savings bonds will find a summary of all matters pertaining to ownership, transfer, payment, and redemption in the Treasury Department's pamphlet *Regulations Governing United States Savings Bonds (Department Circular 530, Seventh Revision,* dated 1952), with the supplements thereto. Three other pamphlets, *Department Circulars 653, 905,* and *906,* each in its current revision, explain the investment details and yield and redemption mathematics for Series E, Series H, and Series J and K bonds respectively. Additional pamphlets on specialized topics such as the legal intricacies of ownership and tax matters are occasionally available.

QUESTIONS AND PROBLEMS

1. Is it conceivable that the present willingness of the American people to bear taxes for the support of the public debt might be replaced by a desire to default? Consider any political and economic trends which might lead in that direction.

2. Do you agree that there is a possibility that government bondholders may be repaid in cheaper dollars? That they may have to submit to ex post facto modification of their rights, because of a paramount public interest?

3. What is the nature of the Federal Reserve System's "management" of the public debt? Could this be done by raising and lowering member bank reserve requirements, without buying or selling any bonds?

4. Are savings bonds regarded as "direct" Federal debt? Define Federal instrumentalities, nonmarketable debt, non-bank-eligible treasury bonds, treasury bills.

5. Explain this sentence: The Treasury 2½s of 1967–72 were quoted yesterday at 100.11 at 100.13, while last week's issue of bills was 1.08% at 1.01%.

6. How do long-term treasury bond issues differ? What features would an individual investor probably seek?

7. As an individual investor, would you choose Series E, Series H, or

Series K bonds for a $3,000 investment? Explain. If you had $50,000 to invest, would you choose one of the above, or a treasury bond?

8. If you had a friend who wished to invest $20,000 in governments, but who insisted on cash income every six months, could you work out a combination of Series E bonds and 2 per cent postal savings deposits (these accrue ½ per cent interest quarterly) which would earn more than Series K bonds and still make cash available as earned? Or would Series H bonds be better?

9. If you directed a $10,000,000 savings and loan association which had $9,000,000 in installment mortgages, $200,000 in a working bank balance, and $800,000 to be kept in government bonds as a seldom-used secondary reserve, what kinds of governments would you choose?

10. What form of ownership would you select for the savings bonds you and your wife buy? Explain.

11. Would you regard the market on government bonds as a satisfactory one? Are governments traded on the exchanges?

12. Is there enough difference in yield between governments and good corporate bonds to justify investment in corporates by small investors? Consider the risk, time to maturity, commission costs, taxes, legal ownership factors, price stability, and liquidity.

13. Will the Federal Reserve System's program for stabilizing the market in long-term governments also tend to stabilize good corporate bonds? Explain.

14. Look up the Treasury 2½s of 1967–72 and determine their principal features.

15. What type of government security would you recommend to an elderly couple with $250,000 net worth who wish to provide liquid resources for $25,000 of state inheritance taxes and $25,000 of Federal estate taxes, but to obtain the maximum income meanwhile? Assume that the Treasury 2½s of 1967–72 are selling at 97.

REFERENCES

Badger, Ralph E., and Harry G. Guthmann: *Investment Principles and Practices,* Prentice-Hall, Inc., New York, 1951, Chap. 18.

Childs, C. F.: *Concerning U.S. Government Securities,* C. F. Childs and Company, Chicago, 1947.

Grodinsky, Julius: *Investments,* The Ronald Press Company, New York, 1953, Chap. 17.

Jordan, David F., and Herbert E. Dougall: *Investments,* Prentice-Hall, Inc., New York, 1952, Chap. 19.

Pickett, Ralph R., and Marshall D. Ketchum: *Investment Principles and Policy,* Harper & Brothers, New York, 1954, Chaps. 12, 13.

Piser, Leroy M.: *U.S. Government Bond Market Analysis,* New York Institute of Finance, New York, 1952.

Robbins, Sidney M.: *Managing Securities,* Houghton Mifflin Company, Boston, 1954, Chaps. 14, 15.

Chapter 22: STATE AND MUNICIPAL BONDS

Approximately 32.3 billion dollars of state and municipal bonds were held by American investors in 1953. While this sum is not large compared with the huge amounts of Federal and corporate bonds outstanding, it represents a very important part of the investment market to investors who are interested in a combination of safety and tax avoidance. Most state and municipal bonds are high grade, and the interest they pay is exempt from Federal income tax.

Public obligations issued by the states and their political subdivisions are roughly classified as "state" and "municipal" bonds. Neither classification represents a homogeneous group, for state obligations vary as to the nature of the promise and the sources of funds for repayment, and the municipal group contains these variations plus others due to the heterogeneous nature of the cities, counties, school districts, improvement districts, and other units which comprise the borrowers. For the sake of brevity bond dealers often refer to all types of state and municipal bonds collectively as "municipals."

State and municipal public bodies in the United States derive their powers from the sovereign authority of the states, through the provisions of the state constitutions, state statutes, and state-granted municipal charters. The powers of each state and its municipalities are unique to that state and need not be closely parallel to those found in other states. It is therefore necessary for an investor in state or municipal bonds to examine the powers and limitations of the borrower as well as the nature of the promises made on the bond, if he is to understand his investment. To facilitate this task it seems necessary to classify the bonds into four general types and the borrowers into five.

Types of Bonds

State and municipal bonds may be roughly classified as (1) full faith and credit bonds, (2) revenue bonds, (3) assessment bonds, and (4) hybrids between the above groups. It is important, in considering these classifications, to remember that they are only rough groupings of many issues of bonds. The bonds within the groups will be similar in many respects, but there will also be great differences in both the legal and the financial positions of different issues.

Full faith and credit bonds, which are also referred to as general obligations or as fully tax-supported obligations, are those whose pay ment is unconditionally promised by a governmental unit which has the power to levy taxes. The majority of state, county, city, town, school district, and road district obligations are of this sort, though the types of taxes which these units may use vary considerably. In general, fully tax-supported public obligations are highly regarded and command the highest prices and lowest yields in the public bond group.

Revenue bonds are bonds issued by publicly owned business agencies such as water departments, electric power departments, toll bridge authorities, and the like, on which payment is promised only from the earnings of the business. The borrowing agency promises to establish rates and operate the business in a manner which will enable it to make payment, and state statutes usually provide for court enforcement of this promise. Because most revenue bonds have been the obligations of monopoly utilities serving growing demands the record of the bonds has been very good, and in general they are highly regarded. In scattered instances revenue bonds based on transit systems, irrigation water systems, and other unstable enterprises have fallen into default, but the weaknesses were usually due to earnings instability, not to the legal nature of the bonds.

Assessment bonds are bonds issued to finance improvements such as pavements or sewers and which are payable from the proceeds of specific assessments levied upon each lot or field in the benefited area. The assessment district in its simplest form has no taxing power; it may collect from each lot only its proportionate share of the original total assessment necessary to finance the improvement. Most such assessments are apportioned on a per lot or per square foot basis, since these improvements cost just as much in front of a vacant lot as they would if the lot were used for a building. The assessment is usually collected in annual installments over a period ranging from 10 to 20 years, to provide the district with money to pay each year's interest and (usually) serial maturities as they come due. Assessment bonds are very reliable investments when the assessed property is highly valuable compared with the size of the assessments; but many defaults occurred during the period 1930–1935 in districts in which heavy assessments had been levied on vacant lots or other low-value property.

Hybrid types of bonds are found in instances where revenue bonds are guaranteed as to payment by the state or municipality which owns the borrowing department; when revenue bonds are further supported by assessments or taxes, as, for example, when irrigation district water revenues are supplemented by taxes on the property in the district; when assessment districts are permitted to levy supplementary taxes on all property in the district, to make up deficiencies due to unpaid assessments; or when other such combinations of money sources exist. One peculiar hybrid between a full faith and credit bond and a revenue bond should be particularly noted: a number of borrowers, including state agencies in Colorado, Pennsylvania, and Tennessee, have sold bonds on which payment is pledged only from specified taxes; there is no unconditional promise to pay.

The Debtors

The five types of debtors to be distinguished are (1) the states; (2) municipalities with broad powers, such as counties, cities, and towns; (3) districts with limited powers, such as school districts, road districts, and similar taxing agencies; (4) assessment districts; and (5) departments and authorities.

On the whole the American states must be regarded as high-class credit risks. They have very effective revenue sources available in their sales taxes, gasoline taxes, motor vehicle taxes, income taxes, inheritance taxes, and general property taxes. Their usual expenditures for highways, institutions, aid to schools, and general government have not been so burdensome as the national government's defense outlays or the municipalities' local services, with the result that state budgets have been comfortably balanced and state debts kept small. However, the states are manifesting an increasing tendency to contribute to school and other local costs and to undertake old-age pensions, veterans' bonuses, and welfare work on a large scale. These outlays are pressing increasingly on the states' revenue sources and may ultimately tend to limit their credit standing to some extent, though in most cases no serious impairment is noticeable at present. Naturally, some states are better than others.

Cities, towns, and counties are heavily dependent on the general property tax for revenue, though business license taxes, sales taxes, and even income taxes are used. Expenditures include police and fire protection, health, schools, sanitation, and an increasing list of regulatory and service functions, plus, in the case of the counties, exten-

Table 44. Gross Debt of State and Municipal Governments, 1902–1952

(In millions of dollars)

	Total	States	Cities and towns	Counties	Other municipal
1902	$ 2,195	$ 270	$ 1,612	$ 205	$ 108
1912	4,498	423	3,447	393	235
1922	10,256	1,163	5,810	1,387	1,896
1932	19,576	2,896	9,909	2,775	3,996
1942	19,690	3,211	9,806	1,846	4,827
1945	16,589	2,425	8,411	1,545	4,208
1950	24,191	5,361	10,908	1,707	6,215
1951	27,040	6,373	11,721	1,875	7,071
1952	29,623	7,040	12,437	2,066	8,081

Source: *Statistical Abstract of the United States, 1953*, p. 392.

sive pension, relief, and welfare work. These costs are substantial and appear to be more burdensome on the available revenue sources than those borne by the states. Also, the service on existing city and county debt is often heavier than that borne by the states, since state debt in 1954 was relatively modest. In general, cities, towns, and counties must be classed as good credit risks, with the wealthier and more diversified communities preferred.

Districts with limited powers, such as school districts, road districts, park districts, and drainage districts, are usually completely dependent on the general property tax. The tax rate they may impose is sometimes limited by law, and the rate's effectiveness is often limited by the capacity of the taxpayers. In districts where public expenditures are reasonably limited, where debt service is not too burdensome, where property is valuable, and where taxpayers have substantial and diversified income sources, the bonds are likely to be good. Under contrasting conditions occasional defaults might be encountered.

Assessment districts are usually organized for the purpose of financing a single public improvement such as a paving or street-lighting project. As such they will usually not have offices or officers; all business is transacted by city or county officials, subject to state statutes which outline all procedures in detail. Each lot in an assessment district is obligated to make regular annual payments into a fund from which interest and maturing bonds are paid. Failure to pay obligates the supervising city or county officials to take steps to foreclose the "improvement lien" and sell the lot to recover the sums due, but this process is often delayed, especially if many lot owners fail to pay. Defaults by lot owners naturally cause the district to fall behind on its interest and principal payments, since it has no other funds. In an attempt to simplify the handling of special assessment funds some states authorize the assessment district to issue and sell a separate "bond" for each lot in the district; these bonds are issued for whatever odd amount the lot owner is required to pay and are payable in installments by the lot owner to the county or city collecting agency for immediate transmission to the bondholder. These bonds may be foreclosed like a superior mortgage (the lien is superior to that of any mortgage) if the lot owner fails to pay. Obviously, an installment bond of this kind is most suitable for an investment institution with appropriate accounting facilities.

States, cities, and counties frequently have "departments" which operate water systems, electric power systems, or other publicly owned business ventures. The municipality usually provides some equity capital, and revenue bonds serve as the funded debt. Since the municipal venture is free of almost all taxes and can usually be assured a monopoly, it has every chance to succeed. Sometimes a publicly owned business venture is operated by a specially created "authority" whose powers are detailed by its own statute. The Port of New York Authority, created jointly by the states of New York and New Jersey, and the California Toll Bridge Authority, created by the state of California, are examples of such agencies. Either the department or the authority may be compared to a business corporation; it must try to earn enough to pay its debts, and if it fails to do so the stockholder (the state or municipal owner) must decide whether to provide the money or to permit the bondholders to seek a remedy in the courts. The record of revenue bonds in general is good, and their use is increasing rapidly. They are usually a little lower in price or higher in yield than general obligations of the same municipality, but this is not always the case.

Bond Features

State and municipal bonds are issued pursuant to the constitutional, statutory, and charter powers which govern the borrowers. In most instances these include bond statutes which are explicit and detailed on such matters as the authorization of the issue, the length of maturity, the security if any, and the source of funds for repayment. In fact, the statutes are so complete that they practically outline the terms of the bonds, and when a few administrative details are furnished in the official announcement, no further description is needed. Trust indentures and trustees are seldom used, as officials designated by law carry out the procedures outlined in the bond statutes.

Some of the legal features which affect the investment standing of public bonds, and which are commonly prescribed by bond statutes, are:

1. Maturities. Both straight and serial maturities are common, with the latter commonly used to finance pavements, school buildings, and other depreciating assets.

2. Sinking funds. Large-scale borrowers such as New York City often find straight maturity bonds easier to sell than serials, but provide for debt amortization through sinking funds which purchase or call prescribed amounts of outstanding bonds annually.

3. Call prices. Increasing numbers of bond statutes now provide call prices for both sinking fund and general retirement purposes. Older public bonds are largely non-callable.

4. Pledged revenues. Except for revenue bonds, the great majority of public bonds are debentures which have no lien or preferential rights to any specific property or revenues. However, some states and municipalities sell bonds which have prior claims to specific tax or fee revenues.

5. Debt limits. Statutes which prevent the incurring of public debt in excess of stated percentages of assessed property values or some other reasonable limit are important to bondholders. Debt limit statutes are sometimes evaded by creation of additional overlapping tax districts or by use of revenue bonds which are not included in the calculations.

6. Tax limits. Tax limitation laws which prevent the levying of general property taxes in excess of a stipulated rate are helpful if they prevent extravagant spending without preventing debt service. Most tax limit laws apply only to levies designed for current spending and permit unlimited extra taxes for debt service only. This is an important feature.

7. Tax collection system. A tax collection system which is equitable and efficient, and which is fortified by appropriate penalties on delinquents, is important. It is desirable that taxes for debt service be included in the same levy with those used for ordinary public expenditures, as tax collectors are sometimes indifferent about collecting bondholders' money if funds for current expenditures are separately collected. Furthermore, the law should require that tax money collected for debt service be segregated immediately in separate bond funds and not placed in a general fund from which all public expenditures and debt payments are to be appropriated at later dates.

8. Tax delinquencies. The statutes should provide for prompt and complete tax sales of defaulting property and should require that tax collectors be diligent in selling delinquent property in order to collect back taxes and restore the property to a tax-paying basis for the future.

Default Experience

During the depression of the 1930s an estimated 3,000 public debtors, including counties, cities, towns, taxing districts, and assessment districts, committed some sort of debt default. The total debts of the embarrassed debtors exceeded 2 billion dollars. However, only 200 million dollars of principal and interest remained in arrears 18 months after the banking holiday, and nearly all of the debtors had resumed regular interest payments. Most of the arrears were paid within the next three years, but in some cases the bondholders had to accept new bonds with longer maturities, lower interest rates, and even reduced principal sums. In general, the short duration of defaults and the smallness of the total ultimate losses reflect great credit on state and municipal debtors.

One state, Arkansas, attempted in 1933 to force its creditors to exchange their outstanding 4½ to 6 per cent bonds for new 3 per cent ones by the simple expedient of authorizing interest payments on the 3s and refusing to pay on the others.[1] Since private citizens may not sue a sovereign state without its consent, the bondholders were without a legal redress, but the threats and protests of investors and bond dealers were instrumental in causing Arkansas to rescind its action.

Subordinate political bodies such as cities or school districts can be dealt with in the courts by any unpaid investor who chooses to take action. Groups of bondholders, usually headed by the securities dealer who marketed the bonds, sometimes take such action. Most state laws permit bondholders to obtain writs of mandamus or court orders which force tax or assessment collectors to take positive action to levy taxes, make collections, and hold tax sales of nonpaying property, in order that money may be raised to pay the bondholders. If this proves impossible, some state laws provide for receivership commissions which supervise the debtor's finances and attempt to work out compromise settlements with the bondholders. Other states have a variety of statutory procedures under which unpaid bondholders and debtor communities work out their own compromises, usually with the aid of the courts or county officials.

In general, it may be said that adjustment of serious public bond defaults is slow, awkward, and unsatisfactory in most states. The holders of small amounts of bonds can hardly afford to go to court to press their claims; unless a protective committee comes forward, the small bondholder waits helplessly for something to happen. Investors in public bonds are well advised to avoid bonds in which serious defaults seem even remotely possible. In cases in which the debtor carries on regular governmental services, such as fire departments, schools, health services, and the like, expenditures for these purposes are often given precedence over debt payments when the money supply is limited, even if this means that the bondholders get nothing.

[1] See Moody's *Governments and Municipals* manuals for 1934 and 1935 for a summary of this affair.

Important Guides to Bond Quality

As in the case of the Federal debt, tax-supported state and municipal bonds can best be tested by inquiring as to the debtors' willingness to pay and ability to pay.

Willingness to pay is indexed by the debtor's record and by the observed attitudes of officials and people. In general, it may be said that American states and municipalities are willing to pay their obligations and will levy adequate taxes for the purpose. There are occasional instances in which bitterness over waste, extravagance, or injustice results in tax "strikes" or a widespread refusal to pay special assessments—witness, for example, the Cook County (Chicago) tax confusion of 1928–1936 over inequities in assessment procedures—but careful investors can find and avoid these "sore spots." Also, it appears that overburdened taxpayers and communities are likely to feel that creditors should share their sorrows when depressions strike, as Arkansas did in 1933. Finally, it should be noted that taxpayers do not feel a personal responsibility to pay taxes or special assessments when it appears that the penalties on nonpayment may not be severe or that their property may not be worth the charges, even though they were enthusiastic in incurring the debt. This attitude was manifest in many special assessment, irrigation, and drainage districts in the period 1930–1940. Defaults occurred, and bondholders had to accept long delays and financial compromises. Willingness to pay thus appears to be closely associated with ability to pay without inconvenience.

The ability of a public debtor to pay its debts is dependent upon the financial capacity of its citizens to carry the burden placed upon them. In gauging the situation, it is necessary to note both the financial position of the debtor unit and the total burdens imposed on the taxpayers by state, county, city, school district, and possibly several other overlapping road, park, sanitary, and special improvement districts. The complexity of the problem is indicated by the fact that a 1942 Census Bureau enumeration found 3,050 counties, 35,139 cities and other incorporated places, 108,579 school districts, and 8,299 other districts functioning as permanent governmental units subordinate to the 48 states. These figures do not include special assessment districts. When important bond issues are offered for sale, the bond underwriters usually employ Dun & Bradstreet or some equally experienced firm to make a survey of the overlapping tax and improvement districts, in order to measure the aggregate debt and tax burden to be borne by the area.

Ability to pay may be gauged by studying the following eight factors, and comparing the debtor in question with other like debtors:

1. The debt burden. Is the aggregate tax-supported and assessment debt (a) reasonable in ratio to property valuation, (b) reasonable on a per capita basis, and (c) reasonable in ratio to the aggregate earning power of the community?

2. The tax burden. Are the taxes reasonable in ratio to property valuation, on a per capita basis, and in ratio to aggregate incomes?

3. Tax delinquencies. Are taxes and assessments (a) paid on time, and (b) finally paid in full?

4. Condition of the budget. Is the community budget balanced? Are floating debts accumulated by use of tax anticipation warrants?

5. Is the trend of expenditures reasonable?

6. Is the trend of the public debt reasonable?

7. Is the community financially well to do, stable, and diversified as to property holdings and income sources?

8. Does the population contain a substantial percentage of native-born, educated, income tax paying, propertied citizens?

Statistics and analytical reports covering these points can be found in the financial services or can be supplied by municipal bond dealers. Since the bare statistics are not too meaningful, it is customary to compare the figures of any municipality with those of others of the same size and type; if the figures appear relatively good now, and also compare favorably with the 1928–1930 figures of municipalities which came through the depression unscathed, they are acceptable. It is best to compare only municipalities of the same size and type; larger cities and more populous counties, for example, usually have and can bear higher expense and debt ratios. Vigilance is also necessary in statistical analysis to make sure that all figures are representative and comparable—that overlapping debts and taxes are all included, that property values are stated at actual rather than fractional assessed valuations, that allowance is made for self-supporting debt, etc.

In the analysis of a revenue bond which has no supplementary tax support or municipal guarantee, the main issue is the earning power of the business project. This would be studied in a fashion similar to that used in corporate situations, anticipating sales, costs, earnings, and expansion needs, and contrasting the available earnings with the amounts required to service the bonds. Matters dealing with such

Table 45. Comparative Debt and Tax Statistics of Large Cities, 1952

(Debt figures include proper portion of all country and subordinate units; tax figures include total general property tax levy)

City	Net tax-supported debt *		Default record, 1930–1947	Percentage of taxes, collected when due		Property tax rate per $1,000 actual value
	Per capita	Percentage of property valuation		1935	Latest year	
Baltimore...........	$146	6.5	No	89.9	97.1	$28.20
Boston.............	204	10.3	No	72.7	91.7	70.70
Buffalo.............	76	4.4	No	90.0	99.9	31.52
Chicago............	98	4.0	No	NA	89.6	36.00
Cleveland..........	112	5.1	Temporary	84.4	97.2	18.06
Detroit.............	96	4.0	Temporary	74.6	98.8	39.18
Los Angeles........	194	13.2	No	91.1	98.7	32.78
Milwaukee..........	54	2.4	No	NA	99.4	45.53
New York..........	274	11.3	No	84.2	95.0	33.30
Philadelphia........	210	12.4	No	84.3	97.1	30.25
Pittsburgh..........	154	10.1	No	80.4	94.3	25.00
St. Louis...........	39	2.4	No	80.7	94.7	30.70
San Francisco.......	156	9.3	No	96.7	99.2	31.35
Median...........	150	9.3	...	84.4	97.1	31.52

* Excludes bonds in sinking funds, debt of self-supporting projects, and assessment bonds. Los Angeles figures do not include Metropolitan Water District.

Source: Adapted from Moody's *Governments and Municipals*, 1953.

items as additional debt, depreciation accounting, annual audits, adequate insurance, levels of rates, disposition of excess earnings, and remedies of the bondholders in case of default could be very important to revenue bondholders. Some revenue bonds have mortgage liens, which seem mostly to be intended to make foreclosure possible in case of default. Revenue bonds may not all be of equal priority; that is, one issue may rank ahead of another in its claim on available funds.

Legality

Because the state statutes governing the authorization and issuance of municipal bonds are usually explicit and technical, it appears necessary to use extreme care in creating a new issue, if questions as to its legality are to be avoided. This leads bond buyers to place great stress on the "legal opinion" of a law firm experienced in such matters. A few recognized law firms in each state make a specialty of advising municipalities and securities underwriters on the creation of bonds.

Tax Position

As has been previously noted, the interest on state and municipal bonds is not includable by a taxpayer as gross income in his Federal income tax return. The exemption rests upon specific provisions of present Federal tax statutes, plus the assumption that the sovereignty of the states would make unconstitutional any Federal tax which burdened the borrowing operations of either the states or their subordinate units. There have been suggestions that interest on assessment bonds and revenue bonds might be held taxable on the theory that they are not the *obligations* of governmental agencies, and further that the sale of electric power or the paving of a street at the propertyholders' expense is not a part of the process of government. There have also been proposals for the enactment of a constitutional amendment abolishing all tax-exempt securities. However, Congress has not been willing to accept either idea. The states are of course free to tax the interest paid by their own bonds, by those of other states, and by municipal obligations of all states, when the bonds are held by taxpayers within their jurisdictions.[2]

State and municipal obligations are fully subject to all applicable Federal and state taxes on estates, inheritances, and gifts, and capital gains on them are taxable.

[2] For a brief review of the tax status of all public bonds, see Moody's *Governments and Municipals,* 1953, Special Features Section.

Markets, Prices, Yields

State and municipal bonds have great attraction for high-bracket individuals, private trust funds, and corporations, for obvious reasons. Ownership figures in the 1953 annual reports of the Secretary of the Treasury indicate that in 1953 individuals, partnerships, and personal trusts held 37 per cent of those outstanding, commercial banks held 33 per cent, and insurance companies 10 per cent. Since high-bracket investors obtain greater advantage from the tax-free feature than others could, they customarily bid the bonds up to a price at which few others will buy them.

Although the principal special feature of municipal bonds is their exemption from Federal income taxation, it is sometimes worth while to consider the effect of state income and local property taxation. Such taxes are usually levied on out-of-state municipals, but the local bonds are usually exempt if owned by individuals and often if owned by corporations or banks. This may on occasion be an item of sufficient importance to induce the investor to favor bonds originating in his own state.

New issues of state and municipal bonds are bought by banks, insurance companies, and dealers who specialize in these issues. The dealers and the bond departments of some banks retail the bonds to investors and maintain over-the-counter markets in them. Market prices are usually steady, though there is no Federal Reserve support to stabilize them. Many issues disappear into bank and trust holdings, to be held until maturity, and are thus never quoted in the trading markets.

Though certain dealers are known to specialize in certain issues of municipal bonds and to make markets in them regularly, most dealers buy and sell a wide range of issues as opportunity offers, without attempting to maintain an inventory in them at all times. The most active dealers list their offerings each day in a publication called *The Blue List of Current Municipal Offerings;* this enables all dealers and brokers to locate inventories and asking prices of important issues on a nationwide basis. State and municipal bonds are usually quoted in terms of yield to maturity (*i.e.*, 2.55 per cent bid, offered at 2.50 per cent), though quotations in terms of percentages and eighths are often used. Most transactions between dealers or brokers and their customers are on a "principal" basis, the firm selling to or buying from its customer, with no commission involved; on this basis the "spread" between what a customer would get for municipal bonds and what he would pay for them would normally range between ½ and 2 per cent of the sum involved, the exact

Table 46. State and Municipal Bond Quotations from the Blue List *of August 3, 1954* *

Bond	Type	Yield or price
California 1½s, 1961	General	1.25
California 2s, 1973	General	2.05
Illinois 1¾s, 1969	General	1.60
New York State 1¾s, 1974	General	1.90
Los Angeles School District 2½s, 1974	General	2.15
New Orleans 2s, 1975	General	2.40
New York City 2s, 1973	General	2.55
Columbus, Ohio, 2¼s, 1973	Limited tax	2.15
Mobile, Ala., 3s, 1968	Water revenue	2.75
Los Angeles Dept. 2s, 1968	Electric revenue	2.10
Georgia State School Building Authority 2.8s, 1971	Revenue	102
Indiana Toll Road 3½s, 1994	Revenue	106
Pennsylvania Turnpike 2¾s, 1970	Revenue	104
Chicago Transit Authority 3¾s, 1978	Revenue	92¼
Scranton Housing Authority 2¼s, 1976	Revenue	2.10
Nashville Housing Authority 2¼s, 1976	Revenue	2.05

* *Blue List* quotations are dealers' asking prices subject to a concession to a purchasing dealer; hence they are approximately net cost prices to a private investor. *The Blue List* does not carry dealers' bid prices, but brokers or dealers desiring to sell can list their offerings, or solicit dealers whose offerings disclose an interest in the bonds in question or in similar ones.

amount depending on the size of the transaction, the marketability of the bonds, the quality of the bonds, and the relationships of the parties.

The prices and yields on tax-exempt bonds as a class are dominated by four factors: (1) the yields available on other securities, particularly high-class taxable bonds; (2) the severity of high-bracket tax rates, which of course determines the relative attractiveness of tax-exempt bonds; (3) the number of high-bracket incomes, which measures the need for tax-exempt investments; and (4) the amount of tax-exempt bonds available. The influence of all these factors can be seen in the war and postwar period 1941–1954. During the war the Federal tax rates were greatly increased, at a time when war prosperity was lifting many individuals' incomes into high tax brackets. This caused an increase in the demand for municipals, just when municipalities had ceased to borrow because their construction activities were suspended by the war. Municipals therefore rose sharply in price and declined in yield. After the war the number of high incomes decreased, competing corporate stock and bond yields rose, and both states and municipalities sold new tax-exempt bonds in great quantities. Accordingly, municipals dropped in price and their yields rose. In late 1947 a spectacular drop in the prices of municipals occurred because it became apparent that the Revenue Act of 1948, then in preparation in Congress, would permit married couples to split their income in separate tax returns; this would give each spouse a separate set of tax brackets, keep the (combined) income from reaching into the high-tax brackets, and thus make tax-exempt municipal bonds less necessary. The sharp increase in the price of municipals in 1950 reflects the expected increase in income tax rates at that time, and the relative decline in 1952–1953 reflects the very great volume of municipals then being sold.

Although all forms of state and municipal projects have contributed to the large volume of municipal bonds sold since the war, two notable ones deserve special mention. The first is the Federal Housing Act program. The Federal Housing Act of 1949 authorizes the Federal Public Housing Administration to enter into contracts with state or municipal agencies which desire to build low-rent public housing projects for occupancy by low-income citizens. Under these contracts the Federal government agrees to pay annual cash subsidies equal to the entire sums needed to pay the interest and principal on the serial revenue bonds which finance the projects. These bonds are technically state or municipal revenue bonds, hence have the tax-exempt status of municipals, but, since the Federal subsidy is earmarked for bond service, they have the unimpeachable quality of Federal obligations. Although these bonds are offered at irregular intervals, they usually total several hundred millions per year and afford an especially large volume of long-term bonds.

The second conspicuous recent development in municipals has been the extensive growth of the highway revenue bond. Although

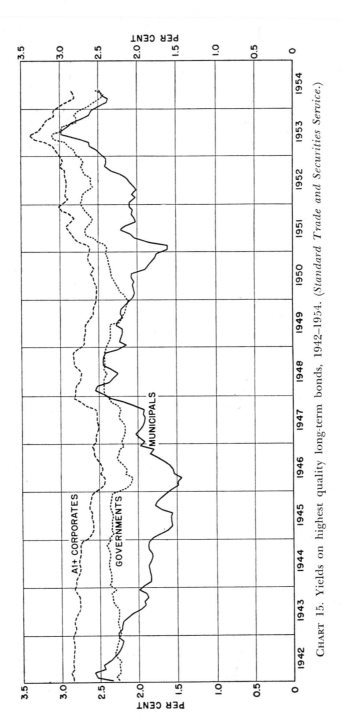

CHART 15. Yields on highest quality long-term bonds, 1942–1954. *(Standard Trade and Securities Service.)*

revenue bonds are in increasing use to finance many types of ventures, the gigantic toll highway developments in Connecticut, New York, Ohio, and other states since 1951 have marked an important trend. In general these bonds have been regarded as very good rather than superb in quality, but their tax-exempt yields of 2.5 to 3.5 per cent have made them very attractive to many investors.

Table 47. Excerpts from Table of Tax-free Yield Equivalents

Individual tax bracket		Gross yield of taxable securities				
Taxable income	Bracket tax rate in 1954	2.00%	2.50%	3.00%	4.00%	5.00%
		Equivalent yield of tax-exempt securities				
$ 2,000	20%	1.60%	2.00%	2.40%	3.20%	4.00%
6,000	26	1.48	1.85	2.22	2.96	3.70
10,000	34	1.32	1.65	1.98	2.64	3.30
20,000	53	.94	1.18	1.41	1.88	2.35
50,000	75	.50	.63	.75	1.00	1.25
100,000	89	.22	.28	.33	.44	.55
Corporation	52%	.96	1.20	1.44	1.92	2.40

The great importance attached to the tax exemption feature leads many dealers in municipal bonds to publish *tables of tax-free yield equivalents,* which are intended to point out the small amount of tax-free interest necessary to equal the posttax remainder from any taxable income. Such tables (see Table 47 for an example) usually assume that the highest tax bracket into which an investor's income reaches is the one which is applicable in determining investment policy. Thus Table 47 indicates that for a man with $20,000 of taxable income, whose top bracket rate is 53 per cent, a 2.35 per cent tax-free yield is as good as a 5 per cent taxable yield. This is weighty reasoning, which probably deserves consideration by many people who know nothing of municipal bonds, but it must also be remembered that other forms of investment also have their advantages—superior liquidity, price-level protection, possibility of lightly taxed capital gains, etc.

One further comment respecting municipal bond yields and taxes must be made. There are many long-term low-coupon municipals which sell at a discount, hence have satisfactory yields to maturity composed partly of cash interest and partly of appreciation of principal. In nearly all such cases only the cash interest is tax-exempt; when the profit on the principal is finally realized by sale or collection of the bond it is a capital gain, subject to both state and Federal income taxes at the low capital gains rates. If a municipal bond is purchased at a premium above par, no tax-reducing capital loss can be realized if the bond is held to maturity and collected at par; in this case the premium is assumed to be amortized against the cash interest, to net a yield below the coupon interest rate.

Sources of Information

The information available to the nonprofessional investor in public bonds is rather sketchy and difficult to understand, compared with the extensive literature on corporate securities. Investors depend on Moody's *Governments and Municipals* manual for useful summaries of available information, though data on overlapping districts is often incomplete. This service also assigns "quality ratings" to the larger issues. Comprehensive prospectuses can be had in only a few instances, and annual reports analogous to corporate reports simply do not exist. Comprehension of the available financial data is also difficult for the amateur, for it requires an understanding of the statutes of each state with respect to municipal bodies, their taxes, debts, and procedures.

Most nonprofessional investors accept the advice of an expert whom they trust, or rely upon conspicuous large borrowers whose standings are easily ascertained, or confine themselves to local issues whose legal features and economic circumstances they know at first hand. The experts have available a detailed analytical service furnished by Dun & Bradstreet covering borrowers and issues of significant size, and also providing special reports on the smaller issues. These, supplemented by the reports of local research agencies in some areas and by the usual reference sources and a general familiarity with the debtor areas, provide the facts upon which decisions can be made.

Important general information for municipal bond buyers is

found in several periodicals, including *The Bond Buyer* and *National Municipal Review,* and in other investment sources. An excellent bibliography on state and municipal finance is contained in the annual *Municipal Year Book.* Extensive statistical data will be found in the Census Bureau's annual reports on *Governmental Debts in the United States, Financial Statistics of Cities,* and *Financial Statistics of States,* and in other census reports; in the *Annual Report* of the Secretary of the Treasury; in the *Statistical Abstract of the United States;* in the *Municipal Year Book;* and in the statistical section of Moody's *Governments and Municipals* manual.

QUESTIONS AND PROBLEMS

1. Explain why state and municipal obligations are so varied in legal background.

2. Distinguish between full faith and credit bonds and revenue bonds. Which would you prefer in a city noted for heavy debt and extravagant political administration, a full faith and credit bond or a water department revenue bond?

3. Why do assessment bonds yield more than general obligations?

4. Look up and classify the bonds of the following debtors as to type and quality: (*a*) Mobile, Alabama; (*b*) Louisiana; (*c*) Imperial Irrigation District, California; (*d*) Los Angeles Department of Water and Power; (*e*) Delaware; (*f*) St. Louis, Missouri.

5. Look up the prices of the bonds studied in Question 4 in the *Bank and Quotation Record.* Does it appear that state bonds sell higher than municipal ones? Are full faith and credit bonds higher than revenue bonds? Do short-term bonds yield less than long-term ones? Interpret your findings.

6. What are the principal revenues and disbursements of your state? Are they increasing faster than the incomes of the population?

7. Would a rapidly growing municipality be as good a credit risk as a well-established and slowly growing one? (Consider the amount of new municipal construction required, the amount of private real estate debt in a new community, and the stability of personal and business income.)

8. Why would state laws prescribe serial maturities or sinking fund bonds for the financing of pavements and school buildings?

9. Explain the use and misuse of debt limitation laws and tax-limitation laws.

10. Which would be best, a very severe penalty for tax delinquency or

a system designed to permit a tax defaulter to pay up in easy installments and thus restore his property to regular tax-paying status?

11. Do state and municipal bonds have a good record since 1930?

12. How would you test a municipal debtor's willingness to pay? Can this be fairly tested prospectively?

13. What are the most important measures of a municipality's ability to pay tax-supported bonds? How could you tell what the fact meant, if you learned that the total tax-supported debt in your city was 8 per cent of the property valuation?

14. Explain the relationship of interest on state and municipal bonds to the investor's personal income tax liability.

15. Would you expect the large numbers of small municipal issues, the obligations of the less important municipalities, to be marketed in distant states? Is it possible, then, that citizens in states having relatively few millionaires, and in which few great trust companies are located, might find good local municipals with attractive yields?

16. Municipal bonds are commonly sold in $5,000 "blocks" rather than in the familiar $1,000 bond unit. What factor in their market appeal probably accounts for this?

REFERENCES

Badger, Ralph E., and Harry G. Guthmann: *Investment Principles and Practices,* Prentice-Hall, Inc., New York, 1951, Chaps. 19, 20.

Dowrie, George W., and Douglas R. Fuller: *Investments,* John Wiley & Sons, Inc., New York, 1950, Chap. 23.

Grodinsky, Julius: *Investments,* The Ronald Press Company, New York, 1953, Chaps. 18, 19.

Hillhouse, A. M.: *Municipal Bonds: A Century of Experience,* Prentice-Hall, Inc., New York, 1936.

Investment Bankers Association of America: *Fundamentals of Investment Banking,* Prentice-Hall, Inc., New York, 1949, Chaps. 11, 12.

Jordan, David F., and Herbert E. Dougall: *Investments,* Prentice-Hall, Inc., New York, 1952, Chaps. 20, 21.

Knappen, L. S.: *Revenue Bonds and the Investor,* Prentice-Hall, Inc., New York, 1939.

Pickett, Ralph R., and Marshall D. Ketchum: *Investment Principles and Policy,* Harper & Brothers, New York, 1954, Chap. 14.

Robbins, Sidney M.: *Managing Securities,* Houghton Mifflin Company, Boston, 1954, Chaps. 17, 18.

Chapter 23: LIFE INSURANCE

Life insurance is one of the major investments of most American families. A 1952 survey under the sponsorship of the Federal Reserve System concluded that 79 per cent of American families owned life insurance, and the 1953 *Life Insurance Fact Book* estimates that in 1953 the average family owned policies in private companies totaling $5,800 in face amount. In addition, government life insurance owned by veterans averaged $700 per American family. Other statistics indicate that the average family's insurance investment had a cash value exceeding $1,300. The total resources invested in American privately operated companies exceeded 78.5 billion dollars at year-end 1953, and the sum was growing at the rate of 5 billion dollars or more annually.

These statistics demonstrate the great importance of life insurance among types of investments. Of course, insurance is seldom purchased solely for investment reasons—in fact, the mortality costs and operating expenses incident to life insurance would usually make the investment unprofitable if the life protection feature were not needed—but as an investment combined with protection, the insurance device is unparalleled in safety, profitableness, and convenience. It therefore occupies an important place in most carefully planned investment programs.

Functions of Life Insurance

Investors include life insurance in their investment plans in order to accomplish a variety of objectives. These objectives are not equally important to all investors, but the following seven need to be considered in connection with almost every investment program.

1. Immediate estate. Perhaps the most widely recognized function of life insurance is to provide an "immediate estate" to the family of a breadwinner who dies before he has had opportunity to accumulate a competent sum for their support. The amount needed to raise a family, provide for emergencies, and afford security to a widow or other dependents is so great that most families find it hard to finance adequate insurance for this purpose, especially while the family and the breadwinner are young. This problem is so important that the average family should make its solution a cornerstone of their investment program. In solving the problem consideration should be given to the adequacy of existing resources, possible social security benefits, probable assistance from relatives, and ultimate inheritances.

2. Savings. Life insurance is one of the great savings systems employed by American families. In a previous chapter it was noted that the typical life insurance policy is designed as a combination of decreasing insurance protection plus increasing savings account, which together equal the face amount of the policy. The policyholder's premium payments are used in part to build up the savings account in his policy, and as the savings account increases the amount of insurance protection which he buys constantly decreases. The ever-increasing savings element in the policy earns between $2\frac{1}{2}$ and 3 per cent in most companies, is kept in safe investments, may be used as collateral if the policyholder needs to borrow against it, may be obtained by "cashing in" the policy if that becomes desirable, and may be exchanged for a retirement income if the policyholder ultimately requests it.

3. Cash resource. Most "ordinary" life insurance policies—that is, those sold in units of $1,000 and up, in private rather than employee-group contracts—contain clauses outlining the terms under which a policyholder may borrow from the company, using his policy as security. The loan may usually amount to almost the entire "reserve" or savings account in the policy, is compulsory on the company, carries a stipulated rate of interest usually between 4 and 6 per cent, and has no definite maturity date. A life insurance policy may also be assigned to a bank or other creditor as collateral, but the convenience of direct borrowing from the company is very great. Surrendering a policy for cash is an equally simple process.

4. Disability income. Few American families are insured against the contingency of long-term disablement of the breadwinner. This is an economic disaster comparable to his early death, but insurance companies have had unfortunate experiences with policies designed to meet the need, and most of them do not now offer adequate contracts. However, some life insurance companies add clauses to insurance policies under which a totally and (apparently) permanently disabled insured may receive an income for life. Assurance of $50 per month under one of these clauses will usually cost the insured $20 to $50 per year, depending mostly upon his age. Some casualty insurance companies also offer disability income policies which partly or wholly meet this need.

5. Retirement income. Most life insurance policies give the insured the option to surrender his policy and receive in return a life annuity equal in value to the cash value of the policy. Some insurance policies are written with this ultimate object in mind. In any case, policyholders who do this are accorded the privileges and choices stipulated in their policies. The annuities may run for the duration of either one or two lives, and they may be guaranteed to pay the annuitants or their heirs either for a minimum period of time or up to a minimum sum. A decision to take an annuity does not have to be made by a policyholder until he is ready for the payments to begin, so the hazard of an early choice which later proves inappropriate does not exist.

6. Clean-up fund. In addition to life insurance earmarked for long-term objectives, families often have use for insurance policies which will pay expenses of last illness, funeral costs, and adjustment costs incident to death. These usually need not be large and may be omitted entirely in cases where the family resources seem adequate to care for possible needs.

7. Business insurance. There are many business situations in which life insurance can contribute convenience and peace of mind. Three typical situations may be noted. In closed corporations or partnerships it is often desirable that the other participants be able to buy out the interest of a deceased member, rather than to admit an heir or a new purchaser into the firm. This can be done if each participant owns insurance on the lives of the others, so that the remaining members are provided with cash when any one of them dies. Second, a business debtor may carry insurance designed to help liquidate his debts in case of his death. Third, any individual whose estate will encounter heavy taxes at his death may find life insurance a convenient means of providing the funds.

Protection and Saving

All life insurance policies are basically combinations of insurance protection and savings account, and the most basic distinction between forms of policies relates to the proportions in which the protection and savings elements are combined. In a low-priced policy all or nearly all of the premiums collected must be used to pay the insured's share of operating expenses and the death claims on the members of his group who die; consequently, little of his premium money remains to go into a savings fund, and the amount of insurance protection for which he is charged remains high, close to the face amount of his policy. On a high-priced policy the premium payment would be large enough to pay the expense and mortality levies and also make a substantial contribution to the reserve or savings fund. In subsequent years the policy would be credited with interest on its reserve fund in addition to the premium paid in and would be charged for insurance protection on only the difference between the face of the policy and the amount of the reserve fund. Thus the remainder to be added to the reserve fund would probably be even larger in succeeding years.

This may be illustrated by the figures of Tables 48 and 49, which compare the results of an ordinary whole life policy with those of a 20-pay life contract. The figures are hypothetical, but they are based on a modern mortality table and on average expense rates and interest earnings.

The tables bring out sharply the fact that the investor who accumulates savings in an insurance policy reduces the complementary life insurance protection feature as his policy reserves grow. If his policies are suited to his needs, this is a proper development, for life insurance protection is less needed as the insured lives to earn and save. Also, most insureds are willing to buy less insurance protection as they get older, for mortality rates rise rapidly at older ages. But the insured who wishes to supplement his savings with insurance protection must realize that in most standard policies he buys less pure protection year by year and that this tendency is most pronounced in the highest priced policies.

*Table 48. Illustration of Protection and Savings Obtained in a
Whole Life Policy Bought at Age 25*

	First year	Tenth year	Twentieth year
Premium paid in..................	$ 16.56	$ 16.56	$ 16.56
Interest on reserves at 2½%.......	.41	3.34	7.08
Total........................	$ 16.97	$ 19.90	$ 23.64
Share of expenses.................	$ 2.00	$ 2.00	$ 2.00
Share of mortality cost.............	2.85	3.78	5.77
Added to reserves.................	12.12	14.12	15.87
Total........................	$ 16.97	$ 19.90	$ 23.64
Face of policy....................	$1,000.00	$1,000.00	$1,000.00
Accumulated reserves to date.......	12.12	131.33	282.81
Insurance protection this year......	987.88	868.67	717.19
Mortality rate per $1,000 this year..	2.88	4.35	8.04

*Table 49. Illustration of Protection and Savings Obtained in a
20-pay Life Policy Bought at Age 25*

	First year	Tenth year	Twentieth year
Premium paid in..................	$ 28.62	$ 28.62	$ 28.62
Interest on reserves at 2½%.......	.61	6.05	13.54
Total........................	$ 29.23	$ 34.67	$ 42.16
Share of expenses.................	$ 4.40	$ 4.40	$ 4.40
Share of mortality cost.............	2.82	3.29	3.61
Added to reserves.................	22.01	26.98	34.15
Total........................	$ 29.23	$ 34.67	$ 42.16
Face of policy....................	$1,000.00	$1,000.00	$1,000.00
Accumulated reserves to date.......	22.01	244.26	551.37
Insurance protection this year.......	977.99	755.74	488.63
Mortality rate per $1,000 this year..	2.88	4.35	8.04

Life Insurance Policy Forms

Insurance companies are constantly alert to devise life insurance policies which meet popular needs or tastes, and as a result most of the contracts now offered for sale have special features which do not fit into simple classifications. However, the basic plans can usually be grouped into four types—term insurance, ordinary life, limited-pay life, and endowment insurance.

Term insurance is very low-priced insurance under which the company's obligation is limited to paying the beneficiary if the insured dies within a stated period of years, usually 1, 5, 10, or 20. Since mortality rates at ages under fifty are not great, term insurance covering such ages can be afforded by almost anyone. The reserves and cash values on such policies are negligible. Many term policies carry clauses permitting the insured to "convert" his term policy into a higher priced permanent form without having to pass a second health examination at the time of conversion. Term insurance is suitable for temporary business protection and for supplementary insurance while children are young or before any significant savings have been made. Convertible term is especially useful for families whose budgets will bear no savings program at the moment but who need immediate protection and an option on permanent insurance in the future.

People who prefer to do their saving independently of insurance companies frequently buy 20-year term insurance and drop portions of it as their accumulated savings convince them that the insurance is no longer needed. Others who carry term insurance as supplementary insurance or to "pay off the home mortgage" follow the same practice of decreasing the amount as the need diminishes.

Whole-life or "ordinary" life insurance is an arrangement under which the company agrees to pay the face of the policy at the insured's death in return for a stipulated premium payable as long as the insured lives. In view of higher mortality rates in the later years, it is obvious that the premium must be high enough to accumulate a reasonable reserve in the earlier years; this reserve provides the usual loan value, cash value, and annuity option features, as well as interest earnings. Ordinary life is the lowest priced form of permanent insurance. It is suitable for most business insurance uses and for family insurance where emphasis is on low premium outlay, long-continued insurance protection, and a limited savings accumulation.

Limited-pay life insurance is a form under which the company agrees to pay the beneficiary when the insured dies, but the insured's premium payments are to be made only for the limited number of years stipulated in the policy, or until his earlier death. The premium-paying term may extend for 20 years, 30 years, until the in-

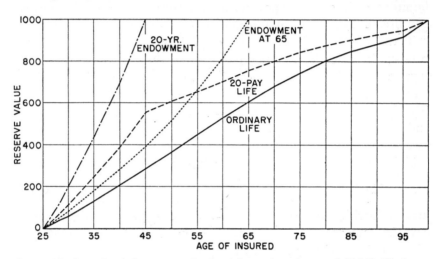

CHART 16. Growth of the reserve (savings) in various forms of $1,000 life insurance policies purchased at age 25 (NLP reserves, CSO 1951 table at 2½ per cent interest).

sured reaches age 60, or for some other limited period. The policy must therefore accumulate a large reserve during the premium-paying period, so that subsequent mortality costs will be small and interest earnings large; this calls for a fairly high premium rate. Limited-pay life policies which call for only 20 or 30 annual payments are therefore important savings vehicles and excellent investments for families whose budgets can carry substantial savings and whose circumstances justify a rapidly diminishing insurance protection feature; but they are not suitable for families not yet able to afford rapid saving, whose budgets can carry only inadequate amounts of high-premium insurance.

Endowment insurance is a form of contract under which the company agrees to pay the beneficiary if the insured dies during the contract period and to pay the insured if he survives to the end of the period. Endowment contracts are mostly written for 20- and 30-year periods and for periods ending when the insured reaches age 60 or 65. A 20-year endowment period naturally calls for a high premium and very rapid reserve accumulation, for the reserve must equal the face of the policy when the 20-year period is complete. A 40-year endowment maturing at age 65, on the other hand, is a relatively modest program which accumulates its reserve slowly but finally matures the full face value at retirement age. Short-period endowments obviously emphasize rapid saving and quickly diminish their insurance protection; longer term ones combine a slow savings program with a slow reduction of the complementary insurance feature.

Chart 16 illustrates the amount of reserve or savings accumulation in policies written on a typical modern mortality table. Since the policy in each case has a $1,000 face value, the amount of insurance protection furnished by a policy at any time is measured by the distance from the curve, which shows the amount of the reserve, to the $1,000 line at the top of the chart.

Ordinary, Industrial, and Group Insurance

Life insurance in private companies is available on three different systems. Ordinary insurance, which accounts for 61 per cent of the amount of insurance in force and about 34 per cent of all policies, is written by practically all companies on any of the plans discussed in the preceding section. It is usually sold in units of $1,000 and larger to applicants able to pass a medical examination or some other selective test. Premiums are payable annually, semiannually, quarterly, or sometimes monthly.

Industrial insurance accounts for 13 per cent of the insurance and 49 per cent of the policies in force. The policies are small, averaging about $340 in amount, are sold without medical examination or extensive investigation of any sort, and premiums are usually collected on a weekly basis by agents who call at the insureds' homes. Industrial policies are useful as burial insurance and for various other purposes, but the relatively high mortality rates and administrative expenses on them cause them to cost much more per $100 of insurance than other types.

Group insurance is insurance purchased through employee or

other groups of which the insured is a member, usually under a plan which is selected and subsidized by an employer. Most group insurance is on a term basis, but endowment or other plans are sometimes used. When employers subsidize group insurance systems, the cost to the insured is often much below the premiums which would be charged for independently purchased ordinary insurance. The

Table 50. *Nonparticipating Premium Rates per $1,000 for Various Policy Forms, Ordinary Department* *

Policy	Age at issue		
	25	35	45
10-year term.........	$ 6.45	$ 8.12	$14.09
Ordinary life.........	15.79	21.65	30.98
20-pay life...........	27.13	33.39	41.63
30-pay life...........	20.40	25.56	33.51
20-year endowment...	46.12	47.12	49.85
30-year endowment...	28.43	30.39	35.84
Endowment at 65....	20.60	30.39	49.85

* Aetna Life Insurance Company rates, as quoted in the *1953 Unique Manual of Life Insurance.*

employee cannot select the particular policy form and terms which he might like, if he participates in a group system, but its economy to him will usually justify arranging his other insurance and savings so the group policy will "fit in" soundly.

Policy Terms and Features

An insurance policy is a contract under which the company and the insured agree on a long list of obligations and privileges. While the basic features of insurance policies are standard, there is no such uniformity about the details, and many of the details are of great importance to individual insureds. The fact that these details are technical makes it nonetheless imperative for the prospective purchaser to study them; unless he carefully plans his insurance purchases he is unlikely to obtain the maximum advantages available in his own particular case.

Among the decisions to be made is to choose between participating and nonparticipating insurance. On a participating policy the insured is charged a premium somewhat higher than the company expects to need. Against this premium are charged a fair share of operating expenses, mortality costs, the necessary addition to the policy reserve, and perhaps some small contribution to the company surplus; the balance can then be returned to the policyholder as a dividend. On a nonparticipating policy the company quotes a definite premium rate, out of which all costs and reserves must be met; the excess, if any, is profit to the company. In general, the premiums on participating policies are much higher than on nonparticipating ones, but the long-run costs are often a little lower. About 70 per cent of life insurance in American companies is on a participating basis. Insureds who choose nonparticipating insurance usually do so because the initial premium costs are lower or because they prefer policies whose net costs are fixed and guaranteed. An occasional insured may choose nonparticipating insurance because he believes that the companies' future mortality or investment experience will be adverse and that participating policies will therefore fare badly. The insureds who choose participating policies probably do so because they hope for lower long-run costs, chiefly as a result of improving national mortality rates.

Most insureds must also decide whether they wish double indemnity and disability waiver of premium clauses in their policies. The double indemnity clause is a simple addition of accidental death insurance to the basic policy, which results in doubling the death benefit if the insured dies as a result of accident. The disability waiver clause is more vital to sound family insurance, as a rule; under it the company agrees to waive all premiums and keep the policy in force in case of the total and (apparently) permanent disability of the insured. This clause does not provide a disability income for the insured, but it is very helpful as a guarantee of uninterrupted insurance and savings accumulation, especially when attached to an endowment or similar policy.

Life insurance policies which build up any significant reserve or savings element must make provision for the insured's rights to his savings. Each policy must therefore clearly state its cash value during each year of the policy term and the arrangements under which this cash value may be obtained, if the insured so desires, through a policy loan or surrender of the contract. Most policies also permit the insured to surrender his policy in return for a full-paid term insurance policy of equal amount or a full-paid whole life policy of lesser amount, in either case equal in value to the cash value of his present policy. Finally, and most important, many policies permit an insured to surrender his policy at a date to be selected by himself, in return for any one of several forms of retirement annuity or for a series of installment payments. All of these options are granted to an insured by express stipulation in his policy, and the sums and privileges granted vary from company to company and policy to policy.

If the proceeds of an insurance policy become payable to the beneficiary by reason of the death of the insured, most policies provide various options as to payment. The insured may select the method of payment in advance, but if he does not the choice will fall to the beneficiary. Payment may be by lump sum, in cash; it may be made in installments, with interest on the deferred sums increasing the total sum to be paid; or any one of several forms of life annuity may be provided to the beneficiary; or the proceeds may simply be left on deposit with the company, to earn interest until withdrawn by the beneficiary. The rates of interest to be allowed by the company, the amounts and types of annuities available, and other features of these beneficiary options are established in each policy.

A great many other important clauses are to be found in insurance policies. Some limit the company's liability if the insured travels by air, engages in hazardous occupations, resides in prohibited areas, serves in the armed forces, or commits suicide. Others limit the company's right to contest the validity of the policy. Others may give the insured special privileges to convert his policy to another form if he so desires. Still others give the insured various options with respect to policy dividends—to take them in cash, in additional insurance, or as an interest-bearing savings account with the insurance company.

Efficiency and Net Cost

A life insurance policy is a sound investment if it provides exactly the features the policyholder needs, is accompanied by efficient administrative and advisory service, and is low in cost. Each of these elements is important. Most insurance policies are the obligations of strong and honest companies, but the insured who does not choose a policy suited to his circumstances does not get his money's worth. Again, life insurance is a complex and technical matter; the average insured will get a better investment in a company whose selling agents are expert and conscientious advisers and in which such matters as policy loans, policy conversions, advice on beneficiary clauses, and service on death claims are handled promptly and sympathetically.

Finally, the cost of an insurance policy is important, since it is usually an investment of major size, on which a small percentage difference can amount to an important sum. It is difficult to measure the cost of insurance fairly, since desirable policy features and good service add to the cost of apparently similar policies. However, some idea of the relative economy of similar policies in different companies can be obtained by comparing their *net costs* over a period of years. Twenty years seems to be an ideal period for this purpose.

Net cost is computed by the formula: Net cost = twenty years' premiums minus twenty years' dividends minus cash value at end of twenty years. This formula simply measures the out-of-pocket cost to the policyholder if he buys insurance, pays the premiums and takes back the dividends for 20 years, and then surrenders the policy for its cash value. The computation can be made either on a historical basis, using the actual histories of policies written 20 years ago, or on a current basis, using present premium rates, dividend rates, and promised cash values. In either instance the company's probable future performance is being gauged by its past or present record.

It will be observed that the larger interest earnings (on larger reserves) and the smaller average insurance protection costs on high-priced policies will inevitably make the net cost on high-priced policies less than that on low-priced ones. This does not prove that high-priced policies are more economical than low-priced ones; it simply proves that net cost comparisons are valid only between similar policies issued at the same age, so that the amounts of reserves held and insurance protection furnished are substantially similar.

Table 51 indicates the sharp differences in net cost for similar insurance in different companies. All the companies whose figures are used in Table 51 are strong, respectable, and sizable concerns; but it appears that a purchaser of a $10,000 whole life policy may save

Table 51. Net Costs per $1,000 of Insurance in Nine Good American Companies

Issued at age 25—Current basis—Policies surrendered after 20 years

Company	Whole life	20-pay life	20-year endowment
A	$17.81	$48.89 *	$159.02 *
B	55.35	28.66 *	130.32 *
C	63.19	8.85	112.65 *
D †	50.80	9.40 *	77.60 *
E	4.47 *	67.05 *	179.23 *
F	13.91	51.86 *	175.65 *
G	47.08	17.47 *	143.61 *
H	7.66 *	80.81 *	179.13 *
I †	66.20	11.20	75.20 *

* Excess of cash value over cost.
† Nonparticipating policies.
Source: Data from the *1953 Unique Manual of Life Insurance.*

$708.50 over 20 years' time if he insures in company H rather than company C. Of course, better policy features or service in company C might make the higher cost worth while, but this must be proved. Actually, the strongest and most accommodating companies seem often to be the lowest cost companies as well.

There are differences in efficiency between insurance companies which affect their net cost results greatly. A company whose underwriting department avoids bad risks will have lower mortality costs to charge against its policies; a company with a skillful investment department will earn more interest and suffer fewer losses; and a well-administered company can keep its operating expenses down. Company progress along each of these lines can be studied by the investor who is willing to make the effort.

Beneficiary Matters

Most life insurance policies direct the company to make payment to a specific beneficiary or beneficiaries upon the death of the insured. This is a sound procedure, for direct payment will make the funds immediately available without subjecting them to the delay and expense of probate, which would be unavoidable if the insurance was payable to the insured's estate. The beneficiary may be a trustee who will administer the funds as directed by the insured.

Insurance payable to any natural person should also be payable to a contingent beneficiary in case the first-named beneficiary does not survive the insured. In fact, the problem is doubly complicated; in most instances in which a common accident or simultaneous illness might result in the first beneficiary's dying shortly after the insured, it would be better to have the insurance go to the contingent beneficiary rather than into the first beneficiary's estate. Various companies have various ways of solving this problem; some permit a clause designating the first beneficiary "if living 30 days after my death, otherwise to the contingent beneficiary"; others suggest payments in installments to the first beneficiary if living on the installment dates, otherwise to the contingent beneficiary.

An earlier section noted that most policies provide several "settlement options" or methods of payment, under which a beneficiary might receive a life annuity, a cash sum, a series of payments, or a withdrawable savings account. The insured usually may either choose the method in advance or leave the choice to the beneficiary when the time comes. The insured who doubts his beneficiary's business acumen will often make the choice in advance; in fact, he may even arrange for the insurance company or a trust company to hold the proceeds in trust, doling out an annuity or periodic sums to the beneficiary but refusing to honor garnishments or other legal process by the beneficiary's creditors.

Life insurance policies usually declare either that the insured retains the right to change the beneficiary or that he does not do so. The insured who retains the right to change the beneficiary retains complete ownership of the policy, hence may cash it in or borrow on it at will. Since it is wholly his, its cash value is also subject to attachment by his creditors. If the insured does not retain the right to change the beneficiary, he will need the beneficiary's consent if he wishes to cash the policy or borrow on it; and since he does not own it outright, his creditors cannot get it. The beneficiary has no effective rights prior to the insured's death.

Annuities

A life annuity is a periodic payment which continues for the duration of the beneficiary's life. It is really life insurance in reverse—insurance against living too long—for its purpose is to make it possible for the annuitant to consume his entire principal plus the interest earnings on it, without risking the embarrassment of outliving his funds. Life insurance companies sell annuitants a monthly income for life at a price which varies with age and sex. Annuities are usually quoted by naming the monthly income which may be purchased for $1,000 in cash. For example, a leading company in 1953 offered a man aged 65 a life annuity of $6.29 per month for every $1,000 invested.

Obviously, an ordinary life annuity will be a great bargain for a long-lived annuitant and a source of loss to a short-lived one, for the insurance company must charge each annuitant enough to finance an average period of payments. The possibility that a $1,000 investment might produce only two or three $6.29 monthly annuity payments before death terminated the bargain causes an ordinary annuity to appear too speculative to many annuity buyers; they therefore ask the company to guarantee monthly payments to the annuitant or his heirs for a minimum period of 5 or 10 years (this is called an annuity certain) or until a stipulated total sum has been paid (this is a refund annuity), with further payments contingent on the life of the annuitant. Since the company's average number of payments to an annuitant group is increased when a period certain or a minimum refund is promised in the contract, the monthly annuity per $1,000 invested is somewhat smaller than it would be on an ordinary basis. Table 52 shows typical 1953 rates for different forms.

Many elderly couples find a joint life annuity attractive. This form of annuity pays as long as either of the annuitant couple lives, though the payment is often reduced in amount after the first death. The cost of the annuity is based upon the two ages.

Annuities may be bought for cash, obtained in return for the cash

surrender values of life insurance policies, or taken by the beneficiary of a life policy under the settlement option provided in the
policy. As a rule it is economical to acquire an annuity through a
life insurance policy, for the rates made available through such
policies are frequently better than cash purchase rates. The great
popularity of the annuity idea since 1930 has led most life insurance

*Table 52. Monthly Annuity Purchasable in 1953 for $1,000 Principal
Amount*

(Annuities obtained as insurance proceeds are usually 3 to 10 per cent greater)

Sex and age of annuitant	Ordinary life annuity	Life annuity 10 years certain	Refund annuity $1,000 guaranteed	Joint annuity equal ages	20 years no life contingency
Male—40.........	$3.29	$3.26	$3.02	$2.70	$5.16
Female—40.......	3.02	3.00	2.83	....	5.16
Male—50.........	4.06	3.96	3.53	3.16	5.16
Female—50.......	3.63	3.57	3.26	....	5.16
Male—60.........	5.34	4.99	4.27	3.92	5.16
Female—60.......	4.62	4.43	3.87	....	5.16
Male—65.........	6.29	5.63	4.75	4.48	5.16
Female—65.......	5.34	4.99	4.27	....	5.16
Male—70.........	7.56	6.32	5.35	5.21	5.16
Female—70.......	6.29	5.63	4.75	....	5.16

Source: Various standard annuity tables as shown in the *1953 Unique Manual of Life
Insurance.*

companies to offer "retirement annuity" insurance policies for sale.
These are generally available in units of "$10 per month" of 10 years
certain life income at age 60 or 65, coupled with $1,000 to $2,000
per unit of death benefit if the insured dies before the annuity
period begins. Retirement annuity policies are virtually endowment
insurance policies, with the endowment proceeds automatically appropriated to buy a life annuity. In 1953 the Pacific Mutual Life
Insurance Company quoted annual premiums on a $10 per month
retirement income contract on a man (income to begin at 65, prior
insurance coverage of $1,000 to $1,500) at $29.47 at age 25, $43.45 at
age 35, or $71.92 at age 45.

Table 52 indicates that annuities bought at moderate ages pay little more per $1,000 of principal than the dividend yield available on good stocks. This leads many people to conclude that annuities are not a satisfactory investment. However, it must be remembered that life annuities are dollar-type investments of very high quality, comparable with bonds yielding less than 3 per cent. For an investor of moderate means who believes that part of his property should be kept in investments of this quality and who is willing to consume part of his principal in his later years, an annuity investment is ideal; it assures him of a substantial and safe dollar revenue as long as he lives and permits him to retain his common stocks and real estate intact for price-level protection and maximum income.

Tax Position of Insurance and Annuities

In general the tax laws deal reasonably with insurance and annuity investments. Practically no general property taxes are levied on them. Most of the states levy an excise tax of 1 to 3 per cent on premiums collected by insurance companies, thus confiscating a portion of the money their citizens attempt to invest through insurance, but this is not a recurring levy on the same money.

Income taxes are not levied on any payments, whether lump sum, installments, or annuities, which may be paid to beneficiaries by reason of the death of the insured; these payments are not income for tax purposes. Dividends paid to the insured on his life insurance policies are not taxable income, either; they are reductions of the premium costs of his policy. However, if the insured surrenders a policy for cash, or receives the proceeds of a matured endowment policy, he has taxable income to the extent that the cash received exceeds the total premium cost of the policy. Life annuity payments received by the insured, either in exchange for a surrendered life policy or bought for cash, are regarded as current taxable income to the extent that the annual payments exceed the total premium cost of the policy divided by the insured's years of life expectancy when the payments begin.[1] If the insured chose installment payments not subject to a life contingency, such as 120 monthly payments of

[1] Thus, if a man aged 68 had an expectation of life of 10 years, and if he surrendered an insurance policy on which his total net premium outlay had been $8,000 in return for a life annuity of $876.30, he would be assumed to receive $800 of principal plus $76.30 of taxable income annually, *regardless of how long he lived.* The

agreed amount, the total cost of the policy would be prorated over the 120 payments, and any excess would be monthly taxable income. The taxable portions of any of these payments may obtain still further tax relief as portions of the "retirement income" of persons over 65 years of age.

All life insurance proceeds payable upon the death of an insured are included in his estate for Federal estate tax purposes, regardless of whether the payments are made to designated beneficiaries or to the estate, if the insurance was owned or controlled by the insured. Because there is some uncertainty whether death taxes should be paid by the general assets of the estate, thus leaving the insurance proceeds intact to the designated beneficiaries, or whether the taxes should be prorated among all heirs and beneficiaries, the point should be covered in every will. The state inheritance tax laws are inclined to exempt fairly substantial amounts of insurance payable to each beneficiary, in addition to the standard exemption provided to the same beneficiary on general inheritances from the estate.

It should perhaps be noted that while family insurance and annuity plans must be made with the tax laws in mind, there is no assurance that the tax laws will remain the same for long periods. Changes made in the tax law revision in 1954 required extensive modification of many investment and insurance plans.

Government Insurance

The United States government has made available to each veteran of World Wars I and II, certain other armed forces personnel, and all servicemen on active duty since 1951 a minimum of $1,000 and a maximum of $10,000 of government-sponsored life insurance. This insurance is the obligation of the government and all operating expenses are borne by the government, thus saving the policyholders the 5 to 15 per cent of their premiums ordinarily absorbed in operating expenses and taxes. Furthermore, gains to policyholders resulting from cashing these policies or collecting endowments for sums in excess of cost are not subject to income taxes.

---

expectation of life figure is actuarially computed if the annuity is joint on two lives or on a period certain or a refund basis. An employee whose annuity is mostly paid for by an employer may regard his annuity as wholly a return of his capital until he gets all of his own contribution back; thereafter his whole annuity is taxable income.

United States Government Life Insurance (World War I) and National Service Life Insurance (World War II and up to 1951) policies are participating contracts, written basically in the form of renewable 5-year term insurance policies but convertible at the option of the insured into standard permanent policies such as ordinary life, 20-pay life, endowment at 65, and others. If the insured continues his original term insurance the premium rate increases with his age at each 5-year renewal date. United States Government Life and National Service Life policies provide the usual settlement options to beneficiaries, including a life income option which is especially attractive. The policies also provide for disability waiver of premiums, and for the addition of a very valuable disability income clause to the policy upon payment of an extra premium.

Since 1951 the government insurance available to discharged servicemen has consisted solely of nonparticipating renewable 5-year term policies issued at favorable rates. Settlement to beneficiaries is made only in 120 monthly installments, and no disability income insurance is provided.

How Much Insurance Is Needed?

Clearly, this is a question which cannot receive a definite answer. Business needs, employers' pension plans, family responsibilities, amount of wealth already available, and a variety of other factors enter into individuals' decisions on this matter. Insurance underwriters sometimes say that the average middle-class family should invest 10 per cent of its income in life insurance and that the face value of policies carried should amount to three to six times the family's annual income. But these are not accurate measures; they disregard the family's special needs, its accumulated savings, and the nature of the policies contemplated. The actual amounts of insurance carried by American families are less than half these suggested sums.

Perhaps the best approach to the "how much" question could be made by tabulating the family's present "estate" and its future savings expectations as a lifetime savings program is pursued. Then the differences between the accumulated estate totals at various times and the amounts necessary for family security in the event of death can be studied, and insurance in suitable amounts and forms can be considered. This is a technical and difficult task, which frequently involves the planning of family wills, trusts, and estate tax matters, as well as simpler decisions on disposition of business enterprises, whether the family savings are to be invested in insurance, and the adequacy of the family budget. Insurance men refer to this task of analyzing insurance needs as "insurance programing." Insurance companies often maintain experts in this field who are available for consultation when investors' problems prove too complicated for the selling agents.

Sources of Information

The best source of life insurance advice and information for the average investor is a thoroughly competent life insurance agent. It costs no more to buy insurance through a competent man than from an uninformed insurance peddler, and it may well cost much less.

For the investor who wishes to study the theory and practice of life insurance there are innumerable textbooks and monographs in every good library, and the U.S. Superintendent of Documents has several informative pamphlets for sale. The most accessible descriptions of policy terms, premium rates, financial practices, net costs, and similar matters will be found in the *Unique Manual,* an annual reference volume published by the National Underwriter Company. This manual is available in most libraries.

Investments of Life Insurance Companies

Life insurance companies are obligated to pay death claims, annuities, surrender values, and policy loan requests to their creditors in dollars. The liabilities of the companies to their policyholders, including special reserves and dividend funds, totaled approximately 73 billion dollars at year-end 1953; to meet these obligations, they had assets valued at about 78.5 billion dollars. However, the companies were not having to liquidate assets to meet their obligations; during 1953 their receipts from interest and premium collections were 14.3 billion dollars, whereas only 9.1 billion dollars was disbursed in expenses and to policyholders and beneficiaries. Even during the worst years of the depression, back in 1931–1933, the insurance companies as a group collected enough premiums and interest to meet all of the calls upon them, including those for policy loans.

The small excess of assets over liabilities, amounting to about 8 per cent, indicates that the life insurance companies should invest chiefly in conservative dollar-sum investments, for they cannot afford investment losses of any great size. On the other hand, liquidity in the short-term sense does not seem to be required of any large percentage of the assets. The companies have therefore aimed their investment policies mainly at security and maximum income, which they have found in long-term bonds and mortgage loans. A considerable degree of liquidity has been obtained by inclusion of serial bonds, sinking fund bonds, salable government bonds, and installment mortgages in the holdings; and, of course, the careful spacing of the maturities of long-term bonds provides a periodic recovery of cash in large amounts.

Because of the decline in bond interest rates since 1934, life insurance companies have been experimenting with stock and real estate holdings to some extent. At the end of 1953 the companies held stocks valued at 2.6 billion dollars, or about 3.3 per cent of their total assets. Of this, about two-thirds was in preferred stocks. Some companies, those operating in states which do not restrict the practice, had several times this percentage in stocks. Real estate in 1953 accounted for 2.0 billion dollars, only about 2.6 per cent of company resources, but was increasing in importance. The real estate consisted of home office buildings, which are held for use plus rental income; large-scale rental housing projects, which are operated for rental income; corporation-occupied business or industrial buildings, which are purchased and leased back to the occupying firms for long periods at rentals sufficient to amortize the purchase costs and yield a satisfactory income; and real estate acquired by foreclosure of loans. The greatest increase in real estate ownership is occurring in the third of these categories; the fourth has been declining. Foreclosed real estate amounting to almost 2 billion dollars was held by the companies in 1936; by 1953 this had fallen to about 27 million dollars.

The average interest rate earned by American life insurance companies on their invested funds rose to 3.36 per cent in 1953. This was reduced to a net rate of 3.15 per cent after payment of Federal income taxes, but even this constituted the best net earnings rate since 1943. The companies averaged 5.07 per cent in the twenties and 4.10 per cent in the thirties, but low general interest rates plus large holdings of low-yielding United States government bonds combined to reduce the figure to low levels in the forties. In 1947 only 2.88 per cent was earned. Since that time, as Table 53 shows, a great increase of higher yielding mortgages and corporate securities has helped to increase earnings. However, the companies are holding firmly to the idea that safety of principal is more important than rate

Table 53. Distribution of Assets, United States Life Insurance Companies

(In billions of dollars)

End of year	U.S. government bonds	State, municipal, and foreign bonds	Corporate securities	Mortgages	Real estate	Policy loans	Other assets	Total *
1924	$ .7	$ .6	$ 2.7	$ 4.2	$ .2	$1.3	$ .6	$10.4
1929	.3	1.0	4.9	7.3	.5	2.4	1.1	17.5
1934	1.9	1.6	5.4	5.9	1.7	3.7	1.7	21.8
1939	5.4	2.3	8.5	5.7	2.1	3.2	2.0	29.2
1944	16.4	2.2	10.7	6.7	1.1	2.1	1.9	41.1
1949	15.3	2.5	23.2	12.9	1.2	2.2	2.2	59.6
1950	13.5	2.6	25.4	16.1	1.4	2.4	2.6	64.0
1951	11.0	2.7	28.2	19.3	1.6	2.6	2.9	68.3
1952	10.3	2.5	31.6	21.3	1.9	2.7	3.1	73.4
1953	9.8	2.6	34.6	23.3	2.0	2.9	3.3	78.5

* Totals may not agree with total of individual items because of rounding.
Source: *Life Insurance Fact Book*, 1953.

of return, and the increase therefore does not seem likely to go far unless basic interest rates increase greatly.

QUESTIONS AND PROBLEMS

1. Review the major functions which life insurance performs. Is it proper to call a life insurance policy an investment?

2. Explain how a policy may act as a cash resource. Is it sound family practice to use a policy loan instead of bank borrowing to finance emergencies?

3. Why does an insured who buys a 20-year endowment policy buy less "insurance protection" than one who buys an ordinary life policy? Does he pay for less?

4. Why does one need less insurance as he grows older? Do insurance policies provide less "protection" as the insured grows older? Explain.

5. Distinguish between ordinary, industrial, and group insurance. Which is the most economical?

6. What kind of insurance would you recommend for a young man without savings or financial resources, who is aged 25 and about to marry? Why?

7. What kind of insurance would you suggest for a professional man aged 45, who has a substantial income and wishes to insure the balance of his earning power up to retirement age at 65?

8. Would you prefer participating or nonparticipating insurance? Why?

9. Distinguish between a disability waiver clause and a disability income clause.

10. Should the insured designate the method of payment of his insurance to the beneficiary? Explain.

11. What is a contingent beneficiary? Why would one be named? How is this done?

12. Explain the calculation of net cost. Should insurance buyers study this factor before buying policies? How would you go about it?

13. Do you think that the idea of using a life annuity as a dollar-sum investment and keeping all of the rest of one's savings in stocks and real estate is a sound one for a retired person? Where is the weak spot?

14. What is a joint life annuity?

15. Should National Service Life Insurance be changed to provide an annuity option for the insured? (A life annuity is available to a beneficiary, but the insured may not surrender his policy at retirement age and obtain one himself.)

16. How would you go about answering the question "how much life insurance" for yourself?

17. What would a decline in interest earnings do to life insurance net costs? Should the companies be encouraged to venture farther into stock and real estate investments?

REFERENCES

Bowe, William Joseph: *Life Insurance and Estate Tax Planning,* Vanderbilt University Press, Nashville, Tenn., 1950.

Donaldson, Elvin F.: *Personal Finance,* The Ronald Press Company, New York, 1948, Chaps. 10–12.

Financial Handbook, The Ronald Press Company, New York, 1948, pp. 340–346.

Maclean, Joseph B.: *Life Insurance,* McGraw-Hill Book Company, Inc., New York, 1951.

Magee, John H.: *General Insurance,* Richard D. Irwin, Inc., Homewood, Ill., 1953, Part V.

Matteson, William J., and E. C. Harwood: *Life Insurance and Annuities from the Buyer's Point of View,* American Institute for Economic Research, Great Barrington, Mass., revised annually.

Mowbray, Albert H.: *Insurance,* McGraw-Hill Book Company, Inc., New York, 1946, Chap. 10.

Pickett, Ralph R., and Marshall D. Ketchum: *Investment Principles and Policy,* Harper & Brothers, New York, 1954, Chaps. 10, 11.

Robinson, C. C., and R. W. Osler: *Guide to Life Insurance,* The Rough Notes Co., Indianapolis, Ind., 1949.

Taxation Affecting Life Insurance, Prentice-Hall, Inc., New York, annual.

Unique Manual of Life Insurance, The National Underwriter Company, Cincinnati, Ohio, annual.

Chapter 24: SAVINGS INSTITUTIONS AND TRUSTS

Although a logical case for combining the discussion of savings institutions and trusts into a single chapter might be made, it seems best to note at the outset that the combination is chiefly one of convenience in time and space. The savings institutions to be described are business organizations whose function is to receive investors' dollars, keep them reasonably liquid and reasonably safe, and return the same number of dollars with interest at a future date. A trust is a legal arrangement under which an individual or an institution takes title to another's property and undertakes to manage it conservatively according to instructions for the benefit of designated beneficiaries. Aside from the fact that savings institutions and trusts are extensively regulated by law and usually conservative in nature, they are more unlike than like in description.

The savings institutions to be described include postal savings, savings departments of commercial banks, mutual savings banks, savings and loan associations, credit unions, and industrial loan companies. These are all familiar agencies in which investors commit very large amounts of money, yet they all have legal limitations, investment practices, and tax positions which affect their usefulness to investors. Many people believe that the average investor does not understand fully either the advantages or the limitations of investments in these institutions. The principal function of this chapter will be to review these advantages and limitations.

Trusts are important to investors as devices for managing property either for short periods, such as during the settlement of a decedent's estate, or for very long periods, such as the entire lifetime of an individual. Even small investors find great advantage in the use of trusts, if they are planned soundly and intelligently. Though the legal details are too technical for discussion here, it is important that every investor know something of trust funds and trust investments. The bare outlines of these matters can be included.

Postal Savings

The United States government accepts the savings deposits of individuals in amounts ranging from $1 to a maximum of $2,500, at over 8,000 post offices scattered throughout the country. These deposits are the unconditional obligation of the government and are returnable to the depositor on demand, except that the post office retains the right to a few hours' notice when large sums are demanded, since it may be necessary to send out for the money. Postal savings deposits earn interest at the rate of 2 per cent per annum; each deposit "certificate" earns one-half per cent for each three calendar months, beginning with the first day of the first month following the date of deposit.[1]

The postal authorities retain 5 per cent of total postal savings deposits in a lawful money reserve fund in Washington and make the balance available for investment. The banks of the depositors' local area may obtain these funds as time deposits if they will secure them with insurance or bond collateral and pay 2½ per cent interest upon them. In recent years the banks have found the receipt of postal savings funds on these terms unprofitable and have accepted less than 2 per cent of them; consequently, the bulk of postal savings money is now invested in government bonds.[2]

The 1952 annual report of the Postmaster General indicated that at June 30, 1952, there were 3,339,378 postal savings depositors whose deposits averaged $783.85 per account.

Postal savings deposits may be made by any competent person over 10 years of age in his or her own name, but no joint, fiduciary, corporation, association, firm, society, or partnership deposits will be received. Each individual may hold certificates of deposit of varying dates and denominations totaling not more than $2,500, but all certificates must be part of a single account in a single post office. Certificates are issued in denominations of $1, $2, $5, $10, $20, $50, $100, $200, and $500. They bear simple interest (compounding is possible by withdrawing principal and interest and immediately redepositing both) and are not transferable or negotiable. Deposits or

[1] Because postal savings accounts do not pay a higher interest rate than the maximum authorized for savings accounts in state banks in the same state, the postal savings rate in a few states has at times been less than 2 per cent per annum.

[2] *Federal Reserve Bulletin,* July, 1954, p. 730.

withdrawals are made in person, through a representative, or by mail. Upon the death of a depositor payment will be made to a properly authorized legal representative of the estate; or if administration of the estate is not required by law, payment will be made to heirs or creditors in accordance with the laws of the state. Lost or destroyed certificates will be replaced upon proper application.

Although there has been little litigation on the subject, it appears that postal savings deposits and the interest paid on them are subject to such state and local property and income taxes as may be levied upon them. The deposits are unquestionably subject to both Federal and state estate and inheritance taxation. Interest earned on money deposited before March, 1941, is exempt from Federal income taxation, but money deposited on and after that date earns fully taxable interest.

As a part of a quick-recourse fund, or as a means of accumulating savings over a period of time, postal savings accounts have much to recommend them. They are completely liquid, perfectly safe, and the 2 per cent yield is better than average for this type of investment. Little interest is lost if withdrawals must be made between quarterly interest dates, and the maximum interest rate of one-half per cent every three months is paid regardless of the duration of the deposit. The $2,500 maximum account is not too small for the convenience of most families, especially since it is applicable to each person, not to the family. There is no form of postal savings ownership in which the account may be made payable to either husband or wife, or in which an account may be transferred without legal formality to a designated beneficiary upon the death of the holder; in this respect postal savings deposits are not so convenient as savings bonds. The tax position of postal savings accounts is identical with that of most savings deposits but lacks the exemption from state income and property taxes which savings bonds have. There are obviously both advantages and disadvantages in postal savings accounts, but the advantages seem important enough to justify many families in making use of this form of investment.

Investors may obtain information about postal savings from two pamphlets issued by the Post Office Department. A very short leaflet, form P.S. 4 (June, 1947), is available at many post offices. A more detailed explanation of the procedure in paying interest entitled *In-*

structions Concerning the Payment of Interest on Postal Savings Certificates (form P.S. 100, dated June, 1941) can be had from the Postmaster General.

Interest-paying Deposits in Commercial Banks

Interest-paying bank deposits constitute a very large portion of the more liquid holdings of American investors. At October 27, 1954, the time and savings deposits in all commercial banks totaled 47 billion dollars. The typical savings account is not large; at June 30, 1945, there were 35.2 million individual holders of 25.1 billion dollars in savings deposits, which would indicate an average of about $713 per account at that time.[3] The average probably exceeded $1,000 by 1954.

The nature and yield of interest-paying deposit accounts are greatly affected by regulations imposed by the Federal Reserve System on all member banks, by the Federal Deposit Insurance Corporation on insured nonmember banks, and by state banking authorities. The Federal Reserve regulations are contained in Regulation Q, which divides all interest-paying deposits into three categories: (1) passbook *savings* accounts, which are available only to individuals, individuals in joint accounts, and nonprofit organizations; (2) *open-account time deposits,* which are passbook accounts available to all depositors; and (3) *time certificates of deposit,* which are interest-bearing promissory notes of the bank, also available to all. Savings accounts must stipulate that the depositor may be required to give 30 days' notice of an intended withdrawal,[4] though the bank may at its own convenience make payment without advance notice. Open-account time deposits and time certificates of deposit must stipulate that the funds may not be withdrawn prior to an agreed maturity date or, alternatively, without 30 days' advance notice to the bank, and the bank may not elect to pay without advance notice. Maximum interest rates which the Federal Reserve members may pay have been limited since 1935 to 2½ per cent on savings accounts and to 2½ per cent, 2 per cent, and 1 per cent, respectively, on certain classes of open-account time deposits and certificates. The banks in

[3] *Annual Report of the Comptroller of the Currency, 1945,* p. 155.

[4] A bank may stipulate a longer notice period but not a shorter one.

a few states are limited to even lower maximums, because Federal Reserve member banks may not pay more than state rules permit state banks to pay.

The rates of interest actually paid by banks on savings and time deposits are much below the maximums permitted by banking regu-

Table 54. Savings Funds in Selected Institutions, December 31, 1920–1953

(In billions of dollars)

Year	Postal savings deposits	Deposits in mutual savings banks	Time and savings deposits in commercial banks	Unpledged shares and deposits in savings and loan associations
1920	$ .2	$ 4.8	$10.5	$ 1.7
1925	.1	7.3	16.6	3.8
1930	.3	9.4	19.0	6.3
1935	1.2	9.8	13.2	4.3
1940	1.3	10.6	15.8	4.3
1945	3.0	15.3	30.2	7.4
1946	3.4	16.8	33.9	8.5
1947	3.5	17.7	35.4	9.8
1948	3.4	18.4	35.9	11.0
1949	3.3	19.3	36.3	12.5
1950	3.0	20.0	36.5	14.0
1951	2.8	20.9	38.1	16.1
1952	2.6	22.6	41.0	19.2
1953	2.6	24.4	44.0	22.8

Source: Data from Banking and Monetary Statistics, the Federal Reserve Bulletin, and the Home Loan Bank Board Statistical Summary 1949.

lations. For the United States as a whole, 1.25 per cent on savings accounts and .5 per cent on time deposits would seem to be typical for 1954, although variations between communities and between banks are marked. Table 55 indicates the average rates paid on all savings and time deposits combined, in recent years. These average rates are probably only a little below the average rate paid on savings accounts, for savings accounts amounted to 92 per cent of total savings and time deposits at a recent date. Most banks pay interest on passbook accounts at semiannual intervals, basing the interest on either the average balance or the lowest balance for the period. Time certificates of deposit usually receive interest for the elapsed time of deposit, with no interest allowed on a deposit of less than 90 days' duration.

The explanation for the low rates of interest paid by banks in recent years can be encompassed in very simple terms. It seems probable that the cost of operating a savings and time department in a bank plus a small allowance for profit would exceed 1½ per cent per annum on the money handled; this estimate would include allowances for salaries, materials, general overhead, credit losses, deposit insurance, and taxes. Income could be earned on about 90 per cent of the funds deposited at rates which would not exceed 2 per cent on bonds and 5 per cent on loans. An average between 2 and 5 per cent would be 3.5 per cent on the earning assets, or 3.15 per cent on the total deposits of the department. With revenues at 3.15 per cent or less and necessary expenses and earnings at 1.5 per cent or more, the margin from which interest can be paid is clearly defined. The outstanding reason for present low interest payments lies in the decline in interest rates during the past twenty years; the greatest hope for increased payments lies in the unlikely contingency of higher general interest rates.

Savings accounts are almost completely liquid, for it is the practice of commercial banks to pay them on demand. They are also reasonably safe, for the high quality of most banks' assets is further supported by bank examinations and by FDIC insurance of every account up to $10,000.[5] Time deposits are somewhat less liquid than

[5] National banks are examined by the Comptroller of the Currency, member state banks by the Federal Reserve System, insured banks which are not in the Reserve System by the FDIC, and all state banks are subject to state banking authorities. The FDIC insures nearly 96 per cent of American commercial banks; the insured banks have over 99 per cent of the interest-bearing deposits in all commercial banks. In the event of weakness in an insured bank the FDIC will endeavor to prevent insolvency by arranging a merger or providing financial aid; if this is not feasible the insured deposits will be made available at once in a solvent bank or a new one, and the FDIC and the uninsured claimants will share equitably in the assets of the failed bank. Finally, it should be noted that the banking laws in a number of states require the segregation of the assets belonging to the savings and time deposit department away from those of the commercial department, in a state bank; and since the loan and investment regulations in such cases are often more stringent on the savings and time deposit funds than on the commercial department funds, the assets are sometimes better grade.

For deposit insurance purposes, all deposits in the same bank owned by one person

savings deposits, since they cannot be withdrawn until maturity or until a notice period has expired, but they may be used as collateral for loans from the bank, and time certificates of deposit are also usually salable. Their liquidity must therefore be rated as very high. Time deposits average much larger in amount than savings deposits, hence are frequently not fully covered by the $10,000 insurance provided to each account by the FDIC, but bank insolvency has been so rare since 1940 that most investors now give it little heed. However, it is well to remember that the safety of any excess over $10,000 in one's bank balance depends on the solvency and liquidity of the bank.

The convenience of bank deposits is a strong argument in their favor. Deposits or withdrawals can be made in person or by mail at conveniently located banking offices and at convenient hours. No fees, commissions, or taxes are involved in making transactions. Related banking services, such as loans, safety deposit, money orders, and checking accounts, are available in the same institution. The possession of a substantial savings or time deposit is an item always reported by a bank to a credit investigating agency; therefore, it improves the depositor's credit standing. Finally, bank deposits can usually be made under a variety of legal titles—by an individual, by a number of individuals but payable to any of them, by a partnership, by a corporation, by a trustee for another, and by individuals in joint-and-survivor accounts. The joint-and-survivor account is one whose balance is payable to any of the participants while all are alive but which is very simply transferred to the survivor or survivors upon the death of one, without being subject to the delay and expense of probate proceedings. The state laws and precedents in each state govern the types of accounts which the banks may accept, but they are usually carefully planned for the convenience of depositors. Investors are well advised to consult with the bank's account expert before selecting the legal form in which they will record their deposits.

Interest earned on bank deposits is subject to all Federal and state income taxes. The deposits themselves are subject to such general property taxes as may be levied upon them, but it is the practice in

---

constitute one account. Joint accounts, partnership accounts, etc., are usually classed as separate accounts.

most states to exempt them or to tax them very lightly. However, the property tax liability should be investigated; even a light tax on principal can make great inroads upon the limited income received. Bank deposits enjoy no exemption of any kind from Federal or state estate, gift, or inheritance taxes.

In summary, it may be said that savings or time deposits in commercial banks are very satisfactory investments from the standpoints of liquidity, safety, and convenience. Their earning power is meager, and they have no tax advantages, hence the investment of large sums for long periods of time in this way seems relatively unprofitable; yet as a means of accumulation, and as an investment for moderate amounts of emergency reserves, bank deposits offer definite advantages.

Mutual Savings Banks

Mutual savings banks are state-chartered deposit institutions whose function is to administer small and medium-size savings deposits with safety and reasonable profit. These institutions have no stockholders or stock capital; they are controlled by elected or self-perpetuating boards of trustees and, in time, accumulate a surplus or corporate net worth by retaining a small portion of their earnings for the purpose. Semiannual "dividend" payments based on the bank's earnings are declared by the directors and paid on the various classes of deposit accounts. Mutual savings deposits are an important form of investment. At October 27, 1954, such deposits totaled 25.9 billion dollars, and the average regular account (excluding school savings, Christmas clubs, etc.) probably exceeded $1,000 in amount. Mutual savings banks are found in 17 states, but their greatest development has occurred in the northeast section of the country, in New York, Pennsylvania, and the New England states.

The laws of various states control the types of deposit accounts which the mutual savings banks may offer and the forms of legal ownership in which the accounts may be carried. In general the accounts are similar to savings accounts in commercial banks, with the further stipulation in eight of the states that accounts may not exceed prescribed sums. In 1954 New York limited single-name accounts to $10,000 and joint accounts to $20,000, with some exceptions. The purpose of the deposit limitations is to prevent the accumulation of large single accounts which might embarrass the bank by large withdrawals.

Mutual savings bank deposits have an enviable record for liquidity. Although the deposit agreement obligates the customer to give the bank 30 to 90 days' notice of an intended withdrawal, the banks in most areas are accustomed to pay on demand. They have usually been able to do so even during depressions. This has required very careful management at times, for the need to maximize earnings has required that the earning assets be principally long-term bonds and mortgage loans. Liquidity has been managed by maintaining small amounts of cash and secondary reserves, spacing the maturities of bonds and mortgages to provide a regular cash inflow, using amortizing mortgages, and cultivating a reputation for strength which avoids "scare" withdrawals. The banks have in recent years also developed cooperative rediscount agencies to which they may sell mortgages or from which they may borrow, and a few have obtained borrowing facilities by joining the Federal Reserve System or the Federal Home Loan Bank System. At December 31, 1953, the combined assets of all mutual savings banks consisted of approximately 4 per cent cash items, 34 per cent government bonds (mostly long-term), 48 per cent loans (mostly mortgages), and 14 per cent other securities and investments.

The safety record of the mutual savings banks has always been excellent. The banks are heavily concentrated in a part of the country which is financially stable, thus reducing their loan losses, but much of the credit for safety must be given to the rigid investment restrictions under which most of them operate. The states which charter savings banks usually limit their loans and investments to conservative and high-grade items and require effective diversification. For example, Massachusetts in 1948 authorized only first mortgage loans on real estate located within 50 miles of the bank; bonds issued or guaranteed by the United States, the state of Massachusetts, and certain other states; certain types of municipal bonds; certain types of railroad and utility bonds; bank stocks; and short-term loans on high-grade collateral security. In Massachusetts and in other states elaborate criteria respecting the size and financial condition of the issuer are prescribed to govern the selection of bonds, and in many states the banking commissioner prepares a list of bonds from which all savings bank bond investments must be chosen.[6] Under such close restriction it is not surprising that the mutual savings banks have remained solvent; neither is it surprising that their earnings have been low. The Massachusetts laws and those of other leading mutual savings bank states have been relaxed since 1948 to permit wider discretion in the choice of mortgages and the use of limited amounts of "nonlegal" bonds and stocks. However, the banks have been very slow to avail themselves of less secure investments when the laws permit them.

Slightly more than 41 per cent of the nation's 528 mutual savings banks were insured in the FDIC at December 31, 1953, but these banks held 75 per cent of all mutual savings deposits. An additional 20 per cent of mutual savings deposits was insured by state deposit insurance funds. All mutual savings banks as a group had surplus accounts exceeding 9.5 per cent of their total assets and amounting to 15.2 per cent of assets at risk; this compared with commercial bank capital accounts of 7.1 and 16.5 per cent, respectively. The mutual savings banks are also comfortably large; the FDIC-insured group averaged 92 million dollars of total assets, while the smaller non-FDIC group averaged 22 million dollars. While the investor may not carelessly assume that every institution has all the advantages of sound assets, strong deposit insurance, large surplus, and the strength commonly associated with size, it appears that most mutual savings banks do have them.

The ratio of total dividends paid to average deposit accounts in FDIC-insured mutual savings banks is shown in Table 55. The Table 55 figures indicate that dividend payments on deposits approximated 2.35 per cent for 1953. However, these figures are based on average deposits and thus include special deposits which obtain a restricted rate and also deposits which lost their dividend privileges because of withdrawal or other activity during the dividend period. It is probable that the average dividend rate on ordinary savings in these banks in the years 1952–1953 was above 2.35 per cent, with most banks paying between 2 and 2.5 per cent. During this period

---

[6] These laws and lists identify the bonds which are generally described as "legal for savings banks" or are referred to simply as "legals." Because the savings bank demand itself is heavy, and because other institutions, trustees, and persons rely on the legal list as a badge of excellence, such bonds usually sell on a low yield basis.

the average savings bank obtained in total income about 3½ per cent on its average assets. Roughly one-fourth of this was paid out in operating expenses, 60 per cent was allocated to dividends, and the other 15 per cent went into loss reserves and surplus. The gen-

Table 55. Average Yields Received on Accounts in Savings Institutions, 1934–1953

Year	Postal savings *	FDIC-insured mutual savings banks †	Commercial bank time and savings deposits †	New York state-chartered savings and loan associations ‡
1934	2.00%	2.56%	2.40%	
1937	2.00	1.92	1.62	3.50%
1940	2.00	1.73	1.30	3.18
1943	2.00	1.65	.93	2.82
1944	2.00	1.60	.87	2.63
1945	2.00	1.49	.87	2.45
1946	2.00	1.47	.84	2.30
1947	2.00	1.53	.87	2.32
1948	2.00	1.57	.90	2.24
1949	2.00	1.79	.91	2.22
1950	2.00	1.84	.94	2.23
1951	2.00	1.88	1.03	2.17
1952	2.00	2.27	1.15	2.39
1953	2.00	2.35	1.23	2.50

* Except in two states in which regulations require state banks to pay less on savings.

† Ratio of interest or dividends paid to average account balances. Inactive accounts and savings (not time) deposits probably received slightly more.

‡ Year ended June 30. Data for 1947 and later are annual rates for half years ended June 30.

Sources: Annual Reports of the Postmaster General, the FDIC, and the New York State Superintendent of Banks.

erous size of their accumulated surplus and loss reserve accounts led a number of banks to increase their dividend rates in the years 1950–1953.

Because of their function as cooperative savings institutions, mutual savings banks pay relatively little income or property taxes. However, the dividends which they pay to their depositors are fully taxable income, and the principal is subject to any state or local taxes which may be laid upon savings deposits. The deposits are fully vulnerable to estate and inheritance taxation.

Mutual savings banks offer many of the same convenience services which commercial banks make available to their depositors. They operate safe deposit vaults, sell money orders, cash checks, furnish data to credit agencies, and transact business in government savings bonds. A number of them also sell life insurance, either in conjunction with savings accounts or independently, at a cost slightly lower than that of ordinary insurance companies because the savings banks make no costly effort to *sell* insurance. They merely take orders for it when an applicant wishes to buy.

Investors are justified in regarding deposits in a typical mutual savings bank as liquid, safe, mildly profitable, and reasonably convenient. All of these qualities may vary with the individual bank, however; so the investor should investigate such matters as the quality of the assets, size of the surplus, management, earning power, dividend policy, deposit insurance, types of deposits and legal form, and convenience services, for himself. If the bank is typical, a deposit in it may have a very useful place in the investor's portfolio.

Savings and Loan Associations [7]

Savings and loan associations are institutions which receive investors' long-term savings accounts and invest the money principally in long-term residence mortgage loans. Most associations are mutual corporations in which the members' savings funds technically are invested in ownership "shares." The quarterly or semiannual earnings distributions on these share accounts are therefore dividends rather than interest. However, there are savings and loan associations in some states which are private business corporations, in which the funds of the general public represent creditors' deposits rather than share purchases; and there are also associations which accept money either as a share investment or as an interest-bearing deposit at the option of the investor.

During the 8 years 1945–1953 the savings and loan associations have shown remarkable growth, as Table 54 indicates. The number of investors has doubled, and the assets of the associations have increased by 200 per cent. An official estimate places the size of the average account in a savings and loan association at $1,471 in 1953.

[7] Also known as building-loan associations, cooperative banks, or homestead associations.

Savings and loan associations are incorporated by the Federal government and by each of the states. At December 31, 1953, there were 1,605 institutions holding Federal charters and about 4,395 holding state charters. In each instance the incorporating agency stipulates the terms upon which investors' funds may be received, the types of investments which may be made by the association, and other essential operating procedures. Savings and loan associations, like all important savings institutions, are audited periodically by the incorporating and insuring authorities, to verify their solvency and general observance of legal requirements. Because it is impossible to describe the rules of all the states in a short space, attention in these pages will be devoted mostly to the Federal association practices; but investors should be aware that state associations may operate somewhat differently.

The Federal associations receive money on two regular investment plans, the savings share account plan and the investment share account plan.[8] There is little real difference between them; the savings share account is a passbook account, to which dividends are credited when declared, while the investment share account is evidenced by $100 par share certificates, on which dividends are paid semiannually by check. The same rate of dividend is payable on the average dollar balance in each type of account. For the purpose of encouraging thrift, the association may pay a slightly higher dividend rate to members who make regular additions to their accounts over a long period. The Federal associations are also permitted to receive cash deposits from people who wish to accumulate funds to pay on their mortgage debts, and they may receive similar deposits by school savings clubs or thrift clubs, but these deposits do not share in the association's earnings and are not regarded as an important part of its operations.

There are few restrictions on the ownership of accounts in Federal associations. The uniform Federal charter (Charter K) states that

Share accounts may be purchased and held absolutely by, or in trust for, any person, including an individual, male, female, adult, or minor, single or married, a partnership, association, and corporation. The receipt or acquittance of any member, including a minor person or a married

[8] New charter forms authorized since 1947 as alternatives to the previous Charter K drop the term "share" from these titles. Most associations continue to use Charter K.

woman, who holds a share account shall be a valid and sufficient release and discharge of the association for any payment to such person on any share account. Two or more persons may hold share accounts jointly in any manner permitted by law.

One of the useful account forms is the so-called "trustee account," in which the individual owner of an account constitutes himself a "tentative trustee" for another who is designated to receive the account at his death. The owner operates the account as his exclusive property during his lifetime, but at his death the designated beneficiary may obtain immediate title to the account, without need for probate orders, by presenting the passbook, proof of the former owner's death, and a release from the inheritance tax authorities to the association.[9]

Savings and loan associations are permitted under Federal law to make loans to members on the security of their share accounts, to make first mortgage loans not exceeding $20,000 in amount on residential properties located within 50 miles of the association's office, to buy government bonds, and to invest in Federal Home Loan Bank securities. (State-chartered associations usually have the right to buy state and municipal bonds also.) In order to permit some latitude, an association is allowed to lend up to 15 per cent of its funds on mortgage security without regard to the 50-mile and $20,000 limits, or on nonresidential property. An association may make FHA-insured and veterans' (GI bill) loans, as well as the higher yielding uninsured types. The latter are ordinarily limited to 75 per cent of appraised value in the case of residences and 50 per cent on other property and must be repaid in monthly installments over not more than 20 years or, if not amortized, must mature in 5 years or less. Certain additional types of loans or investments may be made when authorized by the Federal Home Loan Bank Board.

Since the objects of savings and loan operation are safety and good earnings primarily and liquidity secondarily, the associations usually try to keep most of their funds occupied in mortgage loans. Prior to the war the average association kept 3 to 5 per cent of its assets in cash and a slightly smaller amount in government bonds and invested the balance in mortgages. During the war the influx of new

---

[9] This practice grew up informally in some of the mutual savings banks, particularly in New York, where careful court interpretation has given it standing. See re *Matter of Totten,* 179 N.Y. 112.

savings at a time of diminished building activity gave the associations a surplus of funds which they invested in government bonds. In 1945 such bondholdings amounted to 29 per cent of the assets held by the average association, but by the end of 1953 the bondholdings had been reduced to 7 per cent, as better yielding mortgages were readily available. There is strong sentiment among the associations for the maintenance of greater liquidity than was customary before the war, but each association is free to establish its own policy, subject only to a legal minimum of 6 per cent of its share accounts to be kept in cash or government bonds. With most of its assets in mortgage loans an association should be profitable, but it would not be highly liquid.

Liquidity is sought by savings and loan associations in four different ways. First, they maintain a small liquid reserve, as has been noted. Second, they undertake to obtain a constant inflow of new funds, in both old and new accounts. Third, they lend chiefly on amortizing loans, which assures a steady stream of incoming payments. Finally, they have the right to ask their Federal Home Loan banks for loans on mortgage security in amounts not exceeding 50 per cent of their outstanding share capital.[10] These sources of funds should be adequate to maintain liquidity at practically all times in well-managed associations which have earned the confidence of their investors. Many soundly managed savings and loan associations experienced difficulties in meeting abnormal demands for money between 1930 and 1940 and, as a result, were for a time not held in the esteem they deserved. However, the high liquidity and excellent earnings of most associations since 1946 seem to have dispelled the doubts generated by the great depression, and there seems little reason to expect fear-generated withdrawals in the future.

When a shareholder asks a Federal association for the return of all or part of his money, he may be paid at once or, at the option of

[10] The 11 Federal Home Loan banks are Federal chartered and supervised institutions similar in many respects to the Federal Reserve banks. Mortgage lending institutions may become "members" of a Home Loan Bank by buying small amounts of stock in it. The Home Loan banks obtain additional funds to lend to their members by receiving deposits from members and by selling their bonds to the public. Members may use Home Loan Bank funds both to help satisfy heavy demands for mortgage loans in their communities and to maintain their own liquidity, although excessive dependence on Home Loan Bank funds is discouraged. At the end of 1953 only 68 per cent of savings and loan associations were members, but these members held 94 per cent of all savings and loan resources.

the association, at the end of a 30-day waiting period. Association policies vary on this point; most of them seem to take pride in paying on demand, as the banks do, and this may, indeed, be a good way to earn the confidence of the public. However, some associations prefer to stress their function as custodians of long-term investments and, as a result, demand 30 days' notice of any substantial withdrawal. Savings and loan associations ordinarily expect to meet withdrawal requests at or before the end of the 30-day notice period, but they will not be held insolvent if they are unable to do so. If any Federal association has so many applications for withdrawals that its available funds will not meet them all, it is obligated to set aside at least one-third of its total receipts from account investors and from collections on loans to pay the requests in the order of receipt.[11] There are two exceptions to this rule of repayment in order of request: the association may, at its own option, permit withdrawal of not more than $100 per month from each account without advance notice, even while larger requests are waiting; and while others are waiting, any individual is limited to $1,000 at any one time, after which his additional request is returned to the bottom of the list to await a new turn.

The ultimate safety of a savings and loan account is compounded of two factors, the strength of the association itself and the assurance provided by account insurance in the Federal Savings and Loan Insurance Corporation. There is good reason to expect the average association to be strong. Amortizing home mortgages are highly dependable investments, especially when federally insured. Audits by regulatory bodies should find and correct weaknesses in association practices, and statistics indicate that the average association at the end of 1953 had a comfortable bulwark of reserves and surplus amounting to 7.1 per cent of total assets. Of course, there will be occasional exceptions. Some associations will lack skilled management, some will lack adequate diversification,[12] and some will lack adequate reserves and surplus. However, these deficiencies are more likely to impair earnings than solvency. In the relatively infrequent

[11] The new postwar Federal charter forms which associations are privileged to substitute for their pre-1949 ones would require at least 80 per cent of these receipts to be made available for withdrawals.

[12] Many associations are small. The average size of all the nation's 6,000 associations, including some very large ones, was about $4,400,000 in 1953. The average size of those refusing FSLIC insurance was about $1,100,000.

cases of insolvency which will occur, the investor may still be protected by FSLIC insurance, which at the end of 1953 covered 55 per cent of the savings and loan associations, including all of the Federal chartered ones. The insured associations held 88 per cent of all savings and loan accounts. While the FSLIC insurance does not guarantee that an association will meet withdrawal requests promptly, it does assure each account of ultimate recovery in full up to $10,000; excess amounts participate equitably in the assets of any insolvent association. The insurance contract provides that, if an insured association is proved by examination to have assets worth less than the amount of its share accounts, the FSLIC must offer the insured account holders their choice of (1) a new account equal to the insured amount in a solvent insured association, or (2) 10 per cent in cash plus 45 per cent each in non-interest-bearing debentures of the FSLIC due in 1 year and 3 years.

Federal savings and loan associations are required to make provision out of earnings for actual or impending losses. At least 5 per cent of earnings must be transferred to reserves and undivided profits (surplus) accounts until these are built up to an amount equal to 10 per cent of investors' share accounts. Losses may be charged to these reserves. The balance of earnings is available for dividends. Table 55 indicates the average dividend rates which state-chartered associations in New York have paid in recent years; these are probably typical of the nation as a whole. The rapid decline during the war years reflects the shortage of mortgage investments at that time and the lower earnings due to heavy government bond-holdings. Earnings in the postwar period 1946–1954 rose rapidly, and it appeared in 1954 that average postwar dividend rates would be established somewhere between the low levels of 1946–1947 and the more generous scales of 1940–1941, with most associations paying between 2.50 and 3.50 per cent.

Savings and loan accounts offer many of the conveniences afforded by bank deposits. The facilities for deposit and withdrawal are usually easily accessible, the accounts are good collateral for loans from the association, and many associations operate safe deposit vaults, transact business in savings bonds, cash customers' checks, and furnish credit references. The tax position of savings and loan accounts is usually the same as that of bank savings accounts. The ownership and title features of the accounts are more flexible than those available at banks or in postal savings. The lack of assured liquidity is a drawback, but the good yield is a compensating advantage. Safety is high. It appears desirable that the investor in savings and loan accounts take the trouble to investigate the reputation, liquidity, strength, and earning power of any association in which he contemplates investment, for great variation in these matters exists; but the merit of a long-term investment in a strong association is not to be denied.

Other Savings Depositaries

Two other forms of savings depositaries, credit unions and industrial or Morris Plan banks, should be noted briefly. Credit unions are state or Federal chartered associations, usually of employees in a single business organization. The credit union sells "shares" to its members and sometimes receives interest-bearing deposits also. The funds are used to make relatively short-term installment loans to members, to finance automobiles, furniture, or personal emergencies; if available funds exceed the loan demand they may be invested in savings banks, savings and loan associations, in high-class bonds, or in loans to other credit unions; if loan demands exceed available funds, the union may borrow reasonable sums. Withdrawal procedures are similar to those of savings and loan associations, although there is no provision for solvency insurance and no membership in any central banking institution. The state or Federal incorporating agency prescribes operating rules and makes occasional audits. The solvency record of credit unions is good, though their dividend records are far from uniform. At the end of 1951 there were 11,279 active credit unions in the United States, having over 5 million members and total assets of about 1,200 million dollars.[13] Loans outstanding amounted to 750 million dollars, and for 1951 earnings were 40 million dollars. Despite the heavy use of consumer credit in this postwar period, most credit unions had difficulty in keeping their funds fully occupied. A few large credit unions were

[13] *Statistical Abstract of the United States, 1953,* p. 455. An article in the *United States Investor* for Aug. 7, 1954, estimates the number of credit unions then active at 18,631, with membership of 8,961,500 people, total assets of 2.2 billion dollars, and outstanding loans of 1.7 billion dollars. Data for 1953 in the *Credit Union Yearbook* suggest that the *Investor's* figures are high but not excessively so.

in operation, but about half were reputed to have total assets under $50,000.

Industrial banks are privately owned state-chartered finance companies whose business is to make personal, collateral, automobile, and commercial loans, mostly on an installment payment basis. These institutions are permitted to receive limited amounts of savings or time deposits, typically not more than ten times their own capital accounts, for use in their business. These deposits are repayable after an agreed period of notice, or at a definite maturity date, with interest at a contractual rate which is commonly 2 to 5 per cent. The industrial banks are eligible for deposit insurance and membership in the Federal Reserve System, but most of them have not used the privileges. In general, their safety record is good.

Trusts

A trust is created when an individual, a group of individuals, or a corporation takes legal title to property with the obligation to administer it according to instructions for the good of another. The person having title and control is said to be the trustee; the one who benefits from the property is the beneficiary; and the one who furnished the property and gave the trustee his instructions is the maker, donor, grantor, or trustor of the trust.

There are many forms of trusts used for many purposes. Included among them are cases in which corporate property is held as security for bond issues, escrows and other depositary arrangements, receivership and bankruptcy administrations, executorships of decedents' estates, and court-appointed guardianships to care for the property of children and mental incompetents. However, the trusts to be considered in this chapter are the continuing managerial arrangements under which a trustee manages investments and distributes funds to beneficiaries according to instructions left with him by the trustor. Such trusts are extremely convenient and flexible arrangements; the trustor simply executes a declaration of trust or a will in which he sets forth his instructions to the trustee and provides for delivery of the property. The trustor may instruct the trustee as to the nature of the investments to be used, as to the identity of the beneficiaries and the benefits to be given them, and as to the discretion the trustee may exercise in dealing with emergencies. The trust may be made revocable at the option of the trustor, or once effective, it may be irrevocable; and the trustor may direct that he or others shall or shall not have the right to change the instructions to the trustee at a future date. The trustor may deliver the property to the trustee when the trust is planned, or he may leave it by his will, or he may have life insurance proceeds paid to the trustee.

Trusts do not die with their makers. Indeed, one of their common functions is to administer property and care for two or three generations of beneficiaries. Although trusts for other than charitable purposes are not permitted to continue indefinitely, it is usually possible to maintain them for "the longer of designated lives now in being plus 21 years," or some equally extended period. An individual may, for example, establish a trust which will care for his wife's needs and his own, thereafter care for his children as long as they live, and finally be distributed to his grandchildren. Income or principal or both may be paid out, at such times or under such conditions as the trustor stipulates.

Because of the hazards incident to illness and mortality, long-lasting trusts are usually placed in the care of self-perpetuating boards or of corporations. Endowed hospitals, schools, and charitable foundations are often "owned" by boards of trustees who elect new members to fill vacancies. Other such institutions are organized as nonprofit corporations with self-perpetuating boards of directors. Many trusts created to administer personal or family resources are operated by the trust departments of banks or trust companies. However, many family trusts are administered by members of the family, or by a board consisting of members of the family plus the family attorney, or by a member of the family plus a bank trust department. Trusts established while the trustor is living (living trusts) may be organized and conducted very simply, as private contractual arrangements; but those established by will, inheritance, or court order (court trusts) must in many cases continue indefinitely under judicial scrutiny, making periodic reports to the court about such matters as investments, disbursements, and the measures taken to carry out the instructions of the trustor.

The amount of funds being administered in trust is indeterminable. The Comptroller of the Currency estimates that at December 31, 1952, the 1,513 national banks handling trusts held 10.3 billion dollars in 184,125 living and court trusts, 26.1 billion in 72,725 agency accounts of one sort or another, and 3.2 billion more in other categories, a total of 39.6 billion dollars. This total had grown from 36.1 billion in 1951 and 10.7 billion in 1942. The periodical *Trusts and Estates* (issue of March, 1954) estimates that trust funds held by all banks and trust companies in the United States at year-end 1953 totaled 75 billion dollars. This figure does not include trust funds held by individuals or other nonbank trustees, but it nevertheless compares strikingly with the 26.7 billion total assets of all savings and loan associations or the 78.5 billion total for all life insurance companies on the same date.

The great flexibility of the trust arrangement would make it possible, if there were no laws to prevent, for trustors to immobilize property for long periods and for purposes which might become absurd or obsolete. Consequently, many statutes have been passed to regulate the nature, functions, and duration of trusts and to deny validity to trusts which do not comply with the law. Among the types of statutes commonly passed by the states are those limiting the duration of trusts, discouraging or forbidding trusts which do not pay out income to beneficiaries, forbidding trusts created for the sole benefit of the trustor, and forbidding trusts from which the beneficiary may withdraw principal as well as income at his discretion at any time. Because the state statutes vary, it is necessary for trustors to be sure of the law under which their trusts are established. When trustor, trustee, and beneficiary may all reside in different states, the possibilities of confusion are evident.

The supervision of trusts held by banks and trust companies is basically a matter of state law. However, any bank which is a member of the Federal Reserve System must also obtain a permit from the System before undertaking a trust business. The permit will be issued if the bank appears to be large enough, sound enough, and competent to carry on this type of business, and if there appears to be a need for its services. The bank is required to keep each trust's assets separate from all others and from its own, to keep a separate set of records for each trust, to manage the trust assets diligently and lawfully, to refrain from selling to or buying from the trust, and to execute the trustor's instructions faithfully. Failure of a trustee to execute his duties properly will render him fully liable for any loss sustained by the trust; but losses not due to the trustee's negligence or incompetence are borne by the trust.

The investments in which a trust's assets may be placed are always a matter of concern. If the trustor chooses to stipulate the investment policies to be followed, the trustee must follow instructions. If the trustor grants "full and complete discretion" to the trustee, reasonable policies followed by the trustee are usually acceptable in law. If the trust instrument makes no statement about investments, the trustee is bound to follow the statutes or ruling court decisions of the state whose laws govern the trust. More than three-fourths of the states, including Massachusetts, Michigan, Illinois, California, and New York, observe in varying degrees what is known as the "prudent man" rule; that is, they allow an uninstructed trustee considerable discretionary authority to purchase investments of any type, including common stocks, which an ordinarily prudent man would find suitable in the case at hand. The rest of the states are "legal list" states; that is, they tend to hold that uninstructed trust funds must be rigorously preserved, hence must be conservatively invested in very secure bonds and mortgages of the types prescribed for savings banks. In any case the trustee is obligated, within the scope of his authority, to obtain suitable yield and diversification.

Because reasonable diversification in small trusts is difficult to obtain, 40 states have passed special statutes authorizing banks to combine the funds of small trusts into diversified investment pools. These pools are known as common trust funds; they are operated in a fashion similar to open-end investment companies, except that the only investors in them are the trusts handled by the bank. A bank may operate several common trust funds, possibly one invested entirely in bonds, another entirely in mortgages, and a third holding an assortment of securities; this would permit any trust to have the safety of diversification in a type of security suitable to the needs of the trust. No special charge for either establishment or administration of the common trust fund is made by the bank; it is compensated by the regular fees paid by the trusts. Common trust funds are still new, having been practically unknown in 1937; but in 1954, 170 such funds were in operation, administering more than a billion dollars in assets owned by 50,000 separate individual trusts.

Trust investments are generally handled conservatively. The Comptroller of the Currency reported that at the end of 1952 the national banks had 65.4 per cent of their trust investments in bonds, 23.7 per cent in stocks, 3.7 per cent in mortgages, 3.3 per cent in real estate, and 3.9 per cent in other investments.[14] However, this tabulation included estates in process of settlement, custodianships, agencies, and trusts in which the investments were restricted by law or by the trustors. Another idea of trust department judgment may be obtained in a survey of the investments of 105 discretionary-type common trust funds at year-end 1953.[15] This survey reported that the common trust funds were 25.9 per cent in government bonds, 15.7 per cent in other bonds, 12.4 per cent in preferred stocks, 44.7 per cent in common stocks, and 1.3 per cent miscellaneous. However, this survey may overemphasize common stock holdings; it is probable that many banks keep the high-grade bond holdings in their individual trusts separate, but mingle funds to be less conservatively invested into their diversified common trust funds.

The asset distributions noted in these surveys suggest that most long-term private trusts probably obtain gross incomes amounting to between 3.00 per cent and 4.00 per cent, with the norm about 3.50 per cent. From this must be deducted the trustee's fees and taxes. In a full management trust in which the trustee bears the responsibility of selection of diversified investments, safe deposit, accounting, tax reporting, and some discretionary supervision of beneficiaries' needs, the trustee's fee will fall between .40 per cent and .75 per cent of the principal per annum, with a minimum of $50 per year. If the trustee's functions include management of real estate, supervision of businesses, or other extensive activity, the cost will be greater; if the investments are to consist permanently of government bonds or investment funds chosen by the trustor, or if the trustee is otherwise relieved of work and responsibility, the cost will be less. The trustee's fee would not be greater if he were instructed to keep the entire fund or some stipulated part of it in good stocks, with the objective of maximizing income.

There are no serious tax disadvantages in the use of trusts. General property taxes when applicable are assessed to the trustee and charged to the trust, at the same rates as if assessed to an individual. The income of a revocable trust, or one in which the trustor has control or is the beneficiary, is taxable to the trustor; otherwise, distributed income is taxable to the beneficiaries and undistributed income is taxable to the trust as though it were a person. When the

---

[14] *Annual Report,* 1952, p. 106.
[15] *Trusts and Estates,* January, 1954, p. 16.

trustor dies, any property in a trust in which he had control or an interest is taxed as a part of his estate; and if he creates an irrevocable and completely independent trust during his lifetime, he may be making a taxable gift. But a trust has great probate and death tax advantages; property placed in trust during the trustor's lifetime does not pass through probate at his death; and a trust, once established, may care for successive generations of beneficiaries without further probates or death taxes, if the trust is properly independent of the beneficiaries' control.[16]

The usefulness of trust services is probably little understood by most investors. For an annual fee very little larger than that charged for investment counsel alone, the trustor obtains professional investment management, safe deposit, and accounting services. He may place his trusteed property beyond the reach of his own or his heirs' mistakes, where creditors and importuning relatives cannot get it. He may instruct the trustee as to the normal distribution of benefits and also give him further discretionary authority to assist beneficiaries in unusual situations. All of this may simplify and reduce probate and death tax costs. Finally, these advantages are available to large and small investors. Bank trust departments actively solicit trusts of $50,000 and up, and they will take them as small as $10,000 or $15,000, especially if the bank has a common trust fund which may be used as the means of investment. The charges imposed on a very small trust are proportionately somewhat greater than those on a large one, but they are seldom so high as to be prohibitive.

QUESTIONS AND PROBLEMS

1. What principal advantages do postal savings accounts have as family quick-recourse funds? What is their principal shortcoming?

2. Do commercial bank savings deposits pay enough to justify their use for sums greater than would be needed for quick recourse? What are the chief advantages of bank savings deposits?

3. What are joint tenancy accounts? Are they used in your state?

4. Are all commercial bank savings accounts insured up to $10,000? What happens to a $20,000 account if the bank becomes insolvent?

[16] The cost of probating and settling an estate consisting of securities, including attorneys' and executors' fees, but not including taxes, might typically amount to 10 per cent on $10,000, 6 per cent on $50,000, or 4 per cent on $100,000. Death taxes are considered in Chap. 27.

5. Explain the types of interest-paying commercial bank deposits as defined by the Federal Reserve System. Why do the banks pay less interest than the maximum permitted in Regulation Q?

6. Are any of these forms of deposit accounts exempt from property taxes? From income taxes? From death taxes?

7. What are the most important reasons for the good record of solvency and liquidity established by the mutual savings banks? How are their funds invested at present?

8. Are the earnings of the mutual savings banks satisfactory? Are their dividends satisfactory? How do they compare with those of the savings and loan associations?

9. Could a severe depression threaten the solvency of a savings and loan association which had made large numbers of loans in the years 1950–1954? Is this likely if the loans were carefully made on an amortizing basis?

10. Do you think that a savings and loan association should keep a 25 per cent cash and government bond reserve, with the idea of remaining liquid? Why?

11. Compare the savings and loan "trustee account" with the P.O.D. arrangement on a government savings bond. Are they essentially the same?

12. What is a credit union? Is it in any way similar to an industrial bank? To a savings and loan association?

13. Would it be feasible for a couple aged 65 to place their property in a trust, retaining the right to advise on but not to control the investments, and instruct the trustee (a) to pay them the income and such of the principal as they needed as long as they lived, and (b) to distribute the balance to certain beneficiaries after they died? Would this plan avoid probate costs? Would it prevent investment errors and decisions under family duress in old age? Would it avoid estate taxation? Should this be an irrevocable trust?

14. Could a brother or a son act as trustee for an individual's property? Is this a good idea?

15. If one lived in a "legal list" state, would any trust he might create in that state be limited to investment in bonds and mortgages?

16. Explain the idea of a common trust fund.

17. It is common practice for a trust to provide a life income to one beneficiary and a subsequent distribution of the principal to a second beneficiary. In such cases many trustors instruct the trustee to make emergency payments for the benefit of either, whenever the trustee believes the situation requires it. Is this a sound provision where a bank is the trustee?

REFERENCES

Boehmler, Erwin W., and others: *Financial Institutions,* Richard D. Irwin, Inc., Homewood, Ill., 1951, Chaps. 11, 14.

Financial Handbook, The Ronald Press Company, New York, 1948, pp. 307–323, 609–631.

Institutional Investments, Law and Contemporary Problems, Duke University School of Law, 1952.

Lagerquise, Walter E.: *Balancing and Hedging an Investment Plan,* The Ronald Press Company, New York, 1941, Chap. 18.

Lintner, John: *Mutual Savings Banks in the Savings and Mortgage Markets,* Harvard University Press, Cambridge, Mass., 1948.

Prather, Charles L.: *Money and Banking,* Richard D. Irwin, Inc., Homewood, Ill., 1953, Chap. 27.

Prochnow, Herbert V.: *American Financial Institutions,* Prentice-Hall, Inc., New York, 1951, Chaps. 6, 17.

Shattuck, Mayo Adams, and James F. Farr: *An Estate Planner's Handbook,* Little, Brown & Company, Boston, 1953, Chaps. 4–7.

Stephenson, Gilbert T.: *Estates and Trusts,* Appleton-Century-Crofts, Inc., New York, 1949.

Chapter 25: REAL ESTATE AND
MORTGAGE INVESTMENTS

Real estate holdings bulk large among the investments of American citizens and are widely distributed among a great many people. The Federal Reserve System's 1948 Survey of Consumer Finances [1] indicates that at that time 45 per cent of the nation's spending units (*e.g.,* family groups sharing a home and expenses) owned either homes or farms as compared with 78 per cent owning life insurance, 39 per cent owning checking accounts, and 9 per cent owning corporation stocks or bonds. As a rule, the home or farm owned by an American family is its largest single investment and is of consequent high importance.

This pronounced affinity of investors for real estate is the result of a number of causes. Among them are the social esteem which conventionally attaches to real estate ownership; the feeling of independence and security which the possession of real estate engenders; the enticing propaganda spread by those who believe in real estate; the easy credit which makes the control of properties convenient for many people; the widespread conviction that real estate ownership is profitable; the belief that real estate is a safe investment, perhaps capable of a little fluctuation, but dependably indestructible; and the firm belief of many people that they "understand" real estate, hence will not blunder in buying and managing it. Although the attractions which this recital includes may in some cases be more imaginary than real, they are sufficient to stimulate an ever-increasing number of Americans to buy real property. It is probable that real estate ownership is at present more widely disseminated than it has been for many decades.

By far the most common form of real estate investment is home-ownership; a 1950 survey by the Bureau of the Census indicates that

---

[1] *Federal Reserve Bulletin*, July, 1948, pp. 769, 775.

53.4 per cent of nonfarm American families own their homes.[2] Family farms constitute a second common form of real estate investment; these are 65.7 per cent owned by occupying farmers,[3] and the other 34.3 per cent are mostly the properties of individual investors who rent them to tenants. The third common form of real estate investment is urban residential rentals, including single-family houses, flats, and apartment houses; this is a field in which both small investors and major corporations have holdings. Finally, the general field of business real estate, including both commercial and industrial property, attracts many small investors as well as very large investors.

Mortgage lending is also a form of investment which many people have found attractive. The demand for mortgage money has always been high in this country, for properties are frequently bought and sold and there has always been a large amount of new construction as the nation's wealth and population have grown. Prior to 1933 institutional lenders supplied a large but only slowly growing portion of the demand for mortgage money; subsequent to that date they have greatly increased their relative importance, though individual lenders continue to compete. Individual holdings of farm and nonfarm residential mortgages totaled close to 10 billion dollars in 1952, or more than half as much as their investments in savings and loan associations, and this figure does not include their very substantial investments in mortgages on nonresidential urban property.

Real Estate Values

In general, it appears that reasonably well-chosen improved real estate investments have many similarities to reasonably well-chosen industrial stock commitments. Individual commitments intelligently or luckily chosen may make great gains, and others stupidly or unluckily chosen may deteriorate rapidly in earning power and value. The great majority of properties fluctuate in value and in earning power as business conditions fluctuate and, perhaps, not much out of proportion to the changing values of good industrial stocks. Improved real property seems to be a fair price-level hedge, just as in-

[2] *Statistical Abstract of the United States, 1953*, p. 767.
[3] *Ibid.*

dustrial stocks are; no single piece may be expected to epitomize the average, but the general tendency is for real estate prices to reflect the buying power of the dollar.

Improved real properties fall mainly in the sunk capital category; that is, their location, nature, and purpose are definitely fixed, and their value depends largely on what their services will be worth during the next few decades. Although regional or neighborhood changes may add value, they are even more likely to detract, and the investor must therefore make every effort to foresee the long-term future of any property in which he contemplates investing his money. If the population of a town or city grows, real property in its business district and in its most desirable residential areas normally will be in demand, will earn more, and will sell higher; though it is possible that growth may result in the development of new shopping and residential areas to the disadvantage of the old. In general, community development and style factors have their greatest effects on industrial, commercial, and multiple residence properties, in ways which are directly comparable to the competitive and obsolescence factors which constantly threaten business corporations. Small residential properties and farms seem a little less affected by changing demand and style factors, but even here the investor must be concerned with the problem of future earning power.

One important element which tends to add security to an investment in improved real property must be recalled at this point. It was noted in Chapter 2 that most real estate improvements are of the wasting asset type, which means that the investor-owner progressively recovers his capital through the property's gross earnings, in addition to obtaining whatever net income is earned. Since the operating expense on the average real property is relatively low, the owner is almost certain to recover some of his capital (as a depreciation allowance) and perhaps some net gain out of the annual rents, even if the property is poorly designed or located. The value of the property should reflect the present value of all probable future cash recoveries and earnings, plus any speculative potential which exists. In contrast to this situation, an investment in the stock of a poorly designed and located industrial corporation would probably pay the investor nothing, for depreciation allowances and occasional small earnings would doubtless be needed to modernize the business, in order to prevent poor results from becoming poorer still. In this case only the speculative potential would contribute to market value.

Measuring the Earnings

It is not feasible, in a short chapter such as this, to undertake discussion of the earnings and cost factors which investors encounter on farms, apartment houses, commercial buildings, or industrial property. The situations are hopelessly diverse, both between the groups and within the groups. Consequently, the examples and most of the discussion will be based upon the single-family dwelling, which is the most widely owned form of real property investment.

The most common issue confronting the investor in real property is one involving the soundness of a proposed price—will an investment at this figure pay? The answer may be a difficult one or a very obvious one, if the investor foresees impending price-level changes, population movements, style changes, or other factors which will affect the property. However, the more usual situation calls for a review of the probable average incomes and expenses on the property and a comparison of its earning power with the proposed price. It is not unreasonable to assume that a property which can earn a fair rate of return on its cost, under assumed normal rental conditions, after providing for all reasonable expenses, taxes, and depreciation, is a sound investment. Estimates based on assumed normal conditions in the next five to ten years usually give an indication of these amounts.

In applying this doctrine it will first be necessary to estimate, by comparison or otherwise, what the normal annual rental value of the property for the next few years will be. Neither boom nor depression estimates should be used; a normal or average figure is needed. From this projected annual income must next be deducted (1) expenses of operation, such as heat, water, and janitor service, if furnished to tenants; (2) taxes; (3) depreciation; (4) maintenance; and (5) insurance. Each of these items should be a normal or average estimate based on experience with the given property or others like it. After these items are subtracted from the rental income, the remainder will represent the net earning power of the property. This net earning power expressed as a percentage of the price will provide a measure of the soundness of the investment. The average annual net earning power should be at least 5 per cent. The earnings of the property minus the interest payable on any mortgage debt will of course measure the owner's profit on his invested equity.

These calculations may be illustrated by an example. Assume that a reasonably new single-family dwelling valued at $10,000 is held as an investment, for rental to others, and that a $5,000 mortgage debt at 5 per cent is owed upon it. Assume further that an average rental rate of $100 per month is expected and that a normal average vacancy loss of one month per year is anticipated. If the tenant is to care for lawn and utilities services, but estimated property taxes of $200, depreciation allowance of $200, average maintenance cost of $150, and insurance premiums of $25 are to be borne by the owner, the income statement for the average year in the next ten years might well resemble the following:

Annual Income Statement

Gross income—11 months at $100....		$1,100
Less expenses:		
Operating expenses...............	—	
Taxes—2% on value.............	$200	
Depreciation—2% on value........	200	
Maintenance—1½% on value......	150	
Insurance—¼% on value..........	25	575
Earning power of property...........		$ 525
Less interest on $5,000 mortgage......		250
Net profit.......................		$ 275

This anticipated average income statement indicates that the $10,000 property in question would earn about $525 annually, or 5.25 per cent, which is satisfactory. Its earning power will doubtless decline in the distant future, but by that time the owner will have recovered part of his investment through the annual depreciation allowances, and less net earning power will be needed to justify the remaining capital investment.

An analysis similar to the foregoing is commonly used to justify a familiar "rule of thumb" in testing the soundness of investment in residential property. It has been noted that an average net earning power of 5 per cent is needed to justify the hazards of residential property investment. To this may be added "typical" costs of 2 per cent annually for taxes, 2 per cent for depreciation, 1.5 per cent for maintenance, and .25 per cent for insurance, making a total of 10.75 per cent of value which must be recovered annually in gross rental income, if the investment is to be satisfactorily profitable. Conservative investors then add another 1 per cent for vacancy and credit loss, bringing the total to 11.75 per cent per annum. This is practically 1 per cent per month. The rule of thumb therefore states that a single family property is profitable if its gross earning power approximates 1 per cent of its value per month and, conversely, that it is a sound investment at a price of 100 times its normal monthly rental value.

This rule-of-thumb process is interesting and useful to an investor, but it must be critically qualified. In the first place, it depends on estimates of normal or average rents and expenses, not temporary current ones, and thus must not be applied casually to current rents and prices. Second, the percentage amounts allowed for expenses and depreciation should be based on careful studies of the particular property, not on percentage generalities. In fact, close students of the subject insist that expense and depreciation factors vary so much that single-family residences of various types in various locations can be proved to be promising investments at figures ranging all the way from 70 to 130 times their normal monthly rental values.

A home investment which is owner-occupied is usually much more profitable than a similar property held for rental to others. In the first place, no vacancy or credit loss need ordinarily be expected. Second, an owner who is handy with tools and paintbrush, and whose family is normally careful with family-owned property, can hold maintenance costs to a minimum. Third, the earnings realized from one's equity in his home, which take the form of rent-free occupancy of the premises, are not subject to income tax.[4] Finally, many veterans are now entitled to unusually attractive mortgage loan terms, if they buy their homes; property investments capable of earning 5 per cent are attractive when the capital can be borrowed at 4 or 4.5 per cent.

In the case of residential property over 25 years old, maintenance

---

[4] Homeownership may have other tax advantages. For those who itemize deductions, taxes paid and mortgage interest paid are deductible in computing taxable income for income tax purposes. Also, some states exempt a limited amount of the value of an owner-occupied home from general property taxation.

and depreciation rates sometimes need to be larger in proportion to current values than is the case on new dwellings, and the investment risk is often greater. Consequently, it is sometimes said that while single-family dwellings under 25 years old may sell for 100 to 130 times monthly rental value, those over 25 years will bring only 70 to 100 times monthly rental value. Each figure assumes, of course, that no drastic deterioration of the property or its neighborhood is impending, and as before, each must be regarded as a generality which reflects only general tendencies.

Apartment houses, flats, commercial real estate, farms, and other types of properties may be examined as to earning power by means of the methods just described. These properties vary so much in gross and net earning power, however, that it is not possible to generalize on normal relationships between gross rental income and value. For example, an apartment house which furnishes heat, water, janitor service, and other facilities might readily require an annual gross revenue of 20 per cent of value in order to net a 6 per cent return to its owner; but a neighboring flat providing fewer services might need only 15 per cent. In general, investors expect somewhat higher rates of net return on other forms of urban property than are obtained on investments in single-family dwellings.

Appraisal Methods

There are many methods of appraising real property. Some are applicable to one type of property, some to another. Often different methods are used on the same appraisal, for the sake of verification, or combinations of methods are used.

The appraisal methods most commonly used may be grouped into four general types: (1) those based on comparison of the given property with other properties on which values have recently been established by sale, (2) those based on capitalization of near-term gross or net income, (3) those based on the discounted present value of a series of estimated earnings and capital recoveries over a long term of years, and (4) those based on cost of replacement less depreciation. The first two approaches are used chiefly by individuals and dealers who do not wish to undertake elaborate calculations; they are easy ways to approximate results. The third approach is commonly used in appraising existing office buildings, apartment houses, and similar properties, when the appraiser has access to experience data and engineering estimates which will enable him to forecast probable incomes and expenses over a long period of years. The fourth approach is one very widely employed by lenders on all kinds of improved property but notably, for present purposes, on dwellings.

Appraisals based on cost of replacement usually follow a process which is well worth a review by the investor. The appraiser usually begins by assigning a per-square-foot or per-cubic-foot basic value to the building, based upon the type and size of the structure. These basic values are very carefully estimated on the basis of building costs in the locality. The basic per unit valuation is then multiplied by the number of square feet or cubic feet, to arrive at a basic cost appraisal. Next, the basic cost appraisal is increased or decreased by specific sums, as the appraiser identifies good or deficient fireplaces, bathrooms, kitchen installations, hardwood floors, basement, garage, driveways, and the like. When the building replacement cost estimate is complete, it is then reduced by a percentage representing estimated depreciation; this is based on the age of the building, plus observed deterioration and maintenance factors. To this appraisal of the building is next added the estimated current value of the lot, to obtain a total value applicable to a normal dwelling in a normal neighborhood. However, there are several other factors which might justify arbitrary increases or decreases in the appraisal. Among them are (1) the suitability of the floor plan of the dwelling; (2) the suitability of the external appearance of the building; (3) the appropriateness of the building to the neighborhood, as respects size, quality, and style; (4) the apparent prosperity and durability of the immediate neighborhood; (5) the deed restrictions and zoning ordinances which affect the neighborhood; (6) the convenience of shopping districts, schools, employment opportunities, traffic arteries, and public transportation; and (7) the trends of community growth. This entire appraisal process is based fundamentally on cost of construction and is therefore most accurate on relatively new properties, in relatively new areas, and in situations in which the building is clearly suited to its location and function.

The Importance of Finance

As is true of all investment prices, the prices paid for real estate fluctuate with the supply of properties offered for sale and the demand for them. Real properties are relatively durable, and the total existing supply is capable of augmentation or reduction only at relatively slow rates; consequently, any situation which affects either the buying demand or the normal volume of selling offers is likely to have a noticeable effect on selling prices. One of the most conspicuous factors which influence buying demand or selling offers is the mortgage credit situation.

Prior to 1934 the mortgage loans made in the United States tended to follow a pattern calling for a first mortgage not exceeding 60 or 65 per cent in value, plus a second mortgage for 10 to 20 per cent if the borrower needed it. The first mortgage usually required partial amortization, though not always, and matured typically in 3 to 10 years. The second mortgage would run for 2 to 5 years, with some amortization. Interest rates were usually high, especially on second mortgages, and loans totaling 80 per cent of appraised value or more were difficult to obtain. High percentage loans were hazardous to both lender and borrower, because the maturities were very difficult to refund if they occurred during periods of depression. Furthermore, values were unstable, because defaults on lump-sum maturities during depressions caused foreclosures and forced sales during depressions drove property values down.

Analysis of this situation during the years 1930–1934 led to four important conclusions. First, loans amounting to 80 per cent of property value or more, if consistently available, would widen the real estate market at all times by allowing more people to participate in it and would tend to stabilize values. Second, a single long-term loan of 80 to 90 per cent of value, repayable in equal monthly installments, without a lump-sum maturity at any time, would not often be defaulted. People who cannot manage a lump-sum maturity are often able to make regular small payments, and if they cannot, there are usually others who will buy the embarrassed owner's equity for a small sum and assume the payments. Third, market stabilization plus more secure financing terms will justify lenders in accepting lower interest rates; this will make housing more economical and still further improve the market for properties. Fourth, an option to the borrower to repay his loan at a faster rate than required in the contract will enable him to strengthen both his own and his creditor's position.

These conclusions have played a large part in both Federal and state legislation on housing finance since 1933. The Federal savings and loan program, the home mortgage guarantee provisions of the Servicemen's Readjustment Act of 1944 (the GI Bill), the FHA mortgage insurance program,[5] and amendments to the banking laws have all favored the high percentage, long-term, amortizing type of mortgage. State banking and savings-loan legislation has done likewise. Because this type of mortgage loan has been very popular with borrowers, competition has forced institutions and individual lenders to use it to a major extent on dwellings and to a very considerable extent on multiple housing and business property loans as well.

The loans made on single dwellings, as an example of this type of financing, are likely to allow a period ranging up to 25 or even 30 years for repayment. The interest rate, including mortgage insurance premium, will range from $4\frac{1}{4}$ per cent (on veterans' loans) to 5 or possibly 6 per cent. The amount of loan available will range downward from 100 per cent on some veterans' loans to 80 per cent on FHA-insured mortgages of the less favored types, or to about 60 per cent on certain noninsured loans. The sums required to meet property tax and fire insurance costs, as well as interest and principal amortization, are collected monthly by the lender. The ease of this method of financing is indicated by the fact that the total monthly payment required to pay principal and interest on a 20-year amortizing loan at 5 per cent would be $6.60 per thousand of original loan. That is, an $8,000 loan could be paid off in 20 years for $52.80 per month. To this would be added about $19 per month for taxes and insurance, and the borrower would have to provide for maintenance also, but the total would amount to little more than a normal rent. Of course, a $10,000 property which would support an 80 per cent FHA loan might require a $2,000 down payment, or pos-

[5] The FHA plan is a mortgage insurance arrangement paid for by the borrower, under which the Federal authorities guarantee to the lender that, if foreclosure of an insured loan becomes necessary, they will take title to the foreclosed property and reimburse the lender for the defaulted principal and interest. Lenders are therefore usually willing to make high-percentage loans even in hard times, if the FHA will insure them.

sibly a second mortgage to the seller, but higher percentage first mortgage loans are available on new properties under other provisions of the Housing Act.

Thus far the modern amortizing mortgage has performed very well. The borrowers who have needed to sell have been able to find buyers ready and willing to buy their equities and take over the payments. But there has been no time between 1933 and 1954, except for a brief period in 1937–1938, when consumer incomes have declined importantly or when costs of construction have fallen. Not only has consumer buying power in dollars gone steadily upward during this period, but general prices and construction costs have mounted greatly. Property owners have found that their ability to pay and the market values of their mortgaged homes have both risen, thus making their debts easy to service. Furthermore, there has been no period since 1935 when lenders were unwilling or unable to make mortgage loans. It is implicit in present-day mortgage practices that real estate values shall not be impaired by nonavailability of mortgage loans at any time, for serious declines in property values would cause thousands of properties now mortgaged under high-percentage long-term loans to be worth less than the indebtedness upon them. Government agencies will doubtless be called upon to assist mortgage lenders if ever a serious shortage of mortgage money occurs.

The real test of modern mortgage financing and the property values dependent upon it therefore lies in the future. There were in 1954 many thousands of relatively new mortgage loans, made at high percentages of appraised value during a time of price-level inflation, to veterans and other prosperity-thrilled purchasers whose income sources had not stood the test of time. Whether the alleged merits of the amortizing mortgage will meet the test of 1955–1960 may depend on the stability of general economic conditions during the next few years. The liberality of the FHA loans authorized under various Housing Act amendments since 1945 and the generous financing under the veterans' loan program appear to be setting the stage for a conclusive demonstration.

One interesting aspect of mortgage financing must still be noted. If an owner obtains a generous amortizing loan—a high percentage to value, repayable at long term, carrying a low interest rate—he may sell his equity subject to the loan, and the purchaser thereafter has the advantage of the easy terms. This situation now exists in many cases, especially where borrowers have obtained 4 or 4.5 per cent 25-year veterans' loans. A property financed on such a generous basis offers a subsequent purchaser who buys it the excellent terms originally given to the veteran and is for this reason worth more than an identical property not so financed.

Table 56. Ownership of Urban Residential Mortgages of $20,000 or less and Farm Mortgages, 1945 and 1952

(In millions of dollars)

Ownership	1945	1952
I. Urban residential mortgages......	$18,543	$58,155
A. Savings and loan associations..	5,156	17,590
B. Life insurance companies......	2,258	11,800
C. Mutual savings banks.........	1,894	6,180
D. Commercial banks...........	2,875	11,250
E. U.S. Government agencies.....	859	2,210
F. Individuals and others........	5,501	9,125
II. Farm mortgages.................	4,933	6,300
A. U.S. Government agencies.....	1,756	1,260
B. Life insurance companies......	934	1,525
C. Commercial banks...........	450	980
D. Individuals and others........	1,794	2,533

Source: *Statistical Abstract of the United States, 1953*, pp. 447–448.

Titles and Title Insurance

Investors who buy real property or lend on mortgage security are acutely concerned to obtain a good title or a good lien. To be satisfactory, a title or a lien must not be jeopardized by vague claims of the heirs of former owners, or uncertainty about the release of old mortgages, or the possibility that repairmen may establish mechanics' liens upon the property. There are many such misfortunes which might befall unwary investors or lenders. All states have attempted to assist purchasers and lenders by enacting "recording statutes" which provide that deeds and liens are effective in order of recording in official recorders' offices, but proper evidence may later prove the official records to be incorrect and therefore invalid. Also, there are a number of court and tax offices in which other records affecting the title to property may be found.

Investors who buy property or lend upon it have for many years had the titles investigated by attorneys or title specialists, who reported the situation as shown in the official records and expressed opinions as to the acceptability of the titles. This is still the practice in rural communities and other areas in which real estate activity is not great and in which property histories are well known. However, in major cities the title investigating companies are now willing to write policies of title insurance, guaranteeing to indemnify the owner or lender if a title weakness existing at the date of the search but not then discovered causes loss. It must be admitted that the title companies pay few losses, but their vigilance in searching out weaknesses is probably a major reason for their good record. Because title insurance is not costly, it is a precaution which few investors should omit.

Mortgages, Trust Deeds, Contract Sales

The owner of real property frequently wishes to pledge it as security for a loan. In most states private owners pledge their property by means of a mortgage, which is an instrument establishing the holder's right to have the property sold and the proceeds applied on the debt, if the secured debt is not paid according to its terms. The mortgage must be written, signed by the property owner, and recorded in the official records, if it is to give the mortgagee prior rights ahead of other possible creditors of the property owner. When the mortgage debt has been repaid the mortgage is no longer valid, but an appropriate mortgage release signed by the lender should be recorded, in order to clear the official records.

A properly drawn and recorded mortgage will establish the holder's rights against the property to the full extent of the borrower's title. However, any existing rights of other claimants to the title, and the rights of old mortgages not yet released, cannot be dispossessed by a new mortgage; the new mortgage has a lien only on the maker's rights, which may themselves be junior to old claims. Taxes and special assessments levied on the property have a claim which is prior in lien to any mortgage or title claim; they must be paid by someone, or the entire rights to the property, free and clear of all mortgage claims, may be sold to satisfy the tax bill. It is clear, therefore, that a title search and possibly a policy of title insurance will be essential before a mortgage loan is made.

Once a mortgage has been properly recorded, the holder of the note and mortgage may sell them to another. The purchaser should obtain and record a written assignment of note and mortgage from the original lender; thereafter he may collect payments due on the note, and when it is repaid he may execute an effective mortgage release. The debtor under a mortgage may usually also sell his equity in the property. In this case the purchaser will pay an agreed price for the debtor's equity and should obtain and record a deed to the property; thereafter, as the new owner, he must meet the payments due on the mortgage note to avoid loss of the property through foreclosure. The transfer of the owner's equity does not affect the rights of the mortgagee against the property.

If a mortgage-secured debt is unpaid, the creditor must usually sue the debtor in court, obtain a judgment, and then ask the judge to order the sheriff to sell the mortgaged property at auction to satisfy the debt. After the sale the laws of most states permit the debtor to remain in possession for 9 to 18 months, on the theory that he may within this time be able to pay the debt and recover his property. At the end of this period he must either pay up or yield possession to the purchaser at the foreclosure sale. The entire procedure is somewhat cumbersome and expensive, and because of the postsale delay few good bids are made at the sale; consequently, the unpaid creditor usually has to buy in the property himself, in order to obtain an ultimate fair recovery on his investment.

The trust deed is a substitute for a mortgage, which is used by corporations to secure bond issues and by personal borrowers in a few states. Under this arrangement the borrower deeds his property in trust to a trust company, with instructions to sell the property for the benefit of the creditor if the note is defaulted but to deed it back to the borrower or to his assignee if the note is properly paid off. The legal rights and procedures under the trust deed are much the same as though a mortgage were used, except that no foreclosure suit is necessary and no postsale delay period is usually required.

A contract sale exists when the owner of a property and a prospective purchaser enter into a contract under which the purchaser agrees to make certain payments, usually in installments, and the owner agrees to deliver a valid deed when the payments have been completed. The purchaser usually obtains possession at once. The contract, when properly written and signed, may be recorded in the official records; it will then establish the purchaser's rights ahead of any subsequent deed, mortgage, or other instrument which the seller may execute. Failure of the purchaser to complete the payments will enable the seller to nullify the bargain and recover possession; failure of the seller to produce a valid deed can be rectified by court action. Either the purchaser or seller under a contract of sale may sell his rights during the transaction, without disturbing either the rights or the obligations of the other party. For example, a contract purchaser may assign his rights to a new purchaser, who may then take possession, complete the payments, and receive the deed. If it is the contract seller who sells out, his successor receives a deed subject to the contract, may thereafter collect the remaining payments as they come due, and is finally obligated to deliver a valid deed when the payments are complete.

These procedures and documents are very incompletely described here, but the descriptions will serve to preface several remarks which may be important to investors. First, it is evident that the procedures involved in handling deeds, mortgages, contracts, and other instruments are technical and somewhat confusing, but vital. Large sums are involved, and it is desirable to avoid trouble by employing experts to see that all steps taken are sound and correct. Second, title and title insurance matters are a little difficult to control adequately when mortgages are bought and sold and when contract sales are employed. These matters should be thoroughly understood as they operate under local law. Third, the cumbersomeness of foreclosure proceedings is sufficient notice that real estate loans should not be made except on security which is so good that it will not be allowed to come to foreclosure and except to borrowers who are so strong that they are unlikely ever to default. Fourth, a contract purchase should as a rule be made only from a financial institution which is rather certain to be alive, competent, and willing to complete its bargain after several years have elapsed. In buying on the installment plan from individuals, it is safer to obtain a deed and give back an installment note secured by mortgage. Then, if appropriate receipts for payments have been preserved, it is a simple matter to prove the satisfaction of the mortgage if an issue arises.

Government Regulation and Competition

Investors have learned in the last twenty years that among the very major factors determining the profitableness and soundness of their investments are the policies pursued by state and Federal governments. Taxes, regulation, subsidies, and public competition are important but unpredictable economic forces. They are forces whose importance in the real property field is steadily increasing. Taxes on property are now so heavy that they are always a factor in appraisals and in decisions to build or not to build. Income taxes are also a factor in keeping many individuals out of the traditionally low-yielding rental housing field.

Regulation of rents under the 1942–1952 rent control program was continued so long that the propriety of denying landlords any participation in the price-level expansion of the period, and even of a fair return on their original investments at a time when their properties were in great demand, almost became a part of the national mores. Even the fairness of discriminating between the landlords of "free" and regulated properties at times went unquestioned. The lesson for property owners is that they need never again expect to operate in a completely economic market; when price levels rise, or housing shortages again occur, the political authorities have ample precedent for "freezing" rents at unprofitable levels, if politically powerful groups demand such action. There is, of course, no certainty that this will be done. Federal rent controls were allowed to lapse in 1952 (though a few local regulations persisted longer) and may never be reimposed; but the precedent now stands, and landlords are a minority group.

Subsidies have been won, conspicuously, by farmers and certain limited-dividend housing corporations. Others would like them; cooperative housing associations, for example, would like tax exemption and uneconomic government loans. Even the veterans' housing loan guarantee is a small-scale subsidy. To the extent that the subsidy is irrevocable, as in the case of the veterans' loans, it is an important inducement to investment. But subsidies which are constantly changed in terms, as the farm subsidies are, are difficult to evaluate on a long-term basis. The important and vocal farm group seems certain to receive largesse from the public purse, but to purchase farm land on the assumption that its earning power is underwritten by the government is to assume that government benefits to farmers will continue to be planned to benefit the land instead of the people who work the land. A difference could be made, if Congress cared to do so; and if it occurred to certain groups that absentee landlords were benefiting from the farm program, changes would certainly be suggested.

Finally, public competition must be considered. For some years both Federal and local governments have been dabbling with ideas of public housing. Before the war a number of municipally owned, lightly taxed, federally subsidized low-rent housing projects were constructed by city and county housing authorities. These projects were financed by means of tax-free municipal bonds which were virtually guaranteed by the Federal government, hence had a low money cost; with low property taxes and a Federal subsidy, they have been able to offer apartments at rents far below the essential costs of their privately owned competitors. The Housing Act of 1949 has more recently set in motion a plan to construct 810,000 apartments during the next few years, on much the same basis. This program was originally intended to build more than 12 per cent of the nonfarm housing units constructed in this country during the 8 years 1949–1957. In 1954 its progress was far below this rate, but political decisions on this point are subject to rapid change.

A generously subsidized public housing program intended to house 2 per cent of the nation's population at bargain prices will undoubtedly create a great demand on the part of the excluded citizens for public housing for them too. It will also disparage greatly the self-sustaining housing provided by private investors. Whether the earning power of private properties will be reduced by public competition, or whether enough private investors will suspend their own construction plans so that the total housing supply will remain limited and therefore profitably rented, is a question only the future can answer. At best, the attractiveness of rental housing as an investment has not been improved.

Real Estate Investment: Summary

Investment in real estate is popular and widely practiced. Most improved real estate has some net cash earning power even in hard times and should therefore have a value stability comparable to that of good-grade stocks. In general, real estate values fluctuate with the general price level, and real estate investments may therefore be used as price-level hedges. Real estate financing is now elaborately organized to make major investments easy to finance by means of long-term installment loans. Homeownership is particularly easy to finance and has profit and tax advantages.

Disadvantages in real estate investment include the fact that most real estate purchases must be made in large parcels, thus precluding wide diversification. Real estate is not highly salable, nor is it pledgeable at low cost. Heavily mortgaged properties may be lost entirely if misfortune prevents the maintenance of the regular payments. The present unprecedented number of heavily mortgaged properties owned by debtors of doubtful financial strength is a potential danger to the real estate market. Government regulation, competition, and subsidy are unreliable factors in the situation. Finally, real estate investments require a somewhat greater degree of management effort and skill than do investments in good-grade securities.

Mortgage Loans

It has been observed that the bulk of mortgage lending on homes and farms is done by institutions and, in the case of farms, government agencies. However, there is still an important volume of individual lending in the home and farm mortgage fields. In the case of apartment house and small commercial property loans—for example, store buildings, motels, commercial garages, gasoline stations, vacant lots, and the like—individuals appear to be particularly important as lenders. Most mortgage lending institutions emphasize security in their loan policies, hence are inclined to prefer loans on more stable and marketable security, such as homes or farms, to those on business properties or vacant lots. The lending institutions are also likely to prefer borrowers who have adequate incomes or other resources, so that their loans are likely to be repaid without trouble; this leaves a considerable amount of borrowing by widows, elderly folk, and over-ambitious young people to be financed by private lenders.

But not all private lending is confined to cases in which the loans are speculative in nature. In every community there are individuals who choose to invest their savings by making good mortgage loans. Borrowers find these people through their advertisements, through real estate dealers who know them, and through the word-of-mouth contacts of the community. Again, the sellers of real property often take mortgages on the property as part payment for the property. Speculative builders sell new homes on a similar basis. And a very large part of the total volume of individual mortgage lending doubt-less consists of transactions within families, which are formalized by the use of lien security.

Second mortgage loans [6] form a somewhat unique phase of the mortgage lending field. The major lending institutions do not make second loans, but speculative mortgage companies, mortgage dealers, and individuals are often interested in them. Second mortgages come into existence in various ways. Sometimes a borrower who has or can obtain a first mortgage loan on satisfactory terms is compelled to ob-tain a supplementary second loan on much less attractive terms, to meet his financial needs. Again, the sellers of property often accept in payment the proceeds of the best first mortgage loan the buyer can obtain, plus a cash payment from the buyer's funds, plus a sec-ond mortgage for the balance. Speculative home builders often mort-gage the new home for the maximum amount obtainable on a con-struction loan and then sell their equity for a small cash payment plus a second mortgage for the balance. The interest rate on a nego-tiated second mortgage loan is likely to be 6 to 10 per cent and the term shorter than that of a first lien, often not over five years, whether the loan is amortized or not. A second mortgage arising from a sale

[6] When a real estate owner already indebted on a first mortgage signs a second mortgage he pledges to his creditor just the rights he has left—namely, the right to repay the first mortgagee and continue as owner. If the second mortgagee is unpaid and must force a foreclosure sale, the property is sold *subject to* the first mortgage, on which the buyer must then make the regular payments. If the first mortgage pay-ments are defaulted, a foreclosure sale on its behalf will sell the real estate subject only to unpaid taxes, thus eliminating the second mortgagee's security. Consequently, a second mortgage lender must make sure that the first mortgagee is regularly paid, either by the original debtor, or, in an emergency, by the second mortgagee himself.

An owner obligated on a second (or even a third) mortgage or trust deed continues in possession unless dispossessed after a foreclosure sale.

transaction usually pays 5 or 6 per cent but is also likely to be of reasonably short maturity. A second mortgage may be a safe investment if the property is adequate in value and if the borrower is able to meet his obligations, but it has the disadvantage, if trouble occurs, of requiring the second mortgagee to make sure that proper payments are made on the first mortgage. Default on the first mortgage would permit the first mortgagee to force the sale of the property for his benefit, possibly to the exclusion of the second mortgagee.

In most large communities, and in many small ones as well, there are dealers who buy and sell both first and second mortgages. Their advertisements appear regularly in the classified sections of the newspapers. Most of these dealers expect to assist amateur investors with the technical details incident to transferring title to the mortgages; many of them guarantee their validity (but not their collectibility) as well. The prices quoted are similar to those quoted on bonds; well-secured first mortgages of moderate size, which might be bought by a trust company for one of its trusts or by an individual seeking safety, will sell on a 4½ to 6 per cent yield basis. Small ($500 to $2,000) second liens at 5 or 6 per cent, probably representing the balance of a builder's sale price, may sell at a 20 to 35 per cent discount from face value. Even greater discounts are sometimes found, in cases in which the security is poor or the payments are not regularly met. There are doubtless wonderful opportunities in these markets for astute investors who are familiar with property law, whose appraisal judgments are keen, and who can evaluate the debtor's willingness and ability to pay. However, a mortgage investor who was compelled to make many foreclosures would probably not find his investments profitable.

In summary, it may be said that mortgages offer the investor who is equipped to handle them a satisfactory outlet for his funds. Well-secured loans to good borrowers are safe and yield 1½ times as much as good bonds. The more speculative types, particularly those bought at a discount, offer some element of price-level protection in the appreciation which will occur in their value if property values rise, and in addition, they offer a chance for a speculative profit if wise selection avoids trouble or losses on them. On the other hand, there are disadvantages in mortgage investments. The principal sums are often large, making adequate diversification impossible to people of limited means; and geographic diversification is truly difficult.

Second, most mortgages provide for monthly payments; this makes the bookkeeping a nuisance and returns the lender's capital on a piecemeal basis, so he is very likely to lose some interest on it before he is able to reinvest it. Third, mortgage loans require greater individual effort in making or choosing them soundly, and in watching the security subsequently, than do many other forms of investments. Fourth, the business requires a fund of legal and technical knowledge which is no less formidable than that required for stock investments. Fifth, mortgages are not dependably liquid, for they cannot be readily sold for their true value. They are salable, but only on a negotiated basis, and buyers who will pay fair prices are not always easy to find.

QUESTIONS AND PROBLEMS

1. Which is the most profitable form of equity ownership for a young couple, a home or an assorted stock portfolio? Upon what factors may your answer depend?

2. Explain how the wasting asset feature of improved property investment adds security to an investment in it.

3. Review the method of adding taxes, maintenance, insurance, depreciation, and a fair return on the investment, to obtain the gross income percentage at which residence rental values may be capitalized. Is 100 times the monthly rental value a fair appraisal for a new residence in your community? Should it be?

4. Do the banks and savings-loan associations in your community appraise on a replacement cost basis? What do they regard as a normal relative value of house and lot?

5. What are deed restrictions and zoning ordinances? (These are mentioned but not discussed in the text.)

6. Why are high-percentage, completely amortizing loans regarded as a safeguard against a wave of foreclosures and forced sales?

7. Assuming that most of the properties now mortgaged at high prices and above 80 per cent of value are either mortgaged under FHA or GI loan plans, is it not probable that the Federal agencies would hold foreclosed or abandoned properties off the market rather than risk damage to property values as a result of forced sales during depressions? Does this add further hope for stabilized property values hereafter?

8. Who are the principal lenders on real estate mortgages in your vicinity? Do they use amortizing loans? Can a nonveteran obtain an 80 per cent loan on an existing home? On a newly constructed one?

9. Explain why a house financed with a 95 per cent veteran's loan at 4 per cent brings a good price, if the veteran decides to sell.

10. Why is a search of the official title records not good enough for one who buys or lends upon a $20,000 parcel of city property? What assurance meets the need?

11. What effect does a sale of a parcel of real estate by the mortgage debtor have upon the mortgagee's right to foreclose and dispossess the owner, if the debt is not paid?

12. What effect does the sale of note and mortgage by the original lender to another have on the debtor's obligation?

13. Is there a market in your community through which mortgages are bought and sold? Are mortgages advertised for sale at a discount? Could an investor make money by buying mortgages at a discount?

14. Are second mortgage loans used in your community? Who makes them?

REFERENCES

Badger, Ralph E., and Harry G. Guthmann: *Investment Principles and Practices,* Prentice-Hall, Inc., New York, 1951, Chap. 17.

Boehmler, Erwin W., and others: *Financial Institutions,* Richard D. Irwin, Inc., Homewood, Ill., 1951, Chap. 15.

Donaldson, Elvin F.: *Personal Finance,* The Ronald Press Company, New York, 1948, Chaps. 14, 15.

Dowrie, George W., and Douglas R. Fuller: *Investments,* John Wiley & Sons, Inc., New York, 1950, Chap. 27.

Hoagland, Henry E.: *Real Estate Principles,* McGraw-Hill Book Company, Inc., New York, 1955.

Jordan, David F., and Herbert E. Dougall: *Investments,* Prentice-Hall, Inc., New York, 1952, Chap. 30.

Pease, Robert H. (ed.), and Homer V. Cherrington: *Mortgage Banking,* McGraw-Hill Book Company, Inc., New York, 1953.

Pickett, Ralph R., and Marshall D. Ketchum: *Investment Principles and Policy,* Harper & Brothers, New York, 1954, Chaps. 16, 17.

Prochnow, Herbert V. (ed.): *American Financial Institutions,* Prentice-Hall, Inc., New York, 1951, Chap. 7.

Ratcliff, Richard U.: *Urban Land Economics,* McGraw-Hill Book Company, Inc., New York, 1949.

Chapter 26: FOREIGN SECURITIES
OR PROPERTY

For the past fifty years American investors have paid increasing attention to opportunities outside the boundaries of the United States. Not only has the growing capital supply within this country tended to reduce interest returns here below those obtainable on foreign securities, but American corporations and individual business adventurers have found important outlets for their resources in business projects located abroad. The total value of all privately owned foreign investments was estimated at 13.5 billion dollars in 1946; in 1953 it was 23.7 billion dollars.[1] These figures do not include any of the foreign loans made by the United States government or its wholly owned Export-Import Bank.

Foreign investments available to American citizens may be classified into five groups for study purposes. In descending order of present importance they are (1) foreign branches and subsidiaries of American corporations, (2) securities of foreign corporations, (3) bonds of foreign governments and governmental agencies, (4) individual holdings of foreign real estate or business ventures, and (5) bonds issued by or guaranteed by the International Bank for Reconstruction and Development. Only the first of these groups showed any important growth in the period 1945–1953, though the International Bank still affords some hope for great development when the postwar economic confusion subsides.

American Corporations with Foreign Holdings

Many important American corporations, including such giants as Standard Oil Company of New Jersey, General Electric Company, Armour and Company, and Anaconda Copper Mining Company, have large business investments abroad. Although these holdings

---

[1] *Survey of Current Business*, May, 1954, p. 12.

and others like them represent a major fraction of American foreign investments, the much more important home properties of these corporations cause the stockholders to place only minor emphasis upon the foreign commitments.

Approximately one-third of the foreign investments of American corporations are in branches and subsidiaries in Canada. These outlays have grown rapidly since 1945, in proportion to the enormous economic growth of Canada. Probably the bulk of them are in extractive industries—petroleum, natural gas, iron ore, and general mining have all developed greatly in Canada—but manufacturing and commercial industries have also proved attractive. Favorable commercial laws, a sound currency, a mutual language, and similar business methods make Canadian operations attractive to firms with established operations in the United States.

Although the bulk of American corporate investments abroad is represented by subsidiaries and branches, there are substantial American-controlled corporations whose properties are almost entirely in foreign countries. Among these may be mentioned the Pantepec Oil Company of Venezuela, International Packers, Ltd. (Uruguay and other countries), and International Railways of Central America. Such concerns are acutely subject to the taxes, property laws, currency problems, and foreign-exchange hazards which affect international investments. The owners of their stocks and bonds must be prepared to accept all the ordinary business risks which occur everywhere, plus many added political and economic hazards characteristic of long-term international transactions. Because of the added hazards the price-earnings ratios are likely to be lower and the yields higher than those on strictly American securities of similar quality.

Information about corporations engaged chiefly in foreign activities is found in the usual sources, and the securities are traded on the American listed and over-the-counter markets in the usual manner. The legal devices necessary to organize the business properly do not usually affect the investors—for example, International Packers, Ltd., is an American holding company which controls a number of subsidiaries in various countries, and the American shares of Pantepec Oil are transferable deposit receipts for shares held in trust by a New York bank. Because the corporation or holding company is American-controlled, American-owned, and financially domiciled in the United States, the dividends will be payable in American dollars and stock sales and transfers can be managed in familiar ways in American markets.

Securities of Foreign Corporations

Four-fifths of the 2 billion dollars of foreign-domiciled and foreign-controlled corporate securities owned by Americans are Canadian securities. This is not surprising, in view of the high esteem in which Canada is held by American citizens, and of the similarity of business methods between the two countries. Americans use the Canadian stock exchanges and unlisted markets freely, Canadian securities are marketed in the United States as well as in Canada, and leading Canadian issues are traded on American stock exchanges and unlisted markets. Such corporate names as Canadian Pacific Railway, International Nickel Company of Canada, and Gatineau Power Company are as familiar in the United States as in Canada. Some of these Canadian concerns pay their interest and dividends (and principal, in the case of bonds) in Canadian dollars only, and the checks must then be sold to exchange dealers by securityholders living in the United States; and some of the corporations declare their payments in Canadian funds but remit the equivalent value in United States dollars to payees living south of the border. In the case of bonds, some bond issues are sold payable in United States dollars.

Interest and dividends paid by Canadian corporations to non-Canadians are subject to a 15 per cent income tax collected at the source—*i.e.*, withheld by the corporation. This means that the United States investor in a Canadian corporation will receive only 85 per cent of the payment accrued or declared on his Canadian security, no matter whether payable in Canadian or United States dollars. However, the income tax laws of the United States permit the deduction of a foreign income tax in full from the domestic tax otherwise payable, in most instances, so there is no net disadvantage to United States citizens in this Canadian tax.

The total American investment in foreign-controlled foreign corporations other than Canadian is estimated at about 400 million dollars. These holdings are widely scattered in many countries; Gaumon-British Picture Corporation of Great Britain, O'Okiep Copper Company of South Africa, and Taca Airways of South America are well-known examples. These three concerns have accommodated American shareholders either by depositing their American-held shares in trust in New York, so that American holders may own easily transferable American depositary receipts, or by establishing a stock transfer office in New York. However, most foreign corporations do not do this, and an American holder must accept foreign markets, foreign currencies, and foreign transfer methods.

During the 1920s a number of issues of German, Italian, Japanese, and other corporate bonds were sold in the United States. These were without exception "dollar bonds"—that is, the debtors promised to pay interest and principal in American dollars—and the units were the usual $1,000 bond denomination. Like any corporate security, these bonds are subject to all the commercial hazards which may beset their makers, and to foreign-exchange complications as well when dollars are difficult for the debtors to obtain in their own national exchange markets.

From the foregoing it may be deduced that there are four possible differences between investment in American companies owning foreign properties and investment in foreign-controlled business concerns. First, the managerial group in the foreign-controlled concern may not be primarily interested in the investment welfare of American securityholders. Second, dividends, interest payments, and other payments may be made in the firm's own national currency, not in dollars, and the American payee may experience some trouble and expense in obtaining dollars. Third, foreign taxes on dividends or interest may intercept some of the income. Fourth, foreign markets and transfer methods may be awkward for Americans.

Information about foreign corporations in which Americans hold securities will be found in the usual American financial sources.

Bonds of Foreign Governments and Agencies

Most of the securities distributed in this country as "foreign bonds" have been the bonds of foreign national governments, states, municipalities, and publicly owned corporations. Statistically, these issues have earned the sour reputation they bear. At December 31, 1948, the Institute of International Finance estimated that foreign public debtors plus foreign business corporations had outstanding a total of $4,386,586,652 of bonds payable in dollars, of which a large percentage were American-held.[2] Over $1,997,000,000 of these bonds, or nearly 46 per cent of the total, were in default as to interest or principal or both. Grouping the debtors by geographic regions, the Institute found 59 per cent of Latin American dollar bonds in default, 77 per cent of European bonds, 56 per cent of those from the Far East and Africa, and 0.2 per cent of those from Canada. National governments, municipalities, and government-owned corporations all had black records; state issues looked a little better, but only because the list included a number of characteristically reliable Canadian issues.

Since 1948 a considerable number of defaulting governments or governmental units have resumed payments or have undertaken to negotiate adjustment plans with their creditors. Some of these steps have been taken willingly, as improved economic conditions and postwar restoration have made them possible. Others have been taken after considerable pressure by the Foreign Bondholders' Protective Council and other creditors' agencies, and because the International Bank for Reconstruction and Development does not consider governments which are indifferent to their present obligations to be good risks for new loans. Table 57 notes a number of such adjustments which were in process or in prospect in 1953.

There are of course many foreign nations whose governmental units pay their obligations regularly. Canada, Great Britain, France, Norway, Finland, Guatemala, Argentina, Cuba, the Dominican Republic, Panama, Uruguay, and Australia, among others, have very creditable records. Some units in some of these countries have been in default at times and have even asked their dollar creditors to accept reductions in interest or principal, but that has happened among American public debtors as well.

Foreign public bonds sold in the United States almost always promise payment of principal and interest in dollars. A New York bank is usually designated as the paying agent and administrator of the sinking fund if any. There is no trustee in the usual sense. Sinking funds are common, serial issues are sometimes used, and call provisions are frequently included. Sometimes specific governmental revenues are pledged for debt service; for example, the Republic of

---

[2] *Bulletin* 161, June 20, 1949. A tabulation covering about half the total dollar issues outstanding showed 70 per cent of the bonds in American hands.

Panama once pledged the annual rental paid by the United States for the use of the Canal Zone as security for certain of her dollar bonds.

When foreign public debtors default on their dollar bonds, there is usually no court action which American creditors may take. Un-

Table 57. Price Ranges of Selected Foreign Dollar Bonds, 1948 and 1953

Issue	1948		1953	
	High	Low	High	Low
Antwerp (City) 5s of 1958	99⅛	73	105	101
Australia 3½s of 1966	92	83¾	97¾	88¼
Belgium 6s of 1955	109	103½	106	102
Brazil Stamped Plan A 3.375s of 1979	49½	38	61½	55
Brisbane (City) 5s of 1958	102	94	103¾	100½
Canada 3¼s of 1961	105⅞	103⅛	103¼	99½
Chile 6s of 1960 *	32½	19¼	61¼	55½ †
Colombia 6s of 1961 *	73½	68½	103	98½ †
Cuba 4½s of 1977	118	107⅛	114	107
Denmark 4½s of 1962	82	54⅛	101¾	91¼
Italy 7s of 1951 *	34	20⅛	92	78 †
Mexico 4s of 1954 *	8¼	7	10	8½ †
Norway 4½s of 1956	97⅜	75	101½	99½
Panama 3½s B of 1967	106	101⅝	Retired	Retired
Peru 7s of 1959 *	17	14⅛	56½	48¾ †
Rio de Janeiro Stamped Plan A 2s of 2012	27½	18	32	29½
Uruguay 3½s of 1984	90	70	82	64¼

* Traded flat. Payments in default, uncertain, or in arrears.
† Exchange plan in process or projected in 1953.

less the debtors later become able to pay or wish to rehabilitate their credit by making payments, the bonds remain in default and nothing is done about it. Sometimes well-intentioned debtors pay interest but default on sinking funds and maturities or make partial payments as the funds become available. Others less honorably inclined have on occasion defaulted on interest payments and have later offered to buy the past-due interest coupons at a large discount; still others have defaulted on interest payments, then used their available dollars to buy in and retire their bonds at low prices.[3] Governments which have been compelled to default frequently make adjustment offers to their bondholders under which the old bonds may be exchanged for new ones which pay less interest, call for smaller sinking fund payments, or have later maturities. Conscientious settlements have been made in this manner by a number of nations, among which Brazil is conspicuous; but the indifference of many debtors until circumstances make payment easy or until part payment opens the door to new credits would seem to justify much of the prevailing cynicism.

Because of the great difference in hazard the yields available on foreign public bonds vary widely. On a Canadian or Australian national issue there is little risk, and the yields are comparable to those on high-class American bonds; but on doubtful issues yields of 6 to 10 per cent can be found, and on default bonds very low prices are often quoted. Table 57 shows typical quotations.

Information about foreign public bonds is available in the major financial services, in the financial journals, and in the reports of the Foreign Bondholders' Protective Council and the Institute of International Finance. Investors who wish to invest or speculate in this field should investigate carefully both the debtors' willingness to pay and their ability to pay. The bonds are regularly traded on the stock exchanges and in unlisted markets; hence, quotations will be found in the usual places.

International Bank for Reconstruction and Development

One of the planned instruments for peace and prosperity in the postwar world was an agency whose intervention could reduce the risks of international lending and investing. The International Bank for Reconstruction and Development is such an agency, whose function is to make or facilitate international loans for productive investment. The Bank was planned at the Bretton Woods Conference in 1944 and began business in 1946. Its stockholders are sovereign nations which at June 30, 1952, had subscribed $9,036,500,000 of cap-

---

[3] The actual purchase has often been made by a citizen of the defaulting country, who then repatriates the bond and surrenders it to his government in exchange for one paying interest in local currency.

ital and paid in $1,807,300,000; most of the balance will not be paid in but is subject to call if needed. The United States government owned 35 per cent of the stock, Great Britain had 14 per cent, and others had lesser amounts.

The Bank may lend its own capital funds, it may sell its own debentures to raise additional money, or it may merely guarantee the payment of bonds which eligible borrowers sell to other investors. Eligible borrowers are member governments, states or municipalities within member countries, and private corporations within member countries; but the member national government must guarantee all loans made within its borders. An eligible borrower ordinarily desires a foreign loan either because interest rates are lower than in the home country, or because it needs foreign equipment which it cannot purchase with the home currency because of foreign exchange difficulties. In either case, a loan from the Bank or the sale in a foreign country of the borrower's bonds bearing the Bank's guarantee will solve the problem.

American investors now have opportunity to invest in the dollar debentures of the International Bank; six issues maturing from 1957 to 1980, paying 2 to $3\frac{1}{2}$ per cent coupon rates, and totaling 500 million dollars in amount, have been marketed in the United States. These debentures are high quality. The Bank had less than 2 billion dollars committed to loans in 1953, its borrowings totaled only 556 million dollars, and it has very large uncollected capital subscriptions from the United States and other solvent stockholders which can be used to absorb any losses which may occur. There will be no risk of investor loss in International Bank debentures until many billions of loans are outstanding, and even then the risk should not be great. In mid-1954 the debentures sold on the New York Stock Exchange at 99 for the 3s of 1972 and 103 for the $3\frac{1}{2}$s of 1971.

Causes of Loss

Most of the losses which Americans have sustained in foreign investments are attributable to one or more of eight common situations. These are not listed here in any order which purports to indicate their importance or frequency, but it is suggested that the first five deal with willingness to pay and the remaining three with ability to pay. They are as follows:

1. No recognition of moral obligation. There are probably few other countries in which individuals and governments take as much pride in fulfilling their promises as do those in the United States, Canada, Great Britain, and the Scandinavian countries. In many countries obligations are recognized by the debtors just as long as the advantage of a good credit standing outweighs the burden of making payment. A sense of moral obligation to pay debts is most likely to be present among educated people, people used to commercial transactions, and people who are not in acute poverty. Investors considering foreign commitments can test for this moral hazard by examining the nation's record and present political trends, as well as other pertinent factors. The results will give an indication of the soundness of corporate investments or direct property ownership as well as the reliability of public bonds, for a nation which honors its debts is not likely to expropriate private property without compensation.

2. Jealousy or spite toward Americans. There are a number of foreign countries in which Americans are not popular. Regardless of the cause of such attitudes, they certainly contribute to a willingness to default on American claims and to do things which may injure American property.

3. No immediate need for American cooperation. Debt defaults and adverse legislation toward Americans are much more likely when the nation in question does not need or cannot get American markets or American credits. Even high-quality debtors make a more determined effort to pay when nonpayment jeopardizes something urgently desired.

4. Lack of political stability. Nations addicted to revolutions or to sharp political upheavals are frequently poor credit risks because their governments cannot risk either sufficient taxes or sufficient governmental economy to maintain sound budgets. Furthermore, political turbulence leads to demagoguery and unsound legislation at the expense of foreigners.

5. Misuse of the original funds. This hazard applies only to public bonds, but it is an important hazard in that field. Money borrowed and spent unsoundly by an administration which is later removed from power is sometimes not repaid by successor administrations. It is difficult for a new government to feel obligated to pay for the errors or extravagances of predecessors of which it does not approve.

On the other hand, revolutionary governments often acknowledge prior debts which were incurred to pay for roads, railways, power systems, and similar good assets.

6. Unsound foreign exchange situation. The disturbed state of world trade since 1914 has made international exchange problems very acute for many nations. Wars, booms, depressions, internal disturbances, and trade restrictions have caused trade balances to fluctuate greatly. International lending and capital movements have been sporadic. As a result, international exchange rates have fluctuated greatly, making dollars very expensive at times when foreign debtors wished to buy them to make payments in the United States. Public debtors have sometimes defaulted on dollar bonds because of the high price of dollars, even when they were able to raise normal sums in their own money. In order to keep the dollar at a reasonable exchange rate, and to be able to pay for normal imports from the United States, national governments frequently impose exchange control systems which limit the number of dollars available to transmit interest, dividend, or debt principal payments into the United States. This situation obviously may turn a sound foreign investment into a poor one. Investors are therefore well advised to consider the strength of a nation's foreign exchange position before investing in its securities or in property located within its borders. The diversification, total value, and price stability of the nation's exports, coupled with the amount of its imports, the size of its external debt, and the trend of its current international capital transactions, are important clues to its exchange position. There are signs in 1954 that the disruption of trade and foreign exchange relationships which has persisted so long is abating; if world peace and prosperity enable this trend to continue, international investment conditions will be immeasurably improved.

7. Unsound internal economy. Countries which lack good financial institutions, good laws, or honest government, or which are committed to fanciful economic experimentation are likely to be stagnant and unproductive. Their political units are poor credit risks because of inability to collect revenues or to control expenses, and earnings from properties and business ventures are less dependable than they should be because of uncertain business conditions.

8. Poorly chosen debtors or properties. Even if a national economy is reasonably sound, it is essential that a debtor state or municipality or corporation be financially strong, if its securities are to be good investments. Investors have sustained losses on the bonds of one of the Canadian provinces, for example, despite the strength and stability of Canada as a whole. Admittedly, it is more difficult for an investor to appraise the quality of a municipality or a business property in a distant country than if it were near his home, but failure to make the attempt is an invitation to loss.

Foreign Bondholders' Protective Council, Inc.

This organization was formed in 1933 as an unofficial but governmentally approved body to represent American investors in negotiations with foreign public debtors. Foreign defaults were rife in 1933, yet the United States government found it politically inexpedient to press the debtors for payment or a plan of adjustment; an unofficial agency could do this with better grace. The council is financed by private donations and by small charges levied upon the bondholders it serves.

The council consists of a volunteer committee of leading attorneys, financiers, and statesmen, and a small executive staff. Certain government agencies such as the State Department and the SEC cooperate in collecting information. The function of the council is to approach each defaulting foreign governmental debtor as the representative of the American bondholders, seeking to persuade the debtor to resume payments or to offer an adjustment plan compatible with its ability to pay. If an acceptable solution is reached, the council endeavors to get the bondholders to accept it; if the debtor proposes an unfair plan, the council recommends against it and tries to arrange a better one.

The council has been generally recognized by foreign debtors as the proper American bargaining agency on these matters.

Sources of Information

Information concerning the securities and the economic affairs of foreign nations, municipalities, and corporations can be found in the major financial reference sources. These sources will also give a factual history of defaults and debt adjustments, if any have occurred. The annual reports of the Foreign Bondholders' Protective Council,

Inc., also furnish data on defaults, debt adjustments, and negotiations in progress. Similar material appears in periodic issues of the *Bulletin* of the Institute of International Finance. The institute also publishes occasional appraisals of the economic position of various countries. Periodical articles and occasional studies by securities dealers constitute the remaining best sources for the ordinary investor.

Although the high yields and wide price swings characteristic of foreign securities have attracted many small investors, it is probably fair to say that this is a hazardous and hard-to-understand field for one who cannot study it extensively and constantly. Until the world economy is more stable, it will be best for casual investors to limit themselves to American securities. Bonds issued by or guaranteed by the International Bank are an exception, of course, as are Canadian securities and property.

QUESTIONS AND PROBLEMS

1. Name the types of American privately owned foreign investments in order of importance.

2. Why is American capital being invested abroad?

3. Are American corporations extending their investments abroad at the present time? Are foreign bonds being sold in the United States?

4. Would there be less likelihood of defaults if American-held foreign bonds were payable in foreign money? Would Americans buy the bonds readily under such circumstances?

5. If a foreign government cannot obtain dollars to pay interest on its dollar bonds, can that government honorably permit its citizens to sell export merchandise in America, use the resulting dollars to buy the defaulted bonds at a low price, repatriate the bonds, and then exchange them for interest-paying bonds in the home currency? Consider all the possibilities here.

6. If the American markets trade in interest-paying foreign dollar bonds at 70 cents on the dollar, is it legitimate for the foreign government to encourage its citizens to buy them, repatriate them, and exchange them for home-currency bonds? (The Japanese did this before the war.)

7. Look up the Brazilian Traction, Light, and Power Company stock, and consider its quality and its price.

8. Does the plan for the International Bank seem sound? Should American banks and life insurance companies be permitted to hold its bonds? (Note: Most of them are so permitted.)

9. Which of the causes of loss to American bondholders seems to you to offer the best explanation of the 45-year defaults by the Republic of Mexico? Of the 35-year default by Russia on the Czar's bonds?

10. Explain the nature of the Foreign Bondholders' Protective Council, Inc.

11. Would you buy the dollar bonds of a foreign government which proposed to use the loan "to maintain a satisfactory standard of living temporarily and to build up our capital resources so a satisfactory standard of living can be maintained permanently"?

REFERENCES

Badger, Ralph E., and Harry G. Guthmann: *Investment Principles and Practices,* Prentice-Hall, Inc., New York, 1951, Chap. 21.

Dowrie, George W., and Douglas R. Fuller: *Investments,* John Wiley & Sons, Inc., New York, 1950, Chap. 22.

International Bank for Reconstruction and Development: *Annual Reports,* Washington.

Investment Bankers Association of America: *Fundamentals of Investment Banking,* Prentice-Hall, Inc., New York, 1949, Chap. 13.

Lewis, Cleona: *The United States and Foreign Investment Problems,* The Brookings Institution, Washington, D.C., 1948.

Pickett, Ralph R., and Marshall D. Ketchum: *Investment Principles and Policy,* Harper & Brothers, New York, 1954, Chap. 15.

Prochnow, Herbert V. (ed.): *American Financial Institutions,* Prentice-Hall, Inc., New York, 1951, Chap. 18.

Robbins, Sidney M.: *Managing Securities,* Houghton Mifflin Company, Boston, 1954, Chap. 16.

"Statistical Analysis of Publicly Offered Foreign Dollar Bonds," New York University, Institute of International Finance, *Bulletin* 187, 1954.

United States Department of Commerce: *Foreign Investments,* Washington, 1953.

Chapter 27: TAXES WHICH AFFECT INVESTMENT POLICY

Taxes and assessments for the support of public functions are absorbing more than 25 per cent of the national income in postwar America. This terrific burden is collected in diverse ways by the national government, states, and municipalities, but the levies are so heavy on both property and incomes that taxpayers have need to adapt their investment policies to the conditions created by the tax laws. The phases of investment policy affected are many and various, but among the important ones will be found (1) liquidity of estate, for the purpose of meeting estate and inheritance levies; (2) desirability of tax-exempt versus higher yielding taxable investments, in view of high income taxes; (3) relative attractiveness of secure and hazardous investments, if income is taxed in high brackets; (4) location of residence, safety deposit boxes, family trusts, tangible personal property, and real estate, in view of conflicting state inheritance tax jurisdictions; and (5) method of holding legal title to family property, in view of income tax and estate tax burdens. These problems and other similar ones are matters for experts where the cases are complicated, but most investors, even those in moderate circumstances, are likely to find that a general understanding of tax planning is advantageous.

Tax problems will also bring home to the investor another facet of the increasing complexity of modern times, namely, the necessity for detailed and accurate personal records. The adjusted cost of real estate investments, the actual cash cost of life annuities, the value of inherited property at the time of the previous owner's death, the identification of shares of stock bought at different prices at different times—these and a host of other bits of information may be needed many years after the transactions have faded from memory. Even families with small financial resources need records, for income taxes already reach almost every family, and the taxes of the future will probably require even more detailed reports and calculations.

FEDERAL PERSONAL INCOME TAXES

Because the Federal personal income tax is very complicated, very heavy, and steeply progressive, it probably gives rise to more investment problems than any other tax. Federal income taxes are levied upon every citizen or resident who has any significant income.

Structure of the Federal Income Tax

The Federal income tax is levied annually on the taxpayer's computed taxable income. Taxable income is determined as follows: First, the *adjusted gross income* is found. This sum includes the taxpayer's wages, salary, dividends minus certain exemptions and credits, interest, business profits after business expenses, real estate income after deducting expenses, income from trust funds, certain portions of annuity receipts, and the net balance of profits and losses on sale of investments (*i.e.*, capital gains or losses) as specified by law. It does not include interest on state and municipal bonds, gifts, bequests, social security benefits, most personal insurance benefits, and certain other tax-exempt gains. Second, the *net income* is found. Net income equals the adjusted gross income minus *deductions*. The deductions consist either of an arbitrary 10 per cent of an adjusted gross income (but not exceeding $1,000) or of an itemized total of actual "deductions." The itemized total may include interest paid, taxes paid, losses from property destruction, charitable contributions not exceeding 20 per cent of adjusted gross income, medical and dental expenses in excess of 3 per cent of adjusted gross income, and certain other items, all as specified by law. Third, the *taxable income* is found by subtracting from net income a personal exemption of $600 for the taxpayer (or $1,200 if he is over 65 or blind) and an additional $600 for each dependent. Fourth, the *tax* is determined by applying the current rates to the taxpayer's taxable income. The tax is computed by applying successively higher rates to each "bracket" of taxable income and totaling all of these levies. For example, at the 1954 rates each taxpayer pays 20 per cent on his first $2,000 of taxable income, 22 per cent on the next $2,000, 26 per cent on the next $2,000, and successively more in higher brackets until a maximum rate of 91 per cent is reached.[1]

Federal Personal Income Tax Rates

On taxable income		Tax is		
Over	But not over	This amount	Plus this percentage	Of excess over
$ 0	$ 2,000	$ 0	20%	$ 0
2,000	4,000	400	22	2,000
4,000	6,000	840	26	4,000
6,000	8,000	1,360	30	6,000
8,000	10,000	1,960	34	8,000
10,000	12,000	2,640	38	10,000
12,000	14,000	3,400	43	12,000
14,000	16,000	4,260	47	14,000
16,000	18,000	5,200	50	16,000
18,000	20,000	6,200	53	18,000
20,000	22,000	7,260	56	20,000
22,000	26,000	8,380	59	22,000
26,000	32,000	10,740	62	26,000
32,000	38,000	14,460	65	32,000
38,000	44,000	18,360	69	38,000
44,000	50,000	22,500	72	44,000
50,000	60,000	26,820	75	50,000
60,000	70,000	34,320	78	60,000
70,000	80,000	42,120	81	70,000
80,000	90,000	50,220	84	80,000
90,000	100,000	58,620	87	90,000
100,000	150,000	67,320	89	100,000
150,000	200,000	111,820	90	150,000
200,000	and over	156,820	91	200,000

Note: The total tax is limited to 87 per cent of the individual's net income.

The effective rates established by the Revenue Act of 1953 may be illustrated by the accompanying table, which is applicable to the separate income of an individual. The tax imposed upon a married

[1] This description is too highly condensed to be thorough and may become out of date the next time the tax law is revised. For up-to-date description and analysis adequate to aid in investment planning, see the tax services by Prentice-Hall, Inc., Commerce Clearing House, Inc., or one of the numerous other annual volumes on the subject.

couple may be roughly measured by assigning half of their total income to each and applying the table separately to each half. Special lower rates are applied when the taxpayer is an unmarried "head of a household."

Progressive Rates

It is obvious from the accompanying table that income dollars which are taxed in the higher rate brackets are severely reduced. Taxpayers therefore find it desirable to escape high brackets by (1) dividing family property and income between members of the family, so that as much of the aggregate income as possible falls in the initial low-rate brackets; (2) utilizing investments whose income is not includible in adjusted gross income and therefore is not taxed; (3) timing the receipts of incomes, and particularly of capital gains and losses, to realize such gains and losses at advantageous times; (4) making full use of deductions; and (5) making full use of capital gains and losses.

In considering some of these measures investors will have to weigh their income tax advantages against possible gift or estate tax costs and against legal and administrative disadvantages. In doing so, it seems sound in most cases to hold that the income taxes avoided would have been levied in the investor's top bracket, not at his average rate. For example, if a man earning $30,000 per year sells $10,000 worth of 5 per cent preferred stock at par and invests the proceeds in 2 per cent state bonds, he will reduce his cash income by $300; but the state bond interest is not taxable, and the elimination of the $500 in dividends from his taxable income will take that much off his top bracket, which is taxed at 62 per cent. The tax saving at his top-bracket rate will amount to 62 per cent of $500, or $310, and will therefore exceed the loss in gross income.

Top-bracket taxes also affect decisions with respect to the profitableness of risky investments. The individual who has a $30,000 income is paying a top rate of 62 per cent. That means that a fairly hazardous stock promising 7 per cent if all goes well can actually yield him less than 2.7 per cent. If he can get 2 per cent in a secure tax-free municipal bond, the compensation for risking 100 per cent of his capital is a chance at an extra .7 per cent per year. Of course, there are certain other considerations: there is some price-level protection in stock ownership, there may be a chance for a moderately taxed capital gain (under certain conditions the tax on a capital gain is levied at half rates and is limited to 25 per cent), and the possible capital loss could be partly compensated for by a deduction from taxable income. On the whole, however, it is difficult to see why high-bracket taxpayers are willing to bear business risks, though it appears that they nevertheless do so.

Dividing Family Incomes

Prior to the Revenue Act of 1948 investors often found it desirable to arrange property incomes between husband and wife so as to equalize their separate incomes. Their separate individual tax returns then allowed a complete set of lower brackets to each and avoided pyramiding the income into higher brackets, as a single tax return would have done. However, this device is no longer necessary, since the law now gives the spouses the privilege of combining their incomes and losses advantageously in a joint return. The joint return permits the combining of incomes and deductions and personal exemptions and the allocation of half of the total to each spouse.

But there are still substantial income tax advantages to the high-bracket taxpayer who wishes to give property or income to members of his family or to allocate part of it to family-owned business corporations. Some of the devices used are as follows:

1. Gifts of income-producing property to members of the family will transfer incomes from the top tax brackets of the donor to the presumably lower top tax brackets of the donee. The gifts may be in securities, real estate, partnership interests in family businesses, or shares in a family corporation; they may be direct transfers, or transfers to trusts with the donee as beneficiary. Moderate-sized gifts in trust to minor children, made by donors other than the parents, with the trust income directed to be spent regularly to improve the children's standard of living, can effectively raise the parents' family income at little tax cost, since the children become the taxpayers on the trust income, with full quotas of personal exemptions and lowest tax brackets. Gifts to accomplish these purposes must transfer the property irrevocably, make it substantially free of subsequent control by the donor, and the income must not thereafter be used to meet the legal or moral obligations of the donor. It should also be remembered that these transactions are not all net gain; gift taxes may be encountered, and there may be some disadvantage to

the donor in the loss of control over his principal. However, ultimate estate taxes and probate costs may be reduced.

2. As an alternative to gifts of principal sums, donors may give to others the income from property for periods of 10 years or longer, by irrevocably transferring the property to a trust for that purpose, reserving the right to recover the property subsequently. Gifts of income on a shorter or less absolute basis do not remove it from the donor's taxable income.

3. Family partnerships involving services, or employment in family corporations, may afford means of dividing up large family incomes.

4. Family corporations engaged in business can pay salaries to employed members of the family, which are deductible business expenses to the corporation; if the remaining net income of the business is retained for use in the business, it will be taxed at the corporation tax rates, which may be lower (especially in a small corporation) than the stockholders' personal top brackets. Also, if the business is such as to justify some investments in securities, dividends received by the corporation will be 85 per cent tax-exempt to the corporation. Again, family corporations may under certain circumstances operate pension or annuity plans for the benefit of employees, at a cost which is a tax-deductible expense to the corporation. Family members may share in the benefits as employees.

Nonincludible Income

There is definite advantage in ownership of income which may be excluded in whole or part from adjusted gross income. If it is not included it will not be taxed, and the entire amount will remain available to the owner. Such income need not be cash income. The services of an owner-occupied home, for example, constitute nonincludible investment income. Of course, an investment which is tax-free is not necessarily profitable or suitable for a particular investor. The essential thing is that the investor be familiar with the choices available, so that he may weigh the alternatives for himself. And in view of repeated changes in the tax laws and judicial interpretations thereon, it is desirable to review the situation periodically.

Features of the present laws which permit investors to obtain wholly or partly exempt income include the following:

1. Interest on state and municipal bonds is not includible in adjusted gross income. To a corporation paying a 52 per cent rate or to an indi-

vidual in a high tax bracket it may be profitable to buy a tax-free bond
with a limited yield rather than a taxable security paying much more.
Bond dealers commonly publish tables of "tax-free interest equivalents"
which show how much taxable interest a security must pay to individuals
in various tax brackets in order to give the holder a net remainder equal
to indicated tax-free yields.

2. On corporation bonds bought at a discount only the cash interest
is current income; if the market value rises as time passes, the increase
will be a capital gain when the bond is sold or collected at maturity.
These provisions enable high-bracket taxpayers to report relatively reduced current income and ultimately a capital gain on investments in
such bonds.

3. Undistributed corporate profits are not taxable income to the stockholder, and if he ultimately realizes on such gains by selling his stock, he
will have a capital gain instead of current income. High-bracket stockholders who do not need large dividends therefore find an advantage in
stocks with good earnings but small dividends, if the excess earnings can
be profitably retained in the business.

4. The services of an owner-occupied home and the value of crops consumed where grown are not included in adjusted gross income. It would
thus appear than an individual who owns a home or a garden or an or-
chard which profitably produces services or crops for his own use has a
tax-free income. If his home cost $18,000, and has a rental value of $1,800
per year, and if all taxes, insurance, maintenance, and depreciation total
$900 per year, he has in effect a net income of $900, or 5 per cent; but
since this is not taxable, it is the equivalent of a much larger net income
from securities or rental property.

5. Annuity rights accumulating in employers' pension plans, good will
developing in one's own business, increasing value and earning power
in real estate owned, and interest earnings on one's life insurance reserves
are not taxable income. Some of these may develop into income or capital
gains, but the last three may ultimately pass by inheritance without having been depleted by income taxes. High-bracket taxpayers often find
it advantageous to put liquid funds into 10-pay life insurance policies,
which earn tax-free interest on their reserves, and provide liquidity both
for current purposes and for an ultimate estate.

6. The politically controversial "dividend relief" measure in the
Revenue Act of 1954 entitles each taxpayer to $50 per year in corporate
dividends free of any Federal income tax, and to a tax credit (*i.e.,* an
actual deduction from his computed tax) amounting to 4 per cent of
all additional dividends which are received and included in ordinary

taxable income. If this provision endures, it will provide opportunity to obtain a very limited amount of tax-free income, plus more at a modest tax concession.

Timing the Realization of Gains, Losses, and Deductions

Because the taxpayer's rate of tax is determined each year by the size of his taxable income, it may be important to take taxable gains in low-income years and to realize major losses and deductions during years when income is greatest. There are many ways of doing this, of which a few may be noted:

1. Since neither a loss nor a profit on the capital value of securities, real estate, or other investments is usually "realized for tax purposes" until the item is sold or becomes utterly worthless, the owner can often choose the year in which he "takes" a profit or loss, by choosing the year of sale.

2. When real estate or a business interest is to be sold at a large profit, the gain can be spread over several taxable years by a properly drawn installment sale transaction involving payment in installments. This will prevent the large profit from lifting a small taxpayer into much higher brackets for the year, and give a large taxpayer greater opportunity to offset at least a part of it with possible losses.

3. For a taxpayer who keeps his books on a cash basis—that is, who records incomes and expenses when received or paid, not when earned or incurred—rental incomes, repair costs, and taxes paid may be to some extent cumulated into desired years.

4. Charitable gifts of substantial size may be made in high-income years. Such items are deductible to the extent of 20 (under certain conditions, 30) per cent of the adjusted gross income. Charitable gifts made in property are valued for deduction purposes at market value at the date of gift, but no gain or loss for gross income purposes is realized in making the gift. It may therefore be advantageous to make the gift in property in which a large unrealized profit exists.

Capital Gains and Losses

Capital gains and losses are those arising out of transactions in capital assets. Capital assets consist of securities, residence, personal assets generally, and occasional realty holdings. To be classified as a capital asset an item must be in the nature of an investment, not real estate or equipment used in the taxpayer's business. Profits arising from the sale of any capital asset are capital gains; but capital losses are not recognized on assets held for personal enjoyment, such as residences or automobiles. Real estate and equipment used in the taxpayer's business and investments in real property extensive enough to constitute a business are not considered capital assets, but gains and losses on them have somewhat similar effects on the owner's tax bill.

The provisions of the present tax laws in regard to capital gains and losses are the result of long experimentation by Congress. It was found by test that long-term holders of investments were reluctant to take profits which would be fully taxed or to take losses which were not deductible for tax purposes. Investment markets would not function normally without a reasonable solution on both points. It also seemed desirable to impose heavier taxes on short-term speculative gains than on longer term gains; and experience proved that speculative risk bearers would not take commitments unless losses could be reasonably offset against gains. The capital gains section therefore provides for computing *net long-term* gains or losses by adding algebraically all net gains and losses on assets held more than 6 months; and *net short-term* gains or losses are similarly computed on assets held less than 6 months. The tax plan then involves (1) taxing any net short-term gains by adding them to the taxpayer's ordinary income, and (2) taxing long-term gains (computed as the excess of net long-term gains over net short-term losses if any) at limited rates by either adding half the amount to the taxpayer's ordinary income or taxing them separately at 25 per cent, whichever produces the least tax. Net losses after subtracting all gains regardless of term held, may be subtracted from ordinary income to the extent of $1,000 in the year incurred and in each of the five succeeding years, and may be offset in full against any capital gains which occur within this period. This does not guarantee that all net capital losses will eventually be deducted, but the possibilities are fair.

Since these tax rules result in low-rate taxation of capital gains, high-bracket taxpayers frequently search for ways to obtain capital gains instead of ordinary income. Such ways may include (1) investment in low-dividend but promising concerns whose stock may ultimately be sold at a profit, (2) ventures in oil, mining, timber-growing, or similar developments, and (3) investments in farms or ranches whose land or stock may be built up to great value without realization of income. Corporation executives may take their compensation in part in stock purchase options of limited initial value, which may in time enable them to buy the stock after it has appreciated in value, and thus to obtain a capital gain.

Taxpayers' experiences with capital gain and loss problems in connection with securities have led to a number of widely held beliefs about investment policy, which include the following:

1. Capital assets which rise in value after acquisition should generally be held until the gains become long-term. This will halve the tax rate.

2. Long-term capital gains and capital losses should ordinarily not be taken in the same year. Long-term capital gains are taxable at half rates, whereas a capital loss will offset short-term capital gains or ordinary income in full. It is therefore wasteful to permit long-term capital gains to offset capital losses.

3. If short-term gains have been realized in any year, they should be offset by realizing losses if appreciable unrealized losses exist in the investor's portfolio. This doctrine assumes that taxes not paid may never need to be paid, hence undertakes to postpone them. This is logical if every loss taken saves taxes in amounts substantially greater than the cost of shifting investments.

4. If carried-over losses are about to expire, it may be desirable to take long-term gains to offset them. This is profitable to the extent that the tax savings on the salvaged losses exceed the costs of selling and reinvesting to realize gains.

5. Assets about to become worthless should be sold before they are finally worthless, to establish the year of loss definitely.

The very extensive literature on techniques and accounting rules regarding capital gains and losses includes much practical information which cannot be included in this volume. However, there are three fundamental concepts which should at least be mentioned. First, every capital asset has a *basis* value, which serves as the owner's cost figure when he sells and must compute a profit or loss. In most cases actual cost plus expenses of acquisition constitute this basis. Sometimes the basis must be adjusted, as in the case of stock which pays a liquidating dividend or real estate upon which additions are built. In the case of a gift the donor's basis normally becomes the donee's basis. In the case of an inheritance the new owner's basis is usually the market value at the previous owner's death. Second, any specific asset has its own basis in the investor's hands, if it can be clearly identified; thus, the holder of two U.S. Steel certificates can sell either one and record the gain or loss on it without averaging his costs or otherwise involving the other certificate. Third, every gain or loss transaction must be bona fide; a fictitious transaction with a relative, or a sale at a "loss" which is offset by a purchase of the same security within 30 days before or after, and other such devices, are not legitimate or effective for tax purposes.

STATE PERSONAL INCOME TAXES

In 1953 personal income taxes were being levied by 32 states, at rates which may be described as mildly progressive and not very high. For example, the New York tax, which was typical, allowed certain deductions plus a family exemption of $2,500 or more and imposed a graduated tax which progressed from 2.0 per cent on the first $1,000 of taxable income to a top rate of 7.0 per cent on all over $9,000. Capital gains were taxed at half rates. The burden of these rates is further reduced by the fact that state income taxes are deductible in computing taxable income for Federal income tax purposes. An individual whose top Federal tax bracket is 60 per cent is therefore only out of pocket 40 per cent of the state income taxes which he pays. These facts suggest that state income taxes are as a rule not dominant factors in shaping an individual's investment policy.

Most state income taxes resemble the Federal tax in general structure, though inclusions, deductions, and exemptions all differ in detail. The states usually undertake to tax the entire incomes of their residents and also the portions of nonresidents' incomes which arise from real estate holdings or business activities within the state, but they prevent double taxation by allowing their own residents tax credits on account of taxes paid in other states. A conspicuous difference in income inclusions is the fact that interest on Federal obligations is not taxable by a state, while interest on the obligations of other states and their municipalities is usually taxed. An investor who sought bonds which were exempt from both Federal and state income taxation might therefore find greatest advantage in the state and municipal bonds issued in his home state.

It may be noted that state and local property taxes on intangibles such as stocks, bonds, and mortgages have the same effect on their profitableness to their owners as a tax on their income would have. The methods of assessing and taxing such intangibles are so varied that an inquiry into each individual situation is the only practical approach to an investment policy.

FEDERAL ESTATE TAXES

A Federal estate tax is imposed as an excise upon the transfer of the net estate of every decedent who was a citizen or a resident of the United States. The fact that the tax is an excise upon the transfer of property rather than a levy upon the property itself avoids the constitutional prohibition on direct taxation and also enables state and municipal bonds to be included in the tax base. The Federal government may not levy property or income taxes on state bonds and similar tax-exempt securities, but it can impose an estate tax on the act of transferring them. For practical purposes there are no investments exempt from estate taxation.

Structure of the Estate Tax

The Federal tax is a steeply progressive tax based on the decedent's net estate. It does not affect the majority of families, however, because the net estate is defined as the sum remaining after estate expenses, charitable bequests, the marital deduction, and an exemption of $60,000. The tax is determined as follows:

First, the *gross estate* is computed. This includes the value at date of death or on possible alternative dates of all property owned by the decedent, including his half interest in community property, if any, plus all insurance on his life in which he had some element of ownership, plus his interest in certain types of trusts, plus gifts made "in contemplation of death." Property owned by the decedent is defined to include all property which he held in joint tenancy or tenancy by the entirety with others, except for the portion of such property originally owned or provided by the others. However, real property located outside the United States is excluded from the gross estate.

Second, the *net estate* is found by deducting from the gross estate all funeral expenses, expenses of administration, debts and taxes owed by the decedent, a percentage of any property on which Federal estate or gift tax had been paid within 10 years, property left to charity, the marital deduction, and an exemption of $60,000.

Third, the *gross estate tax* is computed by applying the tax rates specified by law to the net estate. From the gross tax two credits are then deducted: (1) gift taxes previously paid on property included in the gross estate, involving mostly gifts made in contemplation of death, and (2) amounts paid to the states in estate or inheritance taxes, but not in excess of 80 per cent of the "basic estate tax." The gross estate tax minus the two credits determines the amount actually payable, the *net estate tax*.

The accompanying table indicates the amount of estate tax payable on net estates of various sizes under the rates in force in 1954. Each tax is composed of a total of levies in progressively higher rate brackets. This table indicates selected cases; it is not a complete tabulation of all brackets.

Size of net estate after deductions and $60,000 exemption	Gross estate tax	Maximum rate bracket reached	Maximum credit allowable for state taxes
$ 5,000	$ 150	3%	$ 0
20,000	1,600	11	0
50,000	7,000	22	80
100,000	20,700	28	560
200,000	50,700	30	2,640
600,000	180,700	35	16,400
1,000,000	325,700	37	36,560
5,000,000	2,468,200	63	398,320
10,000,000	6,088,200	76	1,076,720
20,000,000	13,788,200	77	2,676,400

Marital Deduction

Since 1948 the tax laws have provided special rules for the application of estate taxation to transfers of property from deceased to surviving spouse. In states having community property laws, the family property accumulated from personal earnings and certain other sources during marriage is regarded as belonging half to one spouse and half to the other. In such cases, only half of this community property is subject to estate or inheritance taxation upon the death of either.[2] To extend this situation equitably to residents of other states, the 1948 Act provided for a marital deduction which excludes from net taxable estate all of the property passing from deceased to surviving spouse, up to a maximum of 50 per cent of the adjusted gross estate. Adjusted gross estate is the gross estate minus debts and estate expenses and minus all community property. The practical effect of the marital deduction is to permit any deceased person to leave half of his noncommunity property to his spouse free of Federal taxes and, in addition, to apply the $60,000 exemption to the remainder of his estate.

Meeting the Tax Problem

Though the estate tax problem is not severe when estates do not exceed $100,000, it is obvious that the burden on large estates requires careful planning. After all, meeting a $6,088,200 tax out of a $10,000,000 estate would be very difficult unless the estate's investments had been made with that in mind. There are also a number of measures which can reduce the total tax load. The various expedients which investors need to consider in framing their policies include:

1. Total tax load may be reduced through avoiding successive taxes and probate costs on the same money, if the original testator or donor places the property in a trust.[3] The trust may then operate without further estate tax or probate costs for many years, with two or three generations becoming the trust's beneficiaries. Alternatively, the testator may bequeath life tenancies and remainder interests to different people; this also transfers the property but once.

2. Gifts made or irrevocable trusts created during a lifetime, if legally effective, may place substantial amounts of property in the hands of members of a family at relatively small gift tax cost, and thus avoid the high estate tax brackets. This will also reduce the probate costs.

3. Charitable bequests will reduce high-bracket estate tax levies, since they are deductible before computation of tax. Since specific property

[2] This was not true of the Federal tax situation in the years 1943–1947.

[3] Because the marital deduction provided in the Revenue Act of 1948 may not be used for property which does not become potentially a part of the surviving spouse's estate, this trust device may require two trusts, one effectively "owned" by the survivor and one independent of his control.

may be left to charities, it is not necessary to keep the estate liquid to pay such bequests.[4]

4. A proper choice between ownership in joint tenancy, as community property, or as separate property, will be profitable for husband and wife. Estate taxes, gift taxes, state inheritance taxes, and probate costs will all be involved here, as well as the details of law in the state of residence. Joint tenancy will generally be useful in estates below $50,000, and separate property is usually preferable in large estates.

5. The estate must always have enough liquid resources, preferably in cash, government bonds, or life insurance, to meet estate expenses and tax liabilities. Certain government bonds are redeemable at par for this purpose, hence are ideal investments for large estates.

6. Business life insurance carried on the lives of partners or stockholders in closely held firms to enable their associates to buy out decedents' shares may be purchased by each participant on the lives of the others. This method of carrying business insurance is advantageous, because if the firm buys the insurance any death may enlarge the share to be bought out, and if each man carries insurance on his life in favor of the others his own estate taxes will be increased.

Tax experts generally advise families against making tax avoidance the major factor in planning the disposition of their estates. The tax loopholes have been so carefully plugged by Congress and the courts that complete escape is possible only at the cost of doing bizarre and foolish things with one's property. For example, individuals have given away property to their families and to charity until their own security or the control over their businesses was jeopardized. Worse yet, they have placed property in irrevocable trusts, only to find that subsequent changes in the tax laws eliminated the tax advantages which they had planned. Or they have made other dispositions which were difficult to reverse and then changed their minds about their entire objectives. Instead of making such desperate efforts to avoid all possible taxes, it is usually conceded to be better policy to (1) determine where the control of and the benefits from the property should be at all times, both before and after the death of the owner; (2) plan for gifts, trusts, and a final will to accomplish these things, keeping always in mind that changes

[4] The bulk of Henry Ford's fortune was left to the Ford Foundation in this manner. The foundation received nonvoting stock in the Ford Motor Company. The family received the voting stock, thus retaining control and property sufficient for their needs.

in the value of properties, in family relations, or in the tax laws may make it desirable to change the plans while the owner still lives; and (3) review the plans to determine whether minor adjustments may minimize the tax costs. This procedure may cost no more in the long run, and it has obvious advantages.

STATE ESTATE AND INHERITANCE TAXES

In 1954 all states except Nevada were imposing taxes upon the transfer of decedents' property. About one-fourth of these states levied estate taxes based upon the size of the estate, as the Federal government does, while the others taxed the heirs' inheritances at rates which usually increased both with the size of the inheritance and the remoteness of relationship between heir and decedent. When the total of the inheritance taxes payable from any estate is less than the available Federal estate tax offset, most states add a supplementary tax to absorb the balance. The inclusions and deductions used in determining the taxable estate or inheritance are of course unique in each state law, but there is a general similarity to the Federal approach except that (1) only property within the state's jurisdiction is includible, (2) life insurance payable to named beneficiaries is often exempted up to very generous amounts, and (3) property exemptions are much smaller.

At the present time a state tax on the transfer of decedents' property seems to be able to reach (1) real estate and tangible personal property if located within the taxing state, (2) intangible personal property wherever located if the decedent is domiciled in the taxing state, (3) intangibles located within the taxing state regardless of the domicile of the owner, and (4) intangibles wherever owned or located if they must be transferred on the books of a corporation incorporated by the taxing state. Double taxation under item 1 is not likely, and the states do not now impose taxes based on item 4. The greatest hazards of double taxation lie in state laws under which an investor might have domicile in more than one state (item 2) or in which intangibles stored or in trust in a state other than his domicile might be taxed in both (item 3). Double taxation can practically always be avoided by taking proper care, since the state laws are not intended to set traps of this nature.

State estate or inheritance taxes commonly exact moderate sums from small estates and fairly large sums from large estates. However, the taxes imposed by the average state on its medium and large estates usually will not greatly exceed the available Federal estate tax credit for state taxes paid and will very rarely do so if the beneficiaries are in Class A and if there are several of them. The following table shows the inheritance tax rates effective in Indiana in 1953. These are average and typical; a low-rate state might cut these rates in half, and a high-rate state might add a half more:

Beneficiaries:
  Class A: Husband, wife, lineal ancestor, lineal descendant, adopted or acknowledged child or descendant thereof
  Class B: Brother, sister, or descendant of either, wife or widow of son, or husband of daughter
  Class C: Others
Exemptions:
  Class A: Wife $15,000; child under 18 $5,000; others $2,000
  Class B: $500
  Class C: $100
  Life insurance payable to named beneficiaries is entirely exempt.

Tax Rates on Each Inheritance

Successive brackets	Class A	Class B	Class C
First $25,000 less exemption...	1%	5%	7%
$25,000–$50,000.............	2	5	7
$50,000–$100,000............	3	5	7
$100,000–$200,000...........	3	8	10
$200,000–$300,000...........	4	10	12
$300,000–$500,000...........	5	10	12
$500,000–$700,000...........	6	12	15
$700,000–$1,000,000.........	7	12	15
$1,000,000–$1,500,000........	8	15	20
Over $1,500,000.............	10	15	20

If the total state tax payable under these rates is less than the available Federal estate tax credit for state taxes, the total Indiana state tax is automatically increased to the amount of the available Federal credit.

The investor's principal object in meeting state death taxes is to keep the state taxes down to or below the offset credit allowed on his Federal estate tax. If this can be accomplished, the state taxes will cost nothing extra. Useful devices for keeping state taxes down include (1) care in avoiding double state taxation, as previously noted;

(2) use of (exempt) life insurance payable to named beneficiaries, especially to Class C or Class D heirs; [5] (3) use of bequests to many heirs, for example, to wife, children, and grandchildren, to avoid large (high-bracket) bequests to a few individuals; and (4) ownership of real property in other states, which may place this property in lower initial tax brackets in those states instead of in top brackets in the home state.

FEDERAL GIFT TAXES

The Federal gift tax is an excise imposed upon the transfer of gifts made by a citizen or resident of the United States. The taxpayer is the donor, not the donee. The tax was enacted in 1932 as a means of taxing transfers made during a donor's lifetime, because such transfers normally escape the estate taxes imposed at his death. The gift tax rates are 75 per cent of the estate tax rates charged in corresponding brackets. No deductions are allowed on account of state gift taxes. Like the estate tax, the gift tax is levied upon the transfer of all kinds of property; tax-exempt securities do not exist.

Structure of the Tax

The gift tax is a progressive tax, imposed annually on the *cumulative total* of taxable gifts made by the donor since June 6, 1932. The amount payable in any year is determined as follows: (1) apply the present tax rates to the cumulative total of taxable gifts; (2) apply the present tax rates to the cumulative total of taxable gifts up to the end of the preceding year; (3) the difference is the tax for the current year.

The gifts to be taxed include all gratuitous transfers of property, except that the first $3,000 of value transferred to each donee in any year is "excluded" from all calculations. Larger amounts are so excluded for years preceding 1943. Subsequent to the enactment of the Revenue Act of 1948, gifts made by husband and wife to others may be regarded as being made half by each.

Deductions which may be made by the donor from his cumulative total of gifts include (1) a single "lifetime" exemption of $30,000, (2) all charitable gifts, and (3) a "marital deduction" equal to half

---

[5] Most of the states classify heirs into three groups, but several use four classifications, and at least one state, Minnesota, uses five.

of any gift made by one spouse to the other after April 2, 1948. Gifts to the other by either spouse of portions of his or her half interest in community property are not eligible for the marital deduction.

The gift tax is thus based on the cumulative total of nonexempt gifts minus the deductions. The detailed rules of computation are complex, and the definitions of items to be included, excluded, and deducted are matters for professionals.

Tax Policy

Judicious use of gifts may result in a number of tax advantages. The most obvious advantages lie in economies in estate expenses and estate and inheritance taxes. If gifts are made to a number of donees over a period of years, the $3,000 annual exemption to each donee plus the $30,000 lifetime exemption will permit tax-free disposition of a large amount of property. Additional gifts subject to tax will be taxed beginning at the lowest gift tax brackets; yet all sums thus removed from the estate will come off the estate's top bracket. Since the estate will be smaller, its administration costs will also be less. Charitable gifts made while living reduce the donor's income taxes, escape gift taxes, and do not appear in the estate to swell the administrative costs.

It may be noted that complete and irrevocable gifts of property also transfer the subsequent income from donor to donee. Since it is probable that the donee will have a lower top income tax bracket than the donor, a saving of income taxes will subsequently occur.

Gifts are extremely useful between the spouses in equalizing separate property holdings and in creating and dissolving joint tenancies and tenancies by the entirety.

STATE GIFT TAXES

State gift taxes are definitely in the experimental stage. Only 12 state statutes were in force in 1953, and the statutes themselves were diverse in nature. In general, the state laws have tended to follow the structural plan of the Federal gift tax, but with inclusions and exclusions patterned after the state estate or inheritance tax. The rates imposed on taxable gifts are generally related to or identical with those of the estate or inheritance tax and are high enough to merit careful tax planning when large gift transfers are contemplated. State gift taxes may not be offset against Federal gift or income taxes; so their impact is usually 100 per cent effective against the taxpayer.

Specific measures for minimizing state gift taxes are often similar to those employed in dealing with Federal gift taxes and state estate or inheritance taxes.

The Tax Experts

Because tax planning is a complex and extensive field, experts capable of advising on such matters should be consulted by anyone having substantial amounts of income or property. The cost will usually be far less than the amount of unnecessary taxes for which the amateur will become liable.

Income tax advice can be obtained from attorneys, accountants, brokerage house analysts, investment counselors, and bank trust officers, although it must be remarked that not all who give such advice are competent to do so. However, the simpler income tax problems are widely understood, because so many people are forced to study them. Estate and gift tax planning, and estate planning in general, is a much less widely understood matter. Accountants and attorneys who specialize on estate problems, a few investment counselors, trust officers, and an occasional life insurance agent are the people most likely to be competent.

For the individual who wishes to do his own studying and planning, the income tax field is reasonably well equipped with elementary books and pamphlets, but the estate tax and planning field is, on the whole, lacking in easy and introductory material. A few pamphlets and articles are available, however, and good technical books intended for experts can be had.

QUESTIONS AND PROBLEMS

1. Name several instances in which family bookkeeping records would be needed many years after a transaction had taken place.

2. What are the most important types of investments whose incomes do not contribute to taxable income for Federal income tax purposes? Is life insurance among these?

3. Is there a Federal income tax advantage in homeownership if the home is not fully paid for? (Note: Consider the deductions used in determining net income.)

4. If an individual's taxable income was $150,000 per year, how high a yield would a mortgage or a bond have to offer in order to be as attractive to him as a 2 per cent municipal bond issued in his home state? Is the situation the same on a stock investment? Would it be worth while for this man to select his municipals chiefly from his own state?

5. Should a high-bracket investor confine himself entirely to state and municipal bonds? Why not? Should he take serious business risks in developing new enterprises? Analyze what happens if the $150,000 per year man buys stock in a speculative oil company and makes $50,000. What if he loses $50,000? Are the possible results offsetting?

6. Explain the "capital gain or loss" provision in the income tax law. Does this apply to investment companies and other corporations also? What is meant by "basis"?

7. Are state income taxes major factors in shaping investment policies?

8. Explain the nature of the Federal estate tax. What kinds of property are exempt from it? How large an estate would a married couple have to have in order to be subject to the Federal estate tax at the first death? At the second death, assuming that all the property then remained in the survivor's estate?

9. Why is excessive emphasis on tax avoidance undesirable in planning estates?

10. Explain the general nature of state estate and inheritance taxes. Are they important enough to require consideration in estate planning?

11. How much would Indiana tax a $660,000 estate left to the widow of a decedent's son? Would this tax exceed the maximum credit available against the Federal estate tax? If the widow had two small sons (grandchildren of the property owner), what would you suggest?

12. Explain the nature of the Federal gift tax and the annual and lifetime exemptions.

13. Is there a Federal tax on charitable gifts? Is there a tax advantage in making such gifts? Explain.

14. Are state gift taxes important? Are the taxes paid capable of offset against Federal gift taxes?

15. How many middle-class investors know enough of income, estate, inheritance, and gift taxes to plan their affairs wisely? How would you suggest that an individual obtain a sound plan for himself?

REFERENCES

Badger, Ralph E., and Harry G. Guthmann: *Investment Principles and Practices,* Prentice-Hall, Inc., New York, 1951, Chap. 24.

Bowe, William Joseph: *Tax Planning for Estates,* Vanderbilt University Press, Nashville, Tenn., 1952.

Butters, J. K., and others: *Effects of Taxation; Investments by Individuals,* Harvard University Press, Cambridge, Mass., 1953.

Casey, William J., and J. K. Lasser: *Tax Shelter for the Family,* Business Reports Inc., New York, 1953.

Casey, William J., and J. K. Lasser: *Tax Sheltered Investments,* Business Reports Inc., New York, 1951.

Dowrie, George W., and Douglas R. Fuller: *Investments,* John Wiley & Sons, Inc., New York, 1950, Chap. 11.

Federal Tax Handbook, Prentice-Hall, Inc., New York, annual.

Gordon, George Byron: *You, Your Heirs, and Your Estate,* Business Reports Inc., New York, 1952.

Grodinsky, Julius: *Investments,* The Ronald Press Company, New York, 1953, Chap. 25.

Handbook of Tax-Saving Ideas, The Tax Digest, New York, 1952.

Jordan, David F., and Herbert E. Dougall: *Investments,* Prentice-Hall, Inc., New York, 1952, Chap. 18.

Pickett, Ralph R., and Marshall D. Ketchum: *Investment Principles and Policy,* Harper & Brothers, New York, 1954, Chap. 30.

Polisher, Edward N.: *Estate Planning and Estate Tax Saving,* Geo. T. Basil Co., Philadelphia, 1948.

Robbins, Sidney M.: *Managing Securities,* Houghton Mifflin Company, Boston, 1954, Chap. 36.

Shattuck, Mayo Adams, and James F. Farr: *An Estate Planner's Handbook,* Little, Brown & Company, Boston, 1953, Chaps. 3, 8, 9.

Tax and Business Insurance Course, Insurance Research & Review Service, Inc., Indianapolis, Ind., annual.

United States Master Tax Guide, Commerce Clearing House, Inc., Chicago, annual.

Chapter 28: ADMINISTERING THE
PERSONAL PORTFOLIO

The first chapter of this book was assigned the task of proving that an individual or a family needed a planned investment program and of outlining the principles upon which one could be constructed. The next twenty-six chapters were devoted to describing many of the types of investments available, the markets in which they are bought and sold, and the factors which determine their value. There remains for this final chapter a discussion of some of the problems involved in establishing personal investment policies and carrying them out. Since these are to a great extent matters of opinion it is probable that the author's own convictions will emerge more strongly in this chapter than they have been permitted to do heretofore, and to the extent that they do the statements must be regarded as personal advice rather than as presentations of fact.

It seems well to preface discussion of these final topics with the comment that an investment program which does not contribute to the happiness, security, and income of its owners is ill-designed. A plan of procedure which keeps the investor distraught and uncertain, which fails to carry assurance of old-age security and other high-priority objectives, or which does not contemplate at least reasonable income or profit is not soundly conceived. Either the investor needs to mend his viewpoint or tactics, or he should resort to professional investment administration or counsel. Possibly he should do both.

The practical suggestions to be advanced in this chapter are intended mainly for individuals who are aware that they are amateurs in the highly technical business of investing and who are humble enough to accept advice. Competent professionals are obviously informed to an extent which exceeds the pretensions of this book. But this chapter is also intended as a plea to reckless investors, especially young ones. Every investment dealer is acquainted with numerous men who have had no success but who are convinced that "next time" they will make marvelous profits or who simply enjoy the excitement of extensive speculation. Almost without exception the dealers report that the reckless amateurs do not do well, that they all too often conclude their investment operations after the manner of the famous Casey at the bat. Since life is too short to permit many investment strike-outs without the hazard of an aftermath of poverty, it is hoped that the conservative gospel to be here expressed may reach a few of the wayward.

A Lifetime Financial Plan

Any individual who undertakes to frame a logical investment policy for himself will shortly realize that his investment plan must have a definite purpose. It must be designed to meet certain needs, to satisfy certain objectives. To determine what these needs and objectives are, the individual must examine his own future. And, since the future is largely a matter of hope and conjecture, it will be desirable for him to map out his financial future as it seems most likely to develop and to make his investment policies accordingly.

Skeptics may ridicule the idea that a systematic lifetime financial plan has any merit. Admittedly, one made at age 25 is likely to undergo many modifications before 65, and the investment policies based upon it may have to be modified accordingly. But the individual who refuses to try to look into the future has no financial guideposts at all. He does not know how to buy life insurance, because he does not know whether he wishes to buy the long-lasting protection of ordinary life or an endowment which will accumulate his dollar savings and ultimately provide him a generous retirement annuity. He does not know whether to buy a home, and if he does, he has no plan to tell him whether to pay down his amortizing loan as rapidly as possible or simply to meet its 20-year terms and make other investments elsewhere. Other instances might be cited, but the argument is clear: the development of a logical investment program requires the making of a definite lifetime financial plan, tentative though it may be. Revisions of both financial plan and investment policies can be made as the planned-for future unfolds.

A lifetime financial plan should tabulate, as of certain future dates, the entire probable family assets and liabilities. Essential items to be noted would be the insurance investment, home and related

debt, the family business if any, funds earmarked for special purposes, and the dollar and equity investments in the general investment fund. A second part of the table should show the family in-

Table 58. Illustration of a Lifetime Financial Plan

	Age				
	25	35	45	55	65
Assets and Liabilities					
$15,000 ordinary life insurance, age 25:					
Protection......................	$15,000	$13,031	$10,758	$ 8,307	$ 5,906
Insurance reserve...............	0	1,970	4,242	6,693	9,095
$15,000 endowment at 65, age 30:					
Protection......................	0	13,481	9,977	5,727	0
Insurance reserve...............	0	1,520	5,024	9,273	15,000
Value of home...................	0	18,750	18,750	15,000	12,000
Mortgage debt...................	0	15,000	6,750	0	0
Value of business................	0	3,000	7,500	12,000	15,000
General investments—dollar items....	0	3,000	3,000	12,000	15,000
General investments—equities.......	0	0	1,500	7,500	30,000
Children's education fund—dollar					
items..........................	0	0	3,000	0	0
Miscellaneous debts...............	0	0	0	0	0
Potential estate *...............	15,000	39,750	57,000	76,500	102,000
Net worth †....................	0	13,239	36,266	62,466	96,095
Income and Outgo					
Business earnings.................	4,500	7,410	9,450	9,600	9,300
Interest and dividends.............	0	90	300	900	1,950
Living expenses...................	3,750	5,400	6,750	7,500	7,500
Insurance premiums...............	248	630	630	630	630
Other saving.....................	503	1,470	2,370	2,370	3,120

* Consists of property owned, less debts, plus insurance protection.
† Consists of property owned, including insurance reserves, less debts.

comes, expenses, and the budgeted amounts necessary to accumulate
the expected savings. Tables of this sort will show very clearly what
is needed to achieve financial security and retirement income and
may therefore contribute greatly to sound decisions on financial
matters.

Table 58 is hypothetical but may be visualized as the plan of the
owner-operator of a small insurance agency. Since this individual

is self-employed, he does not have the promise of an employer pension and, except for his relatively modest social security expectation, is managing his resources and financial future himself. This plan is tentative, crude, and not very specific; yet if it is assumed to be the effective plan at age 35 or at any other of the ages shown, it will provide evidence on many likely issues, such as the adequacy of the life insurance, the need for disability insurance, the soundness of a proposed speculative venture, the adequacy of the savings program, and the like. This sample plan indicates, for example, that the individual can look forward to ownership of his home, $24,095 in insurance reserves, a $15,000 business, $15,000 in bonds, and $30,000 in stocks, at age 65. At that age social security would provide about $1,500 per year for himself and his wife, and his insurance reserves would provide a joint-and-survivor annuity of about $1,350 more. Income from the stocks and bonds would amount to $1,950, and if the business could earn another $1,500 when operated by employees, a retirement income of $6,300 would be available without consuming any of the principal. If these figures do not please our financial planner, he is on notice to change his plan of procedure. He is definitely on notice; the table spreads the prospective results of his present policies before him.

A Personal Investment Policy

The main function of a lifetime financial plan is to determine how the individual will live, how much he will save, and for what general purposes. If he determines to save certain amounts, there next arises the problem of investing the savings logically and soundly, of building them into a comprehensive investment program.

An investment program may be compared to a house, in that it is normally a structure composed of many separate parts. The structure itself is planned to give maximum protection and comfort to the occupants, and the separate parts of the building—the foundation stones, window frames, shingles, rafters, and the like—are of types and sizes which work together to make a sound whole. The architect plans the structure and indicates the types of materials which will be acceptable; the builder chooses the specific materials, after a methodical inspection of available items and consideration of their cost.

The analogy of the house serves to introduce a major tenet of this chapter, which is that every investment program should have a fairly definite architectural design. Chapter 1 outlined a four-step plan for organizing an investment portfolio and also enumerated eight factors to be considered in planning its general nature, but these are not definite enough for present purposes. The situation calls for a statement of policy which is carefully written out and which is explicit enough to direct new investments into planned channels and to guard against hasty ill-fitting choices. It may seem a little ridiculous to recommend that an investor write out a statement of principles for his own guidance, but the recommendation is made because of the many anomalies which the author has found in reasonably well-planned portfolios—anomalies representing pointless deviations from sound tactics which would not have been made if the investors had tested their choices against a set of clearly written policies. If any further argument is needed, it may be stated that banks, insurance companies, investment companies, and trust officers all usually follow written investment policies, and if these professionals find the procedure desirable, it is probable that amateurs will also.

When the policies respecting the types and proportions of investments to be used are all complete, the next step is to add a definite procedure for choosing and managing the individual items. This corresponds to the builder's job in the house-construction analogy. These procedural policies will cover such matters as the use of investment counselors and financial periodicals, the choice of a broker, the routine of studying individual investments, the constant supervision of holdings, and the physical storage of securities. Again it may seem foolish to reduce these matters to a planned routine. Skeptics may even argue that the methodical man will miss good chances for profits, because he is too slow; but it is probable that he will more often miss good chances to make mistakes.

For what it may be worth, the following statement of investment policy is submitted for the reader's consideration. It was written for the use of a middle-class professional man whose business is remote from the investments field but who is keenly interested in managing his own financial affairs. The principles established will not be universally applicable, but they will serve to indicate the issues which each investor must meet for himself.

POLICIES AND PROCEDURES

1. Estate tax problems negligible; all property and deposit accounts will be in joint ownership with wife.

2. Life insurance protection plus all savings to total $30,000 at marriage, to be increased to total of $50,000 when possible. Beyond this point insurance protection not needed to maximize estate, but may be retained.

3. Two life policies totaling $30,000 face value earmarked tentatively to surrender for life annuities at age 65. Cash value then will be $24,095.

4. Life insurance plus checking accounts plus bonds plus borrowing power now provide adequate cash reserves.

5. Disability income policies promising $150 per month to be carried to age 60.

6. Home valued at 2 years' income to be paid for as soon as convenient; no point to paying 5 per cent on mortgage and making large general investments elsewhere. No additional real estate investments planned during active business career.

7. Investment proportions: bonds, savings accounts, cash value life insurance, etc., total 40 per cent; home and diversified high-class common stocks, total 40 per cent; business not counted; remaining 20 per cent flexible, to be in cash, bonds, good stocks, or speculative stocks as conditions warrant.

8. Cycle policy: No attempt to shift funds to restore or adjust 40–40–20 ratios as market conditions change, except that when new funds are added or necessary withdrawals made they will be applied to restore the ratios between the funds.

9. Except for home, life insurance, and United States bonds, not more than 20 per cent of resources to be in any one industry and not more than 10 per cent in any one concern. No single investment under $500. No more than 20 corporate securities at any one time.

10. Bond investments to be high grade, chiefly Series E. All Series E bonds to be in joint ownership, payable to either self or wife.

11. Common stocks to be bought only when the Dow-Jones Industrials sell below 15 times earnings and yield at least 4 per cent and when industrial production is rising or reasonably steady. Common stock money to be held in savings bank until conditions met.

12. No common stock to be bought unless it appears worthy of indefinite retention and unless it appears substantially undervalued. Know and keep watch on a list of desirable stocks, as well as those owned.

13. No corporate security to be bought except after 3 days' reflection, nor without reading the review in at least one good reference service and

at least one good advisory service. Also desirable to see the last annual report and to study the industry.

14. Read all annual reports as they are received. Each industry and each company to be studied at least twice annually, using a good financial service. Advantageous switches from stocks held to others more promisingly situated to be sought, but consider brokerage cost and income tax factors.

15. Use stockbroker with good library facilities. Seek capable and accommodating salesman.

16. Stocks and bonds to be physically acquired and stored in safety deposit box (or possibly fireproof safe if not payable to bearer).

17. Margin accounts to be used only temporarily and occasionally, for opportune purchases of investments which can soon be paid for. No margin purchases with quick resale in mind.

The Risks to Be Undertaken

The discussion of investment risks in Chapter 1 expressed the author's belief that no one of the four types of investment risks—the business risk, the market risk, the money rate risk, and the price-level risk—can reasonably be disregarded in framing an investment program. This belief led to the conclusion that well-selected high-grade common stocks or real estate parcels merit the label "investment" and the accolade of inclusion in very conservative personal portfolios, because they bear much less of the price-level risk than bond investments do, even if they bear more of certain other risks. These are positions which are not fully shared by leading authors and legislators, although the modern trend seems to be toward agreement.

The case for those who would direct all widows, people of limited means, retired individuals, and investment novices into high-class bonds and life insurance investments rests chiefly on the fact that stock or real estate pays only 2 to 4 per cent more, which is held to be inadequate compensation for the risking of principal. This argument completely ignores the price-level risk, which has been considerable ever since 1914, and also ignores the urgency of maximizing income for people who need all the income they can get. It also overlooks the oft-proven fact that over long periods of years reasonably diversified stock portfolios have absorbed their occasional losses and by virtue of higher income and compensating gains have shown better total results than bond portfolios. Instead of directing people who need the advantage of stock and real estate investments away from them, it seems more logical to attempt solutions to the principal problems of proportioning, selection, and diversification, so that these investment mediums may be used with some degree of safety.

Earlier chapters have touched upon most of these problems, with one exception; as yet no conclusions have been drawn with respect to the wisdom of undertaking admittedly risky commitments. Admittedly risky commitments as the author views them are of two types: those which are risky because they are of poor or uncertain quality, acutely subject to such hazards as obsolescence, excessive competition, or destructive legislation; and second, high-quality investments in which the price risk is great because the market is anticipating future incomes from the investment in question on a scale which is as yet unproven. A decision with respect to these risks is part and parcel of every planned investment program. For what it is worth, the following opinion is advanced: (1) small portfolios should avoid both these admittedly risky types, except for small amounts which may be owned indirectly through investment company stocks, until the general fund amounts to at least $10,000 of good-grade items; (2) larger portfolios might well contain a fraction of risky items, but not in excess of the fraction on which a heavy price shrinkage or an almost complete cessation of income for a time would be tolerable.

Some investors who wish to combine security with attempts to earn substantial stock market profits do so by investing a large percentage (possibly 90 per cent) of their funds conservatively at all times and using the other 10 per cent for commitments in dynamic speculations where the percentage of gain could be very high. Even more conservative investors follow similar logic in investing 90 per cent of their funds in high-grade fixed-income securities and 10 per cent in the common stocks of high-leverage investment companies; in case of great inflation the gains on the high-leverage stocks might offset the loss of purchasing power on the bonds, and in a deflation the opposite might be true. Either of these approaches to investment risk bearing has some logic, though it must be admitted that both skill and luck would be required to make the most of them.

It is often stated by young people that they can afford speculative risks while they are young, with plenty of time ahead in which to repair the damage if they sustain losses. Middle-aged men also seem to believe that the "businessman's risk" is an acceptable investment form as long as their earning power is high. Only in old age do these groups concede the importance of conservatism. For most people, and especially with respect to a general fund of investments, this is an unsound philosophy. It is only the individual whose future is well settled, who knows that his resources are adequate to assure his well-being for the rest of his life, who can afford to be casual about "flyers." The young man cannot know whether he can afford to take chances. The earlier savings accumulated by any man are the most important of his whole life. They provide a lifetime emergency reserve, they may finance great business opportunities, and they have time, before he reaches retirement age, to grow double or treble in amount. They deserve to be treated with the utmost care.

This argument against youthful speculation should not be construed as an argument against accepting necessary risks in developing one's own future. It is often very desirable for a man to take major risks in developing his own business or his own career; such risks are an unavoidable counterpart of progress, and they are presumably taken in a field in which the individual is informed and to which he will give constant attention. But this is not true of the general investment of surplus savings; this area will get part-time and probably amateur supervision at best, and it is just as hazardous as any other. It will be better for the young man to invest his surplus funds sanely, and if he must have a speculative thrill occasionally, to get it at the local race track or in a friendly poker game where the stakes are not so prohibitively high.

Viewpoints toward the Investment Markets

Investment dealers are familiar with two completely divergent viewpoints toward market prices, as exemplified by customers who have definite plans of procedure. As might be expected, each viewpoint has in it much that is sound and practical; also, each is deficient to the extent that it tends to ignore the other. The two viewpoints may be labeled the subjective and the market value viewpoints, for lack of better terms.

The subjective attitude toward investments emphasizes the fact that each investor has or should have certain personal objectives in making his investments, which are not necessarily those of his fellow men. He may be determined upon freedom from the business risk, or freedom from care, or price-level protection, or a steady dividend income, or in the location of his holdings in some specific tangible form. Whatever his desires, the emphasis is certainly not upon obtaining market appreciation, which after all is but an accidental consensus brought about by his demands and those of others. Satisfaction of his objectives is the thing.[1]

This viewpoint is sound and wholesome, to the extent that it permits investors to achieve their ends without worry or concern over incidental matters. After all, it is of no overwhelming concern to the holder of good bonds that the investment market fluctuates; his bonds will continue to pay the agreed rates of interest, and the principal will be regained at maturity. Again, the long-time holder of American Telephone stock is little affected when the price moves between 200 and 150; the dividend rate has been unchanged since 1923. Of course, it would make a difference if a fundamental change in earning power or in economic hazard took place; investments must be constantly watched anent this possibility. The old remark that sound investing means to "buy something good and forget it" is as stupid as it is fallacious. But it certainly is not necessary to live and fret with the vagaries of the investment markets. Many successful investors do not even watch the financial pages. They choose their investments with reference to personal needs, recheck them periodically with reference to fundamental soundness, and go about their normal business. Market prices are likely to affect investors with this point of view under only three conditions: (1) when they decide initially that the investment is "worth" its cost, (2) when they decide that the price justifies selling out, or (3) when they de-

[1] One of the impressive manifestations of the subjective viewpoint in investment selection is found in recent mass preferences for low-yield high-quality investments. Ever since the depression of the early 1930s a large percentage of new savings has sought outlets in life insurance, trust funds, savings deposits, government securities, and other safe dollar-sum commitments. The attributes sought in these investments have been sought regardless of low yields in them and much higher yields available elsewhere. The mass movement has been so heavy that the historic proportion between the interest yield on high-class bonds and the dividend yield on good stocks has been materially altered. In 1954 and 1955 there is indication that this mass pressure is to some extent reversing its course.

cide that market prices justify a "switch" from one investment to another.

To the considerable number of investors who take the market value viewpoint toward investments the daily quotations on the financial page and the unending gyrations of the real estate market provide the final measure of investment success or failure. And it is a definite and purposeful measure, for he who buys at a low price and sells at a higher one has assuredly increased his substance. The emphasis on market prices has increased greatly among stock investors in recent years, for the heavy taxes laid on ordinary income make market profits, which are usually less burdensomely taxed, relatively more attractive objectives.

Careful seekers after market profits do not neglect the fundamentals of earning power and security, but they add an elaborate consideration of market supply and demand factors to their calculations. Securities and real estate values are, after all, simply *prices,* which are established by supply and demand. These prices are acutely sensitive to changes in supply and demand, for relatively small fractions of the nation's total stock of securities or real estate constitute the entire market in any given day or week. Consequently, such prices are often sharply unstable, both from day to day and over longer terms of months and years. The individual who has both a keen insight into fundamental values and a knowledge of market behavior can sometimes make highly advantageous purchases or sales. Opportunities for such advantage are found in specific investments, which are frequently priced out of line with the general market; in specific industries or regions, where values are changing or about to change; or in almost the entire market for stocks or real estate, when changes are occurring in business conditions or in the general price level.

Market value changes should not, however, be regarded as the highroad to affluence for the average investor. The best informed and best equipped analysts the investment companies have been able to gather together have seldom been able to surpass the performance record of the market averages in dividend income plus market profits combined.[2] For a layman the obtaining of consistent profits or even a substantial average of profits over a period of years requires a highly infrequent combination of knowledge, judgment, diligence,

2 See Table 34, Chap. 19.

and luck. It requires a degree of concentration on market and economic affairs which would interfere seriously with the pursuit of the average man's profession. And attempts to gain large profits often lead to excessive risk taking, since maximum gains are to be had in ventures with risky commitments or by trading heavily with borrowed money. Neither process is recommended for the amateur or for one who cannot afford to lose.

Seeking Appreciation

In Chapter 1 the idea was advanced that portfolio selections should always be made with some thought of capital appreciation, at least to the extent consistent with other objectives, but at that time no attempt was made to be specific about the methods of doing this. Suggestions along these lines are now in order.

The most important principle to be followed by investment-minded profit seekers (and loss avoiders as well) is that of purchasing only investments which appear to be very attractively priced for long-run holding, even when an early resale is contemplated. Much has been said in previous chapters about the appraisement of industries, corporations, securities, and real estate, and about reasonable price-earnings ratios and yields. This technique deserves application in every instance, as the first determinant of the decision to buy or reject. The investment markets offer many opportunities to commit one's money, and it is not usually necessary, in order to obtain a satisfactory equity investment, to pay more than a reasonable long-run appraisal price. In fact, when purchasing either common stocks or real estate, it is seldom desirable to pay more than 80 per cent of a fair long-term appraisal; for if attractive individual investments cannot be found at bargain prices, it is probable that the entire market is too high for safety.

The second principle is a corollary of the first. It is desirable to sell any equity investment which can be sold for more than 20 per cent above the capitalized value of prospective earnings and dividends, and it is also desirable to "switch" from any holding into any other suitable one which offers substantially greater value. Income tax factors and brokerage costs will have to be considered in making any decision of this type, but frequent review of the entire portfolio in search of items which should be sold will usually pay. It is as desirable to eliminate unattractive holdings at a loss as it is to sell those which have risen to obvious peaks in value.

The third principle requires that high-quality investments be emphasized when business conditions are weakening or uncertain but permits lower quality holdings when the market is low and business is improving or vigorous. This principle requires the eschewing of promising speculative opportunities in many cases and may occasionally force sales at a loss, but these are not great sacrifices. Possibly the rule should require that all equities be liquidated when conditions are uncertain, but this would produce a badly unbalanced portfolio on frequent occasions and would, therefore, be a rather drastic policy when the investor cannot be sure that his forecast is correct. And business conditions are notoriously hard to predict. The best forecasters have been wrong so often that their efforts are normally received with skepticism and humor, even by people who are vitally concerned. Because of this uncertainty many people have turned to formula plans as a means of adapting their investment policies to business conditions. This is in part a defeatist attitude—an attempt to substitute a mechanical process for reasoned analysis which has proved difficult—yet the formulas themselves may be sound enough in conception to throw some light on the central problem of forecasting business conditions. From this viewpoint they may be very useful.

Portfolio Supervision

As has been repeatedly stated before, investment management does not stop after a portfolio has been planned and the initial group of investments purchased. Most investments do not manage themselves. It will be desirable to keep fairly constant watch on the holdings, to make occasional changes as conditions warrant, and to plan for additional investments or withdrawals. All of this requires some attention to economic conditions, a fairly faithful reading of a good financial page and preferably a financial periodical also, close attention to annual reports and other communications about the investments, and a two to four times yearly review of the entire portfolio with the help of good financial reference and advisory services. A good review means just that—a thorough study of industry and company, including competitive position, financial position, outlook, price-earnings ratios, yields, and attractiveness as compared with other possible investments. The financial services can be used in a public library, in a brokerage office, or they can be obtained by subscription, but regardless of inconvenience or expense, their use for this purpose is normally essential.

Diligent supervision of the type necessary for best results is clearly a burden to many people. Very commonly, through ignorance or less excusable neglect, they just do not undertake it, and the consequences are losses or, at best, lack of success. People who do not wish to exercise much investment supervision, and who are also unwilling to pay others to do it for them, should confine their investments to life insurance, bank deposits, government bonds, conservative investment companies, a diversified few of the very finest conservative stocks, and homeownership. The items can be chosen in consultation with friends and experts, and an occasional review of the holdings can be accomplished in the same way. With rigorous insistence upon quality throughout, this type of "buy and hold" investment policy should usually be satisfactory. However, it is not proof against fundamental economic changes, as many holders of "gilt-edge" railroad stocks discovered in 1932 and as the secure holders of high-grade bonds learned in 1941–1952.

The alternatives to personal investment management have all been discussed before. The most promising for individual use were (1) reliance on the advice of a securities firm or salesman, (2) dependence upon the "standard portfolios" recommended by financial periodicals or services, (3) employment of an investment counselor, (4) use of investment companies, at least for funds to be invested in stocks, or (5) the use of trusts. Each of these alternatives is acceptable in its proper place, as the preceding discussions have shown, and the discussions leading to this conclusion need not be repeated here. However, one passing remark will bear repetition: the use of trusts to care for property during its owners' old age, and particularly during the ownership of a widow unskilled in business affairs, is a wise expedient too little availed of by American investors. Such trusts may even be created by will, so that they do not come into being unless the exact contingency they were designed to meet—in this instance, the death of the husband while his wife still lives—should occur.

Title and Safekeeping

Although a discussion of the available methods of taking title to property is beyond the proper scope of this book, the choice of the most convenient method is an essential part of investment management. Each state makes available by statute or common law an extensive collection of tenancies which may be used for real estate and tangible property within its borders and by its citizens for intangible property generally. Among these ownership devices will be found separate property, tenancy in common, joint tenancy or tenancy by the entirety, community property, life tenancies, remainder interests, trusts, and tentative trusts. It is well worth an investor's while to study all the ownership devices which are available to him on different forms of property and to include in his plans for investment management the receipt of all titles in the most useful and convenient form. The choice of the most useful and convenient form would be based first of all on the technical fact of ownership, but matters of administrative convenience, estate settlement, and estate and tax planning would all be of high importance. To illustrate: families making gifts of property to minor children will usually do well to transfer the property to an adult member of the family as trustee rather than directly to the child, for a subsequent desirable sale of the property might be a cumbersome matter with title in the possession of a minor.

Many investors who take title to stocks and registered bonds find it convenient to order dividend and interest checks made payable to and sent to others. This is not an assignment of the money; it simply permits the income to go to the owner's bank for deposit, or to some other person for any purpose, as the owner wishes; and the owner may terminate the arrangement when he wishes. Securities held in trust may in this way be caused to pay income to the beneficiaries directly.

Previous chapters have noted the importance of keeping stock and bond certificates safe from loss or destruction. Savings bonds, postal savings certificates, insurance policies, and similar documents may be replaced at small cost if lost or destroyed, but even in these instances the effort and trouble would be a burden. Consequently, safekeeping is important. Most of these things are not negotiable by delivery, hence may be conveniently kept at home or in a business office in a fireproof safe—the convenience of having them available for inspection or sale is an argument for this practice—but a safe is a natural target for a burglar, and the investor is therefore driven to choose between storage in an excessively expensive safe, use of a commercial safe deposit vault, or storage of securities with a broker. This is perhaps a minor point, but the investor should be sure of what he is doing when he selects one of these storage plans. In many states, safe deposit boxes are instantly closed by the safe deposit company upon the death of the holder or of any joint holder and may not be opened, even for inspection, without inheritance tax office or probate court approval. This may take a few days or several weeks. If insurance policies, wills, savings bonds, or the property of others happens to be stored in this way, unnecessary delays may occur. There are many ways of meeting these problems, one of which the investor may choose after reviewing his own situation.

Living on Principal

The pressing investment problem encountered by most investors in their later years is that of managing an estate whose earnings are inadequate to maintain a reasonable standard of living for them. Social security annuities plus retirement pensions plus interest and dividend and rental incomes are not ordinarily enough. The situation seems to call for a program recognizing four definite needs. First, it is necessary to plan for convenient inroads upon principal, in ways which will retain the income as long as possible. Second, it will be necessary to maximize income to the greatest degree possible, without taking unnecessary risks. Third, it is desirable to stress safety, income stability, and value stability, in order to have assurance of both income and principal for the needs which will occur. Finally, it must be conceded that the need for price-level protection in this situation is as great or greater than in the case of the young investor, for here the price-level connection afforded by personal earning power no longer exists.

It would be idle to assume that elderly persons solve their investment problems solely in the light of what they have and what they need, in terms of arithmetic and economics. They do not. Most of them have families, to whom they wish to leave property and upon whom, in hard extremity, they could depend. Consequently, the use of life annuities to guarantee an income to the end and the willingness to endow old folks' homes generously in return for lifetime care are not so common as good logic would suggest that they should be. Instead, a limited use of life annuities is supplemented by grudging and fearful consumption of the principal upon which the bulk of income usually depends.

The ideal solution to the problem would be joint and survivor annuities amounting in value to nearly half the available property, if need be, plus a moderate quick-recourse fund in savings account or savings bonds, with the balance in high-quality high-dividend common stocks and residential real estate. The common stocks and residential realty would provide price-level protection, and in addition the real estate would place both its net income and the recovered principal of depreciation allowances in the owner's hands. Needless to say, the stocks should be those of large, stable, low-leverage concerns in stable industries, and the real estate should be free and clear of debt and not located in areas likely to be burdened with assessments for improvements. The stocks could then be liquidated one by one, if need be, to provide the extra money needed for living; but it would be a comfortable situation if the annuities plus the rental income plus the dividends could balance the household budget. In that way a considerable portion of principal—the cost of the annuities plus the depreciation of the real estate—could be consumed during the investors' lifetimes without any shrinkage in their monthly receipts and with a minimum amount of risk taking.

There are, of course, many alternatives to which an investor may resort. Series E bonds purchased at intervals for the last 10 or 15 years preceding retirement provide a convenient and economical post-retirement means of consuming principal, as well as emergency reserves. A trust established in a bank which operates a common trust fund can distribute quarterly sums from principal with very little loss of income. And a simple assortment of $500 holdings in good-grade preferred stocks would be available without loss most of the time, and savings accounts could be drawn upon at times when the stocks were not salable at good prices.

QUESTIONS AND PROBLEMS

1. Do you find any merit for yourself in the idea of a lifetime financial plan? Would such a plan disclose the adequacy of your provision for a widow at age 35?

2. Does Table 58 make enough provision for insurance?

3. Can you think of actual cases of investment anomalies in your own family or among your friends? Or are all their investments in this category?

4. Criticize the 17-point investment policy statement shown on page 634. Do you disapprove of any of the policies adopted?

5. Would you approve of stock ownership by a widow of limited means? What kinds of stocks?

6. What advantages and disadvantages can you find in a policy of owning 90 per cent good bonds and 10 per cent speculative stocks?

7. Do you agree that young people should avoid speculative "flyers"? Consider this pro and con. How about a purchase of Allis-Chalmers stock for speculative profit, at a price of 50?

8. Can you reconcile the "subjective" and the "market value" viewpoints toward stock investments into a practical policy for yourself?

9. If you held International Harvester stock and felt that it was time you reviewed the entire situation respecting your investment, what would you do? What sources would you consult?

10. What plan of safekeeping do you employ for fire insurance policies, life insurance policies, will, bank deposit passbooks, savings bonds, other bonds, stocks? Is this entirely satisfactory?

11. How do you intend to organize your savings for living after retirement?

REFERENCES

Badger, Ralph E., and Harry G. Guthmann: *Investment Principles and Practices,* Prentice-Hall, Inc., New York, 1951, Chap. 28.

Dowrie, George W., and Douglas R. Fuller: *Investments,* John Wiley & Sons, Inc., New York, 1950, Chaps. 12, 32.

Engel, Louis: *How to Buy Stocks,* Little, Brown & Company, Boston, 1953.

Graham, Benjamin: *The Intelligent Investor,* Harper & Brothers, New York, 1954.

Grodinsky, Julius: *Investments,* The Ronald Press Company, New York, 1953, Chap. 26.

Investment Bankers Association of America: *Fundamentals of Investment Banking,* Prentice-Hall, Inc., New York, 1949, Chap. 24.

Jordan, David F., and Herbert E. Dougall: *Investments,* Prentice-Hall, Inc., New York, 1952, Chaps. 8, 11.

Lagerquist, Walter E.: *Balancing and Hedging an Investment Plan,* The Ronald Press Company, New York, 1941, Parts II, III.

Pickett, Ralph R., and Marshall D. Ketchum: *Investment Principles and Policy,* Harper & Brothers, New York, 1954, Chap. 32.

Ryals, Stanley D., and E. C. Harwood: *How to Invest Wisely,* American Institute for Economic Research, Great Barrington, Mass., 1954, revised annually.

Sauvain, Harry C.: *Investment Management,* Prentice-Hall, Inc., New York, 1953, Chaps. 14, 15.

INDEX